FEMINIST THEORY
A Critique of Ideology

Edited by Nannerl O. Keohane,
Michelle Z. Rosaldo, and Barbara C. Gelpi

FEMINIST THEORY
A Critique of Ideology

The University of Chicago Press

The articles in this volume appeared in the Summer 1981 (Volume 6, number 4), Autumn 1981 (Volume 7, number 1), and Spring 1982 (Volume 7, number 3) issues of SIGNS: JOURNAL OF WOMEN IN CULTURE AND SOCIETY.

The University of Chicago Press, Chicago 60637
The University of Chicago Press, Ltd., London
89 88 87   5 4 3

Library of Congress Cataloging in Publication Data
Main entry under title:

Feminist theory.

   Includes index.
   1.   Feminism—United States—Addresses, essays,
lectures.   I.   Keohane, Nannerl O., 1940–
II.   Rosaldo, Michelle Zimbalist.   III.   Gelpi, Barbara
Charlesworth.
HQ1426.F474   305.4'2   82-6953
                                    AACR2

ISBN 0-226-43163-0 (pbk.)

Contents

Foreword

All the arts and sciences strive to understand lived human experience, its simple dailiness a continued mystery. Those engaged in the attempt to explain it realize that while experience is ungraspable in one sense, it is also a human construct. Feminist theory brings the added awareness that the construction of women's experience has never been adequate. Whether that experience was made trivial or enviable, sanctified or mystified, it was peripheral, described and explained primarily not by women themselves, but by men. Since women's experience was so rarely a direct focus for theoretical consciousness, a whole range and spectrum of human life remains to be explored, depicted, and understood.

For this reason, feminist theory is fundamentally experiential. Its subject is women's lives, past or present, historically recorded or known only by inference, experienced in association with men of the dominant culture or with men who are also oppressed. Feminist theory reconsiders historical, economic, religious, biological, artistic, and anthropological constructs and explanations. It brings to consciousness facets of our experience as women that have hitherto escaped attention because they have not been part of, and may even have contradicted, predominant theoretical accounts of human life. For to conceive our women's lives as actual often modifies or fractures the constructs that left those lives out of account.

Thus consciousness raising is the essential first step in feminist theory. It is, as Catharine MacKinnon points out in this volume, "the major technique of analysis, structure of organization, method of practice, and theory of social change of the women's movement" (p. 5). At one level, all women's experience must be embraced by our statements about women; and yet as Mary O'Brien puts it, "There is no Woman but real flesh and blood female creatures with brains and pains and aspirations" (p. 101). As individual women we become conscious of our situation by a personal re-vision of the economic practices, sexual mores, and political realities that have assigned that situation to us. As feminist theorists, we must come to terms with the ideological constructs that form our milieu, and with the theorists who first produced those constructs as living thought—Marx, Confucius, Freud, Saint Paul. We must

vii

scan the beacons that flare along the horizon of all culture, asking whether any one of them is *our* lighthouse.[1]

With such a spirit this collection of essays in and about feminist theory considers several systems of thought developed by master theorists. Two beacons to which we restlessly return most often, seeking our light, are those of Marx and Freud. We sense the tantalizing possibilities of reconstruction here: ideas devised in male-centered systems nonetheless offer promise of a new centering in women's lives.

In MacKinnon's essay and in O'Brien's, this promise works itself out through parallels: Marxist argument about production and reproduction, value and class structure, becomes available for rethinking sexuality and desire, power and powerlessness, as well as for reconsidering the creative labor of women giving birth. For Julia Kristeva and for Jean Elshtain, the challenge is the recovery of Freud, who offers entry into the world of the symbolic, the understanding of desire, and the complex play of language.

Other essayists work within other traditions in which they have been trained, struggling to sort out which ideas, lines of argument, and pieces of intellectual equipment can be freed from their pervasive bias toward male experience and used for feminist inquiry. Sometimes, as in Jane Marcus's "Storming the Toolshed," the tone of this struggle is that of battle, scornful and angry. At other times, as in Evelyn Keller's discussion of "Feminism and Science," the critique of familiar constructs dwells on how much these disciplines can learn from, and be refreshed by, feminist ideas.

Whether distrustful or optimistic, the dialogue with the traditions in which feminist scholars were trained inevitably raises the question, How far can we use these theories, these languages? Are they irrecoverably centered in male experience, so that we must somehow begin from the beginning and devise our own languages, our own discourse? Yet what would it mean to do such a thing? Like the Ellen Jamesians in *The World according to Garp,* we would be cutting out our own tongues, absolutely denying ourselves access to the rich possibilities of discourse devised in all cultures of humankind. Such an impoverishing self-denial, even assuming it were possible, would be a denial of self. Instead, like Susan Griffin, we begin with an internal monologue that is a dialogue, sometimes a discordant choir, of voices from different parts of past experience and training, reworking them in painful and painstaking self-scrutiny to fashion them into the matter for a new voice, a woman's voice. Like Myra Jehlen, we confront the "great traditions" of literature, science, and political and economic theory, and, finding ourselves unable to create an Archimedean point outside the world, we devise an internal standpoint that slowly becomes our own. And in the course of doing this,

1. The image is Adrienne Rich's, made in a personal communication.

as Jehlen tells us, feminism, as rethinking, must "rethink thinking itself" (p. 189).

Asking how far we must defer to the authority of the fathers, the masters of past discourse who have so far shaped our voices, raises also the question of how far we must embrace the achievements of our mothers and our sisters as our own. How much must feminism, in its attempt to discover and recover women's work, thereby rethinking traditional canons of judgment, be predisposed to think that work good? How much leeway have we in criticizing one another within the developing voice of feminist scholarship? As Marilyn Boxer's account of the growth of women's studies courses makes apparent, and as Elshtain and Kristeva demonstrate in their essays as well, there is abundant disagreement within the ranks of feminist scholars. Such argument, indeed, is carried on in our own minds as part of the internal dialogue, as part of what it means to find our voices.

Feminist theory as critique of ideology must also criticize itself and counter the tendency to congeal into a new ideology. Ideologies encompass unexamined thoughts about our lives; they are frozen theory, adopted as convenient or embraced fervently as dogma, unquestioned. Susan Griffin offers an eloquent description of the process we must resist: "When a theory is transformed into ideology," she says, "it begins to destroy the self- and self-knowledge. . . . It organizes experience according to itself, without touching experience. . . . Slowly, it builds a prison for the mind" (p. 254). To remain true to our own vision of the truth, we must continue to test thinking against experience, making sure that it remains rooted in the real lives of women. In this endeavor, it is useful to identify different forms of the consciousness of women and consider them as source and subject matter for our theorizing.

One form of women's consciousness is what we might call "feminine consciousness." More often for feminists an object of analysis rather than a source of insight, it involves consciousness of oneself as object of the attention of another; it arises from the sensation of being looked at and brings to one's own awareness what one appears to be in someone else's eyes. This form of awareness is that of the "Other," in Simone de Beauvoir's terms, the woman as defined by male gaze, construct, and desire. The consciousness of this person who is an "Other," the feminine consciousness, is normally castigated in feminist theory as false consciousness, and with reason. Yet the nuances of sensitivity to appearances, the fine distinctions in the observance of one's behavior and that of others, the silent exploration of the consciousness in which one functions as an "Other" deserve our attention as means toward understanding human motivation and psychology, as well as our condemnation as the product of asymmetrical power. So many attributes of women's experience, past and present, have been rooted in this form of "feminine consciousness" that we can hardly remain true to our goal of understanding woman's lived reality if we dismiss this form of consciousness as unworthy of theoretical attention.

A more promising source for new and vibrant theory is what Temma Kaplan in this volume calls "female consciousness" (p. 55). This consciousness, which also encompasses the areas explored at the end of Jean Elshtain's essay, is the deep-rooted, age-old experience of women in giving and preserving life, nurturing and sustaining. Profoundly conservative, it is also resonant with radical possibilities. The notion of women as "close to nature," distorted sometimes to discount the abilities of women to reason and to speak, here becomes the basis for a more fruitful line of argument. Women as life-givers and life-sustainers, bonded together by this common capacity and obligation, have made noble sacrifices and achieved splendid works throughout history. Some theorists have denied reality or legitimacy to this form of "female consciousness" because of the possibilities of abuse that lurk so readily about it. But once again, if we fail to recognize this as a fundamental form of the consciousness of women, we fail to be true to women's lived experience in history.

A third form of the consciousness of women is "feminist consciousness." This is a consciousness developed and defined as we reflect on women's experience, and on the asymmetries in power, opportunity, and situation that have universally marked the fortunes of women. Without denying the importance of "female consciousness," or the reality of "feminine consciousness," our "feminist consciousness" draws attention to the pervasive patterns of subordination, limitation, and confinement that have hampered and crippled the development of the female half of humankind as far back as the species can remember. Concerned about the worldwide situation of women now as well as throughout the past, it develops a vision of an alternative way of living, in which individuals of both sexes can flourish in diverse ways, without restraints imposed by rigid and impersonal sex/gender roles.

Feminist consciousness also explores the construction, deconstruction, and reconstruction of sexuality as a central terrain for the definition and self-definition of women. As Ann Ferguson, Jacquelyn Zita, and Kathryn Addelson make clear, the definition of what it means to be a lesbian and of the relation between lesbian consciousness and feminist consciousness is an important part of this exploration. Their exchange of ideas on the usefulness of Adrienne Rich's concept of a "lesbian continuum" involves questions of whether definition of the term "lesbian" should be weighted toward the political or toward the sexual and whether, if feminist theory uses a phrase like "lesbian continuum" with an essentially political meaning, that usage does not, ironically, make for the erasure once again of lesbian sexuality. Such considerations, merging as they do with a historical argument on the political significance of lesbianism for the feminist movement, shed light as well on the structures of heterosexuality. The discussion also poses the issue of a counter-community, and thus implicitly that of feminist separatism—one of the most strongly argued topics within feminist consciousness, as Kristeva's critique of the separatist impulse demonstrates.

Another division occurs between those engaged in the improvement of women's situation and those working toward a scholarly assessment of it. Boxer recounts the continuing struggle aroused by these different emphases. In fact, feminist consciousness necessarily encompasses both activism and understanding. The tension between them is probably inevitable; we can hope that it also continues to be fruitful. Thinking about women's experience draws attention to the varied injustices and disadvantages imposed on women, the multiple barriers to development as full persons that women have experienced, and this experiential thinking opens a commitment to work for removal of those barriers and redress for injustices.

Thus feminist consciousness invokes self-understanding, as individuals and as women, but not as the only or the final goal. It also raises general questions about the nature of power. As Zillah Eisenstein's essay makes clear, feminists should be alert to political configurations and consider opportunities that can be used to work effectively for change. To give but one example, a factor noted by several essayists in this volume: Motherhood is no longer a synonym for bland, unthinking goodness, nor does it designate the guardian of an irrelevant domestic backwater, or an untouchable area of sanctity. Motherhood is a political battleground, a contested area for control—of women's bodies, of the fortunes of families, of the obligations of community support, of the constraints on choice.

Strategies devised by women for dealing with oppression and injustice run the full gamut from subtle persuasion to terrorism, as Kristeva reminds us in discussing contemporary Europe. Disagreements about the effectiveness—and rightfulness—of these several choices will also continue to mark the movement. The assertion that we can work through such conflicts to advance our common goals as women is audacious and may even be overly optimistic. What makes it nonetheless possible is a shared will for its fulfillment. There are, for that matter, equally bold feminist projects outlined in these theoretical essays: the hope to encompass the experience of all women and yet be true to the lives of individuals, the testing of the strengths and limitations of separatism, the commitment to self-critique so that theory does not harden into ideology, and the hope that we can devise new ways of being powerful without aggressively destructive domination over others.

Perhaps the most audacious and most important goal of all has been eloquently described by the friend and colleague whose work and wit, intelligence and spirit, inform every aspect of this volume: Shelly Rosaldo. As coeditor of these essays before her tragic death, she was responsible for keeping before us the goals of feminism that move beyond injustices against women and deal with oppression and inequality in all areas of human life. As Shelly put it in an article in *Signs* several years ago, "A crucial task for feminist scholars emerges, then, not as the relatively limited one of documenting pervasive sexism as a social fact—or showing how we can now hope to change or have in the past been able to survive it. Instead, it seems that we are challenged to provide new ways of linking the particulars of women's lives, activities, and goals to inequalities wherever they exist."[2]

Yet as Shelly's words make clear, even as we recognize and respond to the need to extend our range of vision to "inequalities wherever they exist," our work as feminists enjoins us to achieve this extension not by generalized statements and vague incantations but by paying close attention to "the *particulars* of women's lives, activities, and goals." Here lies our major source of insight, the rootedness in human experience that allows us to rethink, redirect, and ultimately to reshape our constructions of the world.

Many people helped us in the gathering and editing of these essays, which, in the main, are taken from a special issue of *Signs* on feminist theory, and we are deeply grateful to them. We turned constantly for advice and editorial suggestions to our fellow associates at *Signs:* Estelle Freedman, Carol Jacklin, Myra Strober, and Margery Wolf. When this volume was in preparation Nancy Hartsock was a guest associate editor of *Signs* and was of invaluable help. Carolyn Lougee, a member of our editorial board, as well as the then managing editor of *Signs,* gave us fine editorial advice on the essay by Julia Kristeva.

The very cataloging of these names is pleasure, recalling as it does hours of shared thought and work. We are especially grateful to two who had a transformative effect on this volume: the managing editor and the editorial associate of *Signs.* The authors who worked with them know as we do how great their contribution was and join us, I am sure, in the wish to give them the recognition they deserve.

NANNERL O. KEOHANE
BARBARA C. GELPI

2. Michelle Z. Rosaldo, "The Use and Abuse of Anthropology: Reflections on Feminism and Cross-cultural Understanding," *Signs: Journal of Women in Culture and Society* 5, no. 3 (Spring 1980): 389–417, esp. 417.

Feminism, Marxism, Method, and the State: An Agenda for Theory

Catharine A. MacKinnon

Sexuality is to feminism what work is to marxism: that which is most one's own, yet most taken away. Marxist theory argues that society is fundamentally constructed of the relations people form as they do and make things needed to survive humanly. Work is the social process of shaping and transforming the material and social worlds, creating people as social beings as they create value. It is that activity by which people become who they are. Class is its structure, production its consequence, capital its congealed form, and control its issue.

Dedicated to the spirit of Shelly Rosaldo in us all.

The second part of this article, which will appear in a forthcoming issue of *Signs* as "Feminism, Marxism, Method, and the State: Toward Feminist Jurisprudence," applies the critique developed here to theories of the state and to legal materials. Both articles are parts of a longer work in progress. The argument of this essay on the relation between marxism and feminism has not changed since it was first written in 1973, but the argument on feminism itself has. In the intervening years, the manuscript has been widely circulated, in biannual mutations, for criticism. Reflecting on that process, which I hope publication will continue (this *is* "an agenda for theory"), I find the following people, each in their way, contributed most to its present incarnation: Sonia E. Alvarez, Douglas Bennett, Paul Brest, Ruth Colker, Robert A. Dahl, Karen E. Davis, Andrea Dworkin, Alicia Fernandez, Jane Flax, Bert Garskoff, Elbert Gates, Karen Haney, Kent Harvey, Linda Hoaglund, Nan Keohane, Duncan Kennedy, Bob Lamm, Martha Roper, Michelle Z. Rosaldo, Anne E. Simon, Sharon Silverstein, Valerie A. Tebbetts, Rona Wilensky, Gaye Williams, Jack Winkler, and Laura X. The superb work of Martha Freeman and Lu Ann Carter was essential to its production.

Implicit in feminist theory is a parallel argument: the molding, direction, and expression of sexuality organizes society into two sexes—women and men—which division underlies the totality of social relations. Sexuality is that social process which creates, organizes, expresses, and directs desire,[1] creating the social beings we know as women and men, as their relations create society. As work is to marxism, sexuality to feminism is socially constructed yet constructing, universal as activity yet historically specific, jointly comprised of matter and mind. As the organized expropriation of the work of some for the benefit of others defines a class—workers—the organized expropriation of the sexuality of some for the use of others defines the sex, woman. Heterosexuality is its structure, gender and family its congealed forms, sex roles its qualities generalized to social persona, reproduction a consequence, and control its issue.

Marxism and feminism are theories of power and its distribution: inequality. They provide accounts of how social arrangements of patterned disparity can be internally rational yet unjust. But their specificity is not incidental. In marxism to be deprived of one's work, in feminism of one's sexuality, defines each one's conception of lack of power per se. They do not mean to exist side by side to insure that two separate spheres of social life are not overlooked, the interests of two groups are not

---

I have rendered "marxism" in lower case and "Black" in upper case and have been asked by the publisher to explain these choices. It is conventional to capitalize terms that derive from a proper name. Since I wish to place marxism and feminism in equipoise, the disparate typography would weigh against my analytic structure. Capitalizing both would germanize the text. I also hope feminism, a politics authored by those it works in the name of, is never named after an individual. Black is conventionally (I am told) regarded as a color rather than a racial or national designation, hence is not usually capitalized. I do not regard Black as merely a color of skin pigmentation, but as a heritage, an experience, a cultural and personal identity, the meaning of which becomes specifically stigmatic and/or glorious and/or ordinary under specific social conditions. It is as much socially created as, and at least in the American context no less specifically meaningful or definitive than, any linguistic, tribal, or religious ethnicity, all of which are conventionally recognized by capitalization.

1. "Desire" is selected as a term parallel to "value" in marxist theory to refer to that substance felt to be primordial or aboriginal but posited by the theory as social and contingent. The sense in which I mean it is consonant with its development in contemporary French feminist theories, e.g., in Hélène Cixous, "The Laugh of Medusa: Viewpoint," trans. Keith Cohen and Paula Cohen, *Signs: Journal of Women in Culture and Society* 1, no. 4 (Summer 1976): 875–93; and in works by Gauthier, Irigaray, LeClerc, Duras, and Kristeva in *New French Feminisms: An Anthology*, ed. Elaine Marks and Isabelle de Courtivron (Amherst: University of Massachusetts Press, 1980). My use of the term is to be distinguished from that of Gilles Deleuze and Felix Guattari, *Anti-Oedipus: Capitalism and Schizophrenia* (New York: Viking Press, 1977); and Guy Hocquenghem, *Homosexual Desire* (London: Allison & Busby, 1978), for example.

obscured, or the contributions of two sets of variables are not ignored. They exist to argue, respectively, that the relations in which many work and few gain, in which some fuck and others get fucked,[2] are the prime moment of politics.

What if the claims of each theory are taken equally seriously, each on its own terms? Can two social processes be basic at once? Can two groups be subordinated in conflicting ways, or do they merely crosscut? Can two theories, each of which purports to account for the same thing—power as such—be reconciled? Or, is there a connection between the fact that the few have ruled the many and the fact that those few have been men?

Confronted on equal terms, these theories pose fundamental questions for each other. Is male dominance a creation of capitalism or is capitalism one expression of male dominance? What does it mean for class analysis if one can assert that a social group is defined and exploited through means largely independent of the organization of production, if in forms appropriate to it? What does it mean for a sex-based analysis if one can assert that capitalism would not be materially altered if it were sex integrated or even controlled by women? If the structure and interests served by the socialist state and the capitalist state differ in class terms, are they equally predicated upon sex inequality? To the extent their form and behavior resemble one another, could this be their commonality? Is there a relationship between the power of some classes over others and that of all men over all women?

Rather than confront these questions, marxists and feminists have usually either dismissed or, in what amounts to the same thing, subsumed each other. Marxists have criticized feminism as bourgeois in theory and in practice, meaning that it works in the interest of the ruling class. They argue that to analyze society in terms of sex ignores class divisions among women, dividing the proletariat. Feminist demands, it is claimed, could be fully satisfied within capitalism, so their pursuit undercuts and deflects the effort for basic change. Efforts to eliminate barriers to women's personhood—arguments for access to life chances without regard to sex—are seen as liberal and individualistic. Whatever women have in common is considered based in nature, not society; cross-cultural analyses of commonalities in women's social conditions are seen as ahistorical and lacking in cultural specificity. The women's movement's focus

---

2. I know no nondegraded English verb for the activity of sexual expression that would allow a construction parallel to, for example, "I am working," a phrase that could apply to nearly any activity. This fact of language may reflect and contribute to the process of obscuring sexuality's pervasiveness in social life. Nor is there *any* active verb meaning "to act sexually" that specifically envisions a woman's action. If language constructs as well as expresses the social world, these words support heterosexual values.

upon attitudes and feelings as powerful components of social reality is criticized as idealist; its composition, purportedly of middle-class educated women, is advanced as an explanation for its opportunism.

Feminists charge that marxism is male defined in theory and in practice, meaning that it moves within the world view and in the interest of men. Feminists argue that analyzing society exclusively in class terms ignores the distinctive social experiences of the sexes, obscuring women's unity. Marxist demands, it is claimed, could be (and in part have been) satisfied without altering women's inequality to men. Feminists have often found that working-class movements and the left undervalue women's work and concerns, neglect the role of feelings and attitudes in a focus on institutional and material change, denigrate women in procedure, practice, and everyday life, and in general fail to distinguish themselves from any other ideology or group dominated by male interests. Marxists and feminists thus accuse each other of seeking (what in each one's terms is) reform—changes that appease and assuage without addressing the grounds of discontent—where (again in each one's terms) a fundamental overthrow is required. The mutual perception, at its most extreme, is not only that the other's analysis is incorrect, but that its success would be a defeat.

Neither set of allegations is groundless. In the feminist view, sex, in analysis and in reality, does divide classes, a fact marxists have been more inclined to deny or ignore than to explain or change. Marxists, similarly, have seen parts of the women's movement function as a special interest group to advance the class-privileged: educated and professional women. To consider this group coextensive with "the women's movement" precludes questioning a definition of coalesced interest and resistance[3] which gives disproportionate visibility to the movement's least broadly based segment. But advocates of women's interests have not always been class conscious; some have exploited class-based arguments for advantage, even when the interests of working-class *women* were thereby obscured.

For example, in 1866, in an act often thought to inaugurate the first wave of feminism, John Stuart Mill petitioned the English parliament for women's suffrage with the following partial justification: "Under whatever conditions, and within whatever limits, men are admitted to suffrage, there is not a shadow of justification for not admitting women under the same. The majority of women of any class are not likely to differ in political opinion from the majority of men in the same class."[4] Perhaps Mill means that, to the extent class determines opinion, sex is

3. Accepting this definition has tended to exclude from "the women's movement" and make invisible the diverse ways that many women—notably Blacks and working-class women—have *moved* against their determinants.

4. John Stuart Mill, "The Subjection of Women," in *Essays on Sex Equality,* ed. Alice S. Rossi (Chicago: University of Chicago Press, 1970), pp. 184–85.

irrelevant. In this sense, the argument is (to some persuasively) narrow. It can also justify limiting the extension of the franchise to women who "belong to" men of the same class that already exercises it, to the further detriment of the excluded underclass, "their" women included.[5]

This kind of reasoning is confined neither to the issue of the vote nor to the nineteenth century. Mill's logic is embedded in a theoretical structure that underlies much contemporary feminist theory and justifies much of the marxist critique. That women should be allowed to engage in politics expressed Mill's concern that the state not restrict individuals' self-government, their freedom to develop talents for their own growth, and their ability to contribute to society for the good of humanity. As an empirical rationalist, he resisted attributing to biology what could be explained as social conditioning. As a utilitarian, he found most sex-based inequalities inaccurate or dubious, inefficient, and there-fore unjust. The liberty of women as individuals to achieve the limits of self-development without arbitrary interference extended to women his meritocratic goal of the self-made man, condemning (what has since come to be termed) sexism as an interference with personal initiative and laissez-faire.

The hospitality of such an analysis to marxist concerns is problematic. One might extend Mill's argument to cover class as one more arbitrary, socially conditioned factor that produces inefficient de-velopment of talent and unjust distribution of resources among individ-uals. But although this might be in a sense materialist, it would not be a class analysis. Mill does not even allow for income leveling. Unequal distribution of wealth is exactly what laissez-faire and unregulated per-sonal initiative produces. The individual concept of rights that this theory requires on a juridical level (especially but not only in the eco-nomic sphere), a concept which produces the tension between liberty for each and equality among all, pervades liberal feminism, substantiating the criticism that feminism is for the privileged few.

The marxist criticism that feminism focuses upon feelings and at-titudes is also based on something real: the centrality of consciousness raising. Consciousness raising is the major technique of analysis, struc-ture of organization, method of practice, and theory of social change of the women's movement.[6] In consciousness raising, often in groups, the

5. Mill personally supported universal suffrage. As it happened, working-class men got the vote before women of any class.

6. Feminists have observed the importance of consciousness raising without seeing it as method in the way developed here. See Pamela Allen, *Free Space: A Perspective on the Small Group in Women's Liberation* (New York: Times Change Press, 1970); Anuradha Bose, "Consciousness Raising," in *Mother Was Not a Person,* ed. Margaret Anderson (Montreal: Content Publishing, 1972); Nancy McWilliams, "Contemporary Feminism, Consciousness-Ráising, and Changing Views of the Political," in *Women in Politics,* ed. Jane Jaquette (New York: John Wiley & Sons, 1974); Joan Cassell, *A Group Called Women: Sisterhood & Symbolism in the Feminist Movement* (New York: David McKay, 1977); and Nancy

impact of male dominance is concretely uncovered and analyzed through the collective speaking of women's experience, from the perspective of that experience. Because marxists tend to conceive of powerlessness, first and last, as concrete and externally imposed, they believe that it must be concretely and externally undone to be changed. Women's powerlessness has been found through consciousness raising to be both internalized and externally imposed, so that, for example, femininity is identity to women as well as desirability to men. The feminist concept of consciousness and its place in social order and change emerge from this practical analytic. What marxism conceives as change in consciousness is not a form of social change in itself. For feminism, it can be, but because women's oppression is not just in the head, feminist *consciousness* is not just in the head either. But the pain, isolation, and thingification of women who have been pampered and pacified into nonpersonhood—women "grown ugly and dangerous from being nobody for so long"[7]—is difficult for the materially deprived to see as a form of oppression, particularly for women whom no man has ever put on a pedestal.

Marxism, similarly, has not just been misunderstood. Marxist theory *has* traditionally attempted to comprehend all meaningful social variance in class terms. In this respect, sex parallels race and nation as an undigested but persistently salient challenge to the exclusivity—or even primacy—of class as social explanation. Marxists typically extend class to cover women, a division and submersion that, to feminism, is inadequate to women's divergent and common experience. In 1912 Rosa Luxemburg, for example, addressed a group of women on the issue of suffrage: "Most of these bourgeois women who act like lionesses in the struggle against 'male prerogatives' would trot like docile lambs in the camp of conservative and clerical reaction if they had the suffrage. Indeed, they would certainly be a good deal more reactionary than the male part of their class. Aside from the few who have taken jobs or professions, the bourgeoisie do not take part in social production. They are nothing but co-consumers of the surplus product their men extort

---

Hartsock, "Fundamental Feminism: Process and Perspective," *Quest: A Feminist Quarterly* 2, no. 2 (Fall 1975): 67–80.

7. Toni Cade (now Bambara) thus describes a desperate Black woman who has too many children and too little means to care for them or herself in "The Pill: Genocide or Liberation?" in *The Black Woman: An Anthology,* ed. Toni Cade (New York: Mentor, New American Library, 1970), p. 168. By using her phrase in altered context, I do not want to distort her meaning but to extend it. Throughout this essay, I have tried to see if women's condition is shared, even when contexts or magnitudes differ. (Thus, it is very different to be "nobody" as a Black woman than as a white lady, but neither is "somebody" by male standards.) This is the approach to race and ethnicity attempted throughout. I aspire to include all women in the term "women" in some way, without violating the particularity of any woman's experience. Whenever this fails, the statement is simply wrong and will have to be qualified or the aspiration (or the theory) abandoned.

from the proletariat. They are parasites of the parasites of the social body."[8] Her sympathies lay with "proletarian women" who derive their right to vote from being "productive for society like the men."[9] With a blind spot analogous to Mill's within her own perspective, Luxemburg defends women's suffrage on class grounds, although in both cases the vote would have benefited women without regard to class.

Women as women, across class distinctions and apart from nature, were simply unthinkable to Luxemburg, as to most marxists. Feminist theory asks marxism: What is class for women? Luxemburg, again like Mill in her own context, subliminally recognizes that women derive their class position, with concomitant privileges and restrictions, from their associations with men. For a feminist, this may explain why they do not unite against male dominance, but it does not explain that dominance, which cuts across class lines even as it takes forms peculiar to classes. What distinguishes the bourgeois woman from her domestic servant is that the latter is paid (if barely), while the former is kept (if contingently). But is this a difference in social productivity or only in its indices, indices which themselves may be products of women's undervalued status?[10] Luxemburg sees that the bourgeois woman of her time

8. Rosa Luxemburg, "Women's Suffrage and Class Struggle," in *Selected Political Writings,* ed. Dick Howard (New York: Monthly Review Press, 1971), pp. 219–20. It may or may not be true that women as a group vote more conservatively than men, on a conventional left-right spectrum. The apparently accurate suspicion that they do may have accounted for left ambivalence on women's suffrage as much as any principled view of the role of reform in a politics of radical change.

9. Ibid., p. 220.

10. This question is most productively explored in the controversy over wages for housework. See Margaret Benston, "The Political Economy of Women's Liberation," *Monthly Review,* vol. 21, no. 4 (September 1969), reprinted in *From Feminism to Liberation,* ed. Edith Hoshino Altbach (Cambridge, Mass.: Schenckman Publishing Co., 1971), pp. 199–210; Peggy Morton, "Women's Work Is Never Done," in *Women Unite* (Toronto: Canadian Women's Educational Press, 1972); Hodee Edwards, "Housework and Exploitation: A Marxist Analysis," *No More Fun and Games: A Journal of Female Liberation,* issue 4 (July 1971), pp. 92–100; and Mariarosa Dalla Costa and Selma James, *The Power of Women and the Subversion of the Community* (Bristol: Falling Wall Press, 1973). This last work situates housework in a broader theoretical context of wagelessness and potential political power while avoiding support of wages for housework as a program; its authors have since come to support wages for housework, deducing it from the perspective presented here. See also Sylvia Federici, *Wages against Housework* (Bristol: Falling Wall Press, 1973). Wally Seccombe, "The Housewife and Her Labor under Capitalism," *New Left Review* 83 (January–February 1974): 3–24; Carol Lopate, "Women and Pay for Housework," *Liberation* 18, no. 9 (May–June 1974): 11–19; Nicole Cox and Sylvia Federici, *Counter-Planning from the Kitchen—Wages for Housework: A Perspective on Capital and the Left* (Bristol: Falling Wall Press, 1975); Wendy Edmond and Suzi Fleming, eds., *All Work and No Pay: Women, Housework and the Wages Due* (Bristol: Falling Wall Press, 1975); Jeanette Silveira, *The Housewife and Marxist Class Analysis* (Seattle, Wash.: By the author, 1975) (pamphlet available from the author, P.O. Box 30541, Seattle, Wash. 98103); Jean Gardiner, "Women's Domestic Labor," *New Left Review* 89 (January–February 1975): 47–55; Beth Ingber and Cleveland Modern Times Group, "The Social Factory," *Falling Wall Review,* no. 5 (1976), pp. 1–7;

is a "parasite of a parasite" but fails to consider her commonality with the proletarian woman who is the slave of a slave. In the case of bourgeois women, to limit the analysis of women's relationship to capitalism to their relations through men is to see only its vicarious aspect. To fail to do this in the case of proletarian women is to miss its vicarious aspect.

Feminist observations of women's situation in socialist countries, although not conclusive on the contribution of marxist theory to understanding women's situation, have supported the theoretical critique.[11] In the feminist view, these countries have solved many social problems, women's subordination not included. The criticism is not that socialism has not automatically liberated women in the process of transforming production (assuming that this transformation is occurring). Nor is it to diminish the significance of such changes for women: "There is a difference between a society in which sexism is expressed in the form of female infanticide and a society in which sexism takes the form of unequal representation on the Central Committee. And the difference is worth dying for."[12] The criticism is rather that these countries do not make a priority of working for women that distinguishes them from nonsocialist societies. Capitalist countries value women in terms of their "merit" by male standards; in socialist countries women are invisible except in their capacity as "workers," a term that seldom includes women's distinctive work: housework, sexual service, childbearing. The con-

---

Joan Landes, "Wages for Housework: Subsidizing Capitalism?" *Quest: A Feminist Quarterly* 2, no. 2 (Fall 1975): 17–30; Batya Weinbaum and Amy Bridges, "The Other Side of the Paycheck: Monopoly Capital and the Structure of Conscription," *Monthly Review* 28, no. 3 (July–August 1976): 88–103.

11. These observations are complex and varied. Typically they begin with the recognition of the important changes socialism has made for women, qualified by reservations about its potential to make the remaining necessary ones. Delia Davin, "Women in the Countryside of China," in *Women in Chinese Society,* ed. Margery Wolf and Roxane Witke (Stanford, Calif.: Stanford University Press, 1974); Katie Curtin, *Women in China* (New York: Pathfinder Press, 1975); Judith Stacey, "When Patriarchy Kowtows: The Significance of the Chinese Family Revolution for Feminist Theory," *Feminist Studies* 2, no. 2/3 (1975): 64–112; Julia Kristeva, *About Chinese Women* (New York: Urizen Books, 1977); Hilda Scott, *Does Socialism Liberate Women? Experiences from Eastern Europe* (Cambridge, Mass.: Beacon Press, 1974); Margaret Randall, *Cuban Women Now* (Toronto: Women's Press, 1974) (an edited collation of Cuban women's own observations); and *Cuban Women Now: Afterword* (Toronto: Women's Press, 1974); Carollee Bengelsdorf and Alice Hageman, "Emerging from Underdevelopment: Women and Work in Cuba," in *Capitalist Patriarchy and the Case for Socialist Feminism,* ed. Zillah Eisenstein (New York: Monthly Review Press, 1979).

12. Barbara Ehrenreich, "What Is Socialist Feminism?" *Win* (June 3, 1976), reprinted in *Working Papers on Socialism and Feminism* (Chicago: New American Movement, n.d.). Counterpoint is provided by feminists who have more difficulty separating the two. Susan Brownmiller notes: "It seems to me that a country that wiped out the tsetse fly can by fiat put an equal number of women on the Central Committee" ("Notes of an Ex-China Fan," *Village Voice,* quoted in Batya Weinbaum, *The Curious Courtship of Women's Liberation and Socialism* [Boston: South End Press, 1978], p. 7).

cern of revolutionary leadership for ending women's confinement to traditional roles too often seems limited to making their labor available to the regime, leading feminists to wonder whose interests are served by this version of liberation. Women become as free as men to work outside the home while men remain free from work within it. This also occurs under capitalism. When woman's labor or militancy suits the needs of emergency, she is suddenly man's equal, only to regress when the urgency recedes.[13] Feminists do not argue that it means the same to women to be on the bottom in a feudal regime, a capitalist regime, and a socialist regime; the commonality argued is that, despite real changes, bottom is bottom.

Where such attitudes and practices come to be criticized, as in Cuba or China, changes appear gradual and precarious, even where the effort looks major. If seizures of state and productive power overturn work relations, they do not overturn sex relations at the same time or in the same way, as a class analysis of sex would (and in some cases did) predict.[14] Neither technology nor socialism, both of which purport to alter women's role at the point of production, have ever yet equalized women's status relative to men. In the feminist view, nothing has. At minimum, a separate effort appears required—an effort that can be shaped by revolutionary regime and work relations—but a separate effort nonetheless. In light of these experiences, women's struggles, whether under capitalist or socialist regimes, appear to feminists to have more in common with each other than with leftist struggles anywhere.

Attempts to create a synthesis between marxism and feminism,

13. Stacey (n. 11 above); Janet Salaff and Judith Merkle, "Women and Revolution: The Lessons of the Soviet Union and China," *Socialist Revolution* 1, no. 4 (1970): 39–72; Linda Gordon, *The Fourth Mountain* (Cambridge, Mass.: Working Papers, 1973); Richard Stites, *The Women's Liberation Movement in Russia: Feminism, Nihilism, and Bolshevism* (Princeton, N.J.: Princeton University Press, 1978), pp. 392–421.

14. See Fidel Castro, *Women and the Cuban Revolution* (New York: Pathfinder Press, 1970); but compare Fidel's "Speech at Closing Session of the 2d Congress of the Federation of Cuban Women," November 29, 1974, *Cuba Review* 4 (December 1974): 17–23. Stephanie Urdang, *A Revolution within a Revolution: Women in Guinea-Bissau* (Boston: New England Free Press, n.d.). This is the general position taken by official documents of the Chinese revolution, as collected by Elisabeth Croll, ed., *The Women's Movement in China: A Selection of Readings, 1949–1973*, Modern China Series, no. 6 (London: Anglo-Chinese Educational Institute, 1974). Mao Tse-Tung recognized a distinctive domination of women by men (see discussion by Stuart Schram, *The Political Thought of Mao Tse-Tung* [New York: Praeger Publishers, 1969], p. 257), but interpretations of his thought throughout the revolution saw issues of sex as bourgeois deviation (see Croll, ed., pp. 19, 22, 32). The Leninist view which the latter documents seem to reflect is expressed in Clara Zetkin's account, "Lenin on the Woman Question," excerpted as appendix in *The Woman Question* (New York: International Publishers, 1951), p. 89. Engels earlier traced the oppression of women to the rise of class society, the patriarchal family, and the state, arguing that woman's status would be changed with the elimination of private property as a form of ownership and her integration into public production (Friedrich Engels, *Origin of the Family, Private Property and the State* [New York: International Publishers, 1942]).

termed socialist-feminism, have not recognized the depth of the antagonism or the separate integrity of each theory. These juxtapositions
emerge as unconfronted as they started: either feminist or marxist, usually the latter. Socialist-feminist practice often divides along the same
lines, consisting largely in organizational cross-memberships and mutual
support on specific issues.[15] Women with feminist sympathies urge attention to women's issues by left or labor groups; marxist women pursue
issues of class within feminist groups; explicitly socialist-feminist groups
come together and divide, often at the hyphen.[16]

Most attempts at synthesis attempt to integrate or explain the appeal
of feminism by incorporating issues feminism identifies as central—the
family, housework, sexuality, reproduction, socialization, personal
life—within an essentially unchanged marxian analysis.[17] According to

15. Sheila Rowbotham, *Hidden from History: Rediscovering Women in History from the
Seventeenth Century to the Present* (New York: Random House, 1973); Mary Jo Buhle,
"Women and the Socialist Party, 1901–1914," in Altbach, ed. (n. 10 above); Robert Shaffer,
"Women and the Communist Party, USA, 1930–1940," *Socialist Review* 45 (May–June
1979): 73–118. Contemporary attempts to create socialist-feminist groups and strategies
are exemplified in position papers: Chicago Women's Liberation Union, "Socialist
Feminism: A Strategy for the Women's Movement," mimeograph (Chicago, 1972) (available from Women's Liberation Union, Hyde Park Chapter, 819 W. George, Chicago, Ill.
60657); Berkeley-Oakland Women's Union, "Principles of Unity," *Socialist Revolution* 4, no.
1 (January–March 1974): 69–82; Lavender and Red Union, *The Political Perspective of the
Lavender and Red Union* (Los Angeles: Fanshen Printing Collective, 1975). Rosalind Petchesky, "Dissolving the Hyphen: A Report on Marxist-Feminist Groups 1–5," in Eisenstein,
ed. (n. 11 above), and Red Apple Collective, "Socialist-Feminist Women's Unions: Past and
Present," *Quest: A Feminist Quarterly* 4, no. 1 (1977): 88–96, reflect on the process.

16. Many attempts at unity began as an effort to justify women's struggles in marxist
terms, as if only that could make them legitimate. This anxiety lurks under many synthetic
attempts, although feminism has largely redirected its efforts from justifying itself within
any other perspective to developing its own.

17. While true from a feminist standpoint, this sweeping characterization does
minimize the wide varieties of marxist theories that have produced significantly different
analyses of women's situation. Juliet Mitchell, *Woman's Estate* (New York: Random House,
1971); Sheila Rowbotham, *Women, Resistance and Revolution: A History of Women and Revolution in the Modern World* (New York: Random House, 1972); Zillah Eisenstein, "Some Notes
on the Relations of Capitalist Patriarchy," in Eisenstein, ed. (n. 11 above); Eli Zaretsky, "Socialist Politics and the Family," *Socialist Revolution* 19 (January–March 1974): 83–99; Eli Zaretsky, "Capitalism, the Family and Personal Life," *Socialist Revolution* 3, nos. 1 and 2 (January–April 1973): 69–126, and no. 3 (May–June 1973): 19–70; Virginia Held, "Marx, Sex
and the Transformation of Society," in *Women and Philosophy: Toward a Theory of Liberation,*
ed. Carol C. Gould and Marx W. Wartofsky (New York: G. P. Putnam's Sons, 1976), pp.
168–84; Mihailo Marković, "Women's Liberation and Human Emancipation," ibid., pp.
145–67; Hal Draper, "Marx and Engels on Women's Liberation," in *Female Liberation,* ed.
Roberta Salper (New York: Alfred A. Knopf, Inc., 1972), pp. 83–107. No matter how
perceptive about the contributions of feminism or sympathetic to women's interests, these
attempts cast feminism, ultimately, as a movement *within* marxism: "I want to suggest that
the women's movement can provide the basis for building a new and authentic American
socialism" (Nancy Hartsock, "Feminist Theory and the Development of Revolutionary

the persuasion of the marxist, women become a caste, a stratum, a cultural group, a division in civil society, a secondary contradiction, or a nonantagonistic contradiction; women's liberation becomes a precondition, a measure of society's general emancipation, part of the superstructure, or an important aspect of the class struggle. Most commonly, women are reduced to some other category, such as "women workers," which is then treated as coextensive with all women.[18] Or, in what has become near reflex, women become "the family," as if this single form of women's confinement (then divided on class lines, then on racial lines) can be *presumed* the crucible of women's determination.[19] Or,

---

Strategy," in Eisenstein, ed. [n. 11 above], p. 57). Attempts at synthesis that push these limits include Gayle Rubin, "The Traffic in Women: Notes on the 'Political Economy' of Sex," in *Toward an Anthropology of Women*, ed. Rayna R. Reiter (New York: Monthly Review Press, 1975), pp. 157–210; Sheila Rowbotham, *Women's Liberation and the New Politics*, Spokesman Pamphlet, no. 17 (Bristol: Falling Wall Press, 1971); Annette Kuhn and AnnMarie Wolpe, "Feminism and Materialism," in *Feminism and Materialism: Women and Modes of Production*, ed. Annette Kuhn and AnnMarie Wolpe (London: Routledge & Kegan Paul, 1978); Ann Foreman, *Femininity as Alienation: Women and the Family in Marxism and Psychoanalysis* (London: Pluto Press, 1977); Meredith Tax and Jonathan Schwartz, "The Wageless Slave and the Proletarian," mimeograph (1972) (available from the author); Heidi I. Hartmann, "Capitalism, Patriarchy, and Job Segregation by Sex," *Signs: Journal of Women in Culture and Society* 1, no. 3, pt. 2 (Spring 1976): 137–69, and "The Unhappy Marriage of Marxism and Feminism: Towards a More Progressive Union," *Capital and Class* 8 (Summer 1979): 1–33; advocates of "wages for housework" mentioned in n. 10 above; and work by Linda Gordon, *Woman's Body, Woman's Right: A Social History of Birth Control in America* (New York: Grossman Publishers, 1976), pp. 403–18. Also see Linda Gordon, "The Struggle for Reproductive Freedom: Three Stages of Feminism," in Eisenstein, ed. (n. 11 above). Charlotte Bunch and Nancy Myron, *Class and Feminism* (Baltimore: Diana Press, 1974) exemplifies, without explicitly articulating, feminist method applied to class.

18. This tendency, again with important variations, is manifest in writings otherwise as diverse as Charnie Guettel, *Marxism and Feminism* (Toronto: Canadian Women's Education Press, 1974); Mary Alice Waters, "Are Feminism and Socialism Related?" in *Feminism and Socialism*, ed. Linda Jenness (New York: Pathfinder Press, 1972), pp. 18–26; Weather Underground, *Prairie Fire* (Underground, U.S.A.: Red Dragon Collective, 1975); Marjorie King, "Cuba's Attack on Women's Second Shift, 1974–1976," *Latin American Perspectives* 4, nos. 1 and 2 (Winter–Spring 1977): 106–19; Al Syzmanski, "The Socialization of Women's Oppression: A Marxist Theory of the Changing Position of Women in Advanced Capitalist Society," *Insurgent Sociologist* 6, no. 11 (Winter 1976): 31–58; "The Political Economy of Women," *Review of Radical Political Economics* 4, no. 3 (July 1972). See also Selma James, *Women, the Unions and Work, or What Is Not to Be Done* (Bristol: Falling Wall Press, 1976). This is true for "wages for housework" theory in the sense that it sees women as exploited because they do work—housework.

19. Engels (n. 14 above); Leon Trotsky, *Women and the Family*, trans. Max Eastman et al. (New York: Pathfinder Press, 1970); Evelyn Reed, *Woman's Evolution: From Matriarchal Clan to Patriarchal Family* (New York: Pathfinder Press, 1975); Lise Vogel, "The Earthly Family," *Radical America* 7, nos. 4–5 (July–October 1973): 9–50; Kollontai Collective, "The Politics of the Family: A Marxist View" (paper prepared for Socialist Feminist Conference at Yellow Springs, Ohio, July 4–6, 1975); Linda Limpus, *Liberation of Women: Sexual Repres-*

the marxist meaning of reproduction, the iteration of productive relations, is punned into an analysis of biological reproduction, as if wom-
en's bodily differences from men must account for their subordination
to men; and as if this social analogue to the biological makes women's
definition material, therefore based on a division of *labor* after all, therefore real, therefore (potentially) unequal.[20] Sexuality, if noticed at all, is,
like "every day life,"[21] analyzed in gender-neutral terms, as if its social
meaning can be presumed the same, or coequal, or complementary, for
women and men.[22] Although a unified theory of social inequality is
presaged in these strategies of subordination, staged progression, and
assimilation of women's concerns to left concerns, at most an uneven

---

sion and the Family (Boston: New England Free Press, n.d.); Marlene Dixon, "On the
Super-Exploitation of Women," *Synthesis* 1, no. 4 (Spring 1977): 1–11; David P. Levine and
Lynn S. Levine, "Problems in the Marxist Theory of the Family," photocopied (Depart-
ment of Economics, Yale University, July 1978). A common approach to treating women's
situation as coterminous with the family is to make women's circumstances the incident or
focus for a reconciliation of Marx with Freud. This approach, in turn, often becomes more
Freudian than marxist, without yet becoming feminist in the sense developed here. Juliet
Mitchell, *Psychoanalysis and Feminism: Freud, Reich, Laing and Women* (New York: Pantheon
Books, 1974); Eli Zaretsky, "Male Supremacy and the Unconscious," *Socialist Revolution* 21,
no. 22 (January 1975): 7–56; Nancy Chodorow, *The Reproduction of Mothering: Psychoanalysis
and the Sociology of Gender* (Berkeley: University of California Press, 1978). See also Herbert
Marcuse, "Socialist Feminism: The Hard Core of the Dream," *Edcentric: A Journal of Educational Change,* no. 31–32 (November 1974), pp. 7–44.

20. Sometimes "reproduction" refers to biological reproduction, sometimes to the
"reproduction" of daily life, as housework, sometimes both. Political Economy of Women
Group, "Women, the State and Reproduction since the 1930s," *On the Political Economy of
Women,* CSE Pamphlet no. 2, Stage 1 (London: Conference of Socialist Economists, 1977).
Family theories (n. 19 above) often analyze biological reproduction as a part of the family,
while theories of women as workers often see it as work (n. 18 above). For an analysis of
reproduction as an aspect of *sexuality,* in the context of an attempted synthesis, see Gordon,
"The Struggle for Reproductive Freedom: Three Stages of Feminism" (n. 17 above).

21. Henri Lefebvre, *Everyday Life in the Modern World* (London: Penguin Books, 1971);
Bruce Brown, *Marx, Freud and the Critique of Everyday Life: Toward a Permanent Cultural
Revolution* (New York: Monthly Review Press, 1973).

22. Herbert Marcuse, *Eros and Civilization: A Philosophical Inquiry into Freud* (New
York: Random House, 1955); Wilhelm Reich, *Sex-Pol: Essays, 1929–1934* (New York: Random House, 1972); Reimut Reiche, *Sexuality and Class Struggle* (London: New Left Books,
1970); Bertell Ollman, *Social and Sexual Revolution: Essays on Marx and Reich* (Boston: South
End Press, 1979); Red Collective, *The Politics of Sexuality in Capitalism* (London: Red Collective, 1973). This is also true of Michel Foucault, *The History of Sexuality,* vol. 1, *An Introduction* (New York: Random House, 1980). Although Foucault understands that sexuality
must be discussed at the same time as method, power, class, and the law, he does not
systematically comprehend the specificity of gender—women's and men's relation to these
factors—as a primary category for comprehending them. As one result, he cannot distinguish between the silence about sexuality that Victorianism has made into a noisy discourse
and the silence that has *been* women's sexuality under conditions of subordination by and to
men. Lacan notwithstanding, none of these theorists grasps sexuality *(including desire itself)*
as social, nor the content of its determination as a sexist social order that eroticizes potency
(as male) and victimization (as female).

combination is accomplished. However sympathetically, "the woman question" is always reduced to some other question, instead of being seen as *the* question, calling for analysis on its own terms.

Socialist-feminism stands before the task of synthesis as if nothing essential to either theory fundamentally opposes their wedding—indeed as if the union had already occurred and need only be celebrated. The failure to contain both theories on equal terms derives from the failure to confront each on its own ground: at the level of method. Method shapes each theory's vision of social reality. It identifies its central problem, group, and process, and creates as a consequence its distinctive conception of politics as such. Work and sexuality as concepts, then, derive their meaning and primacy from the *way* each theory approaches, grasps, interprets, and inhabits its world. Clearly, there is a relationship between how and what a theory sees: is there a marxist method without class? a feminist method without sex? Method in this sense organizes the apprehension of truth; it determines what counts as evidence and defines what is taken as verification. Instead of engaging the debate over which came (or comes) first, sex or class, the task for theory is to explore the conflicts and connections between the methods that found it meaningful to analyze social conditions in terms of those categories in the first place.[23]

23. Marxist method is not monolithic. Beginning with Marx, it has divided between an epistemology that embraces its own historicity and one that claims to portray a reality outside itself. In the first tendency, all thought, including social analysis, is ideological in the sense of being shaped by social being, the conditions of which are external to no theory. The project of theory is to create what Lukács described as "a theory of theory and a consciousness of consciousness" (Georg Lukács, "Class Consciousness," in *History and Class Consciousness: Studies in Marxist Dialectics* [Cambridge, Mass.: MIT Press, 1968], p. 47). Theory is a social activity engaged in the life situation of consciousness. See Jane Flax, "Epistemology and Politics: An Inquiry into Their Relation" (Ph.D. diss., Yale University, 1974). In the second tendency, theory is acontextual to the extent that it is correct. Real processes and thought processes are distinct; being has primacy over knowledge. The real can only be unified with knowledge of the real, as in dialectical materialism, because they have previously been separated. Nicos Poulantzas, *Political Power and Social Classes* (London: Verso, 1978), p. 14. Theory as a form of thought is methodologically set apart both from the illusions endemic to social reality—ideology—and from reality itself, a world defined as thinglike, independent of both ideology and theory. Ideology here means thought that is socially determined without being conscious of its determinations. Situated thought is as likely to produce "false consciousness" as access to truth. Theory, by definition, is, on the contrary, nonideological. Since ideology is interested, theory must be disinterested in order to penetrate myths that justify and legitimate the status quo. As Louis Althusser warned, "We know that a 'pure' science only exists on condition that it continually frees itself from ideology which occupies it, haunts it, or lies in wait for it" (*For Marx* [London: Verso, 1979], p. 170). When this attempt is successful, society is seen "from the point of view of class exploitation" (Louis Althusser, *Lenin and Philosophy* [New York: Monthly Review Press, 1971], p. 8). A theory that embraced its own historicity might see the scientific imperative itself as historically contingent. (On the objective standpoint, see text, pp. 537–42.) The problem with using scientific method to understand women's situation is that it is precisely unclear and crucial what is thought and what is thing, so that

Feminism has not been perceived as having a method, or even a central argument, with which to contend. It has been perceived not as a systematic analysis but as a loose collection of factors, complaints, and issues which, taken together, describe rather than explain the misfortunes of the female sex. The challenge is to demonstrate that feminism systematically converges upon a central explanation of sex inequality through an approach distinctive to its subject yet applicable to the whole of social life, including class.

Under the rubric of feminism, woman's situation has been explained as a consequence of biology[24] or of reproduction and mothering, social organizations of biology;[25] as caused by the marriage law[26] or, as

the separation itself becomes problematic. The second tendency grounds the marxist claim to be scientific; the first, its claim to capture as thought the flux of history. The first is more hospitable to feminism; the second has become the dominant tradition.

24. Simone de Beauvoir, *The Second Sex* (New York: Alfred A. Knopf, Inc., 1970). Her existential theory merges, in order to criticize, social meaning with biological determination in "anatomical destiny": "Here we have the key to the whole mystery. On the biological level a species is maintained only by creating itself anew; but this creation results only in repeating the same Life in more individuals. But man assures the repetition of Life while transcending Life through Existence; by this transcendence he creates values that deprive pure repetition of all value. . . . Her misfortune is to have been biologically destined for the repetition of Life when even in her own view Life does not carry within itself its reasons for being, reasons that are more important than life itself " (p. 59). She does not ask, for example, whether the social value placed upon "repetition of life," the fact that it is seen as iterative rather than generative, or the fact that women are more identified with it than are men, are themselves social artifacts of women's subordination, rather than existential derivations of biological fiat. Shulamith Firestone substitutes the contradiction of sex for class in a dialectical analysis, but nevertheless takes sex itself as presocial: "Unlike economic class, sex class sprang directly from a biological reality; men and women were created different, and not equally privileged. . . . The biological family is an inherently unequal power distribution" (*The Dialectic of Sex: The Case For Feminist Revolution* [New York: William Morrow & Co., 1972], p. 3). Her solutions are consistent: "The freeing of women from the tyranny of their reproductive biology by every means available, and the diffusion of childbearing and the childrearing role to the society as a whole, men as well as women" (p. 206). Susan Brownmiller (in *Against Our Will: Men, Women and Rape* [New York: Simon & Schuster, 1976]) expresses a biological theory of rape within a social critique of the centrality of rape to women's subordination: "Men's structural capacity to rape and woman's corresponding structural vulnerability are as basic to the physiology of both our sexes as the primal act of sex itself. Had it not been for this accident of biology, an accommodation requiring the locking together of two separate parts, penis and vagina, there would be neither copulation nor rape as we know it. . . . By anatomical fiat—the inescapable construction of their genital organs—the human male was a natural predator and the human female served as his natural prey" (pp. 4, 6). She does not seem to think it necessary to explain why women do not engulf men, an equal biological possibility. Criticizing the law for confusing intercourse with rape, she finds them biologically indistinguishable, leaving one wondering whether she, too, must alter or acquiesce in the biological.

25. Adrienne Rich, *Of Woman Born: Motherhood as Experience and Institution* (New York: W. W. Norton & Co., 1976); Chodorow (n. 19 above); Dorothy Dinnerstein, *The Mermaid and the Minotaur: Sexual Arrangements and Human Malaise* (New York: Harper & Row, 1977); Suzanne Arms, *Immaculate Deception: A New Look at Women and Childbirth in America* (Boston: Houghton Mifflin Co., 1975).

26. I take Mill's "The Subjection of Women" (n. 4 above) to be the original articulation

extensions, by the patriarchal family, becoming society as a "patriarchy";[27] or as caused by artificial gender roles and their attendant attitudes.[28] Informed by these attempts, but conceiving nature, law, the family, and roles as consequences, not foundations, I think that feminism fundamentally identifies sexuality as the primary social sphere of male power. The centrality of sexuality emerges not from Freudian conceptions[29] but from feminist practice on diverse issues, including abortion, birth control, sterilization abuse, domestic battery, rape, incest, lesbianism, sexual harassment, prostitution, female sexual slavery, and pornography. In all these areas, feminist efforts confront and change women's lives concretely and experientially. Taken together, they are producing a feminist political theory centering upon sexuality: its social determination, daily construction, birth to death expression, and ultimately male control.

Feminist inquiry into these specific issues began with a broad unmasking of the attitudes that legitimize and hide women's status, the ideational envelope that contains woman's body: notions that women desire and provoke rape, that girls' experiences of incest are fantasies, that career women plot and advance by sexual parlays, that prostitutes are lustful, that wife beating expresses the intensity of love. Beneath each of these ideas was revealed bare coercion and broad connections to woman's social definition as a sex. Research on sex roles, pursuing Simone de Beauvoir's insight that "one is not born, one rather becomes a woman,"[30] disclosed an elaborate process: how and what one learns to become one. Gender, cross-culturally, was found to be a learned quality, an acquired characteristic, an assigned status, with qualities that vary independent of biology and an ideology that attributes them to nature.[31]

---

of the theory, generalized in much contemporary feminism, that women are oppressed by "patriarchy," meaning a system originating in the household wherein the father dominates, the structure then reproduced throughout the society in gender relations.

27. In her "notes toward a theory of patriarchy" Kate Millett comprehends "sex as a status category with political implications," in which politics refers to "power-structured relationships, arrangements whereby one group of persons is controlled by another. . . . Patriarchy's chief institution is the family" (*Sexual Politics* [New York: Ballantine Books, 1969], pp. 32, 31, 45).

28. Sandra L. Bem and Daryl J. Bem, "Case Study of Nonconscious Ideology: Training the Woman to Know Her Place," in *Beliefs, Attitudes and Human Affairs,* ed. D. J. Bem (Belmont, Calif.: Brooks/Cole, 1970); Eleanor Emmons Maccoby and Carol Nagy Jacklin, *The Psychology of Sex Differences* (Stanford, Calif.: Stanford University Press, 1974); and Shirley Weitz, *Sex Roles: Biological, Psychological and Social Foundations* (New York: Oxford University Press, 1977).

29. Nor does it grow directly from Lacanian roots, although French feminists have contributed much to the developing theory from within that tradition.

30. De Beauvoir (n. 24 above), p. 249.

31. J. H. Block, "Conceptions of Sex Role: Some Cross-cultural and Longitudinal Perspectives," *American Psychologist* 28, no. 3 (June 1973): 512–26; Nancy Chodorow, "Being and Doing: A Cross-cultural Examination of the Socialization of Males and Females," in *Women in Sexist Society,* ed. V. Gornick and B. K. Moran (New York: Basic

The discovery that the female archetype is the feminine stereotype exposed "woman" as a social construction. Contemporary industrial society's version of her is docile, soft, passive, nurturant, vulnerable, weak, narcissistic, childlike, incompetent, masochistic, and domestic, made for child care, home care, and husband care. Conditioning to these values permeates the upbringing of girls and the images for emulation thrust upon women. Women who resist or fail, including those who never did fit—for example, black and lower-class women who cannot survive if they are soft and weak and incompetent,[32] assertively self-respecting women, women with ambitions of male dimensions—are considered less female, lesser women. Women who comply or succeed are elevated as models, tokenized by success on male terms or portrayed as consenting to their natural place and dismissed as having participated if they complain.

If the literature on sex roles and the investigations of particular issues are read in light of each other, each element of the female *gender* stereotype is revealed as, in fact, *sexual*. Vulnerability means the appearance/reality of easy sexual access; passivity means receptivity and disabled resistance, enforced by trained physical weakness; softness means pregnability by something hard. Incompetence seeks help as vulnerability seeks shelter, inviting the embrace that becomes the invasion, trading exclusive access for protection . . . from the same access. Domesticity nurtures the consequent progeny, proof of potency, and ideally waits at home dressed in saran wrap.[33] Woman's infantilization evokes pedophilia; fixation on dismembered body parts (the breast man, the leg man) evokes fetishism; idolization of vapidity, necrophilia. Narcissism insures that woman identifies with that image of herself that man holds up: "Hold still, we are going to do your portrait, so that you can begin looking like it right away."[34] Masochism means that pleasure in violation becomes her sensuality. Lesbians so violate the sexuality implicit in female gender stereotypes as not to be considered women at all.

Socially, femaleness means femininity, which means attractiveness

---

Books, 1971); R. R. Sears, "Development of Gender Role," in *Sex and Behavior,* ed. F. A. Beach (New York: John Wiley & Sons, 1965).

32. National Black Feminist Organization, "Statement of Purpose," *Ms.* (May 1974): "The black woman has had to be strong, yet we are persecuted for having survived" (p. 99). Johnnie Tillmon, "Welfare Is a Women's Issue," *Liberation News Service* (February 26, 1972), in *America's Working Women: A Documentary History, 1600 to the Present,* ed. Rosalyn Baxandall, Linda Gordon, and Susan Reverby (New York: Vintage Books, 1976): "On TV a woman learns that human worth means beauty and that beauty means being thin, white, young and rich. . . . In other words, an A.F.D.C. mother learns that being a 'real woman' means being all the things she isn't and having all the things she can't have" (pp. 357–58).

33. Marabel Morgan, *The Total Woman* (Old Tappan, N.J.: Fleming H. Revell Co., 1973). "Total Woman" makes blasphemous sexuality into a home art, redomesticating what prostitutes have marketed as forbidden.

34. Cixous (n. 1 above), p. 892.

to men, which means sexual attractiveness, which means sexual availability on male terms.[35] What defines woman as such is what turns men on. Good girls are "attractive," bad girls "provocative." Gender socialization is the process through which women come to identify themselves as sexual beings, as beings that exist for men. It is that process through which women internalize (make their own) a male image of their sexuality *as* their identity as women.[36] It is not just an illusion. Feminist inquiry into women's own experience of sexuality revises prior comprehensions of sexual issues and transforms the concept of sexuality itself—its determinants and its role in society and politics. According to this revision, one "becomes a woman"—acquires and identifies with the status of the female—not so much through physical maturation or inculcation into appropriate role behavior as through the experience of sexuality: a complex unity of physicality, emotionality, identity, and status affirmation. Sex as gender and sex as sexuality are thus defined in terms of each other, but it is sexuality that determines gender, not the other way around. This, the central but never stated insight of Kate Millett's *Sexual Politics*,[37] resolves the duality in the term "sex" itself: what women learn in order to "have sex," in order to "become women"— woman as gender—comes through the experience of, and is a condition for, "having sex"—woman as sexual object for man, the use of women's sexuality by men. Indeed, to the extent sexuality is social, women's sexuality *is* its use, just as our femaleness *is* its alterity.

Many issues that appear sexual from this standpoint have not been seen as such, nor have they been seen as defining a politics. Incest, for example, is commonly seen as a question of distinguishing the real evil, a crime against the family, from girlish seductiveness or fantasy. Contraception and abortion have been framed as matters of reproduction and fought out as proper or improper social constraints on nature. Or they are seen as private, minimizing state intervention into intimate relations. Sexual harassment was a nonissue, then became a problem of distinguishing personal relationships or affectionate flirtation from abuse of position. Lesbianism, when visible, has been either a perversion or not, to be tolerated or not. Pornography has been considered a question of freedom to speak and depict the erotic, as against the obscene or violent. Prostitution has been understood either as mutual lust and degradation or an equal exchange of sexual need for economic need. The issue in rape has been whether the intercourse was provoked/mutually

35. Indications are that this is true not only in Western industrial society; further cross-cultural research is definitely needed.

36. Love justifies this on the emotional level. Firestone (n. 24 above), chap. 6.

37. Millett's analysis is pervasively animated by the sense that women's status is sexually determined. It shapes her choice of authors, scenes, and themes and underlies her most pointed criticisms of women's depiction. Her explicit discussion, however, vacillates between clear glimpses of that argument and statements nearly to the contrary.

desired, or whether it was forced: was it sex or violence? Across and beneath these issues, sexuality itself has been divided into parallel provinces: traditionally, religion or biology; in modern transformation, morality or psychology. Almost never politics.

In a feminist perspective, the formulation of each issue, in the terms just described, expresses ideologically the same interest that the problem it formulates expresses concretely: the interest from the male point of view. Women experience the sexual events these issues codify[38] as a cohesive whole within which each resonates. The defining theme of that whole is the male pursuit of control over women's sexuality—men not as individuals nor as biological beings, but as a gender group characterized by maleness as socially constructed, of which this pursuit is definitive. For example, women who need abortions see contraception as a struggle not only for control over the biological products of sexual expression but over the social rhythms and mores of sexual intercourse. These norms often appear hostile to women's self-protection even when the technology is at hand. As an instance of such norms, women notice that sexual harassment looks a great deal like ordinary heterosexual initiation under conditions of gender inequality. Few women are in a position to refuse unwanted sexual initiatives. That consent rather than nonmutuality is the line between rape and intercourse further exposes the inequality in normal social expectations. So does the substantial amount of male force allowed in the focus on the woman's resistance, which tends to be disabled by socialization to passivity. If sex is ordinarily accepted as something men do *to* women, the better question would be whether consent is a meaningful concept. Penetration (often by a penis) is also substantially more central to both the legal definition of rape and the male definition of sexual intercourse than it is to women's sexual violation or sexual pleasure. Rape in marriage expresses the male sense of entitlement to access to women they annex; incest extends it. Although most women are raped by men they know, the closer the relation, the less women are allowed to claim it was rape. Pornography becomes difficult to distinguish from art and ads once it is clear that what is degrading to women is compelling to the consumer. Prostitutes sell the unilaterality that pornography advertises. That most of these issues codify behavior that is neither countersystemic nor exceptional is supported by women's experience as victims: these behaviors are either not illegal or are effectively permitted on a large scale. As women's experience blurs the lines between deviance and normalcy, it obliterates the distinction between abuses *of* women and the social definition of what a woman *is*.[39]

38. Each of these issues is discussed at length in the second part of this article "Toward Feminist Jurisprudence"), forthcoming.

39. On abortion and contraception, see Kristin Luker, *Taking Chances: Abortion and the Decision Not to Contracept* (Berkeley: University of California Press, 1975). On rape, see Diana E. H. Russell, *Rape: The Victim's Perspective* (New York: Stein & Day, 1977); Andrea

These investigations reveal rape, incest, sexual harassment, pornography, and prostitution as not primarily abuses of physical force, violence, authority, or economics. They are abuses of sex. They need not and do not rely for their coerciveness upon forms of enforcement other than the sexual; that those forms of enforcement, at least in this context, are themselves sexualized is closer to the truth. They are not the erotization *of* something else; eroticism *itself* exists in their form. Nor are they perversions of art and morality. They *are* art and morality from the male point of view. They are sexual because they express the relations, values, feelings, norms, and behaviors of the culture's sexuality, in which considering things like rape, pornography, incest, or lesbianism deviant, perverse, or blasphemous is part of their excitement potential.

Sexuality, then, is a form of power. Gender, as socially constructed, embodies it, not the reverse. Women and men are divided by gender, made into the sexes as we know them, by the social requirements of heterosexuality, which institutionalizes male sexual dominance and female sexual submission.[40] If this is true, sexuality is the linchpin of gender inequality.

A woman is a being who identifies and is identified as one whose sexuality exists for someone else, who is socially male. Women's sexuality is the capacity to arouse desire in that someone. If what is sexual about a woman is what the male point of view requires for excitement, have male requirements so usurped its terms as to have become them? Considering women's sexuality in this way forces confrontation with whether there is any such thing. Is women's sexuality its absence? If being *for* another is the whole of women's sexual construction, it can be no more escaped by separatism, men's temporary concrete absence, than eliminated or qualified by permissiveness, which, in this context, looks like women emulating male roles. As Susan Sontag said: "The question is: *what* sexuality are women to be liberated to enjoy? Merely to remove the onus placed upon the sexual expressiveness of women is a hollow victory if the sexuality they become freer to enjoy remains the old one that converts women into objects. . . . This already 'freer' sexuality mostly reflects a

Medea and Kathleen Thompson, *Against Rape* (New York: Farrar, Straus & Giroux, 1974); Lorenne N. G. Clark and Debra Lewis, *Rape: The Price of Coercive Sexuality* (Toronto: Women's Press, 1977); Susan Griffin, *Rape: The Power of Consciousness* (San Francisco: Harper & Row, 1979); Kalamu ya Salaam, "Rape: A Radical Analysis from the African-American Perspective," in his *Our Women Keep Our Skies from Falling* (New Orleans: Nkombo, 1980), pp. 25–40. On incest, see Judith Herman and Lisa Hirschman, "Father-Daughter Incest," *Signs: Journal of Women in Culture and Society* 2, no. 1 (Summer 1977): 735–56. On sexual harassment, see my *Sexual Harassment of Working Women* (New Haven, Conn.: Yale University Press, 1979). On pornography, see Andrea Dworkin, *Pornography: Men Possessing Women* (New York: G. P. Putnam's Sons, 1981).

40. Ellen Morgan, *The Erotization of Male Dominance/Female Submission* (Pittsburgh: Know, Inc., 1975); Adrienne Rich, "Compulsory Heterosexuality and Lesbian Existence," *Signs: Journal of Women in Culture and Society* 5, no. 4 (Summer 1980): 631–60.

spurious idea of freedom: the right of each person, briefly, to exploit and dehumanize someone else. Without a change in the very norms of sexuality, the liberation of women is a meaningless goal. Sex as such is not liberating for women. Neither is more sex."[41] Does removing or revising gender constraints upon sexual expression change or even challenge its norms?[42] This question ultimately is one of social determination in the broadest sense: its mechanism, permeability, specificity, and totality. If women are socially defined such that female sexuality cannot be lived or spoken or felt or even somatically sensed apart from its enforced definition, so that it *is* its own lack, then there is no such thing as a woman as such, there are only walking embodiments of men's projected needs. For feminism, asking whether there is, socially, a female sexuality is the same as asking whether women exist.

Methodologically, the feminist concept of the personal as political is an attempt to answer this question. Relinquishing all instinctual, natural, transcendental, and divine authority, this concept grounds women's sexuality on purely relational terrain, anchoring women's power and accounting for women's discontent in the same world they stand against. The personal as political is not a simile, not a metaphor, and not an analogy. It does not mean that what occurs in personal life is similar to, or comparable with, what occurs in the public arena. It is not an application of categories from social life to the private world, as when Engels (followed by Bebel) says that in the family the husband is the bourgeois and the wife represents the proletariat.[43] Nor is it an equation of two spheres which remain analytically distinct, as when Reich interprets state behavior in sexual terms,[44] or a one-way infusion of one sphere into the other, as when Lasswell interprets political behavior as the displacement

41. Susan Sontag, "The Third World of Women," *Partisan Review* 40, no. 2 (1973): 180–206, esp. 188.

42. The same question could be asked of lesbian sadomasochism: when women engage in ritualized sexual dominance and submission, does it express the male structure or subvert it? The answer depends upon whether one has a social or biological definition of gender and of sexuality and then upon the content of these definitions. Lesbian sex, simply as sex between women, does not by definition transcend the erotization of dominance and submission and their social equation with maculinity and femininity. Butch/femme as *sexual* (not just gender) role playing, together with parallels in lesbian sadomasochism's "top" and "bottom," suggest to me that sexual conformity extends far beyond gender object mores. For a contrary view see Pat Califia, *Sapphistry: The Book of Lesbian Sexuality* (Tallahassee, Fla.: Naiad Press, 1980); Gayle Rubin, "Sexual Politics, the New Right and the Sexual Fringe," in *What Color Is Your Handkerchief: A Lesbian S/M Sexuality Reader* (Berkeley, Calif.: Samois, 1979), pp. 28–35.

43. Engels (n. 14 above); August Bebel, *Women under Socialism*, trans. Daniel DeLeon (New York: New York Labor News Press, 1904).

44. Reich (n. 22 above). He examines fascism, for example, as a question of how the masses can be made to desire their own repression. This might be seen as a precursor to the feminist question of how female desire *itself* can become the lust for self-annihilation.

of personal problems into public objects.[45] It means that women's distinctive experience as women occurs within that sphere that has been socially lived as the personal—private, emotional, interiorized, particular, individuated, intimate—so that what it is to *know* the *politics* of woman's situation is to know women's personal lives.

The substantive principle governing the authentic politics of women's personal lives is pervasive powerlessness to men, expressed and reconstituted daily *as* sexuality. To say that the personal is political means that gender as a division of power is discoverable and verifiable through women's intimate experience of sexual objectification, which is definitive of and synonymous with women's lives as gender female. Thus, to feminism, the personal is epistemologically the political, and its epistemology is its politics.[46] Feminism, on this level, is the theory of women's point of view. It is the theory of Judy Grahn's "common woman"[47] speaking Adrienne Rich's "common language."[48] Consciousness raising is its quintessential expression. Feminism does not appropriate an existing method—such as scientific method—and apply it to a different sphere of society to reveal its preexisting political aspect. Consciousness raising not only comes to know different things as politics; it necessarily comes to know them in a different way. Women's experience of politics, of life as sex object, gives rise to its own method of appropriating that reality: feminist method.[49] As its own kind of social analysis,

45. Harold Lasswell, *Psychoanalysis and Politics* (Chicago: University of Chicago Press, 1930).

46. The aphorism "Feminism is the theory; lesbianism is the practice" has been attributed to TiGrace Atkinson by Anne Koedt, "Lesbianism and Feminism," in *Radical Feminism*, ed. Anne Koedt, Ellen Levine, and Anita Rapone (New York: New York Times Book Co., 1973), p. 246. See also Radicalesbians, "The Woman Identified Woman," ibid., pp. 24–45; TiGrace Atkinson, "Lesbianism & Feminism," *Amazon Odyssey: The First Collection of Writings by the Poiitical Pioneer of the Women's Movement* (New York: Links Books, 1974), pp. 83–88; Jill Johnston, *Lesbian Nation: The Feminist Solution* (New York: Simon & Schuster, 1973), pp. 167, 185, 278. This aphorism accepts a simplistic view of the relationship between theory and practice. Feminism reconceptualizes the connection between being and thinking such that it may be more accurate to say that feminism is the epistemology of which lesbianism is an ontology. But see n. 56 below on this latter distinction as well.

47. Judy Grahn, *The Work of a Common Woman* (New York: St. Martin's Press, 1978). "The Common Woman" poems are on pp. 61–73.

48. Adrienne Rich, "Origins and History of Consciousness," in *The Dream of a Common Language: Poems, 1974–1977* (New York: W. W. Norton & Co., 1978), p. 7. This means that a women's movement exists wherever women identify collectively to resist/reclaim their determinants as such. This feminist redefinition of consciousness requires a corresponding redefinition of the process of mobilizing it: feminist *organizing*. The transformation from subordinate group to movement parallels Marx's distinction between a class "in itself " and a class "for itself." See Karl Marx, *The Poverty of Philosophy* (New York: International Publishers, 1963), p. 195.

49. In addition to the references in n. 1, see Sandra Lee Bartky, "Toward a

within yet outside the male paradigm just as women's lives are, it has a distinctive theory of the *relation* between method and truth, the individual and her social surroundings, the presence and place of the natural and spiritual in culture and society, and social being and causality itself.

Having been objectified as sexual beings while stigmatized as ruled by subjective passions, women reject the distinction between knowing subject and known object—the division between subjective and objective postures—as the means to comprehend social life. Disaffected from objectivity, having been its prey, but excluded from its world through relegation to subjective inwardness, women's interest lies in overthrowing the distinction itself. Proceeding connotatively and analytically at the same time, consciousness raising is at once common sense expression and critical articulation of concepts. Taking situated feelings and common detail (common here meaning both ordinary and shared) as the matter of political analysis, it explores the terrain that is most damaged, most contaminated, yet therefore most women's own, most intimately known, most open to reclamation. The process can be described as a collective "sympathetic internal experience of the gradual construction of [the] system according to its inner necessity,"[50] as a strategy for deconstructing it.

Through consciousness raising, women grasp the collective reality of women's condition from within the perspective of that experience, not from outside it. The claim that a sexual politics exists and is socially fundamental is grounded in the claim of feminism *to* women's perspective, not from it. Its claim to women's perspective *is* its claim to truth. In its account of itself, women's point of view contains a duality analogous

---

Phenomenology of Feminist Consciousness," in *Feminism and Philosophy*, ed. Mary Vetterling-Braggin et al. (Totowa, N.J.: Littlefield, Adams & Co., 1977). Susan Griffin reflects/creates the process: "We do not rush to speech. We allow ourselves to be moved. We do not attempt objectivity. . . . We said we had experienced this ourselves. I felt so much for her then, she said, with her head cradled in my lap, she said, I knew what to do. We said we were moved to see her go through what we had gone through. We said this gave us some knowledge" (*Woman and Nature: The Roaring Inside Her* [New York: Harper & Row, 1978], p. 197). Assertions such as "our politics begin with our feelings" have emerged from the practice of consciousness raising. Somewhere between mirror-reflexive determination and transcendence of determinants, "feelings" are seen as both access to truth—at times a bit phenomenologically transparent—and an artifact of politics. There is both suspicion of feelings and affirmation of their health. They become simultaneously an inner expression of outer lies and a less contaminated resource for verification. See San Francisco Redstockings, "Our Politics Begin with Our Feelings," in *Masculine/Feminine: Readings in Sexual Mythology and the Liberation of Women*, ed. Betty Roszak and Theodore Roszak (New York: Harper & Row, 1969).

50. Fredric Jameson, *Marxism and Form* (Princeton, N.J.: Princeton University Press, 1971), p. xi. Jameson is describing dialectical method: "I have felt that the dialectical method can be acquired only by a concrete working through of detail, by a sympathetic internal experience of the gradual construction of a system according to its inner necessity."

to that of the marxist proletariat: determined by the reality the theory explodes, it thereby claims special access to that reality.[51] Feminism does not see its view as subjective, partial, or undetermined but as a critique of the purported generality, disinterestedness, and universality of prior accounts. These have not been half right but have invoked the wrong whole. Feminism not only challenges masculine partiality but questions the universality imperative itself: Aperspectivity is revealed as a strategy of male hegemony.[52]

"Representation of the world," de Beauvoir writes, "like the world itself, is the work of men; they describe it from their own point of view, which they confuse with the absolute truth."[53] The parallel between representation and construction should be sustained: men *create* the world from their own point of view, which then *becomes* the truth to be described. This is a closed system, not anyone's confusion. *Power to create the world from one's point of view is power in its male form.*[54] The male epistemological stance, which corresponds to the world it creates, is ob-

51. This distinguishes both feminism and at least a strain in marxism from Freud: "My self-analysis is still interrupted and I have realized the reason. I can only analyze my self with the help of knowledge obtained objectively (like an outsider). Genuine self-analysis is impossible, otherwise there would be no [neurotic] illness" (Sigmund Freud, Letter to Wilhelm Fleiss, #71, October 15, 1887, quoted in Mitchell, *Psychoanalysis and Feminism: Freud, Reich, Laing and Women* [n. 19 above], pp. 61–62, see also p. 271). Given that introspection is not analytically dispositive to Freud, the collective self-knowledge of feminism might be collective neurosis. Although it is interpersonal, it is still an insider to its world.

52. Feminist scholars are beginning to criticize objectivity from different disciplinary standpoints, although not as frontally as here, nor in its connection with objectification. Julia Sherman and Evelyn Torton Beck, eds., *The Prism of Sex: Essays in the Sociology of Knowledge* (Madison: University of Wisconsin Press, 1979); Margrit Eichler, *The Double Standard: A Feminist Critique of Feminist Social Science* (New York: St. Martin's Press, 1980); Evelyn Fox Keller, "Gender and Science," *Psychoanalysis and Contemporary Thought* 1, no. 3 (1978): 409–33. Adrienne Rich, "Toward a Woman-centered University," in *Woman and the Power to Change*, ed. Florence Howe (New York: McGraw-Hill Book Co., 1975).

53. De Beauvoir (n. 24 above). De Beauvoir had not pursued the analysis to the point I suggest here by 1979, either. See her "Introduction," in Marks and de Courtivron, eds. (n. 1 above), pp. 41–56.

54. This does not mean all men *have* male power equally. American Black men, for instance, have substantially less of it. But to the extent that they cannot create the world from their point of view, they find themselves unmanned, castrated, literally or figuratively. This supports rather than qualifies the sex specificity of the argument without resolving the relationship between racism and sexism, or the relation of either to class. Although historically receiving more attention, race and nation are otherwise analogous to sex in the place they occupy for, and the challenge they pose to, marxist theory. If the real basis of history and activity is class and class conflict, what, other than "false consciousness," is one to make of the historical force of sexism, racism, and nationalism? Similarly, positing a supra-class unit with true meaning, such as "Black people," is analytically parallel to positing a supra-class (and supra-racial) unit "women." Treating race, nation, and sex as lesser included problems has been the major response of marxist theory to such challenges. Any relationship *between* sex and race tends to be left entirely out of account, since they are considered parallel "strata." Attempts to confront the latter issue include Adrienne Rich,

jectivity: the ostensibly noninvolved stance, the view from a distance and from no particular perspective, apparently transparent to its reality. It does not comprehend its own perspectivity, does not recognize what it sees as subject like itself, or that the way it apprehends its world is a form of its subjugation and presupposes it. The objectively knowable is object. Woman through male eyes is sex object, that by which man knows himself at once as man and as subject.[55] What is objectively known corresponds to the world and can be verified by pointing to it (as science does) because the world itself is controlled from the same point of view.[56]

"Disloyal to Civilization: Feminism, Racism and Gynephobia," in *On Lies, Secrets and Silence: Selected Essays, 1966–1978* (New York: W. W. Norton & Co., 1979); Selma James, *Sex, Race and Class* (Bristol: Falling Wall Press, 1967); R. Coles and J. H. Coles, *Women of Crisis* (New York: Dell Publishing Co., Delacorte Press, 1978); Socialist Women's Caucus of Louisville, "The Racist Use of Rape and the Rape Charge" (Louisville, Ky., ca. 1977); Angela Davis, "The Role of Black Women in the Community of Slaves," *Black Scholar* 3, no. 4 (December 1971): 2–16; The Combahee River Collective, "A Black Feminist Statement," in Eisenstein, ed. (n. 11 above); Karen Getman, "Relations of Gender and Sexuality during the Period of Institutional Slavery in the Southern Colonies" (working paper, Yale University, 1980); E. V. Spelman, "Feminism, Sexism and Racism" (University of Massachusetts, 1981); Cherríe Moraga and Gloria Anzaldúa, eds., *This Bridge Called My Back: Writings of Radical Women of Color* (Watertown, Mass.: Persephone Press, 1981).

55. This suggests a way in which marxism and feminism may be reciprocally illuminating, without, for the moment, confronting the deep divisions between them. Marxism comprehends the *object* world's *social* existence: how objects are constituted, embedded in social life, infused with meaning, created in systematic and structural relation. Feminism comprehends the *social* world's *object* existence: how women are created in the image of, and as, things. The object world's social existence varies with the structure of production. Suppose that wherever the sexes are unequal, women are objects, but what it means to be an object varies with the productive relations that create objects as social. Thus, under primitive exchange systems, women are exchange objects. Under capitalism, women appear as commodities. That is, women's sexuality as object for men is valued as objects are under capitalism, namely as commodities. Under true communism, women would be collective sex objects. If women have universally been sex objects, it is also true that matter as the acted-upon in social life has a history. If women have always been things, it is also true that things have not always had the same meaning. Of course, this does not explain sex inequality. It merely observes, once that inequality exists, the way its dynamics may interact with the social organization of production. Sexual objectification may also have a separate history, with its own periods, forms, structures, technology, and, potentially, revolutions.

56. In a sense, this realization collapses the epistemology/ontology distinction altogether. What is purely an ontological category, a category of "being" free of social perception? Surely not the self/other distinction. Ultimately, the feminist approach turns social inquiry into political hermeneutics: inquiry into situated meaning, one in which the inquiry itself participates. A feminist political hermeneutics would be a theory of the answer to the question, What does it mean? that would comprehend that the first question to address is, To whom? within a context that comprehends gender as a social division of power. Useful general treatments of hermeneutical issues (which nevertheless proceed as if feminism, or a specific problematic of women, did not exist) include Josef Bleicher, *Contemporary Hermeneutics: Hermeneutics as Method, Philosophy and Critique* (London: Routledge & Kegan Paul, 1980); Hans-Georg Gadamer, *Philosophical Hermeneutics,* trans. David E. Linge (Berkeley: University of California Press, 1976); Rosalind Coward and John Ellis,

Combining, like any form of power, legitimation with force, male power extends beneath the representation of reality to its construction: it makes women (as it were) and so verifies (makes true) who women "are" in its view, simultaneously confirming its way of being and its vision of truth. The eroticism that corresponds to this is "the use of things to experience self."[57] As a coerced pornography model put it, "You do it, you do it, and you do it; then you become it."[58] The fetish speaks feminism.

Objectification makes sexuality a material reality of women's lives, not just a psychological, attitudinal, or ideological one.[59] It obliterates

---

Language and Materialism: Developments in Semiology and the Theory of the Subject (London: Routledge & Kegan Paul, 1977). Mary Daly approaches the ontological issue when she says that ontological theory without an understanding of sex roles can not be "really ontological" (*Beyond God the Father: Toward a Philosophy of Women's Liberation* [Boston: Beacon Press, 1973], p. 124). But both in this work, and more pervasively in *Gyn/Ecology: The Metaethics of Radical Feminism* (Boston: Beacon Press, 1978), the extent of the *creation* of women's *reality* by male epistemology, therefore the extent and nature of women's damage, is slighted in favor of a critique of its lies and distortions. Consider her investigation of suttee, a practice in which Indian widows are supposed to throw themselves upon their dead husband's funeral pyres in grief (and to keep pure), in which Daly focuses upon demystifying its alleged voluntary aspects. Women are revealed drugged, pushed, browbeaten, or otherwise coerced by the dismal and frightening prospect of widowhood in Indian society (Daly, *Gyn/Ecology*, pp. 113–33). Neglected—both as to the women involved and as to the implications for the entire diagnosis of sexism as illusion—are suttee's deepest victims: women who want to die when their husband dies, who volunteer for self-immolation because they believe their life is over when his is. See also Duncan Kennedy, "The Structure of Blackstone's Commentaries," *Buffalo Law Review* 28, no. 2 (1979): 211–12.

57. Dworkin (n. 39 above), p. 124. Explicitness is the aesthetic, the allowed sensibility, of objectified eroticism. Under this norm, written and pictured evocations of sexuality are compulsively literal. What it is to arouse sexuality through art is to recount events "objectively," i.e., verbally and visually to re-present who did what to whom. On the "dynamic of total explicitness" as stylization, explored in the context of the "foremost insight of the modern novel: the interweaving, the symbolic and structural interchange between economic and sexual relations," see George Steiner, "Eros and Idiom: 1975," in *On Difficulty and Other Essays* (New York: Oxford University Press, 1978), p. 100: "Chasteness of discourse [in George Eliot's work] acts not as a limitation but as a liberating privacy within which the character can achieve the paradox of autonomous life" (p. 107). This connects the lack of such liberating privacy for women—in life, law, or letters—with women's lack of autonomy and authentic erotic vocabulary.

58. Linda Lovelace, *Ordeal* (Secaucus, N.J.: Citadel Press, 1980). The same may be true for class. See Richard Sennett and Jonathan Cobb, *The Hidden Injuries of Class* (New York: Alfred A. Knopf, Inc., 1972). Marxism teaches that exploitation/degradation somehow necessarily produces resistance/revolution. Women's experience with sexual exploitation/degradation teaches that it also produces grateful complicity in exchange for survival and self-loathing to the point of the extinction of self, respect for which makes resistance conceivable. The problem here is not to explain why women acquiesce in their condition but why they ever do anything but.

59. The critique of sexual objectification first became visibly explicit in the American women's movement with the disruption of the Miss America Pageant in September 1968. Robin Morgan, "Women Disrupt the Miss America Pageant," *Rat* (September 1978), reprinted in *Going Too Far: The Personal Chronicle of a Feminist* (New York: Random House, 1977), pp. 62–67. The most compelling account of sexual objectification I know is con-

the mind/matter distinction that such a division is premised upon. Like the value of a commodity, women's sexual desirability is fetishized: it is made to appear a quality of the object itself, spontaneous and inherent, independent of the social relation which creates it, uncontrolled by the force that requires it. It helps if the object cooperates: hence, the vaginal

---

tained in the following description of women's depiction in art and the media: "According to usage and conventions which are at last being questioned but have by no means been overcome, the social presence of a woman is different in kind from that of a man. . . . A man's presence suggests what he is capable of doing to you or for you. By contrast, a woman's presence expresses her own attitude to herself, and *defines what can and cannot be done to her.* . . . To be born a woman has been to be born, within an allotted and confined space, into the keeping of men. The social presence of women has developed as a result of their ingenuity in living under such tutelage within such a limited space. But this has been at the cost of a woman's self being split into two. A woman must continually watch herself. She is almost continually accompanied by her own image of herself. . . . she comes to consider the surveyor and the surveyed within her as the two constituent yet always distinct elements of her identity as a woman. She has to survey everything she is and everything she does because how she appears to others, and ultimately how she appears to men, *is of crucial importance for what is normally thought of as the success of her life.* Her own sense of being in herself is supplanted by a sense of being appreciated as herself by another. One might simplify this by saying: men act; women appear. *Men look at women. Women watch themselves being looked at.* This determines not only most relations between men and women but also the relation of women to themselves. The surveyor of woman in herself is male: the surveyed, female. Thus she turns herself into an object—and most particularly an object of vision: a sight" (John Berger, *Ways of Seeing* [New York: Viking Press, 1972], pp. 46, 47 [my emphasis]). All that is missing here is an explicit recognition that this process embodies what the sexuality of women is about and that it expresses an inequality in social power. In a feminist context, aesthetics, including beauty and imagery, becomes the most political of subjects. See Purple September Staff, "The Normative Status of Heterosexuality," in *Lesbianism and the Women's Movement,* ed. Charlotte Bunch and Nancy Myron (Baltimore: Diana Press, 1975), pp. 79–83, esp. pp. 80–81.

Marxist attempts to deal with sexual objectification have not connected the issue with the politics of aesthetics or with subordination: "She becomes a sexual object only in a relationship, when she allows man to treat her in a certain depersonalizing, degrading way; and vice versa, a woman does not become a sexual subject simply by neglecting her appearance. There is no reason why a women's liberation activist should not try to look pretty and attractive. One of the universal human aspirations of all times was to raise reality to the level of art. . . . Beauty is a value in itself" (Marković [n. 17 above], pp. 165–66). Other attempts come closer, still without achieving the critique, e.g., Power of Women Collective, "What Is a Sex Object?" *Socialist Woman: A Journal of the International Marxist Group* 1, no. 1 (March/April 1974): 7; Dana Densmore, "On the Temptation to Be a Beautiful Object," in *Toward a Sociology of Women,* ed. C. Safilios-Rothschild (Lexington, Mass.: Xerox Publication, 1972); Rita Arditti, "Women as Objects: Science and Sexual Politics," *Science for the People,* vol. 6, no. 5 (September 1974); Charley Shively, "Cosmetics as an Act of Revolution," *Fag Rag* (Boston), reprinted in *Pink Triangles: Radical Perspectives on Gay Liberation,* ed. Pam Mitchell (Boston: Alyson Publication, 1980). Resentment of white beauty standards is prominent in Black feminism. Beauty standards incapable of achievement by any woman seem to fulfill a dual function. They keep women buying products (to the profit of capitalism) and competing for men (to be affirmed by the standard that matters). That is, they make women feel ugly and inadequate so we need men and money to defend against rejection/self-revulsion. Black women are further from being able concretely to achieve the standard that no woman can ever achieve, or it would lose its point.

orgasm;[60] hence, faked orgasms altogether.[61] Women's sexualness, like male prowess, is no less real for being mythic. It is embodied. Commodities do have value, but only because value is a social property arising from the totality of the same social relations which, unconscious of their determination, fetishize it. Women's bodies possess no less real desirability—or, probably, desire. Sartre exemplifies the problem on the epistemological level: "But if I desire a house, or a glass of water, or a woman's body, how could this body, this glass, this piece of property reside in my desire and how can my desire be anything but the consciousness of these objects as desirable?"[62] Indeed. Objectivity is the methodological stance of which objectification is the social process. Sexual objectification is the primary process of the subjection of women. It unites act with word, construction with expression, perception with enforcement, myth with reality. Man fucks woman; subject verb object.

The distinction between objectification and alienation is called into question by this analysis. Objectification in marxist materialism is thought to be the foundation of human freedom, the work process whereby a subject becomes embodied in products and relationships.[63] Alienation is the socially contingent distortion of that process, a reification of products and relations which prevents them from being, and being seen as, dependent on human agency.[64] But from the point of view of the object, objectification *is* alienation. For women, there is no

60. Anne Koedt, "The Myth of the Vaginal Orgasm," in Koedt et al., eds. (n. 46 above), pp. 198–207; TiGrace Atkinson, "Vaginal Orgasm as a Mass Hysterical Survival Response," in *Amazon Odyssey* (n. 46 above), pp. 5–8.

61. Shere Hite, *The Hite Report: A Nationwide Study of Female Sexuality* (New York: Dell Publishing Co., 1976), "Do you ever fake orgasms?" pp. 257–66.

62. Jean-Paul Sartre, *Existential Psychoanalysis*, trans. Hazel E. Barnes (Chicago: Henry Regnery Co., 1973), p. 20. A similar treatment of "desire" occurs in Deleuze and Guattari's description of man as "desiring-machine," of man in relation to the object world: "Not man as the king of creation, but rather as the being who is in intimate contact with the profound life of all forms or all types of beings, who is responsible for even the stars and animal life, and who ceaselessly plugs an organ-machine into an energy-machine, a tree into his body, a breast into his mouth, the sun into his asshole; the eternal custodian of the machines of the universe" (Deleuze and Guattari [n. 1 above], p. 4). Realizing that women, socially, inhabit the object realm transforms this discourse into a quite accurate description of the feminist analysis of women's desirability to man—the breast in his mouth, the energy machine into which he ceaselessly plugs an organ machine. Extending their inquiry into the extent to which this kind of objectification of woman is specific to capitalism (either as a process or in its particular form) does little to redeem the sex blindness (blind to the sex of its standpoint) of this supposedly general theory. Women are not desiring-machines.

63. Peter Berger and Stanley Pullberg, "Reification and the Sociological Critique of Consciousness," *New Left Review*, vol. 35 (January–February 1966); Herbert Marcuse, "The Foundation of Historical Materialism," in *Studies in Critical Philosophy*, trans. Joris De Bres (Boston: Beacon Press, 1972); Karl Klare, "Law-Making as Praxis," *Telos* 12, no. 2 (Summer 1979): 123–35, esp. 131.

64. Istvan Meszaros, *Marx's Theory of Alienation* (London: Merlin Press, 1972); Bertell Ollman, *Alienation: Marx's Conception of Man in Capitalist Society* (London: Cambridge University Press, 1971); Marcuse, *Eros and Civilization* (n. 22 above), pp. 93–94, 101–2.

distinction between objectification and alienation because women have not authored objectifications, we have been them. Women have been the nature, the matter, the acted upon, to be subdued by the acting subject seeking to embody himself in the social world. Reification is not just an illusion to the reified; it is also their reality. The alienated who can only grasp self as other is no different from the object who can only grasp self as thing. To be man's other *is* to be his thing. Similarly, the problem of how the object can know herself as such is the same as how the alienated can know its own alienation. This, in turn, poses the problem of feminism's account of women's consciousness. How can women, as created, "thingified in the head,"[65] complicit in the body, see our condition as such?

In order to account for women's consciousness (much less propagate it) feminism must grasp that male power produces the world before it distorts it. Women's acceptance of their condition does not contradict its fundamental unacceptability if women have little choice but to *become* persons who freely choose women's roles. For this reason, the reality of women's oppression is, finally, neither demonstrable nor refutable empirically. Until this is confronted on the level of method, criticism of what exists can be undercut by pointing to the reality to be criticized. Women's bondage, degradation, damage, complicity, and inferiority—together with the possibility of resistance, movement, or exceptions—will operate as barriers to consciousness rather than as means of access to what women need to become conscious of in order to change.

Male power is real; it is just not what it claims to be, namely, the only reality. Male power is a myth that makes itself true. What it is to raise consciousness is to confront male power in this duality: as total on one side and a delusion on the other. In consciousness raising, women learn they have *learned* that men are everything, women their negation, but that the sexes are equal. The content of the message is revealed true and false at the same time; in fact, each part reflects the other transvalued. If "men are all, women their negation" is taken as social criticism rather than simple description, it becomes clear for the first time that women *are* men's equals, everywhere in chains. Their chains become visible, their inferiority—their inequality—a product of subjection and a mode of its enforcement. Reciprocally, the moment it is seen that this—life as we know it—is not equality, that the sexes are not socially equal, womanhood can no longer be defined in terms of lack of maleness, as negativity. For the first time, the question of what a woman *is* seeks its ground in and of a world understood as neither of its making nor in its image, and finds, within a critical embrace of woman's fractured and alien image, that world women have made and a vision of its wholeness.

65. Rowbotham, *Women's Liberation and the New Politics* (n. 17 above), p. 17.

Feminism has unmasked maleness as a form of power that is both omnipotent and nonexistent, an unreal thing with very real consequences. Zora Neale Hurston captured its two-sidedness: "The town has a basketfull of feelings good and bad about Joe's positions and possessions, but none had the temerity to challenge him. They bowed down to him rather, because he was all of these things, and then again he was all of these things because the town bowed down."[66] If "positions and possessions" and rulership create each other, in relation, the question becomes one of form and inevitability. This challenges feminism to apply its theory of women's standpoint to the regime.[67]

Feminism is the first theory to emerge from those whose interest it affirms. Its method recapitulates as theory the reality it seeks to capture. As marxist method is dialectical materialism, feminist method is consciousness raising: the collective critical reconstitution of the meaning of women's social experience, as women live through it. Marxism and feminism on this level posit a different relation between thought and thing, both in terms of the relationship of the analysis itself to the social life it captures and in terms of the participation of thought in the social life it analyzes. To the extent that materialism is scientific it posits and refers to a reality outside thought which it considers to have an objective—that is, truly nonsocially perspectival—content. Consciousness raising, by contrast, inquires into an intrinsically social situation, into that mixture of thought and materiality which is women's sexuality in the most generic sense. It approaches its world through a process that shares its determination: women's consciousness, not as individual or subjective ideas, but as collective social being. This method stands inside its own determinations in order to uncover them, just as it criticizes them in order to value them on its own terms—in order to *have* its own terms at all. Feminism turns theory itself—the pursuit of a true analysis of social life—into the pursuit of consciousness and turns an analysis of inequality into a critical embrace of its own determinants. The process is transformative as well as perceptive, since thought and thing are inextricable and reciprocally constituting of women's oppression, just as the state as coercion and the state as legitimizing ideology are indistinguishable, and for the same reasons. The pursuit of consciousness becomes a form of political practice. Consciousness raising has revealed gender relations to be a collective fact, no more simply personal than class relations. This implies that class relations may also be personal, no less so for being at the same time collective. The failure of marxism to realize this may connect the

66. Zora Neale Hurston, *Their Eyes Were Watching God* (Urbana: University of Illinois Press, 1978), pp. 79–80.

67. In the second part of this article, "Feminism, Marxism, Method, and the State: Toward Feminist Jurisprudence" (forthcoming in *Signs*), I argue that the state is male in that objectivity is its norm.

failure of workers in advanced capitalist nations to organize in the socialist sense with the failure of left revolutions to liberate women in the feminist sense.

Feminism stands in relation to marxism as marxism does to classical political economy: its final conclusion and ultimate critique. Compared with marxism, the place of thought and things in method and reality are reversed in a seizure of power that penetrates subject with object and theory with practice. In a dual motion, feminism turns marxism inside out and on its head.

To answer an old question—how is value created and distributed?—Marx needed to create an entirely new account of the social world. To answer an equally old question, or to question an equally old reality—what explains the inequality of women to men? or, how does desire become domination? or, what is male power?—feminism revolutionizes politics.

Stanford Law School
Stanford University

Women's Time

Julia Kristeva

Translated by Alice Jardine and Harry Blake

The nation—dream and reality of the nineteenth century—seems to have reached both its apogee and its limits when the 1929 crash and the National-Socialist apocalypse demolished the pillars that, according to Marx, were its essence: economic homogeneity, historical tradition, and linguistic unity.[1] It could indeed be demonstrated that World War II, though fought in the name of national values (in the above sense of the term), brought an end to the nation as a reality: It was turned into a mere illusion which, from that point forward, would be preserved only for ideological or strictly political purposes, its social and philosophical coherence having collapsed. To move quickly toward the specific problematic that will occupy us in this article, let us say that the chimera of economic *homogeneity* gave way to *interdependence* (when not submission to the economic superpowers), while *historical* tradition and *linguistic* unity were recast as a broader and deeper determinant: what might be called a *symbolic denominator,* defined as the cultural and religious memory forged by the interweaving of history and geography. The variants of this memory produce social territories which then redistribute the cutting up into political parties which is still in use but losing strength. At the same time, this memory or symbolic denominator, common to them all, reveals beyond economic globalization and/or uniformization certain characteristics transcending the nation that sometimes embrace an entire continent. A new social ensemble superior to the nation has thus been

This article was originally published as "Le Temps des femmes" in *34/44: Cahiers de recherche de sciences des textes et documents,* no. 5 (Winter 1979), pp. 5–19.

1. The following discussion emphasizes Europe in a way which may seem superfluous to some American readers given the overall emphasis on deterritorialization. It is, however, essential to the movement of an article that is above all devoted to the necessity of paying attention to the place from which we speak.—AJ, TRANS.

constituted, within which the nation, far from losing its own traits, rediscovers and accentuates them in a strange temporality, in a kind of "future perfect," where the most deeply repressed past gives a distinctive character to a logical and sociological distribution of the most modern type. For this memory or symbolic common denominator concerns the response that human groupings, united in space and time, have given not to the problems of the *production* of material goods (i.e., the domain of the economy and of the human relationships it implies, politics, etc.) but, rather, to those of *reproduction,* survival of the species, life and death, the body, sex, and symbol. If it is true, for example, that Europe is representative of such a sociocultural ensemble, it seems to me that its existence is based more on this "symbolic denominator," which its art, philosophy, and religions manifest, than on its economic profile, which is certainly interwoven with collective memory but whose traits change rather rapidly under pressure from its partners.

It is clear that a social ensemble thus constituted possesses both a *solidity* rooted in a particular mode of reproduction and its representations through which the biological species is connected to its humanity, which is a tributary of time; as well as a certain *fragility* as a result of the fact that, through its universality, the symbolic common denominator is necessarily echoed in the corresponding symbolic denominator of another sociocultural ensemble. Thus, barely constituted as such, Europe finds itself being asked to compare itself with, or even to recognize itself in, the cultural, artistic, philosophical, and religious constructions belonging to other supranational sociocultural ensembles. This seems natural when the entities involved were linked by history (e.g., Europe and North America, or Europe and Latin America), but the phenomenon also occurs when the universality of this denominator we have called symbolic juxtaposes modes of production and reproduction apparently opposed in both the past and the present (e.g., Europe and India, or Europe and China). In short, with sociocultural ensembles of the European type, we are constantly faced with a double problematic: that of their *identity* constituted by historical sedimentation, and that of their *loss of identity* which is produced by this connection of memories which escape from history only to encounter anthropology. In other words, we confront two temporal dimensions: the time of linear history, or *cursive time* (as Nietzsche called it), and the time of another history, thus another time, *monumental time* (again according to Nietzsche), which englobes these supranational, sociocultural ensembles within even larger entities.

I should like to draw attention to certain formations which seem to me to summarize the dynamics of a sociocultural organism of this type. The question is one of sociocultural groups, that is, groups defined according to their place in production, but especially according to their role in the mode of reproduction and its representations, which, while bearing the specific sociocultural traits of the formation in question, are *diagonal* to it and connect it to other sociocultural formations. I am thinking in particular of sociocultural groups which are usually defined as age groups (e.g., "young people in Europe"), as sexual divisions (e.g., "European women"), and so forth. While it is obvious that "young people" or "women" in Europe have their own particularity, it is nonetheless just as obvious that what defines them as "young people" or as "women" places them in a diagonal relationship to their European "origin" and links them to similar categories in North America or in China, among others. That is, insofar as they also belong to "monumental history," they will not be only European "young people" or "women" of Europe but will echo in a most specific way the universal traits of their structural place in reproduction and its representations.

Consequently, the reader will find in the following pages, first, an attempt to situate the problematic of women in Europe within an inquiry on time: that time which the feminist movement both inherits and modifies. Second, I will attempt to distinguish two phases or two generations of women which, while immediately universalist and cosmopolitan in their demands, can nonetheless be differentiated by the fact that the first generation is more determined by the implications of a national problematic (in the sense suggested above), while the second, more determined by its place within the "symbolic denominator," is European *and* trans-European. Finally, I will try, both through the problems approached and through the type of analysis I propose, to present what I consider a viable stance for a European—or at least a European woman—within a domain which is henceforth worldwide in scope.

Which Time?

"Father's time, mother's species," as Joyce put it; and, indeed, when evoking the name and destiny of women, one thinks more of the *space* generating and forming the human species than of *time*, becoming, or history. The modern sciences of subjectivity, of its genealogy and accidents, confirm in their own way this intuition, which is perhaps itself the result of a sociohistorical conjuncture. Freud, listening to the dreams and fantasies of his patients, thought that "hysteria was linked to place."[2] Subsequent studies on the acquisition of the symbolic function by children show that the permanence and quality of maternal love condition the appearance of the first spatial references which induce the child's laugh and then induce the entire range of symbolic manifestations which

---

2. Sigmund Freud and Carl G. Jung, *Correspondance* (Paris: Gallimard, 1975), 1:87.

lead eventually to sign and syntax.[3] Moreover, antipsychiatry and psychoanalysis as applied to the treatment of psychoses, before attributing the capacity for transference and communication to the patient, proceed to the arrangement of new places, gratifying substitutes that repair old deficiencies in the maternal space. I could go on giving examples. But they all converge on the problematic of space, which innumerable religions of matriarchal (re)appearance attribute to "woman," and which Plato, recapitulating in his own system the atomists of antiquity, designated by the aporia of the *chora,* matrix space, nourishing, unnameable, anterior to the One, to God and, consequently, defying metaphysics.[4]

As for time, female[5] subjectivity would seem to provide a specific measure that essentially retains *repetition* and *eternity* from among the multiple modalities of time known through the history of civilizations. On the one hand, there are cycles, gestation, the eternal recurrence of a biological rhythm which conforms to that of nature and imposes a temporality whose stereotyping may shock, but whose regularity and unison with what is experienced as extrasubjective time, cosmic time, occasion vertiginous visions and unnameable *jouissance.*[6] On the other hand, and perhaps as a consequence, there is the massive presence of a monumental temporality, without cleavage or escape, which has so little to do with linear time (which passes) that the very word "temporality" hardly fits: All-encompassing and infinite like imaginary space, this temporality reminds one of Kronos in Hesiod's mythology, the incestuous son whose

3. R. Spitz, *La Première année de la vie de l'enfant* [First year of life: a psychoanalytic study of normal and deviant development of object relations] (Paris: PUF, 1958); D. Winnicott, *Jeu et réalité* [Playing and reality] (Paris: Gallimard, 1975); Julia Kristeva, "Noms de lieu" in *Polylogue* (Paris: Editions du Seuil, 1977), translated as "Place Names" in Julia Kristeva, *Desire in Language: A Semiotic Approach to Literature and Art,* ed. Leon S. Roudiez, trans. Thomas Gora, Alice Jardine, and Leon Roudiez (New York: Columbia University Press, 1980) (hereafter cited as *Desire in Language*).

4. Plato *Timeus* 52: "Indefinitely a place; it cannot be destroyed, but provides a ground for all that can come into being; itself being perceptible, outside of all sensation, by means of a sort of bastard reasoning; barely assuming credibility, it is precisely that which makes us dream when we perceive it, and affirm that all that exists must be somewhere, in a determined place . . ." (author's translation).

5. As most readers of recent French theory in translation know, *le féminin* does not have the same pejorative connotations it has come to have in English. It is a term used to speak about women in general, but, as used most often in this article, it probably comes closest to our "female" as defined by Elaine Showalter in *A Literature of Their Own* (Princeton, N.J.: Princeton University Press, 1977). I have therefore used either "women" or "female" according to the context (cf. also n. 9 in "Introduction to Julia Kristeva's 'Women's Time' " [this issue; hereafter cited as "Introduction"]). "Subjectivity" here refers to the state of being "a thinking, speaking, acting, doing or writing agent" and never, e.g., as opposed to "objectivity" (see the glossary in *Desire in Language*).—AJ.

6. I have retained *jouissance*—that word for pleasure which defies translation—as it is rapidly becoming a "believable neologism" in English (see the glossary in *Desire in Language*).—AJ.

massive presence covered all of Gea in order to separate her from Ouranos, the father.[7] Or one is reminded of the various myths of resurrection which, in all religious beliefs, perpetuate the vestige of an anterior or concomitant maternal cult, right up to its most recent elaboration, Christianity, in which the body of the Virgin Mother does not die but moves from one spatiality to another within the same time via dormition (according to the Orthodox faith) or via assumption (the Catholic faith).[8]

The fact that these two types of temporality (cyclical and monumental) are traditionally linked to female subjectivity insofar as the latter is thought of as necessarily maternal should not make us forget that this repetition and this eternity are found to be the fundamental, if not the sole, conceptions of time in numerous civilizations and experiences, particularly mystical ones.[9] The fact that certain currents of modern feminism recognize themselves here does not render them fundamentally incompatible with "masculine" values.

In return, female subjectivity as it gives itself up to intuition becomes a problem with respect to a certain conception of time: time as project, teleology, linear and prospective unfolding; time as departure, progression, and arrival—in other words, the time of history.[10] It has already been abundantly demonstrated that this kind of temporality is inherent in the logical and ontological values of any given civilization, that this temporality renders explicit a rupture, an expectation, or an anguish which other temporalities work to conceal. It might also be added that this linear time is that of language considered as the enunciation of sentences (noun + verb; topic-comment; beginning-ending), and that this time rests on its own stumbling block, which is also the stumbling block of that enunciation—death. A psychoanalyst would call this "obsessional time," recognizing in the mastery of time the true structure of the slave. The hysteric (either male or female) who suffers from reminiscences would, rather, recognize his or her self in the anterior temporal modalities: cyclical or monumental. This antinomy, one perhaps embedded in psychic structures, becomes, nonetheless, within a given civilization, an antinomy among social groups and ideologies in which the radical positions of certain feminists would rejoin the discourse of marginal groups of spiritual or mystical inspiration and, strangely enough, rejoin recent scientific preoccupations. Is it not true that the problematic of a time indissociable from space, of a space-time in infinite expansion, or rhythmed by accidents or catastrophes, preoccupies both space science and genetics? And, at another level, is it not

7. This particular mythology has important implications—equal only to those of the oedipal myth—for current French thought.—AJ.

8. See Julia Kristeva, "Hérétique de l'amour," *Tel quel,* no. 74 (1977), pp. 30–49.

9. See H. C. Puech, *La Gnose et la temps* (Paris: Gallimard, 1977).

10. See "Introduction."—AJ.

true that the contemporary media revolution, which is manifest in the storage and reproduction of information, implies an idea of time as frozen or exploding according to the vagaries of demand, returning to its source but uncontrollable, utterly bypassing its subject and leaving only two preoccupations to those who approve of it: Who is to have power over the origin (the programming) and over the end (the use)?

It is for two precise reasons, within the framework of this article, that I have allowed myself this rapid excursion into a problematic of unheard of complexity. The reader will undoubtedly have been struck by a fluctuation in the term of reference: mother, woman, hysteric. . . . I think that the apparent coherence which the term "woman" assumes in contemporary ideology, apart from its "mass" or "shock" effect for activist purposes, essentially has the negative effect of effacing the differences among the diverse functions or structures which operate beneath this word. Indeed, the time has perhaps come to emphasize the multiplicity of female expressions and preoccupations so that from the intersection of these differences there might arise, more precisely, less commercially, and more truthfully, the real *fundamental difference* between the two sexes: a difference that feminism has had the enormous merit of rendering painful, that is, productive of surprises and of symbolic life in a civilization which, outside the stock exchange and wars, is bored to death.

It is obvious, moreover, that one cannot speak of Europe or of "women in Europe" without suggesting the time in which this sociocultural distribution is situated. If it is true that a female sensibility emerged a century ago, the chances are great that by introducing *its own* notion of time, this sensibility is not in agreement with the idea of an "eternal Europe" and perhaps not even with that of a "modern Europe." Rather, through and with the European past and present, as through and with the ensemble of "Europe," which is the repository of memory, this sensibility seeks its own trans-European temporality. There are, in any case, three attitudes on the part of European feminist movements toward this conception of linear temporality, which is readily labeled masculine and which is at once both civilizational and obsessional.

Two Generations

In its beginnings, the women's movement, as the struggle of suffragists and of existential feminists, aspired to gain a place in linear time as the time of project and history. In this sense, the movement, while immediately universalist, is also deeply rooted in the sociopolitical life of nations. The political demands of women; the struggles for equal pay for equal work, for taking power in social institutions on an equal footing with men; the rejection, when necessary, of the attributes traditionally considered feminine or maternal insofar as they are deemed incompatible with insertion in that history—all are part of the *logic of identification*[11] with certain values: not with the ideological (these are combated, and rightly so, as reactionary) but, rather, with the logical and ontological values of a rationality dominant in the nation-state. Here it is unnecessary to enumerate the benefits which this logic of identification and the ensuing struggle have achieved and continue to achieve for women (abortion, contraception, equal pay, professional recognition, etc.); these have already had or will soon have effects even more important than those of the Industrial Revolution. Univeralist in its approach, this current in feminism *globalizes* the problems of women of different milieux, ages, civilizations, or simply of varying psychic structures, under the label "Universal Woman." A consideration of *generations* of women can only be conceived of in this global way as a succession, as a progression in the accomplishment of the initial program mapped out by its founders.

In a second phase, linked, on the one hand, to the younger women who came to feminism after May 1968 and, on the other, to women who had an aesthetic or psychoanalytic experience, linear temporality has been almost totally refused, and as a consequence there has arisen an exacerbated distrust of the entire political dimension. If it is true that this more recent current of feminism refers to its predecessors and that the struggle for sociocultural recognition of women is necessarily its main concern, this current seems to think of itself as belonging to another generation—qualitatively different from the first one—in its conception of its own identity and, consequently, of temporality as such. Essentially interested in the specificity of female psychology and its symbolic realizations, these women seek to give a language to the intrasubjective and corporeal experiences left mute by culture in the past. Either as artists or writers, they have undertaken a veritable exploration of the *dynamic of signs,* an exploration which relates this tendency, at least at the level of its aspirations, to all major projects of aesthetic and religious upheaval. Ascribing this experience to a new generation does not only mean that other, more subtle problems have been added to the demands for sociopolitical identification made in the beginning. It also means that, by demanding recognition of an irreducible identity, without equal in the opposite sex and, as such, exploded, plural, fluid, in a certain way nonidentical, this feminism situates itself outside the linear time of identities which communicate through projection and revindica-

11. The term "identification" belongs to a wide semantic field ranging from everyday language to philosophy and psychoanalysis. While Kristeva is certainly referring in principle to its elaboration in Freudian and Lacanian psychoanalysis, it can be understood here, as a logic, in its most general sense (see the entry on "identification" in Jean LaPlanche and J. B. Pontalis, *Vocabulaire de la psychanalyse* [The language of psychoanalysis] [Paris: Presses Universitaires de France, 1967; rev. ed., 1976]).—AJ.

tion. Such a feminism rejoins, on the one hand, the archaic (mythical) memory and, on the other, the cyclical or monumental temporality of marginal movements. It is certainly not by chance that the European and trans-European problematic has been posited as such at the same time as this new phase of feminism.

Finally, it is the mixture of the two attitudes—*insertion* into history and the radical *refusal* of the subjective limitations imposed by this history's time on an experiment carried out in the name of the irreducible difference—that seems to have broken loose over the past few years in European feminist movements, particularly in France and in Italy.

If we accept this meaning of the expression "a new generation of women," two kinds of questions might then be posed. What sociopolitical processes or events have provoked this mutation? What are its problems: its contributions as well as dangers?

Socialism and Freudianism

One could hypothesize that if this new generation of women shows itself to be more diffuse and perhaps less conscious in the United States and more massive in Western Europe, this is because of a veritable split in social relations and mentalities, a split produced by socialism and Freudianism. I mean by *socialism* that egalitarian doctrine which is increasingly broadly disseminated and accepted as based on common sense, as well as that social practice adopted by governments and political parties in democratic regimes which are forced to extend the zone of egalitarianism to include the distribution of goods as well as access to culture. By *Freudianism* I mean that lever, inside this egalitarian and socializing field, which once again poses the question of sexual difference and of the difference among subjects who themselves are not reducible one to the other.

Western socialism, shaken in its very beginnings by the egalitarian or differential demands of its women (e.g., Flora Tristan), quickly got rid of those woman who aspired to recognition of a specificity of the female role in society and culture, only retaining from them, in the egalitarian and universalistic spirit of Enlightenment Humanism, the idea of a necessary identification between the two sexes as the only and unique means for liberating the "second sex." I shall not develop here the fact that this "ideal" is far from being applied in practice by these socialist-inspired movements and parties and that it was in part from the revolt against this situation that the new generation of women in Western Europe was born after May 1968. Let us just say that in theory, and as put into practice in Eastern Europe, socialist ideology, based on a conception of the human being as determined by its place in *production* and the *relations of production,* did not take into consideration this same human being according to its place in *reproduction*, on the one hand, or in the *symbolic order*, on the other. Consequently, the specific character of women could only appear as nonessential or even nonexistent to the totalizing and even totalitarian spirit of this ideology.[12] We begin to see that this same egalitarian and in fact censuring treatment has been imposed, from Enlightenment Humanism through socialism, on religious specificities and, in particular, on Jews.[13]

What has been achieved by this attitude remains nonetheless of capital importance for women, and I shall take as an example the change in the destiny of women in the socialist countries of Eastern Europe. It could be said, with only slight exaggeration, that the demands of the suffragists and existential feminists have, to a great extent, been met in these countries, since three of the main egalitarian demands of early feminism have been or are now being implemented despite vagaries and blunders: economic, political, and professional equality. The fourth, sexual equality, which implies permissiveness in sexual relations (including homosexual relations), abortion, and contraception, remains stricken by taboo in Marxian ethics as well as for reasons of state. It is, then, this fourth equality which is the problem and which therefore appears *essential* in the struggle of a new generation. But simultaneously and as a consequence of these socialist accomplishments—which are in fact a total deception—the struggle is no longer concerned with the quest for equality but, rather, with difference and specificity. It is precisely at this point that the new generation encounters what might be called the *symbolic* question.[14] Sexual difference—which is at once biological, physiological, and relative to reproduction—is translated by and translates a difference in the relationship of subjects to the symbolic contract which *is* the social contract: a difference, then, in the relationship to power, language, and meaning. The sharpest and most subtle point of feminist subversion brought about by the new generation will henceforth be situated on the terrain of the inseparable conjunction of the sexual and the symbolic, in order to try to discover, first, the specificity of the female, and then, in the end, that of each individual woman.

A certain saturation of socialist ideology, a certain exhaustion of its potential as a program for a new social contract (it is obvious that the

12. See D. Desanti, "L'Autre Sexe des bolcheviks," *Tel quel*, no. 76 (1978); Julia Kristeva, *Des Chinoises* (Paris: Editions des femmes, 1975), translated as *On Chinese Women*, trans. Anita Barrows (New York: Urizen Press, 1977).

13. See Arthur Hertzberg, *The French Enlightenment and the Jews* (New York: Columbia University Press, 1968); *Les Juifs et la révolution française*, ed. B. Blumenkranz and A. Seboul (Paris: Edition Privat, 1976).

14. Here, "symbolic" is being more strictly used in terms of that function defined by Kristeva in opposition to the semiotic: "it involves the thetic phase, the identification of subject and its distinction from objects, and the establishment of a sign system" (see the glossary in *Desire in Language*, and Alice Jardine, "Theories of the Feminine: Kristeva," *Enclitic*, in press).—AJ.

effective realization of this program is far from being accomplished, and I am here treating only its system of thought) makes way for . . . Freudianism. I am, of course, aware that this term and this practice are somewhat shocking to the American intellectual consciousness (which rightly reacts to a muddled and normatizing form of psychoanalysis) and, above all, to the feminist consciousness. To restrict my remarks to the latter: Is it not true that Freud has been seen only as a denigrator or even an exploiter of women? as an irritating phallocrat in a Vienna which was at once Puritan and decadent—a man who fantasized women as sub-men, castrated men?

Castrated and/or Subject to Language

Before going beyond Freud to propose a more just or more modern vision of women, let us try, first, to understand his notion of castration. It is, first of all, a question of an *anguish* or *fear* of castration, or of correlative penis *envy;* a question, therefore, of *imaginary* formations readily perceivable in the *discourse* of neurotics of both sexes, men and women. But, above all, a careful reading of Freud, going beyond his biologism and his mechanism, both characteristic of his time, brings out two things. First, as presupposition for the "primal scene," the castration fantasy and its correlative (penis envy) are hypotheses, a priori suppositions intrinsic to the theory itself, in the sense that these are not the ideological fantasies of their inventor but, rather, logical necessities to be placed at the "origin" in order to explain what unceasingly functions in neurotic discourse. In other words, neurotic discourse, in man and woman, can only be understood in terms of its own logic when its fundamental causes are admitted as the fantasies of the primal scene and castration, even if (as may be the case) nothing renders them present in reality itself. Stated in still other terms, the reality of castration is no more real than the hypothesis of an explosion which, according to modern astrophysics, is at the origin of the universe: Nothing proves it, in a sense it is an article of faith, the only difference being that numerous phenomena of life in this "big-bang" universe are explicable only through this initial hypothesis. But one is infinitely more jolted when this kind of intellectual method concerns inanimate matter than when it is applied to our own subjectivity and thus, perhaps, to the fundamental mechanism of our epistemophilic thought.

Moreover, certain texts written by Freud (*The Interpretation of Dreams,* but especially those of the second topic, in particular the *Metapsychology*) and their recent extensions (notably by Lacan),[15] imply

15. See, in general, Jacques Lacan, *Ecrits* (Paris: Editions du Seuil, 1966) and, in particular, Jacques Lacan, *Le Séminaire XX: Encore* (Paris: Editions du Seuil, 1975).—AJ.

that castration is, in sum, the imaginary construction of a radical operation which constitutes the symbolic field and all beings inscribed therein.
This operation constitutes signs and syntax; that is, language, as a *separation* from a presumed state of nature, of pleasure fused with nature so
that the introduction of an articulated network of differences, which
refers to objects henceforth and only in this way separated from a subject, may constitute *meaning*. This logical operation of separation (confirmed by all psycholinguistic and child psychology) which preconditions
the binding of language which is already syntactical, is therefore the
common destiny of the two sexes, men and women. That certain
biofamilial conditions and relationships cause women (and notably hysterics) to deny this separation and the language which ensues from it,
whereas men (notably obsessionals) magnify both and, terrified, attempt
to master them—this is what Freud's discovery has to tell us on this issue.

The analytic situation indeed shows that it is the penis which, becoming the major referent in this operation of separation, gives full
meaning to the *lack* or to the *desire* which constitutes the subject during
his or her insertion into the order of language. I should only like to
indicate here that, in order for this operation constitutive of the symbolic
and the social to appear in its full truth and for it to be understood by
both sexes, it would be just to emphasize its extension to all that is
privation of fullfillment and of totality; exclusion of a pleasing, natural,
and sound state: in short, the break indispensable to the advent of the
symbolic.

It can now be seen how women, starting with this theoretical apparatus, might try to understand their sexual and symbolic difference in
the framework of social, cultural, and professional realization, in order
to try, by seeing their position therein, either to fulfill their own experience to a maximum or—but always starting from this point—to go
further and call into question the very apparatus itself.

Living the Sacrifice

In any case, and for women in Europe today, whether or not they
are conscious of the various mutations (socialist and Freudian) which
have produced or simply accompanied their coming into their own, the
urgent question on our agenda might be formulated as follows: *What can
be our place in the symbolic contract?* If the social contract, far from being
that of equal men, is based on an essentially sacrificial relationship of
separation and articulation of differences which in this way produces
communicable meaning, what is our place in this order of sacrifice
and/or of language? No longer wishing to be excluded or no longer
content with the function which has always been demanded of us (to
maintain, arrange, and perpetuate this sociosymbolic contract as

mothers, wives, nurses, doctors, teachers . . .), how can we reveal our place, first as it is bequeathed to us by tradition, and then as we want to transform it?

It is difficult to evaluate what in the relationship of women to the symbolic as it reveals itself now arises from a sociohistorical conjuncture (patriarchal ideology, whether Christian, humanist, socialist or so forth), and what arises from a structure. We can speak only about a structure observed in a sociohistorical context, which is that of Christian, Western civilization and its lay ramifications. In this sense of psychosymbolic structure, women, "we" (is it necessary to recall the warnings we issued at the beginning of this article concerning the totalizing use of this plural?) seem to feel that they are the casualties, that they have been left out of the sociosymbolic contract, of language as the fundamental social bond. They find no affect there, no more than they find the fluid and in-finitesimal significations of their relationships with the nature of their own bodies, that of the child, another woman, or a man. This frustra-tion, which to a certain extent belongs to men also, is being voiced today principally by women, to the point of becoming the essence of the new feminist ideology. A therefore difficult, if not impossible, identification with the sacrificial logic of separation and syntactical sequence at the foundation of language and the social code leads to the rejection of the symbolic—lived as the rejection of the paternal function and ultimately generating psychoses.

But this limit, rarely reached as such, produces two types of coun-terinvestment of what we have termed the sociosymbolic contract. On the one hand, there are attempts to take hold of this contract, to possess it in order to enjoy it as such or to subvert it. How? The answer remains difficult to formulate (since, precisely, any formulation is deemed frus-trating, mutilating, sacrificial) or else is in fact formulated using stereotypes taken from extremist and often deadly ideologies. On the other hand, another attitude is more lucid from the beginning, more self-analytical which—without refusing or sidestepping this sociosym-bolic order—consists in trying to explore the constitution and function-ing of this contract, starting less from the knowledge accumulated about it (anthropology, psychoanalysis, linguistics) than from the very personal affect experienced when facing it as subject and as a woman. This leads to the active research,[16] still rare, undoubtedly hesitant but always dis-sident, being carried out by women in the human sciences; particularly those attempts, in the wake of contemporary art, to break the code, to

16. This work is periodically published in various academic women's journals, one of the most prestigious being *Signs: Journal of Women in Culture and Society,* University of Chicago Press. Also of note are the special issues: "Ecriture, féminité, féminisme," *La Revue des sciences humaines* (Lille III), no. 4 (1977); and "Les Femmes et la philosophie," *Le Doctrinal de sapience* (Editions Solin), no. 3 (1977).

shatter language, to find a specific discourse closer to the body and emotions, to the unnameable repressed by the social contract. I am not speaking here of a "woman's language," whose (at least syntactical) existence is highly problematical and whose apparent lexical specificity is perhaps more the product of a social marginality than of a sexual-symbolic difference.[17]

Nor am I speaking of the aesthetic quality of productions by women, most of which—with a few exceptions (but has this not always been the case with both sexes?)—are a reiteration of a more or less euphoric or depressed romanticism and always an explosion of an ego lacking narcissistic gratification.[18] What I should like to retain, nonetheless, as a mark of collective aspiration, as an undoubtedly vague and unimplemented intention, but one which is intense and which has been deeply revealing these past few years, is this: The new generation of women is showing that its major social concern has become the sociosymbolic contract as a sacrificial contract. If anthropologists and psychologists, for at least a century, have not stopped insisting on this in their attention to "savage thought," wars, the discourse of dreams, or writers, women are today affirming—and we consequently face a mass phenomenon—that they are forced to experience this sacrificial contract against their will.[19] Based on this, they are attempting a revolt which they see as a resurrection but which society as a whole understands as murder. This attempt can lead us to a not less and sometimes more deadly violence. Or to a cultural innovation. Probably to both at once. But that is precisely where the stakes are, and they are of epochal significance.

17. See linguistic research on "female language": Robin Lakoff, *Language and Women's Place* (New York: Harper & Row, 1974); Mary R. Key, *Male/Female Language* (Metuchen, N.J.: Scarecrow Press, 1973); A. M. Houdebine, "Les Femmes et la langue," *Tel quel*, no. 74 (1977), pp. 84–95. The contrast between these "empirical" investigations of women's "speech acts" and much of the research in France on the conceptual bases for a "female language" must be emphasized here. It is somewhat helpful, if ultimately inaccurate, to think of the former as an "external" study of language and the latter as an "internal" exploration of the process of signification. For further contrast, see, e.g., "Part II: Contemporary Feminist Thought in France: Translating Difference" in *The Future of Difference*, ed. Hester Eisenstein and Alice Jardine (Boston: G. K. Hall & Co., 1980); the "Introductions" to *New French Feminisms*, ed. Elaine Marks and Isabelle de Courtivron (Amherst: University of Massachusetts Press, 1980); and for a very helpful overview of the problem of "difference and language" in France, see Stephen Heath, "Difference" in *Screen* 19 no. 3 (Autumn 1978): 51–112.—AJ.

18. This is one of the more explicit references to the mass marketing of "écriture féminine" in Paris over the last ten years.—AJ.

19. The expression *à leur corps défendant* translates as "against their will," but here the emphasis is on women's bodies: literally, "against their bodies." I have retained the former expression in English, partly because of its obvious intertextuality with Susan Brownmiller's *Against Our Will* (New York: Simon & Schuster, 1975). Women are increasingly describing their experience of the violence of the symbolic contract as a form of rape.—AJ.

The Terror of Power or the Power of Terrorism

First in socialist countries (such as the USSR and China) and increasingly in Western democracies, under pressure from feminist movements, women are being promoted to leadership positions in government, industry, and culture. Inequalities, devalorizations, underestimations, even persecution of women at this level continue to hold sway in vain. The struggle against them is a struggle against archaisms. The cause has nonetheless been understood, the principle has been accepted.[20] What remains is to break down the resistance to change. In this sense, this struggle, while still one of the main concerns of the new generation, is not, strictly speaking, *its* problem. In relationship to *power,* its problem might rather be summarized as follows: What happens when women come into power and identify with it? What happens when, on the contrary, they refuse power and create a parallel society, a counter-power which then takes on aspects ranging from a club of ideas to a group of terrorist commandos?[21]

The assumption by women of executive, industrial, and cultural power has not, up to the present time, radically changed the nature of this power. This can be clearly seen in the East, where women promoted to decision-making positions suddenly obtain the economic as well as the narcissistic advantages refused them for thousands of years and become the pillars of the existing governments, guardians of the status quo, the most zealous protectors of the established order.[22] This identification by women with the very power structures previously considered as frustrating, oppressive, or inaccessible has often been used in modern times by totalitarian regimes: the German National-Socialists and the Chilean junta are examples of this.[23] The fact that this is a paranoid type of counterinvestment in an initially denied symbolic order can perhaps explain this troubling phenomenon; but an explanation does not prevent its massive propagation around the globe, perhaps in less dramatic forms than the totalitarian ones mentioned above, but all moving toward leveling, stabilization, conformism, at the cost of crushing exceptions, experiments, chance occurrences.

20. Many women in the West who are once again finding all doors closed to them above a certain level of employment, especially in the current economic chaos, may find this statement, even qualified, troubling, to say the least. It is accurate, however, *in principle:* whether that of infinite capitalist recuperation or increasing socialist expansion—within both economies, our integration functions as a kind of *operative* illusion.—AJ.

21. The very real existence and autonomous activities of both of these versions of women's groups in Europe may seem a less urgent problem in the United States where feminist groups are often absorbed by the academy and/or are forced to remain financially dependent on para-academic/governmental agencies.—AJ.

22. See *Des Chinoises.*

23. See M. A. Macciocchi, *Elements pour une analyse du fascisme* (Paris: 10/18, 1976); Michèle Mattelart, "Le Coup d'état au féminin," *Les Temps modernes* (January 1975).

Some will regret that the rise of a libertarian movement such as feminism ends, in some of its aspects, in the consolidation of conformism; others will rejoice and profit from this fact. Electoral campaigns, the very life of political parties, continue to bet on this latter tendency. Experience proves that too quickly even the protest or innovative initiatives on the part of women inhaled by power systems (when they do not submit to them right off) are soon credited to the system's account; and that the long-awaited democratization of institutions as a result of the entry of women most often comes down to fabricating a few "chiefs" among them. The difficulty presented by this logic of integrating the second sex into a value system experienced as foreign and therefore counterinvested is how to avoid the centralization of power, how to detach women from it, and how then to proceed, through their critical, differential, and autonomous interventions, to render decision-making institutions more flexible.

Then there are the more radical feminist currents which, refusing homologation to any role of identification with existing power no matter what the power may be, make of the second sex a *countersociety*. A "female society" is then constituted as a sort of alter ego of the official society, in which all real or fantasized possibilities for *jouissance* take refuge. Against the sociosymbolic contract, both sacrificial and frustrating, this countersociety is imagined as harmonious, without prohibitions, free and fulfilling. In our modern societies which have no hereafter or, at least, which are caught up in a transcendency either reduced to this side of the world (Protestantism) or crumbling (Catholicism and its current challenges), the countersociety remains the only refuge for fulfillment since it is precisely an a-topia, a place outside the law, utopia's floodgate.

As with any society, the countersociety is based on the expulsion of an excluded element, a scapegoat charged with the evil of which the community duly constituted can then purge itself;[24] a purge which will finally exonerate that community of any future criticism. Modern protest movements have often reiterated this logic, locating the guilty one—in order to fend off criticism—in the foreign, in capital alone, in the other religion, in the other sex. Does not feminism become a kind of inverted sexism when this logic is followed to its conclusion? The various forms of marginalism—according to sex, age, religion, or ideology— represent in the modern world this refuge for *jouissance*, a sort of laicized transcendence. But with women, and insofar as the number of those feeling concerned by this problem has increased, although in less spectacular forms than a few years ago, the problem of the countersociety is

24. The principles of a "sacrificial anthropology" are developed by René Girard in *La Violence et le sacré* [Violence and the sacred] (Paris: Grasset, 1972) and esp. in *Des choses cachées depuis la fondation du monde* (Paris: Grasset, 1978).

becoming massive: It occupies no more and no less than "half of the sky."

It has, therefore, become clear, because of the particular radicalization of the second generation, that these protest movements, including feminism, are not "initially libertarian" movements which only later, through internal deviations or external chance manipulations, fall back into the old ruts of the initially combated archetypes. Rather, the very logic of counterpower and of countersociety necessarily generates, by its very structure, its essence as a simulacrum of the combated society or of power. In this sense and from a viewpoint undoubtedly too Hegelian, modern feminism has only been but a moment in the interminable process of coming to consciousness about the implacable violence (separation, castration, etc.) which constitutes any symbolic contract.

Thus the identification with power in order to consolidate it or the constitution of a fetishist counterpower—restorer of the crises of the self and provider of a *jouissance* which is always already a transgression—seem to be the two social forms which the face-off between the new generation of women and the social contract can take. That one also finds the problem of terrorism there is structurally related.

The large number of women in terrorist groups (Palestinian commandos, the Baader-Meinhoff Gang, Red Brigades, etc.) has already been pointed out, either violently or prudently according to the source of information. The exploitation of women is still too great and the traditional prejudices against them too violent for one to be able to envision this phenomenon with sufficient distance. It can, however, be said from now on that this is the inevitable product of what we have called a denial of the sociosymbolic contract and its counterinvestment as the only means of self-defense in the struggle to safeguard an identity. This paranoid-type mechanism is at the base of any political involvement. It may produce different civilizing attitudes in the sense that these attitudes allow a more or less flexible reabsorption of violence and death. But when a subject is too brutally excluded from this sociosymbolic stratum; when, for example, a woman feels her affective life as a woman or her condition as a social being too brutally ignored by existing discourse or power (from her family to social institutions); she may, by counterinvesting the violence she has endured, make of herself a "possessed" agent of this violence in order to combat what was experienced as frustration—with arms which may seem disproportional, but which are not so in comparison with the subjective or more precisely narcissistic suffering from which they originate. Necessarily opposed to the bourgeois democratic regimes in power, this terrorist violence offers as a program of liberation an order which is even more oppressive, more sacrificial than those it combats. Strangely enough, it is not against totalitarian regimes that these terrorist groups with women participants unleash themselves but, rather, against liberal systems, whose essence is, of course, exploitative, but whose expanding democratic legality guarantees relative tolerance. Each time, the mobilization takes place in the name of a nation, of an oppressed group, of a human essence imagined as good and sound; in the name, then, of a kind of fantasy of archaic fulfillment which an arbitrary, abstract, and thus even bad and ultimately discriminatory order has come to disrupt. While that order is accused of being oppressive, is it not actually being reproached with being too weak, with not measuring up to this pure and good, but henceforth lost, substance? Anthropology has shown that the social order is sacrificial, but sacrifice orders violence, binds it, tames it. Refusal of the social order exposes one to the risk that the so-called good substance, once it is unchained, will explode, without curbs, without law or right, to become an absolute arbitrariness.

Following the crisis of monotheism, the revolutions of the past two centuries, and more recently fascism and Stalinism, have tragically set in action this logic of the oppressed goodwill which leads to massacres. Are women more apt than other social categories, notably the exploited classes, to invest in this implacable machine of terrorism? No categorical response, either positive or negative, can currently be given to this question. It must be pointed out, however, that since the dawn of feminism, and certainly before, the political activity of exceptional women, and thus in a certain sense of liberated women, has taken the form of murder, conspiracy, and crime. Finally, there is also the connivance of the young girl with her mother, her greater difficulty than the boy in detaching herself from the mother in order to accede to the order of signs as invested by the absence and separation constitutive of the paternal function. A girl will never be able to reestablish this contact with her mother—a contact which the boy may possibly rediscover through his relationship with the opposite sex—except by becoming a mother herself, through a child, or through a homosexuality which is in itself extremely difficult and judged as suspect by society; and, what is more, why and in the name of what dubious symbolic benefit would she want to make this detachment so as to conform to a symbolic system which remains foreign to her? In sum, all of these considerations—her eternal debt to the woman-mother—make a woman more vulnerable within the symbolic order, more fragile when she suffers within it, more virulent when she protects herself from it. If the archetype of the belief in a good and pure substance, that of utopias, is the belief in the omnipotence of an archaic, full, total, englobing mother with no frustration, no separation, with no break-producing symbolism (with no castration, in other words), then it becomes evident that we will never be able to defuse the violences mobilized through the counterinvestment necessary to carrying out this phantasm, unless one challenges precisely this myth of the archaic mother. It is in this way that we can understand the warnings against the recent invasion of the women's movements by paranoia,[25] as

25. Cf. Micheline Enriquez, "Fantasmes paranoiaques: différences des sexes, homosexualité, loi du père," *Topiques,* no. 13 (1974).

in Lacan's scandalous sentence "There is no such thing as Woman."[26] Indeed, she does *not* exist with a capital "W," possessor of some mythical unity—a supreme power, on which is based the terror of power and terrorism as the desire for power. But what an unbelievable force for subversion in the modern world! And, at the same time, what playing with fire!

Creatures and Creatresses

The desire to be a mother, considered alienating and even reactionary by the preceding generation of feminists, has obviously not become a standard for the present generation. But we have seen in the past few years an increasing number of women who not only consider their maternity compatible with their professional life or their feminist involvement (certain improvements in the quality of life are also at the origin of this: an increase in the number of day-care centers and nursery schools, more active participation of men in child care and domestic life, etc.) but also find it indispensable to their discovery, not of the plenitude, but of the complexity of the female experience, with all that this complexity comprises in joy and pain. This tendency has its extreme: in the refusal of the paternal function by lesbian and single mothers can be seen one of the most violent forms taken by the rejection of the symbolic outlined above, as well as one of the most fervent divinizations of maternal power—all of which cannot help but trouble an entire legal and moral order without, however, proposing an alternative to it. Let us remember here that Hegel distinguished between female right (familial and religious) and male law (civil and political). If our societies know well the uses and abuses of male law, it must also be recognized that female right is designated, for the moment, by a blank. And if these practices of maternity, among others, were to be generalized, women themselves would be responsible for elaborating the appropriate legislation to check the violence to which, otherwise, both their children and men would be subject. But are they capable of doing so? This is one of the important questions that the new generation of women encounters, especially when the members of this new generation refuse to ask those questions, seized by the same rage with which the dominant order originally victimized them.

Faced with this situation, it seems obvious—and feminist groups become more aware of this when they attempt to broaden their audience—that the refusal of maternity cannot be a mass policy and that

26. See Jacques Lacan, "Dieu et la jouissance de la femme" in *Encore* (Paris: Editions du Seuil, 1975), pp. 61–71, esp. p. 68. This seminar has remained a primary critical and polemical focus for multiple tendencies in the French women's movement. For a brief discussion of the seminar in English, see Heath (n. 17 above).—AJ.

the majority of women today see the possibility for fulfillment, if not entirely at least to a large degree, in bringing a child into the world. What does this desire for motherhood correspond to? This is one of the new questions for the new generation, a question the preceding generation had foreclosed. For want of an answer to this question, feminist ideology leaves the door open to the return of religion, whose discourse, tried and proved over thousands of years, provides the necessary ingredients for satisfying the anguish, the suffering, and the hopes of mothers. If Freud's affirmation—that the desire for a child is the desire for a penis and, in this sense, a substitute for phallic and symbolic dominion—can be only partially accepted, what modern women have to say about this experience should nonetheless be listened to attentively. Pregnancy seems to be experienced as the radical ordeal of the splitting of the subject:[27] redoubling up of the body, separation and coexistence of the self and of an other, of nature and consciousness, of physiology and speech. This fundamental challenge to identity is then accompanied by a fantasy of totality—narcissistic completeness—a sort of instituted, socialized, natural psychosis. The arrival of the child, on the other hand, leads the mother into the labyrinths of an experience that, without the child, she would only rarely encounter: love for an other. Not for herself, nor for an identical being, and still less for another person with whom "I" fuse (love or sexual passion). But the slow, difficult, and delightful apprenticeship in attentiveness, gentleness, forgetting oneself. The ability to succeed in this path without masochism and without annihilating one's affective, intellectual, and professional personality—such would seem to be the stakes to be won through guiltless maternity. It then becomes a creation in the strong sense of the term. For this moment, utopian?

On the other hand, it is in the aspiration toward artistic and, in particular, literary creation that woman's desire for affirmation now manifests itself. Why literature?

Is it because, faced with social norms, literature reveals a certain knowledge and sometimes the truth itself about an otherwise repressed, nocturnal, secret, and unconscious universe? Because it thus redoubles the social contract by exposing the unsaid, the uncanny? And because it makes a game, a space of fantasy and pleasure, out of the abstract and frustrating order of social signs, the words of everyday communication? Flaubert said, "Madame Bovary, c'est moi." Today many women imagine, "Flaubert, c'est moi." This identification with the potency of the imaginary is not only an identification, an imaginary potency (a fetish, a belief in the maternal penis maintained at all costs), as a far too norma-

27. The "split subject" (from *Spaltung* as both "splitting" and "cleavage"), as used in Freudian psychoanalysis, here refers directly to Kristeva's "subject in process / in question / on trial" as opposed to the unity of the transcendental ego (see n. 14 in "Introduction").—AJ.

tive view of the social and symbolic relationship would have it. This identification also bears witness to women's desire to lift the weight of what is sacrificial in the social contract from their shoulders, to nourish our societies with a more flexible and free discourse, one able to name what has thus far never been an object of circulation in the community: the enigmas of the body, the dreams, secret joys, shames, hatreds of the second sex.

It is understandable from this that women's writing has lately attracted the maximum attention of both "specialists" and the media.[28] The pitfalls encountered along the way, however, are not to be minimized: For example, does one not read there a relentless belittling of male writers whose books, nevertheless, often serve as "models" for countless productions by women? Thanks to the feminist label, does one not sell numerous works whose naive whining or market-place romanticism would otherwise have been rejected as anachronistic? And does one not find the pen of many a female writer being devoted to phantasmic attacks against Language and Sign as the ultimate supports of phallocratic power, in the name of a semi-aphonic corporality whose truth can only be found in that which is "gestural" or "tonal"?

And yet, no matter how dubious the results of these recent productions by women, the symptom is there—women are writing, and the air is heavy with expectation: What will they write that is new?

In the Name of the Father, the Son . . . and the Woman?

These few elements of the manifestations by the new generation of women in Europe seem to me to demonstrate that, beyond the sociopolitical level where it is generally inscribed (or inscribes itself), the women's movement—in its present stage, less aggressive but more artful—is situated within the very framework of the religious crisis of our civilization.

I call "religion" this phantasmic necessity on the part of speaking beings to provide themselves with a *representation* (animal, female, male, parental, etc.) in place of what constitutes them as such, in other words, symbolization—the double articulation and syntactic sequence of language, as well as its preconditions or substitutes (thoughts, affects, etc.). The elements of the current practice of feminism that we have just brought to light seem precisely to constitute such a representation which makes up for the frustrations imposed on women by the anterior code (Christianity or its lay humanist variant). The fact that this new ideology has affinities, often revindicated by its creators, with so-called matriar-

28. Again a reference to *écriture féminine* as generically labeled in France over the past few years and not to women's writing in general.—AJ.

chal beliefs (in other words, those beliefs characterizing matrilinear societies) should not overshadow its radical novelty. This ideology seems to me to be part of the broader antisacrificial current which is animating our culture and which, in its protest against the constraints of the sociosymbolic contract, is no less exposed to the risks of violence and terrorism. At this level of radicalism, it is the very principle of sociality which is challenged.

Certain contemporary thinkers consider, as is well known, that modernity is characterized as the first epoch in human history in which human beings attempt to live without religion. In its present form, is not feminism in the process of becoming one?

Or is it, on the contrary and as avant-garde feminists hope, that having started with the idea of difference, feminism will be able to break free of its belief in Woman, Her power, Her writing, so as to channel this demand for difference into each and every element of the female whole, and, finally, to bring out the singularity of each woman, and beyond this, her multiplicities, her plural languages, beyond the horizon, beyond sight, beyond faith itself?

A factor for ultimate mobilization? Or a factor for analysis?

Imaginary support in a technocratic era where all narcissism is frustrated? Or instruments fitted to these times in which the cosmos, atoms, and cells—our true contemporaries—call for the constitution of a fluid and free subjectivity?

The question has been posed. Is to pose it already to answer it?

Another Generation Is Another Space

If the preceding can be *said*—the question whether all this is *true* belongs to a different register—it is undoubtedly because it is now possible to gain some distance on these two preceding generations of women. This implies, of course, that a *third* generation is now forming, at least in Europe. I am not speaking of a new group of young women (though its importance should not be underestimated) or of another "mass feminist movement" taking the torch passed on from the second generation. My usage of the word "generation" implies less a chronology than a *signifying space,* a both corporeal and desiring mental space. So it can be argued that as of now a third attitude is possible, thus a third generation, which does not exclude—quite to the contrary—the *parallel* existence of all three in the same historical time, or even that they be interwoven one with the other.

In this third attitude, which I strongly advocate—which I imagine?—the very dichotomy man/woman as an opposition between two rival entities may be understood as belonging to *metaphysics.* What can "identity," even "sexual identity," mean in a new theoretical and scientific space where the very notion of identity is challenged?[29] I am not simply suggesting a very hypothetical bisexuality which, even if it existed, would only, in fact, be the aspiration toward the totality of one of the sexes and thus an effacing of difference. What I mean is, first of all, the demassification of the problematic of *difference,* which would imply, in a first phase, an apparent de-dramatization of the "fight to the death" between rival groups and thus between the sexes. And this not in the name of some reconciliation—feminism has at least had the merit of showing what is irreducible and even deadly in the social contract—but in order that the struggle, the implacable difference, the violence be conceived in the very place where it operates with the maximum intransigence, in other words, in personal and sexual identity itself, so as to make it disintegrate in its very nucleus.

It necessarily follows that this involves risks not only for what we understand today as "personal equilibrium" but also for social equilibrium itself, made up as it now is of the counterbalancing of aggressive and murderous forces massed in social, national, religious, and political groups. But is it not the insupportable situation of tension and explosive risk that the existing "equilibrium" presupposes which leads some of those who suffer from it to divest it of its economy, to detach themselves from it, and to seek another means of regulating difference?

To restrict myself here to a personal level, as related to the question of women, I see arising, under the cover of a relative indifference toward the militance of the first and second generations, an attitude of retreat from sexism (male as well as female) and, gradually, from any kind of anthropomorphism. The fact that this might quickly become another form of spiritualism turning its back on social problems, or else a form of repression[30] ready to support all status quos, should not hide the radicalness of the process. This process could be summarized as an *interiorization of the founding separation of the sociosymbolic contract,* as an introduction of its cutting edge into the very interior of every identity whether subjective, sexual, ideological, or so forth. This in such a way that the habitual and increasingly explicit attempt to fabricate a scapegoat victim as foundress of a society or a countersociety may be replaced by the analysis of the potentialities of *victim/executioner* which characterize each identity, each subject, each sex.

What discourse, if not that of a religion, would be able to support this adventure which surfaces as a real possibility, after both the achievements and the impasses of the present ideological reworkings, in which feminism has participated? It seems to me that the role of what is usually called "aesthetic practices" must increase not only to counterbalance the storage and uniformity of information by present-day mass

29. See Seminar on *Identity* directed by Lévi-Strauss (Paris: Grasset & Fasquelle, 1977).

30. Repression (*le refoulement* or *Verdrangung*) as distinguished from the foreclosure (*la foreclusion* or *Verwerfung*) evoked earlier in the article (see LaPlanche and Pontalis).—AJ.

media, data-bank systems, and, in particular, modern communications technology, but also to demystify the identity of the symbolic bond itself, to demystify, therefore, the *community* of language as a universal and unifying tool, one which totalizes and equalizes. In order to bring out— along with the *singularity* of each person and, even more, along with the multiplicity of every person's possible identifications (with atoms, e.g., stretching from the family to the stars)—the *relativity of his/her symbolic as well as biological existence,* according to the variation in his /her specific symbolic capacities. And in order to emphasize the *responsibility* which all will immediately face of putting this fluidity into play against the threats of death which are unavoidable whenever an inside and an outside, a self and an other, one group and another, are constituted. At this level of interiorization with its social as well as individual stakes, what I have called "aesthetic practices" are undoubtedly nothing other than the modern reply to the eternal question of morality. At least, this is how we might understand an ethics which, conscious of the fact that its order is sacrificial, reserves part of the burden for each of its adherents, therefore declaring them guilty while immediately affording them the possibility for *jouissance,* for various productions, for a life made up of both challenges and differences.

Spinoza's question can be taken up again here: Are women subject to ethics? If not to that ethics defined by classical philosophy—in relationship to which the ups and downs of feminist generations seem dangerously precarious—are women not already participating in the rapid dismantling that our age is experiencing at various levels (from wars to drugs to artificial insemination) and which poses the *demand* for a new ethics? The answer to Spinoza's question can be affirmative only at the cost of considering feminism as but a *moment* in the thought of that anthropomorphic identity which currently blocks the horizon of the discursive and scientific adventure of our species.

Female Consciousness and Collective Action: The Case of Barcelona, 1910–1918

Temma Kaplan

Female Consciousness and Collective Action

Female consciousness, recognition of what a particular class, culture, and historical period expect from women, creates a sense of rights and obligations that provides motive force for actions different from those Marxist or feminist theory generally try to explain. Female consciousness centers upon the rights of gender, on social concerns, on survival. Those with female consciousness accept the gender system of their society; indeed, such consciousness emerges from the division of labor by sex, which assigns women the responsibility of preserving life. But, accepting this task, women with female consciousness demand the rights that their obligations entail. The collective drive to secure those rights that result from the division of labor sometimes has revolutionary consequences insofar as it politicizes the networks of everyday life.

Various people sparked ideas they may not wish to endorse. I am especially grateful to Renate Bridenthal, Nancy Cott, Estelle Freedman, Linda Gordon, Claudia Koonz, Charles Maier, David Montgomery, Rayna Rapp, Ellen Ross, Gavin Smith, Meredith Tax, Gaye Tuchman, Daniel Walkowitz, Annette Weiner, and John Womack, Jr.

As part of being female, women learn to nurture, a task with social as well as psychological effects.[1] Women of the popular classes perform work associated with the obligation to preserve life; such jobs range from shopping for necessities to securing fuel and to guarding their neighbors, children, and mates against danger. The lives of women in the lower classes revolve around their work as gatherers and distributors of social resources in the community, whether or not they also work for wages outside their households. Women who have money simply hire other women to do for them the work of sustaining life that they do not want to do themselves. (Thus before refrigeration and running water, urban women went to fountains and markets every day, while those who could afford servants sent them.) But all classes of women understand what their society's division of labor by sex requires of them: the bedrock of women's consciousness is the need to preserve life. Now as in the past, women judge themselves and one another on how well they do work associated with being female.

Recognition of the existence of female consciousness necessitates reorientation of political theory: by placing human need above other social and political requirements and human life above property, profit, and even individual rights, female consciousness creates the vision of a society that has not yet appeared. Social cohesion rises above individual rights and quality of life over access to institutional power. Thus female consciousness has political implications, as women's collective actions have shown, although women themselves along with historians of their movements have remained ignorant about the motivations for female mass action.

Theories of consciousness attempt to explain causality in history. Modern theories of consciousness began with G. W. F. Hegel's *Philosophy of History*, which analysts such as Karl Marx attempted to rescue from abstraction. Whereas Hegel viewed consciousness as the effect of transcendent Reason operating inexorably through history, Marx restored human consciousness and intentional action as central objects of inquiry.[2] Feminist consciousness, understood from this Marxist perspec-

1. Nancy Chodorow explores the psychological dimensions of the fact that women nurture and men do not in her book, *The Reproduction of Mothering: Psychoanalysis and the Sociology of Gender* (Berkeley and Los Angeles: University of California Press, 1978). Although she does not stress the social requirements for women to nurture, Dolores Hayden examines women's work and describes the efforts of a group she calls "materialist feminists" to transform physical space by collectivizing laundries and kitchens, thereby making women's work more efficient. See Hayden, *The Grand Domestic Revolution: A History of Feminist Designs for American Homes, Neighborhoods, and Cities* (Cambridge, Mass.: MIT Press, 1981).

2. Even the leading early twentieth-century work on consciousness, George Lukács's *History and Class Consciousness* (Cambridge, Mass.: MIT Press, 1971), dwells on ideas rather than movements.

tive, is about power relationships and access to institutions. Feminism attempts to win for women full rights and powers both in the context of class and in the dominant political system. There may be differences among feminists by virtue of the priorities they give to different forms of oppression: radical feminists oppose the gender system solidified in the division of labor by sex; socialist feminists oppose gender and class systems and all power relations based on sexual differences or forms of work.[3] However, all feminists attack the division of labor by sex because roles limit freedom, and to mark distinctions is to imply superiority and inferiority.

The study of female mass movements calls attention to female consciousness. It is possible to examine a range of motivation in the everyday lives of women that might lead them to act collectively in pursuit of goals they could not attain as individuals. Women's movements follow common patterns; they focus on consumer and peace issues and they oppose outside aggressors. Accepting and enforcing the division of labor by sex, therefore, can bring women into conflict with authorities. Women may even attack their rulers when food prices rise too high for suspicious reasons, when sexual harassment brings women's dignity into question, or when the community of women appears to be under attack.

A sense of community that emerges from shared routines binds women to one another within their class and within their neighborhoods. The degree to which women carry out their work in community settings that bring them into contact with each other also influences what and how they think. Physical proximity—such as occurs in plazas, wash houses, markets, church entries, beauty parlors, and even female jails—contributes to the power of female community. These loose networks facilitate the tight bonds that exhibit their strength in times of collective action.

Female solidarity, a manifestation of consciousness, clearly changes in relationship to improvements in women's household working conditions. Thus middle-class women who work for a wage and who pay another woman to perform their housekeeping tasks do not have to go to public laundries or markets. Unlike women in the popular classes, middle-class women have more time for other activities. But they see fewer women on a daily basis. The sense of shared work as women that contributes to female communal consciousness is diminished. The com-

3. Most recent attention to the class implications of the division of labor can be found in feminist work about the impoverishment of welfare systems under late capitalism. It considers how the work women and minority men do in the public sector resembles the service work women do in their households and communities. See Laura Balbo, "The Servicing Work of Women and the Welfare State," mimeographed (Milan: University of Milan, Department of Sociology, 1980); and Temma Kaplan, "A Marxist Analysis of Women and Capitalism," in *Women and Politics,* ed. Jane Jaquette (New York: John Wiley & Sons, 1974), pp. 257–66.

munal work women do influences the way they think, especially about government obligation to regulate necessary resources.

Gossip exchanged during shared work, for example, provides an opportunity for women to think out loud.[4] It may be the means by which women enforce the division of labor upon one another, but it is also the means by which they explore their obligation to sustain life in the midst of difficult conditions. Through gossip, women both express and find reinforcement for their thoughts, which then influence what they do.

When social disorder breaks or endangers daily routines, women of the popular classes sometimes work to reestablish them, even by attempting to seize power themselves. But it is impossible to prove their motivations, as they seldom leave evidence in their own words about the reasons for their actions. This paucity of evidence has caused many who study crowd behavior to focus on acts rather than thoughts. It has led others to associate irrationality and spontaneity with collective action. In the case of female collective action, the thesis that women of the popular classes fight to preserve the sexual division of labor invites a reductionist view that what women do determines what they think. But women reflect upon their lives; they do not act mechanistically.[5]

Still other views of consciousness, those that stress strikes and the development of unions, either leave women out or focus on female worker militance without considering the ways in which women of the popular classes either supported or rejected such efforts.[6] The advantage of relating rise in consciousness with propensity to unionize is that such analysis stresses the importance of self-generating organizations developed by the working class. But these analyses imply that unions alone are the agencies of the working class; they ignore other forms of associational life in the family, the church, workers' circles, cooperatives, and women's groups. Mass support, particularly from women, comes precisely from such organizations. Preserving the networks that connect their associations galvanizes women to act in mining and textile strikes when community survival is at stake.

4. Susan Harding studies the relationship between gossip and female gender identity in "Women and Words in a Spanish Village," in *Toward an Anthropology of Women*, ed. Rayna Reiter [Rapp] (New York: Monthly Review Press, 1975), pp. 283–308.

5. There is no totally convincing explanation of the relationship between consciousness and action. In *The German Ideology* of 1844, Karl Marx presented three contradictory notions of consciousness. The first was that "as individuals express their life, so they are. What they are therefore coincides with their production, both with *what* they produce and with *how* they produce." He amplified this argument when he said that "consciousness can never be anything else than conscious existence, and the existence of men is their actual life-process." Yet he also claimed that humans develop "ideological reflexes and echoes of this life-process." See Karl Marx, *The German Ideology* (New York: International Publishers, 1966), pp. 7, 14.

6. Among the best treatments of strikes are Michelle Perrot, *Les Ouvriers en grève: France 1871–1890*, 2 vols. (Paris: Mouton, 1974); and Rolande Trempé, *Les Mineurs de Carmaux, 1848–1914*, 2 vols. (Paris: Editions Ouvriers, 1971).

The problem associated with viewing female consciousness from the perspective of women's participation in strikes is that it does not explain why men dominate even textile strikes, though the majority of textile workers are women; and why women strike less frequently than men when the issues emphasize working conditions rather than communal survival. Such a perspective cannot explain why so many strikes in which women engage expand into mass strikes that absorb people from the larger community. Even when exploitation at work and drives for unionization precipitate struggles in which women engage, female participants broaden demands to include social reforms.

Another approach considers political parties to be the measure of political consciousness and uses the number of women in leadership positions as an index of women's consciousness. According to this view, great women in male-dominated parties contribute to the general effort and thereby demonstrate class consciousness. Leaders instill consciousness into the popular class and direct its struggles for state power. Women who do not participate in such parties but act according to female consciousness often pursue the same goals as the parties that act in their names. They simply do not follow the dictates of leaders or a previously established program. The teleological view that consciousness exists only if it leads to the seizure of power telescopes all other forms of collective action and associational life into a single "prepolitical" stage, which cannot reveal the changes that arise out of developing consciousness. Most women appear as unconscious auxiliaries who act without thought even when they do precipitate movements such as the Russian Revolution of February 1917.[7]

By viewing consciousness as the creation of party leaders, who are seldom women with female consciousness, this party-centered view underestimates mass organization and self-generating class struggle.[8] It overlooks the contributions made by militants and others who are not party members but who, like women, struggle in the larger community around social issues of food supply, health, and pacifism. The party-centered view brands all nonparty political organization—neighborhood committees, for example—as prepolitical. It cannot explain how women's consciousness develops in the course of struggle; consciousness is seen as a quantum of matter rather than a process.

There are approaches, however, that view consciousness as just another word for women's culture as it extends itself through networks. Thus far, most studies of women's culture have focused upon middle-

---

7. Paolo Spriano takes consciousness to be nearly synonymous with party formation. See Spriano, *Socialismo e classe operaia a Torino dal 1892 al 1913* (Turin: Einaudi, 1958), and *Storia del Partito Comunista Italiano*, 4 vols. (Turin: Einaudi, 1967–76).

8. For a preliminary study of communalism and its political expression, see Temma Kaplan, "Class Consciousness and Community in Nineteenth-Century Andalusia," *Political Power and Social Theory* 2 (1981): 21–57.

class women because they have left evidence of their activity in letters and in contributions to printed literature.[9] But cultural traditions, with their own networks and institutions, also enable women of the popular classes to mobilize against oppressors and work toward an alternative society, the conception of which is well articulated and widely shared. Consciousness appears as the expression of communal traditions altered in response to economic developments and political conflict. Culture, in this case, emerges as solidarity built around networks—a form of solidarity that carries out the division of labor by sex. Communal rituals, regularized processions, songs, and stories passed on through oral tradition constitute a cultural world for women of the popular classes. Consciousness emerges as women reflect upon culture and work—two aspects of the division of labor.

During periods of social mobilization, as in the mass strikes that occurred throughout the world from the 1880s through the 1920s, women's neighborhood networks galvanized into political action groups. Women participated in public meetings and began to organize their own. They demonstrated with men and without them. They transformed their physical neighborhoods, particularly the public squares, in political ways. They moved beyond their neighborhoods, where they carried out women's work, to the seats of power in other sections of the city. They took a message they had developed schematically, a message that assumed even deeper meaning as they continued to make their demands. Thus, a historically rooted analysis that moves from action to thought must work inductively and examine a variety of movements in which women participated.[10]

This paper is a study of one such movement. It describes three kinds

9. See the general debate, "Politics and Culture in Women's History: A Symposium," *Feminist Studies* 6, no. 1 (Spring 1980): 26–64, in which Ellen DuBois, Mari Jo Buhle, Temma Kaplan, Gerda Lerner, and Carroll Smith-Rosenberg refine arguments about women's culture.

10. Charles Tilly uses the phrase "collective action" to describe social movements at incipient stages, long before anyone would consider them revolutionary. See Tilly, *From Mobilization to Revolution* (Reading, Mass.: Addison-Wesley Publishing Co., 1978). The new social history has examined group behavior, radical ideology, religious commitments, and popular culture, among other topics. Its leading practitioners and their pivotal works are Natalie Z. Davis, *Culture and Society in Early Modern France* (Stanford, Calif.: Stanford University Press, 1975); Eric J. Hobsbawm, *Primitive Rebels* (New York: W. W. Norton Co., 1959), and *Labouring Men: Studies in the History of Labour*, 3d ed. (London: Weidenfeld & Nicolson, 1966); and E. P. Thompson, *The Making of the English Working Class* (New York: Vintage Books, 1963). The best argument for the use of inductive reasoning appears in the work of the Italian cultural historian, Carlo Ginzburg. See Ginzburg, *The Cheese and the Worms: The Cosmos of a Sixteenth-Century Miller* (Baltimore: Johns Hopkins University Press, 1980), "Clues: Roots of a Scientific Paradigm," *Theory and Society* 7 (1979): 273–88, and "Morelli, Freud, and Sherlock Holmes: Clues and Scientific Methods," trans. Anna Davin, *History Workshop* 9 (Spring 1980): 5–36. This branch of social history attempts to explain motivation and discover the causes of collective action.

of female mobilization in Barcelona between 1910 and 1918. The events that occurred there show that women's defense of the rights accorded them by the sexual division of labor, although fundamentally conservative, had revolutionary consequences. Conscious that their government was not aiding them to fulfill their role as nurturers, women in Barcelona and elsewhere confronted the state to demand their rights as mothers and potential mothers.

Mass strikes (actually locally rooted, popular insurrections) engaged tens of thousands of women in Spain and elsewhere until the 1920s. Following waves of strikes and rebellions that began with the Barcelona General Strike of 1902, the women's networks in the popular quarters acquired a political character. Networks devoted to preserving life by providing food, clothing, and medical care to households became instruments used to transform social life. Examination of female collective action in 1910 following a case of child molestation, in the 1913 Constancy textile strike, and in the 1918 Barcelona women's war demonstrates how women's consciousness of broader political issues emerged in their defense of rights due them according to the division of labor.

Collective Action: Barcelona, 1910

Community solidarity forms in opposition to a ruling class whose power is supported by army and police. Common antagonism, even more than shared values, welds people together, and consciousness among women that they constitute a community often appears when they share outrage. When they perceive some violation of the norms they uphold according to the sexual division of labor, they gain consciousness of themselves as a community.

Against the background of a long metallurgist and machinist strike, a scandal gripped Barcelona's female working-class community in October 1910. Male workers were fighting for the nine-hour day and against forced layoffs and unemployment. These were obviously matters of concern for their female relatives and for the few females who shared their particular trades. But there seems to have been a sexual division of concern. Male workers preoccupied themselves with the labor situation. Women were outraged by child molestation.[11]

The widow of a police inspector and mother of six children who were all ill in some way had placed the two youngest girls, aged seven and four, in a convent orphanage. On October 10, 1910, she received a letter from the Mother Superior telling her that her seven-year-old was ill and should return home. The child suffered excruciating pain in her

11. Information about this incident appeared in Barcelona's republican newspaper, *El diluvio* (October 18, 1910), pp. 8–9 (morning ed.).

genital area due to internal and external lesions. The nuns said she had a contagious disease. After some delay, the physicians from the clinic admitted that she had venereal disease, the result of rape by a strange man who had promised to bathe her.

The female community of Barcelona took the victim as their own. On October 17, a local festival on the vigil before Saint Luke's Day, large numbers of humble women, described as "mujeres del pueblo," and market women from the Borne and Barceloneta markets of the old city gathered in front of the little girl's house. They bypassed the church; few of them engaged in the anticlerical demonstrations that the men organized. What seems to have been at issue for the women was solidarity with the mother and her sick child rather than rancor at the church. Throughout the marketplaces women talked of nothing else. The female neighbors lamented with the mother as it gradually dawned on all of them that the child had been sexually molested. When the police put pressure on the mother and child, the neighbors carried on a vigil and acted as chorus. The police tried to persuade the mother that her child engaged in immoral acts outside the convent school, but the women became as outraged as the mother, who proclaimed her child's innocence. Despite the far-flung publicity and talk, however, women did not participate in demonstrations beyond the confines of their neighborhood, the physical embodiment of their communal consciousness. They did not leave their neighborhood to attack the convent as the men did. They solidified their bonds as women, as mothers, and as neighbors through talk, support, and small financial contributions to the impoverished family of the victim.

Only when the case went to court for an official inquiry, thereby moving out of the neighborhood into the public realm, did the women act politically. They planned demonstrations at the Plaza of Bishop Urquinaona (a square just down from the central Plaza of Catalonia) and at a big park in the victim's neighborhood. When the women attempted to unite as women, they alarmed authorities, and the governor banned the meeting.[12] An increasing consciousness that officials, not they, would determine how the victim and her family were treated outraged the women. The officials' response amounted to a violation of women's rights to protect children and other women. For, apart from the violence itself, sexual harassment indeed challenges women's authority over other women and over their collective sexuality, the norms of which they enforce through gossip. The use of force against any woman brings into focus contradictions between the rights women believe are theirs according to the division of labor and their inability to enforce those rights against male encroachment.

12. Ibid. (October 30, 1910), p. 15 (morning ed.).

Collective Action: Barcelona, 1913

Political consciousness among women sometimes emerges from female consciousness, as it did in 1913 in Barcelona during the Constancy textile strike. In that action women of the popular classes took their grievances to the governor rather than to their bosses. The fortunes of the textile industry and working conditions in it affected almost all the women in Barcelona's working class. In 1913, 16–18 percent of all women over fourteen in and immediately around Barcelona labored in textile factories and related industries. These figures do not include women who did garment work, embroidery, and whitework in cottage industries. The spinning and weaving factories were often workshops, and they generally employed fewer than forty women. The women worked an eleven- or twelve-hour day, although male laborers usually worked only ten hours. In 1913, the average male wage in textiles was between 3 pesetas and 3 pesetas 75 céntimos a day; the average female wage was between 1 peseta 75 céntimos and 2 pesetas 50 céntimos. Few women, however, earned more than 2 pesetas a day. A shirtmaker, who worked at home, earned about 2 pesetas 50 céntimos for a dozen men's shirts, which took her twelve hours to complete.

For many of the anonymous women who did work at home manufacturing corsets, paper boxes, artificial flowers, shoes, and garments, only a community-wide strike offered the opportunity to attack their oppressors—the jobbers who provided them with piecework. Women organized by neighborhood, not by trade. In their neighborhoods they experienced the power of networks created through years of shared tasks.[13] There was a good reason for female factory workers and women in the community, most of whom earned a living in cottage industry at some time in their life, to unite as they did in 1913.[14]

Many of these women who were mothers watched their children die in the first part of the twentieth century in Barcelona. Dead fetuses and foundlings near starvation were left on the streets of the working-class districts almost every day in the winter and spring of 1913. During that year a family of four, eating three meals a day, consumed coffee and bread in the morning, salt cod and rice at midday dinner, and potatoes and salt pork at night. On the average, this cost 1 peseta 54 céntimos a day, of which 76 céntimos went for bread alone. (The rising cost of

13. A provocative treatment of urban space and consciousness appears in Henri Lefèvre, *La Production de l'éspace* (Paris: Anthropos, 1974).

14. The only detailed description of the Constancy strike of 1913 and its social background appears in Albert Balcells, "La mujer obrera en la industria catalana durante el primer cuarto del siglo XX," *Trabajo industrial y organización obrera en la Cataluña contemporánea (1900–1936)* (Barcelona: Editorial Laia, 1974), pp. 9–121. José Elías Molins, *La obrera en Cataluña, en la ciudad y en el campo. Orientaciones sociales* (Barcelona: Imprenta Barcelonesa, 1915), reported on the oppression of women from a Catholic perspective.

living, due to the intensification of Spain's war against Moroccan gueril-
las and to bad grain harvests throughout the world between 1904 and
1912, contributed to high bread prices.) With the immigration of peasants to the city following the wine blight, rent in the poorest working-
class districts of Barcelona had skyrocketed. The cost of an apartment in
these districts was 50 céntimos a day or 14 pesetas a month. In 1910,
clothing, blankets, and soap came to 25 céntimos a day, and fuel came to
another 20 céntimos.[15] Women helped nurse one another's children,
thereby forming tight bonds. When the government raised hopes for
cheap housing, working-class women demonstrated in favor of such
projects, but few new apartments were built.

In Spain, as elsewhere, housewives had sometimes organized sections of strong political parties in their villages or districts. Female
anarchists did the same throughout Spain.[16] Male leftists had long recognized that women—through neighborhood organization of laundries,
clinics, and food kitchens—supported men during strikes. But little had
been done to win better wages for female workers. In October 1912, the
Constancy Union was formed to organize unskilled men, women, and
children in the textile industry. Organizers called a general meeting of
Constancy on February 17, 1913, and two thousand people, mostly
women, showed up. Only one woman spoke, a textile worker and
socialist from Madrid named María García. Those who shared the platform and chaired the meeting were generally union activists. Speakers
from the floor included anarcho-syndicalists and some socialists from a
variety of trades. Few were women. The speakers discussed the need to
end the unbearable workdays women suffered in factories, but they
never discussed cottage industry or life in the neighborhoods; the Constancy Union, while leading the strike in the name of female workers,
was as slow as contemporary historians to recognize the noneconomic

15. Molins, p. 23; and "Sucessos," *La publicidad* (Barcelona) (January 28–30, February
5, and April 21, 1913), gave just a few examples of how many foundlings and dead fetuses
appeared in the streets of working-class neighborhoods. The labor situation was covered in
"Vida sindicalista," *La voz del pueblo* (Tarràsa) (February 22, 1913); "La vida obrera en
Barcelona," *El socialista* (Madrid) (April 18, 1913); and "Contra el trabajo nocturno," *El
socialista* (July 19, 1913). A. López Baeza, "Acción social: El trabajo en Barcelona," *El
socialista* (November 25, 1913), discussed the statistical unreliability of *Anuari d'estatística
social de Catalunya,* edited by the Museo Social de Barcelona. Most Spanish statistics should
be regarded as approximations. The prices come from the report of a seamstress who
testified before the Bishop of Barcelona. Dolors Moncerdá de Maciá, a leading Catalan
Catholic feminist, reported on conditions in the garment trades on March 16, 1910, in an
address to a Catholic group called Popular Social Action. It was reprinted as a pamphlet,
"Conferencia sobre L'Acció Católica social femenina" (Barcelona: L'Acció Católica, 1910),
pp. 13–14.

16. See Temma Kaplan, "Spanish Anarchism and Women's Liberation," *Journal of
Contemporary History* 7, no. 2 (1971): 101–10, and "Women and Spanish Anarchism," in
Becoming Visible: Women in European History, ed. Renate Bridenthal and Claudia Koonz
(Boston: Houghton Mifflin Co., 1977), pp. 400–421.

aspects of the strike. The organizers agreed to boycott the biggest companies in the districts of Sans, San Andrés, San Martín, Pueblo Nuevo, and Clot, new working-class suburbs immediately contiguous to the factories and to the old city.

There is no way to document how the women's networks grew out of female consciousness and helped intensify that consciousness as the situation deteriorated during the spring of 1913, but the networks had just that effect. Women carried on support work and established food kitchens for female strikers in the silk industry, who were striking against piece rates and fines. The local dairies, where women bought milk or simply congregated, served as information centers. Neighborhood women in Clot and San Andrés and San Martín targeted the company of Fábregas y Jordá, which conveniently had factories in all three districts. They carried on demonstrations in the main squares of each of those neighborhoods to publicize their demands.

The summer of 1913 approached, and prices continued their steady rise. Women, whether they worked outside the home or not, found it difficult to put food on the table. Despite widespread unemployment in the region—an estimated eighty thousand people were out of work—women pushed for a strike in the textile industry.[17] Apart from demands for a nine-hour day and an eight-hour night shift, Constancy called for a 40 percent increase in piece rates and a 25 percent hike in day wages. From the beginning, the governor sought one group among the owners to bargain with workers, but he was unsuccessful. The workers gave employers one month to decide.

In the meantime, women activated their networks in the working-class community. In a general meeting in San Martín, under the auspices of Constancy, women from throughout the city discussed strategies to spread their demands and to organize the strike they knew would come. They decided to send representatives to all the major food markets to talk with women who gathered there daily. Many of the people at this meeting had undoubtedly been involved in the anti–Moroccan War demonstrations of mid-June 1913, which had led to the arrest of socialist leaders.

On the night of July 27, people from throughout the popular neighborhoods of Barcelona and the surrounding textile towns gathered at the Socialist House of the People, on Aragon Street in the Clot district of Barcelona, to discuss the employers' failure to act on their demands. More than a thousand women attended the meeting. By all accounts, they led the demand to strike. On July 30, almost twenty thousand workers in Barcelona, of whom thirteen thousand were women and children, went out on strike. Countless others, including garment work-

17. "Las huelgas," *El socialista* (July 26, 1913); "De la Vaga textil. El Seny," *La campana de Gracia* (Barcelona) (August 9, 1913).

ers, seem to have joined them in street demonstrations. As a liberal journalist explained, "The spirit of women has spoken with enough eloquence to launch the entire working population and, as in other campaigns for social justice, the women excite the exaltation. It will be necessary to negotiate with them, because they will never accept a settlement short of their goals."[18] The goals had emerged in the course of struggle; action promoted new levels of consciousness among ordinary women.

Mass activity centered in the Sans area on the southwest edge of the old city, and in the San Martín, San Andrés, Clot, and Pueblo Nuevo areas throughout the industrialized northern sections. The women of these neighborhoods were particularly suited to lead the struggle. Sans, a village absorbed into Barcelona along with San Martín and San Andrés at the end of the nineteenth century, had its own distinct plazas and daily markets. All the "new" districts were linked to the downtown area by coach and trolley lines. By the time they officially joined Barcelona, they had become popular districts of the old city. But women generally went at least once a week to one of the old markets. When the open street market of the Plaza of Padró, near the first cotton mills of the old city, moved to the covered iron-work market of San Antonio iñ 1879, the women of Sans and of District V of the old town met there either daily or weekly. The Plaza of Padró was contiguous to the streets where the first steam-driven factories were established in 1835. Many of the new spinning mills grew up just twenty blocks away in Sans. The young women and children of old Barcelona and Sans provided the labor power for these mills into the twentieth century. These first mills grew up in the old, settled working-class districts whose squares became rallying places during subsequent demonstrations.[19]

The women of the Sans factories began the strike by demanding that a 1900 law about night work be enforced. Their employers had locked them out. With their female neighbors, the workers began to frequent the leftist centers, but they preferred the Plaza of Catalonia, the city's civic center. Four or five hundred met in groups at the large plaza. Not all the women were factory workers, an issue that later caused much controversy among authorities. On August 5, they began what was to become a daily female community ritual. Instead of gathering at the San José market along the Ramblas, the promenade to the sea, they marched from the Plaza of Catalonia, down the Ramblas, across Columbus Way,

18. "Las huelgas de Barcelona," *El imparcial* (Madrid) (July 30 and August 1, 1913); "El conflicto del Arte Fabril en Cataluña," *El socialista* (July 31, 1913); "Contra la violencia," *El imparcial* (August 2, 1913).

19. Tomás Cabellé y Clos, *Costumbres y usos de Barcelona. Narraciones populares* (Barcelona: Casa Editorial Seguí, 1947), p. 416; Jacques Valdour, *La Vie ouvrière. L'ouvrière espagnol. Observations vécues par Jacques Valdour, vol. 1, Catalogne* (Paris: Arthur Roussea, 1919), pp. 21–22.

and on to the governor's office at the Plaza of the Palace.[20] It is significant that the female community went to the governor rather than to their employers to voice their general grievances and that they did not attempt to build the strength of the Constancy Union. They seem to have been conscious more of communal than of trade union goals.[21]

For four days, the women carried on the same procession, which took about fifteen minutes. They marched at three o'clock in the afternoon, just as the normal crowds swelled the Ramblas after the dinner break. It was hard to distinguish these women from other poor women who frequented the Ramblas. There was a comic element to the scene as the number of undercover police increased; the government was growing nervous about street agitation. On August 8, as the women began their daily march, police stopped them and ordered them to disperse. The women sent the men, who sometimes accompanied them, away to avoid violence. They tried to outsmart the police by regrouping along the predetermined path. Approximately two hundred women reached the governor's office, but the police prevented them from entering. The governor sent word that he had already presented their union representatives with proposals to end the strike. The committee had one day to consider the plan.[22]

Constancy called an assembly to discuss the proposals, scheduling the meeting for seven o'clock at a downtown theater the next evening, August 10. The women, instead of meeting in the Plaza of Catalonia, gathered at the theater at three o'clock that afternoon. Their assembly included women from throughout the city, not just textile workers. They remained until the night meeting began. Luis Serra, who acted as chair, announced that the meeting was an assembly of the community rather than a union meeting; all were welcome and could speak as equals. Debate about the accords ensued, but the assembly voted overwhelmingly to continue the strike. Railroad workers were among those who attended, and they agreed to discuss calling a sympathy strike. Foundry workers in the city had been agitating since mid-July, and they continued their strike. By the night of the tenth, the general strike had begun.[23]

20. "Huelga en el Arte Fabril," *Diario de Barcelona* (Barcelona) (August 5, 1913), pp. 10, 603 (night ed.).

21. "Gobierno Civil. Cuestiones obreras," *La publicidad* (April 12, 1913); "Las operarias en seda. En Barcelona. Las batallas del proletariado. Ecos de la lucha," *El socialista* (April 10, 1913); and "Las obreras triunfan," ibid. (April 11, 1913).

22. "De la Vaga textil. El Seny," *La campana de Gracia* (August 9, 1913); *Diario de Barcelona* (August 4, 1913), pp. 10, 532–34; (August 7, 1913), pp. 10, 653; (August 8, 1913), pp. 10, 712; (August 9, 1913), pp. 10, 796.

23. T. Herros, "Feminismo en actividad," *Almanaque de "Tierra y Libertad" para 1914* (Barcelona: Imprenta 'Germinal,' 1913), pp. 98–99; *Diario de Barcelona* (August 11, 1913), pp. 10, 837–38 (morning ed.); (August 12, 1913), pp. 10, 873 (morning ed.).

Through street demonstrations, women activated female consciousness about the relationship between social life and economic reforms. Some male leaders of Constancy begged them to stop their street action, but the women answered with catcalls. On the afternoon of August 11, a massive demonstration of about fifteen hundred women and eight hundred men gathered in the Plaza of Catalonia and marched down the Ramblas and Columbus Way to the governor's offices. As they approached the Plaza of the Palace, they sent a sixteen-woman committee ahead to meet the governor and explain that they would not return to work. They retraced their steps up Columbus Way. As they reached the Gate of Peace, below the statue of Columbus at the mouth of the Ramblas, the police charged and tried to disperse them. Some strikers broke through to the Ramblas of Santa Mónica and regrouped. Others fought the police. They all reassembled at the Plaza of Catalonia.[24]

On August 12, the women began their march from the Plaza of Catalonia an hour earlier than usual, at two o'clock. But police clearly had orders to stop them without using direct force. The women retreated through the neighboring streets to Pelayo, to the Plaza of Bishop Urquinaona, and to the Plaza of the University in order to approach the Ramblas by the back streets. Most headed down toward the Royal Plaza where mounted police drove them off. The police, with some experience in riot control, blocked all streets that opened onto the Ramblas, and drove them to the nearest back streets. The women and police spent the afternoon battling for control of the Ramblas. Meanwhile the railroad workers, who met nearby, voted three to one to join the battle and extend the general strike.[25]

Throughout the rest of the strike—which was not completely over until September 15—the women continued to hold their demonstrations on the Ramblas. They also held daily meetings throughout the streets and markets of the old city, especially those of Sans, San Andrés, San Martín, Pueblo Nuevo, and Clot. The main focus shifted to the Plaza of Spain, where the old city meets Sans. The women and the new strike committee that had been elected at the August 10 assembly were not cordial. Even the militant labor leaders disapproved of the unruly women's demonstrations. They opposed the tactics women used against female scabs—cutting their hair to mark them as traitors. Female strikers warned the scabs to think of their beauty rather than their stomachs next time. They suggested selling the hair to wigmakers to raise money for the food kitchens. Constancy denounced the women as a mob, and tried to persuade them to stop demonstrating. The women assembled at the Plaza of Spain on August 20 and attempted to march from there down

24. *Diario de Barcelona* (August 12, 1913), pp. 10, 904 (night ed.).
25. Ibid., pp. 10, 905.

the Paralelo, the main street leading from the Plaza of Spain to the harbor where the governor's offices were, to explain that they would not abide by agreements made by the strike committee. The police persuaded them not to march. The women then went to the strike committee offices on Vista Alegre 12, in the heart of District V. They insisted that it was they and not the strike leadership who spoke for the community, and that they would not agree to end the strike.[26]

The governor published the Royal Decree early. It included the sixty-hour week, or a maximum of three thousand hours of work per year in the textile industry. Women could arrange their work day, so long as they managed to work sixty hours a week. The flexibility was meant to permit them a half-day of five hours on Saturdays, so that they could catch up with their housework.[27] In the end, the Royal Decree accomplished nothing for the strikers. Employers refused to abide by a law that interfered with their right to run their factories as they chose.

Nevertheless, the strike had important positive consequences for the women of the city. The street demonstration, especially that which proceeded down the Ramblas to the governor's office, gave physical evidence of their political consciousness; it amounted to a political theory in motion. As the critic John Berger has written: "A mass demonstration can be interpreted as the symbolic capturing of a capital. . . . The demonstrators interrupt the regular life of the streets they march through or of the open spaces they fill. They 'cut off' these areas, and, not yet having the power to occupy them permanently, they transform them into a temporary stage on which they dramatise the power they still lack."[28]

Mass strikes are more than labor struggles over wages and working conditions. What distinguishes them from other strikes is that they carry struggle over into the normal activity of society. They demonstrate the power of those who produce goods and services over those who manage them. During such struggles, daily life becomes a problem that the entire community must solve. Feeding people becomes more than the responsibility of individual women. Providing medical care for wounded strikers becomes a political act. General strikes close down cafes and restaurants where unmarried male workers congregate. The Barcelona community in struggle in 1913 had to create alternative places for them. All mass strikes invariably affect living conditions because privatized "women's work" becomes a public responsibility. Women become increasingly aware of the essential though invisible services they perform. But they also learn that the power they allegedly wield in their own sphere requires struggle if it is to become theirs in practice.

26. Ibid. (August 20, 1913), pp. 11, 238 (night ed.).
27. Ibid. (August 21, 1913), pp. 11, 245 (morning ed.).
28. John Berger, "The Nature of Mass Demonstrations," *New Society* (May 23, 1968), pp. 754–55.

Collective Action: Barcelona, 1918

The effect of subsistence issues upon the development of female consciousness became only too obvious during World War I when Spain was a nonbelligerent. Inflation and war shortages afflicted civilian populations in Barcelona in 1917 and 1918 and exacerbated the normal difficulties working-class women experienced in providing food, fuel, and shelter for their communities. The inability of Spanish authorities to regulate necessities caused women to use direct action in placing social need above political order. A government that fails to guarantee women their right to provide for their communities according to the sexual division of labor cannot claim their loyalty. Experiencing reciprocity among themselves and competence in preserving life instills women with a sense of their collective right to administer everyday life, even if they must confront authority to do so.

Under normal circumstances, women's networks allocate resources ranging from goods and fuel to consciousness and culture. During wartime, food and fuel are removed from women's control to become matters of state concern. So long as authorities regulate supplies, housing, and fuel when they are in short supply or when prices rise above the limitations of normal budgets, women will accept reduced provisions and governmental regulation, as they did in England during World War I. In other situations they may oppose authority, as they did between 1917 and 1923 in Russia, Italy, and Mexico.

The women's insurrection in Barcelona began in early January 1918, during one of the coldest winters on record. Lack of gas and electric power due to coal shortages had forced more than ten thousand workers out of the factories. Bread prices had been inching upward since October 1917. Rumors circulated in early January that they would rise another 5 céntimos. The city established a price board to investigate fuel and food prices. Bakers complained that they needed price hikes to break even, and coal merchants complained that they could not stay in business if they sold coal at prices the board suggested. The shortage and high price of coal used to heat houses triggered the Barcelona movement. By January 9, more than five hundred women began to attack coal trucks throughout the five major districts of Barcelona. About a thousand women attacked a big coal retailer on Parliament Street in the old downtown section of the city and auctioned off the coal at the lowest stipulated price.[29]

The second phase of the growing movement began on January 10,

29. Here, as in the coverage of the 1913 Constancy strike, I have attempted to include accounts from as many different newspapers as possible in order to accumulate detailed evidence about the events. *La Veu de Catalunya* (Barcelona) (January 2–12, 1918); *Diario de Barcelona* (January 10, 1918), p. 459 (night ed.).

when a crowd of about two hundred housewives from the old working-class districts of Barceloneta circulated through the city to the textile factories, where the work force was largely female. They called women workers out. They carried signs that read: "Down with the high cost of living. Throw out the speculators. Women into the streets to defend ourselves against hunger! Right the wrongs! In the name of humanity, all women take to the streets." Have women the right to speak for humanity? These women believed they did, so long as they acted to preserve the division of labor, to do what women do—that is, to act female.

Gathering their forces, housewives and female workers marched down to the governor's offices at the Plaza of the Palace. As the crowd shouted, "Long live this" and "Down with that," a delegation of six young women, led by Amalia Alegre and Amparo Montoliu, climbed the stairs to present the women's grievances to the governor. They asked that coal prices be regulated along with the prices of bread, olive oil, meat, and potatoes.[30] Elsewhere in the city, women continued to attack coal yards, and the mayor dispatched police to guard coal transports. In Gracia, with its well-developed radical political culture, women marched on the slaughterhouse and tried to auction meat. Near Tetuan Plaza, where new metallurgical factories had gone up, women urged men to go on strike.[31]

In an apparent effort to reduce fuel consumption, women from the harbor districts marched on the music halls. The splendor of these palaces of leisure attracted attention throughout Europe; Barcelona had become known as the "Paris of the South." Up and down the streets of pleasure, in from the avenue of the Marquis of Duero, popularly known as the Paralelo, women with sticks broke down doors, smashed mirrors, and sometimes succeeded in persuading bar girls and cabaret dancers to join them. When necessary, as in the Eden Palace, women and owners engaged in physical fights over women's assumed right to control the use of electricity in the music halls.

Women's consciousness became apparent in the patterns of mobilization they chose and the way they defined their movement. They wandered from coal yard to coal yard to gather supporters. Throughout the six-week-long mobilization, women revealed a female urban network. They began with the lines in front of coal dealers and moved later to the San José, Santa Catalina, San Antonio, Sans, Gracia, and Clot markets. Processions and consciousness of community were closely associated in Catholic life. The secular networks of women adopted this old connection, but the markets substituted for shrines and churches along the processional route.

30. *Diario de Barcelona* (January 11, 1918), pp. 467–68 (night ed.); *El diluvio* (January 11, 1918), p. 7 (morning ed.), and (January 11, 1918), p. 2 (afternoon ed.); *La Veu de Catalunya* (January 12, 1918).

31. *Diario de Barcelona* (January 12, 1918), p. 505 (night ed.).

Naming things, including oneself, promotes consciousness. The meaning of the term "vecindaria" was transformed in the course of the uprising. The masculine "vecino" simultaneously means "inhabitant," "head of household," and "citizen." But the feminine correlate is "hembra," or simply, "female." "Vecindaria" is a village term, which denotes a member of a tightly knit community. It is as close to a kinship term as the contemporary language could muster for a civic relationship. It roughly translates as "female comrade" or "sister." The term did not transcend the period of the uprising, but its use during the uprising indicates a sense of female self-awareness and solidarity that grew throughout January and February of 1918. On January 10, in the harbor section, a woman affixed a wall poster that called upon the "vecindaria" to protest the increased cost of living.

Female neighborhood commissions sent informal delegates to one another. On January 12, two separate women's delegations visited the exasperated governor. The group, which seems to have been dominated by younger women, told the governor that they hoped "to stop all work of women in Barcelona until the authorities rolled back prices on all primary necessities."[32] Women excluded men from their daily activities, including visits to the governor.

The delegation that approached him on January 14 demanded that no food or fuel leave the province. By six o'clock that evening, another women's delegation called for a rollback on all prices to pre–World War I levels. Moderate women demurred, visited the governor's office at midnight, and claimed they would be satisfied with more reductions of food and fuel costs.[33] The governor complained that with all the visits from women's delegations, he could not get any work done. A crowd of about a thousand women had gathered at the Plaza of Catalonia and had marched to the governor's office with the regular delegation of women at their head. When the women heard the governor's exasperated comment, they grew angry. They attempted to surge up the stairs, but the police cut them off, panicked, and shot nineteen women.[34]

Female consciousness, which may lack predetermined doctrine and structure, develops rather quickly when rulers resort to force. The shooting on the stairwell seems to have marked the governor's decision to repress rather than receive delegations of women. When women attempted to hold a demonstration on the afternoon of January 15 in the Plaza of Catalonia, the police dissolved the meeting. They shot into the air as women congregated in the nearby Ramblas. They cordoned off the Royal Plaza, another public area that had become a regular gather-

    32. *El diluvio* (January 13, 1918) (night ed.).

    33. *Diario de Barcelona* (January 14, 1918), p. 516 (morning ed.), and p. 573 (night ed.).

    34. Ibid. (January 14, 1918), pp. 573–74 (night ed.), (January 15, 1918), p. 586 (morning ed.), and pp. 621–22 (night ed.); *El diluvio* (January 15, 1918), p. 7 (morning ed.); *La hormiga de oro:Ilustración católica* (Barcelona) (January 19, 1918), p. 31.

ing place for female dissidents. The women grew angry and began to whistle and jeer. A journalist remarked that "repressive action of the police exacerbated the women's rebellious spirit."[35]

Female consciousness united housewives in the working-class districts with female factory workers. From January 15 on, most of the female workers went on strike and forced shops to close, while about seventeen hundred male laborers also refused to work.[36] Women of the popular classes continued to interrupt daily routines. They marched on El Siglo, Barcelona's first department store, where they called saleswomen to join their demonstration. By mobilizing around the sexual division of labor and the common female obligation to distribute resources through their networks, women of the popular class were united, whether or not they worked for a wage.

Women's networks had assumed leadership of a social struggle they pursued in the name of the entire female community. Their attacks on food stores throughout the city increased, as did periodic attempts by police to repress them through armed force. They adopted a committee structure, not unlike the soviets developed in Russia in 1917, to regulate attacks on grocery stores. In the process of solidifying their networks, they formulated new programs for action. These in turn brought the women to new levels of political consciousness about their rights to act according to the division of labor by sex.

Despite official opposition, thousands of Barcelona's women gathered at the Globe Theater for a public meeting. A female weaver presided. The women called for rollbacks on prices of all basic commodities to pre–World War I levels. They demanded rent reductions and lower railroad costs, which they believed were a major element in the general increase in the cost of living, and they demanded that six thousand male railroad workers be rehired. Large numbers of women participated in the general discussion.[37]

Officials in Madrid, though unfamiliar with female networks, were always wary about social strife in Barcelona. Irregular food supplies and fuel shortages, the causes of the struggle, promoted lockouts at those factories that still remained open. The governor tried to reestablish order by calling workers back to their jobs, but he lacked the cooperation of employers. Women sought to air their grievances at the governor's offices on January 21, but they were intercepted by the police.

Fearing civil war, authorities in Madrid recalled the governor. Women continued to attack commercial property in an effort to win control over food distribution. On January 25, the new military governor declared a state of siege and suspended civil rights. Nevertheless, strikes in the textile industry continued until February. Despite military

35. *El diluvio* (January 16, 1918), pp. 7–8 (morning ed.).
36. *Diario de Barcelona* (January 18, 1918), p. 769 (morning ed.).
37. *El diluvio* (January 18, 1918), p. 9 (morning ed.).

repression, women refused to acquiesce to the greed of speculators and the irregularities of the market. As late as February 15, price increases for salted cod at the Gracia market led to political mobilizations.[38]

Conclusion

The 1918 women's war reveals how closely social welfare and female consciousness are linked. The insurrection was a revolution of direct democracy in which everyday life became a political process, and through that process women's awareness grew. Disorders of war brought into view networks responsible for daily distribution of social resources. Breaks in routine raised questions about the quality of life women achieved through the networks they had formed to carry out the division of labor by sex. Women recreated these networks in political ways when merchants, governors, and states impeded their efforts to provide for their community. Women's growing familiarity with government offices, where they went to present proposals, brought them to physical spaces in the city where working-class women had seldom previously appeared. Their own movement through space, from the popular neighborhoods where housewives worked to the buildings where the men of power ruled, represented a flight in consciousness that revealed how the sexual division of labor fit into a larger political schema.

The capacity of local female networks to transcend the purposes for which they were originally formed appeared as women moved further and further away from their own neighborhoods and into the spaces occupied by the government and commercial groups. In 1910, women made forays out of their neighborhoods only at the time of the inquest to show their outrage about the molested child. Otherwise they remained in their own neighborhoods. By 1913, what appeared to be a labor struggle became a ritualized battle over social policy between the popular community, led by women, and the authorities. The street became the stage for this conflict, proof that female consciousness moves women to take radical action in defense of the division of labor.

The logic of female collective action in early twentieth-century Barcelona demonstrates an implicit language of social rights that emerges from commitment to the sexual division of labor. In defending the notion of separate rights based on separate work, women violated the self-same notion. They beseeched and then confronted government officials in the urban plazas and offices that were symbolic of the political and commercial power men wield. Ideas about how daily life and social stability dovetail propelled women to collective action to preserve their routines. They disrupted what was left of orderly life in their neigh-

38. *El sol* (Madrid) (January 9–February 2, 1918); *Almanaque de el Diario de Barcelona para el año 1919* (Barcelona: Imprenta de Diario de Barcelona, 1918), pp. 24–25.

borhoods and, in the course of movement, shocked police and authorities. Dramatization of their place in society wakened female consciousness as well as government fears.

By taking action, women of the popular classes promoted further thought. Shared sensibilities about rights and obligations took political shape in large assemblies of women, in processions, and in visits to the governor's offices. These shared goals, largely unformed until the experience of collective action created understanding, entailed supplying social need in spite of the requirements of war and statecraft. Networks defined themselves more sharply when solidarity found expression in words like "vecindaria" and in physical contact outside familiar neighborhood centers in new physical spaces. Consciousness about the syncopation between power and social need dawned upon female activists because it reproduced in the political arena the division of labor that governed female consciousness in the community. Welfare and inflation shattered social order even in nonbelligerent countries. Preoccupied with providing for themselves and their neighbors, women assumed revolutionary positions in order to defend everyday life and the female rights they needed in order to carry out their obligations.

To understand female consciousness in the popular classes one must comprehend the degree to which working-class women uphold the sexual division of labor because it defines what women do and therefore provides a sense of who they are in society and culture. The women incorporate social expectations with their particular notions of femininity. Their attempts to act according to notions held by their class and in their historical period about what women do sometimes leads them to a reactionary stance, as in the French Vendée and in Salvador Allende's Chile. But whether they act to serve the left or the right, women's disruptive behavior in the public arena appears incompatible with stereotypes of women as docile victims. The common social thread is their consistent defense of their right to feed and protect their communities either with the support of government or without it. Their conviction grows from their acceptance of the sexual division of labor as a means of survival.

Insofar as some feminist theory stresses the need to transform society so that men as well as women attribute high value to nurturance, such theory incorporates female consciousness into feminism. The degree to which women in political parties tend to find themselves channeled toward areas of health, education, and welfare also represents unconscious recognition that women have special prerogatives and socialized skills in these areas. But the insights of female consciousness, which place life above all other political goals, have never found expression in a major state or even a political party. Consider the implications of this for political programs, especially feminism: women's most conservative self-image could potentially convince them to demand that states place life above other goals.

Although the content of the division of labor varies enormously, the process of marking the differences it entails has cultural as well as material and psychological implications. In the course of struggling to do what women in their society and class were expected to do, women in Barcelona became outlaws. To fulfill women's obligations, they rebelled against the state. Their double duty as defenders of community rights and as law-abiding citizens became a double bind, which they forcibly ruptured through direct action.

Female consciousness, though conservative, promotes a social vision embodying profoundly radical political implications that feminist theorists have scarcely recognized. To do the work society assigns them, women have pursued social rather than narrowly political goals. When it appears that the survival of the community is at stake, women activate their networks to fight anyone—left or right, male or female—whom they think interferes with their ability to preserve life as they know it.

The nature of the sexual division of labor into which women are socialized predisposes them to political arguments about social issues. Reactionary political groups have often appealed to women on these grounds. Feminists, who value women's work, seldom argue that a just society would allocate its major spiritual and material resources to the tasks all women have learned to do. Pessimistic in the face of legislation like the Family Protection Act, which threatens the rights women have won in the past decade, feminists may abandon discussion of feminism's social vision to focus on more limited political defense of past gains that are now in jeopardy. That would be a mistake. Incorporating female consciousness into feminist arguments about programs for future economic and social democracy may be the only way to keep the content and spirit of what we have won and could promote a more broadly based social movement than any feminists have previously achieved.

Department of History
University of California, Los Angeles

The Sexual Politics of the New Right: Understanding the "Crisis of Liberalism" for the 1980s

Zillah R. Eisenstein

This essay will explore the New Right's analysis of the "crisis of liberalism" both as an economic philosophy and as a political ideology. Its critique of liberalism, which amounts to an indictment of the welfare state, attributes this crisis to the changed relationship between the state and the family. Therefore the fundamental thrust of present New Right politics is directed at redefining this relationship. In some sense, the New Right thinks that the welfare state is responsible for undermining the traditional patriarchal family by taking over different family functions. The health, welfare, and education of individuals, it believes, should be the purview of the family. The New Right's critique of the welfare state in this way becomes closely linked to its understanding of the crisis of the family. I intend to ask whether this analysis is not a misreading of history. If, as I believe, the growth of the welfare state is as much a response to changes in family structure as it is a cause of those changes, then the New Right has wrongly identified the source of the crisis and as a result has provided us with anachronistic models of the family and the state for the 1980s.

From the perspective of the New Right, the "problem" of the family—defined as the married heterosexual couple with children, the

I wish to thank Beau Grosscup and Rosalind Petchesky for their reading and helpful suggestions on earlier drafts of this article.

husband working in the labor force, and the wife remaining at home to rear the children—stems from husbands' loss of patriarchal authority as their wives have been pulled into the labor force. Richard Viguerie (the major fund raiser of the New Right), Jerry Falwell (a leading evangelist and head of the "Moral Majority"), and George Gilder (the economist whom David Stockman consults and the author of *Wealth and Poverty*) argue that in order to revitalize the capitalist economy, create a moral order, and strengthen America at home and abroad, policymakers must aim to reestablish the dominance of the traditional white patriarchal family. Because black women have always worked outside the home in disproportionate numbers to white women, whether in slave society or in the free labor market, the model of the traditional patriarchal family has never accurately described their family life. Yet today with white married women's entry into the labor force this nuclear model no longer describes the majority of white families either.[1] This is why the "problem" of the family has become more pronounced and why the issue of the married wage-earning woman has now been finally brought to center stage by the New Right. In this fundamental sense the sexual politics of the New Right is implicitly antifeminist and racist: it desires to establish the model of the traditional white patriarchal family by dismantling the welfare state and by removing wage-earning married women from the labor force and returning them to the home.

The New Right's attack is directed so forcefully against married wage-earning women and "working mothers"[2] because, as I argue in *The Radical Future of Liberal Feminism,* it is these women who have the potential to transform society. The New Right correctly understands this. The reality of the wage-earning wife's double day of work uncovers the patriarchal bias of liberalism and capitalist society.[3] As these women begin to understand the sexual bias in the marketplace (where a woman earns 58 cents to the male worker's $1.00) and continue to bear the responsibilities of housework and child care as well, they begin to voice feminist demands for affirmative action programs, equal pay, pregnancy

1. The criticism of female wage earners' effect on family life first emerged in Patrick Moynihan's 1965 report "The Negro Family, the Case for National Action," in *The Moynihan Report and the Politics of Controversy,* ed. Lee Rainwater and William Yancey (Cambridge, Mass.: MIT Press, 1967), pp. 39–124. Moynihan, using the model of the traditional (white) patriarchal family, argued that the deterioration of the Negro family was in large part due to the emasculation of the black male by his female counterpart who was working in the labor force and/or heading a household. Moynihan, believing that "the very essence of the male animal, from the bantam rooster to the four-star general, is to strut" (p. 62), thought that the challenges to the black male's authority by black women made a stable family relationship impossible.

2. The New Right's attack on the married woman wage-earner is at one and the same time a criticism of what it terms the "working mother."

3. See Zillah R. Eisenstein, *The Radical Future of Liberal Feminism* (New York: Longman, Inc., 1981), for a fuller accounting of this point.

disability payments, and abortion rights. They press for the equal rights promised by liberal ideology. The New Right focuses its attack on both liberalism *and* feminism precisely because mainstream feminist demands derive from the promises of liberalism as an ideology—individual autonomy and independence, freedom of choice, equality of opportunity, and equality before the law—and because they threaten to transform patriarchy, and with it capitalism, by uncovering the "crisis of liberalism." Feminist demands uncover the truth that capitalist patriarchal society cannot deliver on its "liberal" promises of equality or even equal rights for women without destabilizing itself.

The New Right's antifeminism is projected as profamily. It seeks to build a politics around questions of family life, a position the Left has always rejected as ineffective. Now that the New Right has effectively brought questions of family life into mainstream politics—a verification of the feminist movement's early appreciation of the political nature of the family—it remains for feminists to try to use this new electoral focus on family politics for our own purposes. The issue is no longer whether one can build a family politics that crosses lines of economic class and race, but rather what kind of family politics will prevail.

Developing a policy for the family or for different forms of the family is as central to the politics of the 1980s as finding a remedy to inflation. Clearly this is the focus, as we shall see below, of the Reagan-Stockman 1981 budget. What is not clear is whether feminists, left-liberals, and leftists will be able to build a coalition around these issues, to agree in particular on the necessity of promoting a nonpatriarchal form of the family. One can only be skeptical about this possibility when one sees that Mark Green, former director to Ralph Nader's Congress Watch, still believes that "the issue of the 1980's is economic: how to generate and distribute wealth in a new era."[4] Until left-liberals and

---

4. Mark Green, "The Progressive Alternative to Cowboy Capitalism," *Village Voice* (March 18–24, 1981), p. 10. One also remains skeptical about this possibility given the Left's analysis of family life provided by Christopher Lasch in *Haven in a Heartless World* (New York: Basic Books, 1977) and his failure to recognize feminism as a progressive political force for the 1980s (see his "Democracy and the Crisis of Confidence," *Democracy* 1, no. 1 [January 1981]: 25–40). The denial of the importance of the feminist movement in guiding, or at least participating in, a progressive coalition is evident in several leftist or left-liberal journals. For example, neither of the first two issues of *Democracy,* the new journal which was founded to address the present antidemocratic tendencies in the United States, has discussed feminism's role in fighting antidemocratic forces. Also see *Radical America, Facing Reaction,* vol. 15, nos. 1–2 (Spring 1981), especially Barbara Ehrenreich's "The Women's Movements: Feminist and Anti-Feminist" (pp. 93–104), which denies the viability of the feminist movement in fighting the right-wing reaction. See the interesting discussion by Stacey Oliker, "Abortion and the Left: The Limits of Pro-Family Politics," *Socialist Review* 11, no. 2 (March–April 1981): 71–96, about the Left's wavering support for reproductive rights. Also see Michael Walzer, *Radical Principles—Reflections of an Unreconstructed Democrat* (New York: Basic Books, 1980), for an example of a leftist analysis of the challenges to liberalism to the exclusion of feminism.

leftists recognize that New Right politics is fundamentally about the familial and sexual structuring of society, they will remain ineffective in the politics of the 1980s. And it will be feminists who will have to "fight the Right."

The New Right versus the "Liberal Takeover" of Government

The New Right represents a coalition of political, religious, and antifeminist groups that hope to dismantle the welfare state and reconstruct the traditional patriarchal family. The New Right's major fund raiser is Richard Viguerie, who started his mail-order company in 1965.[5] Several New Right organizations focus on election campaigns and governmental legislation: the Conservative Caucus, led by Howard Phillips (a former Nixon appointee chosen to dismantle the Office of Economic Opportunity); the Committee for the Survival of a Free Congress, led by Paul Weyrich; and the Conservative Political Action Committee, led by Terry Dolan. Key senators identified with the New Right are Orrin Hatch of Utah, Paul Laxalt of Nevada, Jesse Helms of North Carolina, and James McClure of Idaho. Another major segment of the New Right, the "Electronic Church," is dominated by the Evangelical Right, headed by Moral Majority and Jerry Falwell. The third sector of the New Right comprises the antifeminist "pro-life," "profamily" groups led by Phyllis Schlafly's Eagle Forum and Connie Marshner's Library Court. Although these three sectors of the New Right intersect and function as a coalition, this is not to say that they form one cohesive group, for they do not.

According to Viguerie's book *The New Right: We're Ready to Lead,* the New Right's goal is to organize the conservative middle-class majority in America: citizens concerned about high taxes and inflation; small businessmen angry at government control; born-again Christians disturbed about sex in television and movies; parents opposed to forced busing; supporters of the "right to life" who are against the federal funding of abortion; middle-class Americans tired of Big Government, Big Business, Big Labor, and Big Education; prodefense citizens; and those who believe America has *not* had her day and does not need to tighten her belt.[6]

5. Viguerie started his mail-order company with lists made up of contributors (of $50 or more) to the Goldwater campaign. According to Viguerie, the New Right became politically mobilized in 1974 when Ford chose Rockefeller for vice-president because it identified Rockefeller with the "liberal" establishment of the eastern Trilateral Commission. See Richard Viguerie, *The New Right: We're Ready to Lead* (Falls Church, Va.: Viguerie Co., 1980).

6. Ibid., pp. 15–16. For interesting discussions of New Right politics, see Alan Crawford, *Thunder on the Right* (New York: Pantheon Press, 1980); William Hunter, *The New Right: A Growing Force in State Politics* (Washington, D.C.: Conference on Alternative State and Local Policies and Center to Protect Worker's Rights, 1980); and Thomas McIntyre and John Obert, *The Fear Brokers* (New York: Pilgrim Press, 1979).

Ultimately this list of concerns can be summarized as a criticism of what the New Right terms the "liberal takeover" of government that started with the election of Franklin D. Roosevelt in 1932.[7] According to Viguerie and the New Right, the "liberals" have made the United States a second-rate military power; given away the Panama Canal; created the massive welfare state; lost Iran, Afghanistan, Vietnam, Laos, and Cambodia; crippled the FBI and CIA; encouraged American women to feel like failures if they want to be wives and mothers; and fought for preferential quotas for blacks and women.[8] They identify Adlai Stevenson, Walter Reuther, George Meany, Martin Luther King, Nelson Rockefeller, Hubert Humphrey, and Robert Kennedy as the leaders responsible for the liberal takeover of government. They identify the National Organization of Women, Planned Parenthood, Gay Rights National Lobby, National Abortion Rights Action League, and Women Strike for Peace as the leading single-issue political groups of the "liberal establishment" that are responsible for the liberal takeover of the family. And they identify Andrew Young, William Sloane Coffin, Martin Luther King, and Father Robert Drinan as the religious leaders of the liberal establishment.[9] The New Right has therefore developed its politics to counter the liberal takeover of the state, the family, and the church.

Neoconservatism and the Crisis of Liberalism

In order to understand fully present-day New Right politics one must place those politics within the neoconservative stance of the state today, which is a carry-over from the Carter administration. The elitism of neoconservatives and the pseudopopulism of the New Right are very different ideologically, appealing to different constituencies. However, both these groups believe liberalism is in crisis and share a basic indictment of the welfare state. As we shall see, the New Right utilizes the neoconservative critique of the welfare state but centers this problem in the crisis of the traditional patriarchal family. In the end, neoconservatives want to make the welfare state a conservative one, whereas the New Right says it seeks to dismantle it altogether.

7. Viguerie identifies the major victories of the "liberal" establishment as (1) Johnson's Elementary and Secondary Education Act of 1965, which shifted decision-making power from parents and local school boards to teacher unions and state and federal bureaucracies; (2) the congressional endorsement of the ERA in 1972; (3) the 1973 decision of the Supreme Court to make abortion legal; (4) the creation of the Department of Education in 1979, which extended federal control over education (*The New Right,* p. 202).

8. Ibid., pp. 5, 9.

9. Ibid., p. 105. Viguerie argues that the New Right's use of religion in politics is nothing new because the National Council of Churches has always taken political stands. It advocated admission of Red China to the United Nations as early as 1958, spoke out against prayer in public schools and against the Vietnam War, and endorsed the need for a guaranteed national income.

Leading neoconservatives today—like Daniel Bell, Irving Kristol, Norman Podhoretz, Nathan Glazer, Edward Banfield, James Q. Wilson, and Daniel Moynihan—reject the "Great Society" version of the welfare state because they think it has created what they term the "excesses of democracy."[10] They criticize the present welfare state for trying to create equality of conditions rather than equality of opportunity, for destroying the difference between liberty and egalitarianism. Liberty is the freedom one should have to run the race of life.[11] But there can be no guarantee that each competitor in the race should or will win. A truly liberal society allows everyone to compete, but a race in and of itself requires winners and losers. According to the neoconservatives, the problem is that everyone today claims the right to win. This has led people (particularly women and blacks) not only to expect equality of opportunity, but to expect equality of outcomes or conditions. The neoconservative believes these expectations destroy true liberty—which is about freedom, not equality. Daniel Bell articulates this position when he states, "One has to distinguish between treating people equally and making them equal."[12]

This is why neoconservatives are so critical of affirmative action programs that supposedly predetermine the outcome of a competition. The "excess of democracy" implies that the promises of liberal society have been carried too far; liberty has been redefined as equality. Peoples' desires become insatiable because they expect, and as a result demand, too much from the government. According to the neoconservative analysis, the welfare state is in crisis because it cannot and will never be able to satisfy the demand for equality, which only breeds more demands for greater equality. Hence, the neoconservative believes that only when expectations are lowered will government be able to satisfy the people again.[13] In other words, if people expect less of government, government will be able to perform better. This of course has a certain logic because the welfare state cannot create an egalitarian society and protect capitalist patriarchy at the same time. However, I would argue that the welfare state has never attempted to create equality of conditions and that the crisis of liberalism reflects the incapacity of the welfare state to

10. Peter Steinfels, *The Neoconservatives: The Men Who Are Changing America's Politics* (New York: Simon & Schuster, 1979), p. 51.

11. See Isaac Kramnick, "Religion and Radicalism: English Political Theory in the Age of Revolution," *Political Theory* 5, no. 4 (November 1977): 505–34, for an excellent discussion of equality of opportunity in bourgeois thought. Also see Moynihan, "The Negro Family," for an example of the neoconservative distinction between liberty and equality.

12. Daniel Bell, *The Cultural Contradictions of Capitalism* (New York: Basic Books, 1976), p. 260.

13. See Nathan Glazer and Irving Kristol, eds., *The American Commonwealth* (New York: Basic Books, 1976), esp. Samuel Huntington, "The Democratic Distemper" (pp. 9–38), for a full statement of this argument.

create even equality of opportunity for most white and black women and black men.

The major attack on the welfare state is leveled against what Irving Kristol calls the "new class": "scientists, lawyers, city planners, social workers, educators, criminologists, sociologists, [and] public health doctors" who work in the expanding public sector of the welfare state as "regulatory officials." Kristol sees this class as the people "whom liberal capitalism has sent to college in order to help manage its affluent, highly technological, mildly paternalistic, 'post-industrial society.' "[14]

According to Kristol, the welfare state does not just support the nonworking population, it actually supports the "middle-class professionals who attend to the needs of the nonworking population (teachers, social workers, lawyers, doctors, dieticians, civil servants of all descriptions)."[15] A review of the Reagan 1981 budget cuts clearly shows that they are aimed as much against the members of this supposed new class as they are aimed against the working and nonworking poor.

It is important to note that Kristol does not want to do away with the welfare state, but rather seeks to create a conservative welfare state based on the American values of self-reliance and individual liberty: "Wherever possible, people should be allowed to keep their own money—rather than having it transferred (via taxes) to the state—on condition that they put it to certain defined uses."[16] He wants to reconcile the purposes of the welfare state with the maximum amount of individual independence and the least amount of bureaucratic coercion.

Both Daniel Bell and Kristol recognize that with liberalism in crisis, capitalism needs a new moral vision. Kristol argues that "the enemy of liberal capitalism today is not so much socialism as nihilism. Only liberal capitalism doesn't see nihilism as an enemy, but rather as just another splendid business opportunity."[17] Bell contends that the crisis of liberalism lies in the cultural contradiction of capitalism, which reflects "the disjunction between the kind of organization and the norms demanded in the economic realm, and the norms of self-realization that are now central in the culture." Hedonism, pleasure as a way of life, has replaced the protestant ethic and the puritan temper of "sobriety, frugality, sexual restraint, and a forbidding attitude toward life."[18] Bell criticizes the consumer mentality of immediate gratification in capitalism that corrupts society with rampant individualism and leaves little sense of community or public purpose.

14. Irving Kristol, *Two Cheers for Capitalism* (New York: New American Library, 1978), pp. 14, 17.

15. Ibid., p. 169.

16. Ibid., p. 119.

17. Ibid., p. 61.

18. Bell, pp. 15–16, 21, 55.

Neoconservatives must recognize that the elitist liberalism they espouse will not work any better than the supposed egalitarian liberalism they so fear. Liberal democracy, with its egalitarian promises, functioned well as an ideology for competitive capitalism, but it functions less well for advanced monopoly capitalism. Once one is forced to emphasize the elitist bias of liberalism—liberty rather than equality, equality of opportunity and not egalitarianism—the very ideological force of liberalism is undermined. In actuality liberalism has always been elitist. But once one seeks to protect and further articulate liberalism's elitist (economic, sexual, racial) nature rather than its democratic qualities, one no longer has an ideology that is both liberal *and* democratic. Kristol might learn from himself when he criticizes a politics of nostalgia: "There is no more chance today of returning to a society of 'free enterprise' and enfeebled government than there was, in the sixteenth century, of returning to a Rome-centered Christendom. The world and the people in it have changed. One may regret this fact; nostalgia is always permissible. But the politics of nostalgia is always self-destructive."[19] In the end, the neoconservative criticism of the welfare state is a criticism of the democratic aspects of liberalism and the potential of its ideology to promise egalitarianism. The neoconservatives seek to protect liberalism (and with it capitalist patriarchy) by replacing the democratic potential of its ideology with authoritarianism. Doing so, they attack liberal democracy itself.

The New Right, Liberalism, and the Welfare State

The New Right's indictment, on the other hand, reduces liberalism to the policies, programs, and elected officials of the welfare state. In other words, the New Right's analysis of the "crisis of liberalism" does not extend to the neoconservative critique of liberalism itself as an ideology. Instead, the New Right continues to utilize much of the ideology of liberalism in its rhetoric (which has often been described as populist) at the same time that it supposedly rejects liberalism.

Much of the New Right's ideology is liberal in that it adopts the values of individualism and equality of opportunity. Viguèrie documents this point when he argues that he accepts the vision of the American dream but not the welfare state's role in trying to bring it about for individuals. Phyllis Schlafly embodies the liberal individualist spirit perfectly in the attitudes underlining her anti-ERA position: "If you're willing to work hard, there's no barrier you can't jump. . . . I've achieved

19. Kristol, p. 230.

my goals in life and I did it without sex-neutral laws."[20] Liberal ideology can also be seen in the New Right's "Right to Work Campaign," built on the argument that the individual should have the right to choose whether or not to join a union. This same liberal issue—an individual's right to choose—presents problems for the New Right's antiabortion campaign, which denies this individual right of choice to the woman. One can also see the deference to liberal ideology when President Reagan and Phyllis Schlafly carefully distinguish between their support for the equal rights of women—which recognizes the liberal individualist rights of a woman—and their lack of support for the Equal Rights Amendment, which they argue encourages state intervention into an individual's private life. One can, obviously, reject the welfare state and still be committed to liberal values, as the New Right is.

The New Right uses liberal ideology selectively and inconsistently, not recognizing how the ideology necessitates the welfare state, whereas neoconservatives argue that the ideology itself needs redefinition. Hence, the New Right is caught in the same dilemma that created the welfare state in the first place: an ideology of equal opportunity and individual freedom coupled with a structural reality of economic, sexual, and racial inequality. By dismantling the welfare state the New Right will do nothing about the needs that instigated this form of the state in the first place.

Instead of constructing a new vision of the welfare state, the New Right seeks to construct a society built around the traditional self-sufficient patriarchal family. By doing so it hopes to establish the autonomy of the family from the state. In order to do this the family must be relieved of its heavy tax burden *and* inflation. This will then release the married woman from work in the labor force. "Federal spending eats into the family's income, forcing mothers to go to work to pay for food, clothing, shelter and other family basics."[21] The New Right argument is this: Welfare state expenditures have raised taxes and added to inflation, pulling the married woman into the labor force and thereby destroying the fabric of the patriarchal family and hence the moral order of society.

By reasserting the power of the family against the state, the New Right more accurately intends to reestablish the power of the father. According to Jerry Falwell in *Listen America,* government has developed at the expense of the father's authority: "The progression of big government is amazing. A father's authority was lost first to the village, then to the city, next to the State, and finally to the empire."[22] Falwell is also angry and critical of the inflationary economy because it has under-

20. Carol Felsenthal, *The Sweetheart of the Silent Majority: The Biography of Phyllis Schlafly* (New York: Doubleday & Co., 1981), pp. 55, 58.

21. Viguerie, p. 207.

22. Jerry Falwell, *Listen America!* (New York: Doubleday & Co., 1980), p. 26.

mined the father's authority. He states that children should have the right "to have the love of a mother and a father who understand their different roles and fulfill their different responsibilities. . . . To live in an economic system that makes it possible for husbands to support their wives as full time mothers in the home and that enables families to survive on one income instead of two."[23] He wants to create a healthy economy and limit inflation in order to establish the single-wage-earner family. "The family is the fundamental building block and the basic unit of our society, and its continued health is a prerequisite for a healthy and prosperous nation. No nation has ever been stronger than the families within her."[24] Thus Falwell's fight against inflation is also a fight to reestablish the father's authority and to put women back in the home.

One sees this argument further developed in George Gilder's *Wealth and Poverty,* the book that Reagan has distributed to members of his cabinet. According to Gilder, the economy has become sluggish because the welfare state has created an imbalance between security (investment) and risk by creating an insurance plan for joblessness, disability, and indigent old age. This reduces work incentives, cuts American productivity, and in the end perpetuates poverty.[25] If the welfare state perpetuates poverty, Gilder sees the deterioration of family life as an apparent cause. Welfare benefits destroy the role of the father: "He can no longer feel manly in his own home." In welfare culture, money becomes, not something earned by men, "but a right conferred on women by the state." The male's role is undermined, and with it the moving force for upward mobility "has been cuckolded by the compassionate state."[26] Welfare erodes both the work ethic and family life and thus keeps poor people poor; unemployment compensation only promotes unemployment; Aid for Families with Dependent Children (AFDC) only makes families dependent and fatherless.[27] According to Gilder, "the only dependable route from poverty is always work, family, and faith," not the welfare state.[28]

A principle of upward mobility for Gilder is the maintenance of monogamous marriage and the family. Disruption of family life creates disruption in the economy because men need to direct their sexual energies toward the economy, and they only do so when they are connected to family duty. Marriage creates the sense of responsibility men need: "A married man . . . is spurred by the claims of family to channel his otherwise disruptive male aggressions into his performance as a provider for wife and children." This is not true for women, however. "Few

23. Ibid., p. 148.
24. Ibid., p. 121.
25. George Gilder, *Wealth and Poverty* (New York: Basic Books, 1981), p. 67.
26. Ibid., pp. 114, 115.
27. Ibid., pp. 127, 111.
28. Ibid., p. 68.

women with children make earning money the top priority in their lives," whereas men's commitment to children and to this sense of future spurs them to new heights. "These sexual differences alone . . . dictate that the first priority of any serious program against poverty is to strengthen the male role in poor families" and to maintain it in middle- and upper-class families.[29]

One can discern from Gilder's discussion of the poor family that the model of the successful family is one in which only the male earns wages. Woman's involvement in the labor force has challenged man's position of authority in the family, reduced his productivity at work, and thereby "caused a simultaneous expansion of the work force and a decline in productivity growth."[30] As a result, the husband's drive to succeed in his career has been deterred because "two half-hearted participants in the labor force can do better than one who is competing aggressively for the relatively few jobs in the upper echelons."[31] In the end Gilder believes that it is *familial anarchy,* not capitalism, that causes poverty by creating a nonproductive economy.[32] Women's participation in the labor force promotes family dissolution either by facilitating divorce or by challenging the patriarchal authority necessary to a "productive" economy. This leads to Gilder's indictment of the welfare state, which has only created the higher taxes and inflation that have pulled the married woman into the work force.[33] One can stabilize the family by reasserting the authority of the father in the family and by removing women from the wage labor force, and this can be done if taxes and inflation are reduced.

The antifeminism and racism of the New Right operate on two levels here. First, the presentation of the traditional patriarchal family as the desired model denies the realities of the black family *and* of the married wage-earning woman in both the black and white family. It is interesting to note that while the neoconservatives want to restructure the "new class" in their revision of the welfare state, members of the New Right have targeted wage-earning women to be the agents of the family's social services once they are returned to the home. Thus the attack on the welfare state becomes antifeminist and not merely anti–"new class." Second, the indictment of the welfare state and its "Great Society" programs is being used to turn back whatever gains have been made by black men and women and white women. The move against welfare state administrators is also racist in that many members of the new class who are currently being "declassed" and purged from government are black. Dismantling the welfare state is not only intended to redirect surplus

29. Ibid., p. 69.
30. Ibid., p. 14.
31. Ibid.
32. Ibid., p. 71.
33. Ibid., p. 14.

into the private sector in a period of declining United States industrial power, but it is also supposed to make clear that equality of opportunity for minorities, as well as women, is a privilege reserved for times of plenty.[34]

According to Viguerie, Falwell, and Gilder, married women have entered the labor force because of the high taxes and inflation caused by the continued growth of the welfare state. And married women's entrance into the labor force has eroded the traditional (white) patriarchal family structure necessary to the moral fabric of society and economic vitality. There is, however, another analysis to be considered: the argument that the welfare state is as much a consequence of changes in the economy and in the family (for example, women's entrance into the labor force, new sexual mores, and higher divorce rates) as it is a causal factor. If this is true, then one cannot restabilize the traditional (white) patriarchal family by dismantling the welfare state, because the welfare state developed out of the dissolution of the traditional patriarchal family. The New Right's vision of the state and its vision of the family, then, are both outmoded forms.

Capitalist Patriarchy and the Married Wage-earning Woman

The United States is as patriarchal as it is capitalist. This means that the politics of society is as self-consciously directed to maintaining the hierarchical male-dominated sexual system as to upholding the economic class structure. The forms of order and control in both systems remain mutually supportive until changes in one system begin to erode the hierarchical basis of the other. For example, such erosion in the patriarchal system began to occur when structural changes in the marketplace, changes in the wage structure, and inflation required white married women to enter the labor force.

When I say that there have been structural changes in the economic marketplace, I mean that the service and retail trade sectors of the economy have grown at the expense of the industrial sector. According to Emma Rothschild, 43 percent of all Americans employed in the private nonagricultural part of the economy in 1979 worked in services and retail trade.[35] From 1973 to 1979 the major growth sectors of the economy, which supplied more than 40 percent of the new private jobs, were eating and drinking fast-food places, business services (personnel supply services and data processing), and health services (including pri-

34. I am indebted to Rosalind Petchesky for helping me develop this part of my analysis.

35. Emma Rothschild, "Reagan and the Real America," *New York Review of Books* (February 5, 1981), pp. 12–18, esp. p. 12. Also see Harry Braverman, *Labor and Monopoly Capital* (New York: Monthly Review Press, 1978).

vate hospitals and nursing homes). These new jobs have been the primary source of employment for married women. Some of the women in this service sector supplement their husbands' earnings, but many are single parents. Either way, their labor force participation is essential to maintaining their families *and* this sector of the economy.

Women accounted for 41 percent of all wage earners in 1979: 31 percent of all manufacturing workers, 56 percent of all employees in eating and drinking places, 43 percent in all business services, 81 percent in all health services.[36] "Waiting on tables, defrosting frozen hamburgers, rendering services to buildings, looking after the old and the ill, is 'women's work.' "[37] And this work is low hour and low pay work. Wages in the private service sector averaged $9,853 in 1979 (measured in 1972 dollars); in the industrial sector they averaged $21,433.[38] In nursing and personal service work, in which 89 percent of the workers are women, the average wage in 1979 was $3.87 per hour compared to the average hourly wage of $16.16 in the entire private economy.[39] Most private service sector jobs are also dead ends that offer no possible advancement to a supervisory level; for example, 92 percent of the jobs in eating and drinking places are nonsupervisory. "The United States, in sum, is moving toward a structure of employment ever more dominated by jobs that are badly paid, unchanging, and unproductive."[40]

But what is really interesting about the private service sector is that its growth reflects the market's response to changes in the family, as well as changes in the relation between the state and the family. Increases in state welfare services, nursing homes, and fast-food restaurants all reflect new trends in family life, particularly the changes in woman's place within the family *and* within the market. Work once done in the home has been increasingly shifted to the market, and particular responsibilities of the family have been shifted to the state. We shall see, however, that Reagan's plan is to redirect these shifts. How can he do this, given the present realities of the family, the economy, and the intersection of the welfare state and the economy? And *why* do he and the New Right want to redirect the relationship between the state and the family? I think it is because they believe this will ultimately remove married women from the labor force.

The capitalist need for women workers has developed along with the not always successful attempt to protect the system of patriarchal hierarchy through the sexual segregation of the labor force. Women have been relegated to the low-productivity sector of the market, and their pay is unequal to men's even when the work is of the same or of

36. Rothschild, p. 12.
37. Ibid., pp. 12–13.
38. Ibid., p. 14.
39. Ibid., pp. 12–13.
40. Ibid.

comparable worth. Some women may accept the patriarchal organization of their family life, considering it "natural" that women cook the meals or do the laundry (although many do not), but I have yet to hear one of the secretaries in my office say that she does not have the right to earn the same as a man. Women as workers come to expect equal treatment in the market whether they expect it in their familial relations or not. Relations at home are supposedly regulated by love and devotion; the wage regulates woman's relations at the workplace. Her boss *is not* her husband. In other words, even though capitalism has reproduced a patriarchal structure within the market, the liberal ideology of the bourgeois marketplace—equality of opportunity, equality before the law, individual aggressiveness and independence—remains. As the working woman internalizes and applies these values to herself as she operates within the market's patriarchal structure, she develops a consciousness critical of her dead-ended work life. In the market, one's sex is supposed to be irrelevant. People are supposedly individuals, not members of a sexual class. Hard work is supposed to be rewarded. To the extent that the married wage-earning woman accepts these values when she enters the market, she becomes a contradiction in terms. As a worker she is supposedly an individual, and as a married woman she is a member of a sexual class. Her sexual class identity is highlighted in the market specifically because it is not supposed to matter there.

This highlighting of woman's differentiation from men in the market begins to create a consciousness one can term feminist. We are back to the point that because the majority of married women work in the labor force today and expect equality—even if it is only equality in the workplace—the promises of liberalism are being challenged. The New Right's objection is not merely that equalizing pay between men and women would cost billions of dollars, although the cost to the capitalist or profit maintenance is always at issue. More important is the fact that establishing equality in the workplace would erode a major form of patriarchal control presently maintained in the market as much as it is in the family and the home.

Here then is the contradiction: advanced capitalism, because of structural changes and inflation, has required married women to enter the labor force. Although the structure of the capitalist market is patriarchal, its ideology is definitely liberal. Married wage-earning women have the potential to perceive the conflict between liberalism as an ideology about equality and the sexual inequality of patriarchy as a structural requisite of the capitalist market. In their discontent, however limited, they can begin to recognize and reject this patriarchal structuring of opportunities in the market. When you put this awareness together with a married woman's double day of work—the work of her home and children as well as her outside job—the *possibilities* for feminist consciousness increase. The New Right attack on married wage-earning women lies in this reality: in demanding equality before the law and in wages, wage-earning women have begun to challenge the patriarchal organization of the market. Therein lies the crisis for liberalism: an ideology of (liberal) equality and a contradictory reality of patriarchal inequality is being uncovered by the married wage-earning woman.

The New Right's attack on married wage-earning women also reflects women's greater unification as a sexual class. First of all, white married women have joined black married women in the labor force. Although racial divisions still exist, black and white women share the world of the market more than ever before, and their attitudes reflect this. In 1972 a Harris poll for Virginia Slims cigarettes found that black women outscored white women 62 to 45 percent in support of efforts to change the status of women and 67 to 35 percent in sympathy with women's liberation groups.[41]

Second, married middle-class *and* working-class women find themselves sharing the service sector of the economy. A majority of wage-earning women find themselves in the low paying service and clerical fields, with only a small minority of women occupying professional jobs. The notion that feminism or feminist consciousness is limited to the white middle-class woman has never been more untrue than it is today. As Philip S. Foner has documented so well in *Women and the American Labor Movement*, working-class wage-earning women often define themselves as feminists.[42] The redefinition of women's lives, given the increasing number of women in the labor force, has actually made it necessary for feminism to address the needs of wage-earning women. And the reality of married wage-earning women cuts through traditional economic class lines.

In actuality, the increasing number of poor in our country are women. For unmarried women—divorced, separated, lesbian, never married, widowed—economic class and sexual class seem to merge under advanced capitalism. One might argue that these women are increasingly visible as an economic class through the "feminization of poverty." Three out of every five persons with incomes below the poverty level are women. Two out of every three older persons living in poverty are women. Female-headed families with no husband present comprise only 15 percent of all families but 48 percent of all poverty-level families. The median income of all women aged fourteen and above is well below half that of their male counterparts.[43] This reality is accentuated when a woman's economic inequality and dependence are not mediated through a husband, and her family's needs increasingly have to be met by the state. Economic class differences still exist among women, par-

41. Philip S. Foner, *Women and the American Labor Movement*, vol. 1, *From World War I to the Present* (New York: Free Press, 1980), p. 488.

42. Ibid., p. 478.

43. "Impact on Women of the Administration's Proposed Budget," prepared by the Women's Research and Education Institute for the Congresswomen's Caucus, April 1981, p. 5. Available from: WREI, 400 South Capitol Street S.E., Washington, D.C. 20003.

ticularly when one focuses on both their familial realities as well as their work in the labor force. The point is that the economic class reality of women's lives is very much in flux today because family forms are themselves in flux. Serious rethinking and study remain to be done in this area, given the changing nature of the family and the impact this has on understanding women's economic class.

Changes in the structure of the economy and in the family both reflect and create changes in the system of capitalist patriarchy. Although the state seeks to develop policy that protects the totality of capitalist patriarchy, I am arguing that present conflicts have developed between capitalism and patriarchy that will ultimately undermine the future of liberalism and the welfare state. The question is whether the New Right and the neoconservatives can use these conflicts to indict liberalism and create a "friendly fascism"[44] or whether feminists and leftists can develop a politics out of these conflicts that will lead to a more democratic and feminist state. In order for feminists and leftists to achieve this end, mainstream feminism will have to deal more self-consciously with the capitalist expression of patriarchy, and left-liberals and leftists will have to recognize the patriarchal structure of capitalism.

Although capitalism and patriarchy function as a mutually dependent totality,[45] they also operate as differentiated and conflictual systems. As such they remain two systems that are *relatively* autonomous from each other,[46] never totally separate today and yet always differentiated in purpose. Sexual life, which is what patriarchy ultimately must regulate, and economic life, which capitalism must ultimately regulate, cannot be conflated into one system; yet at present they are not separate, dual systems.[47] They are differentiated, relatively autonomous, and dialectically related. If they were not separate *and* connected to each other, one would not face the irreconcilable conflict of the married wage-earning woman today.

Reagan Administration Policies on the Family and the Welfare State

Although the New Right analysis of the family appears to dominate the state today, there is an earlier view of family life that does not con-

44. Bertram Gross, *Friendly Fascism* (New York: M. Evans & Co., 1980).

45. See my "Developing a Theory of Capitalist Patriarchy and Socialist Feminism," in *Capitalist Patriarchy and the Case for Socialist Feminism,* ed. Zillah Eisenstein (New York: Monthly Review Press, 1979), pp. 5–40, for a discussion of the mutual dependence of capitalism and patriarchy.

46. See my *Radical Future of Liberal Feminism,* esp. chaps. 9 and 10.

47. See Iris Young, "Socialist Feminism and the Limits of Dual Systems Theory," *Socialist Review* 10, no. 2–3 (March–June 1980): 169–88, for what I think is an incorrect assessment of my concept of capitalist patriarchy as reflecting a "dual system."

sider state involvement as an unwanted intrusion. The 1978 report of the commission on Families and Public Policies in the United States compiled during Carter's term argues that social services need to be upgraded for the family, that income maintenance programs are needed given the economic needs of families, and that a pluralistic view of family life should structure policymaking.[48] In this view, state involvement in the family is seen as necessary to enable the family to fulfill its responsibilities.

The commission specifically recommended a national employment policy that would legally enforce one's right to a job; the greater use of flextime, shared work, and other arrangements for full-time jobs; the support of part-time work arrangements to make possible the care of children and the elderly; and increased career counseling with special emphasis on programs for women.[49] These policy guidelines clearly recognize the changing nature of the family, particularly in relation to the two-wage-earner family.

Recent legislation introduced by David Durenberger, Mark Hatfield, and Bob Packwood and endorsed by Patrick Moynihan attempts to follow through on some of these recommendations related to the two-wage-earner family. Their Economic Equity Act (S. 888) tries to counter "policies in the public and private sector that are completely at odds with work patterns determined by the realities of women's dual wage-earning and parenting" by proposing tax credits to employers who hire women entering the work force after divorce or death of a spouse, equal tax status for heads of households and for married couples, employer-sponsored child care that would be provided as a tax-free fringe benefit similar to health insurance, and tax credits to offset the cost of child care.

Both the Commission Report of 1978 and the Economic Equity Act recognize the changing nature of the family and the unresolved conflicts between capitalism and patriarchy that these changes embody. Although this proposed legislation, in and of itself, cannot resolve the contradictions in the married wage-earning woman's life, it can begin to initiate necessary policy changes. As such, it is a beginning in the process of utilizing liberal feminist reforms to instigate progressive change. By virtue of the nature of the problem—the irresolvable conflict between liberalism and patriarchal society—one must move beyond such legislation. But it is through the struggle to pass such legislation that one builds a consciousness of the need for more progressive changes.

The importance of liberal feminist legislation becomes clear when it is compared to policy proposals of the New Right that seek to enforce the

48. *Families and Public Policies in the United States, Final Report of the Commission* (Washington, D.C.: National Conference on Social Welfare, 1978). Available from: National Conference on Social Welfare, 1730 M Street N.W., Suite 911, Washington, D.C. 20036.

49. Ibid., pp. 22–23.

model of the traditional male-headed household. The Laxalt-Jepsen Family Protection Act, as one example of New Right legislation, recommends that textbooks belittling the traditional role of women in society not be purchased with federal money; that tax exemptions of $1,000 be extended to households with dependents over the age of sixty-five; that a wage earner's contributions to a savings account for his nonworking spouse be tax deductible, up to $1,500 per year; that the current marriage tax penalizing married couples with two incomes be eliminated; that legal services corporation money be denied for abortions, school desegregation, divorce, or homosexual rights litigation.

The concerns of the Family Protection Act are spelled out even more starkly in $41.4 billion Reagan-Stockman budget cuts, which are primarily in the area of social services. One-third of the budget reduction comes from just two programs: health and income security. These programs specifically address the poor. And it is women who are the poor today.

Budget cuts are proposed in medicaid, food stamps, child nutrition, fuel assistance, and Aid to Families of Dependent Children. The family is supposed to be the social unit now responsible for all these aspects of health and welfare. Medicaid, a joint federal and state program, was designed to provide medical assistance to low-income persons who cannot afford medical care. In 1979, 61 percent of all medicaid recipients, 11 million people, were women. Thirty-four percent of all medicaid recipients were under the age of fifteen. Thirty-six percent of all households covered by medicaid were headed by females with no spouse present. And about 40 percent of all medicaid expenditures went for nursing-home care.[50] The cuts in medicaid will hit women and children directly, specifically those women heading households. The cuts will also make nursing-home care inaccessible to many, and therefore the care of the aged will be forced back onto women in the family.

Food stamps subsidize food purchases for households that have a net income below the poverty level and assets of less than $1,500. Some 2–3 million people (400,000–600,000 families) may be dropped from food stamp rolls if the proposals are enacted. Six out of ten food stamp households are headed by women.

Child nutrition programs include the national school lunch program, the breakfast program, the special milk program, the child care and summer feeding program, and the special nutrition program. As many as 700,000 women may be eliminated from the "Women, Infant and Child" (WIC) program that provides food packages to pregnant low-income women, infants, and children.[51]

50. Ibid., p. 2.
51. Ibid.

Aid to Families of Dependent Children provides cash benefits to needy families with dependent children. Over 90 percent of the AFDC recipients are women and their children. Over 80 percent of all single-parent households are headed by women, and one-third of these households are in poverty. According to administration estimates, the cutbacks and changes in AFDC would deny benefits to 400,000 families and would reduce benefits to 250,000. Presumably persons who are forced off AFDC rolls will enter the work force, even though 40 percent of all poverty-level women heading families alone already had some work experience in 1979.[52] These are precisely the women who need training in order to get jobs, and the Comprehensive Employment and Training Act (CETA) program, designed for this purpose, is also being cut.

These budget cuts take on even more significance when one sees that the fastest-growing form of the family today is the single-parent woman-headed family. Whereas the total number of families increased by 12 percent between 1970 and 1979, the number maintained by female householders grew by 51 percent.[53] The median income in 1978 of families maintained by a woman was $8,540, or slightly less than one-half (48 percent) of the $17,640 median income of families overall.[54] In 1977, 7.7 million families were headed by women. Almost one female-headed family in three is poor; about one in eighteen families headed by a man is poor.[55]

Two points stand out clearly. The two-wage-earner family has become the most common family form in the society. Fifty-seven percent of two-parent families today have two wage earners.[56] The single-parent woman-headed family is now as common as the traditional patriarchal family. The former presently accounts for 15 percent of the families today, whereas the latter comprises 14 percent.[57] Neither the two-wage-earner family nor the single-parent female-headed family fits the model of the "profamily" policy of the New Right. The budget cuts and their attack on the welfare state presume to protect the traditional patriarchal family from intrusion of the state. But by protecting this form of the family, it creates hardship for other forms of the American family that are as common.

In essence, then, the Reagan-Stockman budget tries to restabilize

52. Ibid., p. 1.
53. Bureau of the Census, "Families Maintained by Female Householders, 1970–79," Current Population Reports, Series P-23, no. 107 (October 1980), p. 5.
54. Ibid., p. 33.
55. "Facts We Dare Not Forget—Excerpts from a Neglected Government Report on Poverty and Unemployment to Which the New Administration Will Surely Pay No Attention," *Dissent* 28, no. 2 (Spring 1981): 166. Also see "Families Maintained by Female Householders, 1970–79."
56. *Families and Public Policies in the U.S.*, p. 14.
57. "Impact on Women of Proposed Budget," p. 5; Ehrenreich, p. 100.

patriarchy as much as it tries to fight inflation and stabilize capitalism. The government's cutbacks in the social services budget while the military budget increases are an attempt to redefine the responsibilities and purview of the state. Individuals and hence the family are supposed to be responsible for their health, education, and welfare. The state will be responsible for defense. Social services have been labeled the "excesses of democracy" and therefore must be curtailed. Neoconservatives want people to understand that the state cannot and should not create equality of conditions for them. And the New Right hopes to reestablish the power of the father in the family by asserting the role and purposes of the family *against* the state.

But let us examine these assumptions for a moment. Neoconservatives and the New Right believe that state intervention must be decreased in order to limit public expectations *and* inflation. But only state intervention in the social service realm is being cut. State spending in the military realm will be increased. As a matter of fact, Reagan initially intended to increase the defense budget from 12.4 percent to 14.6 percent by 1982. Reagan's newest budget proposal to reduce military spending by $2 billion by 1982 only reduces the initial buildup by 1 percent. These cuts will not jeopardize the overall goal of increased military spending at all. According to Lester Thurow, Reagan's military buildup will be the largest in American history, three times as large as the one that took place during the Vietnam War.[58] At the same time, Reagan proposes to cut taxes 30 percent. It is also important to remember that Johnson's refusal to raise taxes to pay for the Vietnam War was largely responsible for the increased inflation rate in this country. This time around, however, we will be adding to an inflation rate of 11 percent, whereas Johnson began the Vietnam War with around a 2 percent inflation rate.[59]

If Thurow's analysis is correct, the present cuts in social services *and* taxes will not limit inflation but rather increase it. In terms of the New Right's own analysis of inflation's impact on the family, this will further increase the burdens on married wage-earning women and families, particularly on the families of the working and nonworking poor. It may even increase the number of nonworking poor. In the end, the New Right's attack on the welfare state appears contradictory at best. First, it criticizes state expenditures only in the social service realm, not in the military and defense sector. Second, its support for cuts in the social service budget may only increase the need for social services, particularly for the working poor. Last, the demand to get government "off our backs" is completely contradicted by its profamily legislation. Basically, when the

58. Lester Thurow, "How to Wreck the Economy," *New York Review of Books* (May 14, 1981), pp. 3–8, esp. p. 3.
59. Ibid., p. 31.

New Right argues against state intervention in the family, it is criticizing economic aid to the family. It actively supports state involvement in legislating sexual matters like abortion and teenage pregnancy
counseling, in limiting venereal disease programs, and in curtailing sex
education. The Family Protection Act and the "Human Life" Bill are two
cases in point of such legislation.

This contradiction in New Right policy between a noninterven-
tionist state (cutting social services) and an interventionist state (legislating family morality) poses serious problems for its profamily program[60] and has slowed enactment of much of its legislation. First of
all, 72 percent of the American public reject the idea of a human life bill
that would consider the fetus a person and make abortion and some
forms of birth control illegal.[61] A majority of the American public does
not believe that this issue should be regulated by government or that
anyone but the woman and her doctor should decide whether she should
have an abortion or not. Second, to the extent that a majority of Americans do not live in the family form that will benefit from the New Right's
profamily policies, the New Right will have difficulty enacting its legislation, if a politics rooted in the other family forms can be articulated and
politically mobilized.

The welfare state has its problems, given its own contradictory nature. Irving Howe has defined at least two functions of the welfare state:
"It steps in to modulate the excesses of the economy, helping to create
rationality and order, and thereby to save capitalism from its own tendency to destruction. And it steps in to provide humanizing reforms, as a
response to insurgent groups and communities."[62] The problem, however, is not the welfare state, although that is a problem. The problem is
rather the kind of society we live in, which is both patriarchal and
capitalist, which would return individuals to self-reliance while maintaining structural barriers related to economic, racial, and sexual class
that limit and curtail the individual. It is up to feminists of all political
persuasions, left-liberals, and leftists to shift the critique from the welfare state to the patriarchal society that creates it. As feminists we need to
marshal the liberal demands for individual self-determination, freedom
of choice, individual autonomy, and equality before the law to indict

60. See Allen Hunter, "In the Wings: New Right Organization and Ideology," *Radical
America* 15, nos. 1–2 (Spring 1981): 113–40, for a similar discussion which he terms selective antistatism.

61. Documented in a February 1981 *Newsday* poll that was conducted nationwide and
reported in *The National NOW Times* (April 1981), p. 2. See also Frederick Jaffe, Barbara
Lindheim, and Philip Lee, *Abortion Politics, Private Morality and Public Policy* (New York:
McGraw-Hill Book Co., 1981), for a full discussion of public opinion about abortion.

62. Irving Howe, "The Right Menace," published in *Dissent* pamphlet no. 1, *The Threat
of Conservatism*, p. 29 (available from *Dissent*, 505 Fifth Avenue, New York, New York
10017).

capitalist patriarchal society. This use of liberal ideology by feminists will permit us to direct the public's consciousness to a critique of capitalist patriarchy, not merely of the welfare state.

The New Right assault is aimed against feminism precisely because it is women's liberal feminist consciousness about their rights to equality that is the major radicalizing force of the 1980s. Liberalism is in crisis today not merely because the welfare state is in crisis as the New Right believes, or because liberalism contains cultural contradictions as the neoconservatives argue, or because capitalism itself is in crisis, as Marxists and left-liberals contend. The "crisis of liberalism" is a result of the conflict between the traditional white patriarchal family, advanced capitalism, and the ideology of liberalism. The married wage-earning woman, black and white, and the potential of her feminist consciousness demonstrates this reality. Hence the New Right assault against her and the feminist movement in general.

Department of Politics
Ithaca College

VIEWPOINT

Feminist Theory and Dialectical Logic

Mary O'Brien

Feminist strategy and feminist scholarship at this moment in their development are hampered by the absence of solid theoretical perspective. It is a commonplace feminist complaint that the history of male supremacy has bequeathed to us a set of cultural and symbolic forms that view human experience from the distorted and one-sided perspective of a single gender. This skewing creates conceptual and theoretical problems that are inseparable from practical and strategic questions as well as from the need to understand in a systematic way both our history and our here and now. Such a theoretical understanding, I would argue, is

This essay is developed from "Marxism, Motherhood, and Metatheory," a paper presented at the Canadian Association of Learned Societies, Saskatoon, 1979. The material is developed in *The Politics of Reproduction* (London: Routledge & Kegan Paul, 1981).

the inescapable prelude to creating a future. All controlled social change is a unity of thought and action, of theoretical perspective interacting dynamically with coherent strategy based on the material reality of lived lives.

The analysis broached in this essay owes a great deal to Marx, especially to the idea of praxis developed by him and his successors. It also owes to both Marx and Hegel the thought that alienation is an epistemological as well as an experiential concept that has nothing at all to do with feeling but has a great deal to do with the actual process in which consciousness opposes itself to Otherness. Nevertheless, this is not a "Marxist" analysis in the orthodox sense, for I want to suggest that Marx's metatheory cannot make sense of the oppression of women, which clearly transcends class, even though the theory did appear to make sense within the historical boundaries within which Marx worked.

Marx developed his materialist science just a little more than a century ago, when millions of women and men in industrial countries were enduring the hardships visited on traditional ways of life by the economics and technology of the Free Market. Theorists met the social ills accompanying industrial revolution with an array of prescriptions for reform, sometimes socialist and frequently utopian. Marx and Engels, attempting in the Hungry Forties to express a complex theory of history in terms comprehensible to working people, criticized utopian socialism and analyzed the historical conditions which bred it with a theory significant also for women in our times.[1] Utopian thought arises, they argue, when people are able to see the defects and injustices of a society but are confronted with a socioeconomic reality not yet mature enough to create the revolutionary conditions by which it will self-destruct. Frustrated by this lack of ripeness, and not yet able to enunciate the social laws at work, such thinkers put imagination rather than science to work in the search for new social laws. They tend to pursue personal initiatives and to preach the rhetoric of radical systematic change while chasing after limited reformist goals. They attack the whole existing value system in an indiscriminate way, sweeping the present out of sight under the roseate carpet of an ideal future. They do everything, in fact, except engage in that disciplined collective activity unified with adequate theoretical understanding that constitutes the only route to rational and purposeful social reconstruction. Nonetheless, Marx and Engels concede, these utopian activities are useful: they publicize problems and arouse and heighten criticism. What they cannot do is initiate radical social change, which must anticipate and precipitate the historical dynamo of class struggle.

This situation has some striking contemporary parallels. Feminism

1. Karl Marx and Frederick Engels, *The Communist Manifesto* (New York: International Publications Co., 1948).

is currently seeking theories that express the historical and the present realities of female experience, but this enterprise is fraught with difficulties, not only in its relation to women's oppression and to class struggle but also in its evaluation of all previous theory. On the one hand, we have abstract and ultimately idealist efforts to uncover the "essence" of domestic labor,[2] and on the other, attempts to make over Marx or Freud or Aristotle or whomever. An additional impediment to such attempts is the lowly status of theory in general: the bourgeois world of the "self-made" capitalist distrusts theory, as does the empirical tradition of liberal scholarship, while the communist world, blithely disregarding Marx's own insight that history is continuous praxis and continuous process, makes the grave of Marx the stopping point for all theoretical activity.

Our urgent task is to analyze the inadequacies of male theory, a critical task that alone can create the theoretical foundations of its own development. Women cannot simply ignore the history of thought because it is, among other things, misogynist. We have to understand why men have created the abstraction Woman, with a capital W, just as they have created generalized abstract Man with a capital M, and why these are differentiated. Generalized, abstract woman, moreover, is a product of male praxis: thought about women, to be sure, but thought unified with very concrete and practical action to create the social conditions under which this abstract being must inhabit her body and her world. The activity that defines the Nature of Woman has been and is speculative and ideological. The activity that defines the lived conditions of women has been political and legal. Male supremacy typifies historical praxis at its most effective: a long-standing but vital unity of thought and action.

It thus comes as no surprise that political theorists have devoted considerable energy to elaborating concepts of Woman.[3] The universally ambivalent view that such concepts develop, seen, for instance in the dichotomy between Eve and Mary, is widely recognized and has been consistently attacked in feminist polemics.[4] Thus, we can argue simply that women are not like that; that there is no Woman but real flesh-and-blood female creatures with brains and pains and aspirations; that such dichotomies are an excuse to oppress and exploit women. Nonetheless polemic against institutionalized male chauvinism has severe analytical

2. For a recent contribution and annotated bibliography, see Bonnie Fox, ed., *Hidden in the Household: Women's Domestic Labour under Capitalism* (Toronto: Women's Press, 1980).

3. Such theorizing starts in Western culture with Plato. See, e.g., *The Republic*, book 5, and especially *The Symposium*, where Socrates argues that intellectual intercourse between men is more nobly creative than sexual intercourse between men and women. It should be noted that the analysis in this paper is biased in that it considers only the Western tradition; I am not qualified to deal with other traditions.

4. I do not use this word pejoratively. Polemic plays as important a part as utopian thought in the dynamics of social change. It identifies issues and excoriates conventional values.

limitations in that it is itself ultimately abstract, yet another fixed dogma about the "Nature of Man" with all the defects of such arbitrary generalization. We must look at the sources of the generalizations themselves.

This definition of Nature, for instance, and its attendant conceptualization are central to any understanding of male-stream thought.[5] The Nature of Woman appears to differ from the Nature of Man precisely because she is somehow more "Natural." Men are as ambivalent about Nature as they are about Woman, and these are, clearly, related ambivalences. Male conceptions of the nature of Nature have varied historically. The orchestration of a harmony of Man and Nature was a recurring motif of Classical thought, revived in the modern world by Hegel and Marx. Yet despite the real concern of dialectics to mediate and cancel alienation, Marxism has joined male metatheory in general in perceiving the fundamental opposition of Man and nature as an invitation to cancel Man's alienation from nature in a praxis of domination and control. One thing remains constant in all the differential formulations of the nature of Nature which embellish male-stream thought: women are inescapably entwined with Nature, and incapable, as de Beauvoir puts it, of transcendence. Woman may be ambivalent in the contrast she experiences between sexuality and maternity, but ambivalence is neither dualism nor contradiction: it is more generally perceived as merely perverse resistance to Woman's inevitable singularity, her ontological oneness with Nature. Men, on the other hand, appear to have two natures as against women's single one. Man's second nature is the one he makes himself, the offspring of his fraternal historical praxis. Idealist concepts of Man are concepts about this free-floating second nature, which, through the artificially created realms of civility, of politics, of philosophy, and, above all, of freedom, has transcended the contingencies of biological being.

This dual Nature of Man, seen as standing opposed to the single Nature of Woman, is not mere philosophical fantasy. It manifests itself concretely in the separation of public and private life. Dualist man lives in both of these realms, but, as Hannah Arendt has been not the first but the most recent to argue, he lives *humanly* only in the public realm.[6] The private realm is the realm of man's animality, the public realm that of his humanity. The first is governed by necessity and is where Woman lives. The second is created in freedom, and is the realm in which man's first

5. This terminology has been developed in earlier works and found useful. See Mary O'Brien, "The Politics of Impotence," in *Contemporary Issues in Political Philosophy*, ed. William R. Shea and John King-Farlow (New York: Watson Academic Publications, 1976), and "The Dialectics of Reproduction," *Women's Studies International Quarterly* 1, no. 3 (1979): 233–39.

6. Hannah Arendt, *The Human Condition* (Chicago: University of Chicago Press, 1958), chap. 2. For a critique of Arendt's analysis of ontological dualism, see Mary O'Brien, *The Politics of Reproduction*, chap. 3.

nature is transcended by his second. To be sure, all men do not perform in both spheres, for necessity ensures that only an elite core of the best of men can acquire the leisure needed to perform those acts of nobility and heroism that constitute the individual and collective splendors of political creativity. All aristocratic and elitist thought believes that such hierarchicalism is inevitable, and it is certainly the case historically that the separation of public and private life has as little meaning to the man on the assembly line as it did for the medieval serf. Nonetheless, the separation, abstract and problematic though it in some ways may be, is an important one, both for ordinary man, for whom it is unreal but consoling, and for all women, for whom it is unreal but exploitive. Women's realm has been fixed theoretically and actually in the private realm, the realm of Nature, Necessity, and Nonfreedom.

Class analysis in the Marxist tradition has given a partial explanation of why only some men have access to the public realm. This realm is the social space in which a ruling class is free to perpetuate the praxis of its own survival qua ruling class. Marxists accept the clear relation between ruling-class praxis and the ownership of private property—property understood here as specifically the ownership of the means of production. Capitalist production thus blurs the lines between public and private life. Though such modes of production as cottage industry have largely vanished, Marx's elaborate analysis of the dialectics of Use Value and Exchange Value can be interpreted as a dialectic between private household production and the production of private enterprise organized in public corporations.[7] When Engels tries to link the oppression of women to social class and private property, however, he returns to a very simplified analysis about an earlier mode of property (households, livestock, primitive tools, and so forth) in societies in which the reality of a public realm is rudimentary, as are class divisions.[8] The analysis is polemical rather than critical, and is certainly not dialectical, for no attempt is made to analyze the contradictions within reproductive as opposed to productive processes nor between the social relations of production on the one hand and the social relations of reproduction on the other.

Other explanatory metatheories, from the putative determinants of psychic structure spun from the clinical genius of Sigmund Freud to the crude animal fantasies of the Tigers of the academic jungle, are equally speculative and unsatisfactory; men are ultimately claimed to be superior to women "by nature." However, and this is important, all of these theories would reject the charge that they are insecurely grounded. They believe themselves to be solidly grounded, and what they are

7. Karl Marx, *Capital: A Critique of Political Economy,* trans. Ben Fowkes (New York: Random House, 1977), 1:125–77.

8. Frederick Engels, *The Origin of Family, Private Property, and the State,* ed. Eleanor B. Leacock (New York: International Publications Co., 1972).

grounded in is the brute fact of women's reproductive function. Women are evidently tied to nature by the a-human act of giving birth to humans.

The unanimity and harmony of the male-voiced choir of intellectual history on this point has had some curious and damaging effects. De Beauvoir, for example, despite the power and integrity in her work, accepts without question the evaluation of childbirth as an inferior animal activity and the biological curse of femininity.[9] Shulamith Firestone pursues this theorem to its logical conclusion; if the subjection of women rests on the low value of the reproductive function, then the liberation of women depends on the capacity to evade this function, to rely on cybernetic technology to guarantee the survival of the race.[10]

Reliance on technology to advance productive development is now sufficiently suspect to make us question the wisdom of proceeding blithely toward general technological reproduction, a process quite different from that in which individual women choose to control their own bodies by technological means. What men (and some women) have done is to let the low social value ascribed by male supremacist ideology to women's reproductive function obscure the sociohistorical necessity for species persistence. This low value and its material base have to be subjected to critical analysis, and that base lies in the nature of the process of biological reproduction itself.[11] While Marx's historical model gives great significance to the dialectical structure of the productive labor process—that unity of thinking and doing by which workers cancel the separation between themselves and the natural world, and in so doing create the world anew—male-dominated culture has not given a high value to the creative power of reproductive labor and the act of giving birth.[12] It has been argued that while we consciously experience our hungers and are consciously aware that we must die, we do not remember or in a real sense experience our birth. This is specious. To be sure, neither men nor women remember clearly the act of being born, but women experience birth as such in an *immediate* way. Men, on the other hand, do not: biologically alienated from birth process at the moment of the ejaculation of semen, men are mere spectators during that process. They must take mediative action to reestablish their relation to biological continuity, to cancel the Otherness, this separation of men from natural genetic continuity. Both men and women know about

9. Simone de Beauvoir, *The Second Sex* (New York: Vintage Books, 1974), p. 24.

10. Shulamith Firestone, *The Dialectic of Sex* (New York: Bantam Books, 1971), p. 199. As Juliet Mitchell has noted (*Woman's Estate* [New York: Random House, 1973], pp. 33–35), Firestone's analysis is dualist rather than dialectical, a simplistic materialism.

11. De Beauvoir, p. xxviii.

12. For an early flight of male biological fancy, see *De generatione animalium*, in which Aristotle argues that men contribute life and soul to the child while women merely contribute "material."

birth, think about it, experience it as real, but experience it differently. There is, in other words, such a thing as *reproductive consciousness*, and the theoretical analysis and comprehension of this form of consciousness, its material roots and its gender differentiation, is an urgent task when developing a comprehension of women's worldly experience.

The first fact to be noted is that biological reproductive *process* is unified with human reproductive *consciousness* precisely because this process, like all human mediation of experience and thought, is a dialectical process. Human reproduction incidentally brings with it a bonus in the sense that it helps to elucidate the far from simple notion of dialectic. As far as I have been able to determine, the dialectical structure of reproductive process was apprehended only by that master dialectician, Hegel himself.[13] Explanations of the Hegelian dialectic usually eviscerate the man's thought in mystifying oversimplification (thesis, antithesis, synthesis) or lapse into a linguistic ambiguity that surpasses Hegel's own; Marx's dialectic is often enough thought to be adequately summed up in the proposition that all history is the history of class struggle. Dialectic is for both thinkers the science which captures the laws of historical process, which is to say the science which comprehends all human experience, for all experience is process. Thus, the forms of subjective and collective consciousness, the forms of objective lived experience, and the praxis which mediates the opposition between thought and action on a personal or collective level are dialectically structured, because, infinitely varied though the content of the experience and thought may be, it all moves: it is formally *process*, it is a series of alienations, contradictions, and mediation. It is, in fact, what we call history, and the laws of its movement are dialectical.

Conventional explanations of what this process is actually like and how it works quite often trail off into opaque gobbledygook about negations and so forth. We can, however, come to terms in a preliminary way with dialectical logic by examining, as Hegel does as a young man, the dialectics of reproduction.

Hegel notes that reproduction is a process of "unity, separated opposites, reunion."[14] What he is referring to is the unity of the man and woman in copulation, which he discreetly calls "love," and the separation and reunion of the respective seed of the lovers, creating a new entity that is both part of but separate from its progenitors. The new seed both

13. The key passages may be found in the fragment "On Love," in *Early Theological Writings*, trans. T. M. Knox and R. Kroner (Philadelphia: University of Pennsylvania Press, 1971), and in the very obscure reworking of his 1803–4 lectures which Hegel published as "System der Sittlichkeit," recently translated by T. M. Knox and H. S. Harris. See also my own extended treatment of Hegel's theory of reproduction in "Man, Physiology, and Fate: Hegel," Grant for Research on Women (GROW) Paper no. 12, mimeographed (Toronto: Ontario Institute for Studies in Education, 1977).

14. Hegel, "On Love," p. 307.

is and *is not* the unity of the parents. It "embodies" that unity but ultimately transcends it: it "negates" the particularity and opposition of male and female. The unified seed then grows and develops and begins to realize its own uniqueness; there is a transformation from quantity (1 + 1 = 3) into quality, a new being who is at least potentially independent. Finally, the matured unity of the seed "breaks free" from its underworld maturation, transformed from mere seed to actual baby, a higher form of the embodied unity and negated separateness of the parents, or, if you will, a negation of a negation.

There are, however, some aspects of this process about which Hegel is prejudiced, evasive, or simply wrong. In the first place, the mature infant does not "break free"; it is brought into the world by human, female *labor*. Given the emphasis which both Marx and Hegel place upon labor as an active form of mediation between Man and his natural environment, this is an important point. Neither thinker appears to have realized that parturitive labor is a crucial factor in the development of reproductive consciousness. This does not mean, of course, that women who have not borne children are somehow incomplete, with no little baby to salve the genital mutilations visited upon them by phallic absence. Reproductive consciousness, like all other forms of consciousness, is not the atomic and subjective affair which individualist ideologies cherish. Reproductive consciousness is *cultural*. It nonetheless rests on a biological substructure, the process of reproduction. Hegel and Marx, however, presumably believe that because childbearing women cannot avoid doing what they are doing they are incapable of experiencing and thinking about what they are doing. The "necessity" to labor reproductively does not have for Marx the ontological significance of the necessity to produce, and is therefore excluded from the substructure of his historicist metatheory.

Further, the separations of which Hegel speaks are differentiated by gender. Man's seed, once alienated, is permanently estranged, and he has no way of knowing whether or not it immediately or ever takes root. Women part from a whole child, but this alienation is mediated by labor. By her labor, the woman confirms two very important things. One, obviously, is the knowledge of this child as in a concrete sense *her* child, the product of her labor, a *value* that her labor has created. The second is the experience of an integration with the actual continuity of her species. Women are in a unity with nature that is biological but not immediate. The birth of the child is an alienation just as much as the loss of the sperm is an alienation. The difference is that the first is mediated involuntarily and naturally in reproductive labor, while the second mediation becomes, as it were, a historical project for men. These separations and mediations are the particular aspect of the dialectics of reproduction, the individual experience, over against which particularity stands, as always in dialectical logic, the Universal. Female reproductive consciousness, mediated by labor, negates the separation between women and genetic continuity: women stand in a relation to *time* mediated by experience. For men, such transcendence of alienation is accessible only to knowledge, specifically to the knowledge of the relationship between sexual intercourse and conception that came, we may assume, as a historical discovery. Unmediated by involuntary action, paternity is essentially idea—fundamentally abstract, passive, and, while it remains unmediated, productive of an alienated consciousness. For men, in a real sense, physiology is fate. Nonetheless, paternity partakes of "universality" not only in the sense that any man may have fathered this child,[15] but in the sense that the male solution to the problem of the uncertainty of paternity has been a universal oppression of women.[16]

Is this important? Why should such a situation bother men? The first answer is that it obviously has done so. The historical record is replete with men's efforts to overcome the uncertainty of paternity. A salient example of such effort is the institution of marriage: the creation of the private realm reserves access to one woman by one man. History also shows us the efforts men have made to create, as social substitutes for the actual genetic continuity from which they are experientially estranged, principles of continuity, social institutions, and self-regenerating ideologies that transcend individual life spans and symbolize the continuity of the race. Some of the more obvious of these are law, political constitutions, gods who are blessedly eternal, constitutional and hereditary monarchy, heritable property, and the Idea of the State. All of these phenomena require careful analysis, but here I simply want to assert, first, that there is evidence that by the unceasing creation of modes, principles, and symbols of continuity men have obscured the fact that the material base of human history is human reproduction. Second, I want to suggest that the actual process of reproduction provides a theoretical framework from which we can view all this male historical praxis constructively.

I am not positing here some notion of psychic need or existential yearning for fatherhood. The dialectics of reproduction permit the evasion of fatherhood, a freedom often enough exploited. Dialectics, however, insists that the structure of human consciousness proceeds by the negation of alienation. Both Hegel and Marx take this view of consciousness, though for Hegel the process is in the first instance a subjective one, developing by means of continuing negation and transcendence to a unity with metaphysical and universal Reason. Hegel then sees Reason as objectified through practice in the world and concretized

15. A difficulty, I believe, which led Plato to attempt a solution by making motherhood as uncertain as fatherhood in book 5 of *The Republic*.

16. "Universal" is used here in the dialectical sense of standing opposed to particularity. It does not mean that every known society is patriarchal, simply that societies which have a record of historical change and dynamism become patriarchal.

in history. For Marx, the dialectical process involves a universal class consciousness seeking to abolish the alienation of labor and the particularity of ruling classes in a more humane universality. Neither of these thinkers deals with reproduction in a dialectical way; rather they retreat ignominiously to the sort of crude empiricism that both despise. For Hegel, women cannot transcend particularity and thus constitute a hazard in the path of Universal Reason: they therefore must have their ethical being, limited as it is, in the household. For Marx, they can only find the transcendence of particularity in social labor. Both men no doubt are reflecting a misogynist attitude toward women that prevailed not only in their time but through recorded history. Indeed, the question of why women did not resist either the appropriation of their children or the development of the marriage relation as a property relation is one that perplexes many modern women. I do not think it should. In the first place, the birth of patriarchy was a historical event about which little evidence has survived. We simply do not know if women fought back. Engels has no evidence at all to support his contention that "the world-historical defeat of the female sex" was the greatest revolution of all time but was a peaceful one—an odd view for a theorist of history-as-struggle.[17] However, we do know that, whether they fought or not, women lost, and the consequent cultural and ideological bastions raised on the substructure of differentiated male and female reproductive experience and resultant consciousness have maintained their strength through frequent recourse to violence. They can only be disarmed when women experience a change in reproductive consciousness comparable in scope to the discovery of paternity. Such a change would be constituted by the transformation of involuntary reproductive labor to voluntary reproductive labor, and its technological beginnings lie in recent historical events.

The dialectical model of consciousness receives a great deal of support from the process of human reproduction, when that process is analyzed seriously. Female "passivity" is not passivity at all, but the fruit of a strenuous and laborious mediation of women with the world and time. Male "virility" is neither instinctive push nor personal valor but is rooted firmly in men's *need to act* to cancel the alienations built into reproductive experience. Potency, far from being simply natural or sexual, is essentially political and ideological. The most obvious mode of mediation, and the most commonly practiced from early times, is the simple appropriation of a child: the assertion first of a right to the child, and eventually the buttressing by custom and law of its problematic legitimacy. Male "potency" is far more than participation in the creation of a new life: it is the ability to resist alienation, a triumph over nature's indifference to the particularity of paternity and man's postejaculatory

17. Engels, p. 20.

fate, and an imposition of man's positive will on natural negativity. The physiology that is fate spurs men to patriarchal praxis, to the assertion of a *right* to the child that, as it is not self-evident, must be asserted and symbolized and socially confirmed. It must be raised, in dialectical terms, from the level of particularity to that of universality.

This praxis is political in a wider sense than that contained in the mere equation of potency and power—potency as the power to appropriate both the child and the labor of the mother which produced the child. In the complexities of reproductive dialectics, men have a series of experiences to cope with. Primordially, they have freedom in a double sense; they have freedom from labor, and freedom to claim or not to claim a paternal right to the child. At the same time, their freedom is an alienation from natural process and genetic time. Additionally, the objectification of ideal paternity in actual, recognized paternity is threatened by other potencies. Any man, as I noted, can claim with equal force that he is the biological father. Paternal uncertainty forces men into social forms of agreement to cooperate with one another; you leave my woman alone and I will return the courtesy. This is the sociopolitical aspect of reproductive dialectic, a necessary cooperation between men to encompass a clearly defined social objective. Marriage in its primeval form is not a contract between a man and a woman, but a treaty among men, a mutual back scratching that restores integrity to male reproductive consciousness. Male potency is an amalgam of the power to appropriate, supported by the socially bestowed right to do so, and dependent on suspicious cooperation between men.

The importance of knowledge about the causal aspects of impregnation is that it confirms human reproduction as historical process rather than as brute biological accident. Paternity is not, like motherhood, an experienced relation to the natural world mediated in labor, but an idea dependent upon the development of human mental powers to a level that can adduce the notion of cause and effect. Fatherhood cannot be confirmed by immediate experience, but only by *knowing;* therefore, we must understand the idea of paternity as historical discovery and the significant implications that follow. In the first place, reproductive process is a dialectical relation of knowledge and experience differentiated by gender. In the second place, reproductive process is not only material and dialectical, it is historical. The historical discovery of physiological paternity was a determinate transformation in reproductive process, initiating a male praxis that necessarily and radically transformed the social conditions in which this discovery could be expressed. The *idea* of paternity necessarily demands collective *action* to objectify it in the world.

But, one may legitimately ask, even if this is the case, so what? One small change millions of years ago is hardly anything to get excited about, especially as we have very imperfect knowledge of the nature of these changes. We should remember, though, that Marx, weaving his theory of history around transformations in modes of production, was able to posit only a couple of such transformations and analyzed in detail only one: the transformation from feudalism to capitalism. Such a recognition only surprises us because, living as we do in the constant motion and change which marks technological innovation and the capitalist passion for expansion, we tend to see our disturbed and fractured lives as arenas of constant change. In a historical sense, changes like these are relatively superficial, making small impact on the value system that they consolidate. They are not, of course, without hazard: we may, for example, find that the perceived need to conquer Mother Nature has killed the old lady off for good. Further, it is easy, in the midst of technological diversity, to overlook the fact that one technological development is qualitatively different from all others. Reproductive technology has its major impact on the social relations of reproduction rather than production, but more important, it is grounded in reproductive rather than productive processes.

It is because contraceptive technology actually transforms both the process and the social relations of reproduction that it constitutes, in Hegel's terminology, a world-historical event. In the first place, it provides a heretofore nonexistent material base for gender equality, rescuing the notion of equality from the dubious justifications of rhetoric and placing it firmly on a material basis. Men and women are now both in the position of having to mediate the separation of copulation and reproduction. The material and conceptual base of the "double standard" no longer exists, and women are currently beginning to explore the ramifications of sexual freedom and control.

Nonetheless, the elusiveness and ambivalence of the male discovery of sexual freedom made so long ago teach us that the separation of sexuality and reproduction is likely to be much more complex than a simple plunge into exuberant instinctual gratification. The banner of the conquering clitoris differs very little from the standard of the penis rampant, for both obscure the fact that at the core of sexuality "liberated" from reproduction lies the alienation of the individual from the continuity of the species. For the first time in history we are forced to ask how important this is. Man's choice of fatherhood and his claim to the right of paternity always carried with it that obverse side of right, the notion if not always the practice of responsibility. Motherhood has been a duty without rights, and in this sense is easily perceived as a form of exploitation to be rejected. So "motherhood," no longer a euphemism for the banal and harmless, is about to become a major political issue. As a result, parenthood may well develop a new and true social value, created by people who see it as an authentic human and social project, freely chosen and rationally controlled. Hardly an issue confined to the choices of individuals, it will also have to be a choice made by the species.

As such it entails radical metamorphoses in social relations, and it is probably not too soon to start thinking about how these are going to be developed. The question is not one to be abdicated to any kind of fatalistic determinism, be it biological, economic, political, or whatever. It is a question of praxis, one central to the strategies of feminism. Women are, in the Marxist sense, the progressive force within these historical developments, just as men were revolutionaries in the discovery of physiological paternity.

We need a sociohistorical model that does not simply consign reproduction to the animal world, perceived as standing opposed to but at the same time as a necessary component of a "man-made" world. Such a new model must recognize that production and reproduction are the necessary substructures of human survival, but that they are different structures grounded in different processes. Even from the present crude adumbration of what such a model might be, it is clear that the integration of women on equal terms in the productive realm is only one half of the journey to equality. The other is the integration of men into the relations of reproduction and into the active care of the next generation. For many women, such a partnership may seem utopian; yet we must note that the choice by women of motherhood as a project removed from the realm of the merely accidental becomes cooperation between free human male and female beings undertaken collectively—a revolutionary idea.

Nonetheless, the problems are immense, and prescriptions are still premature. Where is the understanding of such momentous choices to come from? Here, we note again that contraceptive technology is not just one more technology *comme les autres*. The impact is upon family institutions that have persisted for a very long time. Reproductive technology is revolutionary in a similar but different sense to that in which productive technology was revolutionary in the seventeenth century. That change, we may note, produced a new science: political economy. The current transformation in reproductive process also demands a new science. It is exactly this science that is currently being sought under the indeterminate rubric of "Women's Studies." Still at a rudimentary stage of development, such studies are now confronting those engaged in them with the realization that, as Marx famously remarked, the point is not to describe the world but to change it. For this we need praxis, a new praxis emerging from analysis of the actual process that has historically grounded the relations of men, women, and children.

It is not yet clear what form this new science will take, though it will necessarily break down the disciplinary walls of male-stream thought, so often and so depressingly raised to shut out the difficult critical questions. It is not even clear what such a science might be called. However, the object of such a science, already beginning to appear, is nothing less than the rational control of human reproduction and the creation of the free and humane social relations which can embody this control. The possession of such control by the ruling class of societies dominated by men can already be seen to be pernicious. Contraceptive control can be used by the apostles of potency to accomplish acts of genocide against politically unreliable peoples, or to balance the law of supply and demand as it applies to the ratio between possible productive capacity and the number of mouths to be fed. It can also be used to create a new class division: women who breed and women who do not. There are some signs that all of these things are happening. We have had, after all, the capacity to control production in a rational way for some time but have so far chosen to abdicate this true potency to the mechanical and anti-human laws of the marketplace. Yet we also know that those countries that have transformed productive relations have not appreciably changed the status of women. This failure may well lie precisely in our inability to grasp and articulate the bipolar and dialectical structure of necessity, the relation between production and reproduction. Human emancipation cannot emerge from only one realm of necessity, one set of social relations. It cannot come from a transformation in the public realm that expects a merely reflexive transformation in the private realm. It must emerge from an understanding of the dialectical movement within and between the relations of reproduction and production that makes it entirely possible for historical change to be initiated within the social relations of reproduction. History only now presents us with the possibility of understanding this idea, and developing from it an autonomous feminist praxis with entirely original theoretical premises. It is an enormous challenge.

Ontario Institute for Studies in Education

Feminism and Science

Evelyn Fox Keller

In recent years, a new critique of science has begun to emerge from a number of feminist writings. The lens of feminist politics brings into focus certain masculinist distortions of the scientific enterprise, creating, for those of us who are scientists, a potential dilemma. Is there a conflict between our commitment to feminism and our commitment to science? As both a feminist and a scientist, I am more familiar than I might wish with the nervousness and defensiveness that such a potential conflict evokes. As scientists, we have very real difficulties in thinking about the kinds of issues that, as feminists, we have been raising. These difficulties may, however, ultimately be productive. My purpose in the present essay is to explore the implications of recent feminist criticism of science for the relationship between science and feminism. Do these criticisms imply conflict? If they do, how necessary is that conflict? I will argue that those elements of feminist criticism that seem to conflict most with at least conventional conceptions of science may, in fact, carry a liberating potential for science. It could therefore benefit scientists to attend closely to feminist criticism. I will suggest that we might even use feminist thought to illuminate and clarify part of the substructure of science (which may have been historically conditioned into distortion) in order to preserve the things that science has taught us, in order to be more objective. But first it is necessary to review the various criticisms that feminists have articulated.

The range of their critique is broad. Though they all claim that science embodies a strong androcentric bias, the meanings attached to this charge vary widely. It is convenient to represent the differences in meaning by a spectrum that parallels the political range characteristic of feminism as a whole. I label this spectrum from right to left, beginning somewhere left of center with what might be called the liberal position. From the liberal critique, charges of androcentricity emerge that are relatively easy to correct. The more radical critique calls for correspondingly more radical changes; it requires a reexamination of the underlying assumptions of scientific theory and method for the presence of male bias. The difference between these positions is, however, often obscured by a knee-jerk reaction that leads many scientists to regard all such criticism as a unit—as a challenge to the neutrality of science. One of the points I wish to emphasize here is that the range of meanings attributed to the claim of androcentric bias reflects very different levels of challenge, some of which even the most conservative scientists ought to be able to accept.

First, in what I have called the liberal critique, is the charge that is essentially one of unfair employment practices. It proceeds from the observation that almost all scientists are men. This criticism is liberal in the sense that it in no way conflicts either with traditional conceptions of science or with current liberal, egalitarian politics. It is, in fact, a purely political criticism, and one which can be supported by all of us who are in favor of equal opportunity. According to this point of view, science itself would in no way be affected by the presence or absence of women.

A slightly more radical criticism continues from this and argues that the predominance of men in the sciences has led to a bias in the choice and definition of problems with which scientists have concerned themselves. This argument is most frequently and most easily made in regard to the health sciences. It is claimed, for example, that contraception has not been given the scientific attention its human importance warrants and that, furthermore, the attention it has been given has been focused primarily on contraceptive techniques to be used by women. In a related complaint, feminists argue that menstrual cramps, a serious problem for many women, have never been taken seriously by the medical profession. Presumably, had the concerns of medical research been articulated by women, these particular imbalances would not have arisen.[1] Similar biases in sciences remote from the subject of women's bodies are more

---

1. Notice that the claim is not that the mere presence of women in medical research is sufficient to right such imbalances, for it is understood how readily women, or any "outsiders" for that matter, come to internalize the concerns and values of a world to which they aspire to belong.

difficult to locate—they may, however, exist. Even so, this kind of criticism does not touch our conception of what science is, nor our confidence in the neutrality of science. It may be true that in some areas we have ignored certain problems, but our definition of science does not include the choice of problem—that, we can readily agree, has always been influenced by social forces. We remain, therefore, in the liberal domain.

Continuing to the left, we next find claims of bias in the actual design and interpretation of experiments. For example, it is pointed out that virtually all of the animal-learning research on rats has been performed with male rats.[2] Though a simple explanation is offered—namely, that female rats have a four-day cycle that complicates experiments—the criticism is hardly vitiated by the explanation. The implicit assumption is, of course, that the male rat represents the species. There exist many other, often similar, examples in psychology. Examples from the biological sciences are somewhat more difficult to find, though one suspects that they exist. An area in which this suspicion is particularly strong is that of sex research. Here the influence of heavily invested preconceptions seems all but inevitable. In fact, although the existence of such preconceptions has been well documented historically,[3] a convincing case for the existence of a corresponding bias in either the design or interpretation of experiments has yet to be made. That this is so can, I think, be taken as testimony to the effectiveness of the standards of objectivity operating.

But evidence for bias in the interpretation of observations and experiments is very easy to find in the more socially oriented sciences. The area of primatology is a familiar target. Over the past fifteen years women working in the field have undertaken an extensive reexamination of theoretical concepts, often using essentially the same methodological tools. These efforts have resulted in some radically different formulations. The range of difference frequently reflects the powerful influence of ordinary language in biasing our theoretical formulations. A great deal of very interesting work analyzing such distortions has been done.[4] Though I cannot begin to do justice to that work here, let me offer, as a single example, the following description of a single-male troop of animals that Jane Lancaster provides as a substitute for the familiar concept of "harem": "For a female, males are a

2. I would like to thank Lila Braine for calling this point to my attention.
3. D. L. Hall and Diana Long, "The Social Implications of the Scientific Study of Sex," *Scholar and the Feminist* 4 (1977): 11–21.
4. See, e.g., Donna Haraway, "Animal Sociology and a Natural Economy of the Body Politic, Part I: A Political Physiology of Dominance"; and "Animal Sociology and a Natural Economy of the Body Politic, Part II: The Past Is the Contested Zone: Human Nature and Theories of Production and Reproduction in Primate Behavior Studies," *Signs: Journal of Women in Culture and Society* 4, no. 1 (Autumn 1978): 21–60.

resource in her environment which she may use to further the survival of herself and her offspring. If environmental conditions are such that the male role can be minimal, a one-male group is likely. Only one male is necessary for a group of females if his only role is to impregnate them."[5]

These critiques, which maintain that a substantive effect on scientific theory results from the predominance of men in the field, are almost exclusively aimed at the "softer," even the "softest," sciences. Thus they can still be accommodated within the traditional framework by the simple argument that the critiques, if justified, merely reflect the fact that these subjects are not sufficiently scientific. Presumably, fair-minded (or scientifically minded) scientists can and should join forces with the feminists in attempting to identify the presence of bias—equally offensive, if for different reasons, to both scientists and feminists—in order to make these "soft" sciences more rigorous.

It is much more difficult to deal with the truly radical critique that attempts to locate androcentric bias even in the "hard" sciences, indeed in scientific ideology itself. This range of criticism takes us out of the liberal domain and requires us to question the very assumptions of objectivity and rationality that underlie the scientific enterprise. To challenge the truth and necessity of the conclusions of natural science on the grounds that they too reflect the judgment of men is to take the Galilean credo and turn it on its head. It is not true that "the conclusions of natural science are true and necessary, and the judgement of man has nothing to do with them";[6] it is the judgment of woman that they have nothing to do with.

The impetus behind this radical move is twofold. First, it is supported by the experience of feminist scholars in other fields of inquiry. Over and over, feminists have found it necessary, in seeking to reinstate women as agents and as subjects, to question the very canons of their fields. They have turned their attention, accordingly, to the operation of patriarchal bias on ever deeper levels of social structure, even of language and thought.

But the possibility of extending the feminist critique into the foundations of scientific thought is created by recent developments in the history and philosophy of science itself.[7] As long as the course of scientific thought was judged to be exclusively determined by its own logi-

5. Jane Lancaster, *Primate Behavior and the Emergence of Human Culture* (New York: Holt, Rinehart & Winston, 1975), p. 34.

6. Galileo Galilei, *Dialogue on the Great World Systems,* trans. T. Salusbury, ed. G. de Santillana (Chicago: University of Chicago Press, 1953), p. 63.

7. The work of Russell Hanson and Thomas S. Kuhn was of pivotal importance in opening up our understanding of scientific thought to a consideration of social, psychological, and political influences.

cal and empirical necessities, there could be no place for any signature, male or otherwise, in that system of knowledge. Furthermore, any suggestion of gender differences in our thinking about the world could argue only too readily for the further exclusion of women from science. But as the philosophical and historical inadequacies of the classical conception of science have become more evident, and as historians and sociologists have begun to identify the ways in which the development of scientific knowledge has been shaped by its particular social and political context, our understanding of science as a social process has grown. This understanding is a necessary prerequisite, both politically and intellectually, for a feminist theoretic in science.

Joining feminist thought to other social studies of science brings the promise of radically new insights, but it also adds to the existing intellectual danger a political threat. The intellectual danger resides in viewing science as pure social product; science then dissolves into ideology and objectivity loses all intrinsic meaning. In the resulting cultural relativism, any emancipatory function of modern science is negated, and the arbitration of truth recedes into the political domain.[8] Against this background, the temptation arises for feminists to abandon their claim for representation in scientific culture and, in its place, to invite a return to a purely "female" subjectivity, leaving rationality and objectivity in the male domain, dismissed as products of a purely male consciousness.[9]

Many authors have addressed the problems raised by total relativism;[10] here I wish merely to mention some of the special problems added by its feminist variant. They are several. In important respects, feminist relativism is just the kind of radical move that transforms the political spectrum into a circle. By rejecting objectivity as a masculine ideal, it simultaneously lends its voice to an enemy chorus and dooms women to residing outside of the realpolitik modern culture; it exacerbates the very problem it wishes to solve. It also nullifies the radical potential of feminist criticism for our understanding of science. As I see it, the task of a feminist theoretic in science is twofold: to distinguish that which is parochial from that which is universal in the scientific impulse,

8. See, e.g., Paul Feyerabend, *Against Method* (London: New Left Books, 1975); and *Science in a Free Society* (London: New Left Books, 1978).

9. This notion is expressed most strongly by some of the new French feminists (see Elaine Marks and Isabelle de Courtivron, eds., *New French Feminisms: An Anthology* [Amherst: University of Massachusetts Press, 1980]), and is currently surfacing in the writings of some American feminists. See, e.g., Susan Griffin, *Woman and Nature: The Roaring Inside Her* (New York: Harper & Row, 1978).

10. See, e.g., Steven Rose and Hilary Rose, "Radical Science and Its Enemies," *Socialist Register 1979*, ed. Ralph Miliband and John Saville (Atlantic Highlands, N.J.: Humanities Press, 1979), pp. 317–35. A number of the points made here have also been made by Elizabeth Fee in "Is Feminism a Threat to Objectivity?" (paper presented at the American Association for the Advancement of Science meeting, Toronto, January 4, 1981).

reclaiming for women what has historically been denied to them; and to legitimate those elements of scientific culture that have been denied precisely because they are defined as female.

It is important to recognize that the framework inviting what might be called the nihilist retreat is in fact provided by the very ideology of objectivity we wish to escape. This is the ideology that asserts an opposition between (male) objectivity and (female) subjectivity and denies the possibility of mediation between the two. A first step, therefore, in extending the feminist critique to the foundations of scientific thought is to reconceptualize objectivity as a dialectical process so as to allow for the possibility of distinguishing the objective effort from the objectivist illusion. As Piaget reminds us:

> Objectivity consists in so fully realizing the countless intrusions of the self in everyday thought and the countless illusions which result—illusions of sense, language, point of view, value, etc.—that the preliminary step to every judgement is the effort to exclude the intrusive self. Realism, on the contrary, consists in ignoring the existence of self and thence regarding one's own perspective as immediately objective and absolute. Realism is thus anthropocentric illusion, finality—in short, all those illusions which teem in the history of science. So long as thought has not become conscious of self, it is a prey to perpetual confusions between objective and subjective, between the real and the ostensible.[11]

In short, rather than abandon the quintessentially human effort to understand the world in rational terms, we need to refine that effort. To do this, we need to add to the familiar methods of rational and empirical inquiry the additional process of critical self-reflection. Following Piaget's injunction, we need to "become conscious of self." In this way, we can become conscious of the features of the scientific project that belie its claim to universality.

The ideological ingredients of particular concern to feminists are found where objectivity is linked with autonomy and masculinity, and in turn, the goals of science with power and domination. The linking of objectivity with social and political autonomy has been examined by many authors and shown to serve a variety of important political functions.[12] The implications of joining objectivity with masculinity are less well understood. This conjunction also serves critical political functions. But an understanding of the sociopolitical meaning of the entire constellation requires an examination of the psychological processes

11. Jean Piaget, *The Child's Conception of the World* (Totowa, N.J.: Littlefield, Adams & Co., 1972).

12. Jerome R. Ravetz, *Scientific Knowledge and Its Social Problems* (London: Oxford University Press, 1971); and Hilary Rose and Steven Rose, *Science and Society* (London: Allen Lane, 1969).

through which these connections become internalized and perpetuated. Here psychoanalysis offers us an invaluable perspective, and it is to the exploitation of that perspective that much of my own work has been directed. In an earlier paper, I tried to show how psychoanalytic theories of development illuminate the structure and meaning of an interacting system of associations linking objectivity (a cognitive trait) with autonomy (an affective trait) and masculinity (a gender trait).[13] Here, after a brief summary of my earlier argument, I want to explore the relation of this system to power and domination.

Along with Nancy Chodorow and Dorothy Dinnerstein, I have found that branch of psychoanalytic theory known as object relations theory to be especially useful.[14] In seeking to account for personality development in terms of both innate drives and actual relations with other objects (i.e., subjects), it permits us to understand the ways in which our earliest experiences—experiences in large part determined by the socially structured relationships that form the context of our developmental processes—help to shape our conception of the world and our characteristic orientations to it. In particular, our first steps in the world are guided primarily by the parents of one sex—our mothers; this determines a maturational framework for our emotional, cognitive, and gender development, a framework later filled in by cultural expectations.

In brief, I argued the following: Our early maternal environment, coupled with the cultural definition of masculine (that which can never appear feminine) and of autonomy (that which can never be compromised by dependency) leads to the association of female with the pleasures and dangers of merging, and of male with the comfort and loneliness of separateness. The boy's internal anxiety about both self and gender is echoed by the more widespread cultural anxiety, thereby encouraging postures of autonomy and masculinity, which can, indeed may, be designed to defend against that anxiety and the longing that generates it. Finally, for all of us, our sense of reality is carved out of the same developmental matrix. As Piaget and others have emphasized, the capacity for cognitive distinctions between self and other (objectivity) evolves concurrently and interdependently with the development of psychic autonomy; our cognitive ideals thereby become subject to the same psychological influences as our emotional and gender ideals. Along with autonomy the very act of separating subject from object—objectivity itself—comes to be associated with masculinity. The combined psycho-

13. Evelyn Fox Keller, "Gender and Science," *Psychoanalysis and Contemporary Thought* 1 (1978): 409–33.

14. Nancy Chodorow, *The Reproduction of Mothering: Psychoanalysis and the Sociology of Gender* (Berkeley: University of California Press, 1978); and Dorothy Dinnerstein, *The Mermaid and the Minotaur: Sexual Arrangements and Human Malaise* (New York: Harper & Row, 1976).

logical and cultural pressures lead all three ideals—affective, gender, and cognitive—to a mutually reinforcing process of exaggeration and rigidification.[15] The net result is the entrenchment of an objectivist ideology and a correlative devaluation of (female) subjectivity.

   This analysis leaves out many things. Above all it omits discussion of the psychological meanings of power and domination, and it is to those meanings I now wish to turn. Central to object relations theory is the recognition that the condition of psychic autonomy is double edged: it offers a profound source of pleasure, and simultaneously of potential dread. The values of autonomy are consonant with the values of competence, of mastery. Indeed competence is itself a prior condition for autonomy and serves immeasurably to confirm one's sense of self. But need the development of competence and the sense of mastery lead to a state of alienated selfhood, of denied connectedness, of defensive separateness? To forms of autonomy that can be understood as protections against dread? Object relations theory makes us sensitive to autonomy's range of meanings; it simultaneously suggests the need to consider the corresponding meanings of competence. Under what circumstances does competence imply mastery of one's own fate and under what circumstances does it imply mastery over another's? In short, are control and domination essential ingredients of competence, and intrinsic to selfhood, or are they correlates of an alienated selfhood?

   One way to answer these questions is to use the logic of the analysis summarized above to examine the shift from competence to power and control in the psychic economy of the young child. From that analysis, the impulse toward domination can be understood as a natural concomitant of defensive separateness—as Jessica Benjamin has written, "A way of repudiating sameness, dependency and closeness with another person, while attempting to avoid the consequent feelings of aloneness."[16] Perhaps no one has written more sensitively than psychoanalyst D. W. Winnicott of the rough waters the child must travel in negotiating the transition from symbiotic union to the recognition of self and other as autonomous entities. He alerts us to a danger that others have missed—a danger arising from the unconscious fantasy that the subject has actually destroyed the object in the process of becoming separate. Indeed, he writes, "It is the destruction of the object that places the

   15. For a fuller development of this argument, see n. 12 above. By focusing on the contributions of individual psychology, I in no way mean to imply a simple division of individual and social factors, or to set them up as alternative influences. Individual psychological traits evolve in a social system and, in turn, social systems reward and select for particular sets of individual traits. Thus if particular options in science reflect certain kinds of psychological impulses or personality traits, it must be understood that it is in a distinct social framework that those options, rather than others, are selected.
   16. Jessica Benjamin has discussed this same issue in an excellent analysis of the place of domination in sexuality. See "The Bonds of Love: Rational Violence and Erotic Domination," *Feminist Studies* 6, no. 1 (Spring 1980): 144–74, esp. 150.

object outside the area of control. . . . After 'subject relates to object' comes 'subject destroys object' (as it becomes external); then may come '*object survives* destruction by the subject.' But there may or may not be survival." When there is, "because of the survival of the object, the subject may now have started to live a life in the world of objects, and so the subject stands to gain immeasurably; but the price has to be paid in acceptance of the ongoing destruction in unconscious fantasy relative to object-relating."[17] Winnicott, of course, is not speaking of actual survival but of subjective confidence in the survival of the other. Survival in that sense requires that the child maintain relatedness; failure induces inevitable guilt and dread. The child is poised on a terrifying precipice. On one side lies the fear of having destroyed the object, on the other side, loss of self. The child may make an attempt to secure this precarious position by seeking to master the other. The cycles of destruction and survival are reenacted while the other is kept safely at bay, and as Benjamin writes, "the original self assertion is . . . converted from innocent mastery to mastery over and against the other."[18] In psychodynamic terms, this particular resolution of preoedipal conflicts is a product of oedipal consolidation. The (male) child achieves his final security by identification with the father—an identification involving simultaneously a denial of the mother and a transformation of guilt and fear into aggression.

Aggression, of course, has many meanings, many sources, and many forms of expression. Here I mean to refer only to the form underlying the impulse toward domination. I invoke psychoanalytic theory to help illuminate the forms of expression that impulse finds in science as a whole, and its relation to objectification in particular. The same questions I asked about the child I can also ask about science. Under what circumstances is scientific knowledge sought for the pleasures of knowing, for the increased competence it grants us, for the increased mastery (real or imagined) over our own fate, and under what circumstances is it fair to say that science seeks actually to dominate nature? Is there a meaningful distinction to be made here?

In his work *The Domination of Nature* William Leiss observes, "The necessary correlate of domination is the consciousness of subordination in those who must obey the will of another; thus properly speaking only other men can be the objects of domination."[19] (Or women, we might add.) Leiss infers from this observation that it is not the domination of physical nature we should worry about but the use of our knowledge of physical nature as an instrument for the domination of human nature. He therefore sees the need for correctives, not in science but in its uses. This is his point of departure from other authors of the Frankfurt

17. D. W. Winnicott. *Playing and Reality* (New York: Basic Books, 1971), pp. 89–90.
18. Benjamin, p. 165.
19. William Leiss, *The Domination of Nature* (Boston: Beacon Press, 1974), p. 122.

school, who assume the very logic of science to be the logic of domination. I agree with Leiss's basic observation but draw a somewhat different inference. I suggest that the impulse toward domination does find expression in the goals (and even in the theories and practice) of modern science, and argue that where it finds such expression the impulse needs to be acknowledged as projection. In short, I argue that not only in the denial of interaction between subject and other but also in the access of domination to the goals of scientific knowledge, one finds the intrusion of a self we begin to recognize as partaking in the cultural construct of masculinity.

The value of consciousness is that it enables us to make choices— both as individuals and as scientists. Control and domination are in fact intrinsic neither to selfhood (i.e., autonomy) nor to scientific knowledge. I want to suggest, rather, that the particular emphasis Western science has placed on these functions of knowledge is twin to the objectivist ideal. Knowledge in general, and scientific knowledge in particular, serves two gods: power and transcendence. It aspires alternately to mastery over and union with nature.[20] Sexuality serves the same two gods, aspiring to domination and ecstatic communion—in short, aggression and eros. And it is hardly a new insight to say that power, control, and domination are fueled largely by aggression, while union satisfies a more purely erotic impulse.

To see the emphasis on power and control so prevalent in the rhetoric of Western science as projection of a specifically male consciousness requires no great leap of the imagination. Indeed, that perception has become a commonplace. Above all, it is invited by the rhetoric that conjoins the domination of nature with the insistent image of nature as female, nowhere more familiar than in the writings of Francis Bacon. For Bacon, knowledge and power are one, and the promise of science is expressed as "leading to you Nature with all her children to bind her to your service and make her your slave,"[21] by means that do not "merely exert a gentle guidance over nature's course; they have the power to conquer and subdue her, to shake her to her foundations."[22] In the context of the Baconian vision, Bruno Bettelheim's conclusion appears inescapable: "Only with phallic psychology did aggressive manipulation of nature become possible."[23]

    20. For a discussion of the different roles these two impulses play in Platonic and in Baconian images of knowledge, see Evelyn Fox Keller, "Nature as 'Her'" (paper delivered at the Second Sex Conference, New York Institute for the Humanities, September 1979).

    21. B. Farrington, "*Temporis Partus Masculus:* An Untranslated Writing of Francis Bacon," *Centaurus* 1 (1951): 193–205, esp. 197.

    22. Francis Bacon, "Description of the Intellectual Globe," in *The Philosophical Works of Francis Bacon,* ed. J. H. Robertson (London: Routledge & Sons, 1905), p. 506.

    23. Quoted in Norman O. Brown, *Life against Death* (New York: Random House, 1959), p. 280.

The view of science as an oedipal project is also familiar from the writings of Herbert Marcuse and Norman O. Brown.[24] But Brown's preoccupation, as well as Marcuse's, is with what Brown calls a "morbid" science. Accordingly, for both authors the quest for a nonmorbid science, an "erotic" science, remains a romantic one. This is so because their picture of science is incomplete: it omits from consideration the crucial, albeit less visible, erotic components already present in the scientific tradition. Our own quest, if it is to be realistic rather than romantic, must be based on a richer understanding of the scientific tradition, in all its dimensions, and on an understanding of the ways in which this complex, dialectical tradition becomes transformed into a monolithic rhetoric. Neither the oedipal child nor modern science has in fact managed to rid itself of its preoedipal and fundamentally bisexual yearnings. It is with this recognition that the quest for a different science, a science undistorted by masculinist bias, must begin.

The presence of contrasting themes, of a dialectic between aggressive and erotic impulses, can be seen both within the work of individual scientists and, even more dramatically, in the juxtaposed writings of different scientists. Francis Bacon provides us with one model;[25] there are many others. For an especially striking contrast, consider a contemporary scientist who insists on the importance of "letting the material speak to you," of allowing it to "tell you what to do next"—one who chastises other scientists for attempting to "impose an answer" on what they see. For this scientist, discovery is facilitated by becoming "part of the system," rather than remaining outside; one must have a "feeling for the organism."[26] It is true that the author of these remarks is not only from a different epoch and a different field (Bacon himself was not actually a scientist by most standards), she is also a woman. It is also true that there are many reasons, some of which I have already suggested, for thinking that gender (itself constructed in an ideological context) actually does make a difference in scientific inquiry. Nevertheless, my point here is that neither science nor individuals are totally bound by ideology. In fact, it is not difficult to find similar sentiments expressed by male scientists. Consider, for example, the following remarks: "I have often had cause to feel that my hands are cleverer than my head. That is a crude way of characterizing the dialectics of experimentation. When it is going well, it is like a quiet conversation with Nature."[27] The difference

---

24. Brown; and Herbert Marcuse, *One Dimensional Man* (Boston: Beacon Press, 1964).

25. For a discussion of the presence of the same dialectic in the writings of Francis Bacon, see Evelyn Fox Keller, "Baconian Science: A Hermaphrodite Birth," *Philosophical Forum* 11, no. 3 (Spring 1980): 299–308.

26. Barbara McClintock, private interviews, December 1, 1978, and January 13, 1979.

27. G. Wald, "The Molecular Basis of Visual Excitation," *Les Prix Nobel en 1967* (Stockholm: Kungliga Boktryckerlet, 1968), p. 260.

between conceptions of science as "dominating" and as "conversing with" nature may not be a difference primarily between epochs, nor between the sexes. Rather, it can be seen as representing a dual theme played out in the work of all scientists, in all ages. But the two poles of this dialectic do not appear with equal weight in the history of science. What we therefore need to attend to is the evolutionary process that selects one theme as dominant.

Elsewhere I have argued for the importance of a different selection process.[28] In part, scientists are themselves selected by the emotional appeal of particular (stereotypic) images of science. Here I am arguing for the importance of selection within scientific thought—first of preferred methodologies and aims, and finally of preferred theories. The two processes are not unrelated. While stereotypes are not binding (i.e., they do not describe all or perhaps any individuals), and this fact creates the possibility for an ongoing contest within science, the first selection process undoubtedly influences the outcome of the second. That is, individuals drawn by a particular ideology will tend to select themes consistent with that ideology.

One example in which this process is played out on a theoretical level is in the fate of interactionist theories in the history of biology. Consider the contest that has raged throughout this century between organismic and particulate views of cellular organization—between what might be described as hierarchical and nonhierarchical theories. Whether the debate is over the primacy of the nucleus or the cell as a whole, the genome or the cytoplasm, the proponents of hierarchy have won out. One geneticist has described the conflict in explicitly political terms:

> Two concepts of genetic mechanisms have persisted side by side throughout the growth of modern genetics, but the emphasis has been very strongly in favor of one of these. . . . The first of these we will designate as the "Master Molecule" concept. . . . This is in essence the Theory of the Gene, interpreted to suggest a totalitarian government. . . . The second concept we will designate as the "Steady State" concept. By this term . . . we envision a dynamic self-perpetuating organization of a variety of molecular species which owes its specific properties not to the characteristic of any one kind of molecule, but to the functional interrelationships of these molecular species.[29]

Soon after these remarks, the debate between "master molecules" and dynamic interactionism was foreclosed by the synthesis provided by

28. Keller, "Gender and Science."
29. D. L. Nanney, "The Role of the Cyctoplasm in Heredity," in *The Chemical Basis of Heredity*, ed. William D. McElroy and Bentley Glass (Baltimore: Johns Hopkins University Press, 1957), p. 136.

DNA and the "central dogma." With the success of the new molecular biology such "steady state" (or egalitarian) theories lost interest for almost all geneticists. But today, the same conflict shows signs of reemerging—in genetics, in theories of the immune system, and in theories of development.

I suggest that method and theory may constitute a natural continuum, despite Popperian claims to the contrary, and that the same processes of selection may bear equally and simultaneously on both the means and aims of science and the actual theoretical descriptions that emerge. I suggest this in part because of the recurrent and striking consonance that can be seen in the way scientists work, the relation they take to their object of study, and the theoretical orientation they favor. To pursue the example cited earlier, the same scientist who allowed herself to become "part of the system," whose investigations were guided by a "feeling for the organism," developed a paradigm that diverged as radically from the dominant paradigm of her field as did her methodological style.

In lieu of the linear hierarchy described by the central dogma of molecular biology, in which the DNA encodes and transmits all instructions for the unfolding of a living cell, her research yielded a view of the DNA in delicate interaction with the cellular environment—an organismic view. For more important than the genome as such (i.e., the DNA) is the "overall organism." As she sees it, the genome functions "only in respect to the environment in which it is found."[30] In this work the program encoded by the DNA is itself subject to change. No longer is a master control to be found in a single component of the cell; rather, control resides in the complex interactions of the entire system. When first presented, the work underlying this vision was not understood, and it was poorly received.[31] Today much of that work is undergoing a renaissance, although it is important to say that her full vision remains too radical for most biologists to accept.[32]

This example suggests that we need not rely on our imagination for a vision of what a different science—a science less restrained by the impulse to dominate—might be like. Rather, we need only look to the thematic pluralism in the history of our own science as it has evolved. Many other examples can be found, but we lack an adequate understanding of the full range of influences that lead to the acceptance or rejection not only of particular theories but of different theoretical orientations. What I am suggesting is that if certain theoretical inter-

30. McClintock, December 1, 1978.

31. McClintock, "Chromosome Organization and Genic Expression," *Cold Spring Harbor Symposium of Quantitative Biology* 16 (1951): 13–44.

32. McClintock's most recent publication on this subject is "Modified Gene Expressions Induced by Transposable Elements," in *Mobilization and Reassembly of Genetic Information,* ed. W. A. Scott, R. Werner, and J. Schultz (New York: Academic Press, 1980).

pretations have been selected against, it is precisely in this process of selection that ideology in general, and a masculinist ideology in particular, can be found to effect its influence. The task this implies for a radical feminist critique of science is, then, first a historical one, but finally a transformative one. In the historical effort, feminists can bring a whole new range of sensitivities, leading to an equally new consciousness of the potentialities lying latent in the scientific project.

Visiting Professor of Mathematics and Humanities
Northeastern University

Feminist Discourse and Its Discontents: Language, Power, and Meaning

Jean Bethke Elshtain

The feminist thinker who wishes to tackle the puzzles of power and take up questions of meaning must consider the nature of language itself. There are several reasons for this. First, debates over whether or not discourse is inevitably or necessarily domination, a form of "power over" others, provides much of the exciting interplay of diatribe and dialectic, polemic and philosophical argumentation, that characterize contemporary debates in social and political theory. Some writers on the text as power are feminists; others are not.[1] But all who explore these issues are intrigued by the peculiar relationship between author-text-reader along some vector of power. A mild version of the thesis that power infuses discourse is stated by Paul Foss: "Discourse has become the arena for the generation and propagation of historically specified norms and socially adequate forms of power."[2] Sheila Rowbotham puts the case more urgently: "Language conveys a certain power. It is one of the in-

1. Of particular interest is the work of the "new French feminism" on the text, writing the body, etc. This body of work will not be treated explicitly but it represents a fascinating and vital contribution to the search for feminist discourse. See Elaine Marks and Isabelle de Courtivron, eds., *New French Feminisms: An Anthology* (Amherst: University of Massachusetts Press, 1980).

2. Paul Foss, "On the Value of That Text Which Is Not One," in *Language, Sexuality and Subversion* (August 1979), p. 180.

struments of domination. . . . The language of theory—removed language—only expresses a reality experienced by the oppressors. It speaks only for their world, from their point of view. Ultimately a revolutionary movement has to break the hold of the dominant group over theory, it has to structure its own connections. Language is part of the political and ideological power of rulers. . . . We can't just occupy existing words. We have to change the meanings of words even before we take them over."[3] And a poem by Margaret Atwood gives a bleakly cynical feminist view of the relationship of language to power:

> We hear nothing these days
> from the ones in power
>
> Why talk when you are a shoulder
> or a vault
>
> Why talk when you are
> helmeted with numbers
>
> Fists have many forms;
> a fist knows what it can do
>
> without the nuisance of speaking:
> it grabs and smashes.
>
> From those inside or under
> words gush like toothpaste.
>
> *Language, the fist*
> *proclaims by squeezing*
> is for the weak only.[4]

Another point of view sees language users as hiding behind a variety of "masks." Discussing this provocative notion, Abigail Rosenthal argues that the project of feminist discourse must refuse, because it cannot operate honestly through, various masks: "Feminism is too serious to become operational behind a mask."[5] Thus the motivation of that feminism committed to the project of rational discourse must be to

3. Sheila Rowbotham, *Woman's Consciousness, Man's World* (Baltimore: Penguin Books, 1973), pp. 32–33.

4. Margaret Atwood, *Power Politics* (New York: Harper & Row, 1971), p. 31 (my emphasis). For a brilliant, troubling treatment of the language of fascism, see J. P. Stern, *Hilter: The Führer and the People* (Berkeley and Los Angeles: University of California Press, 1975).

5. Abigail Rosenthal, "Feminism without Contradictions," *Monist* 51 (January 1973): 28–42, esp. 31.

"stand up to every sort of assault, foremost among them the reactions that may settle in the minds of feminists themselves."[6] Rosenthal gives some examples of masks: The "mask of purity" (presuming the victim's language is untainted by her world); the "mask of orthodox Marxism" (presuming that discourse is nothing but a covering rationalization for exploitative relations); the "mask of militancy" (the language of grim personal renunciation, feminist martyrdom as a modern stigmata). I would add the mask of systematic know-it-allism, best recast as the mask of the overarching *Weltanschauung;* the mask of unquestioned inner authenticity based upon claims to the ontological superiority of female being-in-itself; and, sadly, the masks of various modes of philosophic and academic argumentation in which language may be used to perpetrate illusions, and pieces of palpable nonsense may be "demonstrated" as valid because the propositions in which this half-baked knowledge is borne bear no relation at all to the world of real objects, whether natural or socially constituted.

If, however, one continues to believe in the project of human speech, one must move beyond a view of language as simply or inexorably "power over," discourse as domination, or discourse as unavoidably masked, and toward speech as part of an emancipatory effort, a movement toward social clarity and self-comprehension. This does not and should not require a naive denial that language may be deployed to reinforce consensus and to shore up forms of domination by debasing the meanings of words, displacing our attention from the important to the trivial, or covering up with a smokescreen of obscurantisms that aim to deny and to distance. Still, the project of rational speech, an eyes-open, truth-telling passion against "the powers that be" and "the censors within," can be one emancipatory window into the future.

Feminist thinkers must self-consciously and critically confront various traditions of political discourse, feminist and nonfeminist. There are among us, for example, those who seek solutions to our public and private dilemmas by depriving us of a grammar of moral discourse and forcing all of life under a set of terms denuded of a critical edge. In so doing, they would deprive the human object, female and male, of the capacity to think, to judge, to question, and to act, for all these activities are importantly constituted by an everyday, ordinary language infused with moral terms. We must be alert to such destructive options as we break the silence of traditional political thought on questions of women's historic oppression and the absence of women from the realm of public speech. This means that the nature and meaning of feminist discourse itself must be a subject for critical inquiry. What sort of language, public and private, do feminists propose that women speak? What public and private identities do feminists embrace as alternatives to previous social

6. Ibid., p. 31.

and personal definitions of women? How do feminists redescribe social reality and experience in order to reflect on what makes this reality and experience what it currently is, whether what is must be, or whether dramatic alterations are either possible or desirable? And what models for emancipatory speech are available?

My search for emancipatory speech, or speech with an emancipatory "moment," takes me first, as a political theorist, back to the "great tradition" of Western political thought beginning with Plato. For Plato, women are "silenced": he argued that the private speech of the household, the speech of women, lacked either the form of philosophic argumentation or the form of poetry. It was, therefore, without meaning—unformed, chaotic, evanescent, the speech of *doxa* (mere opinion, not truth). Household speech could be neither heroic ("at the beginning," Socrates reminds us, were "those who have left speeches"),[7] nor part of the philosophic male quest for wisdom through a dialogue of a particular kind. The women of Plato's time were not only excluded from politics but also debarred from participating in the process of becoming what Plato meant by a "good" human being—a process that required a special search for truth within the all-male forum for philosophic discourse, pedagogy, and intimacy that is the *mise en scène* for the Platonic dialogues.

Women historically had no place to bring their thoughts, certainly no public arena to give them voice in the misogynist milieu of Greek antiquity. When they did speak, their language was labeled so much reactive noise, devoid of meaning and significance. Cut off from the philosophic speech of the symposia and the public speech of the agora, women's communications in classical antiquity would have taken on the terms of their enforced isolation. That one sex almost exclusively inhabited a public sphere and the other sex the private may help to explain why so many women and men literally could not "speak" to one another.[8]

Plato inaugurated what was to become, over the centuries, a complex and by no means uniform theoretical and discursive tradition. Not

7. Plato, *The Republic of Plato*, trans. Allan Bloom (New York: Basic Books, 1970), bk. 2, 366A–367a.

8. See George Steiner, *After Babel: Aspects of Language and Translation* (London: Oxford University Press, 1977), p. 38: "In most societies and throughout history, the status of women has been akin to that of children. Both groups are maintained in a condition of privileged inferiority. Both suffer obvious modes of exploitation—sexual, legal, economic—while benefiting from a mythology of special regard. Thus Victorian sentimentalization of the moral eminence of women and young children was concurrent with brutal forms of erotic and economic subjection. Under sociological and psychological pressure, both minorities have developed internal modes of communication and defense (women and children constitute a symbolic, self-defining minority even when, owing to war or special circumstance, they outnumber the adult males in the community). There is a language-world of women as there is of children."

all of Plato's heirs were as implacable and dismissive as he to the speech of female subjects, though there are some who simply ignored both women *and* the question of language. I shall take up below two vital contributors to that tradition and to our understanding, or bafflement, concerning human speech and the role of language in human life and thought. But, first, let me sketch the overall shape of the essay.

What is curious as the story of feminist discourse and its discontents unfolds, and what I hope to demonstrate as my own argument proceeds, is the startling way in which contemporary feminists have, from time to time, recapitulated in their thinking earlier arguments on language that erode the search for emancipatory feminist speech. Indeed, in a few instances, feminist commitment to a particular account of human speech interdicts by definition any possibility that speech might serve liberatory purposes. This is true of important thinkers representing radical and Marxist feminist theories who, in what appears to be an unthinking embrace of Hobbesian or Marxist views (to be explored below), undermine their own explicit liberatory aims.

On the other hand, one also finds prominent liberal feminists embracing a contemporary political language, that of academic social science, in which people become abstract role players, and the social spaces inhabited by real human beings are turned into hollow structures that mysteriously perform decreed functions. Accepting the presumptions of classical liberal market theory, this language reduces human motivation to a utilitarian calculus of self-interest. Neither the discourse of modern social science, then, nor the discursive tradition of Western political thought can, together or singly, serve as the rich, fertile soil in which to sow the seeds of emancipatory speech. No single thinker, no school of thought, no "scientific" model of social life, offers an adequate image of human subjects, nor a compelling account of that speech which is a central human capability, which makes us the creatures we are and holds forth the tantalizing possibility of creative change when language bursts the bonds of social control and, unexpectedly, offers intimations of a life still-in-becoming.

But I jump ahead of my story. My beginning task is one of critique, first of several important Western political theorists, then of contemporary feminist thinkers until, at last, I affirm several discursive modes that seem promising: psychoanalytic discourse informed by feminist sensibilities; the notion of "the ideal speech situation" as articulated by the social theorist Jurgen Habermas; and the discussions of female moral reasoning and maternal thinking in the work of Carol Gilligan and Sara Ruddick, respectively.

The scope and urgency of this complex theoretical matrix cannot be understood outside a context that is both historical and textual. We are never altogether untrammeled in our thinking. The past shapes us. But we can become critically self-aware of those modes of thought and reflection that have helped to constitute our own thought and action. Returning, then, to the tradition of Western political thought as deep background to contemporary feminist discourse, let us consider the work of Martin Luther. In the Western political tradition Luther emerges as a liberator of human speech. Frank, openly vulgar, honest in admitting to human appetites, tweaking the public pomposity of the mighty with irreverent earthiness, Luther ripped the veils of pious denial off subjects previously tabooed or whispered about in prurient secret. He transformed the possibilities of meaningful public and private discourse by demonstrating that serious attention should be paid to important and vital questions through the vehicle of the vernacular, the down-to-earth language of the ordinary person.[9] His unadorned frankness of speech unnerved worldly powers unused to candor in public discourse. Earthy public and private talk: What if a woman attempted it? Once stated, the question jars, for one cannot attribute the absence of such "female talk," whether public or private, to female illiteracy and the widespread absence of education. The language of the vernacular was women's language. Instead one must look to the double standard that shapes, gears expectations for, and guides normative judgments of male and female speech, respectively, along public and private vector alike.

A Martin Luther might boast that he could "cut wind" in Germany, and Rome would "smell" it. No woman, particularly no Christian woman and member of the faithful, could address either worldly secular power or her husband, to whom Luther believed she must defer (though to whom she was not subjugated), with such boldness. The truculent, irrepressible speech of one person (the brave man) is from another (the uncontrollable or slatternly woman) brazen, irrational, immoral speech. Because speech is the central way we come to know ourselves, reveal ourselves to others, and express our own identities, to repress the speech of the vernacular simply because propriety or tradition so dictate—or for individuals to repress such speech (the speech of desire) in themselves because, sadly, they "never knew such things" (shorthand for repressed or denied wishes)—is to impoverish possibilities for transformative human discourse that gives expression to human discontents. Despite Luther's personal defiance, his ambiguous heritage is a voice "silent" to public power. Distinctive private voices are liberated or silenced depending on whether the speaker is male or female. The Christian wife must largely speak in the voice of piety and housewifery, though Luther did allow her, within the privacy of spiritual counsel, to voice the language of frustrated desire.

The power of "the word" that Luther used so brilliantly and powerfully was precisely what troubled Thomas Hobbes, whose *Leviathan* re-

9. Martin Luther, *Three Treatises*, trans. Charles M. Jacobs et al. (Philadelphia: Fortress Press, 1960), p. 58. See also John Dillenberger, ed., *Martin Luther: Selections from His Writings* (Garden City, N.Y.: Doubleday & Co., 1961), p. 147.

mains a disturbing classic on the "restless seeking of power after power" and the means by which to curb, curtail, and contain it. For Hobbes, the power of language was so great and its potential for promoting sedition so high that language must be stripped of that power. Hobbes moves, therefore, to divest us of our linguistic capacities and with them of the social relations and way of life they presuppose. If no subject has a public voice, if only one voice, that of the secular god, is heard in the land, no one can debate the competing worth, purpose, and value of public and private existence. The price of civic and domestic peace is to give up the *power* of individual speech, judgment, and understanding.

What is the Hobbesian basis for the Great Silence, his solution to our public and private travail? All individuals are cursed with "a perpetual and restless desire of power after power, that ceaseth only in death."[10] Though God is the first author of speech, man cannot rely on human words to bring order: "The bonds of words are too weak to girdle men's ambition, avarice, anger, and other passions, without the fear of some coercive power."[11]

Not only are words "too weak," they are a positive inducement to private avarice and public sedition. Human speech is riddled with absurdity and senselessness, a "sort of madness when words have no signification,"[12] when names are full of sound and fury but signify nothing. This accursed abuse of words has no meaning and bears no truth: it is, for Hobbes, babbling and "wandering amongst innumerable absurdities" of metaphor and ambiguity. But to silence seditious speech, public and private language must be controlled. All human beings must be passive subjects and, wholly subjected, must quell the inner voices of passion and disarticulate the connection between thought-speech-action. To defuse the power within, Hobbes would impose upon us a new vocabulary: one disimpassioned, neutral, "scientific."[13]

Hobbes's search for "truth" along radical nominalist criteria erodes meaning to human subjects of their own lives and experience which can no longer be couched in ordinary language but must, like everything else that "can intelligibly be said . . . be reducible to a statement about the motion of a material substance."[14] All children and all citizens must be taught this scientific language, all must be indoctrinated in "the right

10. Thomas Hobbes, *Leviathan,* ed. Michael Oakeshott (New York: Collier Books, 1966), p. 80.

11. Ibid., p. 108.

12. Ibid., pp. 34–37.

13. Norman Jacobson, *Pride and Solace: The Functions and Limits of Political Theory* (Berkeley and Los Angeles: University of California Press, 1978), p. 57. See also the discussion in Albert O. Hirschman, *The Passions and the Interests* (Princeton, N.J.: Princeton University Press, 1978), pp. 31–32.

14. Peter Winch, "Man and Society in Hobbes and Rousseau," in *Hobbes and Rousseau,* ed. Maurice Cranston and Richard S. Peters (Garden City, N.Y.: Doubleday & Co., 1972), p. 234.

ordering of names."[15] Human discourse begins and ends, for Hobbes, not with a restless search for meaning but with correct definitions of words shorn of meaning. The notion that the Hobbesian vocabulary, given its reductive mechanistic quality, is somehow "neutral" is a dangerous view that sanctions the silencing of human speech by the all powerful: those with the power to "name names." To that single will and voice, the mortal God, Hobbes's subjects must surrender their plurality of wills and voices. The poison of seditious doctrines is eradicated. The absurdity of private babbling ceases.

What has been lost along public and private dimensions in the Hobbesian deal? The human subject is deprived of the power of individual speech: a *potentia* destroyed by the external imposition of an absolute external power, *potestatis*. Hobbes's scientific vocabulary is one drained of terms of *public* moral evaluation—duty, justice, right, equality, liberty, legitimacy, resistance—and deprived of terms of *private* moral sentiment and emotion—affection, responsibility, love, mercy, compassion, decency, kindness. Good and evil, central to a Christian evaluative grammar, are defanged and reduced to names that signify no more than human "appetites and aversion." Under the terms of the Hobbesian order, it is possible that women would enjoy the terrible equality of the silenced and subjected and that no individual man in concrete social reality would enjoy a social, economic, or political advantage over her. But we as feminists and moral historic agents cannot accept those terms as terms by which to transform public and private reality.

Nevertheless, there are extant feminist approaches to language that bear a relation to Hobbes's theory of discourse. One is a tough, hard language riddled with fierce evocations of power, exploitation, manipulation, and violence. Another is an overblown ontological discourse that represents the flip side of radical nominalism: the celebration of female "Being" as transcending the speech and knowledge of particular female subjects.

In Susan Brownmiller's hard world, all the central features of the male power structure remain intact, but women come to control these structures coequally. This will mean a cease-fire in the sex war. That war can never end, however, given its location in male being. Brownmiller casually accepts the fact that armies will probably be around for a while and that they, too, "must be fully integrated, as well as our national guard, our state troopers, our local sheriff's offices, our district attorney's offices, our state prosecuting attorney's offices—in short the nation's entire lawful power structure (and I mean power in the physical sense) must be stripped of male dominance and control—if women are

15. Hobbes, p. 36. Hobbesian nominalism dictates that words are nothing but arbitrarily applied, artificial, and external conveniences, having no deeper meaning nor social status.

to cease being a colonized protectorate of men."[16] Women must prepare themselves for combat and guard duty, for militarized "citizenship." Brownmiller began plans for this Brave New World by learning "how to fight dirty" and learning "I loved it."[17] The striking thing about this mode of radical feminist language is its machismo cast: raw power, brute force, martial discipline, uniforms, law and order with a feminist face—and voice.

The metaphysical language of Mary Daly is the best example of radical feminism as ontological discourse, a mode of thinking that asserts the primacy of an a priori female Be-ing over against a historical subject who is, importantly, constituted by speech, in and through knowing and acting. Remember Hobbes's extreme reaction against metaphysical language, which led him to reduce humans to matter in motion and human speech to nothing but a series of arbitrary, external "names" for particulars. Daly's return to the mode of discourse Hobbes rejected is similarly extreme. She sees herself as creating a new language, the old being so male-dominated that it cannot be used since it breaks and alienates every female "I" who must speak and write.[18] She argues for a language that does not differentiate or classify objects of reference but is itself the medium of fusion with some greater whole. Perhaps the apogee of this mistrust of "male" language is Daly's insistence that "Lesbians" must initiate/learn from the language of "dumb" animals "whose nonverbal communication seems to be superior to androcentric speech."[19] Daly cites several conversations she has had with animals and translates a few of these; needless to say, all the animals shared her perspective, and none contested her position.

One final dimension of this troubling issue is the language of much radical feminist description, the characterization of the social world from the way woman is portrayed in it as debased, victimized, deformed, mutilated, as a cunt, a hag, and a piece of ass. Our descriptions always take place from a point of view and hence are evaluative. We describe situations on the basis of those aspects we deem relevant or important. In this way, we always evaluate *under* a certain description.[20] Description as

16. Susan Brownmiller, *Against Our Will: Men, Women, and Rape* (New York: Simon & Schuster, 1975), p. 388. Another example may be found in the work of Ti-Grace Atkinson. In her world of Oppressor and Oppressed the only alternative is to reverse who is oppressing or metaphysically cannibalizing whom. See Ti-Grace Atkinson, "Theories of Radical Feminism," in *Notes from the Second Year: Women's Liberation*, ed. Shulamith Firestone (n.p., 1970), pp. 32–37 (available from P.O. Box AA, Old Chelsea Station, New York, New York 10017).

17. Ibid., p. 403.

18. Mary Daly, *Gyn/Ecology: The Metaethics of Radical Feminism* (Boston: Beacon Press, 1979), p. 19.

19. Ibid., p. 414.

20. Julius Kovesi, *Moral Notions* (London: Routledge & Kegan Paul, 1967), p. 63.

evaluation either opens events up for critical scrutiny or forecloses on our capacity to examine them in this way. A serious problem of choice emerges for the thinker who wishes to describe a situation and simultaneously to condemn it. If the descriptive language is too muted—for example, if workers on an assembly line are described as not "fulfilled"—the moral and political point may be lost. On the other hand, overstating the descriptive case, saying that workers are "hideously enslaved, reduced to robots" may backfire. The overinflated description raises in the reader's mind the suspicion that the describer "protests too much," that things cannot possibly be all that bad. It is troubling also that some feminists who set out to describe in order to condemn may, in their descriptions, embrace the terms of their own degradation. This complicated theoretical point bears vital political implications. Aware of the way our descriptions gear expectations, foreclose options, or create possibilities, we must evaluate feminist discourse by asking ourselves what it would do to us, or other female subjects, if we made a particular characterization of women and their worlds our own, if we internalized *that* view of ourselves compared with other possible alternatives.

For example, slaves may come to see themselves as the master sees them; they may embrace their own enslavement. Similarly, "the woman, by willfully defining herself as 'the exploited,' as 'victim,' by seeing herself as she was reflected in the male's perception of her," may seek thereby to attain some power over man, some measure of control.[21] This process varies from one social epoch to the next as the terms of male perceptions of women change. What is distressing is the repeated evocation in feminist discourse of images of female helplessness and victimization. The presumption is that the victim speaks in a pure voice: I suffer therefore I have moral purity and none can question what I say.[22] But the belief in such purity may itself be one of the effects of powerlessness, and that belief, congealed in language, is endlessly self-confirming. It loses any edge of self-criticism, and a feminism that cannot criticize itself cannot, in the last analysis, serve as the bearer of emancipatory possibilities that can never be fixed and defined, once and for all.

Marxist feminism would seem to promise just such a restlessly critical speech, a language geared toward liberation. The matter, however, is neither so simple nor so clear. To assay why, one must consider the Marxian project. What one finds, as one works through the texts, is a major lacuna and a deep disappointment for seekers after emancipatory speech. The absence of a full and coherent account of human beings as speaking subjects deals a blow to any claim that Marxism can offer a

21. Helen Moglen, *Charlotte Bronte: The Self Conceived* (New York: W. W. Norton, 1976), p. 30. See also Ann Douglas, *The Feminization of American Culture* (New York: Avon Books, 1977), p. 10.

22. Rosenthal, p. 29.

comprehensive social theory, for any such theory, in John Dunn's words, must provide for this "centrally human capability."[23] It seems plausible that Marx omitted language from his general theory of human emancipation because he tied language too closely to the particular relations of class society. Language, for Marx, serves largely to cover up the harsh realities of capitalist exploitation. He drops Hegel's dialectic of self-conscious awareness as a linguistically grounded activity and with it the speaking subject goes too. The result, for women, is that their public silence is no more serious a question for Marx than is the distorted speech of men. If the only voice in which man speaks is one of rationalization or "false consciousness," speech which is inauthentic and alienated, woman's relegation to public silence seems a less important deprivation, a less total denial of her subjectivity, than such silence must be within a theory whose focus is the ordering of the social world through language.

If one's answer to the question "Who is the female subject?" revolves around the centrality of speech, Marx's account poses another major problem. In Marxian thought the eradication of a world of necessity will remove barriers to the full exercise of human powers. Man will be free insofar as his essence is freedom. But where does Marx locate this freedom? What is its substantive content? Marx urges that freedom is realizable in a community of persons who have been restored to themselves as "social beings"; it is the positive transcendence of all estrangement.[24] A diffuse species-being will override the particularity of individuals. But how does one substitute generic man for real individuals? That is, do we simply "take" ourselves to be separate persons? Or are we not, each one of us, individuated beings who exist as particular bodies in time and space? The process of ego development requires that, in order to learn a language and thereby become a social being, a child must first separate, classify, and identify particular objects of reference, including himself or herself. Should the child fail in this task, his or her world would be an inchoate stew, a blur of whirring images. This means that language use, by definition, involves separation and differentiation. Due to the paucity of his references to language and the theoretical thinness of his transcendent future where there is no coherent sense of a speaking subject, Marx ends on a silencing note for that subject, male and female.

Following Marx's lead, Marxist feminists exhibit a tendency to treat political speech and action as epiphenomenal, symptomatic of the social relations of capitalism to be dispensed with in some future classless

23. John Dunn, *Western Political Theory in the Face of the Future* (Cambridge: Cambridge University Press, 1979), p. 106. See also Ludwig Wittgenstein, *Philosophical Investigations,* trans. G. E. M. Anscombe (New York: Macmillan Co., 1978).

24. Bertell Ollman, *Alienation: Marx's Conception of Man in Capitalist Society* (Cambridge: Cambridge University Press, 1973). See also Karl Marx and Friedrich Engels, *Collected Works,* 9 vols. (New York: International Publishers, 1975), 3:186.

order. This leads directly to another cluster of concerns over what might be called the "Marxist feminist subject": Who is she, what does she want, and what sort of action shall she undertake? Is she a human being who can give a spoken account of herself? If so, what language does she speak, according to Marxist feminism? If her language is distorted, how do Marxist feminists propose an alternative, undistorted self-identity and self-comprehension cast in and through language?

Marxist thinkers tend to recast the public and private spheres as the spheres of production and reproduction. Given the characterization of social life and history to which Marxists commit themselves, totally or in part, this translation, or shift from what Ludwig Wittgenstein would call one "language game" to another, is not viewed as a serious loss of meaning.[25] By dropping the notion of the private, Marxist feminists (with a few exceptions) lose a host of related concepts, particularly those clustered around familial imagery, emotions, and ties. This is especially true of those Marxist feminists locked into an econometric model, for they see the family only as a unit defined by its role in "the provision of domestic labor and the reproduction cycle of labor-power through which it relates to the functional prerequisites of capitalism."[26] What of family loyalty? Intimacy? Responsibility? Cross-generational ties? Love? Hate?

The powerful and resonant themes we associate with intimate life, themes conjured up by ordinary understanding of what it means to have a "private life" or an "intimate relation," lose their emotional resonance when one attempts to incorporate them into aggregate, collective nouns. In the case of Marxist thought "class" is the most startling example. It is more difficult to reach for the concrete reality of the human subject if one begins from the great distance that a term like "class" necessitates, even though the term may have powerful purchase within a theoretical system.

The most compelling critique of Marxist feminism's infusion of abstracted or econometric terms into the sphere of family ties and relationships would lie in a question to any mother on whether she would accept "producing the future commodity labor power" as an apt characterization of what she is doing. One's fears and love for children are drained of their meaning, their emotional significance, when they are recast exclusively as relations between "reproducers" and "future labor

25. I am not analyzing works from feminist historical scholarship that use Marxism as a powerful conceptual wedge into the history of women; rather, I am concentrating upon those texts that offer a Marxist feminist political perspective.

26. For a critique of Marxist feminist econometric approaches to the family see Jane Humphries, "The Working Class Family: A Marxist Perspective," in *The Family in Political Thought,* ed. Jean Bethke Elshtain (Amherst: University of Massachusetts Press, in press). Humphries, an economic historian working from a Marxist feminist perspective, offers a discussion of the working-class family based on historic case studies and evidence that is dramatically at odds with the abstracted econometric model.

power." In choosing abstracted, reductionistic terms of discourse, many Marxist feminists can go on to evade the daunting questions that arise when one attempts to express and examine the depth and complexity of family relations. Within the boundaries of abstract, econometric discourse, issues that emerge when one takes the human subject and her relations as a starting point are simply washed away.

Even Sheila Rowbotham, the Marxist feminist thinker most attuned to the problem of language and the private sphere in the emotional lives of human beings, ultimately fails to incorporate her insights into a compelling explanatory theory, perhaps because she is determined to state her case *entirely* in untheoretical language. There is enormous strength in using ordinary language and resisting the move, certainly in some ways a power move, to couch one's arguments in an abstract language unavailable to most social participants. But Rowbotham goes too far in seeing the language of theory simply as an instrument of domination that must be repudiated even as she exhorts the oppressed to take over language and make it their own in order to express their reality.[27] She states: "Language of theory—removed language—only expresses a reality experienced by the oppressors."[28] This cannot be wholly correct unless she wishes to draw Marx himself into her indictment: No ordinary proletarian ever depicted his dilemma in the highly complex theoretical language of *Capital.* Theoretical language is seen by Rowbotham dominantly as a weapon in the hands of the powerful. But at times she seems to claim that the language of everyday reality merely refracts the "words of the powerful" in so thoroughgoing a manner that they alone "define and control reality for themselves."[29]

It is true that those in power have a greater opportunity to compel their assessments of social reality, but it does not follow that all language, including the language of theory, must spring from, or serve only, the dominators. If Rowbotham's claims were true it would follow that once the oppressed gained power they too would deploy language as a tool of domination; they too would impose a view of reality on others—unless she is willing to advocate what she elsewhere calls the "sentimentalism" which assumes that the oppressed are purer and more noble because they have suffered and will therefore behave differently once in power. Rowbotham begins by excluding women "from all existing language" and depicting them as profoundly alienated "from any culture"[30] despite

27. Rowbotham, p. 32.
28. Ibid., pp. 32–33.
29. Ibid.
30. Ibid., p. 34. See also Rosalind Petchesky, "Dissolving the Hyphen: A Report on Marxist Feminist Groups 1–5," in *Capitalist Patriarchy and the Case for Socialist Feminism,* ed. Zillah Eisenstein (New York: Monthly Review Press, 1979). Also see Jane Flax, "The Family in Contemporary Feminist Theory: A Critical Review," in Elshtain, ed., for a wide-ranging critique on the shortcomings of a Marxist feminist approach, particularly Juliet Mitchell's

their identity as language-using, culture-bearing, self-interpreting beings. Such a view suggests that women had nothing to do with the
emergence of language and culture and the passing on of historic tradition, that they remained importantly untainted. This is simply false.

When Rowbotham enjoins women to "change the meanings of
words,"[31] or calls for revolutionary movements to "break the hold of the
dominant group over theory," she proffers an important insight. But she
fails to stress that words are not changed de novo by single persons or
groups. Meanings evolve slowly as changing social practices, relations,
and institutions are characterized in new ways. Over time this helps to
give rise to an altered reality, for language evolution is central to reality.
Speech that seeks power to transform the world, as well as the human
subject, must embrace a political language that moves the subject *into* the
world without locking her into the *terms* of ongoing social arrangements.
It is here that the language of liberal feminism falls short.

The best entry into the world of liberal feminism is through an
exploration of its terms of discourse: How do liberal feminists describe
and explain public and private phenomena? What motivations, potentialities, and desired outcomes are held out for women? One is struck
immediately by the depoliticized language liberal feminists deploy in
characterizing persons, male and female, in their public and private
capacities. The most commonly used term is the notion of "role." No one
would disagree that persons play a number of different parts at different
times to different purposes in their social capacities, but liberal feminists'
exclusionary focus on the notion of *role* carries with it important implications for their social analysis.

In liberal discourse, persons are not essentially mothers, fathers,
lovers, friends, scholars, laborers, eccentrics, dissidents, or political leaders but *role players*. Society is a collection of aggregates, social atoms
performing roles. A flattening out of social life and the human subject
results. Each role seems equal to another in a kind of leveling process, a
homogenization of description and evaluation. Cynthia Fuchs Epstein,
for example, dubs motherhood a "role" like any other, a socially constituted and sanctioned activity with a relatively fixed range of operation.[32] The effect is to distort the full meaning of mothering. Mothering
is *not* a role on a par with being a file clerk, a scientist, or a member of the
air force. Mothering is a complicated, rich, ambivalent, vexing, joyous
activity which is biological, natural, social, symbolic, and emotional. It
carries profoundly resonant emotional and sexual imperatives. A ten-

---

structuralist Marxism, to the family. Flax's essay includes a detailed, lengthy bibliography
of Marxist feminist works.

31. Ibid., p. 33.

32. Cynthia Fuchs Epstein, *Woman's Place: Options and Limits in Professional Careers*
(Berkeley and Los Angeles: University of California Press, 1971).

dency to downplay the differences that pertain between, say, mothering and holding a job not only drains our private relations of much of their significance but also oversimplifies what can or should be done to alter things for women, who are frequently urged to change roles in order to solve their problems.

The language of roles, and those terms and notions clustered and associated with it—functional differentiation, systems maintenance, social deviation, dysfunctional, and so on—is a depoliticized language. Elizabeth Janeway's work gives an excellent example of language that depoliticizes. For example, she explicitly repudiates one resonant term of political discourse, "equality," for, she chides, it is "too small a word" to capture what she has in mind.[33] Her vision is of a small number of exceptional women engaged in intentional role breaking to gain status and a sense of identity and, in the process, mounting an unspecified challenge to the universe. One might suggest an alternative interpretation for Janeway's resistance to the word "equality": it is potentially too highly charged a political term for one who neither seeks nor desires genuine structural change.

There are liberal analysts who openly advocate an explicit political role for women beyond that offered by Janeway. But just as the suffragists were constrained in their articulation of a transformative feminist vision by their absorption of sentimentalist notions as to the correct means and ends of politics, contemporary liberal feminists have conceptual difficulties in part because of their embrace of the liberal presumption that all values, ends, and purposes are simple private values or compounds of such values. Liberal feminists share with other liberal pluralists an insistence on the overall social benefits of self-interest.

The problem—or one of the problems—with a politics that begins and ends with mobilizing resources, achieving maximum impacts, calculating prudentially, articulating interest group claims, engaging in reward distribution functions, and so on, is not only its utter lack of imagination but its inability to engage the reflective allegiance and committed loyalty of citizens. Oversimply, no substantive sense of civic virtue, no vision of the political community that might serve as the groundwork of a life in common, is possible within a political life dominated by a self-interested, predatory individualism.

Finally, what is interesting in yet another aspect of feminist discourse, the psychoanalytic feminist texts, is that thus far psychoanalytic feminists have not put to full use for feminist ends the conceptual categories internal to psychoanalysis—rich, dynamic concepts like projection, displacement, regression, and transference. The "feminist ends"

33. Elizabeth Janeway, *Man's World, Woman's Place: A Study in Social Mythology* (New York: William Morrow & Co., 1971), p. 217.

I have in mind include the articulation of a philosophy of mind that repudiates the old dualism with which we are still saddled in favor of an account that unites mind and body, reason and passion, into a compelling account of human subjectivity and identity, and the creation of a feminist theory of action that, complicatedly, invokes both inner and outer realities. A third feminist end to which psychoanalysis could make a major contribution is the amplification of a theory of language as meaning in order to articulate an interpretive story of female experience.

Freudian language in the hands of disciples thoroughly enamored of the "scientific" dimensions of psychoanalytic theory, and less attuned than Freud to the intuitive, fantastic, expressivist aspects of human experience and language, tends to shrink human experience down to clinical terms. Freud himself extended dramatically the range of what is to count as meaningful human speech. He demonstrated the way in which language, finally, is puzzling, enigmatic, full of paradoxes, irony, jokes, and surprises. It is this Freud—the Freud of "wit and its relation to the unconscious," of slips of the tongue, wild dreams, and the language of desire—who recognized that the human being is infinite and that it is presumptuous to assume that one can exhaustively account for the complexity of any single human subject, even a single dream, and thereby to explain (or to explain away) what it means to be human.[34] And language is central to our humanity. If psychoanalytic feminism begins to move in these directions, it will make contact with speech, identity, and action along the whole range of public and private possibilities. At this point, however, psychoanalytic feminists, in their attempts to derive everything from private imperatives buttressed by social compulsion, are paradoxically and unwittingly creating a patina of defenses against politics or against thinking "the political." Political history gets overassimilated to domestic dynamics and family history.

The two psychoanalytically oriented thinkers I will focus upon briefly—Dorothy Dinnerstein and Nancy Chodorow—insist that there is a relatively tight and concretely specified connection between the particular nature of private social arrangements and public outcomes that is detrimental to women and to possibilities for human liberation. In Dinnerstein's view, the female monopoly of early childhood creates as its inexorable result a fear of female authority that perpetuates destructive

34. Freud's entire corpus can be taken as a contribution to a theory of language and meaning, but see the following as a beginning: "Constructions in Analysis," in *The Standard Edition of the Complete Psychological Works of Sigmund Freud*, trans. and ed. James Strachey, 24 vols. (London: Hogarth Press, 1975): 23:355–70; "Introductory Lectures on Psychoanalysis," ibid., vols. 15 and 16; "New Introductory Lectures on Psycho-analysis," ibid., vol. 22; "On the Sexual Enlightenment of Children," ibid., 9:129–39; "The Psychopathy of Everyday Life," ibid., vol. 6; and "The Unconscious," ibid., 14:166–204.

male control of history making and female domination of the sphere of emotional fulfillment and private life. Immersed in a thoroughly privatized self-identity, her women are not allowed to speak *to* the public world.[35]

Chodorow deploys psychoanalysis to construct what she calls a "sociology of gender" by examining the relationship between male dominance and the sexual division of labor. Like Dinnerstein, she insists that female private and male public identities and activities are congealed in the early stages of childhood development. The only way out of this iron cage is a structurally dictated shift to "more collective child-rearing situations."[36] She assigns no specific role to the language-bearing female subject in this transformation. The subject, in her analysis, is locked into a nearly air-tight system in which mothering (with all its portentous implications) gets reproduced. Chodorow's subjects are so thoroughly determined—"over-socialized"—that the potentially creative, unpredictable, and surprising possibilities of human speech do not figure in her analysis. But feminist thinkers could put psychoanalytic theory to use in the creation of a subject-centered discourse if, as Freud did, they approached that theory as a commitment to truth seeking. The psychoanalyst and philosopher Wolfgang Loch describes truth as the active *construction* of a self-understanding. To reach this truth, with its profound implications for political discourse and political action, a particular sort of dialogue, itself a feature of the truth that emerges, must be undertaken. The means of truth seeking cannot be bifurcated from the ends of truth construction. For Loch, this dialogue's vital end is to reach the truth from, by, and for the subject herself, but within a social frame of uncoerced communication which becomes, as in the Hebrew tradition, a rock to stand on.[37] The dynamic process Loch details includes but is not merely interpretation, the drawing out of a hidden meaning; it implicates both subject and analyst (or political thinker by analogy) in the construction or reconstruction of truths whose trajectory aims toward the future.

Finally, a political discourse directed toward the construction of new meanings, focused on subjects becoming more intelligible to themselves, provides intimations of a future in which human speech and discursive

---

35. Dorothy Dinnerstein, *The Mermaid and the Minotaur: Sexual Arrangements and the Human Malaise* (New York: Harper & Row, 1976).

36. Nancy Chodorow, *The Reproduction of Mothering: Psychoanalysis and the Sociology of Gender* (Berkeley and Los Angeles: University of California Press, 1978), p. 217. Juliet Mitchell's important psychoanalytic treatment, *Psychoanalysis and Feminism* (New York: Random House, 1971), is a rigid, abstract, structuralist rendering of Freud that silences the individual subject entirely.

37. Wolfgang Loch, "Some Comments on the Subject of Psychoanalysis and Truth," in *Truth, Consciousness and Reality,* ed. Joseph R. Smith, M.D. (New Haven, Conn.: Yale University Press, 1974), p. 221.

reflection is undominated, uncoerced, unmanipulated, an approxima-
tion of Jurgen Habermas's "ideal speech situation."[38] The salience of this
ideal for a critical account of women's liberation is that it begins from the
point of view of a subject as one who seeks meaning and purpose.

"To imagine a language," writes Wittgenstein, "means to imagine a
form of life."[39] Similarly, to imagine an ideal speech situation is to envis-
age a way of life. For Habermas, the concept of an ideal speech situation
serves as a *worthy* ideal (never perfectly attainable) which helps us to
assess other alternatives with clarity and force. Within an ideal speech
situation, no compulsion is present other than the force of discourse
itself; domination is absent; and reciprocity pertains between and among
participants. Habermas's indebtedness to Freud for his construct of the
ideal-speech situation opens up possibilities for incorporating feminist
imperatives along a number of salient dimensions into the conceptual
heart of one of the more compelling ideas in contemporary social theory.

Finally, each political thinker must plumb his or her own purposes.
If one's purpose is the search for a political language that does not
silence particular persons or groups, nor proscribe particular topics and
spheres of life from discourse, one must engage the present, the world
of the complex modern subject. The "I" that I am grows out of a past
that I can perceive but dimly, a past that can anger, enlighten, illumine,
or mystify my thinking about what it means to be a female, a human
being, a citizen, and a political theorist in a post-Holocaust, post-
Hiroshima age. I do not think we political thinkers have absorbed our
recent past at all. I think we are benumbed by it, and numbing ushers
into silence or suppressed discourse or furious researches into worlds far
removed and far simpler, or so it seems, than our own. But the distorted
communication of the present provides an *anticipation* and *presupposition*
that things could be different: that truth telling and enhanced awareness
are possible. For Freud and Habermas, our humanness presupposes our
capacity to speak and to communicate. But to create a coherent psycho-
social identity, speech of a particular kind is required: speech that simultaneously taps and touches our inner and outer worlds within a
community of others with whom we share deeply felt, largely inarticulate, but daily renewed intersubjective reality.

For example, if, as Carol Gilligan has argued, it is the case that
women have a distinct moral language, one that emphasizes concern for
others, responsibility, care, and obligation, hence a moral language profoundly at odds with formal, abstract models of morality defined in
terms of absolute principles, then we must take care to preserve the
sphere that makes such a morality of responsibility possible and must

38. Jurgen Habermas, *Legitimation Crisis* (Boston: Beacon Press, 1973).
39. Wittgenstein, para. 19, 83.

extend its imperatives to men as well.[40] If Gilligan is right both when she finds women's inner lives more complex than men's and learns that women have a greater ability to identify with others, to sustain a variety of personal relationships, and to attain a genuine reciprocity in those relationships, and when she locates these qualities and capacities in women's involvement with families and the protection of human life, we must think about what would be lost if the private sphere erodes further or if we seek to alter our intimate relations entirely.

One moral and political imperative that would unite rather than divide women, that would tap what is already there but go on to redeem and transform it, would be a feminist commitment to a mode of public discourse imbedded within the values and ways of seeing that comprise what Sara Ruddick has called "maternal thinking."[41] Such thinking need not and must not descend into the sentimentalization that vitiated suffragist discourse. For women to affirm the protection of fragile and vulnerable human existence as the basis of a mode of political discourse and to create the terms for its flourishing as a worthy political activity, for women to stand firm against cries of "emotional" or "sentimental," even as they refuse to lapse into a sentimental rendering of the values and language that flow from "mothering," would signal a force of great reconstructive potential. It would require of feminists moves toward those women they now tend to classify, along with men, as "other." Feminist should be among the first to recognize that individuals who are put on the defensive and made to feel inadequate—as women who mother now feel—will respond in defensive, even reactionary, ways unless or until others begin to approach them as ends-in-themselves rather than simply pawns in the game or enemies in the war.

I shall conclude with a question that poses a promise and a challenge: How do we set about creating a feminist discourse that rejects domination?

Department of Political Science
University of Massachusetts, Amherst

40. Carol Gilligan, "In a Different Voice: Women's Conceptions of the Self and Morality," *Harvard Educational Review* 47, no. 4 (November 1977): 481–517.

41. Sara Ruddick, "Maternal Thinking," *Feminist Studies* 6, no. 2 (Summer 1980): 342–67.

Feminist Theory : A Critique of Ideology , ed Keohane, Rosaldo, a Gelpi (U Chicago Press, 1981)

VIEWPOINT

On "Compulsory Heterosexuality and Lesbian Existence": Defining the Issues

Ann Ferguson, Jacquelyn N. Zita, and Kathryn Pyne Addelson

Ann Ferguson: Patriarchy, Sexual Identity, and the Sexual Revolution

Adrienne Rich's paper "Compulsory Heterosexuality and Lesbian Existence"[1] suggests two important theses for further development by feminist thinkers. First, she maintains that compulsory heterosexuality is

An earlier version of this paper was read at a philosophy and feminism colloquium at the University of Cincinnati, November 15, 1980. I would like to acknowledge the formative aid of Francine Rainone in the ideas and revision of this paper, as well as the helpful comments made by Kim Christensen, Annette Kuhn, Jacquelyn Zita, and Kathy Pyne Addelson on earlier drafts of this paper (Ferguson).

1. Adrienne Rich, "Compulsory Heterosexuality and Lesbian Existence," *Signs: Journal of Women in Culture and Society* 5, no. 4 (Summer 1980): 631–60. Unless otherwise indicated, page numbers referred to in text and footnotes are from this article.

the central social structure perpetuating male domination. Second, she suggests a reconstruction of the concept *lesbian* in terms of a cross-cultural, transhistorical lesbian continuum which can capture women's ongoing resistance to patriarchal domination. Rich's paper is an insightful and significant contribution to the development of a radical feminist approach to patriarchy, human nature, and sexual identity. Her synthetic and creative approach is a necessary first step to further work on the concept of compulsory heterosexuality. Nonetheless, her position contains serious flaws from a socialist-feminist perspective. In this paper I shall argue against her main theses while presenting a different, historically linked concept of lesbian identity.

Rich develops her insight on the concept *lesbian* from de Beauvoir's classic treatment of lesbianism in *The Second Sex* where lesbianism is seen as a deliberate refusal to submit to the coercive force of heterosexual ideology, a refusal which acts as an underground feminist resistance to patriarchy. From this base Rich constructs a lesbian-feminist approach to lesbian history. As she writes elsewhere: "I feel that the search for lesbian history needs to be understood *politically,* not simply as the search for exceptional women who were lesbians, but as the search for power, for nascent undefined feminism, for the ways that women-loving women have been nay-sayers to male possession and control of women."[2]

To use such an approach as an aid to discover "nascent undefined feminism" in any historical period, the feminist historian has to know what she is looking for. We need, in other words, a clear understanding of what is involved in the concept *lesbian* so as to be able to identify such women. Rich introduces the concepts *lesbian identity* and *lesbian continuum* as substitutes for the limited and clinical sense of "lesbian" commonly used. Her new concepts imply that genital sexual relations or sexual attractions between women are neither necessary nor sufficient conditions for someone to be thought a lesbian in the full sense of the term. If we were to present Rich's definition of lesbian identity it would therefore be somewhat as follows:

1. *Lesbian identity* (Rich) is the sense of self of a woman bonded primarily to women who is sexually and emotionally independent of men.

Her concept of lesbian continuum describes a wide range of "woman-identified experience; not simply the fact that a woman has had or consciously desired genital sexual experience with another woman." Instead we should "expand it to embrace many more forms of primary intensity between and among women, including the sharing of a rich inner life, the bonding against male tyranny, the giving and receiving of practical

2. Quoted by Judith Schwarz, "Questionnaire on Issues in Lesbian History," *Frontiers* 4, no. 3 (Fall 1979): 1–12, esp. p. 6.

and political support; if we can also hear in it such associations as *marriage resistance* . . . we begin to grasp breadths of female history and psychology which have lain out of reach as a consequence of limited, mostly clinical definitions of 'lesbianism' " (pp. 648–49).

Rich, in short, conceives of lesbian identity as a transhistorical phenomenon, while I maintain, to the contrary, that the development of a distinctive homosexual (and specifically lesbian) identity is a historical phenomenon, not applicable to all societies and all periods of history. Her idea that the degree to which a woman is sexually and emotionally independent of men while bonding with women measures resistance to patriarchy oversimplifies and romanticizes the notion of such resistance without really defining the conditions that make for successful resistance rather than mere victimization. Her model does not allow us to understand the collective and social nature of a lesbian identity as opposed to lesbian practices or behaviors. Although I agree with Rich's insight that some of the clinical definitions of lesbian tend to create ways of viewing women's lives in which "female friendships and comradeship have been set apart from the erotic: thus limiting the erotic itself," I think her view undervalues the important historical development of an explicit lesbian identity connected to genital sexuality. My own view is that the development of such an identity, and with it the development of a sexuality valued and accepted in a community of peers, extended women's life options and degree of independence from men. I argue that the concept of lesbian identity as distinct from lesbian practices arose in advanced capitalist countries in Western Europe and the United States in the late nineteenth and early twentieth centuries from the conjunction of two forces. In part it was an ideological concept created by the sexologists who framed a changing patriarchal ideology of sexuality and the family; in part it was chosen by independent women and feminists who formed their own urban subcultures as an escape from the new, mystified form of patriarchal dominance that developed in the late 1920s: the companionate nuclear family.[3]

Defining "Lesbian"

Radicalesbians were the first lesbian-feminist theorists to suggest a reconstruction of the concept *lesbian*.[4] Their goal was not merely to

3. Cf. Michel Foucault, *The History of Sexuality*, vol. 1, *An Introduction*, trans. Robert Hurley (New York: Pantheon Books, 1978); Jeffrey Weeks, *Coming Out: Homosexual Politics in Britain from the Nineteenth Century to the Present* (London: Quartet Books, 1977); Mary McIntosh, "The Homosexual Role," *Social Problems* 16, no. 2 (Fall 1968): 182–92; and Christina Simons, "Companionate Marriage and the Lesbian Threat," *Frontiers* 4, no. 3 (Fall 1979): 54–59.

4. Radicalesbians, "Woman-identified Women," in *Radical Feminism*, ed. A. Koedt, D. Levine, and A. Rapone (New York: Quadrangle Books, 1973).

locate some central characteristic of lesbianism but also to find a way to eliminate the standard, pejorative connotation of the term. They wanted, that is, to rid the term of the heterosexist implications that lesbians are deviant, sick, unhealthy beings—a task important not merely as a defense of the lesbian community but of the feminist community and, indeed, of all women. The problem is that Radicalesbians as well as Rich do not clearly distinguish between three different goals of definitional strategy: first, valorizing the concept *lesbian;* second, giving a sociopolitical definition of the contemporary lesbian community; and finally, reconceptualizing history from a lesbian and feminist perspective. These goals are conceptually distinct and may not be achievable by one concept, namely, the lesbian continuum.

In the remainder of this section I will criticize the definitions of lesbian that have been offered in the literature and in common usage; I will argue that none succeeds completely in achieving any one of these tasks. (In fact, the truth may be that the first task cannot be accomplished at all in the opinion of those espousing values of the dominant culture.) In subsequent sections I will give my own suggestion for a sociopolitical definition of the contemporary lesbian community and some thoughts about transhistorical feminist concepts.

What then are some proposed definitions of the concept *lesbian?* First, let us consider the meaning the concept might have in 1981 for an average lay person not deeply engaged in gay, lesbian, or feminist politics:

2. *Lesbian* (ordinary definition) is a woman who has sexual attractions toward and relationships with other women.

One problem with the use of definition 2 as the instrument for delineating members of the contemporary lesbian community (the second goal) is that its meaning does not exclude practicing bisexual women. In fact, many commonsense usages of the term lesbian do not make the lesbian/bisexual distinction. Many women who have loved men and had sexual relationships with them come later to have sexual relationships with women and to think of themselves as lesbians without bothering to consider the metaphysical significance of the distinction between being a bisexual who loves a woman and a lesbian who loves a woman. What does this ambiguity in the application of the concept *lesbian* suggest about the usefulness of definition 2?

One thing it suggests is that homosexual practices by themselves are not sufficient or definitive constituents of a homosexual identity. A certain kind of political context is required. Therefore, when considering sexual identity, we should be wary of attempts to make oversimplified cross-cultural parallels. Most known societies have had some form of legitimate, or at least expected, homosexual practices in spite of the widespread persistence of culturally enforced heterosexuality; but from this we cannot conclude that individuals within those societies had homosexual identities in our modern understanding of the concept. Thus, among the Mohave Indians, those of either sex who so wished could choose to become socially a member of the opposite sex. The "woman" male might simulate pregnancy and menstruation, and the "man" female play the father role to her chosen partner's child by a biological male. Nonetheless the society distinguished between the two partners in such a homosexual pair. The social but nonbiological male or female was deviant, while the social and biological males and females were unfortunate but normal members of society. This distinction is not present today in society's concept of homosexual identity that would equally stigmatize as deviant both partners in a sexual relationship between two people of the same sex.

We could try to correct definition 2 while still seeking some ahistorical descriptive component of lesbian and say that:

3. *Lesbian* is a woman who is sexual exclusively in relation to women.

This definition certainly captures one important use of the concept *lesbian* in contemporary lesbian politics, in that it describes identified members of the lesbian subculture in such a way as to exclude women who engage in bisexual practices. But it also cuts from lesbian history many women like Sappho, Vita Sackville-West, and Eleanor Roosevelt, whom most lesbian feminists would like to include. Yet should a woman be accepted as a lesbian if she engaged in bisexual practices only if she is a historical personage and is not presently demanding to be included in the lesbian community? Surely, this is rather ad hoc!

The problem is that a strict distinction between lesbian/homosexual and bisexual rules out many commonly accepted historical situations involving homosexual practices, for example, those of Greece and Lesbos, because the aristocratic men and women involved (including Sappho) had same-sex love relations but also formed economic and procreative marriages with the opposite sex.

One further definitional strategy would eliminate genital sexual practices as relevant to the concept *lesbian,* thus at once avoiding the standard, pejorative connotations of the term and extending its meaning to include celibate women who are otherwise excluded by definition 3 from the lesbian sisterhood.[5] It is the trivializing of lesbian relations through emphasis on genital practice, many feel, that continues to stigmatize lesbianism. Instead, we should substitute traits valued highly, at least by the intended audience of feminists, and thus cleanse the concept of its negative implications.

This is the definitional strategy suggested by Blanche Weisen Cook

---

5. See Susan Yarborough, "Lesbian Celibacy," *Sinister Wisdom* 11 (Fall 1979): 24–29.

from which Rich, Nancy Sahli, and other recent writers take their cues.[6] The resulting definition is based on Cook's quoted words but with a clause added on the possibility of sexual love between women as a challenge to people's negative feelings about such love:

> 4. *Lesbian* (Cook) is ". . . . a woman who loves women, who chooses women to nurture and support and to create a living environment in which to work creatively and independently,"[7] whether or not her relations with these women are sexual.

My main criticism of definition 4 is a political one. This extension and reconstruction of the term lesbian would seem to eliminate women like Virginia Woolf, Gertrude Stein, and so on—in fact, all women who were sexually attracted to women but who worked with men or in a circle of mixed male and female friends such as the Bloomsbury group. When juxtaposed to Rich's idea of a lesbian continuum as an indicator of resistance to patriarchy, this definition suggests that female couples like Jane Addams and Mary Rozet Smith or women like Lilian Wald whose community of friends were almost entirely feminist are more important role models for lesbian-feminists than women like Gertrude Stein or Bessie Smith.

This approach also leaves out the historical context in which women live. At certain historical periods, when there is no large or visible oppositional women's culture, women who show that they can challenge the sexual division of labor—that is, who work with and perform as well as men—are just as important for questioning the patriarchal ideology of inevitable sex roles, including compulsory heterosexuality, as are the woman-identified women described by Cook. At certain periods even women who pass for men—such as those adventurers Dona Catalina De Erauso, Anny Bonny, and Mary Read[8]—are just as important as models of resistance to patriarchy as the celibate Emily Dickinson may have been in her time.

For these reasons I reject the political implication of radical feminist theory that there is some universal way to understand "true" as opposed to "false" acts of resistance to patriarchy. Consider that implication as expressed in this quote from Rich's interview in *Frontiers*: "We need also to research and analyze the lives of women who have been lesbians in the most limited sense of genital sexual activity while otherwise bonding with men. Because lesbianism in that limited sense has confused and blocked

---

6. Nancy Sahli, "Smashing: Women's Relationships Before the Fall," *Chrysalis*, no. 8 (1979), pp. 17–28.

7. Blanche W. Cook, "Female Support Networks and Political Activism," *Chrysalis*, no. 3 (1977), pp. 43–61.

8. See Nancy Myron and Charlotte Bunch, eds., *Women Remembered: A Collection of Biographies* (Baltimore: Diana Press, 1974).

resistance and survival."[9] I wonder, for instance, whether it is not racist or classist to urge third world women to bond with white women in "Take Back the Night" marches, rather than with third world men in protest against repressive racial violence toward minority men suspected of violence against white women. On the other hand, Emily Dickinson may have bonded with other women, but it is not clear to me that her life is not the sad case of a victim, rather than a successful resister, of patriarchy. Feminists mindful of the different forms of patriarchal hierarchy, including discrimination based on class and race, ought to be very wary of positing universal formulas and strategies for ending it. Hence, I reject the notion of a lesbian continuum because it is too linear and ahistorical.

My final objection to the reconstruction of the concept *lesbian* suggested in definition 4 is that the definition ignores the important sense in which the sexual revolution of the late nineteenth and twentieth centuries was a positive advance for women. The ability to take one's own genital sexual needs seriously is a necessary component of an egalitarian love relation, whether it be with a man or a woman. Furthermore, I would argue that the possibility of a sexual relationship between women is an important challenge to patriarchy because it acts as an alternative to the patriarchal heterosexual couple, thus challenging the heterosexual ideology that women are dependent on men for romantic/sexual love and satisfaction. Therefore, any definitional strategy which seeks to drop the sexual component of "lesbian" in favor of an emotional commitment to, or preference for, women[10] tends to lead feminists to downplay the historical importance of the movement for sexual liberation. The negative results of that movement—by which sexual objectification replaces material objectification, the nineteenth-century concept of woman as a "womb on legs" becoming the twentieth-century one of a "vagina on legs"—do not justify dismissal of the real advances that were made for women, not the least being the possibility of a lesbian identity in the sexual sense of the term.[11]

I conclude that none of the definitions given above succeeds in accomplishing the tasks which those interested in lesbian history have put forward: first, freeing the concept *lesbian* from narrow clinical uses

9. Quoted by Schwarz, p. 6.

10. See Joyce Trebilcot's discussion of related development of the concept of woman-identified woman in "Conceiving Women," *Sinister Wisdom* 11 (Fall 1979): 43–50.

11. Historical and political reasons lead me to reject Annabel Faraday's suggestion that we should get beyond the theoretical task of defining lesbian to the more important task of researching male methods of theorizing and controlling women's sexuality. We do indeed need to do this, but understanding the historical development of a lesbian identity and of a lesbian community as a potential resistance to male control is one part of this broader task. See Annabel Faraday, "Liberating Lesbian Research," in *The Making of the Modern Homosexual,* ed. K. Plummer (London: Hutchinson Publishing Group, 1981), pp. 112–29.

and negative emotive connotations; second, aiding the development of feminist categories for drawing clear lines among contemporary sexual identities; and finally, illuminating women's history by developing trans-historical categories that give us a better understanding of women's historical resistance to patriarchal domination.

An Alternative Approach: The New Lesbian Identity

Some Methodological Considerations

The major problem with definitions 1 through 4 is that they are ahistorical; that is, they all implicitly assume some universal way to define lesbianism across cultures, classes, and races. But this approach, as I hope I have shown, is bankrupt. Nonetheless, I think we can offer a historically specific definition of lesbian for advanced industrial societies that will meet the second goal listed above. But first we need to consider the prior social conditions necessary for one to be conscious of sexual orientation as part of one's personal identity.

Our contemporary sexual identities are predicated upon two conditions. First, and tautologically, a person cannot be said to have a sexual identity that is not self-conscious, that is, it is not meaningful to conjecture that someone is a lesbian who refuses to acknowledge herself as such. Taking on a lesbian identity is a self-conscious commitment or decision. Identity concepts are, thus, to be distinguished from social and biological categories which apply to persons simply because of their position in the social structure, for example, their economic class, their sex, or their racial classification. For this reason, labeling theorists make a distinction between primary and secondary deviance: One can engage in deviant acts (primary deviance) without labeling oneself a deviant, but acquiring a personal identity as a deviant (secondary deviance) requires a self-conscious acceptance of the label as applying to oneself.

A second condition for a self-conscious lesbian identity is that one live in a culture where the concept has relevance. For example, a person cannot have a black identity unless the concept of blackness exists in the person's cultural environment. (Various shades of brown all get termed "black" in North American culture but not in Caribbean cultures, partly because of the greater racism in our culture.) Connected to this is the idea, borrowed from Sartre, that a person cannot be anything unless others can identify her or him as such. So, just as a person cannot be self-conscious about being black unless there is a potentially self-conscious community of others prepared to accept the label for themselves, so a person cannot be said to have a sexual identity unless there is in his or her historical period and cultural environment a community of others who think of themselves as having the sexual identity in question.

Thus, in a period of human history where the distinctions between heterosexual, bisexual, and homosexual identity are not present as cultural categories (namely, until the twentieth century), people cannot correctly be said to have been lesbian or bisexual, although they may be described as having been sexually deviant. This point is emphasized by Carroll Smith-Rosenberg in her classic treatment of the particularly passionate and emotionally consuming friendships of nineteenth-century middle-class women for other women.[12]

The definition of lesbian that I suggest, one that conforms to the two methodological considerations above, is the following:

5. *Lesbian* is a woman who has sexual and erotic-emotional ties primarily with women or who sees herself as centrally involved with a community of self-identified lesbians whose sexual and erotic-emotional ties are primarily with women; and who is herself a self-identified lesbian.

My definition is a sociopolitical one; that is, it attempts to include in the term lesbian the contemporary sense of lesbianism as connected with a subcultural community, many members of which are opposed to defining themselves as dependent on or subordinate to men. It defines both bisexual and celibate women as lesbians as long as they identify themselves as such and have their primary emotional identification with a community of self-defined lesbians. Furthermore, for reasons I will outline shortly, there was no lesbian community in which to ground a sense of self before the twentieth century, a fact which distinguishes the male homosexual community from the lesbian community. Finally, it is arguable that not until this particular stage in the second wave of the women's movement and in the lesbian-feminist movement has it been politically feasible to include self-defined lesbian bisexual women into the lesbian community.[13]

Many lesbian feminists may not agree with this inclusion. But it may be argued that to exclude lesbian bisexuals from the community on the

12. Carroll Smith-Rosenberg, "The Female World of Love and Ritual: Relations between Women in Nineteenth-Century America," *Signs: Journal of Women in Culture and Society* 1, no. 1 (Autumn 1975): 1–29; Weeks (n. 3 above).

13. Some responses to the recent "vanguardism" of political lesbianism in the women's movement have suggested that we avoid such labels as "heterosexual," "bisexual," and "lesbian feminist" and begin to frame a bisexual or pansexual politics (see Beatrix Cambell, "A Feminist Sexual Politics," *Feminist Review* 5 [1980]). While I agree that we need new ideas to get beyond existing labels, it would be utopian to ignore the ongoing strength of heterosexism, which continues to stigmatize and deprive lesbians more than heterosexual women. We need, then, a clearly defined lesbian oppositional culture of resistance, but as feminists we need also to find ways to strengthen our women's community with other feminists as well as to recruit new members into the feminist community. One way to accomplish both these tasks in part is to accept the inclusive definition of lesbian I offer above.

grounds that "they give energy to men" is overly defensive at this point. After all, a strong women's community does not have to operate on a scarcity theory of nurturant energy! On feminist principles the criterion for membership in the community should be a woman's commitment to giving positive erotic-emotional energy to women. Whether women who give such energy to women can also give energy to individual men (friends, fathers, sons, lovers) is not the community's concern.

The Historical Development of the Sexual Identity Lesbian

In considering some reasons why the cultural concept *lesbian* came to exist in the United States and Western Europe only in the early twentieth century, we must ask what particular preconditions underlay the development in the later nineteenth century of the concept of a homosexual type or personality. If we take a socialist-feminist perspective on preconditions for radical social change—the general assumption is (to paraphrase Marx) that people can change their personal/social identities but not under conditions of their own choosing—we can focus on three factors: material (economic), ideological, and motivational.

In other papers I have developed the argument that the "material base" of patriarchy lies in male dominance in the family and extended kin networks.[14] However brutal its economic exploitation, nineteenth-century industrial capitalism did have one positive aspect for women in that it eventually weakened the patriarchal power of fathers and sons and, thus, the life choices of women increased. This relative gain in freedom was not an instant effect of capitalism, of course; early wage labor for women gave most women too little money to survive on their own. Nonetheless, acquisition of an income gave women new options, for example, sharing boardinghouse rooms with other women; and eventually some work done by women drew a sufficient wage to allow for economic independence. Then, too, commercial capital's growth spurred the growth of urban areas, which in turn gave feminist and deviant women the possibility of escaping the confines of rigidly traditional, patriarchal farm communities for an independent, if often impoverished, life in the cities.

Yet as the patriarchal family's direct, personal control over women weakened, the less personal control of a growing class of male professionals (physicians, therapists, and social workers) over the physical and mental health of women grew in strength. At the same time, a growing percentage of women were being incorporated into sex-

14. See Ann Ferguson, "Women as a New Revolutionary Class in the United States," in *Between Labor and Capital: The Professional-Managerial Class,* ed. Pat Walker (Boston: South End Press, 1979), pp. 279–309; and Ann Ferguson and Nancy Folbre, "The Unhappy Marriage of Patriarchy and Capitalism," in *Women and Revolution,* ed. Lydia Sargent (Boston: South End Press, 1981), pp. 313–38.

segregated wage labor for longer and longer periods. Ehrenreich and English argue that the shift from a patriarchal ideology based in the male-dominated family to a more diffuse masculinist ideology was in no sense a weakening of patriarchy, or male dominance, but simply represented a shift in power from fathers and husbands to male professionals and bosses.[15]

It is my view, on the contrary, that the weakening of the patriarchal family during this period created the material conditions needed for the growth of lesbianism as a self-conscious cultural choice for women—a choice that in turn helped to free them from an ideology that stressed their emotional and sexual dependence upon men. Accelerating the process were the studies in human sexuality made around the turn of the century by Freud, Ellis, Krafft-Ebing, and Hirschfield. The ideological shift in the understanding of human nature that their findings involved set the stage for a new permissiveness in sexual mores and the realization that both men and women have sexual drives. This change legitimated the demand of women to be equal sexual partners with men. It also suggested that women could add another dimension of joy to their already emotionally intense friendships with women. As it developed, the concept of a lesbian identity challenged the connection between women's sexuality and motherhood that had kept women's erotic energy either sublimated in love for children or frustrated because heterosexual privilege often kept women from giving priority to their relations with other women.

Noting the ideological changes that made possible the development of a lesbian identity leaves the deeper motivational questions unanswered. First, what lies behind the creation of a new dominant ideology, creating, in turn, a new way of viewing legitimate and illegitimate sexual behavior and changing the previous distinction between "natural" and "unnatural" sexuality to that between "normal" as opposed to "deviant" sexuality and sexual identity? Second, what motivation leads women to accept a deviant label and adopt a lesbian identity?

The answer to the first question is suggested by Michel Foucault's *Introduction to the History of Sexuality.*[16] The rising bourgeois class gradually creates a new ideology for itself that shifts the emphasis from control of social process through marriage alliance to the control of sexuality as a way of maintaining class hegemony. Jacques Donzelot documents how the developing category of sexual health and its obverse, sexual sickness (e.g., the hysterical woman, the psychotic child, the homosexual invert),

---

15. See Barbara Ehrenreich and Deidre English, *For Her Own Good* (New York: Doubleday & Co., 1979); and Mary Daly, *Gyn/Ecology* (Boston: Beacon Press, 1978), chap. 7. Other work that agrees with and supports this perspective is Stuart Ewen, *Captains of Consciousness* (New York: McGraw-Hill Book Co., 1976); and Heidi Hartmann, "The Unhappy Marriage of Marxism and Feminism: Towards a More Progressive Union," *Capital and Class* 8 (Summer 1979): 1–33.

16. Foucault (n. 3 above).

allow for growing intervention in the family by therapists, social workers, and male professionals as mediators for the capitalist patriarchal welfare state.[17] By providing a clear-cut, publicized line between permissible and illegitimate behavior, these categories enforce the social segregation of "deviants" from "normals," thus keeping the normals pure (and under control).[18]

One thing that Foucault and Donzelot as male leftists fail to emphasize is the way that the ideological reorganization they speak of serves not only the bourgeois class but also men reorganizing patriarchy. Christina Simons's important article documents the fact that self-styled progressive thinkers and humanists of the 1920s and 1930s who developed the ideal of the sexually equal "companionate marriage" did so in order to protect their newly mystified form of the patriarchal family (in which the male is instrumental breadwinner and the female is the expressive, nurturant, but sexy mom-housewife) by protecting young people from the lesbian/homosexual threat.[19]

Foucault also fails to emphasize popular resistance to the ideas and forces of social domination. As Rich points out, women have always resisted patriarchy, but why did women choose the particular avenue of lesbianism in the face of intense social stigma attached to it? A general answer is found in the sociology of normal/deviant categories. Once a particular deviation is identified in popular discourse, those dissatisfied with the conventional options have the conscious possibility of pursuing the deviant alternative. We could then expect that among participants in the first-wave women's movements a growing resentment of male domination in the family and the economy may have led some women to turn from sexual relations with men to sexual relations with women.

There is some evidence that in both the United States and Western Europe the growth of lesbianism among middle- and upper-class women was as closely connected with the first wave of the women's movement as the growth of lesbian feminism is with the second wave of the movement. Marcus Hirschfield claimed that in Germany 10 percent of feminists were lesbian.[20] In England, Stella Browne, the British pioneer in birth control and abortion rights, defended lesbianism publicly.[21] Upper-class women like Vita Sackville-West, Virginia Woolf, and Natalie Barney involved themselves in lesbian relationships. The fact that the lesbian subculture did not develop extensively until the 1930s in most countries, however, indicates how difficult it still was for most single women to be economically independent of men. With the rise of somewhat better wage labor positions for women in the 1920s, 1930s, and onward, the

17. Jacques Donzelot, *The Policing of Families* (New York: Pantheon Books, 1979).
18. McIntosh (n. 3 above).
19. Simons (n. 3 above).
20. Weeks (n. 3 above).
21. Weeks (n. 3 above).

gradual rise of an independent subculture of self-defined lesbians can be seen as a pocket of resistance to marriage. The second-wave women's movement in the 1960s and 1970s made possible a further extension of that subculture and a clearer definition of its counterpatriarchal, strongly feminist nature.

Heterosexual Ideology as a Coercive Force

Rich makes two basic assumptions in her defense of the lesbian continuum as a construct for understanding female resistance to patriarchy. First, she assumes that the institution of compulsory heterosexuality is the key mechanism underlying and perpetuating male dominance. Second, she implies that all heterosexual relations are coercive or compulsory relations. No arguments are given to support these crucial assumptions, an omission which I take as a fundamental flaw. While I agree that lesbian and male-male attractions are indeed suppressed cross-culturally and that the resulting institution of heterosexuality is coercive, I do not think it plausible to assume such suppression is sufficient by itself to perpetuate male dominance. It may be one of the mechanisms, but it surely is not the single or sufficient one. Others, such as the control of female biological reproduction, male control of state and political power, and economic systems involving discrimination based on class and race, seem analytically distinct from coercive heterosexuality, yet are causes which support and perpetuate male dominance.

Targeting heterosexuality as the key mechanism of male dominance romanticizes lesbianism and ignores the actual quality of individual lesbian or heterosexual women's lives. Calling women who resist patriarchy the lesbian continuum assumes, not only that all lesbians have resisted patriarchy, but that all true patriarchal resisters are lesbians or approach lesbianism. This ignores, on the one hand, the "old lesbian" subculture that contains many nonpolitical, co-opted, and economically comfortable lesbians. It also ignores the existence of some heterosexual couples in which women who are feminists maintain an equal relationship with men. Such women would deny that their involvements are coercive, or even that they are forced to put second their own needs, their self-respect, or their relationships with women.

Part of the problem is the concept of "compulsory heterosexuality." Sometimes Rich seems to imply that women who are essentially or naturally lesbians are coerced by the social mechanisms of the patriarchal family to "turn to the father," hence to men. But if a girl's original love for her mother is itself due to the social fact that women, and not men, mother, then neither lesbianism nor heterosexuality can be said to be women's natural (uncoerced) sexual preference. If humans are basically bisexual or transsexual at birth, it will not do to suggest that lesbianism is the more authentic sexual preference for feminists, and that heterosexual feminists who do not change their sexual preference are simply lying to themselves about their true sexuality.

The notion that heterosexuality is central to women's oppression is plausible only if one assumes that it is women's emotional dependence on men as lovers in conjunction with other mechanisms of male dominance (e.g., marriage, motherhood, women's economic dependence on men) which allow men to control women's bodies as instruments for their own purposes. But single mothers, black women, and economically independent women, for example, may in their heterosexual relations with men escape or avoid these other mechanisms.

Rich's emphasis on compulsory heterosexuality as the key mechanism of male domination implies that the quality of straight women's resistance must be questioned. But this ignores other equally important practices of resistance to male domination, for example, women's work networks and trade unions, and welfare mothers organizing against social service cutbacks. The (perhaps unintended) lesbian-separatist implications of her analysis are disturbing. If compulsory heterosexuality is the problem, why bother to make alliances with straight women from minority and working-class communities around issues relating to sex and race discrimination at the workplace, cutbacks in Medicaid abortions, the lack of day-care centers, cutbacks in food stamps, and questions about nuclear power and the arms race? Just stop sleeping with men, withdraw from heterosexual practices, and the whole system of male dominance will collapse on its own!

A socialist-feminist analysis of male dominance sees the systems that oppress women as more complex and difficult to dislodge than does the utopian and idealist simplicity of lesbian separatism. They are at least *dual* systems,[22] and more likely multiple systems, of dominance which at times support and at times contradict each other: capitalism, patriarchy, heterosexism, racism, imperialism. We need autonomous groups of resisters opposing each of these forms of dominance; but we also need alliances among ourselves. If feminism as a movement is truly revolutionary, it cannot give priority to one form of male domination (heterosexism) to the exclusion of others. One's sexual preference may indeed be a political act, but it is not necessarily the best, nor the paradigmatic, feminist political act. Naming the continuum of resistance to patriarchy the lesbian continuum has the political implication that it is.

To conclude, let me agree with Rich that some transhistorical concepts may be needed to stress the continuity of women's resistance to patriarchy. Nonetheless, the concepts we pick should not ignore either the political complexity of our present tasks as feminists nor our histori-

22. Iris Young, "Socialist Feminism and the Limits of Dual Systems Theory," *Socialist Review* 10, no. 50/51 (March–June 1980): 169–88.

cally specific political consciousness as lesbians. Rich's argument, on the one hand that compulsory heterosexuality is the key mechanism of patriarchy, and on the other hand that the lesbian continuum is the key resistance to it, has both of these unfortunate consequences.

Philosophy and Women's Studies
University of Massachusetts–Amherst

Jacquelyn N. Zita: Historical Amnesia and the Lesbian Continuum

Ann Ferguson's paper "Patriarchy, Sexual Identity, and the Sexual Revolution" is a welcome port of entry into a conceptual arena that many of us have encountered in our personal and community lives, but one which few of us as philosophers have given careful study and attention.[23] The discussion is long overdue, and since many of our philosophical dialogues have been sparked by the poetic insight of Adrienne Rich, we have once again to thank our poet-philosopher for generating yet another multitude of thoughts and words within the newly expanding community of feminist philosophers. In my own work I have returned to Rich many times for a regeneration of ideas and for the courage to move with hints of things only dimly seen, which we as philosophers shape by a different kind of language, inscribing a different intention into the words of our craft. The difference in style and language between Adrienne Rich's "Compulsory Heterosexuality and Lesbian Existence" and Ann Ferguson's response demonstrates this difference in intention: The first is poetic and literary; the second, philosophical and analytic. Both works share a personal commitment and passion which belongs to good feminist writing. Both pieces are meant to persuade us, but it would be misleading to suggest that the issue is one of definitions alone. The issue central to these two papers goes much deeper. It concerns the living of lesbian lives and the kind of social and political interpretation that we as women bring to our lesbian existence. Involved is a long process of exploration, dialogue, and community exchange.

The dangers of discussion such as this one are obvious enough.

23. Like others involved in feminist writing and research, I am indebted to many women who found it worthwhile to discuss and criticize the development of these ideas. I would like to give special thanks to Naomi Sheman, Vicky Spelman, Janet Spector, Susan Rogers, Hilary Sandall, Susan Bernick, Hazel VanEvera, Marilou Good, and above all Toni McNaron for their generous exchange and support. Also many thanks to Alison Jaggar, whose work in organizing the Philosophical Issues in Feminist Theory Conference held in Cincinnati on November 13–16, 1980, was instrumental in bringing this discussion into existence, Finally, I wish to extend my appreciation to Ann Ferguson, whose work not only inspires this commentary but also provides an articulate and intelligent balance for the discussion at hand (Zita).

Under patriarchy, the pejorative meaning of lesbian has been used as a scare term, as part of the policing mechanism that teaches women to deny and despise certain "wicked" or "outlawed" desires. The woman-hating, homophobia, and flesh-loathing that result pass into the language as if placed there by nature. There is work to be done here. Decoding that language and reweaving its many parts are tasks shared by poets and philosophers from different quarters of the linguistic map. How to cleanse the word lesbian, how to dislodge its negative and evaluative meaning, how to expand the scope of the term, whom to include, whom to exclude, and why—these are the many questions already set in motion by the process of cultural reconstruction.

The path is only dimly seen. The recreation of language and meaning can easily lead to forms of hierarchy, elitism, and the self-righteous appropriation of the very words we desperately seek to reclaim. Enter the Lesbian Olympics, where competing lesbians are ranked, categorized, accepted, and rejected. The criteria for ranking vary with the community—downward mobility, chemical purity, non-monogamy, proximity to men, number of cats, runs-batted-in, ritualistic obscurity, quality of exotic sexual forays, and others. These categories sometimes get confused with the definition of lesbian and its authenticity. Winners of the Olympics are named the real lesbians; runners-up, lesser lesbians; and losers remain losers—immoral, inauthentic, and politically corrupt. Each community claims the right to use the term in the only correct way. To each community belong the only real, authentic, pure-strain lesbians—the trial of language has ended.

What is it we are doing? What is it behind this urge to define, to establish a meaningful difference, to separate our group from the others? What is the point behind this endless question of difference, the same question that reemerges in Rich's and Ferguson's work? It seems to me that our search for language helps build an alternative culture of resistance. For this reason, the definition of lesbian we are looking for must include not only a descriptive and evaluative dimension but also a political dimension. Rich's notion of *lesbian continuum* as one of woman-centered resistance seems to promise much of what we are looking for, a possibility quickly eclipsed by Ann Ferguson's socialist-feminist approach to the same question. I would like to explore the difference between them from my own lesbian perspective.

There are many things I like in Ann Ferguson's commentary. I could not agree more with her refusal to excise the erotic dimension from the concept *lesbian*[24] to counter the more recent, glossy "women-

24. It reminds one of a pair of disjunctive conditions in her final definition (brackets and parentheses mine): "*Lesbian* ([A woman who has sexual and erotic-emotional ties primarily with women] or [who sees herself as centrally involved with a community of self-identified lesbians whose sexual and erotic-emotional ties are primarily with women]) and [who is herself a self-identified lesbian]." The logical form of the definition is ($p \vee q$) r.

loving-women" definitions, which too often hide the genital homophobia of an otherwise purified and cleansed reconstruction of the term. Many lesbians do enjoy sexuality, and many of us find it far superior to the staid and straight prescriptions of our culture. It follows that the lesbian option includes this sexual component—it is there to provide women with the serious and joyous opportunity to reconsider their genital needs and desires in the absence of phallic hegemony and cultural taboos. Hence, the ecstasy of exorcism! Likewise, I agree with Ferguson's critique of current lesbianography. We are in need of categories that accurately name and categorize the actions and lives of our sisters, both dead and alive, who, within their circumstances, resisted the historically specific forms of oppression that owned their womanly existence. To transfer the assignation lesbian—understood as a concept belonging to a late twentieth-century, largely white, middle-class movement—to women who would be revolted or horrified or uncomprehending of the notion is not only bad historiography but idealist revolutionary fantasy. To label such women as "falsely conscious" of their lesbianism is likewise elitist, out-and-out gynocentric, and if not that, perilously close to becoming a new form of lesbian solipsism.

However, in spite of my agreements with Ann Ferguson's analysis, I still want to defend Adrienne Rich's idea of the lesbian continuum. Unlike Ferguson, I do not find Rich's concept all that ahistorical, static, or falsely universalizing. It would be if it were simply the transfer of Ferguson's redefinition of lesbian to women outside of our culture and our times, but it is not. What I want to argue is that Rich's notion of lesbian continuum must be understood in terms of the political interpretation that Rich brings to her lesbianism, and that the issue of debate between Ferguson and Rich lies not so much in opposing definitions as in conflicting concepts of revolutionary praxis and the role of lesbian women in creating such a revolution. The issue is not whether the historically specific definition of lesbian (developed by Ferguson) correctly names our lesbian existence, but what is being named and why. Nor is the issue one among contenders who covet the prize at the Lesbian Olympics, but one set to dialogue by those concerned with the collective reconstruction of resistance cultures, carved by a truly woman-centered politic.

Defining "Lesbian"

In assessing the various definitions of lesbian, Ann Ferguson develops three criteria for evaluating definitional strategies. An adequate definition must free the concept from its narrow clinical usage and its pejorative constriction; it must be useful in accurately naming a new lineage of women's history, one structured by considerations of sexual identity and sexual allegiance; and finally it must help us develop a better grasp of the underground resistance to patriarchal domination.

Why would we want such a definition? Much of what is required of the definition concerns the use, in this case the community use, that will be made of the term.

Lesbians under the existing mode of patriarchy are an endangered species. It seems more than obvious that one reason we want a definition of lesbian is to regulate and control passages into and out of the lesbian community. "Passing" for straight has always been a strategy of lesbian survival, but the phenomenon of passing points to the coercion and force with which the lesbian option is denied and punished in our culture. Whether a woman is holding on to her class, race, or status privilege, or to her children, husband, and friends, or to her only means of economic survival, passing for straight and the leading of a double life are in practice modes of subscribing to the heterosexist norms that it is shameful for women to love women. Is it any wonder then that lesbians who refuse to pass take care of their fragile community existence? Trust becomes a major concern in accepting a woman as a lesbian, especially when infiltration and exploitation of the lesbian community have been all too common occurrences. Lesbian community is a place where lesbians can relax; where the worry of offending straight women no longer exists; where homophobia is erased; where the women you meet share common interests, and experiences, and desires; where lesbian sensibility and erotic caring are givens. It is the place we feel at home—a radical kinship in the making. Is it any wonder that the definition of lesbian is vital to our survival as lesbians?

I would suspect that throughout our past, we have sought out others like ourselves, and that the needs and strategies for lesbian survival[25] (along with the social patterns of recognition and respect) have been as varied as the historical circumstances that have structured a woman's life situation. However, one thing that is shared by all forms of lesbian existence in all societies where compulsory heterosexuality and male control over female sexuality, fertility, and reproduction have been practiced is the meaning of such an existence. In the context of compulsory heterosexuality, lesbian existence, by definition, is an act of resistance.[26]

25. I think it is much more helpful to examine lesbian existence in terms of the needs women have felt and the strategies they have used to survive as lesbians. This will vary with the specificity of material and ideological circumstance structuring the way in which these needs and strategies are recognized and expressed, as well as with the culturally specific modes of satisfaction available for lesbian desires and interests.

26. It is important to note that Rich's idea of lesbian continuum advances the discussion on the institution of heterosexuality by making visible the coercion with which the channeling of the erotic is enforced. During the 1970s many lesbian feminists discussed "heterosexual privilege" as the key mechanism for maintaining heterosexual hegemony. See, e.g., Charlotte Bunch, "Learning from Lesbian Separatism," *Ms.* 5, no. 5 (November 1976): 60–61, 99–102. Rich's recent work adds the dimension of coercion and "learned" compulsion to the exercise of that privilege, thus raising important questions regarding the motivations and consent that structure our use of the erotic.

All this is lost in Ann Ferguson's definition of lesbian as stated above: "[A] *lesbian* is a woman who has sexual and erotic-emotional ties primarily with women or who sees herself as centrally involved with a community of self-identified lesbians whose sexual and erotic emotional ties are primarily with women; and who is herself a self-identified lesbian." Ferguson's definition of lesbian refers to a rather carefully selected (often privileged) group of lesbian-identified women, living in the subcultures of advanced capitalist societies. This kind of culturally defined lesbianism provides a sense of continuity and "belongingness" by means of a community membership. The stability and continuity of one's lesbian identity rest upon community regard and respect,[27] an identity which pervades regardless of the episodic character of a woman's actual lesbian practices. In Ferguson's words, "homosexual practices by themselves are not sufficient to constitute a homosexual identity."

In contrast, Adrienne Rich's definition of lesbian refers to the continuity of resistance that women have always undertaken in independent, nonheterosexual, and woman-centered ways (p. 635). Continuity (and, hence, the lesbian continuum) is created by naming that struggle a lesbian struggle. The sense of continuity and shared identity is not created by symbolic transactions between self and other within a special linguistic community. It is an ethnographic ascription which depends on the criteria of woman-centered resistance used to separate pockets of lesbian existence from the dominant culture.

Ferguson's definition of lesbian has already cut the roots of this continuity, since her definition refers to a very recent form of lesbian existence. It is clear that this particular articulation of lesbian existence and community is dependent on the historical circumstance of recent capitalist development, but to assume that the scope of the term must be truncated to fit the contours of this self-selected group of lesbian women seems deceptively solipsistic. One side of Ferguson's definition requires that a woman be aware of herself as a lesbian and be recognized by the lesbian community as such. This is automatically exclusive. Not only does it exclude many of our dead sisters, but it also ignores women who, for various reasons, refuse to turn their private lesbian lives into a social issue. All of these women would be excluded from the public sphere of lesbian existence and from the scope of the term lesbian. To remedy this, Ferguson expands her definition to include the option of private sexual practices, but ambiguity remains in the phrase "primarily with women." This results in an insidious circularity, since a lesbian is once again whatever the community decides is lesbian or whatever a woman self-

27. Ferguson's reliance on labeling theorists is unfortunate, since it necessarily lends itself to cultural relativism and historical discontinuity. See Thomas Scheff, *On Being Mentally Ill* (New York: Aldine Publishing Co., 1966); T. Scheff, "The Labeling Theory of Mental Illness," *American Sociological Review* 39 (1974): 444–52; E. Schurr, *Labeling Deviant Behavior: Its Sociological Implications* (New York: Harper & Row, 1971).

proclaims as her "lesbianness." A pillow fight! We fall immediately into the pivotal dangers of the Lesbian Olympics. The relativism is smashing.

If we look at Ferguson's final definition with more scrutiny, we also find that many of the inspirational images of resistance and rebellion, or lesbian-identified lesbianism as a political form of resistance, are lost. The definition becomes one of a countercultural group, a group that, at most, provides an outlet for "runaway" women. We no longer are permitted to see our lesbianism in insurrectionary terms. This is because the continuity and continuum with a history of resistance has been cut short by a parochial definition of lesbianism which has turned it into one more counterculture among many. Continuity has been replaced by discontinuity. The blunt force of empiricism has fragmented our "herstory," breaking its connections into short-lived periods. Obviously, this way of defining lesbian is of little use for our historiographical and political concerns. By Ferguson's own criteria of definitional adequacy, this definition fails to meet our needs and interests.

Rich's notion of the lesbian continuum appears to be much more promising, since it rests on a commonality that links the many aspects of lesbian living into a shared unity. This commonality follows directly from the existence of compulsory heterosexuality as an institution, one based on violent strictures (external coercion and internally induced compulsion) that have been necessary to enforce and maintain women's erotic loyalty and subservience to men. Wherever this institution exists, and I would venture to say that it exists wherever patriarchy exists, a woman who refuses to follow the rules engages in an act of resistance. As Rich has suggested, "We can say that there is a nascent feminist political content in the act of choosing a woman lover or life partner in the face of institutional heterosexuality" (p. 659). The discovery of our love for one another and the courage to act on those feelings, however fleeting and minimal, is an awakening of the lesbian continuum in our lives. It is as if the lesbian continuum exists in the transcendental sense[28] as a series of "hints": a multitude of pulls, tugs, palpitations, and desires surfacing in the intimate episodes between women, in their discovery of mutual powers and attractions, and in the many moments quickly eclipsed by the return of repression. These moments and impulses can be stretched into a continuous lesbian identity, one that not only names these desires but holds to them, an identity that will find its expression within the historical context in which a woman lives out her existence.

What all of these existences share in common is a positive discovery of the beauty, power, and knowledge that can exist among women. Yet

28. Surprising parallels can be found in Kant's idea of history, a conceptual construct used to organize and recollect the meaning of the past. The idea of the lesbian continuum functions theoretically in a similar manner, unbeknownst to Kant, of course. See Immanuel Kant, *On History*, ed. Lewis White Beck (New York: Bobbs-Merrill Co., 1963), esp. "Idea for a Universal History from a Cosmopolitan Point of View."

within the context of heterosexual hegemony, this discovery, and action based on it, can only be named as acts of resistance. Hence, the continuum will always link together the many acts of covert and overt sexual politics that hem the periphery of the nonheterosexual, women-centered ways by which we women have always resisted privileged male access to and control over our bodies. The continuum names a struggle already in existence, but it also deepens and expands the existence of that struggle.

Lesbian Continuum: A Strategic Term

I agree with Ferguson that Adrienne Rich fails to sort "successful resistance" from "mere victimization" by lumping together "many forms of primary intensity between and among women," an idea as diffuse as Audre Lorde's expansive notion of the erotic.[29] As a result, Rich is willing to include in her continuum "the grown woman's experience of orgasmic sensations while suckling her child, perhaps recalling her mother's milk smell in her own, to two women like Virginia Woolf's Chloe and Olivia, who share a laboratory, to the woman dying at ninety touched and handled by women" (pp. 650–51). The idea of lesbian continuum extends the concept without paying dues to the success or failure of these resistances. As a result, it leaves open to discussion the question of what counts as successful or failed resistance in particular historical circumstances.

This omission, however, does not invalidate the usefulness of such a concept. Given Rich's perspective, women resisting the bride-price belong to the same continuum as the modern lesbian-identified dyke ("the revolting hag")—the rebellion is continuously against various historically specific forms of male-dominated control over the female body and its cultural expression. As those historical circumstances change, so too the possibility of resistance and its success or failure.[30]

I will argue in contrast to Ferguson that there are several good reasons for adopting the idea of a lesbian continuum as a strategic term, where by "strategic" I will mean a term that not only elucidates the ways

29. Audre Lorde, *Uses of the Erotic: The Erotic as Power,* Out and Out Pamphlet, no. 3 (New York: Out & Out Books, in press).

30. I think that the central concept of the Rich/Ferguson exchange is resistance. A discussion of the concept and meaning of resistance is urgently needed, especially given the newly fashionable idea that any form of sexual taboo breaking is emancipatory and politically important. This is where conceptual and political work needs to be done prior to any attempts to define the term lesbian or lesbian continuum. In the description of working-class resistance, I have found the work of Andre Gorz and Karl Korsch helpful, but in the description of women-centered forms of resistance, there is little written material to be found. Sarah Hoagland's "Lesbian Ethics" (*Lesbian Insider/Insighter/Inciter* 2 [January 1981], pp. 3, 9, 15, 26–29) and Marilyn Frye's discussion in "Some Thoughts on Separatism and Power" (*Sinister Wisdom* 6 [Summer 1978]: 30–39) are particularly useful tools for the work of cultural reconstruction that lies ahead of us.

in which women have always resisted male tyranny and compulsory heterosexuality, but also ways in which these episodic resistances can be solidified and crystallized into an autonomous culture of resistance. If this cultural practice is to become truly revolutionary, then a sense of continuity with the past and a firm sense of a continuum against which "the quality of a woman's resistance" can be measured (within the specificity of her historically lived circumstance) seem desirable and necessary. The "idea of a lesbian continuum" as a strategic term becomes a tool for articulating and making intelligible our lesbian-feminist living.

1. *Continuity.*—My first reason for adopting the lesbian continuum as a useful term is to stop the hysteria about "the lesbian miracle," that "something" which happens to women out of nowhere and sometimes overnight. Although we might choose to invent the term lesbian continuum, we did not invent lesbian existence. The constant illusion of unique discovery rests upon the constant erasure of past lesbian existence, an ahistorical amnesia that leads to the naive romanticism of modern lesbian egoism. As a result, a firm sense of continuity with the long legacy of resistance strategies, all of which seek to reclaim in woman-centered ways control and access to our bodily domains, is lost. Along with this, the meaning of sexual allegiance is obscured. This erasure can be seen in various political agendas that call for a reorganization of the sex division of bodies,[31] the sex division of gender,[32] the sex division of labor, the sex division of rights and obligations, and the sex division of power and status in our existing society. These programs seem curiously incomplete. Including the politics of lesbian resistance into an agenda for struggle brings to light another division—the sex division of the erotic—that is just as central, if not more central, to the cultural and institutional policing of the female body.[33]

31. Special credit should be given to Margaret O'Hartigan whose work and thinking have raised for me many new questions concerning the polarity of sex ascription (as opposed to gender ascription) and its cultural use. See Margaret O'Hartigan, "The Nomenclature of Sex and Oppression," *Minnesota Daily* (October 6–9, 1980).

32. "Sex division of gender" refers to the ascription of masculine or feminine traits or demeanors to human bodies; "sex division of bodies" refers to the ascription of biological "femaleness" or "maleness" to human bodies. Much attention has been given to the former (see esp. Nancy Chodorow, *The Reproduction of Mothering* [Berkeley: University of California Press, 1978] and Dorothy Dinnerstein, *The Mermaid and the Minotaur: Sexual Arrangements and the Human Malaise* [New York: Harper & Row, 1976]), while little attention has been given to the normative content of biological sex identity. The distinction between sex and gender identity seems to rest on a nature/culture dualism. For a critique of this dualistic thinking, see Ann Palmeri, "Feminist Materialism: On the Possibility and the Power of the Nature/Culture Distinction," paper presented at the midwestern meeting of the Society of Women in Philosophy, Detroit, October 1980.

33. In Rich's critique of Chodorow, Dinnerstein, Ehrenreich, English, and Miller (pp. 631–37), she brings to light the external coercions required to enforce heterosexual allegiance. What is missing in the works she cites is an appreciation of the social production of the sex division of the erotic. Even in theories where every other example of sex division is given serious intellectual consideration, this blindness with respect to erotic power and its use persists.

2. *Continuum and quality of resistance.*—By expanding the meaning of woman-centered resistance, the idea of the lesbian continuum brings into focus the quality of resistance in a woman's life. As Rich has pointed out, we are the ones who make the connection between women resisting bride-prices and the lesbian resisting heterosexual closure: "We begin to observe behavior, both in history and individual biography, that has hitherto been invisible or misnamed; behavior which often constitutes, given the limits of the counterforce exerted in a given time or place, *radical rebellion.* And *we can connect* these rebellions and the necessity for them with the physical passion of woman for woman which is central to lesbian existence: the erotic sensuality that has been, precisely, the most violently erased fact of female experience" (pp. 652–53; italics mine). Likewise, for the nascent feminism of lesbian existence to grow, we are the ones who must make the connection between the erotic choice and a deeply expanded consciousness of woman identification. Who is this "we"? I would hope that it includes all the participating members of the lesbian-feminist communities, those willing to undertake the difficult and rewarding tasks of cultural reconstruction and historical re-membering.

Why does the continuum as an idea help to define the quality of resistance? First, in naming these past resistances lesbian, we define the lesbian option as a form of resistance to patriarchy qualitatively different from other forms because, however obscurely, lesbian resistance does include the sexual component. That is, the lesbian option, as an erotic, emotional, social, and political commitment to other women represents an option that cannot, like the alternatives of androgyny or dual parenting, be contained within the institution of heterosexuality. Likewise, the lesbian option cannot be contained as a simple negation or "reaction to" dehumanized heterosexuality—it is radically other and expansive.

Second, the idea of lesbian continuum allows us to ask a whole new array of questions about the institution of heterosexuality, questions that require further theoretical and political interrogations. If the institution of heterosexuality is a core institution of patriarchy in all its historical manifestations, including that of present-day capitalist patriarchy, then the lesbian continuum provides a background against which various strategies of resistance can be evaluated. In this way, the voids and silences of socialist-feminist solutions can be called into question.

Third, the idea of the lesbian continuum illuminates the inauthenticity with which many women are compelled to live their heterosexual lives. This it does by illuminating the institution of compulsory heterosexuality, against which every woman must begin to question the origin and meaning of her most intimate desires. The existence of coercion and compulsion hints of an alien interest at work behind the seeming free will of our womanly lives. To raise questions about the quality of resistance exemplified within a woman's life is to raise questions concerned with authenticity, honesty, courage—virtues not meant to glorify or romanticize the lesbian option, but virtues that mark the achievements of a fully examined life, regardless of sexual orientation. In the idea of the continuum, quantity is superseded by quality, a truly womanly idea of honor in the making.[34]

3. *False inclusion.*—A further reason for adhering to the idea of lesbian continuum is that it is anticlinical in orientation. Rich's idea of lesbian continuum rids the concept *lesbian* of its clinical fixation (hence its clinical containment), by defining it in political terms. This also helps to differentiate lesbian struggle from its unfathomable reduction to male-defined gay rights struggle. This Rich is able to do without denying the centrality of physical passion for woman as the essential feature of lesbianism at the far end of the continuum (pp. 652–53).

> To separate those women stigmatized as "homosexual" or "gay" from the complex continuum of female resistance to enslavement, and attach them to a male pattern, is to falsify our history. Part of the history of lesbian existence is, obviously, to be found where lesbians, lacking a coherent female community, have shared a kind of social life and common cause with homosexual men. But this has to be seen against the differences: women's lack of economic and cultural privileges relative to men; qualitative differences in female and male relationships, for example, the prevalence of anonymous sex and pederasty among male homosexuals, the pronounced ageism in male homosexual standards of sexual attractiveness, etc. In defining and describing lesbian existence I would hope to move toward a dissociation of lesbian from male homosexual values and allegiances. I perceive the lesbian experience as being, like motherhood, a profoundly female experience, with particular oppressions, meanings, and potentialities we cannot comprehend as long as we simply bracket it with other sexually stigmatized existences. [Pp. 649–50]

The concept of lesbian continuum defines lesbianism as its exists under patriarchy as part of a politics of woman-centered resistance, in contrast to the liberal issues of sex preference or lifestyle choices. Furthermore, Rich's continuum is not entirely a "reactive definition." It includes lesbian existence as a source of power and knowledge available to women (p. 633), as a phenomenon that would continue to exist outside of its present historically necessary mode of resistance to patriarchy.[35]

34. I am not claiming that one's transformation into or proclamation of lesbian allegiance is necessarily more authentic than heterosexual loyalties—the dialogue on erotic authenticity and responsibility is very much in progress. It would seem that lesbian living lends itself to more authentic forms of experimentation and questioning, since it is less corrupted by institutional forms of regulation, norms, and expectations but such authenticity is an achievement, not an orgasm.

35. Many thanks to Sandra Harding for emphasizing this point at the Cincinnati conference. Lesbianism as resistance is not entirely a "reactive concept"—it entails a positive discovery of the erotic, or as Audre Lorde says in *Uses of the Erotic,* "a positive source of power and information within our lives" (p. 1).

4. *False polarity.*—Finally, the idea of lesbian continuum releases our imagination from the either/or clinical categories of patriarchal sexual orientation. By means of a continuum we can begin to appreciate aspects of our straight sisters' lives. The many ways in which women have always cared for each other without caring for men, seen each other without seeing men, and related to each other without relating to men can be enhanced by a shared and guilt-free lesbian sensibility. As lesbian women we can begin to appreciate and nurture this sensibility as it exists in every woman, without denying the desire to question the ideological forces that often encase and harden the edges of its expression. This questioning need not lead to new forms of woman-hating between lesbian and straight women, but it can begin to undermine the differences that define and alienate us before we have found the courage to speak to one another. The idea of a lesbian continuum opens the way for this dialogue, while not lending itself to an easy erasure of the deeper ways in which we differ in struggling for and against one another.

In conclusion, I see several important pragmatic consequences in adopting the lesbian continuum as a strategic term. It provides us with a sense of continuity which guides our appropriations of the past and organizes our strategies of resistance. It also provides an ongoing pattern against which we can collectively and individually open to investigation the quality of resistance in our womanly lives. In this sense, lesbian-identified consciousness parallels indirectly the Marxist notion of class consciousness, an awareness that subsists in latent forms until conditions are right for the emergence of a revolutionary subject.[36] In both cases, radical resistance is always present, while its visibility and success depend upon historical circumstance and the subjective factor of readiness. Third, the lesbian continuum provides a way to demarcate lesbian politics from two male modes of containment: that of male clinicians and male-defined gay rights struggles. Lesbianism is constituted as a profoundly womanly form of resistance to male tyranny, more than an issue of sexual preference for "normal deviants." Likewise, the idea of the lesbian continuum enables us to question the polarity that separates straight and lesbian women. It does so by questioning the meaning of these differences, while recognizing the similarities, a questioning that does not necessarily encourage dishonesty or fear about our mutually discovered differences.

Finally, the idea of lesbian continuum opens to new interrogation the institution of heterosexuality as one of the core institutions in the oppression and exploitation of women's lives. Only against the background of a lesbian continuum does the institution of heterosexuality stand out in sharp relief. A socialist-feminist analysis that does not take compul-

36. For example, see Georg Lukacs, *History and Class Consciousness,* trans. Rodney Livingstone (Cambridge, Mass.: MIT Press, in press).

sory heterosexuality seriously as the central factor in female oppression loses this insight.

The Heterosexist Bias of Socialist-feminist Theory

As I mentioned at the beginning of this commentary, the main difference between Rich and Ferguson emerges from their divergent perspectives on feminism. The vital force behind Rich's notion of the lesbian continuum is one which refashions our categories of thought and action by calling into question the legitimacy of compulsory heterosexuality and the rigid erotic polarities that separate women from one another. One problem I have always had with socialist-feminist theory is its tendency to obscure and occlude an understanding of how central the institution of heterosexuality is to our womanly existences. Although Ferguson seems to recognize its centrality as one of the core institutions in the oppression of women, her socialist-feminist approach undermines the full consideration that should be given to the matrix of institutional coercions and compulsions that enforce women's erotic loyalty to men.

This failing can be seen in her reliance on the work of Michel Foucault—and, by implication, of Herbert Marcuse—since both men share similar institutionalist theories of human sexuality.[37] Such an approach explains the existence of the "lesbian phenomenon" as we know it today in terms of a cultural experience *(une prise de conscience)* made possible by the intersection of recent material and ideological conditions. This kind of theoretical approach is, I believe, on the right track but limited. If one is not careful, both the meaning and the emancipatory interest of a lesbian existence will be easily lost within the framework of class struggle, sex division of labor, and fashionable Freudian theories of sexuality.

According to the positivist thinking of Foucault, history consists in discontinuity, rupture, and the absence of a continuous revolutionary subject.[38] The history of women's revolt against patriarchy is likewise codified into discrete categories, each naming different kinds of resistance, which depend on the historical and ideological possibilities in a given context. Within this framework, lesbian-identified lesbianism becomes a phenomenon specific to late capitalism. If one subscribes to the theories of Foucault and Marcuse, the phenomenon of lesbianism becomes part of a one-dimensional libidinal containment, a form of repres-

37. For discussion of Marcuse and Foucault, see Jacquelyn Zinner (Zita), "M. Foucault, *La Volunté de Savoir,*" *Telos,* 11, no 2 (Summer 1978): 215–26.

38. Foucault, *The History of Sexuality* (n. 3 above) and for discussion on his methodology, see *Archaeology of Knowledge,* trans. A.-M. Sheridan-Smith (New York: Irvington Publishers, 1972).

sive desublimation.[39] Its containment and control are made ideologically possible by the emergence of psychoanalytic categories, which belong to the new mental health sciences legitimated by the new class of male medical professionals. Together with the breakdown of the nineteenth-century family, the new economic autonomy granted to women, and the increasingly permissive genital fanaticism of our society, lesbian subculture acquires a new kind of public presence to be tolerated, but not accepted.

Ferguson's critique of Foucault is partially correct. She writes, "The ideological organization they [Foucault and Donzelot] speak of serves not only the bourgeois class but also men reorganizing patriarchy." However, I would like to push the critique of Foucault one step further by suggesting that both the idea of one-dimensional containment and Foucault's history of epistemic discontinuities may rest upon methodological tools that aid in more subtle ways to reorganize and reinforce male control over women. Both ideas obscure the hard-fought and continuous struggles of women against male tyranny—the struggle against patriarchy and compulsory heterosexuality. One way for us to illuminate the struggle is to reject the category of "repressive desublimation" or "the psychiatrization of difference," to deny the historical discontinuity reflected in these metalinguistic turns of Foucault, and to rename the past in terms of a lesbian continuum. We are the ones to make such a connection in re-collecting our past. We are the ones who have recollected the power to name this as an autonomous struggle.

If on the other hand, one adopts a socialist-feminist analysis of human sexuality, as Ferguson does, sex-linked rebellion, especially that of lesbian resistance, runs a great risk of being falsely absorbed into the one-dimensional expansion of patriarchal capitalism. In her use of Foucault's methodology, discontinuity replaces the long and continuous resistance struggle. This discontinuity is widened by the diminished significance Ferguson gives to the institution of heterosexuality, an institution she considers analytically distinct from other forms of male control over the female body.

To what extent the institution of heterosexuality is "analytically distinct" from the sex division of labor, for example, is not at all clear, since an adequate analysis of the latter must also include the heterosexist coding that pervades and enforces such behavior. Nor is it clear that an analysis of the sex division of the erotic would be a purely additive exercise,[40] since the erotic is one of the most compelling and creative

39. Herbert Marcuse, *One Dimensional Man* (Boston: Beacon Press, 1964) and *Eros and Civilization: A Philosophical Inquiry into Freud* (New York: Vintage House, 1962).

40. I owe much to discussions, etc., with Vicky Spelman on this point. Her recent work, "Feminism, Sexism, and Racism" (*Quest*, in press), makes a similar argument on the racism implicit in the additive analysis of white feminist theory. I am suggesting that the same could be said for the heterosexist blindness implicit in feminist theory, including the

forces at work in the human body. It is not as if we must first analyze the sex division of labor and then include the heterosexist values and norms that further legitimate that division, as if the first is the material base and the second merely ideological. The erotic exists at the very core of our being, in the materiality of our bodies. It informs in deeply important ways how we perceive others, the interests we bring to those others, the demands of our environment, the sensibility and care we give to others, our physiological response to others as well as our identity as sexually and emotionally resourceful and responsible human beings.[41] It is a mistake to think that rejecting the institution of heterosexuality means simply "not sleeping with men," and little more, or that the sex division of labor can be abstractly analyzed outside of the institution of compulsory heterosexuality.

This is only one of the ways in which Ferguson minimizes the power of heterosexuality as an institution. Another is to assume that couples are capable of liberating themselves from the institution. Perhaps so, but Ferguson's analysis does not sufficiently emphasize its ponderous force and its sturdy intractability in the face of all but a few liberated heterosexuals. Finally, Ferguson suggests that a lesbian's genital politic will necessarily occlude her commitment to other important issues, which once again suggests that lesbian existence and lesbian-feminist consciousness can be very narrowly conceived as the negation of institutionalized "heterocoitus" and, thus, a political practice analytically distinct from other kinds of struggle. Such a notion rests upon a misleadingly narrow conception of the institution of heterosexuality which in turn defines lesbian existence as bedtime rebellion against compulsory coitus. This is simply false, as anyone can see from the number of radical lesbians active in the wider political community, women who are activists because they are lesbian feminists.[42] By trivializing the pervasive com-

---

recent dual-systems debate among socialist feminists. Interestingly enough, dual-systems theory rests upon the recognition of gender blindness in Marxist theory, while systematically ignoring the heterosexist blindness lurking within the socialist-feminist framework.

41. We are just beginning to undertake the difficult and creative task of articulating what the lesbian world view is and how this epistemic and moral perspective is affected by class, race, and other factors. Along these lines, I have found Sarah Ruddick's "Maternal Thinking," *Feminist Studies* 6, no. 2 (Summer 1980): 342–67, in which she develops a theory of gender thinking, a promising methodological approach that could be applied to lesbian cultural practice. Following Habermas, she sees thinking/feeling/experiencing as social practices that derive from the environmental demands and interests structuring historically different situations. Such a social origins theory of consciousness could be used to map the transformations of lesbian "embodiment" without ahistoricizing the lesbian body.

42. In "The Unhappy Marriage of Patriarchy and Capitalism" (see n. 14 above) Ferguson and Folbre argue quite persuasively that women share a particular epistemic insight into the workings of capitalist patriarchy because of their relationship to sex-affective labor. If one takes seriously the sex division of the erotic as another cultural

plexity of compulsory heterosexuality and obscuring the nature of lesbian resistance, Ferguson comes very close to encasing and containing
the lesbian option as a matter of preference or a matter of genital pleasure devoid of any more diffuse and expansive meaning. Trimming and
cropping this meaning "closets" our visibility in the public sphere. Lesbian feminism is turned into a caricature of otherness, a lost coin for
political exchange. This is a reading of lesbian existence that fits comfortably into a socialist-feminist framework, where all too often the
utilitarian value of the erotic remains unquestioned.

There seem to be two ways to deny the existence of lesbian continuum in looking at history; one is to deny the deeply felt eroticism of
female love and friendship that has persisted for centuries (women-
loving women)[43] and the second is to trace the history of women's resistance (patriarchal resistance) in all other areas except those that challenge the sex division of the erotic. These two lines have merged in the
modern consciousness of lesbian-feminist resistance, where we can at
once celebrate our personal reshaping of the erotic and fiercely pronounce our right to exist in the public sphere. It is at this point that
women-centered politic becomes deeply threatening to patriarchy, when
at last women assume their rights as subjects of erotic desire.[44] Why then
should we continue to exclude this use of the erotic from our lives and
politics? This is the question that haunts all of our theorizing, and much
of our living.

What is at stake in Ann Ferguson's critique of Adrienne Rich's notion of lesbian continuum is more than a quibble about definitions. The
idea of lesbian continuum opens the way for a radical lesbian critique of
socialist-feminist methodology and its categories of containment. As I
have suggested, it is not the case that lesbian continuum misnames the
past; rather it is meant to illuminate what needs to be named by us. It is
naming into visible existence a long history of sexual/political resistance.
This act of naming is far from fraudulent—it is a politically important
move in our redefinition of personal identities and the raison d'être of

---

division central to the oppression of women, one could by extension argue that lesbians
share another special epistemic insight into the workings of patriarchy. A careful articulation of this lesbian situation and its epistemological value are missing in Ferguson's and
Folbre's analysis. Including it would raise some important questions on the centrality of
labor (the "labor fetish") in analyzing the specificity of women's oppression. I believe that
the use of the erotic and the use of our womanly labor power must be examined in concert
as an inseparable unity.

43. To the now classic readings of Carroll Smith-Rosenberg, Blanche Cook, and
Nancy Sahli can be added Lillian Faderman's *Surpassing the Love of Men* (New York: William Morrow & Co., 1981).

44. Many thanks to Naomi Scheman who helped to crystallize this connection of
thought.

our communities. It is a return of the political to the personal and of the repressed to politics. It speaks to all of us.

Women's Studies
University of Minnesota

Kathryn Pyne Addelson: Words and Lives

Brambles

Defining words is an occupation fraught with dangers.

Defining "lesbian" is especially so fraught.[45] One is constantly tangled in one bramble patch or another—and not simply because of political differences in feminist circles. *Lesbian* is a concept which is, of its nature, to be understood from two perspectives. There is the perspective of the "normal" society in which people who have the authority to give definitions do it clinically and so define the lesbian as deviant. There is the other side, that of the so-called deviant subculture, from which lesbians give positive and admiring definitions, criticizing the normal perspective as pathological. This bramble patch is the one Jacquelyn Zita points out. Unless we are very careful, lesbian existence becomes just another kind of deviant existence, on a par with male homosexual or hippy-counter-culture existence.

It is not simply the clinical definition of lesbian which must be questioned. The normal, heterosexist definition of history must be questioned as well, for to associate the word lesbian with resistance to patriarchy requires a new understanding of the historical past, and a new understanding of the present and future. Without such understanding the lesbian definition of the past will be simply a subcultural attempt at finding forbears, while the normal definition of the past continues as a guide toward the future. I think this is a part of Adrienne Rich's concern when she writes of the lesbian continuum.

Understanding history requires respect for those whose experience constitutes our past, but this is particularly important with regard to women's history, because women's resistances and women's pasts have been distorted and made invisible in the telling of normal history. Recognition of this enters into Ann Ferguson's concern that the definition of lesbian existence be historically rooted. At the same time, history, if properly understood, allows us to criticize those who came before us as

45. This research was supported in part by a grant from the Mellon Foundation to Smith College's Project on Women and Social Change. I would like to thank Pamela Armstrong, Jill Freeland, Ann Ferguson, and Pat Miller for their helpful suggestions. I have previously published under the name Kathryn Pyne Parsons (Addelson).

well as ourselves and our own politics. I believe that Rich's idea of a lesbian continuum permits us such criticism. In fact, it permits a radical criticism of Rich's own feminist position. To explain why I believe this, I will have to wander around some of the bramble patches that Zita and Ferguson and Rich have marked out on our topographical maps of the resistance.

Insiders and Outsiders

In the usage of the term now predominant in the United States, *lesbian* is a "deviance concept."[46] Since the turn of the century at least, people in our own society have used deviance concepts to sort people into types. At one time or another, the mentally retarded or mentally ill, prostitutes, criminals, homosexuals, lesbians, truants, hobos, hippies, and hosts of others have been named "deviant." One particularly complex feature of deviance concepts is that their definition involves an assumed definition of some other life pattern that is considered normal. With such assumptions, professionals and laypeople alike often give "clinical" definitions that ascribe deviance to some specified factor requiring treatment before the deviant can be returned to normal.[47] Sometimes the psychological or genetic or moral characteristics of a person are considered the source of deviance, and cure has involved treating the person individually. At other times, causes are seen to lie in the person's social environment, and social change has been recommended—clearing out slums or redlight districts, instituting or deleting welfare payments or food stamps, and so on. The aim of both sorts of cures is to return the deviant person to a normal life. Because deviance is taken to be the problem, the normal life pattern is taken as unproblematic—as normal, for heaven's sake. The metaphysics of the normal is not questioned when one uses deviance concepts.

46. Interactionist sociologists have given an analysis of the social phenomenon of deviance that is helpful in showing this complexity. My understanding of deviance owes a great deal to their discussion, particularly to Howard S. Becker's *Outsiders* (New York: Free Press, 1963), and to David Matza's *Becoming Deviant* (Englewood Cliffs, N.J.: Prentice-Hall, 1969).

47. Based on the evidence they have about attitudes toward what is taken to be deviant, many sociologists point out that in the opinion of those who consider themselves normal, treatment for deviancy simply makes one a different kind of deviant, e.g., a reformed alcoholic, a former homosexual, etc. Once deviant, one is always suspect, out of a kind of belief in the structure of human character. In an early classic work, Frank Tannenbaum says, "The young delinquent becomes bad because he is defined as bad and because he is not believed if he is good. There is a persistent demand for consistency in character. The community cannot deal with people whom it cannot define. Reputation is this sort of public definition. Once it is established, then unconsciously all agencies combine to maintain this definition even when they apparently and consciously attempt to deny their own implicit judgment" (*Crime and the Community* [Boston: Ginn & Co., 1938]).

There are human states or conditions (e.g., being a godmother, or using heroin, or weighing 119 pounds, or having had the mumps) that lend themselves to definitions based on objective, discernible characteristics shared by all the people in question. But a deviant life pattern is defined, not by objective characteristics shared by those living it, but normatively, as violating the normal life pattern. That is, the definition requires two quite different categories of social agents: the people who are categorized as deviant and the normal people who categorize or label them as deviant. Definition of deviance concepts would thus dissolve into a bout of name-calling but for one important fact: Some people have more power than others. Social and economic matters are arranged with their life patterns in mind. They are able to preserve those life patterns from overthrow, partly because they have the power to attach the label of deviant to anyone who would do things differently. Their way of doing things is instituted as the normal way.

Deviance concepts are used in particular societies through particular historical periods. It may be that women have had sexual relations with each other since the beginnings of our species. But if *lesbian* is understood as a deviance concept, then they were not lesbians, unless their society had a certain sort of power structure and unless people in it used labels to class such women as deviant while taking heterosexual relations as normal. If we are interested in *lesbian* as a deviance concept, then Ann Ferguson is correct in limiting its use to certain sorts of societies. The key question is whether Rich is defining *lesbian* as a deviance concept.

There is another important feature of deviance concepts—and when I call them concepts, I am not talking just about words, for the metaphysics of the normal is something we live out in our lives, not in our heads. Because there are two sorts of people involved in using deviance concepts, there are two perspectives: the normal perspective and the deviant perspective. Clinical definitions are given from the normal perspective. But those who are labeled deviant often learn to participate in a deviant subculture, gaining a different perspective. Howard Becker says, "From a sense of common fate, from having to face the same problems, grows a deviant subculture: a set of perspectives and understandings about what the world is like and how to deal with it, and a set of routine activities based on those perspectives. Membership in such a group solidifies a deviant identity."[48] Ann Ferguson notes above the two perspectives involved in the concept of lesbian identity in our society: "In part, it was an ideological concept created by the sexologists who framed a changing patriarchal ideology of sexuality and the family; in part it was chosen by independent women and feminists who formed their own urban subcultures."

48. Becker, *Outsiders,* p. 16.

Ferguson distinguishes three tasks in regard to the concept *lesbian:* the "valorizing" task by which the term is cleared of its pejorative connotations; the sociopolitical task that achieves the self-definition of a contemporary lesbian, oppositional subculture; and the transhistorical task that compares and categorizes women who have resisted patriarchy. She holds out little hope that the valorizing task can be accomplished—and since *lesbian* is a deviance concept we can see that ridding it of pejorative connotations would require not a change of attitudes but an overthrow of the normal, male-dominated ways of organizing our society. Ferguson herself takes the second task as more important. But her own definition seems to use a deviance concept, even though she does so from the perspective of the deviant. The women who would be called lesbians under her definition are the same women who would be labeled so by the normals. For, in our society, lesbian is used to brand women who have women lovers, women who pay too much attention to other women and not enough to men, or who show self-sufficiency, or who hang out with declared lesbians, or who participate in the lesbian subculture. The clinical definitions of the psychiatrists may be narrower, but they are only used as instruments of power to give the appearance of scientific objectivity to the wider, more general usage and to provide ways of forcing women back into line. Deviance concepts are suited to that kind of political use: the use of those with power to establish their way of doing things as normal and to label other ways of doing things as deviant. Thus, to use a deviance concept to define lesbian existence, even if one wants to do so with a reverse political effect, is to define it from the perspective of a deviant subculture, nestled inside a dominant, heterosexual society. If Ferguson is doing that, then Zita seems correct in saying the definition is "one of a countercultural group, a group that, at most, provides an outlet for 'runaway' women."

Zita claims that Rich, on the contrary, is referring to "the continuity of resistance that women have always undertaken in independent, nonheterosexual, and woman-centered ways." Described in this way, Rich's use of the term seems to be an attempt to fulfill Ferguson's third task: "reconceptualizing history from a lesbian and feminist perspective." How is that different from defining lesbian existence with a deviance concept? Let us see.

A Tradition of Resistance

Using deviance concepts conceals the moral and social ugliness of certain ways of doing things, by classifying those ways as normal. Using them also conceals evidence that there are other ways of doing things and evidence that many people are criticizing and resisting. This double effect results in what Rich calls "the lie of compulsory female heterosexuality." The lie operates by concealing reality.

The concealment is accomplished by surrounding one normal way of doing things with many deviant labels, not just one. For example, women who resist normal heterosexual alliances by refusing to marry have been called spinsters who could not catch a man, lesbians, man haters, or (at the other extreme) sluts and whores. Women who resist by refusing to perform wifely duties have been labeled neurotics, hysterics, shrews, viragos, frigid and unloving creatures, and so on—depending on the course of resistance they chose. Women who resist by having primary friendships with other women escaped labels (provided they fulfilled other duties), but only because, as Rich says, "female friendship and comradeship have been set apart from the erotic, thus limiting the erotic itself" (p. 650).

If these observations draw the topography accurately, a definition that appropriately describes resistance to male dominance cannot be expressed in terms of a deviance concept. More, an appropriate definition must cut across normal-deviant lines. For those lines are drawn in from the perspective of the dominant normal (after all, deviance concepts are used politically to maintain power structures). An appropriate definition must also allow us to show the immorality of the normal way of doing things while revealing the fact that women in the deviant subcultures and dominant superculture have resisted and have created positive, self-affirming ways of doing things. Such a definition would not simply be the self-aggrandizement of a counterculture group.[49]

I believe that Adrienne Rich's lesbian continuum may begin to do this work. Rich says,

> When we turn the lens of vision and consider the degree to which, and the methods whereby, heterosexual "preference" has actually been imposed on women, not only can we understand differently the meaning of individual lives and work, but we can begin to recognize a central fact of women's history: that women have always resisted male tyranny. A feminism of action, often, though not

49. Howard Becker says that deviant groups in general are pushed into rationalizing their positions: "At an extreme, they develop a very complicated historical, legal, and psychological justification for their deviant activity. The [male] homosexual community is a good case. Magazines and books by homosexuals and for homosexuals include historical articles about famous homosexuals in history. They contain articles on the biology and physiology of sex, designed to show that homosexuality is a 'normal' sexual response. They contain legal articles, pleading for civil liberties for homosexuals. . . . Most deviant groups have a self-justifying rationale (or 'ideology'), although seldom is it as well worked out as that of the [male] homosexual. . . . The rationales of deviant groups tend to contain a general repudiation of conventional moral rules, conventional institutions, and the entire conventional world" (ibid., pp. 38–39).

always, without a theory, has constantly reemerged in every culture and in every period. We can then begin to study women's struggle against powerlessness, women's radical rebellion, not just in male-defined "concrete revolutionary situations"[50] but in all the situations male ideologies have not perceived as revolutionary. [P. 652]

Women have rebelled always, but they have done so by living a "double life," of which Rich gives many examples: "This *double life*—this apparent acquiescence to an institution founded on male interest and prerogative—has been characteristic of female experience: in mother-hood, and in many kinds of heterosexual behavior, including the rituals of courtship, the pretense of asexuality by the nineteenth-century wife; the simulation of orgasm by the prostitute, the courtesan, the twentieth-century 'sexually liberated' woman" (p. 654).

I think for analytical purposes it helps to sort out two ways of under-standing "the double life." One way is in terms of the experiences of women that have (until recently) been made invisible in the telling of normal history. The other way of understanding the double life is in terms of the "double consciousness" which women (and people in any subordinate position) have in a society.[51] This double consciousness arises from the fact that to survive, one must understand how those who dominate define the world and oneself. One must be able to know what they think and what they expect and what the limits of freedom are. On the other hand, although one must understand it, their dominant per-spective cannot be one's own, because their social position and their place is different; it is (in this case) male. One knows it is not the univer-sal truth but only a perspective, and that sometimes it is false, or foolish, or cruel, or self-aggrandizing, and most often it is blind. In just this way, women know that the male story about the world and about human nature is scarcely true to the facts.

Awareness of the double life and the double consciousness brings the related knowledge that dominant definitions of human activities, like the normal stories about our past history and present institutions, are just that: stories. The possibility of resistance exists because women are not simply characters in men's stories any more than deviants are characters in the stories of the normals. Women have double lives, dif-ferent experiences, and double consciousnesses. Women have their own

50. Here Rich footnoted Rosalind Petchesky, "Dissolving the Hyphen: A Report on Marxist-feminist Groups 1–5," in *Capitalist Patriarchy and the Case for Socialist Feminism,* ed. Zillah Eisenstein (New York: Monthly Review Press, 1979), p. 387.

51. Martha Ackelsberg, Shawn Pyne, and I discussed double consciousness in these terms in a paper at North Carolina State University in spring 1978. Ackelsburg and I further developed the concept in a paper we read in the Black Rose Lecture Series in Boston in the fall of 1978. Both papers were entitled "Anarchism and Feminism," and I wrote under the name Kathryn Pyne Parsons.

perspectives on the world. This being so, we must ask about the social reality of such "institutions" as the family, the normal heterosexual social order, and patriarchy itself.

Just as asking about deviance necessarily raises questions about those who have the power to label, so asking about these institutions necessarily raises questions about those who feel empowered to define and describe them. We must ask whether concepts like *patriarchy* are suitable for historical descriptions of social reality or whether, like deviance concepts, they are definitions supporting a dominant perspective, mere name-callings that deny reality. This is a different way of asking Ann Ferguson's question about what she calls the radical feminists' "universal" and "ahistorical" approach to patriarchy.

Legitimating Control

Adrienne Rich says, "It will require a courageous grasp of the politics and economics, as well as the cultural propaganda, of heterosexuality to carry us beyond individual cases or diversified group situations into the complex kind of overview needed to undo the power men everywhere wield over women, power which has become a model for every other form of exploitation and illegitimate control" (p. 660). Suppose we ask, Why is the control "illegitimate"?[52] Don't the Constitution and our laws legitimate it? Don't the institutions of the family, government, and economic system legitimate it? If not, what would legitimate anything?

When philosophers and moralists puzzle about questions like legitimacy, they often end up referring to universal moral principles by which one can criticize the legitimacy of social institutions. But to look for universal principles is to look for the universally true names of things, and that is the same kind of thinking that permits exploitation and illegitimate control in the first place. For the basic question is, *Who* is doing the naming? Whose perspective do we take when we describe those institutions that grant legitimacy to certain forms of control? Who is it that names the patriarchal family, and whose story about the world lies under that name?

"Patriarchy," "the family," "bureaucracy," "management" name hierarchical ways of organizing what people do. They name the way groups are supposed to be organized in going about their activities, not

52. To say that it is illegitimate because it is control by force and violence is to miss the point. Force and violence have always existed, and they were and are monstrous. But even if all dominant males throughout history had been perfectly gentle, the control would still be illegitimate and exploitative. Force and violence are, after all, reprehensible under our present laws and moral principles. It is these laws and principles which are taken to legitimate control, and that is what I am philosophically questioning in this section.

the way they actually do, for they describe groups in terms of roles and role relations. Those words describe hierarchical structures, not the real human activities going on under their supposed control. For example, an organizational chart of a corporation shows lines of authority and responsibility. Does the chart serve as a true description of reality? Does it show what part many secretaries really play in the work of the corporation?[53] Does it show who really has influence and how the work really gets done and how plans really get made? Or does it, rather, picture lines of an ideal coercion: What those at the top like to think is the reality—or perhaps, what they want those at the bottom to think is the reality? Isn't it a sketch of the way things "ought to be," the way some people would like them to be, not the way they are?

An organizational chart serves the understanding of those who want decisions and plans made in a certain way. Feminists have said that the organizational chart of patriarchal families serves the interests of the men who head them and is made from a dominant, male perspective. That women have a double consciousness and that there has been a tradition of resistance indicate that the chart does not capture reality. Rather it captures the norms according to which sanctions may "legitimately" be applied. This means that "the family" and "patriarchy" are not neutral terms any more than deviant labels like "hobo" or "homosexual" are. They serve to conceal social reality. Donna Divine says that using the institution of the family to study women leads to bias: "Women are being examined through an institution defined by its male dominance, or through categories generated from assumptions about the predominance of men, for example, the public-domestic dichotomy. An initial assumption about hierarchy provides the lines of analysis whereby such hierarchy is confirmed. The dichotomy between public and private realms is part of a map of the social order which men have constructed, identifying the public and visible with the political community. How valid that mapping is has never been fully ascertained."[54]

To question whether hierarchical concepts like *the family* or *patriarchy* refer to reality is not to deny that abominations have taken place, or that the grossest immorality has lived under the label of the normal and the "good." It is to say that, like deviant labels, hierarchical names play an important part in the lie of compulsory heterosexuality: "The lie keeps numberless women psychologically trapped, trying to fit mind, spirit, and sexuality into a prescribed script because they cannot look beyond the parameters of the acceptable. . . . The lesbian trapped in the

53. For a description that cuts through the organizational charts, see Rosabeth Moss Kanter, *Men and Women of the Corporation* (New York: Basic Books, 1977).

54. Donna Divine, "Unveiling the Mysteries of Islam: The Art of Studying Muslim Women," in *An Endless Waterfall: Studies on Women and Social Change*, eds. Kathryn Pyne Addelson and Martha Ackelsberg (forthcoming).

"closet," the woman imprisoned in prescriptive ideas of the "normal," share the pain of blocked options, broken connections, lost access to self-definition freely and powerfully assumed" (p. 657). The lie is as immoral as it is unscientific, despite the large part it has played in what has often passed as ethics and science.

But if we are not to explain history and the present in terms of hierarchical institutions, what social framework are we to use? I think that Rich's idea of a lesbian continuum may offer the right kind of notion. Far from being ahistorical, such a notion may let us examine the past (and present) not in terms of hierarchical institutions but in terms of women's own understandings within the historical contexts of life patterns they were creating. The historical method stemming from it shows respect for the actions and understandings of other women in precisely the way that the lie of compulsory heterosexuality does not.

There remains the question of whether the lesbian continuum is an historically adequate notion in that it permits amplification and criticism of feminist political positions, including the radical feminist position from which Rich herself formulated it.

The Many Ways of Resisting

Both Zita and Ferguson complain that Rich's concept of a lesbian continuum cannot be used to judge the relative success or failure of different forms of resistance in particular historical circumstances. However, Rich does specify two principal criteria for placing women along the lesbian continuum. The first involves resistance to male dominance, which she associates paradigmatically with lesbian existence: "Lesbian existence comprises both the breaking of a taboo and the rejection of a compulsory way of life. It is also a direct or indirect attack on male right of access to women" (p. 649). The second criterion involves women bonding with women. Jacquelyn Zita describes the paradigmatic case of "the lesbian option," and indicates why she thinks it to be so: "The lesbian option, as a total erotic, emotional, social, and political commitment to other women represents an option that cannot . . . be contained within the institution of heterosexuality." Zita also suggests that the lesbian continuum "provides a background against which various strategies of resistance can be evaluated."

I want to measure the quality of resistance in the fictional life of Edna Pontellier, the hero of Kate Chopin's *The Awakening*.[55] Rich seemed to dismiss the case as mired in the lie of romanticism (p. 657),

---

55. In another paper, I discuss deviance as creativity and as moral and social criticism of the normal state of affairs. Kathryn Pyne Addelson, "Awakening," ibid.

and so testing it against the lesbian continuum should be interesting, for as with all scientific measures, the case itself offers a test of the measuring instrument.

Edna Pontellier has been resisting male dominance all her life, though "apparently acquiescing"—as Rich suggests some women do. Her first outright act of resistance comes on the night she learns to swim. She returns to the family cottage. A short time later her husband follows. He tells her to come into the house. She declines.

> She heard him moving around the room; every sound indicating impatience and irritation. Another time she would have gone in at his request. She would, through habit, have yielded to his desire; not with any sense of submission or obedience to his compelling wishes, but unthinkingly, as we walk, move, sit, stand, go through the daily treadmill of the life which has been portioned out to us.[56]

Mr. Pontellier asks again and again; Edna refuses.

> With a writhing motion she settled herself more securely in the hammock. She perceived that her will had blazed up, stubborn and resistant. She could not at that moment have done other than denied and resisted. She wondered if her husband had ever spoken to her like that before, and if she had submitted to his command. Of course she had; she remembered that she had. But she could not realize why or how she should have yielded, feeling as she did then.
>
>   "Leonce, go to bed," she said. "I mean to stay out here. I don't wish to go in, and I don't intend to. Don't speak to me like that again; I shall not answer you." [Pp. 33–34]

At this time, Edna cannot hold out against the weight of her surroundings—at a family resort, on the porch of a cottage within which her children are sleeping. "Edna began to feel like one who awakens gradually out of a dream, a delicious, grotesque, impossible dream, to feel again the realities pressing into her soul" (p. 34). But her retreat is only for the moment. When they return to New Orleans, Edna stops participating in her marriage. She resigns the roles of manager of her husband's possessions and entertainer of her husband's clients; she resigns her sexual role, she resigns (to a large degree) her motherly role. These refusals free her to go around New Orleans, to become aware of her potential as an artist, to earn a tiny income through painting, to find a lover, and to experience a sexual awakening. To succeed in doing all this, she must avoid being labeled deviant, for then the retributive ma-

---

56. Kate Chopin, *The Awakening and Selected Stories of Kate Chopin,* ed. Barbara H. Solomon (New York: New American Library, 1976), p. 33. All later references are to this text.

chinery of her society would forcibly return her to the normal. Her husband tries (and fails) to get a doctor to label her neurotic or hysterical. It is to his own interest to keep her from being stuck with other labels—wayward wife, loose woman, whore.

The lover Edna finds is male—deviant Alcee Arobin who seduces other men's wives. But after her first night with him, is Edna a dupe? She feels "multitudinous emotions," but "above all there was understanding. She felt as if a mist had been lifted from her eyes, enabling her to look upon and comprehend the significance of life, that monster made up of beauty and brutality" (p. 90). Edna takes knowledge from Alcee, a knowledge he has preserved (at great sacrifice) by becoming deviant. She would like companionship and love from Robert Lebrun. When they finally meet alone, he says that he dreamed that she might be his wife, that her husband might set her free. Edna responds:

> "You have been a very, very foolish boy, wasting your time dreaming of impossible things when you speak of Mr. Pontellier setting me free! I am no longer one of Mr. Pontellier's possessions to dispose of or not. I give myself where I choose. If he were to say, 'Here Robert, take her and be happy; she is yours,' I would laugh at you both." [P. 116]

She realizes that Robert does not understand and that he will never understand. She eventually commits suicide—but not over Robert. She commits suicide because she finally faces the contradiction of her motherhood. She will be nobody's property, but if she lives as a mother, her children will own her.

Edna does not measure up as a successful revolutionary fighting for large-scale social change. But I believe she does satisfy Rich's first condition for women who belong to the lesbian continuum. She broke serious taboos (though not the homosexual one); she rejected a compulsory way of life; she attacked "legitimate" male right of access to women. Her experience was a woman's experience, and her rebellion came directly out of the fact that she understood the oppressiveness of male dominance. But she certainly did not bond with other women and, thus, she probably fails Rich's second condition as completely as one can, short of being misogynist—as Edna definitely is not. Does that mean she does not belong on the lesbian continuum? Or does it mean that we must come to a new understanding of what women's resistance amounts to?

Zita gives an interpretation of Rich's perspective which includes reasons for taking woman-bonding as essential and for judging resistances like Edna's to be of poor quality. She says, "If the institution of heterosexuality is a core institution of patriarchy in all its historical manifestations, including that of present-day capitalist patriarchy, then the lesbian continuum provides a background against which various strategies of resistance can be evaluated. In this way, the voids and silences of socialist feminist solutions can be called into question." To speak of "core institutions" in this way leads Zita into the bramble patch where hierarchical concepts are used as though they are the social reality. Rich's notion of a lesbian continuum, I have argued, helps us to skirt that bramble patch as Zita's transhistorical argument does not.

Without question, Rich is absolutely correct in her criticisms of the many feminist authors who ignore the lesbian option and write from a perspective that takes heterosexuality as normal, never noticing the fact that male dominance is inextricably entwined with that metaphysics of the normal. Rich and Zita both are correct when they insist on the importance of resistance to heterosexual practice. But while one common goal is overcoming compulsory heterosexuality, there are many ways to achieve it, as proved by the many kinds of lives labeled deviant in contrast to the normal life patterns of heterosexuality. If some life patterns are more effective as ways of resistance than others, the reasons for that effectiveness must be sought in the historical context of each life. Strategy and tactics at a historical moment, options open and advantages gained: There and not with a priori measures do we best look for answers. However, if this is so, then mustn't we question Rich's calling it a lesbian continuum?

There seems to be a paradox here. Lesbian existence cannot be defined solely in terms of our contemporary culture without being defined as a deviance concept. Rich and Zita are correct in insisting that lesbian be defined historically. However one cannot simply stipulate definitional conditions for historical concepts to suit the political analysis of a feminist position. Historical concepts must be tested against the living past for their validity—and this, in fact, must be why Rich insists on talking of a lesbian continuum. But if we take the past seriously, we see that there have been many women who courageously resisted patriarchy in conditions that did not involve bonding with other women. There have been women resisters who could not be classed as part of a lesbian continuum at all—unless we construe lesbian so broadly as to bear little relation to lesbian existence today. Rich's and Zita's claim that the bonding of women is crucial to resistance seems based on political, and not on historical, argument; thus their claim is left unsupported.

What then of Ferguson's strategy through which lesbian existence becomes a political concept suitable for our own times? Because compulsory heterosexuality is the norm, lesbians must live in our society as deviants. Because the material conditions of lesbian lives are different from those of nonlesbian lives, lesbians must have their own practices and life ways. In these senses, lesbian existence is countercultural. But the existence of many political lesbians is not merely countercultural. Whether a group is merely countercultural or not depends on whether its members have dropped out or whether they are engaged in effective political battle. It is quite clear that many lesbians are engaged in very effective political battle. However, the terms defining willingness to participate in that battle should not be made into a procrustean bed against which to measure the resistance of women throughout history or throughout our own society.

Department of Philosophy and Project on Women and Social Change
Smith College

Archimedes and the Paradox of Feminist Criticism

Myra Jehlen

I

Feminist thinking is really *re*thinking, an examination of the way certain assumptions about women and the female character enter into the fundamental assumptions that organize all our thinking. For instance, assumptions such as the one that makes intuition and reason opposite terms parallel to female and male may have axiomatic force in our culture, but they are precisely what feminists need to question—or be reduced to checking the arithmetic, when the issue lies in the calculus.

Such radical skepticism is an ideal intellectual stance that can generate genuinely new understandings; that is, reconsideration of the relation between female and male can be a way to reconsider that between intuition and reason and ultimately between the whole set of such associated dichotomies: heart and head, nature and history. But it also creates unusual difficulties. Somewhat like Archimedes, who to lift the earth with his lever required someplace else on which to locate himself

For their numerous helpful suggestions and suggestive objections, I am grateful to Sacvan Bercovitch, Rachel Blau DuPlessis, Carolyn Heilbrun, Evelyn Keller, Helene Moglen, Sara Ruddick, Catharine Stimpson, and Marilyn Young.

and his fulcrum, feminists questioning the presumptive order of both nature and history—and thus proposing to remove the ground from under their own feet—would appear to need an alternative base. For as Archimedes had to stand somewhere, one has to assume something in order to reason at all. So if the very axioms of Western thought already incorporate the sexual teleology in question, it seems that, like the Greek philosopher, we have to find a standpoint off this world altogether.

Archimedes never did. However persuasively he established that the earth could be moved from its appointed place, he and the lever remained earthbound and the globe stayed where it was. His story may point another moral, however, just as it points to another science able to harness forces internally and apply energy from within. We could then conclude that what he really needed was a terrestrial fulcrum. My point here, similarly, will be that a terrestrial fulcrum, a standpoint from which we can see our conceptual universe whole but which nonetheless rests firmly on male ground, is what feminists really need. But perhaps because being at once on and off a world seems an improbable feat, the prevailing perspectives of feminist studies have located the scholar one place or the other.

Inside the world of orthodox and therefore male-oriented scholarship, a new category has appeared in the last decade, the category of women. Economics textbooks now draw us our own bell curves, histories of medieval Europe record the esoterica of convents and the stoning of adulterous wives, zoologists calibrate the orgasmic capacities of female chimpanzees. Indeed, whole books on "women in" and "women of" are fast filling in the erstwhile blanks of a questionnaire—one whose questions, however, remain unquestioned. They never asked before what the mother's occupation was, now they do. The meaning of "occupation," or for that matter of "mother," is generally not at issue.

It is precisely the issue, however, for the majority of feminist scholars who have taken what is essentially the opposite approach; rather than appending their findings to the existing literature, they generate a new one altogether in which women are not just another focus but the center of an investigation whose categories and terms are derived from the world of female experience. They respond to the Archimedean dilemma by creating an alternative context, a sort of female enclave apart from the universe of masculinist assumptions. Most "women's studies" have taken this approach and stressed the global, structural character of their separate issues. Women are no longer to be seen as floating in a man's world but as a coherent group, a context in themselves. The problem is that the issues and problems women define from the inside as global, men treat from the outside as insular. Thus, besides the exfoliation of reports on the state of women everywhere and a certain piety on the subject of pronouns, there is little indication of feminist impact on the universe of male discourse. The theoretical cores of the various disciplines remain essentially unchanged, their terms and methods are as always. As always, therefore, the intellectual arts bespeak a world dominated by men, a script that the occasional woman at a podium can hardly revise. Off in the enclaves of women's studies, our basic research lacks the contiguity to force a basic reconsideration of all research, and our encapsulated revisions appear inorganic (or can be made to appear inorganic) to the universal system they mean to address. Archimedes' problem was getting off the world, but ours might be getting back on.

For we have been, perhaps, too successful in constructing an alternative footing. Our world apart, our female intellectual community, becomes increasingly cut off even as it expands. If we have little control over being shunted aside, we may nonetheless render the isolation of women's scholarship more difficult. At least we ought not to accept it, as in a sense we do when we ourselves conflate feminist thought with thinking about women, when we remove ourselves and our lever off this man's world to study the history or the literature, the art or the anatomy of women alone. This essay is about devising a method for an alternative definition of women's studies as the investigation, from women's viewpoint, of everything, thereby finding a way to engage the dominant intellectual systems directly and organically: locating a feminist terrestrial fulcrum. Since feminist thinking is the thinking of an insurgent group that in the nature of things will never possess a world of its own, such engagement would appear a logical necessity.

Logical but also contradictory. To a degree, any analysis that rethinks the most basic assumptions of the thinking it examines is contradictory or at least contrary, for its aim is to question more than to explain and chart. From it we learn not so much the intricacies of how a particular mode of thinking works as the essential points to which it can be reduced. And nowhere is such an adversary rather than appreciative stance more problematical than it is in literary criticism. This is my specific subject here, the perils and uses of a feminist literary criticism that confronts the fundamental axioms of its parent discipline.

What makes feminist literary criticism especially contradictory is the peculiar nature of literature as distinct from the objects of either physical or social scientific study. Unlike these, literature is itself already an interpretation that it is the critic's task to decipher. It is certainly not news that the literary work is biased; indeed that is its value. Critical objectivity enters in only at a second level to provide a reliable reading, though even here many have argued that reading too is an exercise in creative interpretation. On the other hand, while biologists and historians will concede that certain a priori postulates affect their gathering of data, they always maintain that they have tried to correct for bias, attempting, insofar as this is ever possible, to discover the factual, undistorted truth. Therefore expositions of subjectivity are always both relevant and revelatory about the work of biologists and historians. But as a way of judging the literary work per se, exposing its bias is essentially beside the point. Not that literature, as the New Critics once persuaded us, transcends subjectivity or politics. Paradoxically, it is just because the fictional universe is wholly subjective and therefore ideological that the value of its ideology is almost irrelevant to its literary value. The latter instead depends on what might be thought of as the quality of the *apologia,* how successfully the work transforms ideology into ideal, into a myth that works to the extent precisely that it obscures its provenance. Disliking that provenance implies no literary judgment, for a work may be, from my standpoint, quite wrong and even wrongheaded about life and politics and still an extremely successful rendering of its contrary vision. Bad ideas, even ideas so bad that most of humanity rejects them, have been known to make very good literature.

I am not speaking here of what makes a work attractive or meaningful to its audience. The politics of a play, poem, or story may render it quite unreadable or, in the opposite case, enhance its value for particular people and situations. But this poses no critical issue, for what we like, we like and can justify that way; the problem, if we as feminists want to address our whole culture, is to deal with what we do not like but recognize as nonetheless valuable, serious, good. This is a crucial problem at the heart of feminism's wider relevance. No wonder we have tried to avoid it.

One way is to point out that "good" changes its definition according to time and place. This is true, but not true enough. Perhaps only because we participate in this culture even while criticizing it, we do (most of us) finally subscribe to a tradition of the good in art and philosophy that must sometimes be a political embarrassment—and what else could it be, given the entire history of both Western and Eastern civilizations and their often outright dependence on misogyny? Nor is it true enough, I believe, to argue that the really good writers and thinkers unconsciously and sometimes consciously rejected such misogyny. As couched in the analogous interpretation of Shylock as hero because Shakespeare could not really have been anti-Semitic, this argument amounts to second-guessing writers and their works in terms of a provincialism that seems especially hard to maintain in these linguistically and anthropologically conscious times. For such provincialism not only assumes that our view of things is universal and has always been the substance of reality but also that all other and prior representations were insubstantial. So when Shakespeare depicted bastards as scheming subversives, Jews as merchants of flesh, and women as hysterics, he meant none of it but was only using the local idiom. What he meant, thereby demonstrating his universality, was what we mean.

I want to suggest that we gain no benefit from either disclaiming the continuing value of the "great tradition" or reclaiming it as after all an expression of our own viewpoint. On the contrary, we lose by both. In the first instance, we isolate ourselves into irrelevance. In the second—

denying, for example, that Shakespeare shared in the conventional prejudices about women—we deny by implication that there is anything necessarily different about a feminist outlook. Thus, discovering that the character of Ophelia will support a feminist interpretation may appear to be a political reading of *Hamlet,* but, in fact, by its exegetical approach it reaffirms the notion that the great traditions are all-encompassing and all-normative, the notion that subsumes women under the heading "mankind."

It seems to me perfectly plausible, however, to see Shakespeare as working within his own ideology that defined bastards, Jews, and women as by nature deformed or inferior, and as understanding the contradictions of that ideology without rejecting its basic tenets—so that, from a feminist standpoint, he was a misogynist—and as being nonetheless a great poet. To be sure, greatness involves a critical penetration of conventions but not necessarily or even frequently a radical rejection of them. If, in his villains, Shakespeare revealed the human being beneath the type, his characterization may have been not a denial of the type but a recognition of the complexity of all identity. The kingly ambition of the bastard, the "white" conscience of the Moor, the father love of the Jew, the woman's manly heart: these complexities are expressed in the terms of the contemporary ideology, and in fact Shakespeare uses these terms the more tellingly for not challenging them at the root.

But the root is what feminists have to be concerned with: what it means not to be a good woman or a bad one but to be a woman at all. Moreover, if a great writer need not be radical, neither need a great radical writer be feminist—but so what? It was only recently that the great Romantic poets conned us into believing that to be a great poet was to tell *the* absolute truth, to be the One prophetic voice for all Mankind. As the philosophy of the Other, feminism has had to reject the very conception of such authority—which, by extension, should permit feminist critics to distinguish between appreciative and political readings.

We should begin, therefore, by acknowledging the separate wholeness of the literary subject, its distinct vision that need not be ours—what the formalists have told us and told us about: its integrity. We need to acknowledge, also, that to respect that integrity by not asking questions of the text that it does not ask itself, to ask the text what questions to ask, will produce the fullest, richest reading. To do justice to Shelley, you do not approach him as you do Swift. But doing justice can be a contrary business, and there are aspects of the text that, as Kate Millett demonstrated,[1] a formalist explication actively obscures. If her intentionally tangential approach violated the terms of Henry Miller's work, for example, it also revealed aspects of the work that the terms had masked.

1. Kate Millett, *Sexual Politics* (Garden City, N.Y.: Doubleday & Co., 1970).

But she would not claim, I think, that her excavation of Miller's underlying assumptions had not done damage to his architecture.

The contradiction between appreciation and political analysis is not peculiar to feminist readings, but those who encountered it in the past did not resolve it either. In fact, they too denied it, or tried to. Sartre, for instance, argued in *What Is Literature?* that a good novel could not propound fascism. But then he also recognized that "the appearance of the work of art is a new event which cannot *be explained* by anterior data."[2] More recently, the Marxist Pierre Macherey has hung on the horns of the same dilemma by maintaining that the literary work is tied inextricably to the life that produces it, but, although not therefore "independent," it is nonetheless "autonomous" in being defined and structured by laws uniquely proper to it.[3] (I cite Sartre and Macherey more or less at random among more or less left-wing critics because theirs is a situation somewhat like that of feminists, though less difficult, many would argue, in that they already have a voice of their own. Perhaps for that reason, the position of black critics in a world dominated by whites would more closely resemble that of women. But at any rate, the large category to which all these belong is that of the literary critic who is also and importantly a critic of her/his society, its political system, and its culture.)

My point is simply that there is no reason to deny the limits of ideological criticism, its reduction of texts that, however, it also illuminates in unique ways. As feminists at odds with our culture, we are at odds also with its literary traditions and need often to talk about texts in terms that the author did not use, may not have been aware of, and might indeed abhor. The trouble is that this necessity goes counter not only to our personal and professional commitment to all serious literature but also to our training as gentlemen and scholars, let alone as Americans, taught to value, above all, value-free scholarship.

Doubtless the possibility of maintaining thereby a sympathetic appreciative critical posture is one of the attractions of dealing only or mainly with women's writings. With such material, ironically, it is possible to avoid political judgment altogether, so that the same approach that for some represents the integration into their work of a political commitment to women can serve Patricia Meyer Spacks to make the point that "criticism need not be political to be aware."[4] She means by this that she will be able to recognize and describe a distinct female culture without evaluating either it or its patriarchal context politically. Of course she

2. Jean-Paul Sartre, *What Is Literature?* (New York: Harper Colophon, 1965), p. 40; emphasis in original.
3. Pierre Macherey, *Pour une théorie de la production littéraire* (Paris: Librairie François Maspero, 1966), pp. 66–68.
4. Patricia Meyer Spacks, *The Female Imagination* (New York: Avon Books, 1976), pp. 5, 6.

understands that all vision is mediated, so that the very selection of texts in which to observe the female imagination is judgment of a kind. But it is not ideological or normative judgment; rather it is an "arbitrary decision" that "reflects the operations of [her] imagination," a personal point of view, a "particular sensibility" with no particular political outlook. The important thing is that her "perception of the problems in every case derived from her reading of the books; the books were not selected to depict preconceived problems."

Spacks seeks in this way to disavow any political bias; but even critics who have chosen a woman-centered approach precisely for its political implications reassure us about their analytical detachment. Ellen Moers stipulates in her preface to *Literary Women* that "the literary women themselves, their language, their concerns, have done the organizing of this book." At the same time she means the book to be "a celebration of the great women who have spoken for us all."[5] Her choice of subject has thus been inspired by feminist thinking, but her approach remains supposedly neutral for she has served only as an informed amanuensis. The uncharacteristic naiveté of this stance is enforced, I think, by Moers's critical ambivalence—her wish, on the one hand, to serve a feminist purpose, and her sense, on the other, that to do so will compromise the study as criticism. So she strikes a stance that should enable her to be, like Spacks, aware but not political. Since in posing a question one already circumscribes the answer, such analytical neutrality is a phantom, however; nor was it even Spacks's goal. Her method of dealing with women separately but traditionally, treating their work as she would the opus of any mainstream school, suits her purpose, which is to define a feminine aesthetic transcending sexual politics. She actively wants to exclude political answers. Moers, seeking to discover the feminist in the feminine, is not as well served by that method; and Elaine Showalter's explicitly feminist study, *A Literature of Their Own*,[6] suggests that a political criticism may require something like the methodological reverse.

Showalter wrote her book in the hope that it would inspire women to "take strength in their independence to act in the world" and begin to create an autonomous literary universe with a "female tradition" as its "center." Coming at the end of the book, these phrases provide a resonant conclusion, for she has shown women writing in search of a wholeness the world denies them and creating an art whose own wholeness seems a sure ground for future autonomy. But if, in an effort to flesh out this vision, one turns back to earlier discussions, one finds that there she has depicted not actual independence but action despite dependence—and not a self-defined female culture either, but a sub-

5. Ellen Moers, *Literary Women: The Great Writers* (Garden City, N.Y.: Doubleday & Co., 1976), p. xvi.

6. Elaine Showalter, *A Literature of Their Own: British Women Novelists from Brontë to Lessing* (Princeton, N. J.: Princeton University Press, 1977), pp. 319, 11–12.

culture born out of oppression and either stunted or victorious only at often-fatal cost. Women, she writes at the beginning of the book, form such a "subculture within the framework of a larger society," and "the female literary tradition comes from the still-evolving relationships between women writers and their society." In other words, the meaning of that tradition has been bound up in its dependence. Now, it seems to me that much of what Showalter wants to examine in her study, indeed much of what she does examine, resolves itself into the difference for writers between acting independently as men do and resisting dependence as women do. If her conclusion on the contrary conflates the two, it is because the approach she takes, essentially in common with Spacks and Moers, is not well suited to her more analytical goals.

Like theirs, her book is defined territorially as a description of the circumscribed world of women writers. *A Literature of Their Own* is thus "an attempt to fill in the terrain between [the Austen peaks, the Brontë cliffs, the Eliot range, and the Woolf hills] and to construct a more reliable map from which to explore the achievements of English women novelists." The trouble is that the map of an enclosed space describes only the territory inside the enclosure. Without knowing the surrounding geography, how are we to evaluate this woman's estate, whose bordering peaks we have measured anyway, not by any internal dimensions, but according to those of Mount Saint Dickens and craggy Hardy? Still less can one envision the circumscribed province as becoming independently global—hence probably the visionary vagueness of Showalter's ending. Instead of a territorial metaphor, her analysis of the world of women as a subculture suggests to me a more fluid imagery of interacting juxtapositions the point of which would be to represent not so much the territory as its defining borders. Indeed, the female territory might well be envisioned as one long border, and independence for women not as a separate country but as open access to the sea.

Women (and perhaps some men not of the universal kind) must deal with their situation as a *pre*condition for writing about it. They have to confront the assumptions that render them a kind of fiction in themselves in that they are defined by others, as components of the language and thought of others. It hardly matters at this prior stage what a woman wants to write; its political nature is implicit in the fact that it is she (a "she") who will do it. All women's writing would thus be congenitally defiant and universally characterized by the blasphemous argument it makes in coming into being. And this would mean that the autonomous individuality of a woman's story or poem is framed by engagement, the engagement of its denial of dependence. We might think of the form this necessary denial takes (however it is individually interpreted, whether conciliatory or assertive) as analogous to genre, in being an issue, not of content, but of the structural formulation of the work's relationship to the inherently formally patriarchal language which is the only language we have.

Heretofore, we have tended to treat the anterior act by which women writers create their creativity as part of their lives as purely psychological, whereas it is also a conceptual and linguistic act: the construction of an enabling relationship with a language that of itself would deny them the ability to use it creatively. This act is part of their work as well and organic to the literature that results. Since men (on the contrary) can assume a natural capacity for creation, they begin there, giving individual shape to an energy with which they are universally gifted. If it is possible, then, to analyze the writings of certain men independently—not those of all men, but only of those members of a society's ruling group whose identity in fact sets the universal norm—this is because their writings come into existence independent of prior individual acts. Women's literature begins to take its individual shape before it is properly literature, which suggests that we should analyze it inclusive of its *ur*-dependence.

In fact, the criticism of women writers has of late more and more focused on the preconditions of their writing as the inspiration not only of its content but also of its form. The writer's self-creation is the primary concern of Sandra Gilbert and Susan Gubar's *Madwoman in the Attic,*[7] whose very title identifies global (therefore mad) denial as the hot core of women's art. This impressive culmination of what I have called the territorial approach to feminist criticism does with it virtually everything that can be done. In the way of culminations, it delivers us then before a set of problems that cannot be entirely resolved in its terms but that Gilbert and Gubar have uncovered. My earlier questioning can thus become a question: What do we understand about the world, about the whole culture, from our new understanding of the woman's sphere within it? This question looks forward to a development of the study of women in a universal context, but it also has retrospective implications for what we have learned in the female context.

Gilbert and Gubar locate the female territory in its larger context and examine the borders along which the woman writer defined herself. Coming into being—an unnatural being, she must give birth to herself—the female artist commits a double murder. She kills "Milton's bogey" and the specter Virginia Woolf called the "angel in the house," the patriarch and his wife, returning then to an empty universe she will people in her own image. Blasphemy was not until the woman artist was, and the world of women writers is created in sin and extends to a horizon of eternal damnation. For all women must destroy in order to create.

Gilbert and Gubar argue with erudition and passion, and their projection of the woman writer has a definitive ring. It also has a familiar and perhaps a contradictory ring. The artist as mad defiant blasphemer

7. Sandra Gilbert and Susan Gubar, *The Madwoman in the Attic: The Woman Writer and the Nineteenth-Century Literary Imagination* (New Haven, Conn.: Yale University Press, 1979). The chapter referred to at some length in this discussion is chap. 7, "Horror's Twin: Mary Shelley's Monstrous Eve."

or claustrophobic deviant in a society that denies such a person soulroom is a Romantic image that not only applies also to men but does so in a way that is particularly invidious to women, even more stringently denying them their own identities than earlier ideologies did. That there be contradiction is only right, for when Blake hailed Satan as the hero of *Paradise Lost,* he cast heroism in a newly contradictory mold. Satan is archfiend and Promethean man, individualistic tyrant and revolutionary, architect and supreme wrecker of worlds. It should not be surprising that he is also at once the ultimate, the proto-exploiter of women, and a feminist model. But it does complicate things, as Gilbert and Gubar recognize: Mary Shelley found, in Milton, cosmic misogyny to forbid her creation—and also the model for her rebellion. But then, was her situation not just another version of the general Romantic plight, shared with her friends and relatives, poet-blasphemers all?

No, because she confronted a contradiction that superseded and preceded theirs; she was additionally torn and divided, forbidden to be Satan by Satan as well as by God, ambivalent about being ambivalent. If Satan was both demon and hero to the male poets, he offered women a third possibility, that of Byronic lover and master, therefore a prior choice: feminist assertion or feminine abandon. Here again, women had to act before they could act, choose before they could choose.

But it is just the prior choosing and acting that shape the difference between women's writing and men's that no study of only women's writing can depict. So, for instance, Gilbert and Gubar suggest that the monster in Mary Shelley's *Frankenstein* embodies in his peculiar horror a peculiarly female conception of blasphemy. It may well be, but I do not think we can tell by looking only at *Frankenstein.* At the least we need to go back and look at Satan again, not as a gloss already tending toward *Frankenstein* but as an independent term, an example of what sinful creation is—for a man. Then we need to know what it was for Mary Shelley's fellow Romantics. We might then see the extra dimension of her travail, being able to recognize it because it was extra—outside the requirements of her work and modifying that work in a special way. To reverse the frame of reference, if male critics have consistently missed the woman's aspect of *Frankenstein,* it may be only in part because they are not interested. Another reason could be that in itself the work appears as just another individual treatment of a common Romantic theme. Put simply, then, the issue for a feminist reading of *Frankenstein* is to distinguish its female version of Romanticism: an issue of relatedness and historicity. Women cannot write monologues; there must be two in the world for one woman to exist, and one of them has to be a man.

So in *The Madwoman in the Attic,* building on *Literary Women* and *A Literature of Their Own,* feminist criticism has established the historical relativity of the gender definitions that organize this culture; the patriarchal universe that has always represented itself as absolute has been revealed as man-tailored to a masculine purpose. It is not nature we are looking at in the sexual politics of literature, but history: we know that now because women have rejected the natural order of ying and yang and lived to tell a different tale. I have been arguing that, to read this tale, one needs ultimately to relate it to the myths of the culture it comments on. The converse is also true; in denying the normative universality of men's writing, feminist criticism historicizes it, rendering it precisely, as "men's writing." On the back cover of *The Madwoman in the Attic* Robert Scholes is quoted as having written that "in the future it will be embarrassing to teach Jane Austen, Mary Shelley, the Brontës, George Eliot, Emily Dickinson, and their sisters without consulting this book." Not so embarrassing, one would like to add, as it should be to teach Samuel Richardson, Percy Bysshe Shelley, Charles Dickens, William Makepeace Thackeray, Walt Whitman, and their brothers without consulting a feminist analysis.

Indeed, in suggesting here that women critics adopt a method of radical comparativism, I have in mind as one benefit the possibility of demonstrating thereby the contingency of the dominant male traditions as well. Comparison reverses the territorial image along with its contained methodology and projects instead, as the world of women, something like a long border. The confrontations along that border between, say, *Portrait of a Lady* and *House of Mirth,* two literary worlds created by two gods out of one thematic clay, can light up the outer and most encompassing parameters (perimeters) of both worlds, illuminating the philosophical grounds of the two cosmic models, "natures" that otherwise appear unimpeachably absolute. This border (this no-man's-land) might have provided Archimedes himself a standpoint. Through the disengagements, the distancings of comparative analyses, of focusing on the relations between situations rather than on the situations themselves, one might be able to generate the conceptual equivalent of getting off this world and seeing it from the outside. At the same time, comparison also involves engagement by requiring one to identify the specific qualities of each term. The overabstraction of future visions has often been the flip side of nonanalytical descriptions of the present viewed only in its own internal terms. To talk about then and now as focuses of relations may be a way of tempering both misty fantasies and myopic documentations.

Thus the work of a woman—whose proposal to be a writer in itself reveals that female identity is not naturally what it has been assumed to be—may be used comparatively as an external ground for seeing the dominant literature whole. Hers is so fundamental a denial that its outline outlines as well the assumption it confronts. And such comparison works in reverse, too, for juxtaposed with the masculinist assumption we can also see whole the feminist denial and trace its limits. Denial always runs the risk of merely shaping itself in the negative image of what it rejects. If there is any danger that feminism may become trapped, either in winning for women the right to be men or in taking the opposite sentimental tack and celebrating the feminine identity of an oppressed past as ideal womanhood, these extremes can be better avoided when women's assumptions too can be seen down to their structural roots— from the other ground provided by men's writing.

Lest it appear that I am advocating a sort of comparison mongering, let me cite as a model, early blazing a path we have not followed very far, a study that on the surface is not at all comparative. Millett's *Sexual Politics* was all about comparison, however, about the abysses between standpoints, between where men stood to look at women and where women stood to be looked at. Facing these two at the book's starting point was Millett's construction of yet another lookout where a feminist might stand. As criticism per se, *Sexual Politics* may be flawed by its simplifying insistence on a single issue. But as ideological analysis, as model illuminator and "deconstructor," it remains our most powerful work. It is somewhat puzzling that, since then, so little has been written about the dominant literary culture whose ideas and methods of dominance were Millett's major concerns.[8] It may be that the critical shortcomings of so tangential an approach have been too worrisome. Certainly it is in reading the dominant "universal" literature that the contradictions of an ideological criticism become most acute. There are many ways of dealing with contradictions, however, of which only one is to try to resolve them. Another way amounts to joining a contradiction—engaging it not so much for the purpose of overcoming it as to tap its energy. To return one last time to the fulcrum image, a fulcrum is a point at which force is transmitted—the feminist fulcrum is not just any point in the culture where misogyny is manifested but one where misogyny is pivotal or crucial to the whole. The thing to look for in our studies, I believe, is the connection, the meshing of a definition of women and a definition of the world. And insofar as the former is deleterious, the connection will be contradictory; indeed, as the literary examples that follow suggest, one may recognize a point of connection by its contradictions. It will turn out, or I will try to show, that contradictions just such as that between ethical and aesthetic that we have tried to resolve away lest they belie our argument frequently are our

8. I want to cite two works, one recently published and one in progress, that do deal with the traditions of male writing. Judith Fetterley in *The Resisting Reader: A Feminist Approach to American Fiction* (Bloomington: Indiana University Press, 1978) writes that women should "resist the view of themselves presented in literature by refusing to believe what they read, and by arguing with it, begin to exorcize the male ideas and attitudes they have absorbed." Lee Edwards in her forthcoming *Labors of Psyche: Female Heroism and Fictional Form* expresses the somewhat different but related purpose of reclaiming language and mythology for women. My objections to both these approaches will be clear from the essay. Let me add here only that I also find them nonetheless extremely suggestive and often persuasive.

firmest and most fruitful grounds. The second part of this essay will attempt to illustrate this use of contradiction through the example of the American sentimental novel, a kind of women's writing in which the contradiction between ideology and criticism would appear well-nigh overwhelming.

II

The problem is all too easily stated: the sentimental novels that were best-sellers in America from the 1820s to the 1870s were written and read mostly by women, constituting an oasis of women's writing in an American tradition otherwise unusually exclusively male. But this oasis holds scant nourishment; in plain words, most of the women's writing is awful. What is a feminist critic to do with it? It is not that as a feminist she must praise women unthinkingly, but there is little point either in her just contributing more witty summaries of improbable plots and descriptions of impossible heroines to enliven the literary histories. There hardly needs a feminist come to tell us that E. D. E. N. Southworth's cautionary tales are a caution; and as to whether Susan Warner's *Wide Wide World* does set "an all-time record for frequency of references to tears and weeping,"[9] there are others already counting. We might do best, with Elizabeth Hardwick, to simply let it alone. In her collection of more or less unknown women's writings,[10] Hardwick selected works that were commendable in their own rights and discarded most of what she read as "so bad I just had to laugh—I wasn't even disappointed. The tradition was just too awful in the nineteenth-century."

Still, there it is, the one area of American writing that women have dominated and defined ostensibly in their own image, and it turned out just as the fellows might have predicted. It is gallant but also a little ingenuous of Hardwick to point out that men's sentimental writing was just as bad. For Hawthorne, whose *cri de coeur* against the "damned mob of scribbling women" still resonates in the hearts of his countrymen, did not invent the association between sentimentality and women. The scribbling women themselves did, ascribing their powers to draw readers deep into murky plots and uplift them to heavenly visions to the special gifts of a feminine sensibility. If there is no question of celebrating in the sentimentalists "great women who have spoken for us all," it seems just as clear that they spoke as women to women, and that, if we are to criticize the place of women in this culture, we need to account for the very large place they occupied—and still do; the sentimental mode re-

9. Henry Nash Smith, "The Scribbling Women and the Cosmic Success Story," *Critical Inquiry* 1, no. 1 (September 1974): 49–70.

10. Elizabeth Hardwick, *Rediscovered Fiction by American Women* (New York: Arno Press, 1978).

mains a major aspect of literary commerce, still mostly written and read by women.

Although at bottom either way presents the same contradiction between politics and criticism, the sentimental novel would seem, therefore, to flip the problems encountered in *A Literature of Their Own, Literary Women,* and *The Madwoman in the Attic.* The issue there was to uncover new aspects of works and writers that had more or less transcended the limitations of the patriarchal culture—or failed and found tragedy. Inspired by their example, one had nonetheless to temper admiration with critical distance. Here the difficulty lies instead in tempering rejection with a recognition of kinship, kinship one is somewhat hesitant to acknowledge in that it rests on a shared subordination in which the sentimental novel appears altogether complicitous. For the sentimentalists were prophets of compliance, to God the patriarch as to his viceroys on earth. Their stories are morality dramas featuring heroines prone at the start to react to unjust treatment by stamping their feet and weeping rebellious tears, but who learn better and in the end find happiness in "unquestioning submission to authority, whether of God or an earthly father figure or society in general." They also find some more substantial rewards, Mammon rising like a fairy godmother to bestow rich husbands and fine houses. Conformity is powerful, and Henry Nash Smith's explication of it all has a definitive clarity: "The surrender of inner freedom, the discipline of deviant impulses into rapturous conformity, and the consequent achievement of both worldly success and divine grace merge into a single mythical process, a cosmic success story."[11] If that success is ill-gotten by Smith's lights, it can only appear still more tainted to a feminist critic whose focus makes her acutely aware that the sweet sellout is a woman and the inner freedom of women her first sale. With overgrown conscience and shrunken libido, the sentimental heroine enumerating her blessings in the many rooms of her husband's mansion is the prototype of that deformed angel Virginia Woolf urged us to kill.

To kill within ourselves, that is. Thus we return to the recognition of kinship that makes it necessary to understand the sentimentalists not only the way critics generally have explained them but also as writers expressing a specifically female response to the patriarchal culture. This is a controversial venture that has resulted thus far in (roughly defined) two schools of thought. One of these starts from Hawthorne's charge that the popular novels usurped the place of serious literature. The title of Ann Douglas's *Feminization of American Culture*[12] announces her thesis that the sentimentalists exploited a literary Gresham's law to debase the cultural currency with their feminine coin. But gold is at least hoarded, while this bad money devalued outright Hawthorne's and Melville's good. A tough, iconoclastic, and individualistic masculine high culture,

11. Smith, p. 51.
12. Ann Douglas, *The Feminization of American Culture* (New York: Avon Books, 1978).

the potential worthy successor of the tough Puritan ethos, was thus routed from the national arena by a conservative femininity that chained the arts to the corners of hearths and to church pews. Henceforth, and still today, a stultifying mass culture has emasculated the American imagination. Douglas does not blame women for this, for she sees them as themselves defined by their society. Even in the exploitation of their destructive power, she thinks, they meant well; nor would she wish for an equivalently simpleminded macho replacement to the feminized culture. But the implied alternative is nonetheless definitely masculine—in a good way, of course: strong, serious, and generously accepting of women who have abjured their feminine sensibilities. Not a hard thing to do, for if the choice is between Susan Warner and Melville, why were we not all born men?

That choice, however, is just the problem, its traditional limits generated by the Archimedean bind of trying to think about new issues in the old terms, when those terms do not merely ignore the new issues but deny them actively and thus force one instead into the old ways, offering choices only among them. The terms here are masculine and feminine as they participate in clusters of value that interpret American history and culture. It has been generally understood among cultural and social historians that the creative force in America is individualistic, active . . . masculine. Perhaps to a fault: Quentin Anderson would have liked the American self less imperially antisocial,[13] and before him Leslie Fiedler worried that its exclusive masculinity excluded heterosexual erotic love.[14] These analysts of American individualism do not necessarily come to judge it the same way, but they define it alike and alike therefore project as its logical opposition conformity, passive compliance, familialism . . . femininity. Huck Finn and Aunt Polly. The critical literature has until now mostly concentrated on Huck Finn, and *The Feminization of American Culture* completes the picture by focusing on Aunt Polly.

In the sense that its features are composed from real facts, "Aunt Polly" may well be a true picture. But her position in the composite American portrait, opposed in her trite conventionality to "his" rugged individualism, is not a function of facts alone but also of an interpretive scheme secured by a set of parallel dichotomies that vouch for one another: Aunt Polly is to Huck as feminine is to masculine; feminine is to masculine as Aunt Polly is to Huck. Only if we pull these apart will we be able to question the separate validity of either.

Potentially even more radically, Nina Baym[15] sets out to reconsider the component terms of the generally accepted dichotomy in the nineteenth century between female conformity and manly individu-

13. Quentin Anderson, *The Imperial Self* (New York: Alfred A. Knopf, Inc., 1971).
14. Leslie Fiedler, *Love and Death in the American Novel* (New York: Delta Books, 1966).
15. Nina Baym, *Woman's Fiction: A Guide to Novels by and about Women, 1820–1870* (Ithaca, N.Y.: Cornell University Press, 1978). Page numbers indicated in text.

alism, between female social conservatism and masculine rebellion. Representing the other school of thought about sentimentalism, this one in line with recent historical reconsideration of such ridiculed women's movements as temperance and revivalism, she argues that the women novelists too had their reasons. She answers Smith's accusation that the novels' "cosmic success story" pointed an arch-conservative moral by suggesting that for disenfranchised and property-deprived women to acquire wealth, social status, and some measure of control over their domestic environment could be considered a radical achievement, as ruling a husband by virtue of virtue might amount to subversion. As she sees it, "The issue [for the women in the novels] is power and how to live without it." They do not run their society and never hope to, so, short of revolution, no direct action can be taken. Even from their state of total dependence, however, these women can rise to take practical charge of their lives and acquire a significant measure of power by implementing the conservative roles to which the patriarchal society has relegated them. In this light, what Smith terms their "ethos of conformity" takes on another aspect and almost becomes a force for change, all depending on how you look at it.

Which is precisely the problem of this essay, emerging here with unusual clarity because both Smith and Baym approach the material ideologically. Even their descriptions, let alone their interpretations, show the effects of divergent standpoints. Consider how each summarizes the typical sentimental plot. Smith reports that *Wide Wide World* is the tale of "an orphan exposed to poverty and psychological hardships who finally attains economic security and high social status through marriage."[16] Baym reads the same novel as "the story of a young girl who is deprived of the supports she had rightly or wrongly depended on to sustain her throughout life and is faced with the necessity of winning her own way in the world" (p. 19). The second account stresses the role of the girl herself in defining her situation, so that the crux of her story becomes her passage from passivity to active engagement. On the contrary, with an eye to her environment and its use of her, Smith posits her as passive throughout, "exposed" at first, in the end married. Clearly this is not a matter of right or wrong readings but of a politics of vision.

It is as a discussion of the politics of vision that *Woman's Fiction* is perhaps most valuable. Baym has set out to see the novels from a different perspective, and indeed they look different. The impossible piety of the heroine, for instance, Baym views as an assertion of her moral strength against those who consider her an empty vessel, lacking ego and understanding and in need of constant supervision. Typically the heroine starts out sharing this view, taking herself very lightly and looking to the world to coddle and protect her. With each pious stand she

16. Smith, p. 49.

takes over the course of the novel, she becomes more self-reliant, until by the end she has "developed a strong conviction of her own worth" (p. 19) and becomes a model for female self-respect. Thus, the heroine's culminating righteousness and its concomitant rewards, that from one viewpoint prove the opportunistic virtues of submission, indicate to Baym a new and quite rare emergence of female power manifested in the avalanche of good things with which the story ends. To Smith those cornucopia endings are the payoff for mindless acquiescence, sweets for the sweet ruining the nation's palate for stronger meat. For Douglas they are a banquet celebrating the women's takeover; a starving Melville is locked out. But for Baym the comfort in which the heroine rests at last is her hard-earned just reward, the sentimental cult of domesticity representing a pragmatic feminism aimed primarily at establishing a place for women under their own rule.

In that spirit, she sees a more grown-up kind of sense than do most critics in the novels' prudishness, pointing out that, when they were written, the Richardsonian model they otherwise followed had become a tale of seduction. The women novelists, she suggests, were "unwilling to accept . . . a concept of woman as inevitable sexual prey" (p. 26); in a world where sexual politics hardly offered women a democratic choice, they preferred to eschew sex altogether rather than be raped. Here again, point of view is all. One recalls that Fiedler had a more ominous reading. According to him, the middle-class ladies who wrote the sentimental fiction had "grown too genteel for sex" but, being female, they still yearned "to see women portrayed as abused and suffering, and the male as crushed and submissive in the end";[17] so they desexed their heroes by causing them to love exceptionally good girls with whom sex was unthinkable.

Without sharing Fiedler's alarm over the state of American manhood, one has to concede that the sentimental novel, with its ethereal heroines and staunchly buttoned heroes, was indeed of a rarefied spirituality. That its typical plot traced, instead of physical seduction, the moral regeneration and all-around strengthening of erstwhile helpless women would appear all to the good; it is surely an improvement for women to cease being portrayed as inevitable victims. But the fact is that the sentimental heroines, perhaps rich as models, are rather poor as characters. Those inner possibilities they discover in becoming self-sufficient seem paradoxically to quench any interior life, so that we nod in both senses of the word when such a heroine "looks to marry a man who is strong, stable and safe." For, "she is canny in her judgment of men, and generally immune to the appeal of a dissolute suitor. When she feels such attraction, she resists it" (p. 41). Quite right, except we actually wish she would not: do we then regret the fragile fair who fell instantly

---

17. Fiedler, pp. 259–60.

and irrevocably in an earlier literature, or the "graceful deaths that created remorse in all one's tormentors" (p. 25) and in the story some sparks of life?

Baym is well aware of the problem and offers two possible analyses. In the first place, she says, the women novelists never claimed to be writing great literature. They thought of "authorship as a profession rather than a calling, as work and not art. Often the women deliberately and even proudly disavowed membership in an artistic fraternity." So they intentionally traded art for ideology, a matter of political rather than critical significance. "Yet," she adds (and here she is worth quoting at length because she has articulated clearly and forcefully a view that is important in feminist criticism),

> I cannot avoid the belief that "purely" literary criteria, as they have been employed to identify the best American works, have inevitably had a bias in favor of things male—in favor, say of whaling ships rather than the sewing circle as a symbol of the human community; in favor of satires on domineering mothers, shrewish wives, or betraying mistresses rather than tyrannical fathers, abusive husbands, or philandering suitors; displaying an exquisite compassion for the crises of the adolescent male, but altogether impatient with the parallel crises of the female. While not claiming literary greatness for any of the novels introduced in this study, I would like at least to begin to correct such a bias by taking their content seriously. And it is time, perhaps—though this task lies outside my scope here—to reexamine the grounds upon which certain hallowed American classics have been called great. [Pp. 14–15]

On the surface this is an attractive position, and, indeed, much of it is unquestionably valid; but it will not bear a close analysis. She is having it both ways, admitting the artistic limitations of the women's fiction ("I have not unearthed a forgotten Jane Austen or George Eliot, or hit upon even one novel that I would propose to set alongside *The Scarlet Letter*" [p. 14]) and at the same time denying the validity of the criteria that measure those limitations; disclaiming any ambition to reorder the literary canon, and, on second thought, challenging the canon after all—or rather challenging not the canon itself but the grounds for its selection.

There is much reason to reconsider these grounds, and such reconsideration should be one aim of an aggressive feminist criticism. But it has little to do with the problem at hand—the low quality of the women's fiction—that no reconsideration will raise. True, whaling voyages are generally taken more seriously than sewing circles, but it is also true that Melville's treatment of the whale hunt is a more serious affair than the sentimentalists' treatment of sewing circles. And the latter, when treated in the larger terms of the former, do get recognized—for example, Penelope weaving the shroud for Ulysses surrounded by her suitors, or, for that matter, the opening scene of *Middlemarch* in which two young girls quibble over baubles, situations whose resonance not even the most misogynist reader misses.

The first part of the explanation, that the women did not take *themselves* seriously, seems more promising. Baym tells us that they "were expected to write specifically for their own sex and within the tradition of their woman's culture rather than within the Great Tradition"; certainly, "they never presented themselves as followers in the footsteps of Milton or Spenser, seekers after literary immortality, or competitors with the male authors of their own time who were aiming at greatness" (p. 178). With this we come closer to the writing itself and therefore to the sources of its intrinsic success or failure. I want to stress intrinsic here as a way of recalling the distinction between a work as politics—its external significance—and as art. So when seeking to explain the intrinsic failures of the sentimentalists, one needs to look beyond their politics, beyond their relationships with publishers, critics, or audiences, to their relationship to writing as such. Melville wrote without the support of publishers, critics, and audiences—indeed, despite their active discouragement—so those cannot be the crucial elements. He did, however, have himself, he took himself seriously; as Whitman might have said, he *assumed* himself.

Now, no woman can assume herself because she has yet to create herself, and this the sentimentalists, acceding to their society's definition, did not do. To the extent that they began by taking the basic order of things as given, they forswore any claim on the primary vision of art[18] and saw themselves instead as interpreters of the established ethos, its guardians, or even, where needed, its restorers. My point is that, for all their virtual monopoly of the literary marketplace, the women novelists, being themselves conceived by others, were conceptually totally dependent. This means dependent on Melville himself and on the dominant culture of which he, but not they, was a full, albeit an alienated or even a reviled, member. His novel in the sentimental mode could take on sentimentalism because he had an alternative world on which to stand: himself. And although no one would wish on a friendly author the travail that brought forth *Pierre*, there it is nonetheless, the perfect example of what no woman novelist conceiving of herself not as an artist or maker but as a "professional"—read practitioner, implementor, transmitter, follower of a craft—could ever have written. *Pierre* does not know how to be acquiescently sentimental, it can only be *about* sentimentalism. The issue is self-consciousness, and in self-consciousness, it

18. I am aware that this analysis assumes a modern psychology of art, that "creation" has not always been the artist's mission, or tacit acceptance of the established ethos considered fatal. But we are here speaking of the nineteenth century, not of all time; and writers who did not challenge their society's values would also not have questioned its fundamental construction of artistic identity as individualistic and as authentically creative.

is self. With the example of Melville, we might then reconsider the relationship of the rebel to conventions. The rebel has his conventional definition too—that is, his is one possible interpretation of the conventions—so that he stands fully formed within the culture, at a leading edge. On the other hand, in this society women stand outside any of the definitions of complete being; hence perhaps the appeal to them of a literature of conformity and inclusion—and the extraordinary difficulty, but for the extraordinary few, of serious writing.

Indeed, Baym's defense of the women novelists, like that generally of the lesser achievement of women in any art, seems to me finally unnecessary. If history has treated women badly, it is entirely to be expected that a reduced or distorted female culture, one that is variously discouraged, embittered, obsessively parochial, or self-abnegating, will show it. There is little point then in claiming more than exists or in looking to past achievement as evidence of future promise: at this stage of history, we have the right, I think, simply to assert the promise.

If there is no cause for defensiveness, moreover, it does have its cost. In the case of the sentimental novel, for instance, too much apologia can obscure the hard question Baym implies but does not quite articulate, to wit, why are the ways in which the sentimental novel asserts that women can succeed precisely the ways that it fails as literature? *Is its ideological success tied to its artistic failure?* Is its lack of persuasiveness as art in some way the result of the strong ideological argument it makes for female independence? The issue, it seems, is not merely neglecting art for the sake of politics but actively sacrificing it. Which brings the discussion back to the Douglas thesis that since the sentimentalists universalized (Americanized) a debased feminine culture, the more powerful the women (authors and heroines both), the worse the literature and thereby the consequences for the whole culture. The great appeal of this argument is that it confronts squarely the painful contradiction of women becoming powerful not by overcoming but by exploiting their impotence.

I would like to suggest another possible explanation. The contradiction between the art and the politics of the sentimental novel arises, not surprisingly, at the point where the novelists confronted the tradition in which they were working and, for political reasons, rejected it formally: when they refused to perpetuate the image of the seduced and abandoned heroine and substituted in her stead the good girl who holds out to the happy (bitter or boring) end. The parent tradition is that of the novel of sensibility as it was defined in *Clarissa*. But before *Clarissa*, Richardson wrote *Pamela*, probably the prototype of the female "cosmic success story." Pamela begins powerless and ends up in charge, rewarded for her tenacious virtue (or her virtuous tenacity) by a commodious house, a husband, and all those same comforts of upper middle-class life that crowned the goodness of America's sentimental heroines. Indeed, *Pamela* had helped set up their new world, being the first novel actually printed here—by Benjamin Franklin, who understood both romance and commerce and knew how well they could work together. So did Pamela, of course, a superb pragmatist who not only foils a seducer but also turns him into a very nice husband. She is perhaps not so finely tuned or morally nice as her sentimental descendants, but she is quite as careful and controlled, as certain of her values, as unwilling to be victimized—and ultimately as triumphant. In contrast, Clarissa is helplessly enamored, seduced, destroyed. She is also the more interesting character and *Clarissa* the more complex story—can it be that weak victimized women make for better novels?

In the first part of this discussion, I made the point that the madness into which women artists are characterized as driven by social constraints needs to be compared with the similar state often attributed to male artists. The same need arises here, for male protagonists too are generally defeated, and, of course, Clarissa's seducer Lovelace dies along with her. But he is neither weak (in the helpless sense that she is) nor victimized; nor (to name doomed heroes at random) is Stendhal's Julien Sorel or Melville's Pierre. There is certainly no surprise in the contrast as such; we expect male characters to be stronger than female. The juxtaposition, however, may be suggesting something not already so evident: that as the distinctive individual identity of a male character typically is generated by his defiance, so that of a female character seems to come from her vulnerability, which thus would be organic to the heroine as a novelistic construct.

It seems reasonable to suppose that the novel, envisioning the encounter of the individual with his world in the modern idiom, posits as one of its structuring assumptions (an assumption that transcends the merely thematic, to function formally) the special form that sexual hierarchy has taken in modern times. The novel, we know, is organically individualistic: even when it deals with several equally important individuals, or attacks individualism itself, it is always about the unitary self versus the others. Moreover, it is about the generation, the becoming, of that self. I want to suggest that this process may be so defined as to require a definition of female characters that effectively precludes their becoming autonomous, so that indeed they would do so at the risk of the novel's artistic life.

Pamela represents the advent of a new form to deal with such new problems of the modern era as the transformation of the family and the newly dynamic mode of social mobility. *Pamela* works these out very well for its heroine, but there is something wrong in the resolution. Pamela's triumph means the defeat of Mr. B., who in his chastened state can hardly be the enterprising, potent entrepreneur that the rising middle class needs him to be. Her individualism has evolved at the cost of his; later Freud would develop a special term for such misadventures, but

Richardson must already have known that this was not the way it should be.

At any rate, he resolved this difficulty in his next work simply by raising the social status of his heroine. Since she was a servant, Pamela's quest for independent selfhood necessarily took a public form. To affirm her value and remain in possession of her self, Pamela had to assert her equality publicly; to claim herself, she had, in effect, to claim power. But as an established member of the powerful class, Clarissa is in full possession of its perquisites, notably that of being taken as honorably marriageable by the lords of her world. Though it is true that her family's greed for yet more wealth and status precipitates her crisis, the problems she faces are really not those of upward mobility. Standing at the other end of that process, she is profoundly unhappy with its results and with the internal workings of her society. Her story is about the conflict within, the problems that arise inside the middle-class world; and its marvelously suited theater for exploring these is the self within.

In thus locating itself inside the life of its dominant class, the novel only followed suit after older genres. But what is peculiar to this genre is that it locates the internal problems of its society still deeper inside, inside the self. Richardson's earlier novel had retained an older conception more like that of Defoe, identifying the self externally—hence *Pamela*'s interpretation of romance as commerce. *Clarissa*, on the contrary, now treats commerce in the terms of romance. Pamela had projected her inner world outward and identified her growth as a character with the extension of her power. But this approach tends to vitiate the distinction between the private self and the world out there that is the powerful crux of middle-class identity. *Clarissa* takes that distinction as its theme, and the locale of the novel henceforth is the interior life. I want to propose the thesis that this interior life, *whether lived by man or woman, is female,* so that women characters define themselves and have power only in this realm. Androgyny, in the novel, is a male trait enabling men to act from their male side and feel from their female side.

One common feminist notion is that the patriarchal society suppresses the interior lives of women. In literature, at least, this does not seem altogether true, for indeed the interior lives of female characters are the novel's mainstay. Instead, it is women's ability to act in the public domain that novels suppress, and again Richardson may have shown the way. *Pamela* developed its heroine by reducing its hero (in conventional terms). This compensation was, in fact, inevitable as long as the characters defined themselves the same way, by using and expanding the individualistic potency of the self. Since by this scheme Pamela would be less of a person and a character if she were less active, she had to compete with Mr. B. to the detriment of one of them—to the detriment also of conjugal hierarchy and beyond that, of their society, whose resulting universal competitiveness must become dangerously atomizing and possibly centrifugal. In a middle-class society, however, the family unit is meant to generate coherence, in that the home provides both a base and a terminus for the competitive activity of the marketplace. The self-reliant man necessarily subsumes his family, chief among them his wife, to his own identity; it is in the middle-class society above all that a man's home is his castle. But how can this subsuming be accomplished without denying identity to women altogether and thus seriously undermining their potency as helpmates as well? The problem lies in retaining this potency, that can come only from individualism, without suffering the consequences of its realization in individualistic competition. Tocqueville particularly admired the way this problem had been resolved in America. Women in the New World were free, strong, and independent, but they *voluntarily* stayed home. In other words, their autonomy was realized by being freely abandoned, after which, of course, they ceased to exist as characters—witness their virtual absence from the American novel.

The European novelist, at least the English and the French, either less sanguine about the natural goodness of middle-class values or more embattled with older norms, saw that this voluntary subjugation could be problematical. If women too are people, and people are individualists, might they not rebel? If they succeeded in this, social order would crumble; indeed, they could not succeed because they did not have the power. But the possibility, arising from the most basic terms of middle-class thought and also doomed by the very prevalence of that thought, emerged as the central drama of the modern imagination. It is precisely the drama of the suppressed self, the self who assumes the universal duty of self-realization but finds its individual model in absolute conflict with society. Then as it becomes the more heroically individualistic, the more self-realized, the more it pushes toward inevitable doom. If there is a tragic dimension to the novel, it is here in the doomed encounter between the female self and the middle-class world. This is the encounter Gilbert and Gubar have observed and attributed, too exclusively I think, to women. The lack of a comparative dimension can tend to obscure the distinction between representation and reality, to fuse them so that the female self simply is woman, if woman maligned. But, as Flaubert might have pointed out, many a male novelist has represented at least part of himself as female.

Which is not to suggest that European novelists were champions of women's rights. Their interest lay rather in the metaphorical potential of the female situation to represent the great Problem of modern society, the reconciliation of the private and the public realms, once the cornerstone of the new social and economic order has been laid in their alienation. Such reconciliation is problematical in that the self, granted its freedom, may not willingly accept social control; it may insist on its separate and other privacy, on the integrity of its interior vision. Clarissa wants to be and do otherwise than her world permits, and with that impulse, her inner self comes into view. It grows as she becomes less and less able to project her will, or rather as the incursions against her private self become more ferocious. Who, and what, Clarissa is finally *is* that private world.

I want to stress that in championing her alienated private self, the novel is not taking the side of real women, or even of female characters as female. Recent praise of *Clarissa* as a feminist document, or vindications of its heroine's behavior against her patriarchal oppressors, have not dealt clearly enough with the fact that her creator was a patriarch. If nonetheless he envisioned his heroine in terms with which feminists may sympathize, it is, I believe, because he viewed her as representing not really woman but the interior self, the female interior self in all men—in all men, but especially developed perhaps in writers, whose external role in this society is particularly incommensurate with their vision, who create new worlds but earn sparse recognition or often outright scorn in this one.

It is in this sense, I think, that Emma Bovary was Flaubert, or Anna Karenina, Tolstoy, or Isabel Archer, James. But the way Dorothea Brooke was George Eliot reveals the edge of this common identification between author and heroine, for Eliot, though herself a successful woman, cannot envision Dorothea as equally so.[19] One might suppose that she at least could have imagined her heroine, if not triumphant like Julien Sorel, acting out her doom rather than accepting it. It is one thing for male novelists to assume that women are incapable of effective action, but that women do so as well is more disturbing. I am suggesting that George Eliot was compelled by the form of her story to tell it as she did, that the novel as a genre precludes androgynously heroic women while and indeed *because* it demands androgynous heroes. In other words, the novel demands that the hero have an interior life and that this interior life be metaphorically female. The exterior life, on the other hand, is just as ineluctably male (and the novel has its share of active, manly women). These identifications are not consciously made as being convenient or realistic, in which case they would be vulnerable to conscious change. They are assumed, built into the genre as organic and natural; for, if action were either male or female, we would be back with the potentially castrating Pamela. She, however, bent her considerable force to enter the middle class, endorsing its values wholeheartedly. A similarly active Clarissa, an effective and militant Dorothea, must threaten the entire order of things.

The novel is critical, it examines and even approves the rebellions of

19. For an illuminating discussion of this phenomenon—of women novelists being unable to imagine female characters as strong as themselves—see Carolyn Heilbrun, "Women Writers and Female Characters: The Failure of Imagination," in *Reinventing Womanhood* (New York: W. W. Norton & Co., 1979), pp. 71–92.

Clarissa and Dorothea, but only after signaling its more basic acceptance of an order it locates, beyond political attack, in nature itself. Julien Sorel's alienation, however Napoleonic his aspirations, is associated throughout with the female part of his character; his sensitivity, his inability to accept the life and values his father offers him, these are repeatedly described as feminine traits, and the final act that destroys him bespeaks his feminine nature, much to the dismay of his male friends. In the mirror world of this and other novels, femaleness is not conservative but potentially revolutionary. At the same time, it is by cultural definition incapable of active fulfillment. In taking woman as metaphor for the interior life, then, and—far from suppressing her—expanding hers almost to the exclusion of any other life, the novel both claimed its interior, individualistic, alienated territory and placed the limits of that territory within the structures of the middle-class world it serves. George Eliot could have made Dorothea strong only by challenging these structures or by accepting them and depicting her as manly, thereby telling another story, perhaps *The Bostonians*. And no more than this latter would that story have challenged the conventional notions of feminine and masculine.

There is a third possibility for the novel, which is to return to *Pamela* and close down the alienated interior realm by having Dorothea act not out of internal impulses but in response to social dictates. This is what the sentimental novel does, its heroines realizing themselves in society actively but in full accord with its values and imperatives. This solution to the subversive threat posed by female individualism amounts to reversing the Richardsonian development from *Pamela* to *Clarissa*. We have a precise representation of that reversal—wrought, one is tempted to think, in deference to the greater solidity of the middle-class ethic in this country—in the first American novel, *Charlotte Temple* (1791). Its author, Susanna Rowson, copies the contemporary fashion of *Clarissa*-like stories but then, apparently thinking the better of such downbeat endings, tacks on a *Pamela* conclusion. Charlotte Temple, the disastrously fragile English heroine of the story, is carried off by a soldier en route to America; no sooner carried off than pregnant, no sooner pregnant than abandoned, no sooner abandoned than wandering the icy roads in winter in slippers and a thin shawl. She is charitably taken in to a hospitable fireside only to pass away, leaving an innocent babe and much remorse all around. At this point, however, with one perfectly satisfactory ending in place, Susanna Rowson adds a second.

While neglecting Charlotte, her faithless lover Montraville has fallen in love with New York's most desirable belle, Julia Franklin, an orphaned heiress who is "the very reverse of Charlotte Temple." Julia is strong, healthy, and of independent means and spirit. Her guardian entertains "too high an opinion of her prudence to scrutinize her actions so much as would have been necessary with many young ladies who were not blest with her discretion." Though Montraville has behaved badly toward the hapless Charlotte, he seems to be capable of a New World redemption. Overcome by guilt at Charlotte's death, he fights a duel to avenge her honor and is dangerously wounded but, more fortunate than Lovelace, is nursed back to health by the discreet Julia. A representative of the new American womanhood, far too sensible to be tempted by rakes, far too clear about the uses of romantic love ever to separate it from marriage, Julia has accomplished the "Pamela" reform. She marries Montraville, and he becomes one of New York's most upright (and affluent) citizens, the fallen seducer risen a husband through the ministrations of a woman who is not merely good but also strong—strong, of course, in being all that she should be. Thus in Julia Franklin the private and the public selves are one, and the novel, with no relation between them to explore and therefore no way or need to envision the private, comes to a speedy end. About Charlotte a far better novel could have and has been written, but about Julia really nothing but exemplary tales for young girls and their spinster aunts. Pioneer mother of sentimental heroines, she deeds them an ability to take care of themselves (by taking care) that Baym rightly applauds from a feminist viewpoint but that effectively does them in as literature. This implies a possibility no less drastic than that the novel, evolved to deal with the psychological and emotional issues of a patriarchal society, may not permit a feminist interpretation.

The possibility that an impotent feminine sensibility is a basic structure of the novel, representing one of the important ways that the novel embodies the basic structures of this society, would suggest more generally that the achievement of female autonomy must have radical implications not only politically but also for the very forms and categories of all our thinking. Yet as students of this thinking, we are not only implicated in it but many of us committed to much of it. Literary criticism especially, because it addresses the best this thinking has produced, exposes this paradox in all its painful complexity—while also revealing the extraordinary possibility of our seeing the old world from a genuinely new perspective.

This analysis of novelistic form has been speculative, of course, a way of setting the issues of women's writing in the context of the whole literature in order to illustrate the uses of a comparative viewpoint as an alternative footing at the critical distance needed for re-vision. It has also been an exercise in joining rather than avoiding the contradiction between ideological and appreciative criticism on the supposition that the crucial issues manifest themselves precisely at the points of contradiction. As a method this has further implications I cannot pursue here. Let me suggest only that to focus on points of contradiction as the places where we can see the whole structure of our world most clearly implies the immanent relativity of all perception and knowledge. Thus, what appears first as a methodological contradiction, then becomes a subject in itself, seems finally to be shaping something like a new epistemology. But then, it is only right that feminism, as rethinking, rethink thinking itself.

Humanities Division
State University of New York College at Purchase

Storming the Toolshed

Jane Marcus

I. Feminist Scholars and Literary Theory

Sections II and III of this article reflect their occasions. "Lupine Criticism" was given as a talk at the Modern Language Association (MLA) meeting in San Francisco in 1979. Florence Howe chaired the session with panelists Mary Helen Washington, Sydney Janet Kaplan, Suzanne Juhasz, and Tillie Olsen.[1] There was a large and enthusiastic audience, and the session was remarkable historically for discussion of race, class, and sexual identity, particularly lesbianism, and for vocal criticism and participation from the audience. The sparse audience for feminist sessions the following year in Houston, the current debate in the National Women's Studies Association over the primacy of the issues of racism and lesbian identity,[2] and the concurrent minimization of differences in feminist literary criticism itself by Annette Kolodny and others in recent

1. Two of the papers delivered at that meeting have since been published: Mary Helen Washington, "New Lives and New Letters: Black Women Writers at the End of the Seventies," *College English* 43, no. 1 (January 1981): 1–11; and Florence Howe, "Those We Still Don't Read," *College English* 43, no. 1 (January 1981): 12–16.
2. See *Women's Studies Quarterly* 9, no. 3 (Fall 1981), particularly the reprint of speeches by Adrienne Rich, "Disobedience Is What the NWSA Is Potentially About," pp. 4–6; and Audre Lorde, "The Uses of Anger," pp. 7–10.

issues of *Feminist Studies*, [3] make it imperative that we reexamine our history. It was, after all, a playful but serious prediction made in "Lupine Criticism" that aggressive, historical feminist scholarship on Virginia Woolf might cease if the practitioners became absorbed into the academy and stopped combining political activism and the position of "outsidership" with their-scholarly work.

In "Dancing through the Minefield," Kolodny's liberal relaxation of the tensions among us and the tensions between feminists and the academy reflects a similar relaxation on the part of historians and political activists. What this does is to isolate Marxist feminists and lesbians on the barricades while "good girl" feminists fold their tents and slip quietly into the establishment. There is a battlefield (race, class, and sexual identity) within each one of us, another battlefield where we wage these wars with our own feminist colleagues (as in *Signs*), and a third battlefield where we defend ourselves from male onslaughts both on our work and on the laws that govern our lives as women in society. It is far too early to tear down the barricades. Dancing shoes will not do. We still need our heavy boots and mine detectors.

The most serious issue facing feminist critics today is that which divides the profession as a whole, the division between theory and practice. Leaning on the Greeks, our culture still posits philosophy, music, and mathematics as the highest forms of intellectual endeavor. They have been the fields most zealously guarded against female incursion, the fields where it has been most difficult for women to gain training. The English composer Dame Ethel Smyth defended herself from criticism of her battles for status and position among women musicians: she could not withdraw from the world to compose, to act the artist who simply cultivates her own garden, she said, when someone had locked up all the tools. [4] Literary theory is a branch of philosophy. Its most vigorous

3. See Annette Kolodny, "Dancing through the Minefield: Some Observations on the Theory, Practice, and Politics of a Feminist Literary Criticism," *Feminist Studies* 6, no. 1 (Spring 1980): 1–25; and Judith Gardiner's response, "Marching through Our Field," *Feminist Studies* (in press). Gardiner distinguishes between liberal, radical, and socialist feminist critics. Gayatri Spivak's unpublished "A Response to Annette Kolodny" (Department of English, University of Texas at Austin, 1980) is an even stronger critique of Kolodny's position. She writes: "To embrace pluralism (as Kolodny recommends) is to espouse the politics of the masculinist establishment. Pluralism is the method employed by the *central* authorities to neutralize opposition by seeming to accept it. The gesture of pluralism on the part of the *marginal* can only mean capitulation to the center."

4. Dame Ethel Smyth's story of her struggle against the masculine establishment in music is told in *Female Pipings in Eden* (London: Peter Davies, 1934). A revival of Dame Ethel's work has begun: several papers were delivered at the First National Congress on Women and Music at New York University in March 1981; her memoirs have been reprinted, *Impressions That Remained* (New York: Da Capo Press, 1981), with a new introduction by Ronald Crichton; and De Capo Press (1980) has also reprinted the score of her *Mass in D* for soli, chorus, and orchestra, with a new introduction by Jane Bernstein.

practitioners in the United States have been male. It is no historical accident that the hegemony of the theoreticians and the valorization of theory itself parallels the rise of feminist criticism. While we have been doing literary housekeeping, they have been gazing at the stars. They refuse to bear the burden of the sins of their literary fathers or to make amends for centuries of critical abuse of women writers involving the loss, destruction, bowdlerization, or misevaluation of women's texts, diaries, letters, and biographies.

When feminist critics first forced open the toolshed, they polished and sharpened the rusty spades and hoes and rakes men long since had discarded. They learned history, textual criticism, biography, the recovery of manuscripts. They began to search for and reprint women's works and to study the image of woman in Western art. Many moved into linguistics to get at the origins of oppression in language, while others worked to find the writing of women of color.[5] We were all forced to become historians and biographers and to train ourselves in those disciplines. We devoured theories of female psychology, anthropology, and myth to broaden our grasp of the work of women artists. The more materialist and particular the labor of feminist critics became, the more abstract and antimaterialist became the work of the men (they left in Europe the Marxist origins of structuralism and deconstruction). The more we spoke in moral indignation and anger, the more Parnassian were the whispers of male theorists. If the last conference of the School of Criticism and Theory is any model to go by,[6] soon they will have retreated so far from life and literature that they will be analyzing the songs of birds in the garden of Paradise (Adamic only).

Geoffrey Hartman claims for the theorists that literary criticism is in the wilderness.[7] While one may grant that Hartman's manner is a distinct imitation of John the Baptist, one must point out that the theorists are not in the wilderness at all but in a labyrinthine garden with high hedges they have constructed themselves. The arrogance of the metaphor indicates the cause of their isolation. If there is one true word in literary criticism and they are the precursors of their master's voice, the profession is lost. But historians of our difficult era will have little doubt about the social origins of the idea of born-again literary critics. I am reminded of the words of the Victorian aesthetician, Vernon Lee, in a letter to Ethel Smyth. It was bad enough to be a voice crying in the wilderness, she said, but a female philosopher was a "vox clamans" in the closet.[8]

5. See Gloria T. Hull, Patricia Bell Scott, and Barbara Smith, eds., *But Some of Us Are Brave: Black Women's Studies* (Old Westbury, N.Y.: Feminist Press, 1981).

6. The conference, entitled "A Controversy of Critics," was sponsored by the School of Criticism and Theory at Northwestern University in May 1981.

7. Geoffrey Hartman, *Criticism in the Wilderness: The Study of Literature Today* (New Haven, Conn.: Yale University Press, 1980).

8. Quoted by Ethel Smyth in *Maurice Baring* (London: Heinemann, 1937), p. 206.

There are some feminist theorists of note, among whom one may cite especially the work of Gayatri Spivak in literature and Julia Lesage in film criticism.[9] Lesage and her colleagues on the film journal *Jump-Cut* have, in fact, made the most revolutionary breakthrough in feminist theory and practice by trying to effect a rapprochement between the left and lesbians. The lesbian-feminist special issue of *Jump-Cut* is a tour de force of brilliant and ground-breaking essays and includes an editorial in which the male editors attempt to deal with what we may call "reparations" for the long battles of the sexes. The writing and publication of these essays is a hopeful sign, but not a victory, until feminist critics who are neither left nor lesbian read and debate these issues and bring them into the classroom.

There were no feminist critics speaking at the first meeting of the School of Criticism and Theory at Northwestern University in the spring of 1981, though the intelligent response of Mary Douglas, the anthropologist, to one of the more reactionary papers, was the highlight of the conference.[10] Protest at the omission of feminists was met by the response that there *are* no feminist theorists, at least none whom the men find "interesting." If there is as yet no feminist critical theory that men find interesting, there is no reason to suppose that it is not at this very moment being written, nor is there any reason to suppose that men will ever be as interested as we are in developments in our own field. Recent critical books attacking the hegemony of the theorists ignore both feminists and Marxists or give them a light cuff, while the heavy blows are aimed at theorists of their own sex. We are excluded from their discourse (theorizing is a male activity); consequently no intellectual intercourse can take place. Even a Marxist critic like Frederic Jameson is loyal to the old boys.[11]

9. See Gayatri Spivak, "Feminism and Critical Theory," *Women's Studies International Quarterly* 1, no. 3 (1978): 241–46, "Three Feminist Readings: McCullers, Drabble, and Habermas," *Union Seminary Quarterly Review* 35, no. 1–2 (Fall–Winter 1978–79): 15–38, and "Reading the World: Literary Criticism Today," *College English* (in press). The most important essays by Julia Lesage are "Subversive Fantasy in *Celine and Julie Go Boating*," *Jump-Cut* 24–25 (March 1981): 36–43, which deals with the semiotics of body language and domestic space, "Dialectical, Revolutionary, Feminist," *Jump-Cut* 20 (May 1979): 20–23, and "Artful Racism, Artful Rape: D. W. Griffith's *Broken Blossoms*," *Jump-Cut* 26 (in press). See also the entire lesbian feminist special issue of *Jump-Cut* (24–25 [March 1981]), especially its bibliography, p. 21; Ruby Rich's analysis of the teacher in girls' schools playing the roles of "good cop" and "bad cop" in her study of *Maedchen in Uniform*, "From Repressive Tolerance to Erotic Liberation," pp. 44–50; and Bonnie Zimmerman's discussion of lesbian vampire films, "Daughters of Darkness: Lesbian Vampires," pp. 23–24.

10. Julia Lesage uses Mary Douglas's *Purity and Danger: An Analysis of Concepts of Pollution and Taboo* (London: Routledge & Kegan Paul, 1966) as a theoretical construct for the analysis of *Celine and Julie Go Boating* (see n. 9 above); this theory was also very useful to Marina Warner in her analysis of female heroism in *Joan of Arc* (New York: Alfred A. Knopf, Inc., 1981).

11. See Gerald Graff's *Poetic Statement and Critical Dogma* (Evanston, Ill.: Northwestern

Just as Virginia Woolf predicted both the birth of Shakespeare's sister and our work for her arrival, so one may also predict the birth of the feminist critic of genius. She must reject with Virginia Woolf the patriarchal view of literature as a competition with prizes of "ornamental pots" from the headmaster. The feminist critic is always at odds with the headmaster. She is, as Adrienne Rich argues, "disloyal" to civilization.[12] She must refuse the ornamental pot, even if it is very fashionable and made in France. She must break the measuring rod, even if it is finely calibrated in the literary laboratories at Yale. We shall have a theory of our own when our practice develops it. "Masterpieces are not single and solitary births," Woolf wrote in *A Room of One's Own*, "they are the outcome of many years of thinking in common, of thinking by the body of the people, so that the experience of the mass is behind the single voice." Woolf was discussing Shakespeare as the product of history. But her socialist analysis can be extended to criticism as well. By her analysis one can imagine that there were many little Geoffrey Hartmans before there was one big Geoffry Hartman, as in literature there were many little Shakespeares before the master himself.[13]

We have already produced feminist critics to match their male counterparts: Mary Ellman, Kate Millett, Ellen Moers, Elaine Showalter. Sandra Gilbert and Susan Gubar can outdo Harold Bloom at his own game; Gayatri Spivak speaks as an equal among the French deconstructionists; Julia Lesage challenges film theory. Many lesser-known feminists have worked steadily for new readings and new values in their own fields. But even if we were to construct the feminist super-critic from the collective voice of all of them, it is doubtful that the self-appointed priesthood would find her analysis interesting. I suspect that this literary amazon is even now slouching toward Ephesus to be

---

University Press, 1970), and *Literature against Itself* (Chicago: University of Chicago Press, 1979); Frank Lentricchia's *After the New Criticism* (Chicago: University of Chicago Press, 1980); Frederic Jameson's *The Political Unconscious: Narrative as a Socially Symbolic Act* (Ithaca, N.Y.: Cornell University Press, 1981); and Terry Eagleton's "The Idealism of American Criticism," *New Left Review* 127 (May–June 1981): 53–65, which reviews Lentricchia and Jameson and surveys the field. Eagleton notes that these critics refuse to discuss gender and maintain sexist attitudes, but his own review does not mention the brilliant work done by feminist critics in the United States in the last decade, nor has Eagleton's work itself deviated from male discourse despite its Marxism. If Annette Kolodny's espousal of the pluralist position from the margin may be seen as a capitulation to a misogynist power structure, Jameson's Marxist pluralism, in its refusal to deal with gender, should show those tempted to follow Kolodny's lead that male bonding transcends theoretical enmities and is more primary among American critics than the issues that divide them intellectually.

12. Rich (n. 2 above), p. 5.

13. Virginia Woolf, *A Room of One's Own* (New York: Harcourt, Brace and World 1929; reprint ed. 1957), pp. 68–69, 110.

born—the critic who will deliver us from slavery to the canon, from racist, sexist, and classist misreadings. But one can be sure that, welcome as she will be among us, the chosen critics will see her as a false messiah.

I do not think we should surrender easily. It is they and their fathers who excluded and oppressed us and our mothers, they who decided to exclude women writers from what was taught, women students from who was taught. Our historical losses at their hands are incalculable. It is not up to us to beg them to find our work interesting. It is up to them to make reparations: to establish secure women's studies departments, black studies departments, chairs of feminist literary criticism and women's history, to read the work of women and black writers, and to teach it.

After this digression upon theory I would like to return to the subject of the rest of this article. If "Lupine Criticism" is an example of a battle within a small area of literary criticism, fought among one's peers, "One Cheer for Democracy, or Talking Back to Quentin Bell" is a direct confrontation with Virginia Woolf's nephew, official biographer, and owner of her literary estate. In his essay, "Bloomsbury and the Vulgar Passions," given on a lecture tour of the United States and published in *Critical Inquiry,* Bell once again mocks Virginia Woolf's *Three Guineas* for its feminism and pacifism.[14] He minimizes her contribution to political thought by comparing it unfavorably to a pamphlet by his father, Clive Bell, as well as E. M. Forster's "Two Cheers for Democracy" and *A Passage to India.* I admire Bell's *Bloomsbury*[15] and am grateful, as are other Woolf scholars, for the painstaking work of his biography and for the publication of the letters and diaries. Because we are dependent on the estate for permission to publish, it has been difficult for Woolf scholars to take issue with his analysis without jeopardizing their careers. The year 1982 is the centenary of Virginia Woolf's birth. In the thirties she predicted that in fifty years men would allow women writers free speech. Could she have imagined this deadlock in criticism, this "separate but equal" free speech as it now exists in literary criticism, where feminist critics are excluded from discourse with male theorists?[16] She suffered

    14. Quentin Bell, "Bloomsbury and the Vulgar Passions," *Critical Inquiry* 6, no. 2 (Winter 1979): 239–56.
    15. Quentin Bell, *Bloomsbury* (London: Weidenfeld & Nicolson, 1968).
    16. Recent contributions to feminist critical theory include: Myra Jehlen, "Archimedes and the Paradox of Feminist Criticism," *Signs: Journal of Women in Culture and Society* 6, no. 4 (Summer 1981): 575–601; and Nina Baym, "Melodramas of Beset Manhood: How Theories of American Fiction Exclude Women Authors," *American Quarterly* 33, no. 2 (Summer 1981): 123–39. In press is a special issue of *Critical Inquiry* (8, no. 2 [Winter 1981]) edited by Elizabeth Abel called "Writing and Sexual Difference," with essays by Elaine Showalter, Mary Jacobus, Margaret Homans, Susan Gubar, Nancy Vickers, Nina Auerbach, Annette Kolodny, Froma Zeitlin, Judith Gardiner, Catharine Stimpson, and Gayatri Spivak.

from these same exclusions herself, was chastized for her feminism all
her life, and continues to be chastized after her death. She died, I believe, in an ethical torment over her pacifism in a terrible war. It seems
only natural to take up her weapons. Our first target is the shed where
the power tools of literary theory have been kept. There is no doubt that
in the hands of feminist critics they will transform the study of literature.

II. Lupine Criticism

It is amusing to imagine what Virginia Woolf would think of an
MLA meeting. You know how she despised lectures and did not believe
that literature should be taught to middle-class students. She herself only
lectured to women and working-class people. She gave lectures to
women students and fellow professional women, to the Workers' Education League and the Working Women's Cooperative Guild. She refused
offers to lecture to men, to men's colleges and universities, and to male-
dominated institutions. While she was in Italy, studying Mussolini's fascism first hand, she refused, with a simple and defiant No, her government's offer of a Companion of Honour, wanting no companionship
whatever with the concerns of the British Empire. She refused a degree
from Manchester University, and, much to the horror of the editor of
her letters, Nigel Nicolson, she even refused quite proudly to give the
prestigious Clark Lectures at Cambridge, despite the fact that she was
the first woman invited to do so. Her editor feels that this act "only
weakened the cause of women in general" and confesses he cannot
understand why the only prize she ever accepted was a woman's prize,
the Femina Vie Heureuse prize for *To the Lighthouse*.[17]

We all know why she did it, and why, if she were here today, she
would accept the Florence Howe Award for her essays on women writers
and refuse any other honors. Lecturing, she wrote, "incites the most
debased of human passions—vanity, ostentation, self-assertion, and the
desire to convert." We confess all these sins and more; feminist literary
criticism seems to demand them at the moment just for defense. "Why
not create a new form of society founded on poverty and equality?"
Woolf asked. "Why not bring together people so that they can talk,
without mounting platforms or reading papers or wearing expensive
clothes or eating expensive food? Would not such a society be worth,

17. Nigel Nicolson's introduction to *The Letters of Virginia Woolf, 1932–1935*, vol. 5, *The
Sickle Side of the Moon*, ed. Nigel Nicolson and Joanne Trautmann (New York: Harcourt
Brace Jovanovich, 1979), pp. xi–xvii, is a sustained attack on Woolf's politics and
feminism. Carolyn Heilbrun's feminist review of this volume appears in *Virginia Woolf
Miscellany* 14 (Spring 1980): 4; and Nicolson's reply in *Virginia Woolf Miscellany* 16 (Spring
1981): 5. See also Jane Marcus, review of *Sickle Side of the Moon*, ed. Nicolson and Trautmann, *Chicago Tribune Book World* (November 4, 1979).

even as a form of education, all the papers on art and literature that have ever been read since the world began? Why not abolish prigs and prophets? Why not invent human intercourse?"[18]

In the last decade, the Commission on Women and the Women's Caucus of the MLA, with Florence Howe at the helm, and also a vast community of women scholars working together have undertaken the enormous task of revaluating women's work, uncovering forgotten lives and books, reprinting our own literature. Virginia Woolf is our model for this task. We—I say ostentatiously, self-assertively, with some vanity, and a veritable passion to make converts—in this very room are inventing "human intercourse."

Writers like Tillie Olsen and Adrienne Rich have inspired us, not only with their creative work but with their theoretical and historical essays. They continue the work in which Virginia Woolf as a feminist literary critic was engaged, a historical process she called "thinking back through our mothers."[19] Woolf would take a particular delight in what Mary Helen Washington and her colleagues are doing on black and Third World women writers. She would applaud with Suzanne Juhasz the women poets who tell the truth. Loving Katherine Mansfield as she did, and Elizabeth Robins, the forgotten feminist who influenced both Mansfield and Woolf herself, she would rub her hands with glee that Sydney Kaplan and her feminist colleagues are delivering Mansfield's ghost from the hands of the lugubrious Middleton Murry.

We in a new generation of feminist Virginia Woolf criticism have also had the advantage of collective and collaborative work, and we have sustained each other in many trials. Whenever two or three of us are gathered together sharing notes on manuscripts and letters, we feel what Virginia Woolf described in her meetings with her Greek teacher, Janet Case, and with Margaret Llewelyn Davies of the Working Women's Cooperative Guild; we are at "the heart of the women's republic."[20] It is an open secret that Virginia Woolf's literary estate is hostile to feminist critics. There are two taboo subjects: on one hand her lesbian identity, woman-centered life, and feminist work, and on the other, her socialist politics. If you wish to discover the truth regarding these issues, you will have a long, hard struggle. In that struggle you will find the sisterhood of feminist Woolf scholarship.

It all began with Ellen Hawkes's review, "The Virgin in the Bell Biography." She was duly denounced from the pulpit of the English Institute but, despite excommunication, has had a great influence. A

18. Virginia Woolf, "Why?" in *The Death of the Moth* (New York: Harcourt Brace, 1942), pp. 227–34.

19. Woolf, *A Room of One's Own*, p. 79. See also Jane Marcus, ed., *New Feminist Essays on Virginia Woolf* (London: Macmillan, 1981), pp. 1–30.

20. Virginia Woolf, *The Diary of Virginia Woolf*, ed. Anne Olivier Bell (New York: Harcourt Brace Jovanovich, 1977), p. 146.

group of feminist Woolf scholars protested her expulsion and organized a conference at Santa Cruz. Here Madeline Moore brought together many feminists—Sara Ruddick, Tillie Olsen, and Florence Howe among them. Madeline Moore published many of the papers in a 1977 special issue of *Women's Studies*.[21]

The MLA Woolf Seminar has been notably feminist in its papers during the last five years. At one meeting, for example, Margaret Comstock chaired a session on *Between the Acts* with papers by Judy Little and Diane Gillespie, later published in *Women and Literature*. Feminists, including Kate Ellis and Ellen Hawkes, spoke at the Princeton Woolf Conference organized by Joanna Lipking. And at the Bucknell Woolf Conference in 1977, Carolyn Heilbrun, Eve Merriam, and the late Ellen Moers spoke. (Here let me note that Ellen Moers's death diminishes us all; *Literary Women* has provided us with tools and structures for building feminist literary criticism.) These conferences and seminars cemented scholarly friendships and set new directions for Woolf studies.

The publication of Woolf's letters and diaries has greatly facilitated our work. Yet the manuscripts of the novels retain the utmost fascination. We organized a special issue of the *Bulletin of the New York Public Library* with papers from the MLA Woolf Seminar on *The Years*, including Grace Radin's rendering of "two enormous chunks" of material removed from the galleys just before it went to press, Sallie Sears's essay on sexuality, and Margaret Comstock's "The Loudspeaker and the Human Voice" on the politics of the novel. Woolf's "Professions for Women" turned out to be three times the length and feminist strength of the version published by Leonard Woolf in *Collected Essays*. It has been reprinted by the New York Public Library in Mitchell Leaska's edition of *The Pargiters*.[22]

The original speech "Professions for Women" was delivered in January 1931, to a group of professional women. Preceding Virginia Woolf on the platform was Dame Ethel Smyth, the great English lesbian-feminist composer. Virginia Woolf's pacifism always receded when she spoke as a feminist. Her violent feelings came pouring out in her description of Ethel Smyth: "She is of the race of the pioneers: She is among the ice-breakers, the window-smashers, the indomitable and irresistible armoured tanks who climbed the rough ground; went first; drew the enemy's fire and left a pathway for those who came after her. I never knew whether to be angry that such heroic pertinacity was called for, or glad that it had the chance of showing itself."[23]

21. Ellen Hawkes, "The Virgin in the Bell Biography," *Twentieth Century Literature* 20 (April 1974): 96–113; and Hawkes, "A Form of One's Own," *Mosaic* 8, no. 1 (1974): 77–90.

22. See *Bulletin of the New York Public Library* 80, no. 2 (Winter 1977); and Virginia Woolf, *The Pargiters*, ed. Mitchell Leaska (New York: New York Public Library and Readex Books, 1977).

23. Woolf, *The Pargiters*, p. xxciii.

In our field the ice breakers and window smashers have been Tillie Olsen, Adrienne Rich, Florence Howe, Ellen Moers, Carolyn Heilbrun. Our work has been made possible because they drew the enemy's fire. Like Virginia Woolf, we acknowledge our debt, half in anger that such belligerence is necessary, half in gladness that they have fought so well. For the last five years much feminist work on Woolf has appeared in *Virginia Woolf Miscellany*, edited, among others, by the indomitable J. J. Wilson at Sonoma State University. The Fall 1979 issue of *Twentieth Century Literature* contains splendid and important work by feminists: Ellen Hawkes's edition of Woolf's early utopian feminist fantasy, "Friendships Gallery," written for Violet Dickinson; Susan Squier and Louise De Salvo's edition of an early forty-four-page unpublished story about a woman historian; Madeline Moore's edition of the Orlando manuscripts; and Brenda Silver's edition of two very important late manuscripts called "Anon" and "The Reader."[24]

Doubtless I have left out much new work, but this list itself is an impressive example of the comradeship and collective effort of feminist Woolf scholarship. You will note that all this work is American. We have escaped the domination of the Leavises' point of view that still prevents many British readers from seeing Woolf as anything but "elitist" and "mad." The exception is Michele Barrett's edition of Woolf's *Women and Writing*.[25]

Quentin Bell has announced that the "bottom of the barrel" has been reached in Woolf manuscripts, but we are not finished yet. There is a great deal of literary housekeeping to be done. Virginia Woolf wrote to Ethel Smyth about her own struggle for recognition as a composer, "Somehow the big apples come to the top of the basket. But of course I realize that the musicians' apple lies longest at the bottom and has the hardest struggle to rise."[26] I find these "Granny Smyth" apples to be tart and tasty indeed and am editing Dame Ethel's letters to Virginia Woolf.

What feminist scholars have found in the apples at the bottom of the barrel is a taste of the two taboo subjects, Woolf's socialist politics and her love of women. When the fifth volume of her letters was published, reviewers rushed to reassure readers that Woolf did not really mean it when she wrote to Ethel Smyth, "Women alone stir my imagination."[27] Nigel Nicolson insisted to me that Woolf was only joking. While Quentin Bell is ready to admit privately that *Letter to a Young Poet* and "Thoughts on Peace in an Air Raid" are "more Marxist than the Marx-

24. See *Twentieth Century Literature* 25, no. 3–4 (Fall–Winter 1979). The collection was conceived and edited by Lucio Ruotolo at Stanford University.

25. Virginia Woolf, *Women and Writing*, ed. Michele Barrett (London: Women's Press, 1979), also published in 1980 by Harcourt Brace Jovanovich.

26. Virginia Woolf, *The Letters of Virginia Woolf, 1929–1931*, vol. 4, *A Reflection of the Other Person*, ed. Nigel Nicolson and Joanne Trautmann (New York: Harcourt Brace Jovanovich, 1978), p. 348.

27. Ibid., p. 203.

ists," his public lecture, "Bloomsbury and the Vulgar Passions," dismisses *Three Guineas* as silly and unimportant.[28]

Quentin Bell is not amused by feminist criticism of Virginia Woolf. He has invented a name for us. He calls us "lupines." There is a particular variety of flower, the lupine, that grows in the American West, covering the rocky slopes of the Big Horns, the Tetons, and the Wind River Mountains in July. It is electric blue, startlingly erect, and extremely hardy. Perhaps we feminist Woolf critics can survive the patronizing label of British cultural imperialism by appropriating it ourselves. During the struggle for woman suffrage, a patronizing journalist called the most militant of the activists "Suffragettes." After a few weeks of smoldering rage at the insult, the women simply pinned that badge to their own breasts and wore it proudly.

In *Three Guineas* Virginia Woolf suggests that women might wear a tuft of horsehair on the left shoulder to indicate motherhood, as a response to male military decorations. Lupine criticism is obviously here to stay. We might as well accept the label and wear it proudly. If the proliferation and hardiness of the flower is any indication of our tenacity, we have a great future. We have not yet ceased to be "prigs and prophetesses," but we have made a start at inventing human intercourse.

Yet achievement and even struggle in common do not come easily. The first of our two volumes of feminist criticism on Virginia Woolf was finished in 1977, but we were unable to find an American publisher. The essays have circulated among feminist critics and have been cited in books and articles in print for years. Because University of Nebraska Press bought the book from Macmillan/London, the price in America is very high.[29] These incontrovertible economic facts are not lost on young scholars. Virginia Woolf founded the Hogarth Press in order to publish

28. Bell, "Bloomsbury and the Vulgar Passions," pp. 239–56.

29. See *New Feminist Essays on Virginia Woolf,* ed. Jane Marcus (Lincoln: University of Nebraska Press, 1981). The second volume of *New Feminist Essays on Virginia Woolf,* ed. Jane Marcus (Lincoln: University of Nebraska Press, in press) will contain Martine Stemerick's "The Madonna's Clay Feet," part of a University of Texas Ph.D. dissertation based on unpublished manuscripts, including essays by Julia Stephen. Alice Fox, an Elizabethan scholar, has written an essay called "Virginia Liked Elizabeth." Also included are Beverly Schlack's "Fathers in General: The Patriarchy in Virginia Woolf's Fiction"; "1897: Virginia Woolf at Fifteen" by Louise DeSalvo; Evelyn Haller's "Isis Unveiled: Virginia Woolf's Use of Egyptian Myth"; and "Political Aesthetics: The Feminine Realism of Virginia Woolf and Dorothy Richardson" by Diane Gillespie. Ann McLaughlin contributes "An Uneasy Sisterhood: Woolf and Katherine Mansfield." Emily Jensen's lesbian reading of "Mrs. Dalloway's Respectable Suicide" is included, as is Louise DeSalvo's "Tinder and Flint," a study of Vita Sackville-West and Woolf, and Susan Squier's "A Track of One's Own." Sally Sears adds a close reading of *Between the Acts* in "Theater of War"; and the collection contains Carolyn Heilbrun's "Virginia Woolf in Her Fifties." Political scientist Naomi Black contributes "Virginia Woolf and the Women's Movement"; and I have reprinted "No More Horses: Virginia Woolf on Art and Propaganda" (from *Women's Studies* 4, no. 2–3 [1977]: 265–90) to give a perspective on Woolf's politics.

what she wanted to write. Feminists often feel forced by economic realities to choose other methodologies and structures that will ensure
sympathetic readings from university presses. We may be as middle class
as Virginia Woolf, but few of us have the economic security her aunt
Caroline Emelia Stephen's legacy gave her. The samizdat circulation
among networks of feminist critics works only in a system where repression is equal. If all the members are unemployed or underemployed,
unpublished or unrecognized, sisterhood flourishes, and sharing is a
source of strength. When we all compete for one job or when one lupine
grows bigger and bluer than her sisters with unnatural fertilizers from
the establishment, the ranks thin out. Times are hard and getting
harder.

Being an outsider is a lonely life. Virginia Woolf proposed a *Society
of Outsiders.* Lupine criticism, I think, will only flourish in the collective
and in the wild. In captivity, in the rarefied hothouse atmosphere of
current academic criticism, it may wither and die. From my last climbing
trip in the Wind Rivers, I brought back some wild lupines and carefully
transplanted them. My mother warned me that Chicago clay would stifle
them, and she was right. Garden lupines are very pretty, and doubtless
our colleagues would find us less offensive in the cultivated state. The
British label was meant as an insult, and it might be an adjective as well as
a noun. If we are going to wear it, sister lupines, let us wear it with wild
Woolfian abandon.

III. One Cheer for Democracy, or Talking Back to Quentin Bell

Quentin Bell, largely responsible for making the Bloomsbury bed,
now refuses to lie in it. In his book on Bloomsbury and his biography of
his aunt, he provided readers with the materials for what he now calls
"false generalizations."[30] "Bloomsbury and the Vulgar Passions" is a
deliberately mystifying title that does not clarify the politics of the period
but muddies the waters even more.

Virginia Woolf's clear understanding of the role of the intellectual
in relation to the revolution is evident in her title *Three Guineas.*[31] She
wants women and the working classes to unite against the war, but she
does not presume to speak for any but her own class and sex. In "The
Leaning Tower" and *Letter to a Young Poet*[32] she insists on organization in
one's own class and has faith that the working class can produce its own

30. Bell, *Bloomsbury* (n. 15 above); Quentin Bell, *Virginia Woolf,* 2 vols. (London:
Hogarth Press, 1972); and Bell, "Bloomsbury and the Vulgar Passions" (n. 14 above).
31. Virginia Woolf, *Three Guineas* (London: Hogarth Press, 1939).
32. Virginia Woolf, "The Leaning Tower," in *The Moment and Other Essays* (New York:
Harcourt Brace, 1948), pp. 128–54; and Woolf, *Letter to a Young Poet,* Letters Series no. 8
(London: Hogarth Press, 1939).

leaders. Her title, a deliberate play on Brecht's *Threepenny Opera,* exposes the economic origins of the social problems she discusses. Neither pence nor pounds can accurately describe the contributions expected of a woman in her position. Over the years American academics have shared her frustrating experience, signing petitions and writing checks to help in the civil rights movement and the movement to stop the war in Vietnam. Like her, they sought to relieve social ills by imagining free universities like the one Woolf describes in *Three Guineas.*[33] Current feminism grew out of women's effort to find a place in movements for social change which assumed that race and class and the present war were more important than sex grievances. Woolf was the first to identify the enemy openly as "patriarchy."

Why does Bell choose Keynes's elitist phrase for an essay calculated to reduce the political power of *Three Guineas* to an entirely personal cause? If *Three Guineas* is merely an aunt's elegy for a dead nephew, as Bell argues, is not such ferocious grief a "vulgar passion" too? The phrase is not Bell's; it is the phrase of a man he admires, Maynard Keynes. It is a Victorian upper-class phrase. Few members of Margaret Llewelyn Davies's Working Women's Cooperative Guild would know what it means.[34] The phrase itself is heavy with ambiguity, and it is used by Bell in both positive and negative ways. Curiously, it works to the disadvantage of Virginia Woolf either way. It is men like his father, Keynes, and Forster who remain intellectually above the vulgar passions when Bell considers it correct to be so, and men again who are responsive to the vulgar passions of a nation at war, when this is the attitude he admires.

There is a famous point in Bell's biography of Virginia Woolf when the reader, swept along by the swift flow of prose, brisk and cool like an English trout stream in spring, is suddenly thrown into white water. Bell bursts into capital letters. The reader is on the rocks. "But were we then to scuttle like frightened spinsters before the Fascist thugs? She belonged, inescapably, to the Victorian world of Empire, Class and Privilege. Her gift was for the pursuit of shadows, for the ghostly whispers of the mind and for Pythian incomprehensibility, when what was needed was the swift and lucid phrase that could reach the ears of unemployed working men or Trades Union officials."[35] To the generation of thirties intellectuals (John Lehmann was one, and Woolf wrote her scathing *Letter to a Young Poet* to him), Virginia Woolf was "a fragile

33. See Adrienne Rich, "Toward a Woman-centered University," in *On Lies, Secrets, and Silence: Selected Prose, 1966–1978* (New York: W. W. Norton & Co., 1979), pp. 125–55.

34. Virginia Woolf was a life-long member and shared its socialist, feminist, and pacifist politics. See Marcus, "No More Horses: Virginia Woolf on Art and Propaganda"; and Black, in Marcus, ed., *New Feminist Essays on Virginia Woolf,* vol. 2.

35. Bell, *Virginia Woolf,* 2:186.

middle-aged poetess, a sexless Sappho," and "a distressed gentlewoman caught in a tempest." Bell recalls his "despair" as he urged the Rodmell Labour Party to adopt a resolution supporting the United Front, when Virginia, who was the local party secretary, turned the debate from the question. He does not call her a skilled politician for manipulating the meeting, on pacifist principle, away from patriotic militarism. He says, indeed, that she was closer to the feeling of "the masses" than he was. "I wanted to talk politics, the masses wanted to talk about the vicar's wife."[36]

But, I venture, it was precisely her "swift and lucid phrases" that annoyed him, for she spoke to the Workers' Education Association, and she wrote in the *Daily Worker* of a different kind of united front: while the capitalist, imperialist patriarchs were waging their wars, workers should join women in an assault on culture. "Trespass," she urged them, on the sacred precincts of home front institutions while the warriors are in the field. She was arguing for total subversion of the world of empire, class, and privilege. And among the shadows she pursued most vigorously were upper-class, young, male "missionaries to the masses." Take off those "pro-proletarian spectacles," she urged the generation of Auden, Spender, Lehmann, and Bell; if you really want to make the revolution, you must empty your pockets of your fathers' money, you must convert the men of your *own* class.[37] Virginia Woolf took as hard a line on the role of the intellectual in the class struggle as did Lenin or Trotsky. Its ethical imperative is even improved by the addition of feminism to the socialist-pacifist position. Quentin Bell's objections are honest ones, and there were many who agreed with him. He is infuriated by her feminism and enraged by her pacifism, and he fights back like a man.

It is dirty fighting to be sure. She is dead and cannot respond like the "Lapland Witch" Gerald Brenan says she was.[38] E. M. Forster was a dirty fighter, too. He said in his Rede Lecture that Woolf was not a great writer because "she had no great cause at heart."[39] But we have already put *A Room of One's Own* and *Three Guineas* on the shelf next to Milton, Wollstonecraft, Mill, and Swift, and where is Forster's "Two Cheers for Democracy"? It is an embarrassment. Forster said he would give up his country before he would give up his friend. But that was not at issue. Nobody was asking him to give up his friend. And *Three Guineas* has some antifascist feminist thuggery of its own. One thing it does not have is "Pythian incomprehensibility." It is a Cassandracry in the crowd of thirties political pamphlets. No spinsterish whispers either. The

36. Ibid.

37. Woolf, "The Leaning Tower," p. 154.

38. Gerald Brenan, *Personal Record, 1920–1972* (London: Jonathan Cape, 1974).

39. E. M. Forster, *Virginia Woolf, the Rede Lecture, 1941* (Cambridge: Cambridge University Press, 1942).

loudspeaker blares for all to hear, a withering revolutionary feminist analysis of fascism. The Hitlers and Mussolinis have no monopoly on fascism, she says. The origin of fascism is the patriarchal family. And "the daughters of educated men" had better root it out of the hearts of their English brothers before the latter rush off to fight foreign fascism.

Men on the left were horrified. But the argument that elements of fascism lurk behind patriarchal power struggles is still too radical for people. It was the subject of Lina Wertmuller's shattering feminist film *Seven Beauties,* and all the Bettelheims came out with their battering rams and big guns to remind us of how long it will be before men will "tolerate free speech in women."[40]

During the period covered by the fifth volume of Woolf's letters (1932–35), the political and personal insults that she had received from men were creating the deep sense of grievance that finally burst out in *The Years* and *Three Guineas.*[41] *The Years* itself is the most brilliant indictment in modern literature of the world of empire, class, and privilege, of capitalism and patriarchy. Structurally it is exciting, too, in its portrait of the artist as charwoman of the world. *The Years* was to have been a new form of her opera for the oppressed, alternating chapters of fact and fiction. The documentaries have been reprinted in *The Pargiters.*[42] It is too bad that Leonard talked her out of it. He was fearful of mixing fact and fiction. Her fearlessness went into the writing of both books. But she was justifiably terrified of what the male critics would say.

It is doubtful that she would have predicted her nephew's continuing hostility to *Three Guineas.* I believe there is a direct line in English history from the Clapham Sect to Bloomsbury. The anonymous reviewer in the *Times Literary Supplement* who called Virginia Woolf "the best pamphleteer in England"[43] was (consciously or unconsciously) echoing the very words applied to the antislavery pamphlets of her great-grandfather, James Stephen. That Virginia Woolf should have added feminism to the Stephen family causes is the most natural development in the world.[44] Her pacifism was not a "temporary" phenomenon but a firmly held principle of a tripartite political philosophy. It was largely derived from the important and neglected influence of her Quaker aunt, Caroline Emelia Stephen, described by Quaker historians as almost single-handedly responsible for the revival of the practically moribund

40. See Bruno Bettelheim, "Surviving," in *Surviving and Other Essays* (New York: Alfred A. Knopf, Inc., 1979), pp. 275–314, see also pp. 20–23.

41. See Nicolson's attack on Woolf's politics in the introduction to *The Letters of Virginia Woolf, 1932–1935,* vol. 5, *The Sickle Side of the Moon* (n. 17 above), pp. xi–xvii.

42. Woolf, *The Pargiters.*

43. Virginia Woolf, *A Writer's Diary* (New York: Harcourt Brace Jovanovich, 1953), p. 234.

44. The Stephen family background is discussed in Stemerick (n. 29 above); and in Jane Marcus, "Liberty, Sorority, Misogyny," *Proceedings of the English Institute* (in press).

English Society of Friends in the late nineteenth century.[45] It is true, as Bell says, that she modified her position at the last, actually wanted to join the fire wardens, and appears to have been willing to defend her beleagured country in "Thoughts on Peace in an Air Raid." I have described these changes of attitude elsewhere.[46]

Bell's essay is written in response to yet another season of bad press for Bloomsbury. Virginia Woolf wrote to him during an earlier one, stating "Bloomsbury is having a very bad press at the moment; so please take up your hammer and chisel and sculpt a great flaming Goddess to put them all to shame."[47] There was certainly a family precedent. When Fitzjames Stephen was hounded out of office for prejudicing the jury in the Maybrick case after a lifetime of legal bullying and misogyny as the "Giant Grim," Leslie Stephen took up his hammer and chisel and sculpted a genial friendly giant in his biography of his brother. Virginia Stephen herself had participated in Maitland's biography of her father, largely to offset the influence of her aunt Caroline, who had mountains of evidence that the great man had a terrible temper.[48]

Did Bell perhaps agree with Mirsky's dismissal of Bloomsbury and Virginia Woolf in *The Intelligentsia of Great Britain*,[49] the "bad press" referred to? He took up his hammer and chisel but produced no "great flaming Goddess" but a "sexless Sappho," a "distressed gentlewoman caught in a tempest." I suspect in the end we will all come to see Bell's "sexless Sappho" as a true portrait of the artist who equated chastity with creativity. But she will not do as a portrait of the socialist/pacificist/feminist, the "outsider" who "spat out" *Three Guineas* as an original contribution to an analysis of the origins of fascism in the patriarchal family. If she began the book as an elegy for Bell's brother, Julian, there is nothing unusual to her method in that, for all her work is elegy. Even *A Room of One's Own* is a female elegy written in a college courtyard for the female writers of the past. The narrator has been denied access to the library which contains the manuscripts of the two great male elegies in poetry and prose, Milton's *Lycidas* and Thackeray's *Henry Esmond,* and so

45. Catherine Smith discusses Caroline Stephen in her study of English women mystics (Bucknell University, English Department, in preparation). See also Smith, "Jane Lead: The Feminist Mind and Art of a Seventeenth Century Protestant Mystic," in *Women of Spirit: Female Leadership in the Jewish and Christian Tradition,* ed. Rosemary Reuther and Eleanor McLaughlin (New York: Simon & Schuster, 1979), pp. 184–85. Robert Tod is preparing a biography for the English Society of Friends' Quaker biography series (Haverford College, in preparation); and see also Jane Marcus, "A Nun and Her Niece: Virginia Woolf, Caroline Stephen, and the Cloistered Imagination" (paper presented at the Virginia Woolf Society meeting at the Modern Language Association, New York, 1981).

46. Bell, "Bloomsbury." See also Marcus, "No More Horses: Virginia Woolf on Art and Propaganda" (n. 29 above).

47. Woolf, *Letters,* 5:383.

48. Woolf, *Letters,* 1:148, 151–52, 165, 180.

49. Dmitry Mirsky, *The Intelligentsia of Great Britain,* trans. Alec Brown (New York: Conici, Friede, 1935).

she is driven to invent the female elegy. If grieving for Julian Bell's death in Spain forced her to the conclusion that she must speak directly to women of her class, to the mothers, sisters, and wives of the war makers, the public effect of a private sorrow is impressive.

But *Three Guineas* is a stubbornly feminist elegy, singing the sorrows of women under patriarchy, relentlessly repeating itself as history has repeated itself, trying to establish a feminist ethics. To my mind, and to the minds of other feminists, *Three Guineas* is the pure historical product of the Clapham Sect reform movement. It owes much to the "rational mysticism" of Caroline Emelia Stephen's *The Light Arising*.[50] But if the historian can free himself of sex bias, he will see *Three Guineas* in relation to Bertrand Russell's philosophy and to G. E. Moore's *Principia Ethica*. In fact it might be seen as "Principia Ethica Femina," volume 1.[51]

If Woolf later, in "Thoughts on Peace in an Air Raid," admitted woman's complicity in war and concluded that "we must compensate the man for his gun,"[52] she did not suggest how. Bell thinks she has come close to the vulgar passions (which are now positive) in this essay, and he is disposed to grant her some credit.[53] I thought so too in 1976. But I am now disposed to think that "Thoughts on Peace in an Air Raid" is just what the title suggests, a defensive position taken under extreme pressure. The militant feminism of *Three Guineas,* its equally militant pacifism, socialism, and antifascism, are "saddening" and "exasperating" to Bell. Many European and American feminist historians are studying the forms of Italian and German fascism and their relation to the patriarchal family, marriage, and the treatment of women and children, and they have found Woolf's pamphlet a strikingly original and eerily correct analysis.[54] I believe Bell labors under the misconception that feminism is not political—a major mistake—as well as under minor misconceptions that pacifism in World War II was not a respectable political stance (it was certainly not popular) and that Virginia Woolf could not have been much of a socialist because she did not work in Labour Party Committees or associate with the working classes. Even when Bell imagines a committee meeting he sees only Mr. A, Mr. B, Mr. C, Mr. D, and the chairman. I seem to recall that the committee meeting which caused his admirable prose style to flood the gates was chaired by his aunt, Mrs. W., and she prevented him from passing his resolution. It is a long time to hold a grudge.

50. Caroline Emelia Stephen, *The Light Arising: Thoughts on the Central Radiance* (Cambridge: W. Heffer & Sons, 1908).

51. Jaakko Hintinkka's "Virginia Woolf and Our Knowledge of the External World," *Journal of Aesthetics and Art Criticism* 38, no. 1 (Fall 1979): 5–14 is relevant here.

52. Virginia Woolf, "Thoughts on Peace in an Air Raid," in *The Death of the Moth* (New York: Harcourt Brace, 1942), pp. 243–48.

53. Bell, "Bloomsbury and the Vulgar Passions."

54. See Maria-Antonietta Macciocchi's translated work, "Female Sexuality in Fascist Ideology," *Feminist Review* 1 (1979): 59–82.

It is a failure of the imagination to suppose that all pacifists were, like Clive Bell, ad hoc peaceniks for a particular war. Quakers, like Caroline Stephen and Violet Dickinson, Virginia's early mentors, were opposed to all wars.

It seems oddly un-English and more like an American pragmatist or utilitarian argument to judge the quality of a pamphlet by its contemporary effectiveness. James Stephen turned out antislavery pamphlets that failed to stop the slavers. But it was not until he had been dead many years that his son finally got an antislavery bill through Parliament. How much immediate effect did Mill's *Subjection of Women* have? Women did not get the vote until 1928, and the condition of women is still not by any means satisfactory. *Three Guineas* is still read (and this might be a better measure of "effectiveness") by those who hunger for its message, who feel as guilty as Woolf did about fighting for feminism when atrocities and wars demand one's attention. Seeking for the deepest cause of imperialist and capitalist war, she found it in male aggression. She was saddened, but urged women to stop encouraging aggression. I wish she had been more successful.

If effectiveness is the criterion of a pamphlet's success, is there any way of measuring the success of *Three Guineas* in keeping America out of the war when it was published in the *Atlantic* as "Women Must Weep or Unite against the War"? I suppose it is just as possible to imagine that her pamphlet had that power as to assert that Forster's *A Passage to India* had an immense influence in dissuading Britons from their imperialist passions.[55] I do not share Bell's enthusiasm for *A Passage to India*. It seems so pale and liberal compared to the radical antiimperialism and anticapitalism of *Mrs. Dalloway* or *The Years*. Virginia Woolf once described Mrs. Humphry Ward's novels as hanging in the lumber room of literature like the mantles of our aunts, covered with beads and bugles. Well, there is something about E. M. Forster's novels reminiscent of our unmarried uncles' silk pajamas, something elegant, but rather effete. They have not worn well. And Woolf's novels get harder and tougher year by year, ethically unyielding and morally challenging.

Any member of the Women's International League for Peace and Freedom or the Women's Cooperative Guild, as well as many left wing feminists and many socialists, would have seen Virginia Woolf's ideology as more powerful than the liberalism of Keynes or Forster. For those readers, *Three Guineas* is not forced or unsatisfactory. It was not at the time, as Bell implies, nor is it now, a political irrelevance.[56] It is hard to believe that the world is as neatly divided into hawks and doves as Bell would have us believe and that one changes feathers over every war. Some of us imagine Virginia Woolf as a great blue heron anyway, and

55. Bell, "Bloomsbury and the Vulgar Passions."
56. Ibid.

she describes herself as a misfit, an outsider. As for her ability to feel the vulgar passions, to hear the demotic voice, let him read the song of the caretaker's children in *The Years*. It is the voice of the colonial chickens come home to roost. The full measure of *Three Guineas*'s effect is yet to be weighed, for it deals with older, more universal, and more deeply rooted social ills than the Spanish fascism that prompted it. Her intent reminds me of a surrealist poem by Laura Riding:

> She opens the heads of her brothers
> And lets out the aeroplanes
> "Now," she says, "you will be able to think better."[57]

Department of English
University of Texas at Austin

57. Laura Riding, "In the Beginning," *Collected Poetry of Laura Riding* (New York: Random House, 1938), p. 358.

REVIEW ESSAY

For and About Women: The Theory and Practice of Women's Studies in the United States

Marilyn J. Boxer

In 1977, a decade after the first women's studies courses appeared across the United States, the National Women's Studies Association was founded to promote and sustain "the educational strategy of a breakthrough in consciousness and knowledge" that would "transform" individuals, institutions, relationships, and, ultimately, the whole of society.[1] Insisting that the academic is political and the cognitive is affective, the NWSA's constitution clearly reflected the influence of the women's liberation movement on women's studies. Research and teaching at all educational levels and in all academic and community settings would be not

I would like to thank Holly Smith for assistance in locating materials for this essay and Florence Howe for helpful comments on an earlier draft. My colleagues Pat Huckle, Elyce Rotella, and Bonnie Zimmerman have provided the encouragement and constructive criticism that make a Department of Women's Studies a wonderful place for an academic feminist to work.

1. This definition is taken from the preamble to the constitution of the NWSA, drafted at the Founding Convention in San Francisco, January 13–17, 1977, and published in *Women's Studies Newsletter* 5, nos. 1–2 (Winter/Spring 1977): 6–8.

only *about* but *for* all women, guided by "a vision of a world free not only from sexism, but also from racism, class-bias, ageism, heterosexual bias—from all the ideologies and institutions that have consciously or unconsciously oppressed and exploited some for the advantage of others."[2] Women's studies, then, challenged its practitioners to think beyond the boundaries of traditional sex roles, of traditional disciplines, and of established institutions. By breaking down the divisions that limit perceptions and deny opportunities, by revising pedagogical processes as well as courses and curricula, this educational reform has itself become a social movement.

Given this mission and momentum, "women's studies is everywhere" today: in more than 300 women's studies programs, in some 30,000 courses in colleges and universities, in a dozen national and international scholarly journals as well as countless newsletters, in community groups and centers, and in conferences and programs all over the world.[3] This review essay cannot attempt to cover this phenomenon completely but will survey the literature about women's studies as a field in American higher education: its history, political issues, theories, and structures. Because of the nature of women's studies itself, these categories often overlap, and some literature will be discussed more than once. My task is complicated by the limited number of available books and monographs; most writing about women's studies has appeared as articles and notes in periodical publications. This review is therefore offered as a first step toward integrating this wealth of literature.

History

Women's studies first appeared in the last half of the 1960s when women faculty in higher education, stronger in number than ever be-

2. Ibid. In a discussion of the psychology of women, Mary Brown Parlee makes a useful distinction concerning research centered on women: "Sexist research on women is of course still being done, but its creators do not identify themselves as being in the field of the psychology of women. Feminist psychologists' power to define and name their own field has evidently prevailed, and the psychology of women denotes and connotes research that is feminist in some very broad (and perhaps arguably so) sense of the term. Psychologists who do not want to be associated with this perspective no longer use the label for their work, even if their research is about women" ("Psychology and Women: Review Essay," *Signs: Journal of Women in Culture and Society* 5, no. 1 [Autumn 1979]: 121–33, esp. 121, n. 1). To a large extent this statement applies generally to women's studies, although in some cases women's studies programs must or choose to allow students credits toward women's studies degrees for any course that deals in substantial measure with women.

3. "Women's Studies Everywhere" was the title of the Second Annual Conference of the Pacific Southwest Regional Women's Studies Association held at the University of Southern California, May 19–21, 1978. A useful guide to the literature which supports research and teaching on women is Esther Stineman, *Women's Studies: A Recommended Core Bibliography* (Littleton, Colo.: Libraries, Inc., 1979).

fore, began to create new courses that would facilitate more reflection on female experience and feminist aspiration.[4] Supported and sometimes led by feminist students, staff, or community women, these innovators were often political activists who sought to understand and to confront the sexism they had experienced in movements for the liberation of other oppressed groups.[5] Their efforts at organization and course development were inspired by both the free-university movement and the civil rights movement, which provided the model of black studies courses and programs.[6] The large number of early courses on women in literature can perhaps be attributed to the relative accessibility of that field to women. At the same time, a "passion for women's history" represented "more than just a desire for a female heritage"; it was also a "search for ways in which a successful female revolution might be constructed."[7]

4. In 1966 Cathy Cade and Peggy Dobbins taught a course on women at the New Orleans Free School, as did Naomi Weisstein at the University of Chicago (Sara Evans, *Personal Politics: The Roots of Women's Liberation in the Civil Rights Movement and the New Left* [New York: Alfred A. Knopf, Inc., 1980], pp. 183, 185–86). The same year Annette Baxter taught women's history at Barnard College (Janice Law Trecker, "Women's Place Is in the Curriculum," *Saturday Review* [October 16, 1971], pp. 83–86, 92). Despite their larger absolute numbers, in some fields the proportion of women had decreased. Between the 1920s and 1960s, the percentage of Ph.D.s awarded to women in the social sciences declined, especially in economics, history, and philosophy (see Victoria Schuck, "Sexism and Scholarship: A Brief Overview of Women, Academia and the Disciplines," *Social Science Quarterly* 55, no. 3 [December 1974]: 563–85; on representation of women between 1960 and 1970, see Helen S. Astin, "Career Profiles of Women Doctorates," in *Academic Women on the Move*, ed. Alice S. Rossi and Ann Calderwood [New York: Russell Sage Foundation, 1973], pp. 139–61).

5. Beginning in 1968 and 1969, faculty women also reacted to the discrimination they experienced by forming caucuses in academic professional organizations (Kay Klotzberger, "Political Action by Academic Women," in Rossi and Calderwood, eds., pp. 359–91).

6. According to Florence Howe, the first "political" women's studies course emerged from the student movement and was taught at the Free University of Seattle in 1965 ("Feminism and Women's Studies: Survival in the Seventies," in *Report on the West Coast Women's Studies Conference*, ed. [Joan Hoff Wilson and] Women's Studies Board at California State University, Sacramento [Pittsburgh: Know, Inc., 1974], pp. 19–20). For an excellent summary of the early development of women's studies, see Florence Howe and Carol Ahlum, "Women's Studies and Social Change," in Rossi and Calderwood, eds., pp. 393–423.

7. Trecker, p. 86. Although Sheila Tobias claimed that the feminist movement began on campuses where "the intellectual content of feminist ideology was very high and the challenge to the assumptions of the behavioral sciences significant" (Sheila Tobias, ed., *Female Studies I* [Pittsburgh: Know, Inc., 1970], p. [ii]), Jo Freeman felt that the university—"the most egalitarian environment most women will ever experience"—was not the source of the movement ("Women's Liberation and Its Impact on the Campus," *Liberal Education* 57, no. 4 [1971]: 468–78). Indeed many important works by popular writers appeared on the first women's studies syllabi, whatever the course title: Simone de Beauvoir, *The Second Sex*, trans. H. M. Parshley (New York: Alfred A. Knopf, Inc., 1953); Caroline Bird, *Born Female: The High Cost of Keeping Women Down* (New York: David McKay Co., 1968); Betty Friedan, *The Feminine Mystique* (New York: W. W. Norton & Co., 1963); and Kate Millett, *Sexual Politics* (New York: Avon Books, 1971).

Among the pioneers, the quest for revolution was clear from the beginning. Women's studies was a necessary part of women's "struggle for self-determination"; its goal was "to understand the world and to change it."[8] The paraphrasing of Marx demonstrates the importance placed on radical change in the early years and the leading role played by veterans of the New Left in launching the new feminism as well as women's studies.

In mid-1970, in one of the first essays to discuss the neglect and distortion of women in university courses and curricula, Sheila Tobias called for a new program of "Female Studies" at Cornell University, justifying her stand with an analogy to black studies. Cornell's community had already witnessed the validity and vitality of this innovative approach at a conference on women in the winter of 1969 and in a multidisciplinary course on "female personality" team-taught to some 400 students in the spring of 1970.[9] At the same time, courses on women appeared at a number of universities, including a program of five at San Diego State College (now University). That autumn, *Female Studies I* was published, the first in a ten-volume series through which practitioners of the new teaching shared their syllabi, reading lists, and experiences. Compiled by Tobias and published by the feminist press Know, Inc., it featured outlines of sixteen courses taught or proposed during 1969 and 1970, as well as a ten-course curriculum from San Diego State, which in September 1970 became the first officially established integrated women's studies program in the nation.[10]

In December, Know published *Female Studies II,* an anthology of sixty-six course outlines and bibliographies collected by the Commission on the Status of Women of the Modern Language Association and edited by its chairperson, Florence Howe. With Howe's leadership the commission had begun to function as a "clearinghouse" for information in the new, mushrooming field she then designated as "feminist studies."[11]

8. Roberta Salper, "The Theory and Practice of Women's Studies," *Edcentric* 3, no. 7 (December 1971): 4–8, esp. 8.

9. Sheila Tobias, "Female Studies—an Immodest Proposal," mimeographed (Ithaca, N.Y.: Cornell University, July 20, 1970); Sheila Tobias et al., eds., *Proceedings of the Cornell Conference on Women* (Pittsburgh: Know, Inc., 1969). An analogy with black studies was also developed in Salper.

10. Tobias, ed. Programs were established early also at Portland State University (Oregon), Richmond City College (New York), Sacramento State University (California), and the University of Washington.

11. Florence G. Howe, ed., *Female Studies II* (Pittsburgh: Know, Inc., 1970). The general acceptance of the name "women's studies" rather than "feminist studies" probably represents an implicit recognition that expediency favors maintenance of a token of traditional academic "objectivity." However, it is clear that women's studies means feminist studies. The presence of male bias in allegedly objective science is a fundamental assumption of women's studies and has been documented repeatedly across a wide spectrum of scholarly fields. Although the title "feminist studies" fell out of currency in the early 1970s,

The rapid growth of women's studies reflected the widely shared perception that changing what and how women (and men) study about women could and would affect the way women live. It offered a new opportunity for students and scholars to redefine themselves and their experiences in the world. Between 1970 and 1975, 150 new women's studies programs were founded, a feat that was repeated between 1975 and 1980.[12] The number of courses grew to some 30,000, offered at most of the colleges and universities in the United States. This phenomenal expansion was documented in—as well as facilitated by—the *Female Studies* series and other publications of Know, established in Pittsburgh in 1969, and of the Feminist Press, founded by Howe and Paul Lauter in Baltimore in 1970 and moved to the State University of New York (SUNY) College at Old Westbury in 1972.[13] That year also saw the birth of three cross-disciplinary journals: *Women's Studies* and *Feminist Studies* to publish scholarly articles, and the *Women's Studies*

---

it was recently adopted for a new degree program at Stanford University; and the question of renaming was reopened by Susan Groag Bell and Mollie Schwartz Rosenhan, who object not only to the ungrammatical construction of "women's studies," but also to its implication that it means "the study of any topic whatever . . . performed by women" (Richard West, "Feminist Program at Stanford a First," *Los Angeles Times* [May 12, 1981], p. 3; Susan Groag Bell and Mollie Schwartz Rosenhan, "A Problem in Naming: Women Studies—Women's Studies?" *Signs: Journal of Women in Culture and Society* 6, no. 3 [Spring 1981]: 540–42, esp. 541). A case for "feminology" is made by Nynne Koch in "The Why, When, How and What of Feminology," in *Feminology*, ed. Ragnhild Silfwerbrand-Ten Cate et al. (Nijmegen, Netherlands: University of Nijmegen, 1975), pp. 18–20. See also Margrit Eichler in "Discussion Forum: The Future Direction of Women's Studies," *Canadian Newsletter of Research on Women* 5, no. 3 (October 1976): 10–12; and Marilyn Webb, "A Radical Perspective on Women's Studies," *Women: A Journal of Liberation* 3, no. 2 (1973): 36–37.

12. "Editorial," *Women's Studies Newsletter* 5, no. 3 (Summer 1977): 2; Florence Howe and Paul Lauter, *The Impact of Women's Studies on the Campus and the Disciplines*, Women's Studies Monograph Series (Washington, D.C.: National Institute of Education, 1980), p. 4. The latest count is 330.

13. The rest of the series includes Florence Howe and Carol Ahlum, eds., *Female Studies III* (Pittsburgh: Know, Inc., 1971); Elaine Showalter and Carol Ohmann, eds., *Female Studies IV* (Pittsburgh: Know, Inc., 1971); Rae Lee Siporin, ed., *Female Studies V* (Pittsburgh: Know, Inc., 1972); Nancy Hoffman, Cynthia Secor, and Adrian Tinsley, eds., *Female Studies VI: Closer to the Ground—Women's Classes, Criticisms, Programs 1972* (Old Westbury, N.Y.: Feminist Press, 1972); Deborah S. Rosenfelt, ed., *Female Studies VII: Going Strong—New Courses, New Programs* (Old Westbury, N.Y.: Feminist Press, 1973); Sarah Slavin Schramm, ed., *Female Studies VIII: Do-It-Yourself Women's Studies* (Pittsburgh: Know, Inc., 1975); Sidonie Cassirer, ed., *Female Studies IX: Teaching about Women in the Foreign Languages—French, Spanish, German, and Russian* (Pittsburgh: Know, Inc., 1976); Deborah S. Rosenfelt, ed., *Female Studies X: Learning to Speak—Student Work* (Old Westbury, N.Y.: Feminist Press, 1976). See also Carol Ahlum and Florence Howe, *The New Guide to Current Female Studies* (Pittsburgh, Know, Inc., 1971), and *The Guide to Current Female Studies II* (Old Westbury, N.Y.: Feminist Press, 1972); Tamar Berkowitz, Jean Mangi, and Jane Williamson, eds., *Who's Who and Where in Women's Studies* (Old Westbury, N.Y.: Feminist Press, 1974); and Betty E. Chmaj and Judith A. Gustafson, *Myth and Beyond: American Women and American Studies* (Pittsburgh: Know, Inc., 1972).

Newsletter to serve as a forum for the women's studies movement in the community as well as in schools at all levels.[14] Florence Howe and Carol Ahlum described this abundance as "an intellectual feast long denied," a "classical instance of a movement without unified organization or direction" whose spread followed the geography of the new women's movement.[15] Its roots, however, lay deep in the history of American feminism and the education of American women.

Introducing a symposium on "masculine blinders in the social sciences," Victoria Schuck perceived three "rounds" in the history of the women's movement, of which only the third and present posed a challenge to the social sciences. Contemporary feminism, through women's studies, "aimed at destroying the sexual stereotypes bequeathed by nineteenth-century male academics."[16] To Howe, women's studies represented a third phase in American women's struggle for education. First, in the early and mid-nineteenth century, proponents of improving female education accepted cultural assumptions about women's nature and demanded a higher education appropriate to woman's role as a moral teacher. Next, in the late nineteenth century, they began to stress the identity of male and female intellectual capacities and to call for access to the standard courses of studies that M. Carey Thomas of Bryn Mawr College labeled the "men's curriculum." Only in the current third phase did they challenge the male hegemony over the content of college courses and the substance of knowledge itself.[17]

14. *Women's Studies'* editor Wendy Martin explained in the inaugural issue her premise that "careful and disciplined research, illuminated by a feminist perspective by both women and men, can contribute to effective social change" (*Women's Studies: An Interdisciplinary Journal* 1, no. 1 [1972]: 2). *Feminist Studies* was founded to "encourage analytic response to feminist issues and analyses that open new areas of feminist research and critique" (*Feminist Studies* 1, no. 1 [1972], inside front cover). In addition to reporting events and promoting dialogue, the *Women's Studies Newsletter* has played an important role in raising critical issues and in suggesting solutions to common problems. In 1977, the *Newsletter* was chosen as the official organ of the NWSA; in spring 1981 it became the *Women's Studies Quarterly*, still published by the Feminist Press.

15. Howe and Ahlum, "Women's Studies and Social Change" (n. 4 above), pp. 413–14.

16. While "Round 1" from Seneca Falls to the Civil War challenged widely accepted images of femininity, "Round 2" from the Civil War to 1920 attempted no "social redefinition" of female identity, so that the new disciplines that arose in the late nineteenth century could develop and sustain a view of women derived from "moral philosophy" (Schuck [n. 4 above], p. 563).

17. Howe has developed this scheme in several essays. See "Feminism and the Education of Women," in *Frontiers of Knowledge*, ed. Judith Stiehm (Los Angeles: University of Southern California Press, 1976), pp. 79–93; "Three Missions of Higher Education for Women: Vocation, Freedom, Knowledge," *Liberal Education* 66, no. 3 (Fall 1980): 285–97; "Myths of Coeducation" (lecture delivered November 2, 1978), and "Women's Studies and Women's Work" (lecture delivered September 26, 1979), both available from Wellesley College Center for Research on Women, Wellesley, Mass. 02181.

But in its early years, women's studies remained essentially a centerless, leaderless movement, marked by diversity in aim, content, and style. As the number of courses and programs multiplied, duly noted in the national press, newcomers could begin to draw on the reflections of the pioneers who, conscious of the historical importance of women's studies and committed to the cooperative principle, continued to publish not only syllabi and reading lists but detailed accounts of their experiences, bad along with the good.[18] Essays by these early practitioners—Florence Howe, Carol Ahlum, Catharine R. Stimpson, Sheila Tobias—all raised questions without easy answers about the tensions between academic and political goals of classroom teaching, the responsibility of women's studies to the women's movement, and the implications of organizational structure and program governance for impact on the university.[19]

The double purpose of women's studies—to expose and redress the oppression of women—was reflected in widespread attempts to restructure the classroom experience of students and faculty. Circular arrangement of chairs, periodic small-group sessions, use of first names for instructors as well as students, assignments that required journal keeping, "reflection papers," cooperative projects, and collective modes of teaching with student participation all sought to transfer to women's studies the contemporary feminist criticism of authority and the validation of every woman's experience. These techniques borrowed from the women's movement also were designed to combat the institutional hierarchy and professional exclusiveness that had been used to shut out women.[20] Indeed, collectivity in teaching and in program governance

18. See "Women's Studies," *Newsweek* (October 26, 1970), p. 61; Trecker (n. 4 above); and Cheryl Fields, "Women's Studies Gain: 2,000 Courses Offered This Year," *Chronicle of Higher Education* (December 17, 1973), p. 6. For a summary of reasons for and against establishment of a women's studies program by Penn Women's Studies Planners, see *1972 Summer Project Report: A Descriptive Analysis of a National Survey* (Philadelphia: New Morning Press, 1972).

19. Howe and Ahlum examined the origins of women's studies, its relationship to educational reform and to women's education, its basic assumptions and goals, and its role as a feminist movement for change ("Women's Studies and Social Change" [n. 6 above], pp. 393–423). In "The New Feminism and Women's Studies," Stimpson analyzed her reasons for teaching a women's studies course, stressing the multicausality of social, educational, and political circumstances that favored the development of women's studies and the resulting diversity of aims, styles, and goals the movement encompassed (*Change* 5 [September 1973]: 43–48). Tobias reviewed her experiences teaching women's studies at three universities and shared her expectations for its expansion ("Women's Studies: Its Origins, Organization, and Prospects," in *The Higher Education of Women*, ed. Helen Astin [New York: Holt, Rinehart, & Winston, 1978], pp. 80–94, also in *Women's Studies International Quarterly* 1, no. 1 [1978]: 85–97).

20. On new dynamics in early women's studies classrooms, see discussions by Florence Howe, Lillian Robinson, Maureen Greenwald, and Gerda Lerner in Howe, ed. pp. 1–4, 42–43, 70–73, and 86–88, respectively. See also descriptions of women's studies programs

has been deemed the most radical and vital contribution of the women's movement to educational innovation.[21]

Yet the adaptation of feminist principles to teaching and governance in women's studies soon led to controversy. In a widely circulated essay on the defects of the feminist ideal of "structurelessness," Jo Freeman demonstrated that the rejection of formal leadership with visible lines of responsibility favored the development of informal networks where power flowed through underground channels based on friendship, thus creating the very evil it sought to suppress: control by elites.[22] Among Freeman's readers, some hoped that women's studies would avoid the doctrinaire allegiance to ideologies that had proved so destructive in the women's liberation movement.[23]

The responsibility of women's studies to the larger feminist community also became a debated issue in the early years. At two major women's studies conferences in the early 1970s, bitter conflict developed between factions who weighed differently the political and academic aims of the campus movement. The first was a small, invitational conference held at the University of Pittsburgh in November 1971, which polarized into a "revolutionary feminist caucus" of students and political activists and a group of established academics who had come to discuss theoretical issues about women's studies.[24] The second was the West Coast Women's Studies Conference held at Sacramento State College (now University) in May 1973 on problems of "survival in the seventies." A deep cleavage developed when a highly organized group diverted

---

at SUNY/Buffalo, Cambridge-Goddard Graduate School for Social Change, Portland State University, City University of New York (CUNY)/Richmond College, Sacramento State College, and San Diego State College, in Howe and Ahlum, eds., *Female Studies III*, pp. 142–48, 164–73. See also essays in Showalter and Ohmann, eds., esp. Elaine Showalter, "Introduction: Teaching About Women, 1971," pp. i–xii.

21. Christine Grahl, Elizabeth Kennedy, Lillian S. Robinson, and Bonnie Zimmerman, "Women's Studies: A Case in Point," *Feminist Studies* 1, no. 2 (Fall 1972): 109–20; Sarah Slavin Schramm, *Plow Women Rather Than Reapers: An Intellectual History of Feminism in the United States* (Metuchen, N.J.: Scarecrow Press, 1978); Sheila Tobias, "Teaching Women's Studies: Looking Back over Three Years," *Liberal Education* 58, no. 2 (May 1972): 264; Staff, "Teaching Collectively," *Women's Studies Program: Three Years of Struggle* (San Diego: California State University at San Diego, 1973), pp. 42–44. Despite the emphasis on cooperative and group experience, however, women's studies courses made heavy demands on students and teachers. To preclude accusations of "academic anemia," some instructors resorted to "intellectual overkill" (Wendy Martin, "Teaching Women's Studies—Some Problems and Discoveries," in Showalter and Ohmann, eds., p. 9).

22. Jo Freeman, "The Tyranny of Structurelessness," *Berkeley Journal of Sociology* 17 (1972–73): 151–64, reprinted in *Women in Politics*, ed. Jane S. Jaquette (New York: John Wiley & Sons, 1974), pp. 204–14.

23. Mollie Schwartz Rosenhan, "Women's Studies and Feminism: Ideological Conflict in the Academy" (paper presented at the annual meeting of the American Historical Association, San Francisco, December 30, 1973).

24. Rae Lee Siporin, "Introduction: Women and Education: The Conference as Catalyst," in Siporin, ed., pp. iii–xiv.

scheduled sessions from their announced purposes to discuss issues on its own agenda. Exhibiting deep distrust of conference planners and movement leaders, the group attacked "white, middle-class, hetero-sexual" feminists for attempting to separate women's studies from the radical women's movement. In the face of physical as well as verbal confrontation, some of the 700 participants withdrew.[25]

The *Report on the West Coast Women's Studies Conference* is a remark-able document of a period in women's studies history when difficult lessons about process and pluralism were learned. It includes pro-ceedings as well as postconference statements from both sides. In one interpretive essay, Deborah Rosenfelt characterized "the cleavage in purpose and ideology that ran like a crack in the earth" through con-ference activities as a manifestation of the division within the women's movement between "socialist feminists" and "cultural feminists" ("Marx-ists" and "Matriarchs"), who attacked each other for, respectively, em-ploying "male" modes of analysis and confrontation, and enjoying the rewards of apolitical, middle-class academic privilege. Rosenfelt em-phasized the creative aspects of the struggle.[26]

More fearful that women's studies would be destroyed by internal conflict if not by external opposition, Catharine Stimpson analyzed the source of the internecine quarrels in a perceptive essay that remains pertinent today. In "What Matter Mind: A Critical Theory about the Practice of Women's Studies," she identified the problems as women's acceptance of cultural stereotypes of femininity and their consequent distrust of women in power, as well as ideological conflict among five categories of women's studies practitioners: "pioneers" who had taught about women before women's studies began, "ideologues" who had come to women's studies through the feminist movement, "radicals" who had been politicized by other movements, "latecomers" who became interested after women's studies began, and "bandwagoneers" who found women's studies fashionable and useful for their careers. The fiercest strife arose between the "ideologues" and "radicals." While somewhat pessimistic about the future, Stimpson saw hope for survival in the "buoyancy that comes from sensing that to work for women's studies is to belong to a historical tide." To strengthen the growing community of scholars and teachers, she suggested the establishment of a national organization.[27]

25. See Ann Forfreedom, "Whither Women's Studies?" in *Report on the West Coast Women's Studies Conference*, pp. 110–113, esp. p. 113.

26. Deborah Rosenfelt, "What Happened at Sacramento?" in Women's Studies Board at California State University, ed., pp. 78–83, also in *Women's Studies Newsletter* 5 (Fall 1973): 1, 6–7. See also Betty Chmaj, "Confrontation in Anger and in Pain," ibid., pp. 140–43, also in Chmaj and Gustafson, pp. 24–39,

27. Catharine R. Stimpson, "What Matter Mind: A Critical Theory about the Practice of Women's Studies," *Women's Studies* 1, no. 3 (1973): 293–314, also available from ERIC

The perspective that the radical feminist goals of women's studies made it incompatible with the university system led to a complete change in faculty at the earliest of programs, San Diego State, in 1974.[28] Adrienne Rich addressed this issue of women's studies' possible co-optation within the university system at another troubled conference at the University of Pennsylvania in the same year, "Women's Studies: Renaissance or Revolution?" She expressed the fear that women's studies, if integrated into male-defined and -dominated universities, might become isolated pockets of academic life where a few women could nourish a "false illusion of power."[29] More recently, in the foreword to a collection of her prose, she finds that, despite its tenuous hold on the university, women's studies continues to be a place where women may "claim" rather than "receive" an education, may demand to be taken seriously and taught what they really need to know to live as women in the world.[30] Even if staffed by "tokenists," women's studies might, Rich felt, serve as a catalyst "toward a woman-centered university."[31]

Rich envisioned a university transformed by feminist principles, with competition replaced by cooperation, fragmentation by wholeness, and even the line between campus and community shaded. It was a goal which depended on women learning to use their power constructively, as "power to change." Academic feminists would have to succeed in re-designing not only the women's studies classroom but also the

---

(ED 068078) 1972 and in condensed form, "A Critical View of Women's Studies," *Women's Studies Newsletter* 2 (Winter 1972): 1–4.

28. The entire faculty resigned, stating, "We have realized that professionalizing Women's Studies and the institutionalizing of this program is part of the strategy of those in power in the university. . . . A collective program like San Diego's either must develop into a traditional elitist approach to education, or the women who have maintained the collective approach will be fired and replaced by women who are not committed to student interests or needs. In either case, Women's Studies as we have known it, is incompatible with the institution and is eliminated" (Women's Studies Board, San Diego State College, *Women's Studies and Socialist Feminism* [San Diego: San Diego State College, April 20, 1974], pp. 5–7). On the early development of this program see Roberta Salper, "Women's Studies," *Ramparts* 10, no. 6 (December 1971): 56–60; later history, Marilyn J. Boxer, "Closeup: Women's Studies Department at San Diego," *Women's Studies Newsletter* 6, no. 2 (Spring 1978): 20–23.

29. Adrienne Rich, "Women's Studies—Renaissance or Revolution?" *Women's Studies* 3, no. 2 (1976): 121–26.

30. Adrienne Rich, "Claiming an Education" (lecture delivered at Douglass College, September 6, 1977), and "Taking Women Students Seriously" (lecture delivered at New Jersey College and University Coalition on Women's Education, May 7, 1978), both in Adrienne Rich, *On Lies, Secrets, and Silence: Selected Prose 1966–1978* (New York: W. W. Norton & Co., 1979), pp. 231–35, 237–45 (hereafter cited as *On Lies*).

31. Adrienne Rich, "Toward a Woman-centered University," in *Women and the Power to Change*, ed. Florence Howe (New York: McGraw-Hill Book Co., 1975), pp. 15–46, reprinted in Rich, *On Lies*, pp. 125–55, and excerpted in *Chronicle of Higher Education* (July 21, 1975).

"clockwork of male careers" and the value structure on which the university and society were based. With the resources available now, however, much could be done, and even an activist skeptical of academic feminism could "find happiness" teaching women's studies.[32]

By mid-decade women's studies entered a "second phase," settling in for the long haul, no longer justifying itself as primarily compensatory and ultimately, if successful, self-liquidating. This new consciousness was manifested in a series of reports from the field that appeared in the *Women's Studies Newsletter* under the title, "The Future of Women's Studies."[33] One coordinator pointed out that "in order to change or add to the traditional perspectives of the disciplines, women's studies has to be of them, in them, and about them." A second considered it essential to make women's studies "part of the fundamental structure of our schools." A third gave an indication of how far the movement had come from the search for forgotten women in the suggestion that women's studies "constitutes a genuine discipline, understood as we now understand English or history or physics."[34]

To assess the state of women's studies after seven years, the National Advisory Council on Women's Educational Programs commissioned a study by Florence Howe of fifteen "mature" programs with line budgets; paid administrators; officially recognized curricula; and accredited majors, minors, or certificate programs. The report, *Seven Years Later: Women's Studies Programs in 1976*, stressed the successes: student interest and enrollment growth, the breadth and depth of course offerings, the vitality of women's studies scholarship, and the impact on university faculty and curricula.[35] While demonstrating how effectively women's studies programs used resources, it pointed to insufficient and unstable staffing and funding as key issues affecting the future. It said little about some problem areas, such as program governance and relations with the feminist community, but called for further study of others, including the involvement of minority women, the effectiveness of women's studies teaching, the impact of women's studies on host institutions. Although

32. Florence Howe, "Women and the Power to Change," and Arlie Russell Hochschild, "Inside the Clockwork of Male Careers," in Howe, ed., *Women and the Power to Change*, pp. 127–71, 47–80; Carol Anne Douglas, "Can A Radical Feminist Find Happiness Teaching Women's Studies?" *off our backs* 7, no. 1 (December 1977): 11, 14–15.

33. Gayle Graham Yates, "Women's Studies in Its Second Phase," *Women's Studies Newsletter* 5, nos. 1–2 (Winter/Spring 1977): 4–5; "The Future of Women's Studies," ibid., vol. 3, no. 2 (Spring 1975), ibid., vol. 3, nos. 3–4 (Summer/Fall 1975), ibid., vol 4, no. 1 (Winter 1976).

34. Dana V. Hiller, director of Women's Studies, University of Cincinnati, *Women's Studies Newsletter* 3, no. 2 (Spring 1975): 4; Joan Geetter, acting director of Women's Studies, University of Connecticut, ibid.; and Susan Phipps-Sanger, administrative assistant-advisor, and Toni McNaron, coordinator of Women's Studies, University of Minnesota, ibid., 3, nos. 3–4 (Summer/Fall 1975): 26.

35. Florence Howe, *Seven Years Later: Women's Studies Programs in 1976* (Washington, D.C.: National Advisory Council on Women's Educational Programs, 1977).

the report has been seen as "women's studies dressed in her 'Sunday best,' " it captures the essential shape and spirit.[36]

Placed alongside *Female Studies I* (or *II* or *III*), *Seven Years Later* offers dramatic evidence that women's studies was higher education's success story of the decade. Despite a new era of hard times for public education, new programs continued to appear. They were established in technical institutes, Catholic and Mormon universities, anti-ERA states in the South, some high schools, and many community colleges. Women's studies was germinating in the "grass roots."[37]

With the changing cultural environment and increasing integration of women's studies into the educational establishment, a new constituency of students entered the classroom.[38] Unlike the students of the early 1970s, they were less likely to identify themselves as feminists, or sometimes even to understand such basic concepts as sexism and feminism. Susan Sniader Lanser was startled to find her students not only apolitical but still suffering the burden of traditional sex-role expectations.[39] "Consciousness raising," borrowed from women's liberation to become a teaching device in early women's studies classrooms, took place less often but continued to be perceived as a latent function of the formal educational process.[40] Cheri Register identified four stages in

36. Nancy Hoffman, "Seven Years Later: Women's Studies Programs in 1976: A Review," *Radical Teacher* 6 (December 1977): 54–56.

37. For women's studies programs in diverse settings, see, e.g., *Radical Teacher* (Special Issue on Women's Studies in the 70's: Moving Forward), vol. 6 (December 1977). On Catholic colleges, Betty Burnett, "Grass Roots in Women's Studies: Kansas City, Missouri," *Women's Studies Newsletter* 5, no. 3 (Summer 1977): 3–4; and Barbara B. Stern, "How To Establish a Women's Studies Course When the Administration Is Against It, the Students Think It's Too Hard, Your Department Is Out of Money, and You Are Probably Too Old to Be Teaching Anymore," *International Journal of Women's Studies* 2, no. 1 (January/February 1979): 100–101. On a Mormon university, see Judith Gappa and J. Nicholls Eastmond, "Gaining Support for a Women's Studies Program in a Conservative Institution," *Liberal Education* 64, no. 3 (October 1978): 278–92. On women's studies in the South, see Nancy Topping Bazin, "Expanding the Concept of Affirmative Action to Include the Curriculum," *Women's Studies Newsletter* 8, no. 4 (Fall/Winter 1980): 9–11; Mollie C. Davis, "Grass Roots Women's Studies: Piedmont, North Carolina," ibid., 4, no. 2 (Spring 1976): 1–2; and Linda Todd, "Grass Roots Women's Studies: South Carolina," ibid., 4, no. 3 (Summer 1976): 4. On community colleges, see Allana Elovson, *Women's Studies in the Community Colleges,* Women's Studies Monograph Series (Washington, D.C.: National Institute of Education, 1980).

38. From Portland State came the following dialogue, which aptly expresses some of the internal changes. Nancy: "Do you think our 'constituency' has changed? Are there fewer of us now who tend to see women's studies as coextensive with our egos?" Julie: "Not really, and that's not a good way to put it. We're pretty diverse in our needs and uses for the program. Somehow, though, we're all getting older" (Nancy Porter, Julie Allen, and Jean Maxwell, "From Portland State University—in Three Voices," *Women's Studies Newsletter* 3, no. 2 [Spring 1975]: 5).

39. Susan Sniader Lanser, "Beyond *The Bell Jar:* Women Students of the 1970s," *Radical Teacher* 6 (December 1977): 41–44.

40. Ellen Boneparth, "Evaluating Women's Studies: Academic Theory and Practice," *Social Science Journal* 14, no. 2 (April 1977): 23–31. This special issue of *Social Science*

both the classroom process and the development of women's studies and the women's movement. Moving from compensating, to criticizing, to collecting and constructing, and finally to conceptualizing anew, students and teacher would pass through despair to emerge with a new and positive basis for understanding and living with a feminist perspective.[41] However, after a study of the literature evaluating women's studies teaching and their own investigation of the values expressed by teachers, Nancy M. Porter and Margaret T. Eileenchild found no clear evidence of the changes in attitude and perception often reported by students and teachers. They suggested that future evaluations place the women's studies experience in a broad educational context that would encompass such variables as sex of instructor and student, political perspective and goals of the instructor, and classroom structure. Neither the necessary data nor the measurement instrument appropriate to the task are yet available, although the development by Marcia Guttentag of an evaluation method involving participants in setting objectives may prove particularly appropriate to measuring the impact of women's studies.[42]

New perceptions of women's studies were accompanied by new structures. To facilitate communications among practitioners and to enhance the development of scholarship and teaching, the National Women's Studies Association was founded at San Francisco in 1977.[43] After many months of careful preparation, it was designed to express both professional and feminist values. A complicated structure allowing equitable representation to various constituencies—regional groups,

---

Journal (Women's Studies: Awakening Academe) was also published as Kathleen Blumhagen and Walter Johnson, eds., *Women's Studies* (Westport, Conn.: Greenwood Press, 1978). See also Deborah Silverton Rosenfelt, "Introduction," in Rosenfelt, ed. (n. 13 above), p. viii; Barbara A. Schram, "What's the Aim of Women's Studies?" *Journal of Teacher Education* 26, no. 4 (Winter 1975): 352–53; and Schramm (n. 21 above), pp. 345–46. Ellen Morgan worried lest the consciousness-raising experience leave her students alienated from society but lacking an adequate factual and theoretical basis to live as feminists ("On Teaching Women's Studies," *University of Michigan Papers in Women's Studies* [May 1978], pp. 27–34). Blanche Hersh finds Morgan's analysis a useful guide to fulfillment of women's studies' promise to effect change in consciousness (Women's Studies Program, Northeastern Illinois University, "On Teaching Women's Studies," *Program Notes,* vol. 4, no. 1 [January/February 1979]).

41. Cheri Register, "Brief, A-mazing Movements: Dealing with Despair in the Women's Studies Classroom," *Women's Studies Newsletter* 7, no. 4 (Fall 1979): 7–10.

42. Nancy M. Porter and Margaret T. Eileenchild, *The Effectiveness of Women's Studies Teaching,* Women's Studies Monograph Series (Washington, D.C.: National Institute of Education, 1980); Marcia Guttentag, Lorelei R. Brush, Alice Ross Gold, Marnie W. Mueller, Sheila Tobias, and Marni Goldstein White, "Evaluating Women's Studies: A Decision-Theoretic Approach," *Signs: Journal of Women in Culture and Society* 3, no. 4 (Summer 1978): 884–90.

43. On preparation, see Elsa Greene, "The Case for a National Women's Studies Association," *Women's Studies Newsletter* 4, no. 1 (Winter 1976): 1, 3; Elsa Greene and Elaine Reuben, "Planning a National Women's Studies Association," ibid., 4, no. 2 (Spring 1976): 1, 10–11; Sybil Weir, "Planning Continues for the National Founding Convention," ibid., 4, no. 3 (Summer 1976): 1, 10–11.

students, staff, elementary and secondary teachers, lesbians, Third World women, community women—was designed to counter the tendency toward exclusiveness that characterizes many other professional organizations. Sliding registration fees for conventions would provide funds to equalize transportation costs for residents of nearby and distant places. Widespread participation would be encouraged by eliminating keynote speakers.

The successful outcome of the founding convention and subsequent annual conferences reflected the sensitivity of the planners to the problems that beset earlier gatherings.[44] By the end of the decade, the "room of one's own" for which feminists had fought at the beginning was becoming, in the optimistic words of the NWSA's coordinator Elaine Reuben, a "several-story building."[45] Its future remained, however, contingent on the resolution of fundamental, continuing problems.

Political Issues

In fulfillment of the commitment of women's studies to be inclusive of all women and all women's concerns, programs for the NWSA conferences at the University of Kansas in 1979, Indiana University in 1980, and the University of Connecticut, Storrs, in 1981 included more than 250 sessions. Their titles indicate that the concerns and conflicts manifested in the early 1970s in the *Female Studies* series remain alive, while some new issues have emerged. If women's studies is now established firmly enough to survive a decade that began with the accession to political power of right-wing forces clearly allied with antifeminism, it faces continuing challenges from within.[46] The most extensive debates continue to address the relationship of women's studies to the feminist movement and the integration of activist and academic goals, inside as

44. Florence Howe, "What Happened at the Convention," *Women's Studies Newsletter* 5, 1–2 (Winter/Spring 1977): 3–4; Beverly Watkins, "Feminist Educators Seek to Improve Status of Women's Studies," *Chronicle of Higher Education* (January 31, 1977), p. 8. On the 1979 conference, see *Women's Studies Newsletter* 7, no. 3 (Summer 1979): 15–28 and *Frontiers: A Journal of Women Studies*, vol. 5, no. 1 (Spring 1980): 1–70. On the 1980 conference, see *Women's Studies Newsletter* 8, no. 3 (Summer 1980): 3–24. On the 1981 conference, see *Women's Studies Quarterly* 9, no. 3 (Fall 1981): 4–22, 35–40.

45. Elaine Reuben et al., "Visions and Revisions: Women and the Power to Change," *Women's Studies Newsletter* 7, no. 3 (Summer 1979): 18–22.

46. Phyllis Schlafly considers enrollment in women's studies the worst thing a middle-aged woman can possibly do (*Power of the Positive Woman* [New Rochelle, N.Y.: Arlington House Publishers, 1977], p. 59). See also Linda Gordon and Allen Hunter, "Sex, Family and the New Right: Anti-Feminists as a Political Force," *Radical America* 11, no. 6, and 12, no. 1 (November 1977–February 1978): 9–25. According to Catharine Stimpson, women's studies "now has the maturity to move from a defensive to a stalwart posture" ("The New Scholarship about Women: The State of the Art," *Annals of Scholarship* 1, no. 2 [1980]: 2–14).

well as outside the classroom. Although these debates serve to stimulate and to enrich women's studies, they also provide a source of potential conflict among constituent groups and require that the NWSA perform a delicate "balancing act."[47]

Present from the beginning, the old issue of women's studies' possible co-optation remains unresolved. Over the years numerous observers, pointing to the history of home economics, have expressed a fear that women's studies might be absorbed by the academy, lose its feminist thrust, and become a female ghetto with minimal impact on mainstream education and society.[48] Some programs, however, including those at SUNY/Buffalo and Portland State University in Oregon, have continued to consider the struggle against traditional hierarchical organization, in program governance as well as classroom dynamics, critical to the mission of women's studies.[49] The controversy over an early unsuccessful scheme to integrate academic women's studies into a broad spectrum of educational, social, and community services in Southern California and a current conflict over the location of a women's studies institute in West Germany also reflect this concern within the movement.[50] The Feminist Studies Program at Cambridge-Goddard, dedicated to integrating social research and social action, recently dissolved itself rather than com-

47. Barbara Hillyer Davis and Patricia A. Frech, "Diversity, Fragmentation, Integration: The NWSA Balancing Act," *Women's Studies Quarterly* 9, no. 1 (Spring 1981): 33–35.

48. Ruth Crego Benson, "Women's Studies: Theory and Practice," *AAUP Bulletin* 58, no. 3 (September 1972): 283–86; Ann Snitow and Margaret Mahoney, "Higher Education and Women," *Arts in Society* 11, no. 1 (Spring/Summer 1974): 95–96; Jill K. Conway, "Coeducation and Women's Studies: Two Approaches to the Question of Women's Place in the Contemporary University," *Daedalus* 103, no. 4 (Fall 1974): 239–49; Freeman, "Women's Liberation and Its Impact" (n. 7 above); Greene, "Case for a National Women's Studies Association"; Barbara Sicherman, "The Invisible Woman: The Case for Women's Studies," in *Women in Higher Education*, ed. W. Todd Furniss and Patricia Alberg Graham (Washington, D.C.: American Council on Education, 1974), p. 172; and Tobias, "Teaching Women's Studies" (n. 21 above), p. 263.

49. On Portland State, see Nancy Hoffman, "A Class of Our Own," in Showalter and Ohmann, eds. (n. 13 above), pp. 14–28; "Working Together: The Women's Studies Program at Portland State University," in Hoffman et al., eds. (n. 13 above), pp. 164–228; and Porter et al., p. 5. On SUNY/Buffalo, see Grahl et al. (n. 21 above); also Women's Studies College, SUNY/Buffalo, "Proposal for a College of Women's Studies" (unpublished paper, Fall 1971), "Women's Studies College Charter" (unpublished paper, October 15, 1974), "Women's Studies Struggle Continues . . ." (unpublished paper, Spring 1976); "From SUNY/Buffalo," *Women's Studies Newsletter* 3, nos. 3–4 (Summer/Fall 1975): 5–6; and Abstract 60 in "Selected Abstracts from the First National Conference of the National Women's Studies Association, May 30–June 3, 1979, Lawrence, Kansas," *Frontiers: A Journal of Women Studies* 5, no. 1 (Spring 1980): 12–13.

50. For Southern California, see Salper, "Women's Studies." For West Germany, see Tobe Levin, "Women's Studies in West Germany," *Women's Studies Newsletter* 7, no. 1 (Winter 1979): 21–22; Hanna-Beate Schöpp-Schilling, "Women's Studies Research Centers: Report from West Germany," ibid., 8, no. 2 (Spring 1979): 28–29; Peggy McIntosh, "The Women's Studies Conference in Berlin: Another Chapter in the Controversy," ibid., 8, no. 4 (Fall/Winter 1980): 24–26.

promise its commitment to structural change in the education process. But revolutionary fervor cannot be maintained endlessly, and historical circumstances change. Perhaps in light of the spectacular, and to some extent unforeseen, flowering of feminist scholarship—which has created an increasingly strong foundation and justification for the movement— academic women's studies has become less directly a strategy for institutional change and more specifically an attack on sexist scholarship and teaching.

Yet the conviction remains strong that women's studies must be explicitly political, consciously an academic arm of women's liberation, and actively part of a larger social movement that envisions the transformation of society.[51] Unlike other academic pursuits, it must not separate theory from practice. Since "feminist activity made women's studies possible, women's studies must in turn make feminist activity possible."[52] At the NWSA founding convention, one group charged that university women "have taken much more from the Women's Movement than they have to date returned" and suggested ways in which "academic privilege" might benefit the women's movement.[53] Today women's studies practitioners and programs enter into innumerable community activities in many ways: teachers are taking women's studies to nursing homes and prisons, bringing together mothers and daughters, and transforming academic feminism into grass-roots theater.[54]

51. For a cogent statement of this point of view, see Linda Gordon, "A Socialist View of Women's Studies: A Reply to the Editorial, Volume 1, Number 1," *Signs: Journal of Women in Culture and Society* 1, no. 2 (Winter 1975): 559–66.

52. Melanie Kaye, "Closeup on Women's Studies Courses: Feminist Theory and Practice," *Women's Studies Newsletter* 6, no. 3 (Summer 1978): 20–23.

53. S. Brown, E. Hawkes, F. Klein, M. Lowe, E. B. Makrides, and R. Felberg, "Women's Studies: A Fresh Perspective," *The Longest Revolution* 1, no. 3 (February 1977): 13–14, 16. The opposite perspective was expressed by an academic feminist at the International Women's Year Conference in Houston. Noting that the resolution on education ignored women's studies, Amy Swerdlow asserted that "women's studies has supported the women's movement, now it's time for the movement to support women's studies" (quoted by Elizabeth Baer and Dora Janeway Odarenko, "The IWY Conference at Houston: Implications for Women's Studies," *Women's Studies Newsletter* 6, no. 1 [Winter 1978]: 3–6). Linda Gordon has suggested that "we should take our questions from the movement but not our answers" ("What Should Women's Historians Do: Politics, Social Theory and Women's History," *Marxist Perspectives* 1, no. 3 [Fall 1978]: 128–36).

54. Diane T. Rudnick and Sayre Phillips Sheldon, "Teaching Women's History to Men in Prison," and Dorothy Kilton, "Your Mind—Use It or Lose It: Women's Studies in a Nursing Home," *Women's Studies Newsletter* 8, no. 2 (Spring 1980): 9–12; Cynthia D. Kinnard, "Feminist Teaching in a Women's Prison" (NWSA Session Abstract, NWSA Convention, Indiana University, Bloomington, 1980); Nancy Schniedewind, "Reaching Out to the Community: The Mothers and Daughters Conference at SUNY/New Paltz," *Women's Studies Newsletter* 8, no. 1 (Winter 1980): 28–29; Carol Perkins, "Tricks of the Trade," *Radical Teacher* 14 (December 1979): 23–26. See also Catharine R. Stimpson, "Women's Studies and the Community: Some Models," *Women's Studies Newsletter* 2, no. 3 (Summer 1974): 2–3.

Individuals are experiencing and resolving their personal tensions between academics and activism in various ways. For some, it means leaving the university. Jo Freeman, whose work has contributed to both women's studies and the women's movement, has decided that feminism is compatible with scholarship but not with academic life. Mary Howell, on the other hand, has consciously compromised by applying traditional standards in her professional life and dedicating herself to community feminism and women's culture in her private life. Others seem to temper if not transcend the problem by accepting the emerging consensus that women's studies in the long run implies profound change in the structure of knowledge, the university, and society.[55]

Feminist sensitivity to social process is perhaps manifest most clearly in the ongoing, if not always successful, attempt in women's studies to fight against oppression on the basis of race, class, age, religion, and sexual preference as well as sex. A proposed amendment to the NWSA constitution states that "freedom from sexism by necessity must include a commitment to freedom from racism, national chauvinism, class and ethnic bias, ageism, heterosexual bias." The two most critical current issues involve the integration into women's studies and the NWSA of women of color and lesbians.

The NWSA as an organization has acknowledged widespread neglect of women of color in women's studies courses, materials, programs, and conferences. Although the *Women's Studies Newsletter,* the official journal of the NWSA, has during the past five years published a number of articles on research and resources pertinent to black women, considerably less work has appeared on other women of color.[56] At the found-

55. Jo Freeman, "The Feminist Scholar," *Quest* 5, no. 1 (Summer 1979): 26–36. Freeman's anthology, *Women: A Feminist Perspective* (Palo Alto, Calif.: Mayfield Publishing Co., 1975), is one of the most widely adopted texts for introductory courses, while her essays have illuminated important issues on the women's movement. See also Mary Howell, "Can We Be Feminists and Professionals?" *Women's Studies International Quarterly* 2, no. 1 (1979): 1–7, and the proceedings of women's studies conferences sponsored by the Great Lakes Colleges Association (GLCA): Beth Reed, ed., *The Structure of Knowledge: A Feminist Perspective: Proceedings of the Fourth Annual Great Lakes Colleges Association Women's Studies Conference* (Ann Arbor, Mich.: Great Lakes Colleges Association Women's Studies Program, 1978) (hereafter cited as *Structure of Knowledge*), and *Toward a Feminist Transformation of the Academy: Proceedings of the Fifth Annual Great Lakes Colleges Association Women's Studies Conference* (Ann Arbor, Mich.: Great Lakes Colleges Association Women's Studies Program, 1979) (hereafter cited as *Toward a Feminist Transformation*). Both are available from the GLCA Women's Studies Program, 220 Collingwood, Suite 240, Ann Arbor, Michigan 48103.

56. Barbara Smith, "Doing Research on Black Women," *Women's Studies Newsletter* 4, no. 2 (Spring 1976): 4–5, 7; Michele Russell, "Black-Eyed Blues Connections: Teaching Black Women," ibid., 4, no. 4 (Fall 1976): 6–7, and ibid., 5, nos. 1–2 (Winter/Spring 1977): 24–28; Nancy Hoffman, "White Woman, Black Women: Inventing an Adequate Pedagogy," ibid., 5, nos. 1–2 (Winter/Spring 1977): 21–24; Rita B. Dandridge, "On Novels by Black American Women: A Bibliographical Essay," ibid., 6, no. 3 (Summer 1978): 28–30;

ing NWSA conference in 1977, Third World women formed a caucus and presented a series of resolutions aimed at greater inclusion of women of color. Provisions for permanent status for the caucus and special representation on the NWSA Coordinating Council were incorporated into the initial governance plan, while other proposals (including the guarantee that any resolutions to which the caucus objected would not be passed until after review of a Third World women's position paper) were to become part of the finished constitution.[57] Reacting to complaints of inadequate Third World participation in the first and second national conventions, the NWSA selected "Women Respond to Racism" as the theme of the third annual conference in 1981.[58] By scheduling daily consciousness-raising sessions in which participants could focus on the personal as well as societal effects of racism, the association also demonstrated its intention to move beyond tokenism and abstract discussions of the interaction of sexism and racism in society. It was a way of responding to black women's charge that the more or less institutionalized women's studies of recent years has traded its "radical life-changing vision" for "acceptance, respectability and the career advancement of individuals."[59]

Pioneers of black women's studies, such as Barbara Smith, use "black women" as a metaphor for the essential revolutionary message of women's studies. A women's studies committed to research, writing, and teaching that makes the experience of black women immediately accessible to all women would necessarily "require and indicate that fundamental political and social change is taking place."[60] As Gloria T. Hull writes, the experience of working on—and with—a black female subject

---

T. Cross, F. Klein, Barbara Smith, and Beverly Smith, "Face-to-Face, Day-to-Day, Racism CR," ibid., 8, no. 1 (Winter 1980): 27–28; Ann Cathey Carver, "Building Coalitions between Women's Studies and Black Studies: What Are the Realities?" ibid., 8, no. 3 (Summer 1980): 16–19; Betsy Brinson, "Teaching Black Women's Heritage," ibid., 8, no. 4 (Fall/Winter 1980): 19–20. See also Angela Jorge, "Issues of Race and Class: A Puerto Rican Woman's Thoughts," ibid., 8, no. 4 (Fall/Winter 1980): 17–18.

57. *Women's Studies Newsletter* 5, nos. 1–2 (Winter/Spring 1977): 6.

58. For 1979, see Nupur Chaudhuri, "A Third World Woman's View of the Convention," Rayna Green, "American Indian Women Meet in Lawrence," Barbara Smith's comments in "Visions and Revisions: Women and the Power to Change," all in *Women's Studies Newsletter* 7, no. 3 (Summer 1979): 5–6, 6–7, and 19–20. Smith's presentation is also in *Frontiers: A Journal of Women Studies* 5, no. 1 (Spring 1980): 48–49. For 1980, see Catharine R. Stimpson, "Writing It All Down: An Overview of the Second NWSA Convention," *Women's Studies Newsletter* 8, no. 3 (Summer 1980): 5–7; and Nancy Polikoff, "Addressing Racism," *off our backs* 10, no. 7 (July 1980): 17–19.

59. Barbara Smith, comments in opening panel, in *Structure of Knowledge*, p. 14. See also Pat Miller, "Third NWSA Convention to be Held in Connecticut," *Women's Studies Quarterly* 9, no. 1 (Spring 1981): 30, and report on CR sessions at Storrs in *Women's Studies Quarterly* 9, no. 3 (Fall 1981): 13–16.

60. Smith in *Structure of Knowledge*, p. 13.

in feminist scholarship may summon a researcher to explore the tenets of her own life and work.[61]

Another group of women suffering special oppression in contemporary American society are lesbians. The paucity of literature addressing the treatment of lesbians in women's studies parallels feminists' relatively late decision to make elimination of heterosexual privilege and homosexual oppression a central aim. This commitment offers women's studies an opportunity to affirm its radical vision. However, although the NWSA constitution acknowledged the need for specific representation of lesbian women and conference planners have scheduled numerous lesbian-oriented sessions and cultural events, women's studies practitioners have produced very little relevant literature on research or teaching.[62] Toni McNaron's 1977 account of exploring lesbian experience and culture in a drug treatment center and the guidelines suggested very recently for studies of lesbianism by Peg Cruikshank, J. R. Roberts, and Bonnie Zimmerman are rare exceptions to the rule of silence, which confirms Adrienne Rich's observation that, with regard to lesbians, women's studies (and black studies) have "reinforce[d] the very silence out of which they have had to assert themselves."[63] A survey of texts used widely in introductory women's studies classes confirms the impression that "heterosexism is alive and well in the women's studies textbook market."[64] The lesbian perspective that "enforced heterosexuality is the extreme manifestation of male domination and patriarchal rule" remains largely inarticulated.[65]

61. Gloria T. Hull, "Researching Alice Dunbar-Nelson: A Personal and Literary Perspective," *Feminist Studies* 6, no. 1 (Summer 1980): 314–20, to be included in *Black Women's Studies*, ed. Gloria T. Hull, Patricia Bell Scott, and Barbara Smith (Old Westbury, N.Y.: Feminist Press, 1981). Charles P. Henry and Frances Smith Foster similarly call on black studies to include the history of black female activism and of black feminism in black studies, and they call on women's studies to make more than token efforts to include black women ("Black Women's Studies: Threat or Challenge?" *Western Journal of Black Studies,* in press).

62. Toni White, "Lesbian Studies Flourish at National Women's Studies Conference," *off our backs* 10, no. 7 (July 1980): 16–18.

63. Adrienne Rich, "It Is the Lesbian in Us," in *On Lies,* p. 201 (hereafter cited as "Lesbian in Us"). See also Toni McNaron, "Finding and Studying Lesbian Culture," *Women's Studies Newsletter* 5, no. 4 (Fall 1977): 18–20; Peg Cruikshank, "Lesbian Studies: Some Preliminary Notes," J. R. Roberts, "Black Lesbian Literature/Black Lesbian Lives: Materials for Women's Studies," and Bonnie Zimmerman, "Lesbianism 101," all in *Radical Teacher* 17 (November 1980): 11–25. Both Roberts and Cruikshank offer specific suggestions for course building. Cruikshank is editing *Lesbian Studies* (Old Westbury, N.Y.: Feminist Press, in press).

64. Bonnie Zimmerman, "One Out of Thirty: Lesbianism in Women's Studies Textbooks," in Cruikshank, ed. Zimmerman notes that neither the first (1975) nor the second (1979) edition of Freeman's widely used text, *Women: A Feminist Perspective,* includes an article on lesbianism.

65. Barbara Smith, "Racism and Women's Studies," *Frontiers: A Journal of Women Studies* 5, no. 1 (Spring 1980): 48–49.

The assumption of heterosexuality both reflects and reinforces ignorance about lesbians and lesbian perspectives. As Adrienne Rich points out, even to acknowledge that "heterosexuality may not be a 'preference' at all but something that has had to be imposed, managed, organized, propagandized, and maintained by force" requires the courage to risk shattering confirmed convictions.[66]

In a recent, provocative essay, Marilyn Frye contends that even in women's studies the supposition of heterosexuality remains "so complete and ubiquitous that it cannot be perceived for lack of contrast." Presenting perhaps one pole of contemporary lesbian political thought, while Rich on the other speaks to "the lesbian in us all," she calls for lesbians to withdraw support from women's studies unless heterosexual feminists begin to examine the ground of *their* choice of sexual preference.[67] Whatever their reaction to Frye's proposal, practitioners of women's studies must by now recognize that any effort to educate about and for women must include consideration of lesbian experiences and of a range of lesbian political perspectives. For prior self-scrutiny by women's studies teachers, the CR guidelines offered by Elly Bulkin are helpful.[68] The establishment of a clearinghouse for lesbian feminist materials should also aid in remedying the current neglect.[69]

By the early 1980s, the tension between academics and activists in women's studies had been largely resolved with the answer "both/and."[70] A lingering distrust of leadership remained, as well as some resistance to scrutiny of "congenial truths."[71] Challenges from lesbians and women of color to make women's studies truly inclusive continue. Recent writings, however, suggest that the major thrust of the second decade will be toward directing the movement outward, toward "mainstreaming." Despite a decade of the new scholarship, women's studies has so far made

66. Adrienne Rich, "Compulsory Heterosexuality and Lesbian Existence," *Signs: Journal of Women in Culture and Society* 5, no. 4 (Summer 1980): 631–60.

67. Marilyn Frye, "Assignment: NWSA—Bloomington 1980: Speak on 'Lesbian Perspectives on Women's Studies,' " *Sinister Wisdom* 14 (Summer 1980): 3–7, and "On Second Thought . . . ," *Radical Teacher* 17 (November 1980): 37–38. See also Rich, "Lesbian in Us," pp. 199–202. I am indebted to my colleague Bonnie Zimmerman for this analysis.

68. Elly Bulkin, "Heterosexism and Women's Studies," *Radical Teacher* 17 (November 1980): 28–30.

69. Sample course outlines, bibliographies, and other materials may be obtained from Coralyn Fontaine, Lesbian-Feminist Study Clearinghouse, Women's Studies Program, 1012 Cathedral of Learning, University of Pittsburgh, Pittsburgh, Pennsylvania 15260.

70. This term is used by Peggy McIntosh in her discussion of the community/ university conflict in Berlin (n. 50 above), p. 26.

71. Marlene Mackie suggests that because of their ideological sympathies, women's studies scholars may succumb to the "temptation to demand that science substantiate [their] values" and fail to challenge work that they find pleasing. She calls on practitioners of women's studies to "cultivate skepticism of results congruent with [their] value premises" ("On Congenial Truths: A Perspective on Women's Studies," *Canadian Review of Sociology and Anthropology* 14, no. 1 [February 1977]: 117–28, esp. 122).

little progress toward its "ultimate strategy" of transforming the established male-biased curriculum. The primary impact of women's studies has been the establishment of programs that make feminist scholarship visible and available, but usually only on an elective basis.[72] The failure of affirmative action to add women to existing faculties, the limited prospects for growth expected in the coming decade, and the spreading appeal of "back to basics" all suggest that fundamental change in educational institutions will come only after feminist academics insinuate women's studies into the traditional, and especially the required or general education, curriculum.[73]

In late 1979 the Fifth Annual Great Lakes College Association Women's Studies Conference adopted as its theme "Toward a Feminist Transformation of the Academy." Emphasizing the extent to which the feminist vision challenges the male-centered definition of knowledge, keynote speaker Elizabeth Kamarck Minnich compared the work of women's studies with "Copernicus shattering our geo-centricity, Darwin shattering our species-centricity."[74] While a few male administrators may follow the lead of Louis Brakeman, provost of Denison University, in facilitating the passage of new requirements for courses in women's studies or minority studies, most may be expected to resist change.[75] Feminists must therefore recognize, as Alison Bernstein points out, that "liberal education reform is a women's issue" and find ways to direct the argument.[76]

For example, Florence Howe has prepared an outline of five reasons why women's studies is particularly appropriate to the goals of liberal education: it is interdisciplinary and unifying, it teaches skills in critical analysis, it assumes a problem-solving stance, it clarifies the issue

72. See Florence Howe, "Editorial," *Women's Studies Quarterly* 9, no. 1 (Spring 1981): 2; and Howe and Lauter (n. 12 above), p. vii.

73. At a talk given at the December 1979 meeting of the Modern Language Association in San Francisco, "Writers We Still Don't Read," Howe observed that only women teachers care if women writers are taught. She suggests one strategy for change: accurate labeling of traditional courses, e.g., naming a course on Melville, Whitman, Emerson, and Thoreau "Male Writers of the Nineteenth Century in the United States." For arguments that women's studies has made few inroads into the traditional liberal arts, see Lois Banner, "Women in the College Curriculum: A Preliminary Report," mimeographed (Washington, D.C.: Department of History, George Washington University, 1978); Ann Froines, "Integrating Women into the Liberal Arts Curriculum: Some Results of 'A Modest Survey,'" *Women's Studies Newsletter* 8, no. 4 (Fall/Winter 1980): 11–12.

74. Elizabeth Kamarck Minnich, "Friends and Critics: The Feminist Academy," in *Toward a Feminist Transformation of the Academy* (n. 55 above), p. 7.

75. Louis Brakeman in closing panel, "Curriculum Reform, or What Do You Mean, 'Our College Should Have a Feminist Curriculum?'" in *Toward a Feminist Transformation*, pp. 49–52. On resistance to the elimination of sexism in academia, see remarks of Paul Lauter in closing panel, "The Feminist Critique: Plans and Prospects," in *Structure of Knowledge*, pp. 53–58.

76. Alison Bernstein, comments in closing panel, in *Toward a Feminist Transformation*, pp. 59–61.

of value judgment in education, and it promotes socially useful ends.[77] Nancy Topping Bazin, in describing her successful campaign to convince university administrators that a bias in curriculum is also subject to affirmative action measures, and Carolyn C. Lougee, in her account of general studies revision at Stanford University, agree on another reform strategy: women's studies should be integrated into general education by redefinition and expansion of basic required courses rather than offered as an alternative general education curriculum.[78] Some feminist educators may see this approach as a threat to the survival of separate women's studies courses or question whether content can be abstracted from a feminist framework or taught by faculty at large without sacrificing essential goals. Others may find classroom dynamics transformed by the presence of students seeking mainly to fulfill degree requirements.[79]

Theories

Whatever the possibilities for and implications of integration into the "core" curriculum, it seems certain that the future of women's studies will extend well beyond the five or ten years that some observers once thought its likely life span.[80] Just as many feminists found that the goals of the women's movement could not be fulfilled by the "add-women-and-stir method," so women's studies scholars discovered that academic fields could not be cured of sexism simply by accretion. In one discipline after another, initial "compensatory" scholarship led to the realization that only radical reconstruction would suffice.[81] In terms of a scheme developed by Catharine Stimpson, the deconstruction of error and the reconstruction of (philosophical and scientific) reality from a feminist perspective have now led to a third stage of women's studies

77. Florence Howe, "Toward Women's Studies in the Eighties: Pt. 1," *Women's Studies Newsletter* 8, no. 4 (Fall 1979): 2.

78. Bazin (n. 37 above); and Carolyn C. Lougee, "Women, History and the Humanities: An Argument in Favor of the General Studies Curriculum," *Women's Studies Quarterly* 9, no. 1 (Spring 1980): 4–7.

79. Perhaps feminist educators could press for faculty development programs to accompany general education revision. See Elizabeth Ness and Kathryn H. Brooks, *Women's Studies as a Catalyst for Faculty Development*, Women's Studies Monograph Series (Washington, D.C.: National Institute of Education, 1980); and Boxer (n. 28 above), p. 22.

80. Florence Howe foresees a century of research ("Introduction: The First Decade of Women's Studies," *Harvard Educational Review* 49, no. 4 [November 1979]: 413–21).

81. The expression "add-women-and-stir method" was used by Charlotte Bunch in a panel, "Visions and Revisions: Women and the Power to Change" (NWSA Convention, Lawrence, Kansas, June 1979); excerpts were published in *Women's Studies Newsletter* 7, no. 3 (Summer 1979): 20–21. Bari Watkins summarizes this process of discovery in "Feminism: A Last Chance for the Humanities," in *Theories of Women's Studies*, ed. Gloria Bowles and Renate Duelli-Klein (Berkeley: Women's Studies, University of California, Berkeley, 1980), pp. 41–47.

scholarship, the construction of general theories. Feminist thinkers are now asking a question with far-reaching implications for the future: "Is women's studies a discipline?"[82] Although raised early in the movement, it was pursued little until recently.[83] While the relative lack of theorizing about women's studies may be due to a certain reluctance to engage in what is considered a traditionally male province, it may also reflect the widespread use of the ill-defined term "interdisciplinary" to describe a practice that has been for the most part multidisciplinary and inter-departmental.[84] Given also the history of women's studies; its origins in the women's movement; its dependence on faculty with marginal status in the academy; and its practical, opportunistic, and immensely success-ful method of growth, essential abstract questions have understandably received sustained attention only recently.

Although practice has taken precedence over theory, even those content to define women's studies as "what women's studies' students do" have, with Devra Lee Davis, called for a new perspective from which to develop questions about the "woman in the moon." Women's studies needed a new "unifying framework [to] give it functional integrity within the academy."[85] A relatively simple answer, which received little attention, was Kenneth Boulding's suggestion that women's studies con-stitutes the beginnings of a new science of "dimorphics," which in a hundred years might be able to explain the implications of the human gender system.[86] This seems, however, a way of institutionalizing gender differences that feminists hope to overcome.

Others, beginning with Davis, found considerable powers of expla-nation in Thomas Kuhn's theory of scientific revolutions.[87] Kuhn not

82. Catharine R. Stimpson, "Women's Studies: An Overview," *University of Michigan Papers in Women's Studies* (May 1978), pp. 14–26.

83. See Susan S. Sherwin, "Women's Studies as a Scholarly Discipline: Some Ques-tions for Discussion," in Siporin, ed. (n. 13 above), pp. 114–16. Mollie Schwartz Rosenhan called for recognition of women's studies as a new discipline in "The Quiet Revolution" Xeroxed (Stanford, Calif.: Center for Research on Women, 1978).

84. Gloria Bowles and Renate Duelli-Klein, "Introduction: Creating Women's Studies Theory," in Bowles and Duelli-Klein, eds., pp. i–iv. On feminist reluctance to deal in theories, see also Charlotte Bunch, "Not by Degrees," *Quest: A Feminist Quarterly* 5, no. 1 (Summer 1979): 7–18.

85. Devra Lee Davis, "The Woman in the Moon: Prolegomenon for Women's Studies," in Siporin, ed., pp. 17–28.

86. Kenneth Boulding, "The Social Institutions of Occupational Segregation: Com-ment 1," *Signs: Journal of Women in Culture and Society* 1, no. 3, pt. 2 (Spring 1976): 75–77. Sheila Tobias sees a redefinition of women's studies as dimorphics as a means of attaining academic legitimacy at the possible cost of separation from the women's movement ("Women's Studies: Its Origins, Organization, and Prospects" [n. 19 above], p. 93). Hanna Papanek considers dimorphics useful as a "gender-blind" term to describe a type of re-search on women but inadequate to describe the whole. See her comments in "Discussion Forum: Future Direction of Women's Studies" (n. 11 above), pp. 18–20.

87. Thomas Kuhn, *The Structure of Scientific Revolutions* (Chicago: University of Chicago Press, 1970). Analysts using the Kuhnian model include Sandra Coyner, "Wom-

only presents a model for fundamental change over time that applies even to the allegedly "objective" disciplines of the "hard" sciences, he also describes a process that at several points seems familiar to feminists challenging ideas in the humanities and social sciences. Whenever women seek to apply theories of human behavior based on men's lives to their own experience, they confront what Kuhn terms the "anomalies" that then lead to the challenge to and ultimately the reversal of "paradigms" in "normal science." The fullest feminist analysis of Kuhn, which includes an excellent discussion of the meaning and uses of the concept "discipline," is Sandra Coyner's provocative essay "Women's Studies as an Academic Discipline: Why and How to Do It." Stressing the disadvantages of interdisciplinarity—the denial of autonomy and recognition, the difficulty of transcending disciplinary thinking—Coyner advises women's studies practitioners to abandon the energy-draining and still overwhelmingly unsuccessful effort to transform the established disciplines. Instead they should continue developing the new community of feminist scholars who will eventually discover new paradigms and found a new normative science.

Viewing women's studies in the Kuhnian perspective, Coyner brings a new clarity to the massive resistance against which feminist scholars struggle. Overcoming the sexism of men and institutions is less fundamental a problem than is accomplishing a complete scientific revolution in each discipline women's studies touches. But "scientific revolutions are not simple matters of accumulating or improving the quality of explanation," she points out.[88] They require the passing of a generation. Rather than waste time and effort in battle, feminist scholars should break free and pronounce women's studies a discipline. The new staffing patterns Coyner proposes would perhaps be the most difficult part of her plan to realize; according to this scheme, one faculty member might teach "Women in American History," "Psychology of Women," and "The Family" as well as a women's studies survey or seminar. For Coyner the problem of finding such qualified persons would be solved by future generations of scholar-teachers with Ph.D.s in women's studies based on multidisciplinary graduate training. The appropriate administrative structure for such a program is, of course, a department.

The pole opposite Coyner in this debate over ideal structures is grounded in the feminist philosophy that rejects disciplinarity itself as

---

en's Studies as an Academic Discipline: Why and How to Do It," and Renate Duelli-Klein, "How to Do What We Want to Do: Thoughts about Feminist Methodology," in Bowles and Duelli-Klein, eds., pp. 18–40, 48–64. See also Devra Lee Davis, "Woman in the Moon," in Siporin, ed. (n. 13 above), pp. 17–28; Ginny Foster, "Women as Liberators," in Hoffman et al., eds. (n. 13 above), pp. 6–35; Ann Fitzgerald, "Teaching Interdisciplinary Women's Studies," *Great Lakes Colleges Association Faculty Newsletter* (March 1978), pp. 2–3; Rosenhan, "Quiet Revolution."

88. Coyner, pp. 18–40.

fragmentation of social experience, a male mode of analysis that cannot describe the whole of female—or human—existence. By stressing the indivisible nature of knowledge, women's studies could become a force for liberation from a dehumanizing overspecialization. Co-optation of women into the dominant culture might foreclose humanity's "last chance for radical change leading to survival," says Ginny Foster, who sees women's studies as a means through which women, the majority of the population, might derail a male-driven train to doom.[89] Many analysts have stressed the salutary function of creating totalities from the insights of several disciplines, usually using the term "interdisciplinary" in the sense of "multidisciplinary."[90]

In the first issue of *Signs,* the editors suggested several possible patterns for the new interdisciplinary scholarship: "One person, skilled in several disciplines, explores one subject; several persons, each skilled in one discipline, explore one subject together; or a group, delegates of several disciplines, publish in more or less random conjunction with each other in a single journal."[91] That the interdisciplinary promise proved difficult to fulfill was admitted several years later by Catharine Stimpson. Beyond the "fallacy of misplaced originality," she had encountered unexpected resistance, even within women's studies, to moving outside one field of expertise. She hoped to see women's studies produce "translators," persons equipped to "interpret the languages of one discipline to persons in another."[92]

Taking a middle position, Christine Garside Allen, a scholar trained in philosophy and religious studies, has argued that women's studies should combine introductory and advanced-level "interdisciplinary" courses (for which she suggests "conceptual history" as a method) with intermediate course work in the disciplines.[93] Allen's colleague in English and fine arts, Greta Hoffman Nemiroff, has described their experiences in building and teaching a thematically based introductory course that moves beyond the disciplines. In a very interesting treatment of the meaning and implications of interdisciplinarity, Nemiroff analyzes the difficulties and the value of transdisciplinary work. Because women's

89. Foster.

90. See, e.g., Christine Garside Allen, "Conceptual History as a Methodology for Women's Studies," *McGill Journal of Education* 10 (Spring 1975): 49–58; Annette K. Baxter, "Women's Studies and American Studies: The Uses of the Interdisciplinary," *American Quarterly* 26, no. 4 (October 1974): 433–39; Fitzgerald; Tobias, "Women's Studies: Its Origins, Organization, and Prospects"; Joanna S. Zangrando, "Women's Studies in the U.S.: Approaching Reality," *American Studies International* 14, no. 1 (August 1975): 15–36.

91. Catharine R. Stimpson, Joan N. Burstyn, Domna C. Stanton, and Sandra M. Whisler, "Editorial," *Signs: Journal of Women in Culture and Society* 1, no. 1 (Autumn 1975): v–viii, esp. v.

92. Stimpson, "Women's Studies: An Overview"; also "The Making of *Signs,*" *Radical Teacher* 6 (December 1977): 23–25.

93. Allen, p. 57.

studies challenges the discipline-based categories in which the structure and economy of most universities are grounded, it cannot be easily assimilated within the academy. Despite the disadvantages and even dangers to its faculty, women's studies also offers advantages to all involved: a new inventiveness, an impetus toward fruitful collaboration, a "working model of critical thought." Although present categories of knowledge may limit women's studies in attaining "full 'disciplinehood' within its own interdisciplinarity," practitioners can advance its development by systematic efforts to examine and expand its "interface" with other disciplines.[94]

Dissatisfaction with the limits imposed by the disciplines has led others to speculate on how women's studies might transcend traditional divisions of knowledge. The change might come slowly, through the discovery of questions unanswerable by disciplinary thinking, as Diana Grossman Kahn suggested in her treatment of a hypothetical new science of "grockology." Or after a decade of small changes, the near future might bring the breakdown of currently accepted categories, a possibility foreseen by scientist Anne Fausto-Sterling, whose own interests bridge the biological aspects of development and semiotics. Florence Howe calls for women's studies to concentrate on "breaking the disciplines" so that they release their hold on women and women's studies. According to Howe, the history of the disciplines—from their origins in religious studies through the secularization and professionalization of the nineteenth century—has led to a fragmented contemporary academy that is antithetical to women's studies' holistic view and problem-solving intention. These essential characteristics of the new scholarship, along with a historical perspective, a critical approach, and an empirical practice, might pave the way to the "radical reinvention" of research, teaching, and learning which will characterize the "woman-centered university."[95]

If interdisciplinarity implies transdisciplinarity in a transformed university, what does it mean for the contemporary practice of women's studies? Gloria Bowles has said that "perhaps one day the Renaissance man will be replaced by the interdisciplinary woman," but she admits that this person does not yet exist. Meanwhile, she agrees with Catharine Stimpson that women's studies scholarship "at its best is an act of translation." Although Bowles has pioneered a course on "theories of wom-

94. Greta Hoffman Nemiroff, "Rationale for an Interdisciplinary Approach to Women's Studies," *Canadian Women's Studies* 1, no. 1 (Fall 1978): 60–68.

95. Diana Grossman Kahn, "Interdisciplinary Studies and Women's Studies: Questioning Answers and Creating Questions," in *Structure of Knowledge*, pp. 20–24; Anne Fausto-Sterling, "Women's Studies and Science," *Women's Studies Newsletter* 8, no. 1 (Winter 1980): 4–7; Florence Howe, "Breaking the Disciplines," in *Structure of Knowledge*, pp. 1–10; and Adrienne Rich, "Toward a Woman-centered University," in Howe, ed., *Women and the Power to Change* (n. 31 above), pp. 30–31.

en's studies," she cautions against the potential danger of what Mary Daly calls "methodolatry." Instead of artificially constructing a new system of thought, perhaps women's studies practitioners should find their questions in the women's movement and derive methods appropriate to women's survival needs.[96]

It is precisely this feminist effort to improve women's lives that Renate Duelli-Klein, coeditor with Bowles of the first volume of *Theories of Women's Studies,* considers central to development of women's studies' methodology. The way to avoid sexist methods such as "context stripping"[97] is to ground theory in "feminist action research." Researchers must abandon the pretext of "value-free objectivity" for a "conscious subjectivity" more appropriate to studies explicitly intended to be for as well as about women.[98]

Duelli-Klein's analysis of feminist methodology draws on Marcia Westkott's analysis of how sexist content, method, and purposes affect representations of women in the social sciences. Westkott suggests alternative ways of thinking about social reality that link rather than separate subject and object, forming what she terms an "intersubjectivity" that is expressed in a dialectical relationship of subject and object. Feminist thought characteristically replaces dichotomous with dialectical modes of analyzing self and other, person and society, consciousness and activity, past and future, knowledge and practice. It is "open, contingent and humanly compelling" in contrast to that which is "closed, categorical and human controlling." It also fortifies abstract understanding with active commitment to improve the condition of women.[99] At this stage, Westkott finds, feminist criticisms of content, method, and purpose are "strands" just beginning to emerge; they do not add up to a new discipline. But since the social creation of gender is a basic assumption of women's studies, Westkott's analysis offers more than just a criticism of established social science: it becomes a solid building block for the building of women's studies theory.

Structures

Definitions of women's studies imply relationships to structures. In practice interdisciplinarity within the academic program has led to the

96. Gloria Bowles, "Is Women's Studies an Academic Discipline?" in Bowles and Duelli-Klein, eds., pp. 1–11.

97. See Parlee (n. 2 above).

98. Duelli-Klein provides an example based on a project undertaken by sociologists in Germany who worked with battered women toward analysis of their collective experience.

99. Marcia Westkott, "Feminist Criticism of the Social Sciences," *Harvard Educational Review* 49, no. 4 (November 1979): 422–30.

formation of networks and committees staffed and supported by several disciplines, departments, divisions, or colleges. This is a structure appropriate to the aim of infiltrating the disciplines, professional schools, and other academic units. Since the committee coordinating women's studies usually has limited responsibilities for personnel and budget decisions (which are controlled by departments), it can often include staff, students, and even community women, whose presence highlights and helps to implement the feminist assumption that women's studies is for all women. From the beginning, planners feared that departmental status for women's studies might narrow its focus and limit its impact by reproducing the male model of fragmented knowledge and bureaucratized isolation; it could create a feminist ghetto far from the arena of the women's movement and threaten the implementation of feminist principles.[100]

Given the choice between establishing a separate department that could, like many black studies programs, be forgotten or perhaps eliminated in periods of retrenchment or of creating a decentralized program as a base from which to reach out, most academic feminists might have chosen the latter. The Women's Studies Planners at the University of Pennsylvania recommended against a departmental structure. At San Francisco State, the women's studies governance board opted "to *not* work towards a separate 'Women's Studies' department since our major purpose is the recognition of women's important 'place' at every level in all disciplines rather than its 'special character.' "[101] One study showed that students, who favored the departmentalization of black studies and wanted courses in women's studies, did not favor a department of women's studies.[102] In many cases, however, no deliberate choice was made. Women's studies developed along the lines of least resistance: courses here and there, according to faculty interest and administrative openness; committees composed of whoever was interested and able to participate.

Catharine Stimpson and Florence Howe, from their perspectives as editors of *Signs* and *Women's Studies Newsletter*, respectively, both ob-

---

100. E.g., Gerda Lerner felt that women's studies "implicitly challenges the basic assumptions underlying all of social science, all of our culture—that man is the measure. Such an all-encompassing challenge cannot be approached by a narrow disciplinary focus" ("On the Teaching and Organization of Feminist Studies," in Siporin, ed., pp. 34–37, esp. p. 34). Nancy M. Porter describes how a "shadow department" at Portland State University maintained its commitment to women's studies as action not subject in "A Nuts and Bolts View of Women's Studies," in Hoffman et al., eds., pp. 167–77.

101. Quoted by Howe and Ahlum, "Women's Studies and Social Change," in Rossi and Calderwood, eds. (n. 4 above), p. 420.

102. Michele H. Herman and William E. Sedlacek, "Student Perceptions of the Need for a Women's Studies Program," *College Student Journal* 7, no. 3 (September–October 1973): 3–6.

served that the opposite sides of segregation and isolation were independence and autonomy. Acknowledging the diversity of circumstances and—perhaps in light of the internal conflicts of 1973—the dangers of establishing a single model for women's studies, Stimpson declared that "each program must work out its destiny . . . that women's studies should be seen as a multiplicity of intersecting activities."[103] Howe, strongly influenced by her experience in the "free-university" movement of the 1960s and the apparent decline of black studies during the 1970s, tended to stress the pitfalls of separation or what she called "stuffing women in a corner." Fearing that "women and minority groups [would] rest content with their piece of turf rather than turn their energetic movements into strategies for changing the university as a whole," she stressed the advantages of programs maintained through non-departmental channels.[104]

By the spring of 1974 when the *Women's Studies Newsletter* raised a series of questions about the viability of various structures, the non-departmental pattern was already established. The following year, while noting the network structure's disadvantages to (especially untenured) faculty in allowing joint appointments and divided responsibilities, Howe still felt that the departmental alternative would render women's studies more vulnerable to excision. In her national survey, she found the fifteen "mature" programs she visited "clear about their strategic mission: not to build an empire in one small corner of the campus, but to change the curriculum throughout."[105]

Advocacy of administrative independence in the early years was rare. Although Sheila Tobias felt that departments might be able to put up a stronger fight for resources than programs would, only San Diego State and SUNY/Buffalo developed rationales that geared separation to essential feminist goals.[106] Both groups considered structure more significant than content and emphasized the need for autonomy. At San Diego State, the original women's studies program was designed as one unit in a proposed ten-part women's center that would include components for research, publication, child care, storefront operations, cultural activities, recruitment and tutorials, community outreach, campus women's liberation, and center staff operations.[107] A coordinating committee representing all components and the community would govern

103. Stimpson, "The New Feminism and Women's Studies" (n. 19 above).
104. Florence Howe, "Structure and Staffing of Programs," *Women's Studies Newsletter* 3, no. 2 (Spring 1975): 1–2, and "Introduction," in Howe, ed., *Women and the Power to Change* (n. 31 above), pp. 1–14, esp. p. 9.
105. See also "Editorial," *Women's Studies Newsletter* 2, no. 2 (Spring 1974): 2; "Structure and Staffing of Programs," p. 2; and *Seven Years Later* (n. 35 above), p. 21.
106. Tobias, "Teaching Women's Studies" (n. 21 above), p. 263.
107. Salper, "Women's Studies" (n. 28 above).

the center collectively, fulfilling the founders' belief that "the actual curriculum of the university is less important than the structure of the
education itself. . . . What you learn in school is how to fit into the
structure of domination and power hierarchy which is the basis of all
institutions of class society. . . . Women's studies, based on collective
structure, exists in opposition to the structure of the university."[108]
Within the college where it was established, the women's studies program was responsible directly to the dean and, until three members
achieved tenure, subject to the supervision of a committee of tenured
faculty. Although the program underwent a complete change in faculty
in 1974, it retained its original autonomy within the college and was
recognized as a full-fledged department.[109]

Autonomy at SUNY/Buffalo meant establishing a separate college
within the university system set up in the 1960s to allow students to
develop experimental and innovative programs. Although its faculty
positions and degree-granting power were located in American studies,
the Women's Studies College offered some courses exclusively for credit
in women's studies, while others were cross-listed with a variety of departments. Despite a major controversy with the administration during a
rechartering process in 1974 and 1975, the college continues committed
above all to "organizational struggle," which its separate structure facili-
tates. As a "center of women's lives," it is apparently less concerned about
"ghettoization" than about its ability to maintain collective governance
and educational methods "which develop in our students and instructors
the capabilities and assertiveness necessary to accept the active responsibility for their own educations."[110]

Given the diversity of existing academic units, the forms of women's
studies may be infinite. Noteworthy uncommon types include the Department of Ethnic Studies and Women's Studies at California State
University, Chico, and the consortia for women's studies organized by
the Five Colleges in Western Massachusetts, the Great Lakes Colleges
Association, and the Big Ten.[111] One of the most perceptive statements

108. Women's Studies Board, San Diego State College (n. 28 above), p. 8.
109. See Boxer (n. 28 above). The department now has three tenured as well as three
tenure-track faculty and is no longer subject to an external advisory committee.
110. "Women's Studies College Charter," SUNY/Buffalo (n. 49 above). At present the
collegiate system is being phased out. The Buffalo program is moving to combine its
American studies and women's studies resources into one B.A. program which maintains
as many as possible of the innovative and structural aspects of the Women's Studies College.
111. See Gayle Kimball, "From the California State University, Chico," *Women's
Studies Newsletter* 3, nos. 3–4 (Summer/Fall 1975): 23; Catharine E. Portugues, "From the
University of Massachusetts, Amherst," ibid., pp. 25–26; Beth Reed, "The GLCA Women's
Studies Program: A Consortial Approach," ibid., 6, no. 1 (Winter 1978): 17–19; Gayle
Graham Yates, "Big Ten Forms Women's Studies Permanent Consortium," ibid., 7, no. 1
(Winter 1979): 31.

on the question of structure came from the director of a women's studies department, Juanita Williams of the University of South Florida:

> The establishment of a separate program, as contrasted to the offering of courses about women in existing traditional departments . . . is and probably will continue to be an important administrative and fateful issue, one that will not be resolved soon, and perhaps never. The reason for this, as I see it, is that women's studies, more than any other part of the curriculum at the present time, are emerging in idiosyncratic ways on campuses; the forms that their establishment take are a function of the beliefs, energies, and personalities of the women promoting them, and of the character of the institution and the supporting community.[112]

Williams provides an excellent summary of the evident advantages of separation, which she feels outweigh the potential dangers of isolation: essentially a central structure provides identity, generates research, exercises relative autonomy in selection of faculty and in curriculum development, and indicates a substantial institutional commitment. Noting the many demands on women's studies faculty to sit on university committees, to present guest lectures, and to participate in public relations activities, Williams finds no evidence of insularity. On the contrary, she suggests that "a little occasional isolation would be welcome at times."[113]

Reports from the field since the mid-1970s suggest that the commitment to structural innovation declined as the early ties to community women's liberation weakened and as the practitioners of women's studies on campus began to seek the security of stable course offerings for students, tenure-track appointments for faculty, and continuing and adequate funding for programs. Research revealing both the sexism in the content, methods, and fundamental assumptions of established disciplines and the potential of women's studies for creating a renaissance in the liberal arts seems to have encouraged an ethos that emphasizes obtaining and maintaining resources for the long haul. Programs without a departmental base find this particularly hard. They depend on the "charity of departments," which they routinely have to convince to offer the courses they need. They lack the ability to hire their own faculty; those they borrow from departments often labor under double responsibilities and fear adverse tenure or promotion decisions specifically because of their work in women's studies.[114] One case of a negative

112. Juanita H. Williams, "Administering a Women's Studies Program," *Women's Studies Newsletter* 2, no. 3 (Summer 1974): 5, 11–12, esp. 11.

113. Ibid., p. 12.

114. See comments by Sybil Weir and Dana V. Hiller, *Women's Studies Newsletter* 3, no. 2 (Spring 1975): 4–6, and Greene (n. 43 above), pp. 4–5. Christa Van Daele, "Women's Studies: Time for a Grass Roots Revival," *Branching Out* 5, no. 1 (1978): 8–11, presents a

tenure decision allegedly made on this ground gained nationwide notoriety.[115]

Although it is too early to know what models will prove most enduring or effective, increasingly positive perceptions of the departmental model have appeared. Defusing earlier criticism, Dana Hiller points out that women are no more ghettoized in women's studies than in many other fields.[116] Coyner questions the validity of the home economics and black studies analogies, noting that interdisciplinary departments of biochemistry and linguistics have prospered.[117] Sarah Slavin Schramm asserts that "women's studies is worthy of separate status," which, given its collective orientation and community ties, need not produce "isolation and excision."[118]

Comparing the situation of the Women's Studies Program with that of the Department of Ethnic Studies at the University of California, Berkeley, Gloria Bowles clearly feels the latter has the stronger position. Recognizing explicitly a fact generally obscured in the debate over strategies and structures, she notes that "if Women's Studies had begun in 1969, we might be in the same position [as Ethnic Studies]."[119] For Madeleine Goodman, the key to success is the commitment made by a university when it establishes a separate unit with permanent faculty, space, and support, where women's studies can be the "central professional responsibility of a group of individuals hired and evaluated as professors of women's studies." From this secure base, they can also

gloomy picture of faculty marginality in two Ontario universities, as does R. J. Smith for the University of Michigan ("Women's Studies on Trial," *Michigan Daily* [April 13, 1980], p. 3). Howe discussed faculty problems in *Seven Years Later,* pp. 63–66. Emily Abel and Deborah Rosenfelt focus on the situation of part-time faculty in women's studies ("Women Part-Time Faculty," *Radical Teacher* 17 [November 1980]: 61).

115. On the case of Maija Blaubergs against the University of Georgia, see Lorenzo Middleton, "Academic Freedom vs. Affirmative Action: Georgia Professor Jailed in Tenure Dispute," *Chronicle of Higher Education* (September 2, 1980), p. 1.

116. Dana V. Hiller, "Women's Studies Emerging," *Journal of National Association for Women Deans and Counselors* 41, no. 1 (Fall 1977): 3–6.

117. "The problem is not just separation but continuing racism and sexism" (Coyner, p. 38). Greta Hoffman Nemiroff, however, attributes the survival of biochemistry and other science and computer-based interdisciplinary fields to infusions of money from government and industry (p. 65).

118. Schramm (n. 21 above), pp. 351–55. This analysis appeared earlier as "Women's Studies: Its Focus, Idea, Power and Promise," *Social Science Journal* 14, no. 2 (April 1977): 5–13.

119. Gloria Bowles, interviewed by Deborah Rosenfelt, "Ethnic Studies and Women's Studies at UC/Berkeley: A Collective Interview," *Radical Teacher* 14 (December 1979): 12–18. The Ethnic Studies Department had a budget of over a $1 million and fourteen ladder positions, compared with $30,000 and no regular faculty in women's studies. The autonomous programs at San Diego State, South Florida, and SUNY/Buffalo all date from the early 1970s.

reach out in many directions. Goodman describes many campus and community activities that demonstrate that the program at the University of Hawaii, though separate, "has hardly been a ghetto."[120]

In the economically troubled early 1980s, however, the opportunity to choose "either/or," department or network, may be unlikely. Some universities indeed still provide no resources beyond departmentally based courses and urge faculty "to develop devices to maintain and nurture communication with each other" on their own time.[121] Perhaps the best option will be evolution into "both/and," that is, a core of faculty devoted only to women's studies, perhaps persons trained in more than one discipline to become the "interdisciplinary women," working with interested teachers in whatever places they may dwell.[122] While it appears that by 1980 a network model had become the most common form of women's studies program, at the present time a data base adequate for assessment over time remains unavailable. In any case, clearly the organization must fit the university's existing structure and ambience.[123]

Conclusion

The greatest promise of women's studies and its most enduring problem are inextricably linked. The "exhilaration beyond exhaustion"[124] that moves women's studies flows out of the combination of personal and professional interests it allows and demands. The integration of scholarship and politics provides academic feminism with an endless supply of questions to research, courses to teach, and missions to accomplish. It affects every major issue considered here: the adaptation of feminist principles to the classroom, the conflict between political and academic aims, the attempt to transform academic structures as well as curricula, the interaction of campus and community feminism, the struggles against racism and homophobia inside and outside of women's

---

120. Madeleine J. Goodman, "Women's Studies: The Case for a Departmental Model," *Women's Studies Newsletter* 8, no. 4 (Fall/Winter 1980): 7–8.

121. Barrie Thorne, "Closeup: Michigan State University," *Women's Studies Newsletter* 4, no. 2 (Spring 1976): 8.

122. Some programs have developed majors which use a "core plus" model; faculty appointment may or may not follow the same plan. See, e.g., Boneparth (n. 40 above), p. 25; Hester Eisenstein, "Women's Studies at Barnard College: Alive and Well and Living in New York," *Women's Studies Newsletter* 6, no. 3 (Summer 1978): 4; Elaine Hedges, "Women's Studies at a State College," ibid., 2, no. 4 (Fall/Winter 1975): 5; Yates, "Women's Studies in its Second Phase" (n. 33 above), p. 5.

123. Howe and Lauter (n. 12 above), pp. iv, 4. Judith Gappa and J. Nicholls Eastmond describe a carefully contrived and successful campaign to fit women's studies into a most unlikely structure (n. 37 above).

124. This phrase is borrowed from Minnich (n. 74 above), p. 5.

studies, the difficulties of interdisciplinarity in a discipline-based world, the ambivalence of both autonomous and multidepartmental structures, the search for a new unifying framework and appropriate methodology.

These are all facets of the symbiotic relationship between women's studies and women's liberation, a connection that provides strength to both parts but also allows for a potentially counterproductive confusion. This is evident in the difficulties experienced by the NWSA. Committed to the feminist goal of including all oppressed and underrepresented women, it has built a structure that threatens to produce "an elite of officially-recognized caucuses."[125] Although it thereby strives to deal continuously and substantially with the effects of centuries of economic discrimination and social violence against women of color and lesbians, it nevertheless remains vulnerable to charges of racism and homophobia and to countercharges that communication is inhibited and fragmentation encouraged by pressure to pass as a "true feminist."[126] As a result, delegates at national conventions have felt obliged to promise action that the association's meager resources may not be able to sustain.[127] If inflated expectations and narrow politics combine to prevent open presentation of views deemed unacceptable, and controversy is submerged under waves of consensus, the NWSA may become representative of only a part of the women's studies constituency. The survival of the organization, the profession, and the unfulfilled mission itself requires that women's studies practitioners recognize the complexities of the relationship between education and social change, understand the limitations of their present power, and, while continuing to struggle with difficult issues of current concern, address new questions as well. The building of a discipline—and a better world—takes place through the constructive resolution of disparate ideas, interests, and aims.

While multipurpose gatherings such as the annual NWSA conventions serve many needs, the vast majority of participants who completed the evaluation questionnaire in 1979 rated networking and renewing acquaintances more important concerns than curriculum development or administrative and employment needs, which, however, more

125. Nanette Bruckner, "Dialectics or Diversity" (position paper prepared for the NWSA Coordinating Council to present to the membership, Storrs, Connecticut, Spring 1981). For a more positive view, see Deborah S. Rosenfelt, "A Time for Confrontation," *Women's Studies Quarterly* 9, no. 3 (Fall 1981): 10–12.

126. Davis and Frech (n. 48 above), pp. 33–35. On fragmentation, see also reports on the conferences in Kansas and Indiana in the *Women's Studies Newsletter* 7, no. 3 (Summer 1979): 5–9, and ibid., 8, no. 3 (Summer 1980): 3–9; and the comments of Alice Chai and Helen Stewart as reported in *off our backs* 11, no. 7 (July 1981): 20–21.

127. On the conflict between feminist goals and "fiscal responsibility," see Barbara Hillyer Davis's report on the finance committee (*Women's Studies Newsletter* 7, no. 3 [Summer 1979]: 25) and Alice Henry's report on the 1981 assembly (*off our backs* 11, no. 7 [July 1981]: 2–6).

than half considered very important.[128] Perhaps other ways to foster contemplation and communication need to be developed: shorter, simpler conferences on single issues such as integrating theory and practice in the classroom; moving students beyond the favored courses in health, psychology, and sexuality to the less popular courses on economic and political systems; finding or creating job markets for graduates; opening general education to women's studies; building a major or graduate program; implementing feminism in hiring practices; developing means to produce more women's studies teachers; pioneering cross-disciplinary Ph.D. programs; and surviving "Reaganomics" and New Right attacks on academic freedom. Published proceedings from such meetings would fulfill needs now barely touched for the most part by brief articles and notes of the type surveyed in this essay. Perhaps it is also time for *Female Studies: Series Two,* for practitioners of the second decade to reach out and share, to deliberate over strategies and contend about tactics, but also to celebrate achievements and join hands for the long struggle to reform education and society in the image and interest of us all.

Department of Women's Studies
San Diego State University

128. Patricia A. Frech and Barbara Hillyer Davis, "The NWSA Constituency: Evaluation of 1979 Conference Participation," *Frontiers: A Journal of Women Studies* 5, no. 1 (Spring 1980): 68–70.

The Way of All Ideology

Susan Griffin

And it was then I knew that the healing
of all wounds
is forgiveness
that permits a promise
of our return
at the end.
[ALICE WALKER, "Good Night, Willie Lee/I'll See You In the Morning"]

I

1

I begin thinking about political theory by thinking about the way we think. I speculate about ideology. About form. And then about dialogue. The three phenomena occur to me at once. Forms: the forms of hierarchies, of institutions, of habits, the way things are done; the forms of language, gesture, art, of thought, and equally, of emotion. What we say to one another being often what it is predictable that we will say; what I will say, if you say that: Dialogue.

But a speculation about dialogue is also a speculation about ideology. For so often we speak as if my questions and your answers, my statements and your responses, were all written down somewhere in a great codicil of conversations. As if, in the same code, who "I" believe myself to be, and who I believe "you" to be, were also written; as if it were recorded that there must be an "I" and a "you," the "you" corresponding to the inevitable "other": the enemy.

And now I sit up straighter and glare in the eye of an imaginary "you" who forbids me to have such thoughts as the one I am about to utter, and I ask this "you": What if all our efforts toward liberation are determined by an ideology which despite our desire for a better world leads us inevitably back to the old paradigm of suffering?

2

This is not a question filled with dread, I tell this "you." For now this other half of a continual dialogue in my mind, has become the censor. *She* reduces, maligns, misinterprets my thoughts. *She* challenges, troubles, and unsettles me. And I argue with her. I tell her, this is a question filled with hope. It is filled with the implication that our dialogues can be transformed into real speech, to a liberating conversation; it is a question imbued with the suggestion that we might free ourselves from the old paradigm of warfare, that I may not need an enemy.

3

Who are these two in me? The "I" with whom I identify, the "you" whom I define as the not "I." They always shift; they are never the same two. One day "you" is the nag, the dictator, the time and motion expert, the boss, the destroyer. And on that day "I" am the dreamer, the seeker, the poet, the visionary thinker, the daring questioner nevertheless terrified by this other, who looks over my shoulder, nevertheless afraid of her judgments, even falling silent when I sense her disapproval.

At other times "I" am the authority, the good girl, the stable and predictable one, whereas "you" are a secret thought, a hidden memory, a long-buried desire. When I was a married woman, this "you" remembered all along that I had been in love with women, remembered the passion I felt in my woman's body for another woman, disrupted the comfortable, acceptable image I had of myself.

But now, in my recent thought about thinking, this "you" is the commissar of knowledge. She is politically correct. She is moral. Her ears are pitched for heresy. She hears me, for instance, think about psychology, about the structure of the mind, the structures of emotions, and she whispers to me words to the effect that I am being apolitical, that I am being one of *them*. In my mind, I have become exhausted arguing with her.

4

Yet in and through this exhausting argument I know I am split from myself. I watch the phenomenon in myself. What I think of as myself is actually split in two. A new thought, a new way of seeing—which is at its heart the articulation of a new feeling, and hence a new experience in the world—wishes to be born. In the effort to exist, this thought thrusts away all doubt, all second thoughts. But these second thoughts are thoughts of alarm. They are afraid of change. They would remain the same.

Slowly I begin to identify myself with the new thought. I split away from my doubts, calling this doubting self "you." Now I project the doubting half of my own inner conversation upon another. I supply her with her missing part of the dialogue. As I argue with myself, I imagine I am arguing with her. I have created a figment of my denied self whom *she* has now come to represent.

5

I have encountered the idea of a denied self before. Writing of racism in the 1960s, James Baldwin spoke in *The Fire Next Time* of the creation of the "nigger" in the white mind. The idea of the nigger, he observed, said nothing about black character and everything about white racist character. The nigger is the denied part of the white idea of self, a fantasy of another's being created out of a purposeful ignorance of the self. And I discovered the same delusion, the same denied self, in the pornographer's idea of a woman.

Moreover, as I wrote about the pornographer's mind I discovered that pornography itself was not so much an art form as it was an ideology and an ideology which, like the ideology of racism, *requires* the creation of another, a not-I, an enemy. This is a world view in which the self is irrevocably split so that it does not recognize its other half, and in which all phenomena, experience, and human qualities are also split into the superior and the inferior, the righteous and the evil, the above and the below. What is superior, according to this ideology, is by rights above all that is inferior. For the righteous must have authority over and control of the evil.

And the other, the not-I, bears all those qualities which are lesser and bad; thus the other is the enemy who must be controlled or annihilated.

6

The one and the other. Now, as I think about my own thought, I ask myself if racism and pornography and the unholy warfare in my own mind can have a common origin? For if this were true, I reason, it would bear on my own efforts to liberate myself from the ideologies which oppress me and to free myself from the imprisoning conditions of a society hostile to female being.

7

Images, gestures, facts of history, whole patterns of culture begin to assemble in my mind, and I am reminded once more of the traditional association, in the mind of this civilization, between the other and nature; and between the "one" (the identified self, the white, anglicized man) and culture. How women are said to be closer to nature, more emotional, lacking in intellect or spiritual calling, needing the authority of a man, a man's cool reason, the spiritual control of a male voice, a male God. Peoples of color envisioned as bestial, and superhumanly sexual, as sensual, and overemotional, even dangerous, with natural cunning, needing to be mastered, counseled, told how to live, to speak, to work.

In this ideology the denied self, projected onto the other, embodies all that is part of the natural, sensate life of the body and all of the natural emotions which so often cause one to feel out of control, even frightened of oneself. Through this ideology's fantasy that the other is dangerous, one sees above all a mind which *fears natural life*. The desire to hide from nature is the secret raison d'être of this ideology. Through this ideology the mind imagines that to wish is to command, or that feeling can be replaced by concept.

Because we are natural beings we do not have power over nature; we face physical death, the possibility of injury, the certainty of aging, the continual vulnerability of flesh to pain, the experience of separation, loss, and grief. And our feelings too have a life beyond our conscious control. We want what we are not supposed to want. Remember what it is painful to know. Become overwhelmed with ecstasy or rage or pain and lose our bearings.

The mind would control natural life by denying natural power and by keeping a knowledge of that power apart from itself. Yet knowledge of natural power and the life of natural feeling cannot die; this knowledge, this life persists even with our own hunger, our own breathing. Because of the very persistence of feeling, the mind which wants to deny this life must give it some mode of existence. Thus the mind creates a fantasy of another being, the other, who embodies all the qualities of the denied self.

But now, alongside my thought about this pattern of our culture to deny nature and to associate nature with the other, I consider another cultural pattern. And this is the preponderant hostility within culture to creativity.

In an essay called "Poems Are Not Luxuries," the poet Audre Lorde has made an illuminating connection between this civilization's fear of the associative and musical language of poetry (a language which comes from the depths of reason beneath rational consciousness, from dark, unknown regions of mind) and the same civilization's fear of black skin, of the female, of darkness, the dark other, Africa, signifying an older, secret knowledge.[1]

For, of course, it is not simply inventiveness which is feared. The new machine, the new gadget is worshipped. What is really feared is an open door into a consciousness which leads us back to the old, ancient, infant and mother knowledge of the body, in whose depths lies another form of culture not opposed to nature but instead expressing the full power of nature and of our natures.

This fear of the knowledge of the body has created a dualism between culture and nature, intellect and emotion, spirit and matter. And the same fear has made of women—as it has of peoples of color and of Jews—symbols of feeling, carnality, nature, all that is in civilization's "unconscious" and that it would deny. This is why it is so terrifying to the traditional mind of our culture to confront a woman who is scholarly, or a black political philosopher.

I remember that in Germany the period before the holocaust was remarkable both for the assimilation of Jews into German culture and for an extraordinary burst of creativity among Jewish people. The anti-Semite had regarded Yiddish culture as inferior, and through this denigration he spared himself the recognition of what for him would be an impossible formula. Because within his symbolic reasoning, the existence of a Jew who was "cultured" would mean that nature and culture are not forever separate. Now the anti-Semite had to confront a Jew who could not only speak German but write great poetry in German, write great German music, and expand the boundaries of German science. These accomplishments must have created a terror in the anti-Semite's mind; each of them represented a union between nature and culture. And in this metaphorical system, such a union could only mean that unconscious knowledge—our physical knowledge of the power of nature and the memory of the power of our mothers—will become conscious. The anti-Semite is afraid to know himself.

Should it be a surprise then that this period of history was also

1. Audre Lorde, "Poems Are Not Luxuries," *Chrysalis: A Magazine of Female Culture*, no. 3 (1977), pp. 7–9. See also Audre Lorde and Adrienne Rich, "An Interview with Audre Lorde," *Signs: Journal of Women in Culture and Society* 6, no. 4 (Summer 1981): 713–36, esp. 728–29.

remarkable for the breaking of many other separating paradigms—the breakdown of traditional forms of art, of traditional family structures, of the old Newtonian idea of the structure of the universe which separated matter and energy, of the separation between mind and body? And finally, that the burst of extraordinary creativity in every kind of field was not experienced exclusively by Jews; it was a phenomenon for which later this period as a whole was to be thought remarkable.

8

If before I failed to see that a fear of nature and a fear of creativity must be inextricably associated, it is only because, schooled in my own culture and its paradigms, I have failed to see that nature and creativity share the same origin, are born in the same breath. For I have come to age in a culture which opposes spirit to the flesh and which uses culture as a way to deny the power of the natural.

And now I begin to suspect that all ideology must share a hidden tendency. For beyond a just description of the truth, an ideology holds the promise that one may control reality with the mind, assert the ideal as more real than reality, or place idea as an authority above nature, and even above our sensual experience of nature: what we see, what we hear, what we feel, taste, smell.

And with this promise, always, inevitably, no matter what the ideology, the idea of the other is born. For another must become a symbol and a scapegoat for the ideologist's own denied knowledge that this ideology is not more real than reality and must bow to contradictory natural evidence.

The list is long. The persecution of the Christians. The persecution of the heretics. The Inquisition. The Pogroms. The persecution of Socialists and Communists. The Stalinist purges. (And into this fabric is woven the continual persecution of peoples of color, of women, of Jews, the fear of lesbians, the silencing of our creativity.)

9

Ideology. Ideology, form, and dialogue. One begins as a socialist arguing that matter comes before spirit. One wins a revolution and vanquishes the enemy. But then one discovers the enemy is not yet dead. She is a poet whose words are vaguely unsettling. Who doubts. And then there are the prisons again, the police again, the old terror again. The war is still waging.

10

And there is still a war waging within me. I have been schooled in the ways of this culture. In my own mind unknowingly I choose the same solution to emotional dilemma that my culture has chosen and has taught me to choose. Though I argue against pornography and racism, my own mind splits against itself, creates a "you." Now this "you" is the ideologist, a part of myself I hide from myself. She is afraid of my own creativity. She asks old questions which exclude the possibility of new insights. She has categorical ideas of thought or expression from which she will not deviate. She dismisses my ideas with labels, epithets, catch phrases. She purposely misinterprets me and seizes on small mistakes to humiliate me.

And she is a martinet. She wants me to produce a comprehensive world view so that nothing in the world is unexplained. She is a Prussian soldier in the world of the intellect. She is not interested in unanswered questions, in uncertainties, intuitions, barely grasped insights, hunches. Moreover she wishes every idea to be consistent, to conform to one ideal. She is not familiar with Freud's notion that in the unconscious what seems contradictory to the conscious mind is resolved.[2] She is impatient for resolution.

Moreover, she argues to me that I should not cite Freud. She is given to categorizing everyone as either enemy or not an enemy. To her way of thinking, one cannot agree with some ideas belonging to one thinker and disagree with others. A thinker is either good or bad and one must not quote bad ideas. Indeed, she censors not only my imagination and my thinking but my reading.

And, predictably, she is obtuse to musical, to associative language. Though she lives in my mind alongside a poet, claiming to have respect for poetry, every time a line of poetry begins to be formed, she silences it. It does not fit her idea of what is moral or useful.

And, above all, she values production. She cannot understand a poetry without clear purpose. Before each line is written, it must, to pass her censorship, clearly relate to some moral cause. It must argue for liberation. That a new expression at its birth may have no obvious relationship to liberation, but may, in the end, be more liberating than all her expectations, has not occurred to her. And cannot occur to her. For above all she labors in defense of ideology, in defense of the desire to control reality with the idea and to describe reality as always *predictable*. Thus, it is contrary to her real purpose to let herself know that from the darker, unknown part of my mind great riches might come. She is ashamed of such riches, for such riches speak of a larger reality than she is willing to admit exists.

This is the way of all ideology. It is mind over body. Safety over risk. The predictable over the surprise. Control over emotion. But the history of ideologies is also a tragedy. For in the beginning a political theory is born of genuine feeling of a sense of reality. But in a state of feeling alone, the knowledge of oppression remains mute, and the reality of

2. Sigmund Freud, *Collected Papers*, ed. Ernest Jones, trans. Joan Riviere, 5 vols. (New York: Basic Books, 1959), 5:184.

oppression is explained away by oppressive theories; it is said, for instance, that members of the working class have failed to raise themselves by their own bootstraps or that poverty is a sign of having sinned against God, of lacking God's grace. A theory of liberation must be created to articulate the feeling of oppression, to describe this oppression as real, as unjust, and to point to a cause. In this way the idea is liberating. It restores to the oppressed a belief in the self and in the authority of the self to determine what is real.

But when a theory is transformed into an ideology, it begins to destroy the self and self-knowledge. Originally born of feeling, it pretends to float above and around feeling. Above sensation. It organizes experience according to itself, without touching experience. By virtue of being itself, it is supposed to know. To invoke the name of this ideology is to confer truthfulness. No one can tell it anything new. Experience ceases to surprise it, inform it, transform it. It is annoyed by any detail which does not fit into its world view. Begun as a cry against the denial of truth, now it denies any truth which does not fit into its scheme. Begun as a way to restore one's sense of reality, now it attempts to discipline real people, to remake natural beings after its own image. All that it fails to explain it records as dangerous. All that makes it question, it regards as its enemy. Begun as a theory of liberation, it is threatened by new theories of liberation; slowly, it builds a prison for the mind.

11

As I sit to write, the ideological part of my mind dictates that an essay about political philosophy should not be invaded by emotion. This objection partakes of the duality of literary forms. It rests on the claim that truth is more truthful when it emanates from a disembodied voice. This part of my mind has accepted the illusory possibility of objectivity.

And like the racist or the pornographer, this part of my mind schooled in ideology projects whatever is unacceptable in myself onto others.

12

As I was composing the notes toward this writing, I was forced to confront my own self-denial and projection. Waiting in line to be served in a restaurant, I began to notice an older woman who was sitting at a table alone. She was not eating, and she seemed to be miserable. I assumed she was waiting to be met. Her expression, the paleness of her skin, something in her posture all indicated to me that she might be ill, perhaps even seriously ill, perhaps dying. I imagined then that she was nauseous. I was hungry. Yet as I looked at her I felt my appetite begin to ebb, a nausea seemed about to invade me by virtue of her presence. I was afraid that I might be seated at a table next to her, so that I might become more nauseous, or be contaminated. Slowly, despite another voice in me that urged reason and compassion, I felt an anger toward her. Why was she sick in this restaurant? Why force people who are eating to participate in her misery? I wanted to shout at her that she should go home, but of course, I did not. I was deeply ashamed of my feelings. And because of this shame I hid them away.

Later, seated at a table across the room, after I had eaten breakfast and forgotten the woman, my friend left the table. Then idly I glanced in the woman's direction again. And I saw that she had been joined by an older man, who I felt was her husband, and by a younger man, who I presumed to be her son. Now I imagined the cause of her waiting. In my mind, I saw the older man going to pick up his son; the son being terribly late, leaving his sick mother to wait for him. And I was indignant on his mother's behalf. Not knowing for certain whether he was her son, whether she was ill, or whether he indeed had been late, I began composing a speech in my mind. I felt justified in my anger at him. After all, was he not a man and she a woman? Were not women always waiting for men, being taken for granted, being caused misery? Were not sons as a lot ungrateful and unkind and disrespectful to their mothers? Someone ought to speak to him. *I* ought to. I ought to tell him how ashamed he should be for making his poor mother wait.

But, at last, fortunately, I began to laugh at myself. For, of course, it was I who had been ashamed, ashamed of my own responses to this woman, I who had been unkind in my thoughts toward her. And now I who could assuage my own guilt by being angry at someone else, whom I imagined responsible for her pain. From her persecutor, I had turned myself into her champion. And in all this, I avoided confronting or knowing myself.

And now as I looked at my imagined portrait of her son I saw myself. For according to my ideological explanation of male hostility toward women, men are afraid of women, and most particularly of their mothers, because they fear death. And was not that precisely what I had projected on her, my own fear of my own death, of the possibility that my body might fail me, and instead of giving me hunger, give me nausea?

Because I was ashamed of this feeling in myself, because of the ideologist in me who censored my own feeling and did not let it live long enough to be explored and understood, I was in danger from the most dangerous brand of ignorance, ignorance of myself.

13

This is one of the ways ideology hides the truth. One is only allowed, through the justifying framework of ideas, to acknowledge certain emotions toward certain people. A woman can hate a man for oppressing her. Black can hate white. Working class can feel rage at the ruling class. All of these are made acceptable by theories of liberation. And as such they are liberating angers. But another whole range of emotions exists which ideology defines as unacceptable. Suppose, for instance, one feels a love for the enemy, or a particular member of the enemy class. Suppose one feels anger and hatred toward another of the same oppressed group? Suppose a woman hates a woman? These emotions are defined as "incorrect." And they become hidden. Thus, I become blind toward my own anger and fear of another woman, because this feeling is not correct. In this way by its own denials and blindnesses each new ideology creates its own forbidden, subterranean world of reality.

14

But now another set of questions begins to arise in my mind. Without ideology, someone in me asks, how can one argue for liberation? How can one even think, or see deeper cause, make that analysis which opens out to social change? Is not this writing itself ideological? For I have interpreted conflict as a conflict between idea and nature, culture and nature. Am I arguing that thought itself is dangerous? Am I making an intellectual case against the intellect? Or, in a different light, am I not invalidating all that political theory makes evident?

II

1

In my mind now another couple is forming, another split between two parts of myself. And this is not the old pair, the visionary and the censor. Rather, both of these are ideologists. One of these is my political self. She has always seen things in terms of divisions of power. She knows that there are those who have the power to shape the lives of others. She knows the forms of that power, both visible and subtle: money, social position, language, education, simple physical force.

But now another is born, and she is a psychological thinker. She loves to gossip. She loves to try to understand her own deeper motives and the meanings of the lives of those around her. She is fascinated by the mind itself and by the shape of feelings. The political thinker is suspicious of psychology for, so often, psychologists have obfuscated or denied real political oppression. And yet, the psychological thinker is also suspicious of purely political thinking. For she has begun to notice how often the political mind will disguise and deny personal feelings with correct political rhetoric. I call these two thinkers Rachel and Agnes. The quality of their dialogue has not been illuminating.

2

Rachel the political theorist says: "I'm more worried about being raped than about the danger of ideological thinking. Somehow it seems to be more relevant to my everyday urgent life." Agnes the psychologist says: "Don't you know that your own mind shapes your everyday life?" Rachel says: "Don't you know male, white, capitalist power shapes my life?" Agnes says: "And you have no power to change this?" Rachel says: "I will take the power." Agnes says: "Don't you know your own mind shapes the way you take this power, determines whether you succeed or fail?"

They go on like this. The result is boredom. Agnes wins, then Rachel wins, then Agnes wins. But slowly each has reduced her ideas to the ridiculous. All the subtleties of both, all their perceptions, have been erased in an attempt to erase the truths which they offer each other. Their arguments become sadly predictable.

Here then is another aspect of ideological structure. Dialogue—which is finally perhaps the form of all thought—must become a war. One must lose and the other win. There must be a clear victor. One must be shown to be wrong. And therefore, each kind of thought is pitted against the other. The listener must choose between one and the other, either a truth or a falsity.

And yet Agnes has much insight to offer Rachel, and without Rachel's questions, Agnes's thought is curiously out of touch with reality, even as she argues for a knowledge of reality. For instance, Rachel tells Agnes that to have no political theory is impossible. For having no theory simply implies that one agrees with the political structures that exist, with the status quo. And moreover, Rachel explains, one must be able to name and locate oppression if one is to argue and struggle against oppression. Otherwise, she says, one begins to believe that oppression is simply a state of nature.

On the other hand, Agnes has wisdom to give to Rachel. She says that there are two kinds of anger. The first is accurate and appropriate; it is *known*. But the second is not accurately placed. It is displaced and therefore *unknown*. The first anger, she says, liberates one, both in mind and in body. But the second anger, she warns, imprisons. It becomes obsessive; it turns into bitterness; it leads to self-defeat; it turns us against ourselves. Because this second anger hides another deeper anger, the true anger, of which one is ashamed. Therefore, she tells Rachel, a political theorist who does not explore her own emotions is in danger of turning against herself.

3

As I write I realize that this question of two kinds of anger is essential. For me, it is the missing link between political and psychological understanding. I recall an episode from a case history of a child so severely abused by her parents that for years she never spoke. Finally a therapist broke through her veil of silence, and she began to trust the world again. Just as she was doing well her father, who had almost murdered her by trying to burn her alive, came to visit her. He promised to call her nightly, and to return in a week, to be a kind and loving parent. However he did not call, nor did he come. And the child was angry at him. Yet she could not admit her rage to herself. She was ashamed to admit that she might be abandoned in this way by her father, unwilling to admit her anger. Thus she displaced her anger on those who were close to her, on her friends, on those who had nursed her back to health, whom she had just recently learned to trust. Slowly she became alienated from everyone around her and began to retreat once more into herself, rejecting the world. But finally, she discovered and admitted the real source of her anger. She spoke out her rage against her father and acknowledged that he had left her, failed her, and that he was not capable of loving her. Only when she acknowledged her real anger could she trust herself and the world again.

To escape from genuine sources of anger is to escape from the self. And this escape is shaped and colored by shame, for one hides a feeling only if one is ashamed of that feeling. But ironically, to hide feeling does not get rid of shame; rather it increases one's inner feeling of humiliation, or of dishonor. For the very act of hiding *proves* to the self that what is hidden is terrible. Living in such a deceit, one lives with the constant and inarticulate feeling that one's inner self is evil, wrong, or even repulsive. And moreover, since one is hiding, one is actually lying, and this lie compounds one's feeling of wrongness. It is thus inevitable that displaced anger will lead to self-hatred and even to a desire for self-punishment. (The oppressed attack one another not only because it is safe but also because such an attack is an expression of self-hatred.)

But of course this self-hatred must be veiled, too: it is given another name. Thus the abused child complained of real irritations and difficulties, but these took on momentous proportions.

Ideology is capable of masking many different kinds of appropriate angers. For years I have noticed that male anger at women is often expressed in the name of "revolution." Although it has been almost always women and not men of the upper class who showed any concern for suffering of the poor, it was a woman, Marie Antoinette, who became the symbol in male revolutionary culture for aristocratic callousness. Patricia Hearst and not her father was kidnapped. And similarly white women became the symbol for Southern race privilege. (Though white women are not by any means without blame, one must be suspicious when a woman is chosen to symbolize a predominantly male power system.)[3]

3. Similarly, to picture a black man as the symbol of the rapist is a covert expression of racism, not because black men do not commit rape, but because this is a predominantly

But one is capable of many displaced angers. In the name of female liberation, we attack another woman because she is "incorrect." We say she is identified with males and then associate our anger at her with our anger at male power. Yet through this accusation we can express our anger at women, at our mother perhaps, or at ourselves. On the surface our attacks may be perfectly justified by fact. But this does not belie the other fact that these accusations serve to hide us from our real feelings. These feelings give a certain tone, an inappropriate rage or finality to our expressions. And in the end it is only when feelings are accurately named and explored that we cease ultimately to destroy ourselves, in body and mind, with our anger.

But here is another essential link between psychology and political theory. The secret existence of a hidden anger creates a false anger. And because ideas are intermingled with and even proceed from feeling, this false anger leads to the distortion of political theory. Thus there are two uses for theory. The first purpose of an idea is to explain reality. But a second purpose is to escape or deny reality. The same political theory can be used to arrive at truth or delusion.

I can find no better description of theory as madness than in Isaac Deutscher's portrait of Stalin. Speaking of Stalin's behavior during the period of Soviet industrialization and agricultural collectivization after 1929, Deutscher writes: "He was now completely possessed by the idea that he could achieve a miraculous transformation of the whole of Russia by a single *tour de force*. He seemed to live in a half-real and half-dreamy world of statistical figures and indices of industrial orders and instructions, a world in which no target and no objective seemed to be beyond his and the party's grasp."[4] When Stalin insisted that 17 million tons of pig iron could be produced, certain economists and managers voiced fears that this was impossible. Enraged by their opposition, Stalin labeled these men and women "right-wing" opportunists and "wreckers."

Similarly, Stalin's collectivization of farms turned into a war on the peasants, and the old way of farming was destroyed before the new way of farming was functioning. Again, Deutscher writes vividly of this cast of mind: "The whole experiment seemed to be a piece of prodigious

---

white society and because the image of a black man as a rapist has a history in the racist imagination of this white society. In the same way, a supposedly leftist censure of Zionism often reveals beneath its surface an anti-Semitism. For the same objections to nationalism (or military power, defense, and aggression) is not leveled at the Arab states, or at the Soviet Union, or indeed at France, or at Canada, or any nation that remains sovereign. Moreover an exaggerated fear and censure of Jewish power belongs to the history of anti-Semitism as does the choice of the Jew as the scapegoat for anger at bankers, capitalism, communism, anarchy, racism, and imperialism.

4. Isaac Deutscher, *Stalin: A Political Biography* (London: Oxford University Press, 1961), p. 321.

insanity, in which all the rules of logic and principles of economics were turned upside down. It was as if a whole nation had suddenly abandoned and destroyed its houses and huts, which, though obsolete and decaying, existed in reality, and moved, lock, stock, and barrel, into some illusory buildings."[5] Since the hidden motive behind such ideology is to escape reality and deny real thoughts and feelings, it is predictable that this ideology would destroy the real for "illusory buildings."

And precisely because it exists to disguise hidden thoughts and feelings, such an ideology must be fanatical. It must insist that no other truth than its own is possible. The very idea of an alternative suggests a search. But any search might disclose the original lie. In this atmosphere, anyone who deviates from the correct position is suspect. Now, ironically, ideology creates an atmosphere hostile to ideas. And fanatical ideologists, claiming that they possess the only description of reality possible, become anti-intellectual. Creativity is a threat to those in this frame of mind.

Of course the political theory inspired by delusion must be hostile to knowledge. In place of the development of the soul, self-knowledge, and education, such an ideology substitutes indoctrination. Before Stalinism took hold, the poet Osip Mandelstam accepted the end of democratic forms of education. Of this, Nadezhda Mandelstam writes, "Isn't this the basic error of our times and of each one of us? What do the people need to be indoctrinated for? What satanic arrogance you need to impose your views like this! It was only in Russia that the idea of popular education was replaced by the political concept of indoctrination. When M. himself became a target for it, he was one of the first to revolt."[6] In the same way, movements have been known to turn against their most creative and ingenious members. For example, speaking the correct line of the day, which held that all portraits of black people had to be tragic, Richard Wright accused Zora Neale Hurston of creating "minstrel" characters. "But I am not tragically colored," she responded.[7]

But who or what one really *is,* ceases to matter to ideology. For ideology gives birth to still another deceit: the enemy. The poet Osip Mandelstam, the writer Nadezhda Mandelstam, both once socialists, become enemies. Zora Neale Hurston is an enemy.

And moreover ideology makes over the real, material enemy—one who has actual power over our lives, or who actually poses a danger—into an inhuman entity. Suddenly this enemy ceases to possess any human qualities. No explanation can be offered, psychologically or ma-

5. Ibid., p. 326.
6. Nadezhda Mandelstam, *Hope against Hope* (New York: Atheneum, 1979), p. 114.
7. Cited by Mary Helen Washington in her introduction to "How It Feels to Be Colored Me," in *I Love Myself When I Am Laughing: A Zora Neale Hurston Reader,* ed. Alice Walker (Old Westbury, N.Y.: Feminist Press, 1979), p. 17.

terially, for his behavior. He is evil incarnate, sprung unborn and whole from hell. We refuse to understand him except as a kind of thing, a force. To consider that he may have a soul or that he may have been born innocent becomes a heresy.

And this enemy is oddly generalized. Now everyone male, everyone female, everyone white, everyone black, everyone Chinese, or Jewish is by virtue of biological identification the enemy.

At times the genuine anger of the oppressed also becomes generalized, from the force of experience and time, and for self-protection. But hatred for a delusory enemy has a different quality. It is final and relentless; it renders an irreversible judgment in the form of an idea. This is the idea of a natural, or inborn badness: the enemy becomes a monstrosity by virtue of characteristics acquired at birth. Andrea Dworkin has written of this kind of thinking: "It was this very ideology of biological determinism that had licensed the slaughter and/or enslavement of virtually any group one could name, including women by men. Anywhere one looked, it was this philosophy which justified atrocity. *This one faith which destroyed life with a momentum of its own.*"[8] Moreover, because the enemy serves as a mask for hidden thoughts and feelings, new enemies must always be created. If, for instance, men are the enemy, women who associate with men soon also become enemies.[9] One understands why this idea of an inhuman enemy must lead to violent atrocity. For such an enemy represents an original lie. A lie that is part of the self, always present, always threatening, powerful.

We live in a society which is built upon a prejudice toward women and peoples of color, homosexuals, Jewish people, the disabled. In that society we are the other. If we make those who are not oppressed as we are oppressed into enemies, we do not have the power to make them suffer as we do. What has been called "reverse sexism" or "reverse racism" is impossible, since racism and sexism are institutions which by definition include social, political, and economic sanctions.[10] And yet, if we produce a delusionary enemy in our minds, we do damage ourselves; we sacrifice a part of ourselves to that delusion; we lose part of our own power, the power of consciousness.

8. Andrea Dworkin, "Biological Superiority: The World's Most Dangerous and Deadly Idea," *Heresies* 6 (1978), pp. 47–51, esp. p. 48. Emphasis mine.

9. Andrea Dworkin describes an incident which took place on a public panel in 1977 on lesbianism as a personal politic. Members of the audience shouted at her, "Slut, bisexual, she sleeps with men." Andrea answered their accusations by saying that she did not sleep with men. Of this answer she writes, "All my life I have hated the prescribers, those who enforce sexual conformity. In answering, I had given in to the inquisitors, and I felt ashamed. It humiliated me to see myself then: one who resists the enforcers out there with militancy, but gives in without resistance to the enforcers among us" (ibid., p. 46).

10. I owe this description of racism to Ricky Sherover-Marcuse.

4

"But he fears the inner city of his soul"
[WILHELM STEKEL, *Sadism and Masochism*]

Agnes and Rachel have tried to banish each other from consciousness. But it is the very association of their thoughts and the confrontation between their two visions that is illuminating.

One cannot kill off a part of the self. If I silence my doubts, they
grow larger. If I forget an earlier self, this self haunts me in my dreams
and tries over and over to break through my ordinary consciousness,
even with violence. If I deny my own emotions, I begin to imagine they
exist in another, and this other becomes my enemy. But if I own my
feelings and trace them to their origins, they lead me to a self-knowledge
that is liberating and healing.

5

Every time I deny myself I commit a kind of suicide. And it is, in this
light, interesting to know that Hitler, the prototype of the fascist man,
committed suicide. For his hatred and fear of "the Jew"—and then the
Slavs, and black people, the gay, the disabled—was ultimately a denied
self-hatred. Of this one story comes to mind. When he wrote *Mein Kampf*
Hitler recorded that he became an anti-Semite one day when he saw an
old man dressed in a caftan walking through Vienna. "Is this a Jew?" he
asked, and then said to himself, "Is this a German?" deciding forever
that this Jew could not have been a German and was eternally separate
and different from himself. His biographers reveal that when he was a
young art student he bought his clothes from a Jewish man who sold
second-hand apparel, and the piece of clothing he wore most often was a
caftan purchased from this man. Moreover, what Hitler did not know is
that the Jewish caftan was really German dress from the Middle Ages,
preserved by the Jewish people who were exiled from Germany at that
time.

6

Indeed, the part of myself that I have exiled is essential to me
especially because she asks troublesome questions. There is a reason
Rachel exists. Her abstract ideas, her feeling of righteousness, originated
in my own experience. She is a part of what I have lived and felt; she is
ingrained into my very being. And so too Agnes is a part of my seeing,
my own sense that I know, my ability to perceive. If they disagree, it is, as
Freud suggests, perhaps a fault only of our limited knowledge. For they
are both expressions of myself and somewhere they must meet.

7

And what matters above all, in any dialogue, I begin to see, is intent. Rachel may see what Agnes is forgetting, or Agnes may know what Rachel does not know, yet if either one intends to make the other into an enemy, what they say to one another is distorted. It is not only that a certain intention behind words will make me defensive and thus deaf to reason. This is true. But it is also true that a false intention will distort the speaker's words.

I can be angry. I can hate. I can rage. But the moment I have defined another being as my enemy, I lose part of myself, the complexity and subtlety of my vision. I begin to exist in a closed system. When anything goes wrong, I blame my enemy. If I wake troubled, my enemy has led me to this feeling. If I cannot sleep, it is because of my enemy. Slowly all the power in my life begins to be located outside, and my whole being is defined in relation to this outside force, which becomes daily more monstrous, more evil, more laden with all the qualities in myself I no longer wish to own. The quality of my thought then is diminished. My imagination grows small. My self seems meager. For my enemy has stolen all these.

III

1

My whole outlook upon social life is determined by the question: How can we recognize the shackles that tradition has laid upon us? For when we recognize them we are also able to break them. [FRANZ BOAS]

Difference. Conflict. Trouble. Separation. These exist in and out of our minds. But we need not experience these through the old paradigm of warfare. What I know from the political theory of liberation is that where an old paradigm exists, a new paradigm can come into being.

I think, for example, of the paradigm of diversity instead of the paradigm of struggle. Along with his discovery of the struggle for survival, Darwin discovered that an environment tends to be richer and more sustaining to all the life in its boundaries when many different varieties of life forms exist within that environment. Or I think, for example, of the fact that any art form flourishes when many different artists are creating through that form. I think of an example from modern physics, in which science itself has had to accept two contradictory descriptions of reality as true. For light has been proven equally to be a particle and to be a wave. And modern physics must accept both these theories at the same time, hoping that at some time this paradox will answer a riddle, or that the answer to a riddle will solve this paradox. For the seeming existence of contradiction can be a gift of knowledge in a disguised form. So often in the history of thought a paradox has led to the discovery of a larger and more fundamental truth, even a new paradigm, in the attempt to reconcile two apparently contradictory phenomena. And we may fail to see this more fundamental truth precisely because we have been blinded by our belief in an old paradigm, an ideology.

2

This is the state my mind is in now: contradiction. At one and the same time, I agree with a political description of reality and with a psychological description of reality. At one and the same time, I see that social and economic forces shape human behavior and that human behavior is shaped by the life of the child. At one and the same time, I believe that we are shaped by circumstance and that we shape the circumstance around us. In my own mind I experience the same dualism which haunts civilization between psychological thinking and political thinking. Yet, I cannot give up either vision, because both to me are equally true and experienced as such every day, every moment.

3

Thus I begin to learn to live with questions. With uncertainty. With an unknowingness. At times frightening, at other times this state of suspension makes me fall in love with the world. I find myself laughing. I am surprised, delighted. The universe holds a secret larger than me. I listen.

4

And then it occurs to me that it is a coincidence of perhaps some significance that science should have to hold in its canon two contradictory notions in an age in which modern physics has challenged the old dualities between subjective and objective truth, matter and energy, time and space, in a time in which it is known that nothing in the universe is solid, that everything is mortal, changing, continuing to move, and that the line between one entity and another, myself, for instance, and the air around me, does not exist.[11]

11. It is a significant part of these synchronous events that Einsteinian physics should have aroused a "pitch of fury" in the fascist mind. Einstein, with his self-described "distrust of every form of authority," had unnerved the fascist mind with his suggestion that time is not a fixed and immutable dimension. Bruno Thuring wrote in alarm that now instead of one geometry there might be as many geometries "as one likes!" He described Einstein's theories as a Jewish plot to "relativize all concepts" which must lead to "chaos" (Bruno

5

Everywhere the old either-or begins to break down. The personal is political, the political psychological. Anger and love are part of one another. Hatred becomes compassion. The old idea of who the self is and who the world is becomes too small.

And this bears directly on our condition as women. For the "idea" of a woman is born, if a duality, out of the false concepts of masculine and feminine. The very word "woman" signifies all those qualities which the masculine mind splits off from itself, declaring that one is either male or female. And in the female live all those qualities the male has decided are inferior or suspect.

And this bears on our condition as those who would liberate ourselves. For we who struggle for liberation begin to make enemies of each other. In the struggle we create mutually exclusive categories of being, moral orders, and judge each other righteous or not righteous. We create saints and sinners. And wars.

6

And in all this, do we forget that we have swallowed the old paradigms, been raised in the same woman-hating culture? We ourselves have learned to associate woman with nature, dark skin with dangerous knowledge. In a part of us, we are afraid of all that masculine society fears. We fear female power, in ourselves and in others. And we fear separation. We do not like another woman to think differently than we do. We confuse ourselves and our own integrity with that of other women, whom we confuse with our mothers, whom we confuse with nature. That which in society has created conditions which imprison us also determines the shape of the dialogue we have between us, the shape of our efforts toward liberation. Just as society has separated the idea of "woman" from the idea of "knowledge," we cease to be able to accept our own thoughts, feelings, and sensations as a source of authority. We, too, long for an ideology which will erase our own experience.

7

Thus, we may have to relearn thinking. We have to learn to tolerate questions. Like Jane Goodall, who waited interminably for the trust of the primates she observed, we may have to cultivate patience. We may

---

Thuring, *Albert Einstein's Umsturzversuch der Physik*, cited in Frederic V. Grunfeld, *Prophets without Honor* [New York: McGraw-Hill Book Co., 1979], p. 152). And the Nazi ideologist Alfred Rosenberg used the term "the Albert Einsteins" to refer to Jewish intellectuals and artists (cited in Grunfeld, p. 149).

even have to learn to cultivate paradox, welcome contradiction or a troublesome question. We may have to learn to love knowledge for its own sake, not as a means to power. This is not to argue that one cannot argue. This is not to argue against thought. But rather to argue against the old dualities. Against ideology. And for the intellect. For the clear intellect which explores the self and the world with a genuine desire to know.

8

After all, the two ways of seeing which pose a contradiction in my mind do have a common ground. Both perceive the world as damaged. Both hope to change the world for the better. Both have a passionate desire to heal suffering. And finally, both of these ways of seeing the world, in their most profound visions, are forgiving.

For a deeply political knowledge of the world does not lead to a creation of an enemy. Indeed, to create monsters unexplained by circumstance is to forget the political vision which above all explains behavior as emanating from circumstance, a vision which believes in a capacity born to all human beings for creation, joy, and kindness, in a human nature which, under the right circumstances, can bloom.

When a movement for liberation inspires itself chiefly by a hatred for an enemy rather than from this vision of possibility, it begins to defeat itself. Its very motions cease to be healing. Despite the fact that it declares itself in favor of liberation, its language is no longer liberating. It begins to require a censorship within itself. Its ideas of truth become more and more narrow. And this movement that began with a moving evocation of truth, begins to appear fraudulent from the outside, begins to mirror all that it says it opposed, for now it, too, is an oppressor of certain truths, and speakers, and begins, like the old oppressors, to hide from itself.

9

And finally, as I think about thinking, I begin to know that all original thought—political, scientific, poetic—shares one quality. That is the desire to know the whole truth, to understand and to know what is obscured or what has been forgotten, to take in the unknown. And this desire to know is perhaps finally a way of loving. It is intimately connected to an attitude which honors all that is living. For the desire to know deeply all that is, as part of our outrage over injustice and suffering, accepts the truth, the whole and compassionate being.

Berkeley, California

Index

THE HORSE
Book
of Lists

THE HORSE
Book
of Lists

968 Fascinating
Facts &
Tantalizing
Trivia

By Cindy Hale

Laguna Hills, California

Karla Austin, *Director of Operations and Product Development*
Nick Clemente, *Special Consultant*
Barbara Kimmel, *Editor in Chief*
Lesley Ward, *Consulting Editor*
Kara Smith, *Production Supervisor*
Amy Stirnkorb, *Designer*

Library of Congress Cataloging-in-Publication Data

Hale, Cindy.
  The horse book of lists : 968 fascinating facts and tantalizing trivia / by Cindy Hale.
    p. cm.
  ISBN 978-1-933958-34-7
  1. Horses—Miscellanea. I. Title.

  SF301.H34 2009
  636.1—dc22
                          2008014253

BowTie Press®
A Division of BowTie, Inc.
23172 Plaza Pointe Dr., Ste. 230
Laguna Hills, California 92653

Printed and bound in China
16 15 14 13 12 11 10 09   1 2 3 4 5 6 7 8 9 10

Dedication

For my father, who has always loved both history and horses.

Contents

Acknowledgments

Many professionals in the horse industry contributed to this book by sharing personal anecdotes and their expertise. They include trainers, veterinarians, and tack store owners. Curators and directors of museums also shared their knowledge; without them, I would not have had the pleasure of learning about the glorious past of the horse. Horse show judges accredited by the United States Equestrian Federation also provided insight, so that I gained a better appreciation of how they view competitors. Finally, *The Horse Book of Lists* could not have been completed without the help and support of the many horse lovers who contributed their responses to my surveys and polls.

Introduction

If you're a horse lover, no doubt you're already a fount of equine knowledge. But here are even more fun facts, informative insights, and interesting tidbits that will make you the center of attention whenever you gather at the water trough with your barn buddies. And for those times when you're rubbing elbows with non-horsey folk, the collection of trivia will have them saying, "I didn't know *that* about horses!"

Chapter One

The Horse in History

The hoofprints of the horse are often found alongside the footsteps of humankind. Whether the horse served as a battlefield mount; a workmate in plowing, hunting, and herding; or a recreational diversion, the horse helped make history.

---

5 Fantastic Archaeological Sites Related to Horses

1. Kurgans: Altay Mountains, Siberia

Excavations of kurgans (the Russian word for a burial mound) have uncovered artifacts dating to the fifth-century-BC culture of the Scythians, a nomadic society so dependent on horses that the legendary ancient Greek poet Homer referred to them as "the mare milkers." Female Scythians were as accomplished on horseback as their male counterparts were, leading some historians to theorize that they inspired the legend of the warrior-women Amazons. In fact, a kurgan housing the mummified remains of a woman revealed that she was buried in her riding clothes, alongside several sacrificed horses.

2. Lascaux: Dordogne Valley, France

Lascaux is the site of a world-renowned cave complex that contains the artwork of Paleolithic humans. Dating to approximately 15,000 BC, some 900 animal figures on the cave walls were beautifully created using charcoal and powdered minerals in hues of black, red, and yellow. The most prominent beast depicted is the horse. Over 600 equines gallop across the rough-hewn limestone walls in a prehistoric homage to the horse.

3. St. Mary Reservoir: Alberta, Canada

An archaeological dig at this drained basin unearthed spear-heads approximately 11,000 years old that contained residue determined to be horse protein. That, plus skeletal remains of extinct prehistoric horses, is seen as evidence that early humans and many animal species existed there and that zealous over-hunting, and not climate change alone, led to the demise of the early horse in North America. Not until the arrival of Spanish explorers in the 1500s were horses reintroduced to the continent.

4. White Horse Hill: Wiltshire County, England

The famed "white horses" of England are a collection of giant stylized depictions of horses carved into the hillsides by early civ-

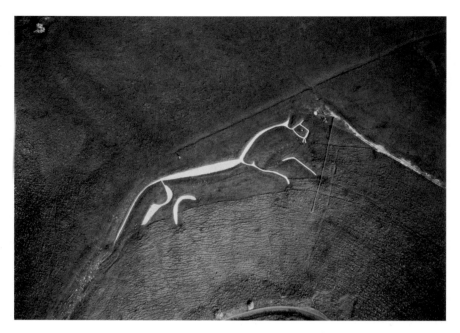
The Uffington Horse, White Horse Hill

ilizations. The oldest white horse can be found on an escarpment of the Berkshire Downs near the town of Uffington; hence, it is known as the Uffington Horse. Modern soil-testing methods date the creation of the Uffington Horse to 1200–800 BC. It was no easy feat for the artists. Like other chalk horses, the Uffington Horse was wrought by first digging a trench into the ground and then filling it with native chalk. With a length of 365 feet, the figure can be viewed from twenty miles away. It remains a mystery whether the white horses served as a totem marking the territory of a particular tribe or as a religious symbol.

5. Zibo: Shandong Province, China

Numerous burial sites of revered rulers from China's feudal past contain the remains of sacrificed horses, as the ancient

Chinese believed that war horses would be needed in the after-life. But most telling, perhaps, is the discovery of the tomb built for himself by Duke Jing, fifty-eighth in a long line of rulers in the state of Qi, a powerful stronghold from 770–476 BC. So passionate was his devotion to his horses that when one of them died, Jing not only buried the horse reverently but also sacrificed the horse's personal handler or groom, presumably so the horse would be handled by a familiar caretaker through-out eternity.

10 Breeds with Ties to History

1. Akhal-Teke: The roots of this lithe, athletic breed date back to 2400 BC in Central Asia, where it became highly prized by nomadic tribesmen known as the Tekes. Although primarily used as a racehorse in its native Turkmenistan, the Akhal-Teke is also known throughout the world for its inherent abilities in dressage and jumping.

2. Arabian: Although it's not possible to pinpoint the origin of the world's oldest purebred riding horse, the Bedouins who came to inhabit the Arabian Peninsula in 2500 BC brought with them the early predecessors of the modern Arabian: a hot-blooded, noble, refined horse known for its beauty and stamina.

An Akhal-Teke stallion

3. Caspian: These small horses with dainty features are prominently displayed on the official seal of King Darius of Persia (500 BC). These are the storied miniature horses of Persia, and the Caspian horse is considered its direct descendant. Extremely rare today, the Caspian was rediscovered in hilly terrain surrounding the Caspian Sea in 1965.

4. Destrier: This is the so-called Great Horse that knights rode into battle during the Middle Ages. Although no longer in existence—it was replaced by a lighter horse more suited to a streamlined cavalry—it is thought to be the ancestor of modern draft horses.

5. Einsiedler: Today this breed has been incorporated into the ranks of the Swiss warmblood, but its origin can be traced

Where Did All the Horses Go?

According to evolutionary theory, the family tree of the modern horse resembles a shrub with many branches. There is no straight line from a single predecessor to today's version of the horse. However, fossil studies point to a dog-size creature known as *Hyracotherium*—also frequently referred to as *Eohippus*, or "dawn horse"—as the earliest ancestor. *Hyracotherium* stood only about eight inches tall and about twenty inches long and roamed the Northern Hemisphere about 45 million years ago. By crossing the land bridge between North America and Siberia, the early horse was able to migrate to Europe, the Middle East, and North Africa. Once that pathway was submerged by ocean waters at the end of the Ice Age, the horses that were left in North America met their demise through climate change and the voracious appetite of early man.

to the tenth century and the Benedictine monastery at Einsiedeln, Switzerland. Although a consummate cavalry mount, thanks to its athletic ability and its trainability, it is used today as a sport horse.

6. Exmoor pony: It is widely believed that the Exmoor pony is descended from the horses that crossed the prehistoric land bridge from North America to Asia and migrated to Europe. The ancient Celts used Exmoor ponies to pull their chariots, and the Domesday Book of 1086 (a survey of England conducted for William the Conqueror) mentions the native ponies. Because of its harsh environment in southwestern Britain, the Exmoor pony was rarely exposed to other breeds, so its ancestral color and conformation have not changed. It is always solid bay or brown and features sturdy bones and a doubly thick coat in winter.

7. Kiger mustang: Differentiated from more common American mustangs, the Kiger mustangs were discovered in 1977 near Kiger Gorge, a remote area of Oregon, during a Bureau of Land Management (BLM) roundup. The herd was predominantly dun-colored and uniform in conformation, evidence that the secluded environment had afforded only limited crossbreeding with other feral horses. DNA testing confirmed that the herd was descended from Spanish horses left behind during the conquest of the New World.

8. Morgan: A true American breed, the foundation sire foaled in 1789 was named Figure and was owned by Justin Morgan, a Vermont schoolteacher. The small yet hardy bay stallion proved incredibly potent, passing on his strength, stamina, and beauty to countless offspring and establishing a new breed of horse for a new country.

9. Przewalski: Also known as the Asiatic or Mongolian wild horse, this stout little horse closely resembles a donkey or zebra but with a brown coat and tan muzzle. Though named for a Russian explorer who encountered herds in 1881, the scruffy equine was actually "discovered" by westerners, perhaps as far back as the fifteenth century. The Przewalski is considered the only true wild horse remaining in the world.

10. Tarpan: A prehistoric breed of horse whose images are found in cave drawings, the Tarpan was first domesticated by the Scythians circa 3000 BC. Unfortunately, as the harsh steppes of Ukraine were settled, farmers saw the herds of native wild horses as a threat to their crops, so the Tarpan was hunted and disposed of. A small horse that was dun or grullo in color, the last of the Tarpans died in 1876 on a Polish game preserve.

8 Dates: A Timeline of the Draft Horse in America

1800: Oxen are the preferred beasts of burden on American farms. Not only are they cheaper than horses, but also they can become a meal when their working days are over.

1830: About this time, European draft horses are imported to America. They work at a faster pace than oxen. Their loft-

Draft horses at work

ier gait and brawny strength are needed to plow and till the heavy soils of the prairie.

1849: The discovery of gold in California means that draft horses and draft crosses are brought west to haul ore wagons. They also move timber from the forest to be used in smelting furnaces.

Heavy-Duty Horses

The term *draft horse* describes a variety of breeds specifically bred for the ability to pull heavy loads as well as farming implements. Each breed boasts a colorful history. For example, the popular Percheron traces its roots to the French province of Le Perche. It is said that French knights exclusively rode gray horses, and those robust animals are thought to be the ancestors of today's Percherons, which are predominantly black or gray in color. When the medieval era ended, the hefty yet elegant Percheron became the horse of choice for pulling heavy coaches. As the United States was settled, the Percheron was in demand as a horse to pull freight. In the 1880s, over 7,500 Percherons were imported to the United States

1880: Trolleys (horse cars) pulled by draft horses operate in major American cities.

1900: Draft crosses are used to pull New York City fire wagons.

1910: The rise of industrialization means the end of the draft horse era, particularly in urban settings.

Percheron draft horses

from Le Perche. Today, the breed is still used on small farms and in logging operations where a draft horse offering both brawn and brains is needed. Percherons are also often crossed with Thoroughbreds to produce hardy but athletic horses for dressage and jumping.

1945: Only 2,000 purebred draft horses remain in the United States.

1980: Thanks to an increase in specialized classes for draft horses at horse shows and a burgeoning interest in natural, non-mechanized modes of farming, draft breeds begin to make a comeback.

8 Examples of the Horse in Myths and Religions

1. Native Americans, particularly tribes of the Southwest, carved small images of animals from semiprecious stones. These fetishes were believed to have magical powers that could be used by the bear-

Zuni horse fetishes

er to overcome threats or problems. A horse fetish was—and still is—popular, as it is thought to possess healing powers and to provide strength and swiftness.

2. Epona, goddess of horses and those who care for them, was worshiped by the Celts until the Roman invasion (222 BC). Epona is the only Celtic deity to find a home in the Roman pantheon of mythology, where she eventually became the protectress of the cavalry.

3. Rhiannon is the goddess who is associated with horses in Welsh mythology, which includes a grand tale about how Lord Pwyll was so smitten with her beauty that he made her his queen after he spied her riding astride a magical and elusive white horse.

4. The Chinese zodiac celebrates the Year of the Horse every twelve years. The next go-round is in 2014. Humans born under that sign are said to be outgoing, adventurous, and energetic. But they're also impetuous and strong willed.

5. The Bible's book of Revelations, chapter 6, describes the appearance of the Four Horsemen of the Apocalypse, generally thought to represent pestilence, war, famine, and death. The horses are colored white, red, black, and "pale," respectively.

6. American folklore of the Old West includes the story of superhuman cowboy Pecos Bill and his horse, Widowmaker. In this tall tale, Widowmaker is so jealous of Bill's new bride, Slue-Foot Sue, that he bucks her off his back, sending her bouncing on her bustle, unable to stop, to the moon and back.

7. In the Hindu religion, a magnificent white horse named Devadatta is ridden by Kalki, an incarnation of the god Vishnu, who brandishes a sword to reestablish righteousness and virtue in a world that has become evil and corrupt.

8. The beautiful unicorn is a legendary creature in world cultures throughout history. In the East, for example, it is known as Kirin (Japan) and Ki-lin (China). Ancient Greek natural historians mentioned the unicorn as a real creature, although the one-horned animal described circa 390 BC was probably a misinterpretation of journal notes describing a rhinoceros.

10 Horsey Phrases from Yesteryear

1. "Chomping at the bit": Also known as "champing" at the bit, the phrase probably dates back to horse riders' earliest use of a bit and bridle. A nervous or spirited horse would chew on the bit or grind its teeth in anticipation of taking off at a gallop. Nowadays the expression connotes a person who is likewise eager to get started.

2. "Don't change horses in midstream": This warning comes from an 1864 speech by Abraham Lincoln on his renomination for president despite considerable criticism of his handling of the Civil War. With this remark, he was metaphorically comparing switching political allegiance to the unwise decision to hop off one horse and climb aboard another in the midst of a swift current.

3. "Feeling your oats": Farmers and ranch owners long ago discovered that horses fed high-energy feeds such as oats and then allowed to remain idle become frisky and rambunctious when put to work later. Therefore, the phrase has become associated with an energetic or playful person.

4. "Hold your horses": The expression, meaning "Be patient," first appeared in print in nineteenth-century American literature. The phrase originally referred to keeping a tight rein on a team of feisty, antsy carriage horses.

5. **"Home, James"**: The second half of this adage is, "and don't spare the horses." It no doubt refers back to the days when people of wealth and high social standing would instruct their carriage drivers to get them home quickly, even if that meant taxing the horses' stamina.

6. **"If wishes were horses, then beggars would ride"**: Taken from a Scottish proverb, this is one line of an extended poem that reminds the reader that it takes more than wishing to get what we want or need.

7. **"She looks like she's been rode hard and put away wet"**: This insult to a woman's appearance (although it could certainly also be leveled at a man) refers to the matted coat and generally fatigued, disheveled look of a horse that has worked up a sweat and then been sent back to the barn without a thorough grooming. As an idiom, the implication is that someone has been driven hard and looks or feels much the worse for wear.

8. **"Straight from the horse's mouth"**: When old-time horse dealers advertised a horse's age, the art of judging the truth of the claim by examining its teeth came in handy. Rather than trusting the dealer, a knowledgeable horseman could verify the horse's age by looking in the horse's mouth. Hence, the

"Straight from the horse's mouth!"

expression came to mean getting inside information or news from a reliable source.

9. "That's a horse of a different color": This phrase harkens back to the early days of racing—no doubt before the time of the tough backstretch steward—when a bettor might discover that the horse he wagered on had been replaced with an imposter. Today this expression generally means "That is a different matter altogether," not necessarily that something fishy is going on.

10. "Wild horses couldn't tear us apart": Although this phrase describes a person's attachment to another (usually romantic), it derives from a gruesome practice. In antiquity, a supreme punishment was dismembering a person by having his limbs tied to several horses that are then sent off at a gallop.

11 Instances of Horses Affected by Wartime Events

1. In 1541, England's King Henry VIII issued his "Bill for the Breed of Horses," which ordered the destruction of all stallions under fifteen hands tall and all mares under thirteen hands tall. This extreme measure was supposed to increase the size of the British Empire's warhorses over a few genera-

No More Fraud at the Race Track

It's understandable that common phrases include references to the nefarious ploy of substituting one racehorse for another. Not until 1946 did the Thoroughbred Racing Protection Bureau mandate tattooing the upper lip of racehorses for identification purposes. Today, all racehorses are tattooed before they are permitted to enter a race. The tattoo, which is a series of numbers preceded by a letter, is stamped on the inside of the horse's upper lip. The letter represents the year the horse was foaled, and the numbers following it are the last five digits of the horse's registration number. Because there are only twenty-six letters in the alphabet, the letters have to be recycled. It helps to know that the letter *A* was used for horses foaled in 1997. The letter *B* then signifies 1998, and so on. At the racetrack, it is the designated horse identifier's job to verify that the horses entered in an upcoming race are not imposters. The horse's lip tattoo is compared with the tattoo number recorded on the horse's registration papers. If everything matches, the horse is permitted to head to the saddling paddock.

tions. However, many of the feral ponies that lived in the remote mountains of Wales eluded their hunters and became the foundation stock for today's phenomenally popular Welsh pony.

2. According to petroglyphs and other archaeological findings, it appears that for a brief period (estimated as 1650–1750) the Comanche of the American Southwest put leather armor on their horses to shield them from spears and arrows as they battled the rival Apache. The practice died out, however, once guns became available.

3. The Battle of Waterloo (June 18, 1815) was costly for the cavalries on both Coalition and French sides. Among Wellington's victorious horsemen and Napoleon's vanquished troops, approximately 45,000 horses were killed or wounded on that fateful day.

4. Napoleon's famed warhorse, Marengo, was captured by the British Army at Waterloo. The horse outlived Napoleon by eight years. Marengo's skeleton is on display at London's National Army Museum.

5. Over 1 million horses died during the American Civil War. In addition to direct losses from artillery wounds, many horses died of respiratory illnesses brought on by exhaustion, inclement weather, and poor stabling conditions.

6. The Australian Waler (named for New South Wales) was the mount of choice for the famed Light Horsemen, the Aussie cavalry who fought in World War I. Walers served honorably in the harsh conditions of the Middle East, but quarantine restrictions prevented the horses from returning home to Australia. The majority were sold to the British cavalry stationed in India. The rest—about 2,000—were shot because they were too old or unsound to be useful. About 200 of the horses in this unlucky group were fed last meals by the Light Horsemen who had ridden them. Then, rather than have the horses dispatched by unfamiliar hands, these soldiers did the deed themselves.

7. Before he became president, Theodore "Teddy" Roosevelt was an officer in the Rough Riders, a volunteer cavalry regiment of the U.S. Army that fought in the Spanish-American War (1898). Because transport space was limited, Roosevelt's men had to leave their horses behind when they shipped out to Cuba (and subsequently had to fight on foot). Roosevelt and his fellow officers were permitted to bring their horses along, but neither this privilege nor Roosevelt's rank could secure the safe landing of one of his horses. The off-loading techniques in Cuba were chaotic and involved hoisting horses overboard in a sling. Roosevelt's big horse, ironically named Rain-in-the-Face, was swamped by a huge swell and drowned. The loss of this horse meant that Roosevelt had to charge into battle on his other horse, an oversize pony named Little Texas.

Campagne de France, 1814, by Jean-Louis-Ernest Meissonier (1815–1891)

8. Approximately 570,000 horses and mules served the United States during World War I. About 70,000 died. In 1919, the U.S. War Department authorized the breeding of horses for wartime use through the Remount Service. Civilian horse breeders participated in the program, which was dissolved in 1949.

9. Although many horses and mules were used by the United States during World War II (1939–1945), the last cavalry charge of the U.S. Army was in 1942, against the Japanese on the Philippine island of Luzon.

10. The home of the Exmoor pony, a forested moor in England, was used as a training ground by British troops during World War II. The troops practiced using live ammunition, which decimated the local herd: only fifty ponies survived to become the foundation for modern breeding stock.

11. Fort Bragg in North Carolina is home to the U.S. Army's Special Forces. Since 9/11, part of their training includes riding lessons and basic horse care, necessary skills for assignments in the Middle East, where agrarian societies still rely on horses. A horse is also often the most reliable and least conspicuous mode of transportation in the region.

10 Items at the International Museum of the Horse

Kentucky Horse Park, Lexington, Kentucky

(Contributed by Bill Cooke, museum director)

1. Concord Coach, manufactured by L. Downing & Sons (circa 1855–1856). This coach held nine passengers and traveled a route between the cities of Keene and Spoffore in New Hampshire.

2. Walnut plow with brass-plated blade and fancy scrollwork brackets on handle. The plow was made in 1845 for Kentucky senator Henry Clay in honor of his long service to his country.

3. Japanese saddle from the Edo period (circa 1665). This fully restored saddle features a design of a dragon among waves. The saddle is an excellent example of the wonderful craftsmanship of Japanese saddle makers during the Edo period. It would have been proudly used by a samurai warrior.

Japanese saddle from the Edo period

4. Triple Crown trophies won by Whirlaway (1941), Citation (1948), Secretariat (1973), Seattle Slew (1977), and Affirmed (1978). The museum is proud to display the Triple Crown trophies of five of the eleven Thoroughbreds to win American horse racing's most elusive prize.

5. B. F. Avery Mowing Machine, made in 1876. This horse-drawn mower features maple inlaid on walnut, with nickel-plated brass and iron. It was made in Louisville, Kentucky, as a demonstration piece for the U.S. Centennial Exposition in Philadelphia.

6. Chinese saddle, circa late 1600s to early 1700s, Qing dynasty. The saddle has a red, white, and blue fabric seat with cloisonné detailing at the front and back. The red paint visible on the underside suggests that the saddle may have been painted completely red to protect it during the Chinese Cultural Revolution (1966–1976). The saddle was originally purchased from a descendant of a Mongolian noble family, who stated that it was presented to his ancestor by the Qing emperor for meritorious military service.

7. Luristan brass harness ring from Iran (1000–700 BC). Because of the harness ring's small size, it is easily missed by patrons of the museum. Museum director Bill Cooke considers it one of the most elegant pieces in the collection, especially considering its age.

8. The Mary A. Littauer Library Collection and Archives. Mary Littauer was revered as the grand dame of equestrian historians. The museum was honored to be chosen as the recipient of her library and archives following her death in 2005.

9. Miniature knight and horse in armor. Crafted by Granger of Paris, France, around 1700, this fully articulated mounted knight was once activated by a keyed mechanism.

10. George III silver goblet. Made in Ireland (circa 1780), this elegant handcrafted goblet was used as the trophy for the 1977

Tremont Stakes, won by Calumet Farm's Alydar. While relatively insignificant as a racing trophy, it is a fine example of the work of eighteenth-century Irish silversmiths.

15 Facts About America's Pony Express

1. The Pony Express was formed to deliver mail between St. Joseph, Missouri, and Sacramento, California. St. Joseph was on the edge of settled territory, and Sacramento was the hub of the gold mining industry. The threat of civil war intensified the need for open communication with the western frontier.

2. The Pony Express operated for only a short time, from April 1860 through October 1861.

3. The Pony Express employed about 400 mounts. Horses were changed at stations set up every ten to fifteen miles along the route. Some of the stations were stagecoach stops, but others were not much more than crude shacks with spartan amenities.

4. A one-way trip required seventy-five different horses.

5. Many of the horses, particularly those procured on the West Coast, were range-bred mustangs.

Pony Express Stables at the Pony Express Museum

6. Horses averaged a pace of ten miles per hour.

7. The route was about 2,000 miles long, much of it over rough terrain.

8. Typically, it took ten days to complete the route one way.

9. The fastest run took just over a week. The reason? It was carrying President Abraham Lincoln's inaugural address.

10. Riders could not weigh over 125 pounds.

11. Because of the harsh conditions of the job and the risks of solitary travel on horseback, recruitment ads sought "expert riders willing to risk death daily."

12. Several riders died on the route after falling from their horses, yet only once did the mail fail to reach its destination. A rider drowned after falling off his horse while crossing a river, and the mailbags were never recovered.

13. Riders used special leather saddlebags, called mochillas, to carry the mail.

14. No one got rich working for the Pony Express. Riders were paid only $10 a day, and the owners never turned a profit. In fact, the owners ended up in bankruptcy.

15. The Pony Express ended when telegraph lines to California were completed on October 24, 1861.

5 Museums That Celebrate the American West

1. Autry National Center
Los Angeles, California

The history of westward expansion and the contributions of various cultures are explored through a trio of institutions: The Southwest Museum of the American Indian, the Museum of the American West, and the Institute for the Study of the American West.

Southwest Museum of the American Indian
234 Museum Dr.
Los Angeles, CA 90065
Telephone: 323-221-2164

Museum of the American West and
the Institute for the Study of the American West
4700 Western Heritage Way
Los Angeles, CA 90027
Telephone: 323-667-2000
Web site: www.autry-museum.org

2. National Cowboy and Western Heritage Museum
Oklahoma City, Oklahoma

Exhibits, art galleries, artifacts and hands-on activities allow visitors to experience what was required to tame the American West.

1700 N.E. 63rd St.
Oklahoma City, OK 73111
Telephone: 405-478-2250
Web site: www.nationalcowboymuseum.org

3. National Cowgirl Museum and Hall of Fame
Fort Worth, Texas

This museum honors the women whose courage and individuality reflected the pioneer spirit.

1720 Gendy St.

Fort Worth, TX 76107

Telephone: 817-336-4475

Web site: www.cowgirl.net

4. National Ranching Heritage Center
Lubbock, Texas

With its forty-seven authentic ranch structures, this museum and historical park gives a representation of the lifestyle of the working ranch as it existed from 1780 through 1930.

3121 Fourth St.

Box 43200

Lubbock, TX 79409

Telephone: 806-742-0498

Web site: www.nrhc.com

Las Escarbadas of the XIT ranch, National Ranching Heritage Center

The Real Annie Oakley

Not everyone is familiar with the name Phoebe Ann Moses Butler, but that was the real name of Annie Oakley (1860–1926), who rode to fame as the only female member of Buffalo Bill's Wild West Show. She was inducted into the National Cowgirl Museum's Hall of Fame in 1984. Incredibly skilled with a firearm, Oakley grew up in a poor Ohio family and learned to shoot in order to hunt down a good meal. She crossed paths with Frank Butler, a flamboyant marksman who traveled the country accepting challenges with other

5. Texas Cowboy Hall of Fame
Fort Worth, Texas

Housed in the original horse barns of the famed Fort Worth Stockyards, where the Texas livestock industry once boomed, the hall features a large collection of wagons and other horse-drawn vehicles.

128 E. Exchange
Fort Worth, TX 76164
Telephone: 817-626-7131
Web site: www.texascowboyhalloffame.com

shooters, in 1875. Oakley bested Butler by hitting all twenty-five of her marks to Butler's twenty-four. He was smitten with the young woman and they married. Their life together included touring with the Wild West Show for sixteen years, where they brought the

Annie Oakley, circa 1887

romance and rowdiness of the Old West to spectators who had never experienced them firsthand.

10 Steps in the Development of Horsemanship

1. The horse was first domesticated around 6000 BC in the area surrounding the Black Sea. Indo-European tribes corralled and maintained horses primarily for their meat and milk.

2. Horse skulls dating from 4000 BC show signs of bit wear, suggesting that horses were being ridden at that time. However, none of these primitive bits exist today. Historians speculate that during this era bits were constructed of hemp, sinew, or rawhide and that, even earlier, riders might have used crude bitless bridles similar to today's hackamore to control a horse.

3. Riders who hopped onto the back of a horse around 2000 BC used a nose ring, placed through the horse's nostrils, to steer the animal. Because this mechanism alone doesn't allow for minor adjustments in course, riders must have influenced their horse's movement by varying their leg pressure and body positions. The first metal bit, a type of snaffle, was created around 1500 BC. Then reins, which were attached to rings on the bit, could be used to steer the horse.

4. Kikkuli, a horsemaster in the Hittite kingdom, composed a training manual for chariot horses in 1345 BC. His concept of so-called interval training, which increases a horse's stamina through a series of prescribed workouts, is still used today in the training of Thoroughbred racehorses.

5. Although a primitive saddle was used around 800 BC, it consisted of little more than an animal hide or cloth tossed onto a horse's bare back. By 200 BC, both Asians and the Romans had produced saddles equipped with wooden trees to alleviate pressure on the horse's spine and reduce discomfort. The metal stirrup, which gave the rider greater stability in the saddle, came to prominence during the fifth century.

6. Greek historian Xenophon composed *On Horsemanship* in 350 BC. This work is considered the first in the Western world to detail the selection, training, and care of horses that are to be ridden.

7. The class of medieval fighting men known as knights arose during the twelfth century. Knights undertook rigorous training that included perfecting their horsemanship skills. In turn, their horses were

The Battle of Castille 1453,
by Charles Philippe Lariviere
(1798–1876)

trained in certain maneuvers on the battlefield, including kicking, biting, and stomping fallen enemies. Prized warhorses, like their knights, were protected by armor; equine armor is known as barding.

8. Today's hunter and jumper riders owe a debt of gratitude to Federico Caprilli (1868–1907), an Italian cavalry officer and gifted horseman. Through experimentation, Caprilli formulated the forward seat. In this innovative position, the rider rises out of the saddle and leans forward with the upper body. This

Telltale Ears

Horse with ears pricked forward, indicating alertness

A significant aspect of natural horsemanship is paying attention to a horse's body language. By doing so, a human can better understand just what a horse is thinking, which in turn improves the opportunity for effective communication. The horse uses its acute sense of hearing to help it navigate its environment. The position of a horse's ears is very revealing, primarily because the equine ear can rotate 180 degrees, allowing for a great deal of expression. For example, when a horse pins its ears flat against the top of its head, it's exerting its dominance over another horse or a person. A bite or kick may come next. Ears that are pricked forward mean that the horse is keenly focused on something, attempting to pick up any faint sound that might aid in identifying an unfamiliar object or figure. And an ear that is singularly cocked off to the side as a horse passes something suspicious forewarns the rider that the horse is on full alert.

way, the rider stays with the motion of the horse as it takes flight over jumps.

9. Western riding developed from the influence of the Spanish conquistadors and became the riding style of choice in the American West by the 1700s. The western saddle even resembles the early Spanish saddles, although a saddle horn was added by cowboys so they could secure a rope to their tack. Because cowboys needed their hands to be as free as possible so they could rope, open fence gates, and shoot a rifle, cow ponies were taught to neck rein, or respond to light pressure when the reins are held in one hand.

10. The natural horsemanship movement gained popularity during the late twentieth century, fostered by a renewed interest in the teachings of Bill and Tom Dorrance, Buck Brannaman, and Ray Hunt. Natural horsemanship promotes communicating with the horse rather than merely breaking and training it. To achieve the desired relationship with one's horse, the human handler must become educated in the horse's natural instincts and behavior patterns.

Chapter Two

Horse Breeds and Colors

According to the most recent statistics (2005) from the American Horse Council, there are more than 9 million horses in the United States, with a wide variety of breeds and colors.

5 Most Popular Horse Breeds in America

1. **American Quarter Horse:** The history of the American Quarter Horse began in the 1600s, when the heavily muscled horse was revered for its ability to sprint distances of about a quarter-mile. That ability led to the breed's early name, the Celebrated American Quarter Running Horse. Once cowboys

discovered the breed's innate talent for working cattle, the breed became a favorite for anyone with a western saddle. The American Quarter Horse registry was officially formed in 1940, and today the breed enjoys tremendous popularity due to its versatility.

2. Appaloosa: Known for their dotted coat patterns and striped hooves, the Appaloosa was originally concentrated in the Palouse prairie region of the American Northwest. Its name is derived from references to the distinctive horse as "a Palouse horse." The Nez Perce tribe is credited with developing the breed in the early 1800s. However, when the U.S. Army Cavalry defeated the Nez Perce, it confiscated the tribe's horses, and the breed fell into obscurity. Fortunately, the Appaloosa Horse Club was founded in 1975 to preserve the breed. Today, the modern Appaloosa is a popular, hardy horse that's at home in English or western tack.

3. Arabian: The modern purebred Arabian horse is no different from its predecessors of the ancient Middle East. The breed first came to prominence in America after Turkey brought forty-five Arabians as a live exhibit for the 1893 Chicago World's Fair. The Arabian Horse Association was formed in 1908 to ensure the preservation and purity of the breed. Today, there are more Arabian horses living in the United States than in all the other countries of the world combined. The breed's appeal is due to its refined beauty, athleticism, and intelligence.

Although the Arabian is capable of performing in equestrian disciplines as varied as dressage and western reining, it is internationally known as the premier mount for endurance competitions, thanks to its stamina and soundness.

4. Paint: Spanish explorer Hernán Cortés brought the first pinto horses to North America in 1519. Some of the descendants of those horses became feral mustangs, which the Comanche captured and trained as their own colorful mounts. It wasn't until 1965, however, that pinto horses with a definite stock horse (western riding horse) conformation had their own registry, known as the American Paint Horse Association

An American Paint Horse

The Modern Sport Horse

Former Thoroughbred racehorses used to head straight to second careers as competition mounts for English riders. That trend changed, however, in the 1980s when American riders began importing warmblood sport horses from Europe. Today, these European imports and their homebred brethren have eclipsed the Thoroughbred as the English riding horse of choice. Just what is a warmblood? The easiest answer is that it is the result of a cross between a spirited, "hot-blooded" breed such as a Thoroughbred and a more laidback, "cold-blooded" breed such as a draft horse. Yet the modern warmblood is actually many generations removed from such rudimentary pairings. Thanks to conscientious breeding, it has developed a reputation as a type of

(APHA). While the spotted coloration known as "pinto" can appear in numerous breeds, to be registered with the APHA, a horse must exhibit one of three acceptable coat patterns and have at least one registered Paint parent. The only other breeds permitted within the pedigree are American Quarter Horses and Thoroughbreds.

horse blessed with size, substance, athletic talent, and a reliable disposition. Each warmblood registry has specific requirements based on conformation and pedigree. The young stock is presented for inspection at annual evaluations called

Olympic medalist dressage duo Debbie McDonald and Hanoverian mare Brentina

keurings. A horse accepted into the registry is branded with the registry's logo, a visible stamp of approval. Some of the more popular warmblood sport horse breeds are the Hanoverian, the Holsteiner, the Dutch Warmblood, and the Trakehner.

5. Thoroughbred: All Thoroughbreds can trace their lineage to three stallions that were imported to England from the Middle East in the seventeenth and eighteenth centuries. These Arabian and Barb stallions were crossed with English mares, and the result was an athletic, refined, and intelligent horse that became the consummate racehorse. The same qualities make the Thoroughbred an excellent sport horse for show jumping and other English riding disciplines. The Jockey Club was formed in 1894 to document the pedigrees of all Thoroughbreds in North America.

5 Unusual Horse Breeds from Around the World

1. Camargue: Born in a marshland habitat in southern France, the silvery white Camargue lives in a feral state until it is broken to ride. Its destiny is that of a pleasure horse or, more traditionally, as a mount for the French version of the American cowboy.

2. Deliboz: The Republic of Azerbaijan is home to this high-spirited horse that's similar to the Arabian. Suitable for many uses, it's used for racing, as a pack animal, and for all-around riding purposes. It has a speedy gait much like the American Saddlebred's rack (an animated four-beat gait). Another unique trait is that, due to a thick fold of tissue down the center line, its tongue appears to be forked.

3. Icelandic: Descended from small, hardy horses brought to Iceland nearly eleven centuries ago, the Icelandic horse was once a workhorse but now is more often used for pleasure

An Icelandic horse

riding, thanks to its surefootedness and its fast yet smooth gaits. Icelandics not only walk, trot, and canter but also perform at the tölt (a gliding four-beat gait) and the flying pace (a gait in which the front and hind legs on the same side move back and forth together).

4. Knabstrupper: This breed shares the same color genes as the American Appaloosa, so its coat is spotted in various arrays of colors. The breed registry began in 1812 in Denmark. Since then the striking horse, which is known for its compliant disposition as well as its color, has been used for both riding and driving.

5. Marwari: Native to India, the Marwari is remarkable for its placid, endearing temperament and its heritage on the battlefield as a noble war mount. Blessed with stamina and sound legs, the Marwari is also known for its ears, which curve and curl inward at the top, forming the shape of a lyre.

18 Breed Registries in North America

1. American Hanoverian Society
Lexington, Kentucky
www.hanoverian.org

2. American Knabstrupper Association
Cypress, Texas
www.knabstruppers.com

3. American Miniature Horse Association
Alvarado, Texas
www.amha.com

4. American Morgan Horse Club
Shelburne, Vermont
www.morganhorse.com

5. American Paint Horse Association
Fort Worth, Texas
www.apha.com

6. American Quarter Horse Association
Amarillo, Texas
www.aqha.com

7. American Saddlebred Horse Association
Lexington, Kentucky
www.asha.net

8. American Shire Horse Association
Effingham, South Carolina
www.shirehorse.org

9. American Trakehner Association
Newark, Ohio
www.americantrakehner.com

10. Appaloosa Horse Club
Moscow, Idaho
www.appaloosa.com

11. Arabian Horse Association
Aurora, Colorado
www.arabianhorses.org

**12. Friesian Horse Association
of North America**
Lexington, Kentucky
www.fhana.com

**13. International Andalusian Lusitano
Horse Association**
Birmingham, Alabama
www.ialha.com

14. Jockey Club (Thoroughbreds)
Lexington, Kentucky, and
New York City
www.jockeyclub.com

15. Percheron Horse Association of America
Fredericktown, Ohio
www.percheronhorse.org

**16. Tennessee Walking Horse
Breeders' and Exhibitors' Association**
Lewisburg, Tennessee
www.twhbea.com

17. United States Icelandic Horse Congress
Anchorage, Alaska
www.icelandics.org

23 Coat Colors, Patterns, and Markings

Coat Colors

1. Bay: The body may be varying shades of brown, from light tan to auburn to deep mahogany, but the bay horse will also have black points. That means its mane, tail, and lower legs will be black.

2. Black: A true black horse does not have any brown or red hairs in its coat. If stabled inside, where the sun cannot have any bleaching effects, a black horse will appear almost midnight blue in color.

3. Brown: Although dark brown horses may appear black, their reddish brown muzzle gives away their true color.

4. Buckskin: Sandy yellow or tan in color, the buckskin has the same black points of a bay. It looks much like a dun, but without the barring or dorsal stripe. A buckskin is genetically a diluted bay.

5. Chestnut: The chestnut color spectrum runs the gamut from golden brown to cinnamon red and near chocolate or liver colored. Sometimes a chestnut can have a flaxen or blond mane and tail.

6. Cremello: A cremello horse is the palest of blondes with a white mane and tail. It also has pink skin and blue eyes. Not quite white, the cremello coloring occurs when a chestnut or sorrel base coat is diluted with the crème gene.

7. Dun: Horses designated as dun colored are tawny yellow to reddish brown with darker lower legs. Often the legs sport dark barring (horizontal striping), somewhat resembling a zebra. Duns also have a dorsal stripe, a line of darker pigmented hair that runs along the spine to the tail.

8. Gray: Dark at birth, the coat of a gray horse becomes more silver or white as the horse matures. Even though older gray horses may appear white, their skin remains black.

9. Grullo: An unusual silver blue or mousey gray coat, it typically has the dorsal stripe and darker lower legs of a dun.

10. Palomino: While palominos are often referred to as having a golden coat, the actual shade of gold can vary from creamy buff or beige to a deep copper. The most prized palomino color boasts a metallic sheen in the sunlight, much like a newly

A grullo horse

minted coin. A palomino results when the chestnut (or sorrel) color gene is diluted by the gene for crème.

11. Sorrel: Though actually interchangeable with the term *chestnut*, some horsemen use the term *sorrel* to specifically identify chestnut horses of light golden hues.

12. White: There aren't any albinos in the horse world, and a true white horse is extremely rare. It will have pink skin but brown eyes. Most often what people refer to as a white horse is actually a gray that has lost all of its dark dapples.

Patterns and Markings

13. Bald face: Horses with a wide blaze that extends to and even past their eyes are said to have a bald face.

14. Blanket Appaloosa: In this pattern, the Appaloosa will be mostly solid colored over much of its body. The hindquarters will then be white, as if blanketed. Inside the white area will be a smattering of leopard-type spots.

15. Blaze: A stripe of white that usually extends the length of the horse's face.

16. Leopard Appaloosa: One of the distinctive patterns of an Appaloosa, the leopard coloration makes the horse appear to be dotted with large polka dots.

Three blazes

THE HORSE BOOK OF LISTS

17. Overo: Also found in pintos and Paints, the white portion of an overo pattern rarely crosses the horse's back. White spots or patches generally have jagged edges. An overo may have a solid-colored head, but its face will often have a bold white marking.

18. Roan: Horses with a lot of white hairs mixed into an otherwise solid-colored coat are referred to as roan. The roaning does not increase with age, as does the whitening of a gray horse.

19. Snip: A snip is a small blip of white located on the horse's muzzle.

20. Sock: Much like a white bootie, a sock is found on the horse's pastern. Bay horses may have black spots in their socks.

21. Star: A star is a small, often diamond-shaped white marking on the horse's forehead.

22. Stocking: Taller than a sock, a stocking can extend past the horse's hock or knee. A horse with several stockings is considered flashy and is often described as having "a lot of chrome."

23. Tobiano: The most common pinto or Paint horse pattern, the tobiano usually has white legs and a solid-colored head, although its face can sport white markings. Clearly defined patches of color typically adorn the tobiano's flank and chest. The mane and tail can be a mix of white and the base coat color.

Chapter Three

Horses at Work

Even in today's mechanized world, horses still work alongside people in unique, important careers.

6 Jobs in Which Horses Help Humans

1. Teaching Tool: Although horses can't earn a degree in psychology, they can be the catalyst for positive psychological change in people. A variety of psychotherapy and personal growth programs integrate horses into their treatment strategies. Equine Assisted Psychotherapy (EAP) is one such specialty. Because horses don't respond to emotional outbursts and can't be manipulated through physical force, horse handling and riding skills are taught to encourage patience, self-discipline, and responsibility. A sense of trust is also achieved.

2. Rehabilitating Wounded War Vets: Soldiers who have lost limbs in the wars in Afghanistan and Iraq have been helped and inspired by several pilot programs using horses. As part of an intense rehabilitation strategy known as hippotherapy (*hippos* is the Greek word for horse), the soldiers learned to regain their balance on the back of a horse. Being able to command a horse's movements also gave the amputees a sense of control and confidence. Included in the program were horses stabled at Fort Hood, Texas, and Fort Myer, Virginia. The Fort Myer Percherons are the noble caisson horses used in military funerals at Arlington National Cemetery.

3. Search and Rescue: Many law enforcement agencies and accredited volunteer groups maintain a unit of skilled riders and trained horses for this special duty. In varied missions such as locating a missing person, hunting for a criminal, or helping victims of natural disasters, members of MSAR (Mounted Search and Rescue) teams work in partnership with their horses. Horses traverse difficult terrain faster than searchers on foot. And the mounted rider has a higher line of sight, which improves visibility over the top of brush and rocks. MSAR horses can also be used to pack equipment such as communication devices into remote areas during an extensive operation.

4. Pet Therapy: Although pet therapy typically involves dogs and cats, Miniature Horses are also making the rounds at nursing homes and hospitals, welcomed because of their petite size

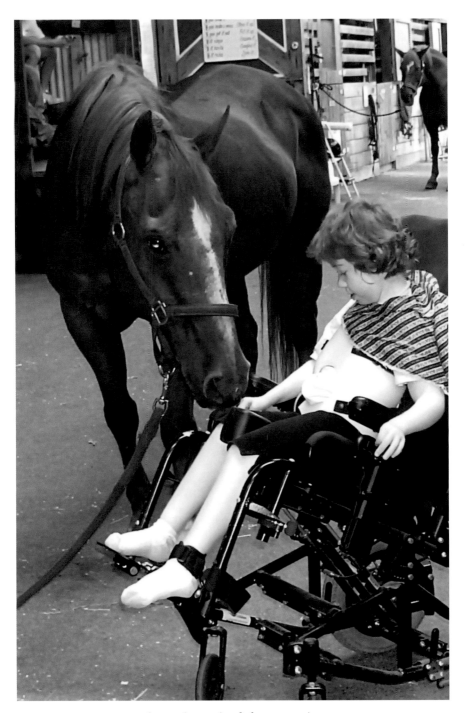

An equine-assisted therapy session

and gentle disposition. Both the elderly and the young respond to the small horses' soft coats, tiny hooves, and inquisitive natures. Senior citizens often have childhood memories of being around horses, and just about every youngster responds positively to the sight of a horse, whatever its size. Hence, a visit by a Miniature Horse is an opportunity for friendly conversation between patient and handler and offers the patient a respite from an institutionalized setting.

5. Special Needs Riding: Horsemanship programs designed specifically for riders with disabilities began in Europe in the 1950s. The concept spread to North America, where the North American Riding for the Handicapped Association (NARHA) was formed in 1969. Today, certified riding centers offer structured therapeutic riding sessions for disabilities as varied as cerebral palsy, visual impairment, and autism. According to the most recent statistics from the NARHA (2006), more than 5,000 horse, ponies, and miniature horses participate in therapeutic riding programs in North America.

6. Police Horse: A uniformed police officer astride a thousand-pound horse creates what has been referred to as "a ten-foot cop." This team of specially trained horse and rider is an imposing force in crowd-control situations. The horse also offers better maneuverability than a patrol car and a chance to relate to civilians in a positive manner. After all, who hasn't wanted to pet a police horse?

The Horse in the Small Package

The American Miniature Horse was derived by crossing the smallest Shetland ponies with ponies used for work in coal mines. Through selective breeding, Miniature Horses registered with the American Miniature Horse Association must stand less than thirty-four inches tall. They typi

An American Miniature Horse

cally weigh 150–250 pounds. Although "Minis" can easily be trained to pull a small cart, they should not be ridden by anyone heavier than seventy pounds, which means they are suitable mounts only for very young children. Thus, Minis are predominantly backyard pets and companions. They also are exhibited at shows specifically for Miniature Horses. There, these tiny equines compete in events in which their obedience, conformation, and athletic ability are on display.

10 Qualities of a Good Police Horse

(Contributed by Officer Bruce Smith, Arcadia, California, Police Dept., California Mounted Officers Association 2003 "Officer of the Year")

1. Soundness: Police work is hard on a horse, given that the majority of the horse's deployment (six to eight hours) is at the walk or standing on hard ground with a rider and equipment on his back.

2. Quiet Temperament: The police horse is a great public relations tool, so he must be able to stand quietly in a crowd. A horse that cannot stand still could be a danger to the public.

3. Age: The most desirable ages are from about eight years old through a horse's teens, and even into the twenties if the horse is sound and healthy.

4. Trainability: The horse must be willing to obey the rider's commands and accept discipline. Some horses are more "teachable" than others.

5. Solid Social Behavior: The ideal mounted police horse must be able to get along with his rider, the general public, and other horses.

Mounted police officers

6. Adaptable: The environment during deployment can be ever-changing, from bright stimuli to crowd control to monotony, so a police horse has to be adaptable. As the environment changes, he must be able to figure out things quickly and trust his rider.

7. A Low Flight Response: Nature gave horses a flight response for their survival. However, some horses have a low flight response. They're less likely to exhibit an instinctive urge to flee a threatening situation.

8. Patience: Police work can require mounts to stand at a crowd control situation or a major sporting event for long periods of time. Police mounts may also spend long periods tied to the trailer, so they must not become impatient while tied.

9. Color: In general, solid-colored horses (such as bay, brown, chestnut, and black) are preferred for use in law enforcement, as they present a more uniform and military appearance. A group of solid-colored horses also provides the riders with a certain degree of anonymity.

10. Appropriate Size: The horse's size should be proportionate to the rider, usually 15.1 to 16.2 hands tall. Police work requires the officer to get in and out of the saddle several times during a deployment, and the rider needs to manage this comfortably.

6 Interesting Lines of Work for Horses

1. Cab Horse: New York City is the urban center most often associated with carriage tours. Although New York's carriage business has a past history of abuse and neglect, stringent rules now regulate working hours and standards of care for workhorses that shuttle humans around Central Park. Credit for improvements goes primarily to the American Society for the

Prevention of Cruelty to Animals (ASPCA), which was founded in 1866 in response to the dismal treatment of the carriage horses. As a side note, although New York's horse-drawn taxis are commonly referred to as hansom cabs, they are not the patented carriage designed by Joseph Hansom in 1834. Instead, they're actually vis-à-vis carriages, a style of French vehicle made so that passengers can sit across from each other.

2. Racetrack Lead Pony: Most racehorses are high-strung and nervous, and they respond to the companionship of a lead pony. Despite their title, lead ponies are actually large, robust geldings around sixteen hands tall. They can be of any breed, but they must be fast enough to canter alongside a racehorse as it warms up on the track. And they must be strong enough to withstand being bumped and bullied by a fractious colt. Good lead ponies may not be glamorous Thoroughbreds, but they are an indispensable part of horse racing.

New York City's horse cabs

A Racehorse's Best Buddy

The excitable temperament of a racehorse is often soothed by putting a calm horse at its side during morning workouts or the nerve-racking walk to the starting gate. These long-suffering horses, which frequently have to endure nips and body slams from their rambunctious charges, are referred to as lead ponies. But they're never actual ponies. A racehorse's sidekick has to be a stout, full-size horse in order to handle the tough task of escorting a feisty racehorse. There have been some memorable lead ponies. Seabiscuit formed an attachment to a small palomino gelding named Pumpkin. Smarty Jones, the winner of the Kentucky Derby and Preakness Stakes in 2004, had the bay gelding Butterscotch as his lead pony. Faithful Butterscotch served as a lead pony until

3. Funeral Assistant: Elegant horse-drawn hearses are widely available for hire. Immaculate in their presentation, they are either restored vintage funeral carriages or detailed replicas, recalling earlier eras like the Old West or Victorian times. The carriage driver and attendants wear period-appropriate garments and are experienced in proper protocol. The hearses are

*A lead pony and rider alongside
a racehorse and jockey*

his retirement at the age of twenty-three. Triple Crown winner Secretariat (1973) was often accompanied by a flashy roan gelding named Billy Silver. A dependable lead pony is often the unsung hero behind the scenes at the racetrack.

pulled by a team of matched black horses, generally Percheron draft horses or high-stepping Friesians, a breed of Dutch harness horse.

4. Lumberjack's Partner: Horse logging is considered less devastating to the environment than is the use of huge trucks and gargantuan clear-cutting machinery. Horses don't compact soil and they don't require wide swaths of roads cut into the forest. A team of stout horses is used to "skid" logs on a heavy-duty carrier called a sled. The freshly cut timber is then off-loaded onto logging trucks. Those who practice horse logging claim it provides a sense of nostalgia and also allows for a closer, more selective inspection of prospective timber.

5. Four-Legged Field Master: Due to rising fuel costs and modern society's yearnings for the past, the popularity of draft horses as an alternative to a gas-powered tractor is growing, especially on smaller farms. There's an ecologically friendly element, too. A draft horse can eat the foodstuff grown on the very ground it works, and its manure becomes compost that is returned to the soil. Proponents of the practice also tout the sense of satisfaction that comes from working the land naturally, behind the steady pace of a gentle giant, rather than in the rigid seat of a noisy mechanized vehicle.

6. Ranch Horse: The life of a modern-day ranch horse isn't much different from that of its predecessors. Today's ranch horse is usually bred from proven working bloodlines, meaning that it's genetically programmed to literally feel at home on the range. There is specialization, though. Some horses, particularly the fast, stout ones, are used for roping steers. The smaller, more agile horses are used for cutting cattle, which is the

Horses at home on the farm

process of separating one wily steer from the rest of the herd for doctoring and branding. Still other horses are best at moving cattle from one grazing area to another. There is always a job for a good "cow pony."

Chapter Four

Cowboys and Trail Horses

Riding the trails either as a real cowboy or as a recreational rider is one of life's great pleasures.

---

10 Cowboy Terms You May Not Know

1. Bell mare: An older, authoritative mare in a string of ranch horses. She wears a bell around her neck to signify her as the leader and to make it easy to locate the group.

2. Buckaroo: A colloquial term for a cowboy from the western and northern regions of the United States. However, calling a

Texas cowboy a buckaroo might be considered to be using "fightin' words."

3. Chinks: Leather leggings that cover a western rider's thighs and knees to protect them on the trail.

4. Dally: To wrap a rope around the saddle horn several times, usually to restrain the calf or steer at the other end.

5. Hoolihan: The tossing of a lariat (rope) with a backhanded flip of the wrist; used specifically for roping horses, as they're less likely to be spooked by the hoolihan's flight path.

Cowboys rounding up a herd of horses

6. Jingle bobs: Small decorative attachments on the rowel of a spur that make a jingling sound when the wearer walks.

7. Ranahan: An old-time term for a top ranch hand or lead cowboy.

8. Remuda: Horses that are kept together in a herd so they can always be at hand for a particular purpose. Often cow ponies are kept in a remuda so that cowboys can catch a fresh horse whenever necessary.

9. Stampede string: A braided string, usually made of horsehair, that is wrapped around the crown of a cowboy hat and then pulled snug beneath the wearer's chin. It keeps the hat in place when riding a fast or rambunctious horse.

10. Woolies: Chaps often worn in winter by cowboys working on the prairie. They're made with Angora goat hair, which insulates the rider's legs.

4 Places to Embrace Your Inner Cowboy

1. Calgary Stampede: Although it has undergone some transformations, the annual Calgary Stampede held in Calgary,

Alberta, Canada, still has the same theme since its inception in 1912: to promote and preserve the heritage of the Old West and its values. The Stampede features so many western-themed performances and agricultural showcases that it takes several days to see all there is to see. Fortunately, it runs for ten days each July. A highlight of the Stampede is a world-class rodeo with over $1 million in prize money at stake. If that doesn't conjure up a cowboy state of mind, perhaps the famed chuck wagon races will: these are hotly contested, raucous events pitting skilled teams of drivers and horses pulling wagons against each other, clearly reminiscent of days on the range. Yee-haw!

2. National Finals Rodeo: This is no small-town, dusty rodeo. It has been held in Las Vegas since 1984 and always showcases the top rodeo performers, who must qualify in their respective events to participate. The indoor stadium is generally sold out, often hosting up to 20,000 spectators for evening performances. Combine the drama of cowboys and cowgirls competing for more than $5 million in total prize money and a setting of bright lights, loud music, and pyrotechnics befitting a Las Vegas venue, and the National Finals Rodeo is a western experience you won't forget. Plus, because it's held in December, you can shop with abandon at the associated Cowboy Christmas trade fair.

3. Guest Ranch: If your idea of enjoying the western mystique is somewhat more bucolic, then consider visiting a working

On a dude ranch trail

guest ranch. There are numerous ranches throughout the west and Southwest, most of which are members of guest or dude ranch associations in their respective states. Though you'll stay in luxurious rooms or cottages far superior to any bunkhouse, during the day you'll saddle up a horse and ride with real cowboys. You'll get an opportunity to tend herds of cattle, scout open trails, and try your hand at chores like roping and branding. This is arguably the best way to learn firsthand just how glamorous and romantic a cowboy's life really is. Or isn't.

4. Cowboy Poetry Readings: What did the cowboys do for entertainment once the sun set and the cattle were down for the night? They gathered around the campfire and played songs on their guitars, told tales, and recited their best efforts at poetry. The same oral tradition is alive at cowboy poetry gatherings, which are equal parts good-natured fun and an homage to a simpler life. Two of the largest events are the National Cowboy Poetry Gathering, held in Elko, Nevada, and the Texas Cowboy Poetry Gathering in Alpine, Texas. Both of these annual festivals take place in the winter.

15 Things a Trail Horse Must Be Able to Do

1. Cross water including puddles and slow-moving streams, which are basic water features in natural terrain.

2. Willingly step over low obstacles on the ground, such as a fallen tree limb.

3. Remain calm when ridden past barking dogs. This can be difficult, as a horse may perceive a dog as a possible predator.

4. Sidepass, or step laterally away in response to pressure from the rider's leg. This allows the rider to remain in the saddle

Crossing water

Extreme Trail Riding

For riders who find that the average trail lacks adventure, a pair of equestrian sports might just provide the zing that they need. They are endurance riding and the fairly new sport known as Ride and Tie. Endurance riding drew an enthusiastic following in the 1950s after a horseman named Wendell Robie rode from Nevada to California along the old Pony Express trail in less than twenty-four hours. This was considered an amazing feat for both horse and rider. As the sport evolved, it has incorporated stringent rules related to the conditioning of the horse. Frequent veterinary checks along the route ensure that the horse is both sound and fit enough to continue. Arabian horses, because of their inherent

when maneuvering to reach something to the side, such as the latch on a gate.

5. Back up on cue to avoid a potential trail hazard.

6. Stand still while a rider mounts and dismounts. No one wants to be left in the dust while the horse gallops off into the sunset!

stamina and soundness, are the predominant choice of endurance-riding participants.

The sport of Ride and Tie, invented in 1971, lingers outside mainstream equestrian competition. Three team members (two humans and a horse of any breed) traverse a cross-country course. The lead team member starts by riding the horse some distance, tying him there to a tree, and then continuing on foot. The second team member catches up to the horse on foot, climbs aboard, rides on past the first team member, and repeats the process of tying the horse and walking on. The rotation continues until the entire team reaches the end of the course, which ranges from twenty to one hundred miles, depending on the competition. Success in both of these long-distance equestrian sports requires dedication, physical conditioning, and solid horsemanship skills.

7. Stand patiently while tied to a hitching post or tree.

8. Walk patiently back to the barn or trailer. A horse that is overeager to go home is called barn sour.

9. Behave in a group. A rambunctious or overly dominant horse will incite bad behavior in the other horses.

Trail riding in English tack

10. Be brave enough to venture out on the trail without the company of another horse. After all, sometimes you want to ride in solitude.

11. Load and unload from the trailer without dramatics.

12. Remain calm around traffic. A horse that is apprehensive around trucks and buses is liable to bolt into the street without thinking of the consequences.

13. Confidently cross a bridge. The hollow sound of hooves clomping across a bridge can unnerve some horses. Once across, they're reluctant to cross back again.

14. Be surefooted on uneven terrain.

15. Possess an inquisitive nature. A horse that is curious about its environment, rather than suspicious, is more likely to enjoy the ever-changing scenery of a trail ride.

Chapter Five

Buying a Horse

Every horse lover dreams of owning a horse, but it's wise to be well informed before making such a major decision.

10 Questions to Consider Before Buying a Horse

1. Can you afford the monthly upkeep? Think beyond the lump-sum initial purchase price. You'll also have to budget for those little recurring expenses that add up: tack, feed supplements, and grooming supplies such as fly spray and shampoo.

2. What about veterinary emergencies? Can you afford to set aside money each month just in case your horse needs an expensive house call from an equine doctor? Simple first aid techniques aren't sufficient for colic, acute illness, or major trauma.

3. For everyday horse care, you'll need to know the basics of equine first aid. Can you bandage a leg? Treat a superficial wound? Take a horse's temperature?

4. In addition to budgeting your money, can you budget time for your horse? Once the novelty of owning a horse wears off,

Applying first aid

will you have the enthusiasm and energy to invest in an animal that needs daily exercise?

5. Are you prepared for the less glamorous aspects of owning a horse? For example, if you keep your horse on your property, how will you dispose of manure? The average one-thousand-pound horse produces fifty pounds of manure a day. Where will you put that?

6. If you plan to stable your horse at a boarding facility, is there a reputable site nearby? Check local facilities for healthy, well-fed horses and fencing that is in good repair.

7. Are you confident in your horse-handling skills? Just about any horse will soon take advantage of a human who is intimidated by a horse's physical size. The horse must respect you as the herd leader.

8. Will your family and significant other support your horse habit? Your passion for all things equine could upset the dynamics of a relationship. It's no fun to be forced to choose between a horse and a person.

9. Are you willing to humble yourself and admit that you will always have something new and insightful to learn about both horses and horsemanship? Seeking advice from experienced professionals will enhance your relationship with your horse.

An owner doing chores

10. How do you see yourself as a rider? Do you envision your-self competing at shows or cruising down the trails? The world of horses offers you opportunities to do both. Select a horse and a riding style that will allow you to achieve your dream.

10 Steps to Buying a Horse Wisely

(Compiled by the editors of Horse Illustrated*)*

1. Accept that you might not be able to afford the perfect horse. Decide which traits are most important to you, and then be willing to compromise on others.

2. Take riding lessons. Mastering basic horsemanship will make owning a horse both a safer and a more personally fulfilling experience.

3. Spread the word that you're in the market for a horse. Local networking might lead to a suitable horse right in your own neighborhood.

4. Don't buy impulsively. Allow yourself time to think over a prospective purchase before you make a decision.

5. Look for the horse you need, not the horse you want. That fuzzy foal may indeed be darling, but weren't you in the market for an older, trail-broke gelding?

6. Shop with your riding instructor or a knowledgeable barn buddy. Objective input from a trusted horseperson could keep you from making a bad decision.

A riding lesson

7. If you find a horse you like, try riding him more than once. You'll get a better idea of the horse's typical behavior.

8. Ride the prospective horse away from its home to see how he behaves in a different environment. Most sellers will allow you to take a horse on trial, at least for a day.

9. Have a prepurchase exam. An equine veterinarian will evaluate the horse's general health and alert you to any potential soundness issues.

10. Get all pertinent information from the seller. Besides a bill of sale, you'll also need your new horse's veterinary and farrier records, plus any tips on his personal tastes in feed. That way, your horse will enjoy a smooth transition from one home to another.

A prepurchase veterinary exam

Vital Signs

Every horse owner should know the normal vital signs of a healthy horse. Such knowledge can help determine whether it's time to summon a veterinarian. First, a horse's normal body temperature ranges from 99–101 degrees Fahrenheit. The temperature must be taken rectally with a heavy-duty animal thermometer. After strenuous exercise, especially in hot summer weather, the horse's temperature may be slightly elevated. A temperature of 103–104 degrees Fahrenheit generally indicates a fever. A feverish horse would also be listless and refuse to eat. Next, a horse's normal pulse is thirty-six to forty-two beats per minute.

7 Issues on Keeping Your Horse at Home

1. How much of your property are you willing to sacrifice for your horses? Unless you have a large expanse of property, keeping a horse—or two or three—at home usually means that you'll have to forgo those plans for a pool, spa, and barbecue pit.

The pulse is taken by listening to the heart on the left side of the chest just behind the left elbow. A horse in pain will have an elevated pulse, although foals and ponies may have a heart rate that is normally a bit faster. Another vital sign is the respiration rate. A healthy horse takes 8–12 breaths per minute. Breathing that requires great abdominal effort or that sounds thick and heavy can signal an emergency such as pneumonia. Finally, the color of a horse's gums can reveal much about his health. Gums should be light pink. A horse with pale or blue-tinged gums is not getting enough oxygen into his system. Yellow or jaundiced gums potentially indicate liver disease. By memorizing normal vital signs a horse owner can be better prepared to spot the early warning signs of health problems.

2. Have you priced the cost of barns, corrals, and fencing? Structures designed to safely house horses are expensive. You may have to scale down those plans for a dream barn.

3. Do you have realistic expectations of the chores involved? There is always something to do when you keep your horses at home, from feeding to general maintenance of fencing. And don't forget the mucking. Horses pass manure about a dozen times a day. That's a lot of poop to shovel!

Mucking the stall

4. Do you mind dust, mud, and flies? No matter how hard you try, it's impossible to keep your home spotless when a stable is just a few steps away.

5. Is there really enough room for your horses to exercise? Cramped corrals wedged into the corner of a backyard are not sufficient. Unless you plan to ride your horse almost daily on local trails, your property should include a round pen or turnout paddock so your horse can stretch his legs and work off excess energy.

6. What about vacations? Forget those spur-of-the-moment getaways. Any out-of-town trips will now require planning. Horse care will become your number-one priority. Will it be hard to find someone who is reliable, comfortable handling horses, and willing to take on that responsibility while you are away from home?

7. Of course, your horses should have access to veterinary and farrier care; however, you should be prepared to handle minor, everyday bumps and scrapes. You'll need an assortment of bandages, leg wraps, salves, and liniments and a secure place to store them.

10 Fun Things to Do with and for Horses

1. Bake homemade horse treats: Easy-to-bake recipes using simple ingredients like rolled oats, molasses, and shredded carrots are available in books and on the Internet.

2. Teach your horse some tricks: You can gradually teach your horse to bow by luring him into stretching his neck down and

Beware the Barbed Wire Fence

The cost of installing fencing can deter the dream of keeping a horse at home. One impulse is to gravitate to the least expensive option, which is often barbed wire. Although it might work well on open ranges to secure cattle, barbed wire is not a wise choice for fencing horses. Barbed wire was first patented in 1874, and its popularity on southwestern cattle ranches helped tame the West, but not before it earned the nickname "the Devil's Rope" for its tendency to snare unsuspecting animals and mangle them. Horses were often the victims of nasty barbed wire wounds. They don't have the tough hide and thick hairy coats of cattle. And unlike cattle, which seem to learn to respect barbed wire, horses instinctively panic when they come in contact with the spiked wire fencing. Once snagged, horses will struggle, ripping holes in their skin and possibly fatally wounding themselves. For these reasons, other fencing choices should be investigated. Round metal pipe fencing is a popular choice. Although it may not be aesthetically pleasing, it is durable and strong. Plain wooden fencing is another alternative, although bored horses have a habit of chewing on wood. That can be prevented by installing low-wattage electrified "hot wires," but these products are battery powered and thus require frequent maintenance to keep them functioning as a deterrent. Finally, modern versions of vinyl fencing are

Barbed wire:
a hazard to avoid

becoming more acceptable. With the appearance of freshly painted wood, white vinyl fencing looks fresh, horses won't chew on it, and if a board does crack or break it's easily replaced. It is, however, quite expensive. As you can see, selecting fencing materials for horsekeeping is not an easy—or cheap—task.

A horse and rider in a parade

to the side for a carrot. Build his repertoire, and you'll be the talk of the riding community!

3. Ride your horse in a parade: Band together with a few of your barn buddies, don some costumes, and wave to the crowds. Just practice first to make sure your horse has the right temperament to willingly strut down a street lined with noisy spectators.

THE HORSE BOOK OF LISTS

4. Schedule a spa day: Break out the shampoo, the mane and tail conditioner, the electric clippers, and a bevy of brushes. Give your horse a beauty school makeover.

5. Go Christmas caroling: Bring cheer to your neighborhood. Who cares if you really can't sing that well? Round up some like-minded friends, saddle up your trail horses, and hit the bridle paths on a December evening.

6. Participate in Show and Tell at a local elementary school: Not every school kid is familiar with horses. Introduce them to your passion by arranging to bring your trusty steed for an informative seminar.

7. Massage: A certified equine massage therapist can help alleviate muscle soreness or just help your horse relax.

8. Organize a drill team: Find a half-dozen or so riders with some free time and freewheeling spirits. Select a team captain. Plan an orchestrated pattern, set it to music, make or buy some costumes (don't forget to color-coordinate your horses and tack), and you'll have yourself a grand time on horseback. If your drill team gets good enough, you can perform at rodeos and charitable events.

9. Volunteer at an equine rescue organization: These are charitable organizations that take in abused, neglected, or unwanted

Riders in a drill team

horses. Some rehabilitate the horses and try to find them new, loving owners. Others serve as a retirement home. By donating your time, your efforts will honor the relationship you have with your horse by making life better for a less privileged animal.

10. Try a different riding discipline: You and your horse will be invigorated by the challenge of something new. Contact a professional trainer or instructor, and ask about riding in a lesson or clinic. Ever want to barrel race? Jump? Dressage, anyone?

Coming to the Rescue

If not for the many reputable equine rescue organizations, many unwanted horses would be transported to slaughterhouses or die of neglect. Horses at rescue facilities are rehabilitated and, if sound enough, adopted into loving homes. Many unwanted horses are by-products of the Thoroughbred racing industry. A racehorse that proves to be too slow or unsound to be profitable to its owners often becomes a liability. Rescue groups such as the Thoroughbred Retirement Foundation and the Exceller Fund work tirelessly to find homes for these horses, many of which will make inexpensive prospects for English riders. Cast-off Standardbreds, which race by pulling a lightweight two-wheeled cart called a sulky, can also find their way to the doorstep of a rescue group. Even though it is known for its speedy trot and pace, rather than a canter or gallop, the sweet-natured Standardbred can be retrained as a versatile riding horse. The Standardbred Retirement Foundation works to meet that goal. Thanks to rescue groups, fewer unwanted horses will meet an inhumane or premature end.

Chapter Six

Tack and Supplies

Owning a horse requires stocking and maintaining a range of equine accessories.

---

12 Training Tack Essentials

1. Longe line

2. Longeing cavesson

3. Longe whip

4. A mild snaffle bit for schooling sessions or longeing

5. A more advanced bit—such as a curb or twisted snaffle—for fine-tuning the horse

6. Surcingle for work on the longe line

7. Set of long lines for ground driving the horse when necessary

8. Side reins for longeing exercises

A smooth snaffle

THE HORSE BOOK OF LISTS

9. Martingale or training fork to help set the horse's head

10. Figure 8, flash, or dropped noseband in case the horse opens his mouth to bit pressure

11. Sturdy practice headstall for training sessions to prevent wear and tear on show tack

12. Several sets of reins in case one set breaks

10 Training Tack Terms Defined

1. Longe line: A sturdy, heavy-duty cotton rope approximately thirty feet in length. Nylon webbing is also used for longe lines, but nylon is more likely to cause rope burns on the handler's hand if the horse should suddenly pull away. The longe line is snapped onto the halter or bridle, and the horse is then worked in a circle. Longeing a horse not only works off the horse's excess energy but also allows a young horse to learn basic commands without having to carry the weight of a rider.

2. Longe whip: Not a device for punishment but a training aid, the longe whip allows the trainer to signal the horse to move forward or to increase his pace on the longe line.

3. Longeing cavesson: While most trainers and handlers longe their horses in a halter or bridle, a longeing cavesson is another option more common among English riding enthusiasts. It's a heavy padded noseband with a metal nosepiece to which swivel-mounted metal rings are attached. The longe line is then snapped onto one of the rings.

4. Surcingle: A wide leather or nylon band that buckles around the horse's body much like a girth or cinch. There are brass or stainless steel rings on both sides of the surcingle, allowing the trainer to attach reins and equipment when necessary. In this manner, a surcingle can substitute for a saddle in work on the longe line.

5. Long lines: A pair of leather, rope, or nylon reins approximately twenty feet long. These extra-long reins are attached to the bit rings of a mild snaffle and run through the rings of a surcingle. The horse is then asked to go through his paces and practice turning while the trainer walks behind the horse holding the long lines in his or her hands. This process, also called ground driving, prepares the horse to be ridden under saddle.

6. Side reins: Short, adjustable leather or nylon straps that are often constructed with a segment of elastic or a stretchable round "donut" so that there is some give-and-take in the side reins. As a longeing exercise, side reins are attached to the surcingle and then to the snaffle bit rings to simulate the rider's hands holding the reins.

7. Standing martingale or tie down: The standing martingale is a single strap that runs directly from the girth, through the horse's front legs, and attaches to the bridle's noseband or to a cavesson. It restricts the horse from tossing his head. Many English show hunters wear standing martingales while jump-

A bridle with a standing martingale

ing. In western riding, the equivalent item is called a tie down. It's a standard piece of equipment on horses used for roping.

8. Running martingale or training fork: The running martingale is a little more complicated than the standing martingale but is also used to restrict a horse's head carriage. The running martingale is a narrow leather strap that is attached to the girth at one end. The other end passes between the horse's front legs and then splits or forks at the horse's chest. There is a ring at the end of each fork. The reins pass through these rings. If the horse raises his head too high, the reins will tighten. In response, the horse lowers his head to seek relief, thereby learning just where to carry his head. In English disciplines, this piece of equipment is called a running martingale; in western riding, it's called a training fork.

9. Figure 8 noseband: When buckled about the horse's face, this special type of narrow noseband does indeed resemble a figure 8. The leather straps criss-cross the bridge of the horse's nose and then buckle under the horse's chin, below the bit. The bit pressure prevents the horse from opening his mouth. It also helps prevent a hard-mouthed horse from pulling on the bit.

10. Flash attachment: The same idea as the figure 8 noseband; however, the flash is attached to a regular noseband. When attached via a buckle, the flash can be applied or removed as the situation warrants.

8 Parts of an English Bridle

1. Bit ring
2. Browband
3. Cavesson
4. Cheek piece

5. Crown piece
6. Noseband
7. Reins
8. Throatlatch

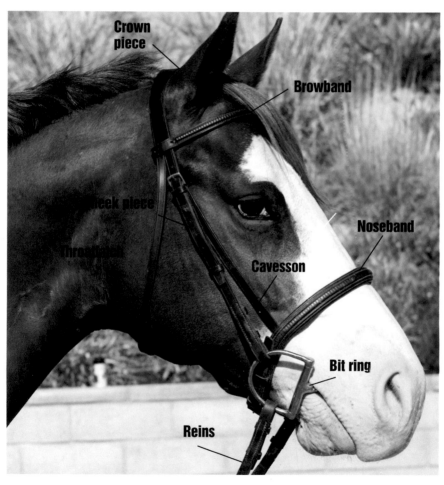

An English bridle

6 Parts of a Western Bridle

1. Cheek

2. Crown

3. Curb strap

4. Ear slot

5. Reins

6. Shank

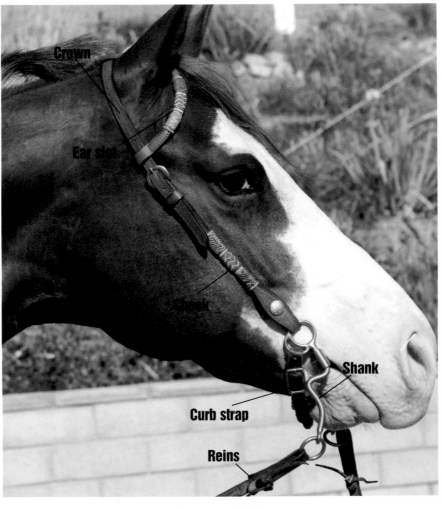

Crown

Ear slot

Cheek

Shank

Curb strap

Reins

A western bridle

15 Types of Bits

1. Curb: A curb bit influences the horse by exerting pressure on several parts of his mouth and head. The lower half of a curb bit includes a shank. The reins are attached to the shank. When the rider pulls back on the reins, the shank adds leverage. The longer the shank, the more severe the leverage action. Pressure from the bit itself is exerted on the horse's mouth. Because of the leverage the shank creates, the horse also feels pressure on the poll (the top of the head) through the crown piece of the bridle, and on the chin, thanks to the curb strap. Most well-trained western horses are ridden in a curb bit, although there are also curb bits for English horses.

2. Eggbutt: A snaffle with oval or egg-shaped rings. The shape of the bit rings prevents the bit from pinching the sensitive corners of the horse's mouth.

A curb bit

The Fit of the Bit and Bridle

Bits and bridles come in several different sizes to accommodate a wide variety of horses. Standard bit width is five inches, which fits comfortably in the mouth of the average-size horse. Pony bits are four and one-half inches wide, whereas warmblood sport horses often require a bit that is slightly wider than the standard bit at five and one-quarter inches. A bit that is too narrow will pinch the horse's mouth and cause sores. When placed on the bridle, the bit should hang so it creates one wrinkle or crease at the corner of the horse's mouth. The cheek pieces of the bridle can be

3. D-Ring: The two rings of this snaffle bit are clearly shaped like the letter *D*. A popular bit choice for use with racehorses, the shape of the ring prevents the bit from being pulled through the horse's mouth when a great deal of rein pressure is applied.

4. Full cheek: This type of snaffle features cheek pieces that extend for several inches from the top and bottom of the bit rings. Frequently used on show hunters, the design of the full cheek aids in turning the horse.

adjusted to make the bit fit. Other adjustments are buckling the throatlatch and noseband properly. The purpose of the throatlatch is to prevent the bridle from slipping off over the horse's head. There should be just enough room to fit a fist between the buckled throatlatch and the horse's jaw. The noseband, which helps keep the horse's mouth closed around the bit, should be tightened so a finger can easily slip between it and the horse's face. Finally, bridles come in four sizes: pony-size, cob (generally for Arabians and petite horses), full-size (for average horses), and oversize (for warmblood sport horses). There is a bit and a bridle just the right size for every horse.

5. Gag: At first glance, a gag bit looks a lot like a snaffle. But on closer inspection, it's apparent that the cheek pieces of the bridle slide through holes in the snaffle bit rings. The reins are then attached to the ends of these extra-long, narrow cheek pieces. The result is a bit that exerts considerable pressure on the horse's mouth and poll. To soften its effect, an additional set of reins is often attached to the outside of the bit rings, giving the rider two sets of reins and the option of employing the gag rein only when necessary. This is not a bit for novice riders; however, it does provide excellent control for tough-mouthed, strong horses. Gag bits are most often used in show jumping and three-day eventing.

6. Hackamore: Actually a bitless bridle, the hackamore nonetheless can be part of a horse's training. It consists of a hard, durable noseband (or bosal) that's usually made of leather wrapped around a cable of tough, braided rawhide. The hackamore works by applying pressure to the sensitive parts of a horse's nose and jaw. While it may look mild, the action of a hackamore can be severe in uneducated hands. Hackamores were traditionally used in the training of western cow ponies; however, there are variations of hackamores specifically designed for show jumping.

7. High port curb: The mouthpiece of a curb bit has a port (a U-shaped curve) in its center to accommodate the horse's tongue. A high port relieves pressure on the tongue. The bit then exerts more pressure on the horse's lower jaw in unison with a leather chin strap or flat chain. This combined pressure applied to the lower jaw makes the horse lower his head.

8. Kimberwicke: Often used on ponies, the kimberwicke is also seen on American Quarter Horses and Paints ridden in English events. It has bit rings similar to a D-ring snaffle, yet also offers some mild leverage action similar to a curb bit. Hence, it works well on a horse or pony that has a tendency to lean on the bit or that is used to being ridden in a western bridle.

A western bosal hackamore

9. Loose ring: Just as its name indicates, the snaffle bit rings are not fixed onto the mouthpiece. This freedom of movement permits the horse to move the bit around inside the mouth somewhat. That makes it a mild snaffle and a good choice for a horse's first bit.

10. Mullen mouthpiece: The Mullen mouthpiece is not jointed in the middle like the typical snaffle bit. Instead, it is a solid bar. This bit is usually slightly curved so it lies gently on the horse's tongue.

11. Pelham: Two sets of reins are used on a Pelham bit, which is considered a curb bit for English horses. One set of reins attaches to rings near the corners of the horse's mouth, simulating the action of a snaffle bit. But the other set of reins attaches near the bottom of the short, straight shank, eliciting a curb response. A curb chain, which lies flat against the horse's chin, is also part of the Pelham bit. Hence, the Pelham bit is designed to integrate aspects of both the snaffle and the curb. It is a common bit on larger show hunters and jumpers that require an optimum amount of control.

12. Rubber snaffle: This bit's mouthpiece is wrapped or coated with thick rubber. That encourages the horse to feel the bit with its lips, tongue, and teeth. It is often a starter bit for young horses with sensitive mouths.

A Pelham bit

An unjointed snaffle bit

13. Snaffle: A ring is attached to each end of a snaffle's mouthpiece. The reins are then attached to the rings. When the rider pulls on the reins, the bit correspondingly applies pressure to the horse's mouth. Although a snaffle is most often associated with English riding, most horses of all riding disciplines begin their training in a snaffle bit.

14. Twisted snaffle: To increase its severity, the metal mouthpiece of this snaffle is slightly twisted so that the horse more readily responds to pressure from the bit. If this snaffle has multiple tight twists, then it is aptly called a corkscrew snaffle.

15. Western correction: Designed with a hinged mouthpiece, loose shanks, a moderate to high port, and long shanks, a correction bit allows a rider to convey requests to the horse with a light touch on the reins. However, it's a bit best left to skilled riders on trained horses. Otherwise, the horse can become confused and frustrated.

12 Parts of an English Saddle

1. Cantle	**5.** Pommel	**9.** Skirt
2. Girth	**6.** Saddle flap	**10.** Stirrup leather
3. Knee roll	**7.** Safety stirrup bar	**11.** Stirrup or "iron"
4. Panel	**8.** Seat	**12.** Twist

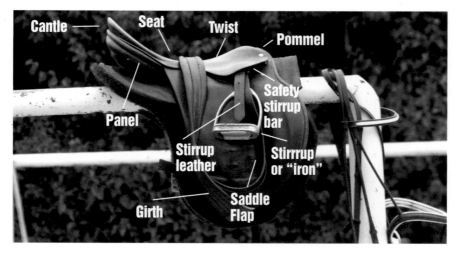

English dressage saddle

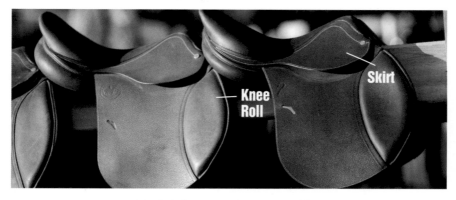

English hunter and jumper saddles

16 Parts of a Western Saddle

1. Cantle
2. Cinch
3. Concho
4. Dee ring
5. Fender
6. Gullet
7. Horn
8. Jockey
9. Latigo
10. Latigo keeper
11. Rigging or cinch ring
12. Seat
13. Skirt
14. Stirrup
15. Strings
16. Swell

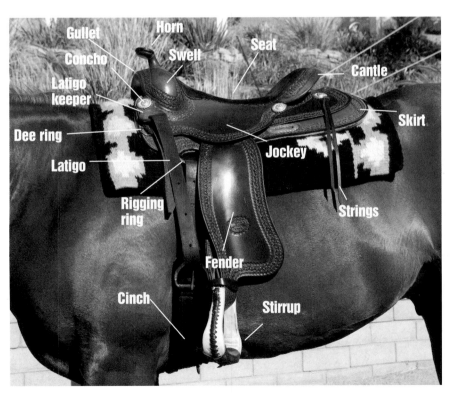

A working cowboy's western saddle.

7 Rider Training Aids and Apparel

1. Boots: Any hard-soled boot with at least a one-inch heel will keep a foot from slipping through a stirrup. Beyond that, boot style is a matter of the wearer's personal taste.

2. Chaps: Full-length leather chaps cover the rider's entire leg and zip over the top of jeans. Half chaps zip or Velcro just above the rider's calf and can be made from faux suede. Both give a greater sense of security in the saddle, helping the rider adhere to the tack.

3. Body protector: Mostly seen in the English riding disciplines of cross-country riding and three-day eventing, body (chest) protectors are also gaining acceptance among professional rodeo cowboys who ride saddle broncs. A body protector can help pad the upper body in case of a fall. Modern designs and materials have reduced some of the bulk and weight of early versions.

4. Crop or bat: Applied to the horse's side, behind the rider's leg, the tap or smack of a crop teaches the horse to respond to pressure from the rider's calf or heel.

5. Gloves: After many hours holding a longe line or a pair of reins, a trainer's hands become brutally chapped and weath-

A young rider wearing a safety helmet

ered. Gloves can help prevent skin damage as well as improve one's grip.

6. Helmet: Perhaps the wisest investment for someone training a young horse—and for any rider—is a helmet that meets or exceeds safety testing standards, as designated by an ASTM/SEI tag. This tag signifies the approval of ASTM International, formerly the American Society for Testing and Materials (ASTM), and the Safety Equipment Institute (SEI). A high-quality helmet can prevent or greatly reduce the severity of head injuries.

Western boots outfitted with spurs

7. Spurs: Available in numerous lengths and designs that increase or modify their intensity, spurs are meant to reinforce the rider's leg aid.

20 Items in a Well-Stocked Tack Box

1. Rubber curry comb to lift dirt and loosen dead hair

2. Stiff brush to help distribute natural skin oils

3. Soft brush for the horse's face and sensitive areas

4. Tail brush to detangle snarls

5. Metal comb for thinning or shortening the mane

6. Terry cloth rub rag for wiping the inside of the horse's ears and nostrils

7. Protective boots (such as splint boots and bell boots) for the horse's legs

8. Hoof pick for removing pebbles and debris from the hooves

9. Hoof oil or emollient to help prevent dry, brittle hooves

10. Fly repellent to shoo away pesky biting insects

11. Shampoo formulated specifically for horses so it doesn't dry the coat

12. Coat polish to get rid of tangles and static cling in manes and tails

13. Hardware that might come in handy in a pinch, such as screw eyes and gate snaps

An organized tack box

14. Duct tape for a multitude of uses, including securing a loose shoe in place until the farrier arrives

15. Scissors to cut baling twine and open feed bags

16. Hole punch so leather tack can be quickly adjusted to a proper fit

17. Topical antibiotic ointment for common scrapes

18. Antibacterial soap for first aid and minor skin irritations

19. Leg bandage and wrap to help reduce swelling and protect a wound on extremities

20. Large-animal thermometer

10 Tack Tips: Selecting and Caring for Gear

1. Bits, headstalls, and halters are available in various sizes: pony, cob (for Arabians or small horses), full (standard horse size), oversize (for warmblood sport horses), and draft. Always choose the appropriate size tack for your horse by checking the tag or the embossed stamp on leather goods.

2. Stay away from trendy gadgets. That newfangled training device could become an object of torture in the wrong hands.

3. Tack made from quality leather with detailed craftsmanship may be pricier, but its durability usually makes it a better investment than cheaper, shoddier equipment.

4. Used tack from a reliable manufacturer can be a bargain. But inspect it carefully. Avoid older tack with frayed or cracked leather and loose stitching.

5. Each riding discipline has very specific tack requirements. If you are planning to compete in horse shows, find out what's required before you make the wrong purchase.

6. If you need additional holes in your tack to adjust it correctly, use a leather punch. Space new holes evenly and be conservative. Too many holes weaken the leather and detract from its appearance.

7. Keep all tack away from the mouths of young horses. They have a tendency to chew leather!

8. After a long ride, wipe the sweat from your tack. This helps prevent the leather from absorbing the salt in the sweat and drying out.

9. Mold and mildew can be problems for leather tack, especially in humid climates. Tack should be stored in a dry, well-ventilated area.

10. When cleaning tack, use only products specifically designed for that purpose. Use leather cleaning agents to help suds away grime and sweat and leather conditioners to restore natural oils. Quality leather tack that is cared for properly will last a lifetime.

Cleaning tack

Chapter Seven

Training the Horse

The average horse weighs one thousand pounds. Such a powerful animal can be handled and ridden safely only when properly trained. And only a properly trained horse can be successfully used for competitive endeavors.

---

7 Steps for Starting a Horse Under Saddle

1. Teach the horse to longe, preferably in a round pen. He should move forward, stop, and reverse based on voice commands and hand signals. Use a longe whip as an aid to help convey your requests.

2. Make sure the horse is comfortable with things touching his body, especially on his flank and around his hind legs. For example, calmly drape the longe line over his back. Bump his lower legs with the end of the lead rope. Reassure the horse that he won't be harmed.

3. Bridle the horse. Use a very mild bit such as a loose ring, egg-butt, or rubber snaffle. Allow the horse to get used to wearing a bridle over several schooling sessions. When longeing, place a halter over the top of the bridle. Do not attach the longe line to the bit rings. That will put too much pressure on a young horse's sensitive mouth.

4. Once the horse is accustomed to wearing a bridle, acquaint him with a saddle blanket and surcingle. Rub the blanket along his neck. Let him sniff it. Set it gently on his back. Do the same with the surcingle. When you tighten the cinch on the surcingle, do it slowly. By tightening it in increments, you avoid suddenly surprising your horse with a constricting strap around his belly.

5. After longeing successfully with the bit and surcingle in place, introduce your horse to a pair of long lines. You can now snap one long line onto each bit ring of the snaffle. Work the horse at the walk and trot in a round pen or small arena with the long lines. This is much like driving a horse, except that you are walking instead of sitting in a wagon or cart. Ask the horse to halt by pulling on the long lines and saying, "Whoa." Turn left and right by pulling gently on the long lines. This simulates the same maneuvers your horse will encounter when he's being ridden.

THE HORSE BOOK OF LISTS

Introducing a saddle blanket to a young horse

6. Now it's time to replace the surcingle with a lightweight saddle. Again, allow the young horse to inspect the saddle before gently placing it on his back and slowly tightening the cinch. Work the horse with the bridle, saddle, and long lines.

7. It's finally time to hop on! Make sure you're wearing a helmet and that the surrounding area is clear of obstacles. While a handler holds the horse, put your foot in the stirrup and mount halfway. Lie across the horse's back so that the horse gets an

More Than Going in Circles

The practice of longeing the horse (also sometimes spelled "lungeing") has been part of horse training for centuries. The famed Spanish Riding School in Vienna, Austria, which came to prominence under the reign of Charles VI in 1735, always included longeing in its program. *Longe* derives from the French word *allonge*, which means to lengthen or stretch out, an appropriate term for encouraging a horse to stretch and become more limber and supple. Unfortunately, in the wrong hands longeing sometimes amounts to urging a frisky horse to work off excess energy by zipping around at dangerous speeds. Instead, longeing should be a valuable exercise to help train and condition the horse. It can also be integrated into riding lessons. Much can be learned when the instructor keeps a rider on the longe line. Because the rider needn't worry about controlling the horse, he or she can experience riding without reins, a significant

initial feeling of weight on his back. Quietly slide to the ground and pat the horse. The next time, have the handler lead the horse while you lie across his back. Repeat this process until you're sure

Longeing a horse

step in developing a sense of balance on the back of the horse. Such an idea has been taken to an artistic level in the sport of vaulting. While a trustworthy horse—usually a wide-backed draft horse—is on the longe line, skillful equestrians perform gymnastic feats that combine horsemanship with acrobatics. Vaulting is yet another example of how longeing can be far more than simply going in circles.

that the horse accepts this new experience. Then it's time to climb into the saddle and have the handler let you be the one holding the reins. Your horse is officially started under saddle!

9 Naughty Habits: Their Causes and Cures

1. Balking: This is the refusal to go forward. The horse may embellish balking by backing up. Although a horse may balk in apprehension of the trail ahead, nonetheless he is disobeying a request from his rider. If confronting a scary object on the trail, the horse should be reassured and given a moment to realize that he is not in danger. Once the horse has calmed down, the rider should once again ask the horse to move forward. If the horse continues to balk, the rider should apply a nudge of the heel or a smack of the crop behind his or her leg to demand that the horse move on. Sometimes turning the horse left or right and encouraging him to take a few steps in either direction will also refocus the horse's attention on the rider.

2. Barn sour: Horses are herd animals, and they enjoy each other's company. However, a horse that is barn sour is either obstinately reluctant to ride away from the barn or so eager to return home that every trail ride ends with the horse dancing sideways or trying to race all the way back to the barn. One solution is to vary the route on the trail so that the horse is less able to predict when he's heading home. Next, the horse should never be fed a treat or a meal as soon as he gets back to the barn. That just increases the allure of returning home. Another tactic is to stop the horse each time he begins to get antsy, turn him around, and head away from the barn again. Winning this battle of wills takes time and patience, but allowing the behavior without any repercussions only reinforces it.

3. Bolting: Usually, bolting is an instinctive response to a perceived threat. Without giving any consideration to traffic, other horses, or people on the ground, the horse raises his head and runs full steam ahead away from what is bothering him. Unfortunately, this can send the horse directly into an even more dangerous situation. To stop this runaway train, the rider must sit deeply in the saddle, lean back with the upper body and pull back on the reins. If the horse is running blindly into a hazardous area, the rider can exert more pressure on one rein in order to turn the horse in a circle. That often breaks the horse's fixation on bolting and allows the rider to bring the horse to a stop.

4. Bucking: A horse that bucks ceases its forward motion, drops its head toward the ground, arches his back and then springs up into the air in an effort to dislodge his saddle or his rider. Occasionally, a fresh horse is so full of excess energy that he will buck as a response to stimuli such as another horse at play or a loud noise. However, a horse that habitually bucks is unpredictable and dangerous. A rider's first response should be to raise the horse's head by pulling up and back on the reins. At the same time, the rider should send the horse forward by squeezing with the legs.

5. Cribbing: Probably the most destructive of stable vices, cribbing is a horse's habit of grabbing a fence or stall door with his teeth, arching the neck, pulling backward, and then sucking in air with an audible grunting sound. Nervous or bored horses are most prone to cribbing, and once the habit is ingrained in a horse's behavior, it is nearly impossible to break. Horses that crib are prone to dental damage and colic. Their relentless cribbing can also quickly destroy property. When a horse first begins to crib, fastening a cribbing collar around his neck may help discourage the behavior. If that fails, then surgery to snip specific neck muscles often yields success.

6. Kicking out: When a rider asks a horse to increase the pace or move laterally by the application of leg pressure, the horse should comply. But some horses have to convey their displeasure by kicking out a hind leg as a response to the rider's request. It's almost like a child throwing a temper tantrum. The rider should correct the horse by applying the crop behind his or her leg, smacking the horse on the side. This reinforces the rider's leg aid and reminds the horse to respond more obediently.

7. Rearing: Similar to balking, rearing is the horse's way of adamantly telling you he doesn't want to go forward. However, rearing carries the avoidance to a dangerous extreme. Although sometimes an overly severe bit can elicit a rear, a horse that rears as a vice is untrustworthy. The offending horse stops and stands up on his hind legs. If the horse loses his balance, he can stumble

Cribbing

Sacking Out

One method of desensitizing a horse that habitually shies or spooks is the practice of sacking out. Although the practice has its roots in western riding and cowboy lore, it can be used on any horse being broke to ride. Sacking out teaches the insecure horse not to be frightened of strange objects and builds his confidence in his handler and rider. In its simplest application, the handler calmly approaches the horse holding an empty burlap bag or feed sack. The horse is permitted to sniff and inspect the sack; the sack should not present any surprises to the inquisitive yet

and fall backward, injuring both himself and the rider. Novice riders should not try to cure a rearing horse; that's best left to professional trainers. Skilled riders can feel when a horse is about to rear and deftly direct the horse into a turn. That usually aborts the rear. They then punish the horse by making him gallop forward, which is exactly what the horse didn't want to do.

8. Shying: It's normal behavior for a horse to shy occasionally. A shadow, a barking dog, a piece of paper on the ground—any scary object could cause a horse to suddenly stiffen his legs and

wary animal. Once the horse is calm, the sack is rubbed against the horse's body, draped over his head, and finally gently slapped against the horse's sides. At first, the horse might flinch or step away from the sack, but with patience and a few soothing words, the horse will soon stand obediently. To increase the intensity of the exercise, a few empty, crushed soda cans may be added to the sack to make a rattling noise. The horse begins to realize that he doesn't have to instinctively jump away from anything unusual that touches her body. That's definitely beneficial to a rider who is about to climb aboard a young, green, or apprehensive horse.

jump away. When the horse whirls in the opposite direction as he shies, he can unseat an unprepared rider. The best way to treat the habitually shying horse is to calmly introduce him to different environments. When the horse shies, the rider must remain calm. Punishing the horse for being afraid compounds the horse's anxiety. With time, the horse should gain confidence in unfamiliar surroundings. But if the shying continues, a veterinarian should examine the horse and check for vision problems such as cataracts. Perhaps the horse is scared simply because he can't see clearly.

9. Weaving and pacing: Stable vices are often signs that the horse is nervous or fretful in his environment. A horse that weaves stands in one place in the stall and sways back and forth for hours. A horse that paces walks up and down the fence line of the corral, wearing a trench in the ground. Both vices expend so much energy that the horse loses weight and condition. Sometimes the problem can be solved by simply moving the horse next to a different neighbor. Sometimes the horse needs more freedom to exercise on his own. In this case, a large pasture may be a better stabling option than a stall or small corral.

5 Reasons for Professional Training

1. Much like attending school, professional training sets specific goals and objectives of increasing difficulty so that your horse's education is based on a solid foundation.

2. A professional trainer has the experience to troubleshoot and deal with equine behavioral issues.

3. With a more detached point of view, professional trainers aren't "barn blind." They care about your horse's welfare, but their judgment isn't clouded by sentimentality, so they can objectively assess your horse and his progress.

4. A training program brings consistency to your horse's work routine. There are no missed rides due to outside distractions or personal commitments. This is your trainer's profession, not a hobby.

5. As your horse is professionally trained, you also will gain knowledge and experience. That strengthens the bond between you and your horse as well as your ability to work together.

A professional training session

8 Qualities of a Successful Training Stable

1. The head trainer has a professional resume that includes references from satisfied clients and experience working under or alongside other professionals.

2. The head trainer continues his or her professional education by attending clinics, reading books, and sharing ideas and theories with peers. This is evidence of an open mind and the willingness to embrace advances in horsemanship.

3. When the head trainer is away at a competition or on vacation, a competent assistant or substitute is readily available to step in.

4. The training regimen is observable. Schooling sessions are conducted in an organized, not haphazard, manner. A chart or notebook records each horse's work schedule.

5. The stable is an efficient business. Clients receive statements and bills on time and are fully informed of charges for extra lessons or show fees so there are no surprises at the end of the billing cycle.

6. Gossiping about clients is not allowed.

A well-kept stable

7. Only humane training methods are used. Horses in training are free of spur marks, rope burns, and whip welts.

8. Horses that have been in the training program for at least several months can perform. Jumpers jump fences, reining horses can work through a reining pattern, and pleasure horses are calm on the trail. The proof of a stable's success is in its horses' performance and reliability.

10 Bits of Advice on Becoming a Horse Trainer

1. Keep regular business hours. Your clients will perceive you as a true professional, and your spouse or significant other will be guaranteed some quality time with you.

2. Have a life away from the barn. Develop a hobby that doesn't involve horses. It makes you a well-rounded person and reduces stress. Make sure you have a retreat when days are rough at the barn, because some days will be rough.

3. Hire good help. You'll need a capable assistant who can ride and teach if you're injured or sick and a groom or stable manager who can help oversee the everyday care and maintenance of the barn.

4. Be candid with your clients. Don't mislead them into thinking they own a future champion if the horse truly doesn't have the talent.

5. Accept that you can't succeed with every horse. It's OK to admit defeat or that you simply aren't the right horseman or horsewoman to deal with a particular horse's issues. Suggest an alternative trainer who might be better suited to the horse. Your clients will respect you more, not less.

A riding instructor and student

6. Always carry insurance. That includes liability insurance in case one of your clients takes a horrendous tumble and health insurance for yourself. You could go years without an injury, but if you're badly hurt, you won't be able to work. Plus, insurance will help pay your medical bills.

7. Realize that good clients—as well as good horses—come and go. The reasons are varied: people lose interest in riding, change jobs and move, or simply want a different environment. Refrain from criticizing the training program at competing barns. Instead, keep your chin up, and don't speak ill of past customers. Your reputation will stay clean, and your clientele will grow.

8. Keep a neat and tidy barn. A first impression is a lasting impression, and if someone wanders in to take a look at your facility and the aisles are dirty and tack is strung about, the impression is that you run a shoddy business.

9. When you meet potential clients, try to get a feel for what they expect from you. Clearly explain your training program. If you get an inkling that you're not the right fit for them or for their horses, tell them so and avoid the inevitable falling-out in the future.

10. Never lose your love of horses. Take a moment each day to reflect on why you chose this profession. You'll be more eager to get up each morning.

6 Suggestions for the Homeschooled Horse

1. Save your pennies and sign up for a clinic. It's an opportunity to ride with some of the world's best horsepeople.

2. Attend horse expos in your region. A variety of professionals will be on hand to share their training tips. Most of them also ride in demonstrations, so you'll get a chance to see their philosophies in action.

A riding class

3. Subscribe to magazines that feature training articles and interviews with accomplished riders.

4. Watch instructional DVDs starring high-profile equestrians. Many of them have wonderful production values. DVDs also have a built-in advantage: you can stop and replay the action as many times as you need to see how something is done.

5. If you live far from a reputable trainer, consider making the trek for a lesson into a weekend getaway. Chances are you can board your horse overnight at the training facility, so be sure to ask. Then you can come home and during the week practice what you've learned.

6. Collect books on horsemanship and training and start your own reference library.

Donkey Neck Tie

Although successful trainers remain open to new techniques for schooling a horse, they also stay true to time-tested methods. One old-time practice still followed on some ranches is the use of a neck donkey to teach colts and fillies how to lead. A wide collar is fitted around a donkey's neck. A soft rope, about eighteen to twenty-four inches long, is attached to the collar. That rope is then snapped onto the halter of a weanling horse. The two animals are paired this way for a couple of days, always under supervision. The objective? To teach the weanling horse that it must accept and yield to pressure from the lead rope. When the donkey wants to eat, he walks to the feed tub. When he wants to drink, he heads to the water trough. When it's time for a nap, he lies down. All the while, the weanling horse has no choice but to acquiesce. After all, the horse is tethered to a donkey, an animal known to be single-mindedly set in his ways. Once the young horse tags along willingly, the weanling is released from the neck donkey and can begin more structured halter training. Of course, the neck donkey method should not be attempted by novice horse handlers, and the concept doesn't appeal to every horse trainer. But it's an interesting technique that some professionals use with great success.

Chapter Eight

The Competitive Horse and Rider

What better way to test the partnership between horse and human than in competition? Whether the prize is a ribbon at a horse show, a trip to the winner's circle, or simply bragging rights among peers, competitive events celebrate our relationship with horses.

---

4 Quirky Equestrian Competitions

1. Buzkashi: This ancient Central Asian game is the national sport of Afghanistan. The word *buzkashi* translates as "goat grabbing," which fairly sums up the objective of the contest. A headless goat (or calf) carcass is placed on the ground in the center of a circle on the playing field. Then teams of riders try to scoop it up and successfully carry it to the scoring area. Although this may sound like an easy—albeit gruesome—task, it is not. This is a fiercely aggressive sport: riders are often tossed, maimed, and bruised, only to climb back on and ride some more, and traditional matches can go on for days.

2. Competitive mounted orienteering: Riders good at finding their way through uncharted territory based on their map-reading skills are attracted to this new equestrian sport, which combines the trail ride and the treasure hunt. Riders read a list of vague clues describing Objective Stations hidden within a designated area. They must then rely on their navigational talents and horsemanship to find the spots. The winning rider—or group if it's a team event—is the one who completes the course with the fastest time.

3. Cowboy mounted shooting: The Wild West lives again in this sport, complete with gunfire. Riders race against the clock as they gallop through a marked course, shooting at balloons. Their weapons are .45 caliber single-action revolvers like those used in the late 1800s. But instead of real bullets, the guns fire black powder blank cartridges that pop the balloons. Both male and female participants are required to dress in authentic western garb, which adds to the rootin' tootin' atmosphere of the competition.

Cowboy mounted shooting

4. Tent pegging: In this sport with ancient Asian origins, riders gallop at top speed with a lance or sword and try to dislodge a

A Pair of Polos

Like buzkashi, the modern game of polo also began as an ancient tribal game, known to have been played in Persia in 200 BC. Organized polo was first played in the United States in 1876. Currently, there are two types of regulated competition. The first is traditional outdoor polo, played on a grass field 300 yards long. It's a game of high speed, extraordinarily well-trained swift horses, and daring riders. An outdoor polo match, played in 6 seven-and-a-half-minute time periods called chukkers, demands such exertion from the horses that each rider requires numerous mounts. Outdoor polo is thus a very expensive sport. The more affordable version of polo is arena polo, played indoors on an enclosed dirt field 300 feet long. Because a match lasts just four chukkers and utilizes a much smaller playing field, arena polo requires fewer horses per player. It is nonetheless an exciting, challenging sport, as the larger arena polo ball, which

series of small pegs partially buried in the dirt. It is believed that this contest evolved from battlefield tactics involving mounted riders who would swoop down upon an enemy encampment

Polo

resembles a small soccer ball, bounces around the dirt and careens off the arena wall. In both versions of polo, the objective is the same: to outride your opponents and, using long-handled mallets, drive the ball through the goalposts.

and yank free the pegs that held the tents upright. Today, tent pegging is popular mostly in India and parts of the Middle East, although interest is growing in the United States.

8 Popular Types of Equestrian Competition

1. Barrel racing: The most popular gymkhana (time-based competition) on horseback, barrel racing, according to contest lore, began in Texas in the 1930s when young female rodeo aspirants demonstrated their riding skills by loping a pattern around a few barrels. Several decades later, barrel racing for women was a mainstay of major rodeos, but it was seen as a diversion during intermission. Yet by 1995, there were more than 800 barrel racing competitions recognized by the sport's governing body, the Women's Professional Rodeo Association. As evidence of the growth of the sport, by 2004, female barrel racers competed for over $5 million in prize money at sanctioned events.

2. Cutting: In this high-octane western performance class, a selected steer is singled out, or cut, from a herd. It is then up to the well-trained horse to prevent the steer from rejoining the herd. Modern-day cutting contests are based on the everyday duties of a working ranch horse, which must routinely corner or capture a calf, cow, or steer. The earliest record of an organized cutting event was in 1898, when a group of Texas ranchers decided to see just who had the most talented cow ponies in the region. Over the next several decades the sport grew, and some large Texas cattle ranches became cutting dynasties that consis-

Barrel racing

tently produced top cutting horses sired by their homebred stallions. The American Quarter Horse, with its legendary "cow sense," or inherent ability to predict a cow's movements, became the most desired mount for the sport. In 1946, the National Cutting Horse Association (NCHA) was formed to standardize judging criteria for competitions and to maintain performance records. Today, the NCHA annually awards more than $40 million in total prize money at sanctioned cutting shows.

3. Dressage: The early Greeks were the first horsemen to recognize that highly trained horses were an asset in battle. In fact, many of the upper-level "high school" movements in dressage have their origins in battlefield maneuvers. The Spanish Riding School in Vienna, organized under the rule of Charles VI in 1735, was one of the first government-supported horsemanship programs to teach classical dressage. Dressage preserved its military connections, as only cavalry officers were permitted to compete in the first Olympic dressage tests held in 1912. However, as cavalries around the world were gradually disbanded after World War II, dressage became an equestrian pursuit strictly for competition. Far more than finessed flatwork, dressage is very much an art form when practiced to its highest level, the grand prix test. Any horse can benefit from dressage training, which teaches the horse to be compliant and obedient under saddle as well as exhibit expressive gaits. In dressage, a horse is brought up through the ranks of competition by successfully mastering tests at levels of increasing difficulty.

4. Hunters: The modern show hunter is a more refined, elegant version of the field hunter, the coarse yet sturdy mount ridden cross-country on a foxhunt. The tradition of foxhunting inspired hunter competition in the show ring. Although early hunter classes were conducted over courses in open fields, the vast majority of today's show hunters compete over a course of eight to ten fences inside an enclosed arena. In such a confined area, competition emphasizes maintaining a slow, rhythmical

Hunter competition

gallop throughout the course rather than the bold, energetic strides of open-field hunting. To be successful, a show hunter must also demonstrate classic jumping style by lifting his knees evenly toward his chin in the air and rounding his back, creating an arc or bascule in flight. Thoroughbreds, culled from the racetrack, used to be the quintessential hunters. Yet that breed's favor has recently been eclipsed by the various warmblood sport horses, thanks to their more mellow demeanor. Very young children often compete on ponies bred and trained specifically for hunter competition. While prize money is offered at some major events, bragging rights and Horse of the Year titles are the primary lures for hunter riders.

5. Reining: As the West was settled, cowboys relied on horses that could turn quickly, stop suddenly, and stand patiently when working around cattle. Cowboys enjoyed showing off the skills of their favorite horses, and these impromptu demonstrations led to the modern sport of reining, in which the western horse works through a pattern requiring him to gallop and slide to a stop, spin (pivot quickly) both left and right, and back up rapidly in a straight line. The rider should be able to control the horse throughout the pattern with very light contact on the reins. The National Reining Horse Association (NRHA) was formed in 1966 to establish patterns, sanction competition, and promote the sport. In 2000, reining was recognized as an international equestrian sport, the same recognition accorded English riding disciplines such as show jumping and dressage. That means that western reining horses now compete at world-class events such as the World Equestrian Games, where teams representing countries from around the world vie for the world championship. Nationally, NRHA competitions award more than $10 million in total prize money each year.

6. Show jumping: The scoring system for show jumpers is entirely objective: the horse that gets over the course in the fastest time, incurring the fewest faults for downed rails, wins. But it wasn't always this way. At the beginning of the twentieth century, European horse shows included "horse lepping [leaping]" contests. Sometimes the contests emphasized crowd-pleasing entertainment more than they did advanced horsemanship. With an obvious need for standardized scoring, the American Horse Shows Association (now the United States Equestrian Federation) was formed in 1917 and the British Show Jumping Association in 1925. Today, riders at all levels have opportunities to compete, with grand prix events as the pinnacle of achievement. As the sport has matured, the courses have become more technically difficult, requiring horses to adjust their stride and navigate around tight turns in order to negotiate the vast variety of obstacles in the modern show arena.

7. Three-day eventing: As its name indicates, three-day eventing takes place over three days, and each horse-and-rider team accumulates points and faults throughout the competition. The first day is devoted to the precision of dressage, the second day comprises negotiating cross-country courses with intimidating obstacles, and the third day culminates in a bold round of show jumping. It takes a well-rounded horse to win at this sport, just the sort of horse originally trained as a military mount. In fact, the earliest version of three-day eventing was a contest for active-duty army officers and their horses, held at the Stockholm Olympics of 1912. By 1924, however, civilians were permitted to compete on privately owned horses, and the sport was transformed to its current status as a popular albeit immensely challenging equestrian competition.

8. Western pleasure: The most popular performance classes for western horses are found in the western pleasure division, which offers events for riders of all ages and levels of riding and for both young and mature horses. Horse shows that are open to all breeds offer western pleasure classes, but often it is the traditional stock horse breeds such as American Quarter Horses, Paints, and Appaloosas that excel, as they tend to embody the classic conformation and low, ground-covering strides that represent the ideal. To counter that trend, breed-specific horse shows offer their own western pleasure classes, so Arabians compete against Arabians, Morgans against other Morgans, and so on. Regardless of the association or the organization hosting the show, all western pleasure horses are evaluated on how well they epitomize the perfect horse to ride on the trails or around a ranch. They must walk, jog, and lope on a loose rein, displaying both comfortable gaits and a compliant attitude.

8 Popular Competitive Associations

1. American Grand Prix Association (AGA)

Bradenton, FL

www.stadiumjumping.com

Supports Olympic-level show jumping by offering the AGA tour, a series of grand prix jumping events in the United States offering over $3 million in prize money

World Class Contests

While a multitude of national and regional riding associations and breed registries offer horse shows for their members, equestrian competitions at the international level are overseen by the FEI (Federation Equestre Internationale), headquartered in Lausanne, Switzerland. The most famous international equestrian competitions occur at the Olympic Games. Horses and riders first participated in the modern Olympics in 1900, when all three equestrian events were jumping contests. Today's Olympic equestrian contests—the only Olympic events in which men and women compete together—are dressage, show jumping, and three-day eventing. The FEI also recognizes endurance riding, reining, vaulting, and driving, and it sanctions world championships for those disciplines. Riders with disabilities gained the opportunity to compete in FEI-sanctioned dressage and driving events beginning in 2006.

2. Federation Equestre Internationale (FEI)

Lausanne, Switzerland

www.horsesport.org

The governing board for equestrian competition at the international level

3. National Cutting Horse Association (NCHA)

Fort Worth, TX

www.nchacutting.com

Maintains performance records of cutting horses as well as sanctions competitions

4. National Reining Horse Association (NRHA)

Oklahoma City, OK

www.nrha.com

Sets standards for reining competition worldwide

5. United States Dressage Federation (USDF)

Lexington, KY

www.usdf.org

Promotes dressage through educational programs and sanctioned competitions in the United States

6. United States Equestrian Federation (USEF)

Lexington, KY

www.usef.org

The national governing body for equestrian sports in the United States; also licenses horse show judges for USEF-sanctioned shows

7. United States Eventing Association (USEA)

Leesburg, VA

www.useventing.com

Promotes and advances the sport of three-day eventing in America

8. Women's Professional Rodeo Association (WPRA)

Kingman, AZ

www.wpra.com

Maintains performance records for barrel racing and sets competition standards

5 Unforgettable Racehorses of the Past 50 Years

1. Kelso (1957–1983): He was a scrawny foal. He didn't have stellar bloodlines. And he was difficult to handle. For these reasons, the dark bay Kelso was gelded at an early age, a perhaps regrettable decision, as he eventually earned $1,977,896. Never a contender for the Triple Crown, he became a veteran of handicap races, where his assigned weight was based on his race record. In the Suburban Handicap, he carried 136 pounds, a staggering weight, and still won the race. Kelso was small in stature, but he was a dynamic force. He drew crowds wherever he raced, buoying the spirits of Americans troubled by the

Cuban missile crisis and the assassination of President John F. Kennedy. He won the Eclipse Award (horse racing's highest honor) as Horse of the Year a record five times, and he finally retired from racing at the age of nine. Not a horse content to hang out in a pasture, Kelso had a second career in the show ring as a hunter and jumper.

2. Secretariat (1970–1989): Ask most people to name a Thoroughbred racehorse, and chances are they'll say Secretariat. His name might have been Scepter or Games of Chance, two other names submitted to the Jockey Club when it came time to register the handsome chestnut colt. Ultimately, Secretariat the colt grew into the big red horse that most racing experts consider the greatest racehorse of all time. His greatness comes not just from winning the elusive Triple Crown in 1973 but also from the way he won. Secretariat wasn't just formidable, he was fast. His thirty-one-length victory in the Belmont Stakes set the world record for one and one-half miles on the dirt (two minutes, twenty-four seconds). His winning margin was so vast that TV cameras were barely able to keep Secretariat and his trounced foes in the same frame. As captivating as a Hollywood matinee idol, the big red stallion was featured on the cover of *Time* and *Newsweek* magazines. Although his record as a sire was nothing to be ashamed of, none of his offspring duplicated his phenomenal career. He was euthanized at the age of nineteen because of complications of laminitis, a circulatory problem affecting the hooves. As further proof

Secretariat winning the 1973 Belmont Stakes and thus the Triple Crown

of his sustained popularity, the United States Postal Service issued a first-class stamp in 1999 bearing his portrait.

3. Ruffian (1972–1975): A filly like Ruffian is rare. She was gorgeous to look at: dainty yet beautifully conformed and nearly ebony in color. She was also royally bred, which along with her astonishing racing record helped earn her the title "Queen of the Fillies." She was undefeated after ten races, virtually annihilating her rivals at both short and long distances. Sadly, the acclaim that accompanied such a record—along with an Eclipse Award for Outstanding Two-Year-Old Filly in 1974—led to her tragic demise. A nationally televised match race that pitted her against the recent Kentucky Derby winner, Foolish Pleasure, was held on July 6, 1975, at Belmont Park. Ahead after a half mile, Ruffian fractured her leg. Although her jockey, Jacinto Vasquez, tried to pull her up, the filly was defiant. She did not want to allow another horse to beat her for the first time. She underwent surgery to repair the leg, but when she awoke from anesthesia, she thrashed about so badly that she fractured the other front leg and had to be euthanized. She was buried near the finish line at Belmont Park. There has never been another official match race since then.

4. John Henry (1975–2007): Neither large nor beautiful, John Henry was nonetheless an imposing figure on the racetrack. The bay gelding exuded the confidence of a cocky prizefighter. That self-assurance also made him the bane of the grooms who had to dodge his teeth back at the barn. But those devilish idiosyncrasies were tolerated because John Henry was the epitome of a professional racehorse. He would often pause during the post parade to acknowledge the crowd or stare at the tote board, as if to consider just how well the bettors were supporting him. Although he was originally purchased as a yearling for a paltry

$1,100, he earned over $6 million during eight years of racing, making him the richest gelding in racing history. The winner of two Eclipse Awards as Horse of the Year, John Henry retired to Kentucky Horse Park, where he lived until his death at the age of 32.

5. Barbaro (2003–2007): He was a classic Thoroughbred in looks. A rich red bay with a finely chiseled head, Barbaro looked like a champion even before he won his first major race, the Laurel Futurity, as a two-year-old. Undefeated going into the 2006 Kentucky Derby, Barbaro won in commanding fashion by more than six lengths. Immediately, media and racing fans hungry for another Triple Crown champion—the first since Affirmed in 1978—saw Barbaro as a serious contender. And he was. But when the game colt fractured his right hind leg shortly after the start of the Preakness Stakes (the second leg of the Triple Crown) on May 20, 2006, their attention quickly refocused on the champion's treatment and prospects for recovery. Almost daily, reports came from New Bolton Center, the surgical unit at the Veterinary School of the University of Pennsylvania. An avalanche of cards, flowers, and horse cookies poured in to the equine hospital from horse lovers and ordinary people touched by the struggle of a brave animal facing the longest odds of his life. Barbaro's struggle was long and extraordinary—he seemed at first to make significant improvement, only to suffer a succession of setbacks that ultimately forced the veterinarians to euthanize him on January 29, 2007.

Kentucky Derby Details

Undeniably the most famous of American horse races, the Kentucky Derby is held the first Saturday in May at Churchill Downs racetrack in Louisville, Kentucky. Considered the most honorable test of three-year-old Thoroughbreds, the first Kentucky Derby was held in 1875 and won by a chestnut colt named Aristides. At that time, the Derby was one and one-half miles long, considered a marathon distance for young horses. In 1896, it was shortened to its current length, one and a quarter miles. The record for the fastest Kentucky Derby belongs to Secretariat, who blazed home in 1:59.40 in 1973. Of course, horses can't participate without a jockey holding the reins. The jockey with the most Derby wins is the late Eddie Arcaro (1916–1997), who won five. Two of the winners he piloted went on to nab the Triple Crown, which includes the Preakness and Belmont Stakes. They were Whirlaway (1941) and Citation (1948). African American jockeys also have their place in Kentucky Derby history. In the inaugural Derby, thirteen of the fifteen riders were

The Kentucky Derby

African American, and fifteen of the first twenty-eight runnings were won by African American jockeys. Once in the winner's circle, the champion horse is traditionally draped with a blanket of red roses, which gives the race its nickname, the Run for the Roses.

6 Champion Horses That Exceeded Expectations

1. Charisma: *Small, muddy, hairy,* and *scraggly* were the words that New Zealander Mark Todd supposedly used to describe Charisma when he first observed the gelding that was a cross between a Thoroughbred and a Percheron draft horse. Yet the diminutive dynamo's expressive dressage performances and courageous jumping efforts made him an unbeatable force in the grueling sport of three-day eventing. Charisma and Mark Todd won back-to-back individual Olympic gold medals in the 1984 (Los Angeles) and 1988 (Seoul) Games.

2. French Flash Hawk: This American Quarter Horse is an example of a high-strung, skittish horse that just needed to find the right outlet for his keen temperament. With his somewhat unpredictable nature and the wide white blaze on his face, he was nicknamed "Bozo" after the famous circus clown. A horse-savvy cowgirl, Kristie Peterson, bought the wary horse for a mere $400. That turned out to be a real deal, as Bozo and Peterson earned more than $1 million in professional barrel racing, including three National Finals Rodeo championships.

3. Khemosabi: This legendary Arabian show horse and sire was almost too flashy for his own good. According to his breeder and owner, Ruth Husband, when she observed the newborn colt's abundant white markings, "I wasn't thrilled." She considered not even registering the colt. Fortunately, her spouse thought otherwise. Khemosabi not only was registered but also became a Legion of Excellence Champion and a Legion of Masters Champion. He also sired over 1,300 foals, making him the most popular Arabian stallion of all time.

4. Pieraz: This little gray Arabian gelding goes by the nickname "Cash" because he cost the whopping sum of $500. Fortunately, owner/rider Valerie Kanavy saw the horse's true worth, because eventually she piloted Cash to a World Championship in Endurance in 1994. Valerie's daughter, Danielle, repeated the win in 1996. Because of his athletic prowess, it was decided to preserve his genetic material. Cash became the second horse in history to be successfully cloned.

5. Snowman: In 1956, New York riding instructor Henry de Leyer went to a local auction looking for school horses. What caught his eye, though, was a placid, big-boned white plow horse that was being loaded onto a truck bound for the slaughterhouse. For just $80 de Leyer purchased the gentle giant, who soon became a show jumping legend. In 1959, de Leyer rode Snowman to a European championship, clearing a seven-foot, two-inch wall. Snowman was eventually retired and lived out his life on the de Leyer farm.

Zippo Pine Bar

6. Zippo Pine Bar: Rancher Norman Reynolds was looking for a utilitarian horse to add to his string of horses on his cattle ranch, so he bought Zippo as a weanling for just $1,000 in 1970. It seemed as if the colt might grow into a useful working cow horse. But when Zippo won ribbons in the show pen, Reynolds realized he had more than the average cow pony. Zippo Pine Bar spent more than a decade as the AQHA Leading Sire of Performance Horses, and his foals won more than $2 million in western pleasure prize money. His bloodlines continue to be an influence in Quarter Horses, Paints, and Appaloosas.

6 Insider Tips on Grooming the Show Horse

1. If your horse has white socks or stockings, dust them with a liberal coating of baby powder or cornstarch, then brush away the excess. You'll be amazed at how white they'll look.

2. Cover up any clipping mistakes by holding the clippers horizontal and then gently working the blades across the growth of the hair. That will help blend in the surrounding hair, making your boo-boos less noticeable.

3. Use inexpensive baby wipes to whisk away grime and secretions from around your horse's nose and eyes. They also work well to remove that carrot-stained slobber from your horse's lips.

4. Is there static cling in your horse's tail? Rub a clothes dryer sheet through the hair.

5. Make your hunter's braids last longer by knotting the yarn ends underneath the braid. If the knot sits atop the braid, you'll likely rub it out after a few classes over jumps.

6. Send stainless steel bits, spurs, and English stirrup irons through a cycle in your dishwasher. Your horse will look even more beautiful when these items are sparkling clean.

Sponging tail clean before a show

15 Dates: A Timeline of Female Firsts

1804: Alicia Meynell of England becomes the first recorded female jockey to ride in an official race, aboard a horse owned by her lover, Colonel Thornton. She apparently proved her mettle because a year later, riding under her married name, Mrs. Thornton, she wins a race against a much-honored male jockey.

1913: New York's venerable National Horse Show is the site where Loula Long becomes the first woman to win a roadster class. In this event, a single, speedy horse is put through his paces while hitched to a small, lightweight cart.

1915: The Thoroughbred filly Regret becomes the first female horse to win the Kentucky Derby. Two others eventually will follow in her hoofprints: Genuine Risk (1980) and Winning Colors (1988).

1915: Eleonora Sears and Marion du Pont become the first women to compete astride—rather than sidesaddle—at the prestigious National Horse Show. This is seen as quite a scandalous escapade by the more traditionally minded spectators.

1943: Judy Johnson petitions the Maryland Racing Commission to allow her to ride in steeplechases held at Pimlico racecourse. After much deliberation, Johnson is

Seasonal Shine

One of the hallmarks of a well-groomed show horse is a shiny coat. But horses normally grow a thicker coat of hair in the fall to prepare for winter, and it's hard to maintain that sleek look. One option is to clip off the offending long coat, but that often reveals a slightly off-colored undercoat. The other choice is to fool the horse's body into thinking it's still summer. As autumn days get progressively shorter, the horse's retina perceives less daylight. This stimulates increased production of melatonin, a hormone that, among other functions, regulates hair growth. The higher level of melatonin triggers the growth of the winter coat. But a 200-watt lightbulb placed outside the horse's stall can work wonders. It must be left on long enough after dark so the horse perceives "daylight" for sixteen continuous hours throughout the show season. There is one drawback to the nightlight program. Because cold-season nighttime temperatures are nippy, the sleek horse will need to wear a blanket to keep cozy.

allowed to ride; however, steeplechase officials are ordered to provide her with a dressing room separate from her male counterparts.

1949: The cowgirls just won't stay home from the rodeo, so the Girls Rodeo Association is formed specifically to give the gals a competitive organization. Eventually, it will grow into the current Women's Professional Rodeo Association.

1952: At the Summer Olympics in Helsinki, female riders are permitted to compete against men in equestrian sports for

A female rodeo competitor

the first time. But they're allowed only in dressage, as show jumping is considered too dangerous. Lis Hartel of Denmark rises to the occasion and wins a silver medal.

1956: The Summer Olympics in Melbourne are the first Games to permit women in show jumping. Great Britain's Patricia Smythe takes home a bronze medal in team competition.

1964: Three-day eventing, considered the most rigorous of the international equestrian sports, finally gets its female standard-bearer when Lana du Pont of the United States competes as a member of the silver medal–winning team at the Tokyo Olympics.

1968: Already a veteran of international equestrian competition in show jumping, Kathy Kusner pursues a lengthy legal battle that ultimately allows her to become the first female licensed professional jockey in the United States.

1970: Diane Crump becomes the first woman jockey to ride in the Kentucky Derby. She finishes a distant fifteenth aboard a horse named Fathom.

2000: Lindy Burch rides a red roan mare to become the first woman to win the National Cutting Horse Association Open World Championship.

2003:: Royal Blue Boon Too becomes the first commercially cloned horse in the United States. The twenty-six-year-old American Quarter Horse mare is already the dam of numerous champion cutting horses that have earned more than $2 million in competition. Although her clone is ineligible for registration, she may be permitted to compete.

2005: The Thoroughbred mare with the odd name Makybe Diva wins her third consecutive Melbourne Cup and becomes a national sports heroine. At the grueling length of nearly two miles, the Melbourne Cup is the Australian equivalent of the Kentucky Derby, at least in the race's social significance: it is referred to as "the race that stops a nation."

2007: Mandy McCutcheon becomes the first woman rider to accumulate over $1 million in winnings at National Reining Horse Association competitions.

6 Stories of What Can Go Wrong at a Show

1. "What can go wrong at a horse show?" a competitor asked. "How about getting to the show and realizing you forgot all the bridles!"

2. A young competitor and her mother were allowing their Thoroughbred to munch some of the grass surrounding the parking lot of a horse show. It was a pleasant break between classes until a cricket jumped up the horse's nose, sending him

scrambling backward. "He sat down on the bumper of another woman's car," the girl recalls. "Needless to say, the woman was not happy, and the insurance company didn't know how to file the claim."

3. Sometimes victory is snatched away. "I was named the winner of a really big class at a really big show. I got the ribbon, had the photo shoot, and then management tracked me down and said, 'Sorry.' The scoring was done wrong, and they took away my prize!"

4. Other show horses can be the agents of fate. "My lovely little mare, with her thick full tail, was stabled next to a rowdy gelding. During the night, he chewed through the vinyl temporary stall wall to visit with her. Well, I get there the next morning to braid, only to discover half of her tail and some of her mane are chewed off."

5. Another rider's jumping performance, not to mention composure, was severely disrupted when a horse in an adjacent arena tossed its rider and then leaped over the railing into her arena. She had to attempt to finish her course with a loose horse cavorting between the obstacles.

6. When nonhorsey family members try to help out, the result can be the stuff of family lore. "My father decided to longe my energetic gelding while I was getting dressed. My horse took off

down the field with dear old Dad hanging on. My horse ran all the way down the field and back to the trailer and, amazingly, my dad never let go."

5 Tips for Keeping Your Horse Sane at a Show

1. Arrive in plenty of time to longe your horse or at least hand-walk him around the show grounds. That will give him time to settle in and become acquainted with the new environment.

2. Scrutinize the footing. Look out for rocks, hard patches, and slick mud. If your horse bruises his sole or twists an ankle, you'll be packing up and going home.

A horse attempting a fast getaway

3. Whether you're stabling overnight or tying up to your trailer between classes, try to make your horse's "break area" a quiet, shady haven away from the hubbub of the show ring. Give him time to relax and a place to decompress.

4. Steer clear of trouble in the warm-up ring or schooling areas. That means you'll have to ride defensively to protect your horse from other equines that might not be totally under control.

5. Choose your classes wisely, according to your horse's experience and level of training. A horse show is not the place to try new things. Your horse will already be distracted by merely being at a strange place. Instead, compete in classes that reflect what you've been practicing at home. That way, your horse will have an opportunity to shine!

Taking a peaceful break

10 Dos and Don'ts from USEF Horse Show Judges

(Advice from judges Andrea Meek and Liza Applebaum)

1. Don't discipline your horse at the back gate, in full view of the judge. It makes a bad first impression that is hard to dismiss once you enter the show ring.

2. Don't enter the show ring wearing dirty or dusty boots. It only takes a few seconds to knock grime off your footwear.

3. Don't ignore directions from the judge. If you're excused from competition for whatever reason, exit immediately.

4. Don't make the judge and fellow riders wait while you chat on your cell phone, finish your lunch, or groom your horse. That's inconsiderate and marks you as an unprepared and undisciplined competitor.

5. Don't show your horse in trendy gadgets, bits, or tack unless you're certain that such items are allowed according to the rule book.

6. Do learn your courses and patterns ahead of time rather than making everyone wait while you memorize them in a panic.

A champion dressage horse and rider

7. Do have a good understanding of class requirements before you fill out an entry form. That will help you select classes appropriate both for your riding skills and for the training level of your horse.

8. **Do** present a neat and tidy appearance to the judge. That means your clothes should fit well and your tack should be clean and in good repair.

9. **Do** keep your horse in excellent condition. That means your horse should be serviceably sound and in good flesh, and his hooves should have been recently trimmed or shod. This demonstrates pride of ownership and good horse management skills.

10. **Do** exude good sportsmanship, even if things go wrong. Often, that is remembered much longer than who won a blue ribbon.

6 Ways to Recycle Horse Show Ribbons

1. Cut off the streamers, arrange them in a pleasing geometric pattern, and sew them into a quilt. Although the fabric used for horse show ribbons isn't particularly sturdy or reliably colorfast, your ribbon quilt will be perfectly suitable for decorative purposes or as a wall hanging.

2. Use a canvas backing for a needlepoint belt project. Then select horse show ribbons based on a color scheme or perhaps the wording on the streamers. Now stitch them onto the canvas backing.

Who Gets to Be the Judge?

According to a 2005 study sponsored by the American Horse Council, there are 2.8 million show horses in the United States and more than 480,000 active competitors. That means that there's a lot of showing going on, and every competition requires the officiating services of a judge. Judges of small shows designed for novice riders and green horses aren't usually required to have formal certification. Instead, they are hired based on their reputation in the local horse community and their own experience as a successful competitor. At larger shows, where horses and riders vie for year-end awards and national championships, judges must hold an official judge's card certifying that they have met specific requirements. Breed registries and major riding associations each have specific criteria for issuing cards; in general, all prospective judges must pass written tests, present letters of recommendation from established

3. For an interesting collection of home decor, gently fold some of your favorite ribbons into large clear glass jars. Heavy-duty jars used for fruit preserves or vintage, apothecary-style con-

A horse show judge

judges, and apprentice under the tutelage of a mentor judge. To keep abreast of trends and rule changes, all horse show judges are also required to attend educational clinics. In light of the time and dedication it takes to obtain and maintain a card, horse show judges take their job seriously and deserve competitors' respect.

tainers work best. Consider adding decorative labels denoting the date, the show, and the horse's name. Display them on a shelf for a great conversation piece.

A horse show ribbon quilt

4. During the holiday season, create a Christmas tree with a horsey theme. Use ribbon rosettes as ornaments.

5. Regardless of the time of year, horse show ribbons woven around a grapevine wreath look unusual yet inviting hung on the door of your tack room, your office, or your home.

6. If you have oodles of ribbons, you can always donate your extras to a therapeutic riding program to be reused as awards in its in-house events. Your ribbons will support a good cause and put a smile on the face of a proud horse lover.

Winning Colors

Horse show competitors always strive to win a blue ribbon, as blue is the color of the first-place award. Or is it? Although blue ribbons are handed out to the winner in the United States, horse show competitors in Canada and Britain are awarded a red ribbon for first place. In the Netherlands, an orange ribbon is often the highest award. International differences aside, American riders learn early on what color signifies which placing in U.S. horse shows. Second place is always red, third yellow, and fourth white. Next comes pink for fifth place, green for sixth, and purple for seventh. Brown, which seems an unlikely color for a horse show ribbon, symbolizes eighth place. Ultimately, a bounty of ribbons in any color is certain to make any horse show competitor happy.

SEABISCUIT

SEABISCUIT

1933 — 1947

Chapter Nine

The Horse in Art

The horse is a creature with an aesthetically pleasing form. Its long limbs, graceful neck, and rounded loins as well as its spirited nature and physical strength have made the horse an appealing subject for artists throughout history.

5 Illustrious Illustrators

1. C.W. Anderson (1891–1971): Distinctive black-and-white illustrations that evoke a sense of calm beauty are trademarks of C.W. Anderson's work. Anderson wrote and illustrated more than forty horse books. His series of children's horse books are collectibles today. They relate the ongoing adventures of Billy and his horse Blaze, and each tale also espouses good basic horsemanship. Aside from his artistic endeavors, Anderson was a noted horseman and a horse show judge for the hunter discipline.

2. Wesley Dennis (1903–1966): It's easy to understand why Wesley Dennis is forever associated with the prolific author Marguerite Henry. Their first venture was Henry's *Justin Morgan Had a Horse* (1945), and they eventually collaborated on fifteen books. Dennis's experience as an avid polo player and as an all-around horseman allowed him to portray each horse's individual personality and expressions without sentimentality. That reputation no doubt led novelist John Steinbeck to select Dennis to illustrate Steinbeck's *The Red Pony*.

3. Charles M. Russell (1864–1926): He always wanted to live the life of a cowboy, so as a young man, Charles M. Russell did just that. He took a job for nearly a dozen years working on a cattle ranch in Montana. His familiarity with the environment, the characters he encountered, and the horses he handled is evident in his drawings and paintings. It is estimated that he created more than 4,000 works of art in his lifetime, including illustrating novels and short story collections about the American West. He was also commissioned to produce cover illustrations for popular periodicals such as *The Saturday Evening Post*.

4. Sam Savitt (1917–2000): A lifelong equestrian, Sam Savitt gained prominence as an illustrator creating cover images for Dell pulp fiction and comic books of the 1950s. Serialized Zane

Cover illustration by Sam Savitt:
Gene Autry's Champion, *issue no. 5 (1952)*

Grey westerns as well as the adventures of Gene Autry and
Champion, Roy Rogers and Trigger, and the Lone Ranger and

Silver all needed an artist who could produce a dramatic cover that would sell books and be true to the conformation and movement of a horse. Savitt would often study a real-life horse, make a quick pencil sketch, and then return to his studio and fill in the details with whichever artistic medium he was using at the time: watercolor, oil, charcoal, or others. He found a wide audience as the illustrator of Gordon Wright's *Learning to Ride, Hunt, and Show*, the seminal handbook of English riding published in 1958. Savitt's style became so popular that his instructional book *Drawing Horses with Sam Savitt* (1991) is still in print. A founding member of the American Academy of Equine Artists, Savitt illustrated more than 150 books.

5. Norman Thelwell (1923–2004): British cartoonist Norman Thelwell was already a regular illustrator for the humor magazine *Punch* when he happened to draw a cartoon featuring a pony in 1953. The cartoon was enormously popular, and his editor encouraged him to draw more. Eventually, Britain's apparently insatiable appetite for pony humor led Thelwell to write *A Leg at Each Corner* in 1961. That book introduced the character of Penelope and her hilariously hirsute pony, Kipper. Soon, a cartoon strip was launched featuring the two characters and their assorted barn buddies. That, in turn, led to several more books. Although Thelwell was also a highly regarded landscape painter, he will perhaps be best remembered—and loved—for delighting horse lovers of all ages with the antics of kids and their ponies.

5 Ways to Add a Horsey Theme to Home Decor

1. Wool saddle blankets woven in colorful geometric designs are referred to as "Navajos." Choose one in colors that complement your home's color scheme, and put it to use as a small area rug or toss it over the back of your sofa. A Navajo also makes a unique wall hanging in a den or guest room that is already accessorized in a southwestern theme.

2. Create a dazzling lucky charm to hang over a doorway. All it takes is a horseshoe, some colored craft wire (20 gauge works best), and an assortment of glass beads. Simply secure the wire through the topmost nail hole in the shoe. Make several loops around the shoe, and then begin stringing the beads onto the wire, continuing to add beads as

A decorative beaded horseshoe

you wrap the wire around the shoe. Finish by using a pair of needlenose pliers to make a tight knot in the wire on the underside of the shoe. Add a narrow piece of satin ribbon as a hanger.

3. Christmas tree ornaments can have a horsey flair. Buy a set of clear glass balls from your local craft store, along with some paint specifically made for use on glass. Remove the hanger from the glass ball, and stuff the inside with material familiar to all horse lovers. Clean wood shavings (stall bedding) or bits of alfalfa, hay, or oats work well. Put the hanger back in place. Then paint a horse design on the outside of the glass ball. Your artwork will be limited only by your creativity. Use a paint pen to add the name of a favorite horse, if you like. As a finishing touch, tie a bow of straw-colored raffia onto the hanger. Give them as holiday gifts to your barn buddies.

4. Western shirts that date from the 1940s through the 1970s have become valuable collectibles, especially if they bear the label of a now-defunct manufacturer such as Rockmount Ranch Wear, H Bar C, or Panhandle Slim. Shirts made by Nudie Cohen, who designed highly embellished shirts for rodeo champions and Hollywood stars, are also highly prized. But rather than wearing such garments, why not display them inside rustic wooden picture frames? Fold them neatly so the embroidered yoke or the pearl snap buttons are featured, and you'll have a unique piece of wall art.

5. Vintage western spurs with rowels—complete with their hand-tooled leather straps—can add to a Home on the Range motif. Set them on the hearth next to a pair of well-worn yet handsomely detailed cowboy boots for a conversation starter.

5 Formidable Equine Painters

1. George Stubbs (1724–1806): Born in England, Stubbs revolutionized the artistic depiction of the horse. Not only did he travel to Italy to study the work of the Renaissance masters, but he also dissected a collection of horse cadavers to methodically inspect equine anatomy firsthand. That enabled him to portray horses that were anatomically correct in their conformation and movement. His landmark book *Anatomy of the Horse* (1766) was filled with his own illustrations.

2. Sir Alfred Munnings (1875–1959): In his earliest works, Munnings painted the English countryside. But when he enlisted in the army and was rejected for active duty because of blindness in one eye, he was assigned to work with the remount horses of the Canadian Cavalry. That association led him to paint portraits of officers and their war steeds and, in turn, to be commissioned to paint scenes of English sporting life, particularly foxhunting. Perhaps due to his background as a landscape artist, the English countryside that forms the background of his paintings is colorfully and lovingly portrayed. Munnings was knighted in 1944 as he began a five-year tenure as president of the Royal Academy.

3. Richard Stone Reeves (1919–2005): An American painter famous for his commissioned portraits of blue-blooded

Thoroughbreds, Reeves developed a love of horses growing up on Long Island near Belmont Park racetrack. During his career, he painted more than 1,000 Thoroughbreds, including Secretariat, Seattle Slew, and John Henry. In 1982, President Ronald Reagan and First Lady Nancy Reagan presented Queen Elizabeth II with a Reeves portrait of her champion racehorse, Dunfermline.

4. Fred Stone (1930–): American Fred Stone's equestrian artwork can be found on posters, calendars, prints, murals, and collectible plates in numbers far greater than any other equine artist. That's quite a feat, considering he didn't pursue painting horses as a career until his midforties. That's when his daughter, who worked in the racing industry, coaxed him into painting the portraits of some of the graceful horses that populated the backstretch. Stone is famous for evoking emotion through his paintings. Sometimes this is achieved through a dual image, as if the horse is recalling its glorious past or dreaming of its hopeful future. In other portraits, Stone captures a poignant expression in the animal's eyes.

5. Tim Cox (1957–): A real-life cattle rancher and accomplished horseman, Tim Cox has become one of the most popular and prolific contemporary western artists in the world. His paintings are reproduced as limited edition prints and later become featured images on calendars and greeting cards. A winner of numerous juried art shows, Cox is not known for

A Legacy of Hope: Barbaro, *by Fred Stone*

commissioned portraits but rather as a gifted artist who paints subject matter with which he is intimately familiar. Hence, he paints realistic ranch scenes of cowboys at work and colorful landscapes of the Southwest blessed with roving herds of horses. Cox's horses are not sleek show horses or Thoroughbreds of royal lineage, but stout, rough-hewn cow ponies and mustangs.

6 Statuesque Horses: A Sampling of Life-Size Bronzes

1. Appeal to the Great Spirit: Utah resident Cyrus Dallis grew up around Native Americans and was forever sympathetic to their struggles to assimilate into a predominantly European culture without losing their own. Many of his bronzes are images of American Indians. Perhaps most memorable is *Appeal to the Great Spirit* (1908). An American Indian sits bareback on his weary pony, beseeching a divine power for guidance and support. Several copies exist in the United States; the original sits at the entrance to Boston's Museum of Fine Arts.

2. Big Ben: One of Canada's most beloved sports heroes is a 17.3-hand Belgian warmblood gelding named Big Ben. The show jumper, ridden by Canadian Ian Millar, won over $1.5 million in prize money. Following Big Ben's death (at age twenty-three) in 1999, Millar's hometown of Perth, Ontario, decided to erect a monument in his memory. What transpired was a community fund-raiser to commission a life-size bronze of Big Ben and Millar in action. Stewart Smith, assisted by Ruth and Jean Abernethy, sculpted the statue, which can be found in downtown Perth.

3. Cowboy: Frederic Remington helped shape the romantic image of the Old West through his artwork. He originally began his artistic career as an illustrator of scenes of western life for covers of magazines popular in the late 1800s and also as a painter. He delved into writing pulp adventure stories about cowboys and gunslingers. That romantic appreciation of the Old West embodies his sculptures. A great example of Remington's work is *Cowboy* (1908), his only large-scale bronze sculpture. Remington captures a cow pony coming to an abrupt stop as its rider pulls tautly on the reins. The original stands in Philadelphia's Fairmount Park.

4. Rugged Lark: One of the most successful American Quarter Horse show horses, Rugged Lark was so versatile in so many different performance classes that he won the coveted Super Horse Award from the American Quarter Horse Association twice (1985 and 1987). He also was honored with the registry's Silver Spur Award (1996) for embodying the positive traits of the breed: a gentle disposition, athleticism, and a solid work ethic. When Rugged Lark died in 2004, artist Marrita McMillian was commissioned to create a life-size bronze of the great horse. In fact, she made two. One stands above the horse's burial site at his home, Bo-Bett Farm near Ocala, Florida. The other, which includes the figure of his owner Carol Harris at his side, is on display at the American Quarter Horse Heritage and Museum in Amarillo, Texas.

5. Seabiscuit: It seems fitting that a bronze statue of Seabiscuit would be found at Santa Anita racetrack in Arcadia, California.

That's where the famous horse raced eleven times, including perhaps his most famous victory, the 1940 Santa Anita Handicap. "The Biscuit" won that race and then retired. In 1941 sculptor Hughlette "Tex" Wheeler presented his artwork. Seabiscuit was even present for the unveiling. The statue, which depicts Seabiscuit at the walk, stands in the racetrack's

Secretariat statue at Kentucky Horse Park

lush gardens. A duplicate statue is installed at the National Museum of Racing and Hall of Fame in Saratoga Springs, New York. Seabiscuit's home and final resting place, Ridgewood Ranch in Willits, California, was bereft of a monument until 2007, when a copy of Wheeler's statue was unveiled there. Now a likeness of the famous racehorse can be seen in the three places he is most closely associated with.

6. Secretariat: An impressive statue of the 1973 Triple Crown winner was unveiled in 2004 at Kentucky Horse Park. Created by Ed Boguki, the life-size bronze depicts Secretariat prancing to the winner's circle after winning the Kentucky Derby. With his neck arched and a lilt to his stride, Big Red seems to be leading his groom, Eddie Sweat, who holds tightly to the reins. Jockey Ron Turcotte sits proudly astride. Another statue of Secretariat is on display at Belmont Park, where it was dedicated in 2006.

5 Tips for Aspiring Equine Artists

(From Jean Abernethy, equine artist and illustrator)

1. Spend time with horses. Let their nature soak into your brain. Notice how they behave, their gaits and gestures, and their responses to each other.

Jean Abernethy

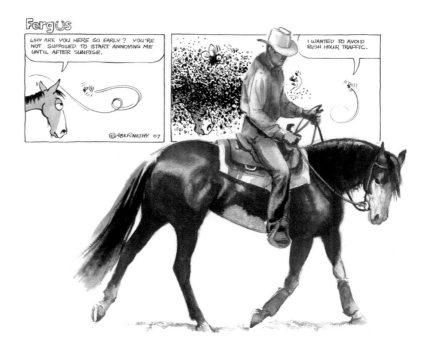

2. Practice. Always have a sketch book handy. Draw from life as much as possible. Draw every day. Understand that some of your drawings are going to turn out very ugly. Draw anyway. Drawing may sometimes frustrate you, but it will never make you worse.

3. Study your subject. Find books on anatomy, conformation, and various breeds. The equestrian artist never has too many horse books. Correct proportion and muscle/bone structure is of critical importance in creating a handsome drawing. Studying pictures of horses will teach you what "looks right."

4. Learn to draw people and inanimate objects, too. Drawing only horses will limit you. Art books, and classes if possible, will help you learn to understand and draw all forms you can see. You will achieve a great deal more when you can put correct tack and a rider on the horse, put them in a landscape setting, and perhaps draw a trailer or cart in a scene as well. (Yes, wheels will drive you crazy. Learn it anyway.)

5. Study the work of other artists. No matter how good you get, there will always be other artists out there who are better than you are. Study their work. Have a mental list of artists whose work you would like to emulate. This will give you joy and drive you half mad at the same time. It will also help you figure out what sort of art you want to create and the techniques necessary to get there.

Sharon Fibelkorn

3. Don't work for free. You are either in business, thus working to make yourself a living, *or* you are a hobbyist, giddy with the pleasure of just seeking praise for your efforts. Either way, it's your choice, but no serious businessperson does anything for free, unless they're donating their time and talent for a charitable cause.

4. A photograph is the sole property of the photographer who took it. In business today, this copyright is extremely valuable, and before you just sign it away, you should be certain you have been compensated fairly. After all, you may or may not be able to shoot those pictures again, but once you sign away your copyrighted images, they will glut the editorial market with free reuse. Eventually, this practice can put photographers out of business. So read your contracts carefully!

5. Never lose or sacrifice your vision. As you gain knowledge of your craft and you head out to the working world, there will be a lot of pressure to produce images. You may worry more about what publishers and editors are demanding rather than how you actually desire to photograph your subject. This is a mistake, so remember to remain true to yourself and allow yourself to develop your own style. Let photography become your art!

Chapter Ten

The Horse in Entertainment

As readers and viewers, we're captivated by the horse. When we're not communing with our own horse, we enjoy living vicariously through the adventures of other horse lovers.

5 Favorite Classic Horse Novels

(From a survey of adult equestrians)

1. *Black Beauty,* by Anna Sewell (1877): One of the first novels to depict the life of an animal, *Black Beauty* is credited with helping improve the plight of carriage horses. Thanks to the traumatic experiences related by the book's equine hero, the use of the check

rein—which during the Victorian era contorted a carriage horse's head into a fashionably high position—was abolished.

2. *National Velvet,* by Enid Bagnold (1935): Protagonist Velvet Brown isn't a girly girl like her sisters. She loves horses, and one day she wins a piebald horse in a raffle and ends up riding "the Pie" in the world's most difficult steeplechase race. It's a story familiar to all horse lovers, but many readers are unaware of the inside story. The author based the famous pinto at the center of the story on a spotted horse her children owned and jumped. And the character of Mi Taylor, the erstwhile jockey who trains young Velvet to ride in the Grand National, was inspired by her family's groom.

3. *My Friend Flicka,* by Mary O'Hara (1941): Thanks to O'Hara's descriptive prose, the rugged beauty of Wyoming ranch land is almost as memorable as the golden-coated filly at the center of this novel. Young Ken Laughlin is a sensitive day-dreamer, not an aspiring ranch hand ready to follow in his father's bootsteps. But as he raises the mustang filly named Flicka—the name means "little girl," according to a Swedish cowpoke—he learns all about personal responsibility and commitment. It's a coming-of-age story with horses. What could be better than that?

4. *The Black Stallion,* by Walter Farley (1941): Although the Black Stallion series eventually comprised twenty-one titles, it is

the stirring initial tale that most readers recall fondly. A young boy, Alec Ramsey, is shipwrecked on a deserted island with an unbroken, spirited stallion, whom he befriends and learns to ride. The two are rescued and gallop to victory in a hotly contested match race. The realistic details of Farley's books are the result of his lifelong relationship with horses. He spent much of his youth alongside his uncle, a professional racehorse trainer. As an adult, Farley rode dressage and owned Arabian horses.

5. *Misty of Chincoteague,* by Marguerite Henry (1947): The tale of Misty, a feral pony from a tiny island off the coast of Virginia, has become a timeless classic for horse lovers. Henry relates the real-life story of how Misty became a member of the Beebe family once the siblings Maureen and Paul captured her. Although the beloved Misty died in 1972, she can still be seen, thanks to the wonders of taxidermy, inside the Beebe homestead on Chincoteague Island.

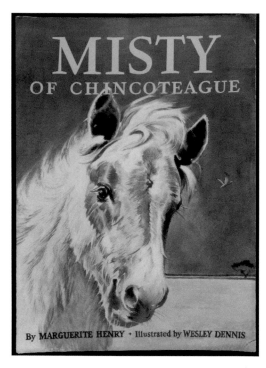

Misty of Chincoteague
*book cover, illustrated by
Wesley Dennis*

10 Songs with Lyrics About Horses

1. "Back in the Saddle Again": Gene Autry's classic cowpoke tells us how good it is to be home on the range once more.

2. "Beer for My Horses": The horses get beer and the men get whiskey in this celebration of good guys who triumph over bad guys.

3. "Cool Water": The dusty trails are proving too much for this saddle tramp and his horse.

4. "Good-Bye Old Paint": An itinerant cowboy bids farewell to a horse he has grown to love.

5. "I Ride an Old Paint": In this folk song, Old Paint is carrying a cowboy on his way to Montana.

6. "Jingle Bell Rock": Originally released in 1957, this upbeat standard has been recorded by dozens of artists who urge that "jingle horse" to giddy-up and pick up his feet.

7. "Run for the Roses": A ballad that lovingly portrays the life of a Thoroughbred racehorse, this 1981 Dan Fogelberg tune has become a modern-day Kentucky Derby theme song.

Strumming a tune

8. "She Rides Wild Horses": A woman escapes from her dead-end life in her nightly dreams of horseback riding.

9. "Tennessee Stud": All is right with the world once the Tennessee stud links up with his Tennessee mare.

10. "Wildfire": A mournful song about a pony that gets lost in a snowstorm and the young girl who follows suit.

7 Rainy-Day Flicks

1. *The Horse in the Gray Flannel Suit* (1968): Helen is a horse-crazy adolescent who begs her widowed father for an English show horse. The bedraggled man is under pressure at work to come up with a new ad campaign for an antacid, so he devises a scheme to please both his daughter and his boss. It's lighthearted family fare from Disney.

2. *Casey's Shadow* (1978): Lloyd Bourdelle is a third-tier Cajun horse trainer, making a meager living at the small tracks for his three sons. He pins their hopes—and their financial future—on a colt they've named Casey's Shadow. Will he make it to the big race? It's a nice family film worth a bowl of popcorn.

3. *The Man from Snowy River* (1982): The action-packed saga of Jim Craig, a young man who has to find his place in the harsh world of Australian horse ranching after his father's tragic death. The plot involves brumbies (the Aussie term for mustangs), a feisty young woman, a prized colt, and a cantankerous cattle baron.

4. *Phar Lap* (1983): Another true-life horsey drama, this tale is a murder mystery, told in flashback. Who killed the Australian racehorse Phar Lap after he won a major contest in Mexico? Phar Lap is a high-strung colt that is first treated harshly and then turned into a winner when he comes under

Phar Lap *(1983)*

Movie Set Watchdog

The Film and TV Unit of the American Humane Association (AHA) has monitored the treatment of horses—indeed, all animals—used in filmed media since 1940. The animal welfare organization became involved after it became known that abusive tactics were employed to create more exciting action scenes. For example, in early westerns, it wasn't unusual for galloping horses to be thrown to the ground with the use of trip wires, causing sometimes fatal injury. Today, AHA monitors more than 1,000 filmed productions a year and is responsible for the tagline at the end credits that reads, "No animals were harmed in the making of this film." Unfortunately, even though all domestic Screen Actors Guild productions are required to give AHA representatives unlimited access to produc-

the care of a young groom who bonds with the fractious horse.

5. *Champions* (1984): A British steeplechase jockey aptly named Bob Champion is diagnosed with cancer and given

tions when animals are used—and even though production companies are urged to follow established guidelines for the treatment of animal actors—accidents, illnesses, and even deaths still befall horses on film sets. Two stunt horses were euthanized because of injuries incurred during the filming of *Flicka* (2006). The same fate befell a stunt horse used in 2007's *3:10 to Yuma*. Full investigations by the AHA found that the deaths of the horses were not due to neglect or abuse. Still, publicity about the accidents quite possibly adversely affected ticket sales. An online rating system for films found on the AHA's Web site (www.americanhumane.org) helps concerned moviegoers decide which movies to attend and which to boycott. A complete description of a film's use and treatment of animals is provided as well as rankings ranging from Outstanding to Unacceptable.

less than a year to live. But instead of hanging up his tack, he struggles through treatment and its side effects to ride in the Grand National. Sound like a manipulative melodrama? It's a true story. The leading role is wonderfully acted by John Hurt. The champion horse, Aldaniti, plays himself.

6. *Sylvester* (1985): Charlie is a cowgirl working in the stock-yards to support herself and her two brothers. Faced with financial woes, she decides to make some money by training a spirited, athletic bronc—Sylvester—into a three-day eventing champion. As Charlie knows next to nothing about the sport, she seeks help from a crusty ex-cavalry officer to teach her the finer points of dressage and show jumping.

7. *In Pursuit of Honor* (1995): The precise historical details are debatable, but the film's emotionally charged plot centers on an order issued by General Douglas MacArthur in 1935 to modernize the U.S. Army. That meant slaughtering some 500 loyal cavalry horses, which a handful of career cavalry officers won't allow. They heroically attempt to lead the herd of horses across the Canadian border to sanctuary, with the U.S. Army in pursuit.

20 Celebrities Who Ride in Real Life

1. Kate Bosworth: Her success as a young rider on the hunt seat show circuit helped land her role in *The Horse Whisperer.*

2. Christie Brinkley: Often a competitor in celebrity cutting horse events, Brinkley also frequents the annual Hampton Classic English horse show on Long Island.

3. Kevin Costner: An actor who truly enjoys working in the western genre, Costner owns horses on his ranch. When he married Christine Baumgartner in 2004, he had extra horses brought in for his guests so they too could enjoy horseback riding.

4. Russell Crowe: Crowe has ridden regularly since childhood and rides frequently on his Australian cattle ranch.

5. Robert Duvall: Duvall is an accomplished horseman in both English and western saddles.

6. Sam Elliott: Often cast in westerns, Elliott has ridden horses for much of his life.

7. Oded Fehr: The Israeli actor learned to ride for *The Mummy* films rather than rely on a stunt double. He has continued to improve his horsemanship skills ever since.

8. Morgan Freeman: Although he doesn't ride as much as in years past, Freeman still owns several horses. His favorite is a gelding named Sable.

9. Richard Gere: Gere favors Appaloosas.

10. Whoopi Goldberg: Goldberg owns several horses and rides for pleasure.

11. Tommy Lee Jones: A longtime Texas horseman, Jones also is an avid polo player.

12. Michael Keaton: Keaton has competed in western events, particularly cutting.

13. Viggo Mortensen: Not only did Mortensen buy his primary mount from *Hidalgo*, but he also purchased a pair of horses from his stint as Aragorn in the *Lord of the Rings* films.

14. Robert Redford: Redford rides horses on his Utah ranch. An advocate for America's feral mustangs, in 2006 Redford also lent his support to the proposed American Horse Slaughter Prevention Act.

15. Julia Roberts: At home in the saddle, Roberts reportedly had the horse Hightower flown via FedEx to the location of *Runaway Bride* for her memorable horseback scene.

16. Kurt Russell: Russell has owned horses for many years. At the conclusion of filming *Dreamer: Inspired by a True Story*, he purchased a palomino gelding as a gift for costar Dakota Fanning.

17. Tom Selleck: Selleck has owned western stock horses for years. His daughter, Hannah, is a promising hunt seat equitation and jumper rider on the West Coast.

William Shatner on horseback

18. William Shatner: Shatner rides for pleasure and in competition. He owns a collection of finely bred American Saddlebreds and American Quarter Horses.

19. Martha Stewart: Stewart owns and rides Friesians.

20. Keifer Sutherland: During a break in his acting career, Sutherland actually joined the rodeo circuit as a roper. He continues to ride.

5 Famous Modern Movie Horses

1. Docs Keepin Time: This black stallion wasn't much of a winner at the racetrack, but he proved to be such a star on film that he won the American Quarter Horse Association's coveted Silver Spur Award in 1994. The award is given to registered American Quarter Horses that embody the versatility and athleticism of the breed. Docs Keepin Time had the title role in the film version of *Black Beauty* (1994). He also played the titular role in the American television series *The Adventures of the Black Stallion* (1990–1993) and appeared as the horse named Gulliver in the movie *The Horse Whisperer* (1998). Docs Keepin Time is particularly adept at working at liberty, meaning he can work without a rider and respond to subtle off-camera cues from his handler.

2. Dollor: At six feet, four inches tall, actor John Wayne needed a tall, substantial horse to ride in his many westerns. His favorite mount was named Dollor. The big sorrel with the white blaze was ridden by Wayne in seven films, including *The Shootist* (1976), Wayne's final big-screen performance. Wayne was so fond of Dollor that he had the horse's name written into the script of *The Shootist*. Dollor, however, wasn't so fond of his equine costars. Reportedly, Dollor was the alpha horse on any movie set: he was known to nip at horses that crossed his path and kick at horses that crowded him from behind. Dollor lived out his final days in retirement on a ranch in Texas.

3. Fighting Furrari: One of ten horses purchased to portray Seabiscuit in *Seabiscuit: An American Legend* (2003), Fighting Furrari (nicknamed "Fred") got the plum roles of portraying Seabiscuit in the winner's circle, in various close-ups, and when the famed racehorse is being rehabilitated back at the farm. He was, essentially, the equine star of the film. Fighting Furrari's laidback disposition, which served him so well in front of the cameras, didn't help him much during his own racing career. He started sixteen times at River Downs, a small track in Ohio, and won just a single race. But his less than impressive performances on the track were eclipsed by his work on film, where he will forever be remembered as Seabiscuit. During racing season, Fred resides at Santa Anita as an equine ambassador. His stall is one of the stops on the track's backstretch tour, where he's always willing to greet visitors in exchange for a pat or a carrot. The rest of the year he enjoys a second career as a successful show jumper.

Fighting Furrari as Seabiscuit (see also page 220)

4. Hightower: Not the fanciest of horses to look at, Hightower is a rather plain sorrel gelding. But he stands sixteen hands tall, an impressive size that is just as impressive onscreen. He is also a reliable performer, able to act scared, threatening, and passive. Hightower starred as Pilgrim, the horse Robert Redford rehabilitates in the film version of *The Horse Whisperer.* Hightower is also the horse that Julia Roberts rides as she gallops away from her wedding in the opening scenes of *Runaway Bride* (1999).

5. TJ: The movie *Hidalgo* (2004) required the use of five chest-nut and white spotted American Paint horses. Each one was ridden at some time during filming by star Viggo Mortensen. However, Mortensen thought one horse in particular was special: a small, nearly pony-size stallion named simply TJ. Mortensen felt that TJ had an abundance of character, as the horse seemed to truly enjoy the role of an equine movie star. When the filming finished, Mortensen purchased the horse.

7 Special Sites for Horse Lovers

1. Kentucky Horse Park: Considered the world's only park dedicated entirely to the horse-human relationship, this sprawling collection of barns, arenas, and pastures also includes a museum featuring artifacts and artwork pertaining to the history of the horse. Located in Lexington's bluegrass countryside, Kentucky Horse Park is home to a host of retired champion show horses and racehorses that reside in the Hall of Champions. The daily Parade of Breeds gives spectators an opportunity to see an assortment of the world's horses performing their specialties, many ridden by riders in native costume. On most weekends, a nationally sanctioned horse show is scheduled. Add to the regular activities and attractions special events like Breyerfest (a convention for model horse collectors

The Stunt Horses of the Steel Pier

Not all stunt horses get to do their work in the glamorous world of Hollywood. From 1929 to 1978, a sideshow act involving diving horses and young women in bathing suits captivated audiences at New Jersey's Steel Pier in Atlantic City. The horses would ascend to a platform as high as forty feet in the air. Then a female rider would climb aboard the bareback horse and grasp a rope attached to the halter. Without much hesitation, but allowing time for the announcer to rile the spectators, the horse would leap off the platform with the rider and plunge into an eleven-foot-deep pool. Performances occurred as often as four times a day, seven days a week. The diving horses of the Steel Pier were seen as a quaint oddity until the animal rights movement began to take notice in the early 1970s. The sideshow was frequently picketed, and questions were raised about the use of electric prods and trapdoors to force the horses into taking the plunge. Those claims were juxtaposed against statements from workers that horses that proved fainthearted were simply culled from the

Atlantic City, New Jersey

troupe. Eventually fate intervened, and the carnival atmosphere of the Steel Pier, including the diving horses, disappeared in 1978 when the site was sold to developers. The final two diving horses, named Gamal and Shiloh, were ushered into peaceful retirement, thanks to the efforts of the Fund for Animals. The 1991 film *Wild Hearts Can't Be Broken* is based on the true story of Sonora Webster, a young girl who performed with the diving horses during the Great Depression.

held every July) and the world-class Rolex Three-Day Eventing competition (held in the spring). In 2010, the park will host the World Equestrian Games. In short, Kentucky Horse Park is a dream vacation destination for horse lovers.

2. Spruce Meadows: This is North America's premier site for enjoying international show jumping. Located on the outskirts of Calgary, Alberta, visitors are treated to both the natural beauty of the Canadian outdoors and the hospitality of the bustling city. The inviting physical environment extends to the showgrounds themselves, immaculately maintained with gardens, picnic areas, and, depending on the season, a miniature world's fair of craftsmen, musicians, and food vendors. Spruce Meadows holds a series of hotly contested show jumping events. The most spectacular is the annual Masters Tournament held in September. It offers over $2 million in prize money and attracts horses and riders from around the world. Spruce Meadows also attracts spectators: crowds of nearly 50,000 are not unusual. The grandstands are thus filled with enthusiastic fans, cheering and sighing over the fortunes and misfortunes of their favorite equestrians.

3. Breeder's Cup Horse Races: Since its inception in 1982, the slate of Breeder's Cup races determines the annual championships for Thoroughbred racing. Although not as steeped in popular culture as the Kentucky Derby, the Breeder's Cup races arguably mean more to racing professionals and Thoroughbred breeders than the Run for the Roses does. Eleven races make up the Breeder's Cup program, with varying conditions such as length of the course and age and sex of the horses. Each race offers a purse of at least $1 million. But not just any Thoroughbred can race for a Breeder's Cup championship. Horses must earn their way to the starting gate by accruing points in qualifying races throughout the year. The Breeder's Cup races are held at a different racetrack each year, making a thrilling day at the races a possibility for people from all over the United States.

4. AQHA World Show: The first world championship horse show exclusively for registered American Quarter Horses was held over a long weekend in 1974. It offered $111,000 in prize money. Today, the same annual show lasts over two weeks, and awards total more than $2.4 million. This truly is a world championship show. Although horses and riders from North America dominate, each year more competitors from around the globe make the trek with their American Quarter Horses to Oklahoma City to vie for titles. The AQHA World Show is a celebration of the American Quarter Horse, complete with exhibitions and an expansive trade show. Competition includes classes for horses shown at halter (where conformation and movement are scored) and a plethora of English and western performance events. There's enough glitz, glamour, and glorious horses to keep every horse lover in attendance entertained for days.

Feral Chincoteague ponies

7. Tournament of Roses Parade: Considered one of the most spectacular parades in the world, the Rose Parade in Pasadena, California, has been a New Year's Day tradition since 1890, when the Valley Hunt Club decided to emulate a French festival of roses. Even then the parade featured floats festooned with floral arrangements in the form of wagons and carriages pulled by beautiful horses. The connection to horses and equestrian units continues. The modern Tournament of Roses Parade includes 300 horses and riders. An effort is made to feature a variety of horse breeds and riding disciplines. Visitors who can get to Los Angeles a few days early can enjoy a treat the parade's worldwide television audience misses: a preparade event called Equestfest at the nearby Los Angeles Equestrian Center. The activities are held in the center's indoor stadium, with its spacious grandstand seating. Spectators can watch the parade's horses and riders perform their routines, which include trick riding, roping, and team drills.

Tournament of Roses Parade

Chapter Eleven

Horse Health

Despite their size and impressive stature, horses are notoriously fragile. They are susceptible to a variety of illnesses and prone to leg injuries. Keeping a horse healthy and happy requires vigilance and dedication.

18 Parts of the Horse

1. Cannon bone
2. Chestnut
3. Coronet band
4. Crest
5. Croup
6. Dock of tail
7. Elbow
8. Fetlock
9. Flank
10. Forearm
11. Gaskin
12. Hock
13. Knee
14. Muzzle
15. Pastern
16. Poll
17. Stifle
18. Withers

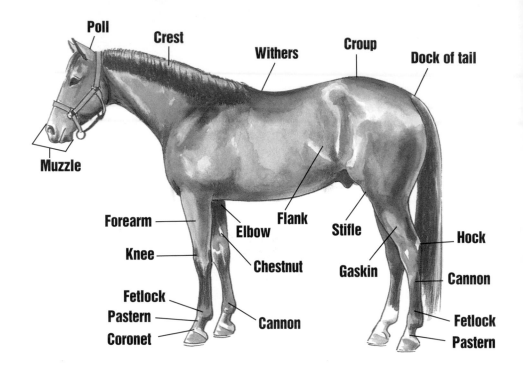

Poll

Crest

Withers

Croup

Dock of tail

Muzzle

Forearm

Elbow

Flank

Stifle

Hock

Knee

Chestnut

Gaskin

Cannon

Fetlock

Pastern

Cannon

Fetlock

Coronet

Pastern

10 Tips on Health and Soundness

(Contributed by Jennifer Voltz, DVM)

1. Every horse needs quality feed and continuous access to clean, fresh water.

2. Create a safe environment with strong fencing, shade and shelter from the elements, and a comfortable place to lie down.

3. Owners who board their horses are still responsible for their horse's care, and they should check on their horses frequently.

Being an absentee owner is no excuse for neglecting a horse's welfare.

4. Feral horses are constantly on the move. This keeps them fit, works off any excess calories, aids in digestion, and contributes to soundness. To keep a domesticated horse healthy, provide regular exercise. But keep in mind that just like human athletes, horses need an exercise routine that includes a warm-up and a cooling-down period. This will help preserve the horse's soundness.

5. Establish a relationship with a local equine veterinarian for routine preventive care, such as annual vaccines, and for emergency situations.

6. Plan a horse budget that includes a little extra stashed away for veterinary emergencies. That way, a horse can receive adequate care in a crisis.

7. Don't forgo regular farrier visits. Pleasure and performance horses need their hooves trimmed and their shoes reset every six to eight weeks. A horse with soundness issues may also need corrective shoes or specialized trims.

8. Colic is the number one cause of death in horses. Any sort of abdominal pain causes the symptoms of colic, so responsible horse owners should be familiar with its symptoms. Pawing at

A farrier at work

4. A good farrier has firsthand experience related to horses. He or she knows how to handle a horse confidently and humanely.

5. Professional demeanor is important. A successful farrier keeps scheduled appointments except in cases of emergency. Not showing up because clients were overbooked is unacceptable.

9 Important Areas on a Horse's Foot

1. Bars

2. Bulbs of heel

3. Frog

4. Heel

5. Hoof wall

6. Quarter

7. Sole

8. Toe

9. White line

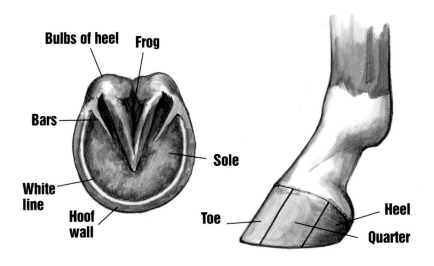

6 Bones in a Horse's Fetlock and Foot

1. Cannon bone
2. Coffin bone
3. Navicular bone
4. Long pastern bone
5. Sesamoid bone
6. Short pastern bone

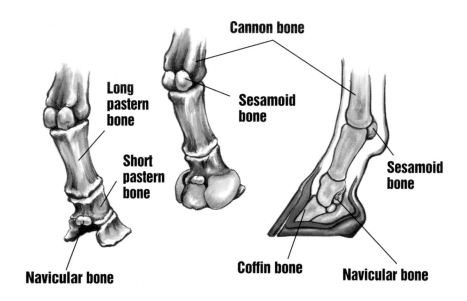

5 Common Causes of Lameness

1. Bowed tendon: A fairly common ailment of horses that perform in high-intensity events such as racing and jumping, a bowed tendon gets its name from the resultant "bowing out" of the damaged, thickened soft tissue. The affected tendon is usually the superficial digital flexor tendon, which runs down the back of the horse's cannon bone. It's prone to injury when the horse overextends its fetlock joint or is repeatedly overworked. Bowed tendons occur predominantly in the front legs and only rarely in the hind legs. When the tendon is acutely inflamed, there is pain, heat, and swelling. The horse is noticeably lame, especially if the tendon fibers are actually torn and not merely inflamed. Treatment for a bowed tendon centers on resting the horse for up to a year and then gradually returning it to exercise.

2. Navicular disease: This is a complicated and not fully understood chronic, degenerative disease process that involves the tiny navicular bone located inside the horse's hoof. The navicular bone and its surrounding soft tissues are part of the horse's locomotive apparatus. That's why inflammation in the navicular area or in the bone itself causes the horse to feel pain with each step, particularly in the heel areas of the front feet. To alleviate the pain, the horse will appear to be walking on his toes with short, stiff steps. The exact cause of navicular disease is unknown, although contributory factors include riding the horse on hard, uneven terrain and poor hoof conformation. Long toes and low heels or very upright hooves put constant strain on the navicular bone and the deep digital flexor tendon, which runs beneath it. Corrective shoeing can help, as can some medical interventions such as oral anti-inflammatory drugs and vasodilators, which increase blood flow to the navicular area. A surgical procedure that cuts the nerve that supplies sensation to the horse's heels is a last resort.

3. Ringbone: Excessive bony growth that invades the pastern joint is called ringbone, as over time the calcification can begin to encircle the entire joint. Though ringbone is most prevalent in the front legs, all four legs can be affected. Faulty conformation such as pigeon toes, splay legs, and upright pasterns predispose a horse to ringbone, as the pastern joint is then in an unnatural, unbalanced position. That places stress on ligaments and tendons that help support the pastern joint, eliciting an inflammatory response that leads to the production of new, unwanted bone in the area. Symptoms of lameness increase as the degenerative disease progresses. The first step in halting ringbone is to have a qualified farrier carefully balance the horse's feet with corrective trimming and, if necessary, shoeing. Anti-inflammatory medications help the horse feel more comfortable and quiet the inflammatory response. Surgically fusing the pastern joint stabilizes the area and in some cases provides permanent pain relief.

4. Stone bruise: If a horse steps on a small rock or pebble or is worked over hard, rough terrain, the sole of the foot can be bruised. A horse with flat feet or thin soles is conformationally prone to bruising. Like a bruise at any place on the body, minute amounts of blood are released into surrounding tissues. That builds up pressure, causing the horse to be lame, especially if he happens to bear weight precisely over the bruised area. Until the bruise resolves, the horse can be made more comfortable by laying him up for several days and stabling him on soft bedding. Topical medications, recommended by a veterinarian or farrier, can help toughen the sole to prevent future bruising. Sometimes rubber pads are added beneath a horse's shoe to cushion the sole of a flat-footed horse. Occasionally, a stone bruise leads to an abscess. If that occurs, the horse may become severely lame. The area over the abscess must be trimmed away with a hoof knife, a delicate procedure to be performed only by a veterinarian or farrier. Once accumulated blood and pus is allowed to drain, the horse will become sound. A poultice applied to the hoof will speed the healing.

5. Thrush: There are plenty of bacteria in a horse's natural environment, including anaerobic bacteria, which thrive in oxygen-poor environments. When a horse's feet become soft from overexposure to moisture or the horse's hooves are not kept trimmed, the bacteria can invade the cleft and folds of the frog. The frog is the horny, V-shaped pad on the underside of a horse's hoof. The first symptom of thrush is a putrid odor noticeable when the hoof is picked clean. A thick, dark material may also ooze from the frog. If the thrush infection is superficial, the horse won't be lame. But if it penetrates deeply into sensitive tissue, the horse will be profoundly sore. Treatment consists of trimming away the infected parts of the

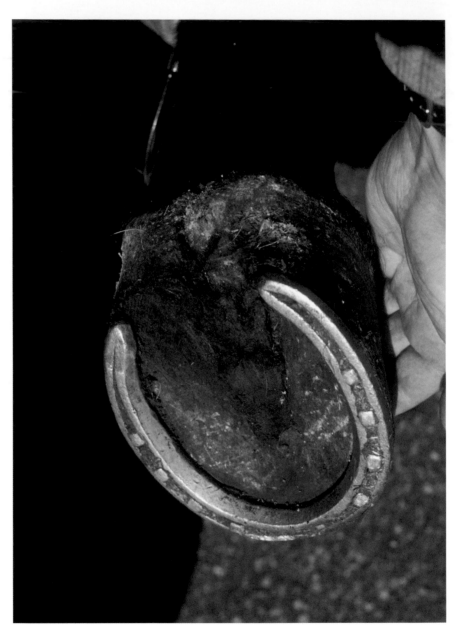

Thrush

frog, applying a topical antiseptic or oxidizer (such as hydrogen peroxide) on the recommendation of a veterinarian or farrier, and meticulous hoof care.

5 Items for a Broodmare Checklist

1. Honestly evaluate your mare's worth as a breeding prospect. This may require an objective outsider who can see faults in conformation, movement, and size that an enamored owner might miss. Soundness problems that could be hereditary should be reason enough to eliminate the mare from any breeding program. Granted, no horse is perfect, but any flaw that is present in the mare may show up in the foal.

2. Consider the motivation for breeding the mare. Creating a performance horse that might not otherwise be affordable is not always feasible. The stud fee, vet fees, and the risk of ending up with a foal that is short of expectations may make buying a young horse already on the ground a more prudent option.

3. Before officially signing a contract to "book" a mare to a stallion, have a veterinarian examine the mare for breeding soundness. This could include an ultrasound of the reproductive tract and cultures of the uterine lining to make sure that the mare is free of infection. A mare with an infected reproductive tract is unlikely to get in-foal.

4. Keep track of the mare's heat cycles. During the spring breeding season, a mare cycles approximately every twenty-one days and will be receptive to a stallion for about five days. Near the end of each cycle, the mare ovulates, releasing an egg. Timing is of the essence, however, as that egg is viable for only about twelve hours. Hence, the mare has a better chance of getting in-foal with the guidance of a veterinarian who can precisely determine when the mare is ready to be bred.

5. Once the mare is declared in-foal, she needs regular exercise and quality feed. A broodmare should enjoy adequate nutrition yet not be allowed to become obese. Being fit and healthy helps ensure a successful breeding and an uneventful foaling.

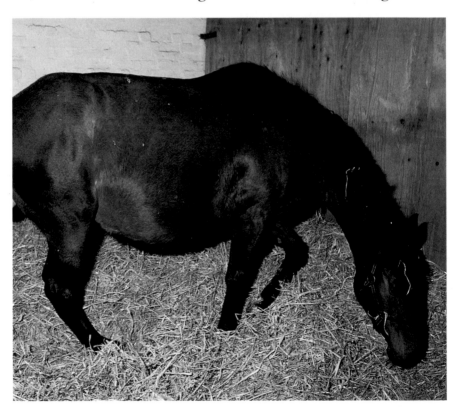

A mare in-foal

10 Things to Know Before Baby Arrives

1. You'll have a long time to plan for the foal's arrival because the average gestation is 340 days, or roughly eleven months. That's a long time to wait, but just think of how many names you can dream up!

2. When the mare rises after giving birth, the umbilical cord will break. You must be ready to disinfect the stump with a solution of iodine or chlorhexidine.

3. Once the foal is born, the show has just begun. A foal can take up to two hours to stand and four hours to begin nursing.

4. Foals must pass the meconium, a hard stool that forms in their digestive tract in utero. If the foal begins to strain, you'll have to gently administer an infant-sized saline enema, available at drugstores.

5. Weather permitting, both mare and foal will need daily access to a large playground. The turnout area must be made foal-proof in advance. Fence rails must be spaced close enough together so that the foal cannot roll or slide out of the enclosure. Heavy-duty mesh wire fencing that prevents such escapes is a good alternative.

A mare and foal

6. Foals don't arrive knowing how to lead. It will be your job to introduce the foal to a halter and lead rope just a couple of days after birth. This is the start of the foal's education.

7. You must also accustom the foal to the grooming process. At first, colts and fillies think all that rubbing and scratching is a game, so be prepared to dodge nips, kicks, and body slams until you teach the baby horse that humans are not two-legged playmates.

THE HORSE BOOK OF LISTS

8. Colts and fillies are typically weaned from their dams at four to six months of age. Some mares are quite glad to be rid of their rambunctious youngsters, and some weanlings quickly adapt to their independence. On the other hand, it's not uncommon for mares to become agitated and for weanlings to mope and whinny balefully. Secure fencing is vitally important at this time.

9. Weanlings and yearlings require meticulous attention to their diet. Nutritional deficiencies can have disastrous effects that result in lifelong soundness issues. Consult your veterinarian to formulate a proper diet for your baby horse before weaning.

10. A young horse needs to learn many skills, from how to stand patiently while tied up to how to load quietly into a trailer. And guess what? You'll have plenty of time to teach him, because a foal needs to mature two to three years before you can climb on his back for serious training.

6 Hereditary Diseases of Horses

1. Severe Combined Immunodeficiency (SCID): A genetic abnormality in the bloodlines of Arabian horses causes this disease. A SCID-affected foal is born with an incomplete or defective immune system. It is unable to fight off infections and

The Orphan Foal

If a mare dies during or shortly after giving birth, the foal will have to be raised as an orphan. But what's the best plan? First, a veterinarian will draw blood to find out whether the foal received antibodies from his dam's milk. Because foals are not born with a fully intact immune system, they must nurse heartily for the first twenty-four hours from their dam. That early milk, called colostrum, is rich in antibodies. If the mare dies before the foal can nurse, then colostrum that has been stored at a milk bank can be fed via bottle to the orphan. Large equine veterinary clinics either maintain a supply of frozen colostrum or can obtain it on short notice. Next, a decision must be made whether to raise the foal on commercially produced formula or put him with a nurse mare. Bottle feeding a foal is neither easy nor fun. The foal needs to be fed every few hours and can become agitated when he spies the handler approaching with the next serving of milk. Moreover, lack of normal socialization with his dam may adversely affect the orphan throughout his life. That is the primary reason for

Bottle feeding a foal

considering the use of a nurse mare. Not only will the foal have ready access to a natural source of nutrition, but he will also have a Momma mare to teach him some manners. Draft breeds and draft crosses are usually the most sought-after nurse mares because of their docile dispositions and their abundant milk production. But placing an orphan foal with an unfamiliar mare could have tragic results if the mare rejects the foal and kicks him. That's why any attempt to play matchmaker should be left to professionals. Ultimately, the most successful adoptions occur when the nurse mare has recently lost her own foal. By pairing a mare bereft of a baby and a foal that's lost a mom, two horses can be made more content.

usually dies within a few months of birth from illnesses such as pneumonia. Because the gene for SCID is recessive, both sire and dam must possess and transmit the SCID gene for their offspring to be stricken. If only one parent transmits the defective gene, the foal will not become ill but will be a carrier of the disease. The SCID cycle continues when two apparently healthy horses are actually carriers of the disease and are inadvertently bred together. There is a one-in-four chance that any offspring of that pair will inherit the SCID gene from both parents and die of the disease. In 1998, genetic testing to identify the presence of the SCID gene became available, and now Arabian breeding stock can be DNA tested so two carriers are not unknowingly bred to each other. Stallions that have been DNA tested and found not to be carriers are promoted for breeding as being "SCID clear."

2. Overo Lethal White Syndrome (OLWS): The overo is one of several colored coat patterns found predominantly in American Paint Horses, though it can occur in several other breeds. In an attempt to increase the odds of having a foal with splashy white markings, uninformed owners sometimes breed their overo mare to an overo stallion. Unfortunately, if both sire and dam carry the recessive gene for Overo Lethal White Syndrome, this practice can produce a foal born with the condition. Foals afflicted with OLWS are totally or almost totally white, with blue eyes. Shortly after birth, they begin demonstrating signs of colic because OLWS results in an undeveloped, contracted intestine unable to pass feces through the digestive tract. Embryonic nerve cells that should develop in the gastrointestinal tract do not. These nerve cells are genetically linked to coat color, hence the combination of the white coat and the defective digestive tract. The condition is always fatal, so foals diagnosed with OLWS are humanely euthanized. There is a test for OLWS. Before breeding, overo stallions are often tested to determine whether they are carriers of the gene,

An overo Paint Horse

and mare owners can make informed decisions before selecting a stallion.

3. Hereditary Equine Regional Dermal Asthenia (HERDA): Also referred to as hyperelastosis cutis (HC), this gruesome malady was first documented in 1971. It can be traced to certain cutting and working cow horse bloodlines found in the pedigree of many American Quarter Horses. Because HERDA causes a defect in collagen, the "glue" that holds layers of skin together, an affected horse develops unsightly lesions, and the skin seems to slide or slough off whenever pressure is applied. This condition makes saddling the horse without trauma impossible. Afflicted horses are usually diagnosed at two and die within a few years, although with meticulous care, some can be maintained as nonrideable pets. Fortunately, a DNA test was developed in 2007 that can determine if a horse is a HERDA carrier, which should eventually help eradicate the disease.

4. Hyperkalemic Periodic Paralysis (HYPP): This is a muscle disease caused by a hereditary imbalance in potassium and sodium levels in the horse's body. Affected horses experience episodes of muscle twitching, temporary paralysis, and collapse. Severe attacks can be fatal. HYPP has been traced to a specific bloodline found primarily in the pedigrees of American Quarter Horses, that of a successful and prolific stallion named Impressive. However, Impressive's bloodline can also occur in Appaloosas and Paints. There is a test for HYPP. Horses can be identified as N/N (meaning they do not possess the defective gene and are "normal"), N/H (signifying that they are heterozygous carriers of the trait, or possess one defective and one normal gene), or H/H (meaning they are homozygous for HYPP; that is, they inherited defective genes from both parents). Because the gene for HYPP is dominant, a horse that inherits the gene from even one parent (N/H) will be affected to some degree. Foals that inherit the defective gene from both parents (H/H) are usually severely afflicted. And because the gene for HYPP is dominant, there is a 50 percent chance that the offspring of a carrier and a normal horse will be affected, a 75 percent chance that the offspring of two carriers will be affected, and a 100 percent certainty that the offspring of a horse identified as HYPP H/H will be affected. In an effort to purge its registry of HYPP-affected horses, the American Quarter Horse Association requires all foals descended from Impressive to be tested. As of January 2007, a foal that has been identified as HYPP H/H is refused registration.

5. Cervical Stenotic Myelopathy (CVM): Also known as Wobblers Syndrome, this disease is most frequently diagnosed in fast-growing male horses under the age of three. Although not proved to be genetically linked, there is a presumed hereditary component in that certain bloodlines within several horse breeds, including Thoroughbreds, seem to be predisposed to CVM. That may be because these bloodlines are likely to produce robust foals that achieve height and growth rapidly. An additional risk factor is nutritional deficiency. Affected horses are referred to as wobblers because they exhibit an unsteady gait and a lack of coordination, especially in their hindquarters. This is due to abnormal bony growth along the cervical vertebrae that compresses the spinal cord. CVM used to warrant euthanasia, but with advances in treatment, this is not always the case. An early diagnosis coupled with drug therapy, intense nutritional management, and perhaps surgical intervention can sometimes halt the progression of the disease and allow the horse to lead a productive life.

6. Chronic Progressive Lymphodema (CPL): A disfiguring disease may lurk beneath the abundant, thick hair—known as feathers—found on the lower legs of many draft horses. What first begin as skin ulcers eventually progress to grapelike clusters of nodules beneath the skin. Once the lymphatic system is compromised, the horse's lower legs become swollen, thickened skin folds develop, and secondary infections set in. The resultant pain causes lameness, and with further infections the horse's life may be cut short. Although the draft breeds most commonly affected are the Shire, Clydesdale, and Belgian, CPL has appeared in other draft horses as well. Based on current research into CPL, heredity does seem to play a role, in that certain breeds or specific bloodlines may transmit a predisposition for the disease. Unfortunately, at this time there is no cure for CPL. However, an early diagnosis offers a chance to manage the disease.

6 Tips for Making the Golden Years Pleasant

1. Consult an equine veterinarian to determine an appropriate exercise routine. Older horses can still lead useful lives, provided that their work routine is adjusted for age-related issues such as arthritis. In fact, it's not unusual for performance horses to compete well into their teens and early twenties, often serving as "schoolmasters" for very young or novice riders.

Enjoying the golden years

2. Adjust feed ration if warranted. Commercial feeds are available that are formulated specifically for older horses. They usually include "good" bacteria that aid digestion and absorption of nutrients.

3. Have teeth inspected annually and floated if warranted. Floating is a procedure in which a veterinarian or equine dentist uses files and drimmels to expertly remodel misshapen teeth. A horse's teeth grow throughout his life, and the average life expectancy of a horse is about twenty-four years. The edges of molars can become worn down and rough from all those years of grinding hay and grain. If an older horse begins to "quid" (drop half-chewed bits of food from its mouth), that's a sign that the teeth need attention.

4. Schedule annual veterinary exams. For example, bloodwork can reveal early warning signs of kidney problems or metabolic disease that might be manageable through dietary changes.

5. Address peculiar changes in the geriatric horse's appearance. A perpetually shaggy coat and a thick cresty neck may signify equine Cushing's disease, a disease of the endocrine system that can lead to laminitis.

6. Ultimately, when the time comes, be prepared for humane euthanasia. An equine senior citizen that has served humans loyally deserves a peaceful end among those who oversaw his care.

Counting the Years

The life span of the average horse is twenty to twenty-five years, although with good nutrition and continuous health care, many horses make it to thirty. Ponies tend to live a bit longer. In fact, the world's oldest equine, according to *Guinness World Records*, was actually a pony. Sugar Puff, of West Sussex, England, died in 2007 at the documented age of fifty-six. A simple math equation won't translate a horse's age into human years, but there are some broad analogies. Horses are considered physically mature at about four years old (comparable to a human at the end of puberty) and in their prime from eight to twelve years old. The term *aged* describes a horse fifteen years and older. A horse becomes a senior citizen at twenty-two years old, roughly analogous to a sixty-five-year-old person. Of course, many people are active and thriving at sixty-five, as are many equine senior citizens. Good genes, good care, and a dose of good luck keep horses and horse lovers full of life well into their golden years.

5 Fateful Endings of Faithful Equines

1. Bucephalus: As a young boy, Alexander the Great tamed the fractious stallion by keeping the horse's head turned toward the sun as he led him. That way, the horse could not see his shadow, which was causing him to spook. Alexander named the horse Bucephalus, literally "Ox Head," because the animal had a large head shaped much like a bull's. Bucephalus was Alexander's mount throughout a decade of military conquest. The horse died in 326 BC of wounds suffered in battle. In his memory, Alexander founded the city of Bucephala, possibly the site of the modern-day city of Jhelum, Pakistan.

2. Comanche: When cavalry reinforcements arrived at the scene of the Battle of Little Bighorn in 1876, they found Lt. Col. George Custer and all of his troops massacred. The only survivor left to greet them was a badly wounded part-mustang gelding named Comanche, the personal mount of Capt. Myles Keogh. Comanche was ferried back to Fort Lincoln via steamboat, where he slowly recovered. Later, he was sent to live at Fort Riley, where he enjoyed the role of both cavalry mascot and four-legged hero. He died at the age of twenty-nine and was given a funeral with full military honors. He wasn't buried, however; he was stuffed and put on display at the University of Kansas, where he still stands at attention.

3. Exceller: Foaled in 1973, this handsome dark bay Thoroughbred was a successful racehorse, winning $1.6 million in the United States and Europe. He wowed legions of racing fans when he won the Jockey Club Gold Cup, beating Affirmed and Seattle Slew, two Triple Crown winners. Unfortunately, Exceller didn't exactly set the world on fire as a breeding stallion. After a mediocre career at stud, during which time he was sold several times, his life ended in a most undignified manner, far from the winner's circle. In 1997, Exceller met his fate at a slaughterhouse in Sweden, where he was killed for human consumption. Fortunately, when Exceller's fate became known, it became the impetus for efforts to rehabilitate and find second careers for ex-racehorses.

Exceller

4. Charisma: A beautiful, talented jumper, Charisma began to falter in the show ring after he was purchased by George Lindemann Jr., a young tycoon with aspirations for the Olympic equestrian team. In 1990, Charisma was surreptitiously killed to collect a $250,000 claim for the highly insured horse. Lindemann was convicted on three counts of wire fraud in 1995, sentenced to thirty-three months in prison, and fined $500,000. Charisma came to symbolize a tiny but ugly subset of the horse show circuit of the late 1980s: owners who would rather dispatch an expensive horse than sell it at a financial loss or admit that they could not ride it successfully. Although the practice was quietly rumored to be more rampant than was ultimately proved, a federal investigation uncovered eleven English show horses that had been killed—mostly by electrocution—in order for their owners to fraudulently claim insurance payouts.

5. Brigadier: In 2006, this handsome chestnut gelding was on duty as a mounted patrol horse with the Toronto, Ontario, police department. The horse and his rider, Constable Kevin Bradfield, approached an irate motorist stopped at an ATM machine. The driver sped away in his van, and Bradfield reined in Brigadier, only to realize that the suspect had made a U-turn and was heading back toward him and his horse. The driver rammed into Brigadier, fracturing the horse's front legs beyond repair, and fled the scene. Bradfield, who sustained non-life-threatening injuries, had to witness his horse being humanely euthanized by being shot on the scene by fellow officers. Outrage at the death of the popular horse in the line of duty was so great that a public memorial service was held in his honor and a bill, informally known as Brigadier's Law, was proposed to amend the Canadian criminal code to better protect law enforcement animals.

5 Ways to Memorialize a Horse

1. A Developed Diamond: At least one company in the United States will create a diamond from the carbon in a horse's cremated remains or a lock of its mane or tail hair. When the carbon is subjected to specific levels of heat and pressure it forms a genuine—albeit not flawless—diamond. Slight imperfections are fitting: they give the lab-created diamond character, much like the horse's idiosyncrasies gave it a unique personality.

2. A Place of Honor: What better place to reflect on the life of a beloved horse than beneath a shady tree next to the barn? A garden bench can literally be a seat of honor when a craftsperson embeds mementos of the horse's life in the bench seat or back. Old horseshoes, medals won in horse show events, halter nameplates, and silver bits can be incorporated into the design.

A horsehair bracelet

3. Hirsute Jewelry: During the Victorian era, jewelry and personal accessories made with locks of hair from family members were considered not only fashionable items but also tributes to loved ones. Making jewelry from horsehair follows in the same tradition. Skilled artisans make tightly woven bracelets, necklaces, watch fobs, belts, barrettes, and rings from hair plucked or snipped from a favorite horse. Such pieces are often embellished with tiny colored glass beads, sterling silver, or 14K gold.

4. A Work of Art: Gifted equine artists can etch, sketch, or paint an heirloom-quality likeness of a beloved horse. Many artists prefer to visit the horse while it is alive to best capture its spirit and personality; however, posthumous portraits are a popular option. They are based on collections of snapshots that reveal the horse's conformation, color, and if possible, some of the animal's behavioral traits.

5. The Gift of Cash: Veterinary schools conduct ongoing research into diseases and injuries that claim the lives of horses. Cash donations to various vet-school research programs are welcomed. By helping fund studies that may contribute to cures and treatments, a grieving owner may take comfort in taking action so other horses might be spared.

5 Signs Your Horse Is Enjoying Life

1. Your horse shows interest in daily activities around the barn rather than sulking in the back corner of the stall or hiding out in the far corner of the paddock.

A healthy American Quarter Horse

Chapter Twelve

Horses Coast to Coast

Whether you live in the area or are just visiting, there are lots of horsey places to see and things to do in the various and varied regions of the United States—from visiting museums to trail riding to watching Thoroughbreds race!

10 Must-See Spots Across America

1. In the Northeast: The National Museum of Racing and Hall of Fame, 191 Union Avenue, Saratoga Springs, New York (www.racingmuseum.org)

2. In the Southeast: The Aiken Thoroughbred Racing Hall of Fame, 135 Dupree Place, Aiken, South Carolina (www.aikenracinghalloffame.com). In the spring, take in the Aiken

Aiken Thoroughbred Racing Hall of Fame

Triple Crown—flat racing, steeplechase racing, and polo—and the annual Aiken Horse Show (www.aikenhorseshow.com)

3. In the South: The Steeplechase at Callaway, 1017 Second Avenue, Columbus, Georgia (www.steeplechaseatcallaway.org)

4. In the Midwest/Great Plains: The International Horse Archery Festival in Fort Dodge, Iowa (www.Krackow.com/horsearchery.html)

5. In the Midwest/Great Plains: The Black Hills Wild Horse Sanctuary, PO Box 998, Hot Springs, South Dakota (www.wildmustangs.com)

6. In the West: The Teton Covered Wagon Train and Horse Adventure, Jackson Hole, Wyoming (www.tetonwagontrain.com)

7. In the West: For great horse-related goodies, shop at the Cabaline Country Emporium & Saddlery, 11313 Hwy 1, Pointe Reyes Station, California and Toby's Feed Barn, 11250 Hwy 1, Pointe Reyes Station, California

8. In the Southwest: The National Cowboy & Western Heritage Museum, 1700 N.E. 63rd Street, Oklahoma City, Oklahoma (www.nationalcowboymuseum.org)

9. In the Southwest: The Wild Wild West Pro Rodeo, in Southwest Horsemen's Park, US 180 East, Silver City, New Mexico (www.silvercity.org)

10. In the Southwest: The Ruidoso Downs Race Horse Hall of Fame, in the Hubbard Museum of the American West, 841 Hwy 70, Ruidoso, New Mexico (www.hubbardmuseum.org)

14 Scenic Places to Ride in the Northeast

1. Connecticut: Natchaug State Forest, Route 98, Chaplin (contact Mashamoquet Brook State Park, Pomfret Center, CT 06259)

2. Connecticut: Pachaug State Forest, Route 49, PO Box 5, Voluntown, CT 06384

3. Delaware: Lums Pond State Park, 1068 Howell School Road, Bear, DE 19701

4. Maine: Acadia National Park, PO Box 177, Eagle Lake Road, Bar Harbor, ME 04609

5. Massachusetts: Boston Area Trails (contact Greater Boston Convention and Visitors Bureau, Two Copley Place, Ste. 105, Boston, MA 02116)

6. New Hampshire: Bear Brook State Park, Route 28, Allenstown, NH 03275

7. New Jersey: Allaire State Park, Box 220, Route 524, Farmingdale, NJ 07727

8. New Jersey: Wharton State Forest, 4110 Nesco Road, Hammonton, NJ 08037

9. New York: Brookfield Trail System, 2715 State Hwy 80, Sherburne, NY 13460

10. New York: Otter Creek Horse Trails, 7327 State Route 812, Lowville, NY 13367

11. Pennsylvania: Allegheny National Forest, PO Box 847, Warren, PA 16365

12. Pennsylvania: Ohiopyle State Park, PO Box 105, Ohiopyle, PA 15470

13. Rhode Island: Lincoln Woods State Park, 2 Manchester Print Works Road, Lincoln, RI 02865

14. Vermont: Merck Forest and Farmland Center, Route 315, Rupert Mountain Road, Rupert, VT 05768

11 Racetracks to Visit in the Northeast

1. Delaware: Delaware Park, 777 Delaware Park Boulevard, Wilmington (www.delpark.com)

2. Massachusetts: Suffolk Downs, 111 Waldemar Avenue, East Boston (www.suffolkdowns.com)

3. Massachusetts: Three County Fair, 41 Fair Street, Northampton (www.3countyfair.com)

4. New Jersey: Meadowlands Racetrack, 50 Route 120, East Rutherford (www.thebigm.com)

5. New Jersey: Monmouth Park, Oceanport Avenue, Oceanport (www.monmouthpark.com)

Lincoln Woods State Park

6. New York: Aqueduct Racetrack, 11000 Rockaway Boulevard, Jamaica (www.nyra.com)

7. New York: Belmont Park, 2150 Hempstead Turnpike, Elmont, Long Island (www.nyra.com)

8. New York: Finger Lakes Gaming and Racetrack, 5857 Route 96, Farmington (www.fingerlakesracetrack.com)

9. New York: Saratoga Race Course, 267 Union Avenue, Saratoga Springs (www.nyra.com)

10. Pennsylvania: Penn National Race Course, 720 Bow Creek Road, Grantville (www.pennnational.com)

11. Pennsylvania: Philadelphia Park, 3001 Street Road, Bensalem (www.philadelphiapark.com)

15 Scenic Places to Ride in the Southeast

1. Kentucky: Daniel Boone National Forest, 1700 Bypass Road, Winchester, KY 40391

2. Kentucky: Mammoth Cave National Park, PO Box 7, Mammoth Cave, KY 42259

3. Kentucky: Taylorsville Lake State Park, PO Box 205, Taylorsville, KY 40071

4. Maryland: Fair Hill National Resources Management Area, 1401 National Park Drive, Manteo, NC 27954

5. Maryland and Virginia: Assateague Island National Seashore and Chincoteague National Wildlife Refuge (Maryland District: 7206 National Seashore Lane, Berlin, MD 21811; Virginia District: PO Box 38, 8586 Beach Road, Chincoteague, VA 23336

6. North Carolina: Cape Hatteras National Seashore, 1401 National Park Drive, Manteo, NC 27954

7. North Carolina: Uwharrie National Forest, Uwharrie Ranger District, 789 NC Highway 24/27 East, Troy, NC 27371

8. South Carolina: Croft State Natural Area, 450 Croft State Park Road, Spartanburg, SC 29302

9. South Carolina: Lakeview Plantation, 875 Cedar Knoll Road, Fairfax, SC 29827

10. South Carolina: The Hitchcock Woods, The Hitchcock Foundation, PO Box 1702, South Boundary and Laurens Street, Aiken, SC 29802

Green River in Mammoth Cave National Park

11. Tennessee: Big South Fork National River and Recreation Area, 4564 Leatherwood Road, Oneida, TN 37841

12. Tennessee and North Carolina: Great Smoky Mountains National Park, 107 Park Headquarters Road, Gatlinburg, TN 37738

13. Virginia: George Washington National Forest, 5162 Valleypointe Parkway, Roanoke, VA 24019

14. **Virginia:** Mount Rogers National Recreation Area, 3714 Highway 16, Marion, VA 24354

15. **West Virginia:** Watoga State Park, HC 82, Box 252, Marlinton, WV 24954

10 Racetracks to Visit in the Southeast

1. **Kentucky:** Churchill Downs, 700 Central Avenue, Louisville (www.churchilldowns.com)

2. **Kentucky:** Ellis Park Race Course, 3300 US Hwy 41, N. Henderson (www.ellisparkracing.com)

3. **Kentucky:** Keeneland, 4201 Versailles Road, Lexington (www.keeneland.com)

4. **Kentucky:** Kentucky Downs, 5629 Nashville Road, Franklin (www.kentuckydowns.com)

5. **Kentucky:** Turfway Park, 7500 Turfway Road, Florence (www.turfway.com)

6. **Maryland:** Laurel Park, Route 198, Laurel (www.maryland racing.com)

7. Maryland: Pimlico Race Course, 5201 Park Heights Avenue, Baltimore (www.marylandracing.com)

8. Virginia: Colonial Downs, 10515 Colonial Downs Parkway, New Kent (www.colonialdowns.com)

9. West Virginia: Charles Town Races and Slots, US Route 340, Charles Town (www.ctownraces.com)

10. West Virginia: Mountaineer Race Track and Gaming Resort, Route 2, Chester (www.mtrgaming.com)

12 Scenic Places to Ride in the South

1. Alabama: Talladega National Forest, Shoal Creek Ranger District, 450 Highway 46, Heflin, AL 36264

2. Alabama: Tuskegee National Forest, 125 National Forest Road 949, Tuskegee, AL 36083

3. Arkansas: Devil's Den State Park, 11333, West Arkansas Highway 74, West Fork, AR 72774

4. Arkansas: Ozark National Forest, 605 West Main, Russellville, AR 72801

13. Missouri: Harry S. Truman Dam and Reservoir, Harry S. Truman Project Office, U.S. Army Corps of Engineers, 15968 Truman Road, Warsaw, MO 65355

14. Missouri: Blue and Gray Park Reserve, 300 S. Bynum Road, Lone Jack, MO 64070

15. Nebraska: Fort Robinson State Park, PO Box 392, Crawford, NE 59339

16. Nebraska: Indian Cave State Park, 65296 720 Road, Shubert, NE 68437

17. North Dakota: Maah Daah Hey Trail, U.S. Forest Service, 240 W. Century Avenue, Bismarck, ND 58503

18. North Dakota: Theodore Roosevelt National Park, Box 7, Medora, ND 58654

19. Ohio: Cuyahoga Valley National Park, 15610 Vaughn Road, Brecksville, OH 44141

20. Ohio: Hocking State Forest, 19275 State Route 374, Rockbridge, OH 43149

21. South Dakota: Badlands National Park, 25216 Ben Reifel Road, PO Box 6, Interior, SD 57750

22. South Dakota: Custer State Park, HC83, Box 70, Custer, SD 57730

23. Wisconsin: Wildcat Mountain State Park, E. 13660 State Highway 33, PO Box 99, Ontario, WI 54651

24. Wisconsin: Chequamegon-Nicolet National Forest, 1170 Fourth Avenue South, Park Falls, WI 54552

Chequamegon-Nicolet National Forest

18 Racetracks in the Midwest/Great Plains

1. Illinois: Arlington Park, 2200 West Euclid Avenue, Arlington Heights (www.arlingronpark.com)

2. Illinois: Fairmount Park, 9301 Collinsville Road, Collinsville (www.fairmountpark.com)

3. Illinois: Hawthorne Race Course, 3501 South Laramie Avenue, Cicero (www.hawthorneracecourse.com)

4. Indiana: Hoosier Park, 4500 Dan Patch Circle, Anderson (www.hoosierpark.com)

5. Indiana: Indiana Downs, 4200 North Michigan Road, Shelbyville (www.indianadowns.com)

6. Iowa: Prairie Meadows, 1 Prairie Meadow Drive, Altoona (www.prairiemeadows.com)

7. Kansas: Anthony Downs, 521 E. Sherman, Anthony (www.anthonydownsraces.com)

8. Kansas: Eureka Downs, 210 N. Jefferson Street, Eureka (www.eurekadowns.com)

Hoosier Park

9. Kansas: Woodlands Race Park, 9700 Leavenworth Road, Kansas City (www.woodlandskc.com)

10. Michigan: Great Lakes Downs, 800 Harvey Street, Muskegon (www.greatlakesdowns.com)

11. Minnesota: Canterbury Park, 1100 Canterbury Road, Shakopee (www.canterburypark.com)

12. Nebraska: Columbus Races, 822 15th Street, Columbus (www.columbusraces.com)

13. Nebraska: Fonner Park, 700 E. Stolley Park Road, Grand Island (www.fonnerpark.com)

14. Nebraska: Horsemen's Atokad Downs, 1524 Atokad Drive, South Sioux City (www.horseracing.state.ne.us)

15. Nebraska: Horsemen's Park, 6303 Q Street, Omaha (www.horsemenspark.com)

16. Ohio: Beulah Park, 3664 Grant Avenue, Grove City (www.beulahpark.com)

17. Ohio: River Downs, 6301 Kellogg Avenue, Cincinnati (www.riverdowns.com)

18. Ohio: Thistledown, 21501 Emery Road, North Randall (www.thistledown.com)

13 Scenic Places to Ride in the Pacific Northwest

1. Alaska: Chugach State Park, Potter Section House, Mile 115 Seward Highway; contact HC 52, Box 8999, Indian, AK 99540

Denali National Park

2. Alaska: Denali National Park, PO Box 9, Denali Park, AK 99755

3. Oregon: Eagle Cap Wilderness, 88401 Highway 82, Enterprise, OR 97828

4. Oregon: Hells Canyon National Recreation Area, 1550 Dewey Avenue, PO Box 907, Baker City, OR 97814

5. Oregon: Nehalem Bay State Park, 9500 Sandpiper Lane, PO Box 366, Nehalem, OR 97131

6. Oregon: Rogue River-Siskiyou National Forest, 333 W. 8th Street, Medford, OR 97501

7. Oregon: Siuslaw National Forest, 4077 S.W. Research Way, PO Box 1148, Corvallis, OR 97339

8. Oregon: Williamette Mission State Park, Oregon Parks and Recreation Department, State Parks, 725 Summer Street NE, Suite C, Salem, OR 97301

9. Washington: Bridle Trails State Park, Washington State Parks and Recreation Commission, 7150 Cleanwater Lane, PO Box 42650, Olympia, WA 98504

10. Washington: Gifford Pinchot National Forest, 10600 N.E. 51st Circle, Vancouver, WA 98682

11. Washington: Mount Rainier National Park, Tahoma Woods Star Route, Ashford, WA 98304

12. Washington: North Cascades National Park, 810 State Route 20, Sedro-Woolley, WA 98284

13. Washington: Olympic National Park, 600 East Park Avenue, Port Angeles, WA 98362

North Cascades National Park

2 Racetracks to Visit in the Pacific Northwest

1. Oregon: Portland Meadows, 1001 North Schmeer Road, Portland (www.portlandmeadows.com)

2. Washington: Emerald Downs, 2300 Emerald Downs Drive, Auburn (www.emdowns.com)

25 Scenic Places to Ride in the West

1. California: Anza-Borrego Desert State Park, 200 Palm Canyon Drive, Borrego Springs, CA 92004

2. California: Jack London State Historic Park, 2400 London Ranch Road, Glen Ellen, CA 95442

3. California: Joshua Tree National Park, 74485 National Park Drive, Twentynine Palms, CA 92277

4. California: Lake Oroville State Recreation Area, 400 Glen Drive, Oroville, CA 95966

5. California: Lassen Volcanic National Park, PO Box 100, Mineral, CA 96063

6. California: Sequoia and Kings Canyon National Parks, 47050 Generals Highway, Three Rivers, CA 93271

7. California: Point Reyes National Seashore, 1 Bear Valley Road, Point Reyes, CA 94956

8. California: Yosemite National Park, PO Box 577, Yosemite National Park, CA 95389

Yosemite Valley

9. Colorado: Arapaho and Roosevelt National Forests, 12150 Centre Avenue, Building E, Fort Collins, CO 80524

10. Colorado: Chatfield State Park, 11500 N. Roxborough Park Road, Littleton, CO 80125

11. Colorado: Pike National Forest, 1920 Valley Road, Pueblo, CO 81008

12. Colorado: Rocky Mountain National Park, Backcountry Office, Rocky Mountain National Park, Estes Park, CO 80517

13. Colorado: San Juan National Forest, 15 Burnett Court, Durango, CO 81301

14. Idaho: Boise National Forest, 1249 S. Vinnell Way, Boise, ID 83709

15. Idaho: Bruneau Dunes State Park, HC 85, Box 41, Mountain Home, ID 83647

16. Idaho: City of Rocks National Reserve, PO Box 169, 3035 Elba Almo Road, Almo, ID 83312

17. Montana: Bob Marshall Wilderness, Rocky Mountain Ranger District, 1102 Main Avenue NW, PO Box 340, Chateau, MT 59422

18. Montana: Glacier National Park, PO Box 128, West Glacier, MT 59936

19. Nevada: Washoe Lake State Park, 4855 E. Lake Boulevard, Carson City, NV 89704

20. Nevada: Great Basin National Park, 100 Great Basin National Park, Baker, NV 89311

21. Nevada: Red Rock Canyon National Conservation Area, 1000 Scenic Loop Drive, Las Vegas, NV 89124

22. Wyoming: Bighorn National Forest, 2013 Eastside 2nd Street, Sheridan, WY 82801

23. Wyoming: Grand Teton National Park, PO Drawer 170, Moose, WY 83012

Grand Teton National Park

24. **Wyoming:** Shoshone National Forest, 808 Meadow Lane, Cody, WY 82414

25. **Wyoming, Montana, and Idaho:** Yellowstone National Park, Backcountry Office, PO Box 168, Yellowstone National Park, WY 82190

10 Racetracks to Visit in the West

1. **California:** Bay Meadows Race Track, 2600 S. Delaware Street, San Mateo (www.baymeadows.com)

2. **California:** Del Mar Thoroughbred Club, 2260 Jimmy Durante Boulevard, Del Mar (www.dmtc.com)

3. **California:** Golden Gate Fields, 1100 Eastshore Highway, Berkeley (www.goldengatefields.com)

4. **California:** Hollywood Park, 1050 South Prairie Avenue, Inglewood (www.hollywoodpark.com)

5. **California:** Santa Anita Park, 285 West Huntington Drive, Arcadia (www.santaanita.com)

6. Colorado: Arapahoe Park, 26000 E. Quincy Avenue, Aurora (www.mihiracing.com/arapahoe_park.shtml)

7. Idaho: Les Bois Park, 5610 Glenwood Road, Boise (www.leboispark.org)

8. Montana: Montana ExpoPark, 400 Third Street NW, Great Falls (www.mtexpopark.com)

9. Montana: Yellowstone Downs, 308 Sixth Avenue N., Billings (www.metrapark.com)

10. Wyoming: Wyoming Downs, 10180 Hwy 89 North, Evanston (www.wyomingdowns.com)

14 Scenic Places to Ride in the Southwest

1. Arizona: Catalina State Park, PO Box 36986, Tucson, AZ 85740

2. Arizona: Grand Canyon National Park, PO Box 129, Grand Canyon, AZ 86023

3. Arizona: Petrified Forest National Park, 1 Park Road, Petrified Forest, AZ 86028

Grand Canyon National Park

4. New Mexico: Carson National Forest, 208 Cruz Alta Road, Taos, NM 87571

5. New Mexico: Gila National Forest, 3005 E. Camino del Bosque, Silver City, NM 88061

6. Oklahoma: Great Salt Plains State Park, Route 1 Box 28, Jet, OK 73749

7. Oklahoma: Robbers Cave State Park, PO Box 9, Wilburton, OK 74578

8. Oklahoma and Arkansas: Ouachita National Forest, Box 1270, Hot Springs, AR 71902

9. Texas: Caprock Canyons State Park and Trailway, PO Box 204, Quitaque, TX 79255

10. Texas: Guadalupe Mountains National Park, HC 60 Box 400, Salt Flat, TX 79847

11. Texas: Hill Country State Natural Area, 10600 Bandera Creek Road, Bandera, TX 78003

12. Texas: Lake Somerville State Park and Trailway, Birch Creek Unit, 14222 Park Road 57, Somerville, TX 77879

13. Utah: Grand Staircase-Escalante National Monument, Bureau of Land Management, Kanab Resource Area Office, 318 North 100 East, Kanab, UT 84741

14. Utah: Zion National Park, SR-9, Springdale, UT 84767

13 Racetracks to Visit in the Southwest

1. Arizona: Rillito Downs Park, 4502 North First Avenue at River Road, Tucson (www.raccom.state.az.us)

2. Arizona: Turf Paradise, 1501 W. Bell Road, Phoenix (www.turfparadise.com)

Zion National Park

3. Arizona: Yavapai Downs, 10501 Hwy 89A, Prescott Valley (www.yavapaidownsatpv.com)

4. New Mexico: The Downs at Albuquerque, 201 California Street NE, Albuquerque (www.abqdowns.com)

5. New Mexico: Sunland Park Racetrack and Casino, 1200 Futurity Drive, Sunland Park (www.sunlandpark.com)

6. New Mexico: SunRay Park, 39 Road 5568, Farmington (www.sunraygaming.com)

7. Oklahoma: Blue Ribbon Downs, 3700 West Cherokee, Sallisaw (www.blueribbondowns.net)

8. Oklahoma: Fair Meadows in Expo Square, 4609 E. 1st Street, Tulsa (www.fairmeadows.com)

9. Oklahoma: Remington Park, One Remington Place, Oklahoma City (www.remingtonpark.com)

10. Texas: Lone Star Park, 1000 Lone Star Parkway, Grand Prairie (www.lonestarpark.com)

11. Texas: Manor Downs, 9211 Hill Lane, Manor (www.manor downs.com)

12. Texas: Retama Park, 1 Retama Parkway, Selma (www.retamapark.com)

Haleakala National Park

13. Texas: Sam Houston Race Park, 7575 N. Sam Houston Parkway West, Houston (www.shrp.com)

2 Scenic Places to Ride in Hawaii

1. Haleakala National Park, PO Box 369, Makawao, Maui, HI 96768

2. Kalaupapa National Historical Park, PO Box 2222, Kalaupapa, HI 96742

Glossary

A Hodgepodge of Horseology

aids: The rider's tools for communicating commands to the horse. Natural aids include the rider's legs and hands. Artificial aids include devices such as spurs and whips.

barren: Describes a mare that was bred but did not get in-foal.

bascule: The natural arc of the jumping horse's body in midair. Talented jumpers display an expressive bascule.

bedding: Material placed on the floor of stalls to cushion horses when they lie down. Bedding also absorbs urine, aiding stall hygiene. Types of bedding include wood shavings and straw.

bell boots: Protective coverings worn around a horse's pasterns.

A bell boot encircles the top of the horse's hoof and shields the heel from bruising during exercise or competition. The name comes from the boots' bell shape.

billet: One of several leather straps for securing the girth to an English saddle.

bitting up: Longeing a horse in a surcingle and side reins. This is one method of getting a young horse accustomed to wearing a bridle and holding a bit in his mouth.

bosal: A braided noseband, usually made of stiff rawhide, sometimes used in addition to the bridle of a western horse.

breeches: Close-fitting pants for English riding, usually with a suede or leather patch on the inside of the knee to help the rider grip the saddle.

broodmare: A mare specifically used for producing foals.

canter: A slow, smooth gallop.

chaps: Leather or suede outer pants worn by a rider. Chaps protect a rider's legs from being scraped by brambles or thorns and improve seat security by enhancing the rider's ability to grip the saddle.

chlorhexidine: A topical liquid antiseptic solution used to clean a horse's wounds and applied to the umbilical stump of newborn foals to prevent bacteria from entering the foal's bloodstream.

conformation: A horse's bone structure, musculature, physical features, and body proportions. Equine authorities recognize correct and ideal conformation standards for each breed of horse.

corral: A fenced outdoor enclosure for stabling a horse.

crow hopping: In this halfhearted buck, the horse humps his back, stiffens his legs, and pops up in the air for several steps. A common cause of crow hopping is a saddle that is cinched too tightly.

dam: A horse's mother. Secretariat's dam was Somethingroyal.

foal: A newborn horse.

foaling: The process of a mare giving birth.

gelding: A castrated male horse. The majority of male horses used for riding are geldings, as the procedure makes them more cooperative and less aggressive.

gymkhana: A variety of games on horseback that utilize standardized patterns run at speed, usually in timed competition.

halter: The head collar worn by horses so they can be handled, led, groomed, and tied up. Halters are constructed of rope, nylon webbing, or leather.

hand: The unit of measurement for the height of a horse or pony. One hand equals four inches.

headstall: The part of a bridle, minus the bit, that fits on the horse's head.

heat cycle: A mare's peak fertility cycle. In general, the breeding season for horses is April through September. During those months, at approximately every twenty-one days a mare will "show heat" for about five days, meaning she will ovulate (produce an egg) and be receptive to a stallion.

hinny: A mule is a cross between a jack (male donkey) and a mare (female horse). A hinny is the offspring of a stallion (male horse) and a jenny (female donkey). Because it's widely believed that foals take after their dam more than their sire and that donkey traits are less desirable than are horse traits, hinnies are less popular than mules.

jog: In western riding, a jog is a very slow trot.

lay-up: To rest and rehabilitate an injured horse.

lope: The western version of a canter, a lope is a very slow, cadenced gallop.

martingale: An item of English tack consisting of a leather strap attached to the girth that exerts pressure either on the reins (a running martingale) or the noseband (a standing martingale) to control the position of the horse's head.

mutton withered: Describes a horse with very low, rounded withers, similar to the withers of a sheep. This conformation makes saddle fitting difficult.

paddock: A large corral typically designed so the horse has room to roam around and enjoy light exercise.

picket line: A rope stretched between two sturdy trees. Horses are then tethered to the line. Often used for overnight horse camping.

poultice: A paste or liquid applied to the horse's hoof or body to relieve soreness. A common poultice is a mixture of warm water and Epsom salts.

pigeon toed: A defect in conformation in which the horse's front feet turn inward.

polo wraps: Long, soft bandages made of cotton knit or fleece that are wrapped around a horse's lower legs to protect the bones and tissue from injury. Originally used on polo horses, these wraps are now popular on all types of performance horses.

rawhide: Hide, or animal skin, that is untanned, thus light in color and extremely tough and stiff. Cut into thin strips, it is used to make some parts of western tack.

round pen: A circular corral, often with solid sides, about fifty feet in diameter. Round pens are used in training horses. The small enclosed area helps keep the horse focused on the trainer or handler.

rowel: The wheel-shaped ornamentation on the end of a spur, often with a scalloped or sharp-toothed edge. The rowel is pressed against the side of the horse when the rider applies leg pressure, eliciting a quicker response to commands.

sire: A horse's father. Bold Ruler was the sire of Secretariat.

splay legged: A defect in conformation in which one or both front legs are turned outward.

splint boots: Protective coverings for the insides of a horse's legs. They can prevent an injury in case a horse happens to strike himself while exercising or working.

stallion: A male horse that has not been castrated.

steward: An official at a horse show or racetrack in charge of enforcing rules.

stride: The length of one entire step of a moving horse. The average riding horse has a galloping stride of about twelve feet; however, a racehorse's galloping stride can exceed twenty feet. Reportedly, Man O'War's stride could open up to twenty-five feet.

surcingle: A secondary girth that wraps around a jockey's saddle. Also, a training girth used in longeing. The longed horse wears a bridle with reins attached to the surcingle, in essence mimicking the sensation of a rider holding the reins.

thrifty: A descriptive term for a horse that maintains his weight and condition on small rations. Hence, a horse that can be inexpensively fed.

wean: To permanently separate colts or fillies from their dams.

weanling: A colt or filly that has been taken from the dam. This marks the beginning of a young horse's life independent of the dam.

Appendix

Where to Go to Learn More

Adoption of Mustangs

Bureau of Land Management Wild Horse and Burro Program

Bureau of Land Management

Washington, D.C.

www.wildhorseandburro.blm.gov

Arranges roundups and adoptions of mustangs; provides statistics on feral horse herds.

Mustang Heritage Foundation

Bertram, Texas

www.mustangheritagefoundation.org

Promotes the adoption of mustangs from the Bureau of Land Management roundups and provides education and resources on how to train a mustang.

Competitive Mounted Orienteering

National Association for Competitive Mounted Orienteering

See Web site for state chapter contact information

www.nacmo.org

Sets rules and organizes competitions for mounted orienteering events.

Cowboy Mounted Shooting

Cowboy Mounted Shooting Association

Scottsdale, Arizona

www.cowboymountedshooting.com

Develops rules and guidelines for the sport; maintains performance records.

Endurance Riding

American Endurance Ride Conference

Auburn, California

www.aerc.org

Encourages and enforces the proper conditioning of the horse for the sport; oversees competitions.

Equine Veterinary Resources

American Association of Equine Practitioners (AAEP)

Lexington, Kentucky

www.aaep.org

Provides continuing education for member veterinarians and provides horse care information to the community; offers an online link to locate an equine veterinarian in any specified region.

Kentucky Derby
Churchill Downs
Louisville, Kentucky
www.churchilldowns.com
Historical home of America's most popular horse race.

Polo
U.S. Polo Association
Lexington, Kentucky
www.us-polo.org
Assigns handicaps to players; standardizes rules for playing both outdoor and arena polo in the United States.

Rare Breeds of Horses
American Livestock Breeds Conservancy
Pittsboro, North Carolina
www.albc-usa.org
Works to protect over 150 breeds of livestock, including some breeds of horses, from extinction.

Rescue Groups
Exceller Fund
Granada Hills, California
www.excellerfund.org

Dedicated to finding homes for unwanted ex-racehorses.

Standardbred Retirement Foundation
Hamilton, New Jersey
www.adoptahorse.org
Seeks adoptive homes for standardbred racehorses; offers year-end awards and competitions for standardbreds trained for horse show events.

Thoroughbred Retirement Foundation
Headquarters in Saratoga Springs, New York
www.trfinc.org
Provides retirement home for ex-racehorses too infirm for second careers; also finds homes for horses that have been rehabilitated. Offers programs aligned with correctional facilities in which prisoners work with rescued horses.

Ride and Tie Competitions
The Ride and Tie Association
Sequim, Washington
www.rideandtie.org
Establishes rules and standards for competitions.

Statistics on the Horse Industry in America
American Horse Council
Washington, D.C.
www.horsecouncil.org

Thoroughbred Racehorses
National Museum of Racing and Hall of Fame
Saratoga Springs, New York
www.racingmuseum.org
Houses horse racing memorabilia, an extensive gallery of racing-themed artwork, and a Hall of Fame honoring inducted horses, jockeys, and trainers.

Trail Riding
North American Trail Ride Conference
Sedalia, Colorado
www.natrc.org
Promotes the selection, conditioning, and training of horses for competitive trail riding.

Vaulting
American Vaulting Association
West Hollywood, California
www.americanvaulting.org
Promotes equestrian vaulting in the United States; provides instructional material and establishes rule book for competitions.

Welfare of Horses
American Humane Association
Los Angeles, California
www.americanhumane.org

Monitors and observes the use of all animals in filmed media; provides an online rating system of movies based on how closely productions follow AHA guidelines.

Fund for Animals
New York City, New York
www.fundforanimals.org
Works in partnership with the Humane Society of the United States to pass laws protecting animals.